NEW YORK REVIEW BOOKS
CLASSICS

W9-AWE-198

THE GRAY NOTEBOOK

JOSEP PLA (1897–1981), the eldest of four children, was born in Palafrugell on the Costa Brava to a family of landowners. He studied law in Barcelona, abandoned law for journalism, and in 1920 moved to Paris to serve as the correspondent for the Spanish newspaper *La Publicidad*. Banned from Spain in 1924 for his criticisms of the dictator Primo de Rivera, Pla continued to report from Russia, Rome, Berlin, and London, before returning to Madrid in 1927. He supported the new Spanish Republic that emerged in 1931, but was soon disillusioned and left the country during the Civil War, returning in 1939. Under the Franco regime, he was internally exiled to Palafrugell and his articles for the weekly review *Destino* were frequently censored. After 1947 his work began to be published in Catalan, and his complete works were published in full in 1966. They comprise forty-five volumes, of which *The Gray Notebook*— begun in 1919, but polished and added to throughout the intervening years—is the first.

PETER BUSH is an award-winning translator who lives in Barcelona. Among his recent translations are Ramón del Valle-Inclan's *Tyrant Banderas* (for NYRB Classics), Teresa Solana's *Crazy Tales of Blood and Guts*, Mercè Rodoreda's *In Diamond Square* and Najat El Hachmi's *The Body Hunter*.

VALENTÍ PUIG is a Catalan poet, novelist, and literary critic who writes in both his native Catalan and in Spanish.

THE GRAY NOTEBOOK

JOSEP PLA

Translated from the Catalan by
PETER BUSH

Introduction by
VALENTÍ PUIG

NEW YORK REVIEW BOOKS

New York

THIS IS A NEW YORK REVIEW BOOK
PUBLISHED BY THE NEW YORK REVIEW OF BOOKS
435 Hudson Street, New York, NY 10014
www.nyrb.com

Originally published in Catalan as *El quadern gris*

LLLL institut ramon llull
Catalan Language and Culture

*The publication of this work has been made possible by grants from the Institut
Ramon Llull and from the Directorate General of Books, Archives, and Libraries
of the Spanish Ministry of Culture.*

Library of Congress Cataloging-in-Publication Data
Pla, Josep, 1897-1981, author.
[Quadern Gris. English]
The Gray Notebook / by Josep Pla ; translated by Peter Bush.
pages cm. — (New York Review Books Classics)
ISBN 978-1-59017-67 1-9 (alk. paper)
1. Pla, Josep, 1897-1981—Diaries. 2. Authors, Catalan—20th century—
Biography. I. Bush, Peter R., 1946- translator. II. Title.
PC3941.P54Q8313 2013
849'.985203—dc23
[B]
   2013028497

ISBN 978-1-59017-671-9
Also available as an electronic book; ISBN 978-1-59017-671-9

Printed in the United States of America on acid-free paper.
10 9 8 7 6 5 4 3 2 1

CONTENTS

INTRODUCTION

TO JOSEP Pla, writing was a question of loyalty towards life. Truth, he said, was the grace of literature. Shrewdness was indispensable. And memory was more important than imagination. He was not interested in metaphor but in the language of things. He sought a comprehensive realism, rich in detail and full of color. He aspired to a literature that represented a form of survival rather than a mere wisp of culture, though of course nothing can stall the annihilating industry of time.

Pla was a classical stylist, with a style that was transparent, almost indiscernible. It's more difficult to describe things accurately than to have an opinion, he insisted—"that's why everyone has an opinion." In his work there is an ongoing tension between description and action that recalls Balzac, though when it comes to people and characters, Pla is more akin to Stendhal, not so much making things up as projecting himself into the story. Pla was committed to the accidental, to the unpredictable glories of the concrete and empirical. Memory triumphs over invention, depiction over episode, scene over plot, in pages of great sensual precision and syntactical richness that are marked everywhere by a meticulous and musical deployment of the adjective. Pla's work is a mirror in which the real is reconstructed, even reimagined, without being pressed into the service of the symbolic.

His finest book is *The Gray Notebook*, which offered a new twist on the old genre of the bildungsroman, and which brought expressiveness, flexibility, and a range of register to the Catalan language that had previously only existed in its poetry. In *The Gray Notebook*, Pla proves himself a master of the cutting turn of phrase, the unexpected adjective. He can deliver the shock of a lightning bolt. He has the speed and nerve of a purebred horse.

The book presents itself as a diary chronicling twenty months in the life of a twenty-one-year-old, beginning in May 1918 and ending in November 1919. From the start of his career as a writer, Pla had drawn on his diaries for his published work, which helped to give them their distinctive style and energy. *The Gray Notebook*, however, wasn't published until 1966, when Pla was sixty-nine. He transformed a document of youth into a—or the—work of his prime, the entries of a diary into an autobiography built of fragments. The addition of descriptions, short stories, landscapes, scenes, reminiscences, and flashes of moral reflection had enhanced it over the years, without Pla worrying overly much about the chronological blunders that might have crept in with the reworking. In the book's pages style becomes a tone of voice, and the reader is held spellbound.

Pla was an empiricist, for whom the only escape from life's inevitable failures lay in literature. He was a memoirist with an aversion to intimacy who was perfectly attuned to the ridiculous, a wanderer who knew how to spin a tale out of his daily round with the gifts of a novelist. Pla can make a serving of grilled sardines the occasion of a lyrical pencil sketch. He has the old Roman sense of equanimity and order, off-setting his skepticism about other people and the world at large with a faith in life, not as we wish it to be but as it is. He rewrote his diary—that is, he wrote *The Gray Notebook*—while sitting before the fireplace of his ancestral home, the stern tramontana blowing outside and making the fire smoke, a cigarette burning on his lips as he sought the mot juste. It is a book in which human memory resists oblivion and the individual, the collective. Where the concrete is valued over the abstract, skeptical awareness over the certainties of the absolute, and the thing over the verb. The prose of *The Gray Notebook* is as alive as common sense.

Spain was neutral during World War I, and *The Gray Notebook* opens with public opinion deeply divided between supporters of the Germans and the Allies. Pla himself was a Francophile. The University of Barcelona, where he had enrolled to study law, had shut down due to the Spanish flu epidemic, leading him to return to his family home in Palafrugell, the small city in the Ampurdan where he had been born. *The Gray Notebook* moves back and forth between coast and capital, with the literary circles of the small town and big city standing in live contrast to each other. Pla preferred the exuberant cynicism of his friends in Palafrugell to the pretentious circle of writers and intellectuals who gathered at the Barcelona Ateneu. (This included two of the greatest figures of the era, the philosopher Eugeni d'Ors, most famous internationally for his *Three Hours in the Prado Museum*, though that is only one of his brilliant books, and Francesc Pujols, a libertine thinker who devised an eccentric system of values that was much admired by Salvador Dalí.) Whether writing about Palafrugell or Barcelona, Pla, who greatly admired the eighteenth-century French literature of conversation, makes a careful record of all the playful and boastful remarks that are exchanged. After all, what is writing for if not to render human conversation intelligible?

As a young reporter on the streets of Barcelona in an era of social conflict, Pla found a city in upheaval. Troubled by the grotesque world of academia and its rickety, anachronistic ways, he apathetically completed his law degree, as described at the end of *The Gray Notebook*, and headed to Paris as a foreign correspondent. He was to write countless pages of journalism in the years to come, later refashioned into his many books, all of them displaying the purring decorum, at once sensual and self-regarding, of a literary cat.

Pla had no fear of freedom, without which there can be no hope of grace. But freedom has to be combined with a sense of continuity. Attentive to both the strictures of form and the limitless possibilities beyond the horizon, a writer must be precise while creating a mood, must honor both the sensual and the rational, all the while aspiring to turn raw life into something sinuous or striking, like the line of a melody or a human profile. This requires the writer to take an active part in the continuing struggle between culture and nature. Pla was well aware of nature's infinite and incalculable capacity for destruction, and yet *The Gray Notebook* is filled with wonderful landscapes. Landscape for Pla was his homeland.

Pla's complete works comprise more than thirty thousand pages.

Catalan literature, after a period of medieval splendor—whose high-lights are the poetry of Ausiàs March and the prose of the philosopher Ramon Llull—went into steep decline; by the time of Montaigne, Pla would say, it had all but disappeared. Until the romantic era, Catalan was reduced to little more than a domestic vernacular. Pla's body of work comprises journals, notebooks, novels, stories, aphorisms, reminiscences, a political history of contemporary Spain, and a picture of mid-century Catalonia, including portraits and biographies of its major figures, which has all the minute detail of a modern digital file. Of his few novels, the best is *La calle estrecha* (1952). Better are his many stories—of the sea, the small world of pensions in Barcelona, and Berlin—which emulate the realism of Dutch painting.

As a literary portraitist, whether of himself or others, Pla owes a great deal to the French moralists of the seventeenth and eighteenth centuries. In this vein, he affirms, "I would never defend the egotism of irresponsibility. I defend the defendable sort of egotism, which converts the era's dead weight into abstraction." Or: "Death is the last sentence in the book of life; what you need to do is make sure its pages aren't blank." His other devotion is to home. On returning from a trip, he writes:

> And now, thank God, we're finally back home! Behave like a prodigal son in today's world or in any other world? Never! Always come home! Come home whether it rains and the trees are growing, or the mistral gathers causing so much damage, or whether we're on the verge of a wretched drought. The land we tread gives us a certain idea of what life is. Everything is unsure, everything uncertain. We have no choice but to accept the land we've been born to, however bitter, poor or fertile it may be. We have nothing else.

For us, too, at the beginning of the twenty-first century, everything remains unsure, everything uncertain. Yet literature creates a bond. Pla is such a bond.

Pla was in Paris for the drafting of the Treaty of Versailles, whose provisions made World War II inevitable. He reported on the League of Nations, of which his most vivid memories were the steaks served in Geneva's restaurants. He wrote about the tragedy of old Europe, soon to be reduced to rubble, from the vantage point of a man left standing on the railway platform while everyone else leaps onto one or another ideological train. He witnessed Mussolini's march on Rome in 1922, traveled to Moscow in 1925 when Trotsky and Stalin were caught in a power struggle, and was in Berlin during the hyperinflation of the Weimar Republic. Like Canetti, he grasped that a currency has a moral value; when its value drops, so does the value of human life. Humanity "shrinks" with inflation. Pla's superb, angst-ridden stories written from Berlin are comparable to those of Isherwood. He describes Hitler reading aloud from *Mein Kampf* in the presence of General Ludendorff and people resorting to suicide as readily as they would eat a peach.

In the 1930s, Pla's attitude toward the Spanish Second Republic veered from confidence to uncertainty about the political stability of the country. His account of events, however, is always lucid. He fled to France when he became the target of death threats from the anarchists. Later he assumed the military coup that brought Franco to power would act as a prelude to the reestablishment of the monarchy, yet the dictatorship would endure until 1975. The fratricide of the Spanish Civil War broke something in Pla, made him more bitter and skeptical. It was hard to be a believer of any kind in such an unsettled country and in such disjointed and chaotic times. Franco confiscated his passport, putting an end to his travels. So he found refuge in the local, living in his ancestral home, writing in the small hours before dawn. The cosmopolitan correspondent posed as a modest rural landowner, and yet even the bucolic can have a cruel edge. What is civilization but frustration, Pla wrote. He thought World War II was "perhaps the time when humanity has come closest to jungle and cave."

It was years before he was free to travel again, when he began writing weekly articles for the magazine *Destino*. His prose has been justly compared to the work of V. S. Naipaul. His *Letters from Italy* was published in 1955, a "book of sensations organized around the fresh green color used to paint the windows of Italy." Pla had been a habitué of the *wagon-lit* from the last hurrah of the belle epoque to postwar Europe. Eventually he discovered the happy solitude of traveling by oil tanker. He visited New York and Israel. It was always from the West that he approached the world.

Whether Pla is describing the passing figure of a young Italian woman, the dampness of Girona in his childhood, or a delicate white wine sipped on the banks of the Rhine, he does so with the sort of unforced style that, in the words of Pascal, astonishes and delights us: Expecting to find an author, we meet instead a man. Nature is disorder for Pla; culture is pitted against it. Ivy will destroy a house that took years of effort to construct. Literature, however, is never an end in itself: It exists to clarify and order our thoughts. How to wrest reality *sub specie aeternitatis* from fleeting everyday life? Though memory can supplant art, there is no art without memory.

—VALENTÍ PUIG
Translated by Valerie Miles

THE GRAY NOTEBOOK

1918

8 March. There is so much influenza about that they've had to shut the university. My brother and I have been at home in Palafrugell ever since. We are a couple of idle students. I only see my brother at mealtimes; he is a very keen football player—despite breaking an arm and a leg on the pitch. He leads his life. I do what I can. I don't miss Barcelona, let alone the university. I like small-town life here with my friends.

At lunch when it is time for dessert, the table is suddenly blessed with a large dish of crème brûlée and a deliciously light, golden sponge cake sprinkled with powdered sugar. "You do realize you're twenty-one today?" asks my mother.

And it would be absurd to quibble: I am twenty-one today. I glance around the table. My father is eating silently, as he always does. My mother seems less fretful than usual. As only saints' days are celebrated in this country, the presence of the sponge cake and crème brûlée puts me on my guard. I wonder if they have really been preparing for my birthday or in fact wanted to remind me that the balance sheet from my early years is very thin, indeed quite blank. That would be natural enough, I imagine! How very disagreeable it must be to have children who are such hazy, unknown quantities. Nonetheless, I am frivolous enough to be unable to resist the challenge to my conscience the sweet pastry poses, and I find the sponge cake extremely tasty and the crème brûlée delicious. When I serve myself a second helping, the chill in the air grows. Twenty-one years old!

Families! Such curious, complicated things . . .

It starts to rain in the late afternoon—a dense, steady drizzle.

There's hardly any breeze. The sky is gray and overcast. I can hear the small raindrops pattering on the trees and the soil in the garden. A dull, distant sound like the sea in winter. Icy cold March rain. Evening falls, the sky changes from gray to a pale and unreal gauzy white. A heavy silence, a silence you can cut with a knife, hangs over the town, weighing down its roofs. The sound of the rain becomes vaguely musical, a monotonous trill. My obsession for the day floats along with it: twenty-one years old!

Watching the endless rain makes me drowsy. I don't know what to do next. Clearly, I should be studying and reviewing my textbooks so as to put the onerous burden of my law degree behind me. Out of the question! I can rarely resist the temptation to read the smallest scrap of paper I find in the street, but textbooks kill my curiosity.

I decide to start this diary. I'll write whatever happens—simply to pass the time—come what may. My mother is clean and tidy. She is obsessed with keeping the house in regimented order. She loves to rip up paper, burn old junk, and sell anything for which she can't find an immediate practical or decorative use to the rag-and-bone man. It will be nigh on a miracle if her admirable domestic virtues spare these sheets of mine. If they don't, it will hardly be the end of the world...

9 March. You are apparently expected to introduce this kind of writing with bits of biography. Memoirs, reminiscences, and diaries, however humble and commonplace, always entertain me. If these jottings do escape the flame, perhaps one day a distant relative or curious individual with time on his hands will deign to glance their way.

I was born in Palafrugell (Lower Ampurdan) on 8 March 1897. My family is entirely from the Ampurdan. The landscape of my life encompasses Puig Son Ric, in Begur, in the east; the Fitor mountains, in the west; the Formigues Islands, in the south; and Montgrí, in the north. I have always felt this is a very old country. All sorts of wandering peoples have passed this way.

My father is Antoni Pla i Vilar. Pla is the name given to the tiny village of Pla de Llofriu, a humdrum spot within the boundaries of

Palafrugell that has its own parish church. Surrounded by poor, dry farming land, these are households of narrow-minded, long-suffering people who have never had very much to look forward to. Vilar is the name of a family from Mont-ras, a municipality on the road from Palafrugell to Palamós that is full of vociferous republicans and is the scene of the fiercest political and personal conflicts. All my father's forebears worked on the land. The Llofriu parish archive starts immediately after the Council of Trent. Mossèn Birba, an enlightened priest who used to be the parish priest, happier reading old documents than hoeing tomato beds, once told me that the presence of my family is recorded in the earliest registers in the archive. My ancestors were poverty-stricken farmers who mainly depended on the cultivation of vineyards.

Between 1860 and 1870 the Vilar family moved from Mont-ras to Barcelona. A great-uncle, Dr. Vilar, the brother of Marieta Vilar, my paternal grandmother (Maria Vilar Colom), set up as a doctor in the old fishing port of the Barceloneta. Dr. Vilar was a political radical, an atheist and materialist who worshipped science. A typical throwback to the revolutionary spirit of 1848, he was an excitable, nervy, highly generous man, with a romantic head of hair and a face so pale it contrasted sharply with the broad, black silk tie he always wore.

Marieta Vilar came to Barcelona at the time of the Second Carlist War to marry my grandfather, Josep Pla Fàbregues. Because roads were so unsafe, she journeyed back by sea, disembarked in Palamós, and traveled home in one of the carts that plied the route daily. It was autumn and they left towards dusk. Before reaching the En Bitlla bridge the horses took fright and started to retreat. There was a dead man in the middle of the road. A green-wood fire was sending up thick white smoke from a dark pine grove nearby. General Savalls's cavalry was camped under the pines. The woman who was to be my grandmother reached home in a state of shock, trembling, her cheeks deathly pale. After loosening her stays and laying her down on the settee, they brought her around by killing a hen and feeding her cups of chicken broth. The memory of this fright remained with Grandmother Marieta throughout her life, and not very long ago, I heard her telling a small farmer, who was complaining about how dangerous life was, "Right you are! The truth is that somebody ought to get on with governing so we won't have to kill a hen every three or four days for the sake of innocent people."

My mother is Maria Casadevall i Llach. Her father, Pere Casadevall, was a blacksmith and owned a forge in Palafrugell. His firstborn son, Esteve Casadevall i Pareres, emigrated to Cuba and made a considerable fortune (for the time) from tobacco. A third of this fortune was inherited by his middle sister, in other words, my mother. As a young man, Grandfather Pere was a liberal and a follower of General Espartero. When his son returned from Cuba, his views grew rapidly more moderate. As he started to mellow, he took out a subscription to *El Brusi* and—after closing the forge—enjoyed a tranquil, placid old age.

The Llachs come from Gavarra in the Fitor mountains and on this side my great-grandfather was a tenant farmer in Cavorca, a remote, solitary farmstead, between heaven and the forest. It was a robust family and they were all long-lived. My grandmother's generation comprised seven youngsters: one boy and six girls. The boy was a deserter, went to Rheims in France, married there, and his son, Gaston, was killed in Verdun, fighting for France. That may seem strange, but it isn't really. Two of the girls married in Sa Bardissa—that is, in Calonge—two in Palamós and two in Palafrugell. Some of these families subsequently emigrated to France. Currently, two brothers, who are my mother's cousins, are direct-action anarchists and considered highly dangerous by the police. They spend their lives in and out of jail, rushing from one hideout to another, and can just as easily be found here as on the other side of the Albera mountains. This is not at all unusual in families in this country: The wealthy, or merely prosperous, branches are usually conformist and Catholic while the poor relations are starving and anarchist. The richer the one side, the more rebellious the other.

Marieta is the only grandparent I have ever known. Grandfather Josep Pla died young, struck by lightning while watching a storm from a window in the farmhouse. Grandfather Pere Casadevall was already dead by the time I came into the world. By the look of a daguerreotype preserved at home, Gràcia Llach i Serra, my maternal grandmother, seems a very gentle soul, with her hair parted over a perfect forehead and a touch of melancholy warmth in her sculpted, open features.

I have the impression that the family held Esteve Casadevall in high esteem for many years because of the fortune he brought back from Cuba. Once he had returned, he married a very pious, distinguished lady, Donya Beatriu Girbal. They didn't have children. As youngsters, this lady and her single sister, Carme, lived in Champagne, in Épernay, where their father owned a champagne cork business. They experienced the Franco-Prussian War and German invasion in person, and one day saw Prince Bismarck ride across the town on a white horse.

Under the influence of Donya Beatriu, Sr. Casadevall gradually drew closer to the church. One year Father Goberna, the famous Jesuit preacher from Barcelona, embarked on a very dramatic mission to Palafrugell. There were spectacularly violent conversions. Sr. Casadevall was moved to become an active, deeply committed Catholic. The mission was still in progress when he went to the notary and dictated a will leaving ten thousand five-peseta gold coins (two-thirds of his fortune in hard currency) to the curia in Girona. His actions as a convert were typical of a renegade. People insinuated that in Cuba he must have been a radical liberal and Freemason. I never did get to the bottom of all that. It is true that religion gave Sr. Casadevall a very public profile. It was during the papacy of Pius IX, and the local republicans appointed him nuncio to His Holiness. He became an unremittingly serious gentleman, at once stern and stolid, of granite-hard convictions. He wore a frock coat, top hat, and patent leather shoes and flourished a black, shiny walking stick with an ivory top like a billiard ball. He had beautiful handwriting. He was tall and thin with a slight stoop.

My parents married at the age of twenty, young and in perfect health. From right after my birth, I was reputed to be a well-built baby. Nowadays newborns are immediately put on the scales (pharmacists have recently begun to make them available with cushion included). That wasn't the case in my time. If it had been, I'd have been a champion heavyweight. My mother used to tell me that when she or the nursemaid took me out in the stroller, the loving couples they encountered would go into raptures over my cheeks. The young ladies caressed me and said the strangest things in that gabble people adopt when speaking to babies. They'd look at the young man by their side and titter, as if to say "One day I hope you'll give me such a bonny babe."

Embarrassed, the young man would look down shyly, very polite, maybe thinking "We'll do our best."

Funny to think that my birth and outings in the local streets sparked these noble ideas and lofty responses in the inhabitants of my birthplace. As an adult, I've never managed to make such a strong impression.

Be that as it may, I was born on carrer Nou—or carrer del Progrés—a very long, sad street, straight as a church candle, that runs from carrer de la Caritat to the Palamós train tracks. The house was a high building that faced north. The rooms looking over the road were freezing in winter. Conversely, the rooms with a southern aspect were very sunny with a view of a walled kitchen garden. Beyond this garden and the low dividing wall, you could see a huge orchard—Joanama's—that was kept just so. It is very likely that my fondness for well-ordered, extremely tidy things—even if I personally have always been untidy—came from the mental pleasure I derived as a child from those terraces that were so well tended, well irrigated, and perfectly laid out.

I remember nothing at all about my childhood. People say I was never sick, apart from the usual childhood illnesses (scarlet fever, chicken pox, etcetera). When I was in diapers, I must have glowed blissfully. Our family life, it's almost certain, was beyond reproach. People have told me they'd love to have had my parents. I must admit that, given the choice, I'd have voted for the individuals who did in fact bring me into the world and rear me. People demand virtuous and villainous things of their parents that generally parents are not in a position to give: money, social status, guile, and nerve. The only thing to ask of parents is physical strength and a healthy body. Everything else is imponderable and at the mercy of happenstance.

All in all, I suspect that the diaper stage is the happiest in our earthly existence. What a wonderful time! What long sleep, what soft pillows, what luscious feasts, and what succulent, delicious liquids one must swallow! To live in a world where hunger is all and you simply watch while everyone strives to feed you—that must be a nonstop epiphany and sheer delight. Can you imagine? I am sure that the unconscious memory of life in the maternal cloister and the protected glade of infancy leads over time to a contrasting sense of discomfort and insecurity. Life becomes nostalgia for that lost warmth and stolen happiness. But I've never been able to conjure up the tiniest genuine memory of that period of quiet pleasures and vegetable well-being... no doubt contributing to the charms of that lost paradise—a paradise on earth—at the breast.

Srta. Enriqueta Ramon lived next door, a small, plump old spinster, who every day squeezed into an elaborate corset, and was ruddy-cheeked, despite her refined sensibility, beneath a steep pile of permed hair. Srta. Enriqueta's vegetable garden—though she'd never have agreed to make concessions to anything so vulgar—was a tiny, flower garden and was linked to ours by a well the two households shared. My mother liked to carry me to the stone bench by the well, where Srta. Enriqueta—I've been told—would make a fuss over me from her side of the well. So dramatic were her demonstrations of affection that sometimes my mother had no choice but to hand me, like a fragile package, across the abyss of the well into her arms. With a well in between, such expressions of feeling are not, I'd say, well-advised. We could all have fallen down the well: the spinster, mother, and I. For obvious reasons, I was most at risk. I didn't know this at the time, but I have since concluded that this toing and froing was done to prepare me for the considerable tensions and perils life held in store. Thinking about it as an adult still gives me goose bumps. It reinforces my sense of the infinite foolishness of humanity.

I am unable to describe how consciousness first dawned in me. I draw a complete blank, total amnesia. My first precise memory is visual: An image flashes up of my father reading the daily newspaper at the table, leaning over the white tablecloth, his entire face stained by the light filtering through the green cloth shade of an oil lamp. I was so astonished by the sight of my father's skin oozing green that I broke into uncontrollable, nervous laughter. My two subsequent memories involve smells: the rather acrid aroma of burnt cork that always floats in the air of Palafrugell and suggests to newcomers with sensitive noses that a fire has just been put out, and the velvety smell of people's clothes—something I have always found unpleasant and tart. Later on I associated this stink with the rubbing noise made by velvet trousers as people walked by. My fourth memory is disagreeable: the anguish from nightmares of walking along the edge of the church belfry parapet. I have always been afraid of heights. I am a flatlands animal, able to tolerate only the slightest undulations—a horizontal beast.

After that my memory harbors a confused tumult of images and memories. Out of this inextricable disorder emerges, with great precision, the surprise I felt the day I urinated and realized the liquid smelled of wild asparagus. Two hours earlier I'd eaten an asparagus omelet. Immediately I grasped the law of cause and effect.

My education began early, at the age of three. I went to the school the Marian brothers had established in the Rajola neighborhood of Palafrugell. The *hermanos* dressed strangely, which may be why I felt such intense spontaneous respect for them. Their habits were tied with a tasseled cord, and they wore capes over their backs that were half the length of those worn by rural landowners in France. They also had small hats that came as a surprise in a country where the majority of priests wore birettas, and sported black linen socks in low-cut shoes. Despite their peculiar attire, the school was excellent, serious, and disciplined. I will never forget Brother Blas, who taught me the basics with such efficiency and speed.

The school also had an excellent location: The classrooms were south-facing and received all the breezy light and warmth from the plains of Calella. The playground was large and sunny. What unforgettably good times I enjoyed there! Each season of the year had its special game: spinning tops, color-flecked marbles, leapfrog and statues, football, hurling sticks. There was a miserable pomegranate tree in one corner of the playground. Despite the knocks it took and the injuries it displayed, the tree still flowered every year, a wonderful mass of crimson flowers and yellow pistils. At my desk I gazed in awe for hours at the pomegranate tree set against a deep blue, pink, or green sky, a blue-green porcelain sky on days when the north wind blew!

On Thursdays we went to the Marquès plantation, a huge garden of pine trees in neat, symmetrical rows against an exuberant backdrop of the old country houses in Ermedàs, framed by avenues of tall pines. That dark, mushroom-scented grove, where a dreamy light shimmered, sent me into ecstasy. At night, I would think about the gray, lonely sound of the wind whistling through the high branches and I'd see the warm, still light floating beneath the golden green of the trees.

In 1904 we went to live in the house my father had built on carrer del Sol. I was seven at the time. My sister Rosa was crawling, but about to walk. When we moved, the painters and wallpaper hangers were still hard at work. In the sitting room a mustachioed local spent several days at the top of a ladder, his neck twisted and his tongue stuck slightly out, painting chubby putti on the ceiling. With a very thin brush he added the final touches to the cherubim bottoms while humming under his mustache, at a slow, old-fashioned tempo: "Sparrow, o sparrow, how you liked to lark when you went to bed..." There was the fresh smell of a new, likable house everywhere. My first memory of reading is linked to this house: It was there on a hot summer evening I read the news of Morral's bomb attack on King Alfonso and Eugenie. It was the first thing I ever sat down to read right through.

And one fine day, I don't know when or prompted by what, I discovered that we ate well at home, objectively speaking, if I might say so. Though perhaps that came later, when I was older. In any case it was quite a discovery. It was my first inkling of how important it is for families of good standing to keep to the tradition of combining a touch of imagination and a well-honed sense of reality when going to the marketplace.

11 March. Today I walked past the house where I was born on carrer Nou—or carrer del Progrés. Its high, cold, sinister façade, striped by rain, suggested nothing; its walls evoked nothing. Not one memory—except for the orchard behind the house. On the other hand, there is nothing in our home on carrer del Sol that doesn't bring back floods of memories of childhood, adolescence, and countless things the passage of time hasn't entirely erased.

As a child I was very shy. I still am, and my innumerable gaffes in polite company are symptomatic: I'm reasonably complex if also rather gauche. I believe that at the time my brother Pere was at least as shy as I was. The village priest, Mossèn Soler de Morell, was a frequent visitor at home. It was an old friendship that dated back to the execution of Sr. Esteve Casadevall's will. The rector carried a copy of the will to the curia in Girona inside a briefcase wrapped in a dark gray cloth. Naturally he was given a triumphant welcome and received with exultant paeans of praise.

Mossèn Soler was a pinkish-white old man with fine straw-colored hair; he was small and well preserved, with a celluloid sheen and as dumpy as a baby rabbit. His bright purplish eyes lacked inquisitorial venom and kept up admirably with the tone of his every sentence. His adorable, highly eloquent gestures made him a delightful gentleman, with a charming, sugary, and affectionate manner. He wore his heart on his sleeve—this fact is not to be denied.

And yet the usual meaning of that phrase has always made me feel extremely uneasy, I'm ashamed to admit. I'm not sure how to put this: I've always felt that phrase to be inseparable from excessive artifice, absurd pretense, and irritating, monotonous sincerity. I've always been averse to wallowing in voluptuous emotion, and am brusque, prickly, and uncouth in my temperament. If I were to say I'm not as sensual as your average man in this country, people would laugh. But the laughter would be even louder—especially from my friends—if I were to claim that I am a voluptuary. I am far from voluptuous, even in my use of adjectives. When I am drinking, I don't want a few exquisite drops. I prefer large, full, elegant glasses.

When Mossèn Soler went for a stroll down local streets or on the outskirts of town, he was always preceded by the rectory dog—a small, fat, stumpy-legged animal, his fur white but for a black spot above his eye. He had no tail and breathed with difficulty. Whenever my brother and I saw that dog, a kind of anguish overcame us. We would dive around the next street corner, break into a run, and flee . . .

Mossèn Soler's fulsome greetings were inevitably accompanied by the gentlest of good advice, and gifts of religious prints and sweets. In the street he struggled to break free from children who rushed in a tumult to be his friend and kiss his hand—they'd knock heads in the race to get to him first. When I bumped into him, I didn't know where to look, what to say, or where to put my hands and feet. One day, when I was at home, the doorbell rang. I went to see who it was. It was Mossèn Soler smiling sweetly, with his dog between his legs. My spirits dropped. I stepped back, swung around, and ran into the garden where I hid behind the woodpile.

This is all very strange, unjustified, and gratuitous. It really is. It would be equally absurd to imagine I didn't feel the greatest respect for that holy man.

When we moved to the new house on carrer del Sol—and this is one of my oldest memories—all father's friends came to visit. In general, the building was a success. One day Dr. Pons came: a doctor for minor ailments. I watched him inspect every nook and cranny, taking his time. Finally, after the usual congratulations, as he was saying his farewells by the storm door, Dr. Pons nudged my father in the arm and said in a voice hoarse with laughter, "It is a fine house, Tonet. One of the best in town. I congratulate you. You have married well!"

Tonet is how all my father's closest friends addressed him. Those who were on less intimate terms called him Sr. Tonet.

Now when you are seven years old, everything is a mystery. But at that age some mysteries have drawbacks and become obsessions you can't get out of your mind. What was Dr. Pons suggesting with those words "You have married well! I congratulate you!"? For ages I tried to fathom what he meant. Much later, in the thick of life's difficulties, I began to have an inkling...

I remember so much from that period. The long, chilly winters that I reckon were much colder than they are now; the impetuous north winds that sometimes blew for a while and left the country in an exhausted, worn-out state of convalescence; the freezing rooms with mosaic tiles that felt like blocks of ice underfoot; the icicles dripping onto the balconies overlooking the street; the pinkish frost on top of the broccoli in the garden; the sound of the wind blowing down chimneys and the acrid smoke they exhaled that made us choke; the days of endless rain that we spent in the attic pretending to say mass, or watching the rain pour down, our noses pressed against the windowpanes, or the magic of our excitement at the silent, restful snow...

On Sunday mornings we went to church in our best clothes. We were stiff with cold. Our mother took us with Aunt Lluïsa, father's sister, a pious spinster, a Daughter of Maria, very much in the know about the gossip concerning the local clergy. Auntie talked about religion, in a vein of homespun piety. She always said, "Our Lord, poor man..."

Obviously she was referring to Jesus Christ our Lord, because our eternal Father stared down from the highest part of the main altarpiece, under the ceiling, with his large white beard, imperious eye, and apparently iron constitution, albeit well preserved, and to call him a "poor man" would have been both improper and inexact. Auntie was a Daughter of Maria, had the run of the church, and excellent taste when it came to the flowers and altar cloths. We liked listening to her. She was pious in a warm, tender, and remarkably self-sacrificing way.

Sunday after Sunday the rosary prayers sounded sweet and gentle in the yellow candlelight. But then there would be a big festival, a time for the triduum or novena, when an outside preacher came and the altar looked magnificent. The resonant, rapturous Churrigueresque altarpiece, bathed in light from candles and the four chandeliers that hung from the ceiling, was splendid to behold. It had been conceived as a great spectacle but was much more than that on the holiest of days: The light would cling to the sacred wood carvings, blur the figures and faces on what appeared to be a huge glossy dish of apple stuffing splashed by shiny golden juice that trickled and ran. Sermons were customarily in Spanish, and the local preachers who usually gave them seemed more Spanish than the genuine item. They were verbose, declamatory, and gesticulated dramatically. They spoke and performed with the violence of conviction. The fashion at the time was to speak in the most convoluted way possible, for long, confused periods. The priests sounded extremely elegant, or at least they thought so. In the bright light, you could see them soaked in sweat, flushed and frenzied. Shocked at first, people then listened in a state of benign satisfaction and pious well-being, comfortable in their pews. When the preacher finally descended from his pulpit, the congregation exchanged glances, anxious that the sermon might have been too short or the preacher too plainspoken.

The town's main holiday was Saint Margaret's Day, July 20. After that, we went to Calella and spent a month by the beach. My mother had inherited the small house Sr. Casadevall and his wife, Donya Beatriu, had built in El Canadell. We enjoyed a delightful month—a month that flew by in no time—fishing, swimming, rowing, and rock-climbing. We owned a small boat called *Nuestra Señora del Carmen* that was registered in Palamós. We really liked rowing. We rowed for hours and hours, and hardly ever got tired. The sun skinned us alive. We roasted and we turned black and brown, and our pupils shrank so much you could hardly see them.

The day after Saint Rose's Day (August 30) we returned to Palafrugell in the cart that also carried our mattresses. Accustomed as we were to fresh air and a life of leisure and freedom, we found the town cramped, its streets oppressive and badly ventilated. Wearing shoes was a trial. Our clothes constrained us. Buttoning our collars was tricky. Everything seemed tight. The first showers fell in mid-September and the country took on a mellow, autumnal hue. The air was pure, the land lost its harshness, and the incandescent skies of summer turned warm light blue. The rain made it easier to fit our buttons in their buttonholes.

In September we spent a few days at the Pla farmstead. Jaume and Francisca, the tenant farmers, would be waiting for us at the entrance. A tall, skinny old man with huge ears, Jaume loved to clown and would take us to eat figs and grapes or stroll among the pines. There he also read to us, usually a Catalan translation of Aesop's *Fables*, a book illustrated with clumsy, stiff woodcuts full of drama. He found the animal stories highly amusing and the morals of the fables were for him rules for life.

Sometimes he picked up his juniper walking stick and suggested we go with him to Mont-ras to see his friends. Martí Macies and Joan Companys were his age, renowned cork peelers who liked good wine and a hand of cards. Macies, small and weedy with sunken cheeks and rotten teeth, smoked a pipe with a reed stem. Weasel-thin, he recounted dubious, labyrinthine stories in a sharp, piping voice. Joan Companys was a stocky, sturdy fellow, pockmarked by smallpox, baldpated, beardless with a pinkish complexion. His voice was loud and gravelly, and he laughed like a child and—perhaps quite unconsciously—acted as the foil in the games set up by Macies, whom he admired. Camaraderie transformed those three men when they got together. They drank huge quantities of wine or anisette, and ate walnuts, a handful of hazelnuts, and a few almonds with a crust of bread to soak up the liquid. They looked like men from classical antiquity.

When we returned to the farmhouse, in the evening we'd sit in a circle by the doorway, separating the wheat from the chaff. Jaume told us endless stories of thieving and adventures from the Second Carlist War. An oil lamp burnt above, projecting monstrous shadows onto the walls and vaulted ceiling. The light was so small and feeble and died so slowly and meekly that we were all almost asleep by the time it went out for good.

Then it was time to go to bed. But when we went upstairs, carrying our candles, a horrendous fear seized us. The house was low and dark, full of odd agricultural implements we weren't used to. Strange, terrifying shapes loomed in the half dark. Doors banged, were locked and bolted. Upstairs we bumped into the corners of wardrobes, cupboards, and the sides of beds. We felt these bumps when we had half shut our eyes and averted our gaze, and tried to hide our terror. It was horrible. Once in bed, once the candles had been snuffed out, in the pitch black our fears vanished. Then sleep took over.

14 March. Now, finally, it's a real joy to live in Catalonia. That's unanimous. Everybody agrees. Inevitably we all have, have had, or will have influenza.

Every day for the last four or five years I have been reading Xènius's *Glosari*. Currently people don't seem as fond as they used to be of the column Eugeni d'Ors writes. Personally I find the *Glosari* affected and at times showy. I always mistrust people who try to be arty.

Sometimes I wonder whether concupiscence—what is normally called concupiscence—isn't one of the most potent human motives for action. Unfortunately I'm not drawn to action. I'm not fascinated by whirlwinds or even curious to imagine what one is like. The river flows, and I want to stay seated on the bank. My reading of Baroja's novels—novels I have devoured eagerly in recent days—has swept away any of my genes for action. Baroja is a very active anti-aphrodisiac. He is a mystic, devoid of the imaginative, whimsical charm mystics often possess. In this sense, his books have done me a lot of harm. Perhaps one shouldn't read such rabidly ascetic books—or at least not without alternating them with pornography.

Honesty in the Ampurdan. The civil guards lead a young lad in handcuffs down carrer Estret. He is swarthy, skinny, with a beautifully combed forelock. Slung over his shoulder is a sackful of rabbits and hens that are moving around. When they walk past us, a woman next to me exclaims, mouth wide open, "What a shock! He seemed so honest."

16 March. Sr. Balaguer, the clerk at the magistrate's court, likes to join my father for a coffee. He is very affable. Whenever he sees me, he says, "Come to court! It will be good practice for your degree. You can read papers and see things of interest."

"The court must be about to open," I respond.

"After ten...that's what I call a reasonable time."

I went to the magistrate's court today, after ten. It occupies a corner of the town hall. Five or six steps up from the street you enter a large, bare, high-ceilinged room lit by a window that overlooks a stiflingly hot inner yard. There are two or three tables, a few chairs, and a coatrack, and on the back wall a crucifix and a photo of the king. A low door, with a single leaf, leads into the magistrate's office. I am familiar with this office from my other visits: It's tiny, with shelves of books and papers, and a stove with a chimney pipe that pokes out of the window over the street.

The lights come on as I walk in. Two bulbs inject a diluted, floury yellow into the dismal, opaque glow from the inner yard. The air is acrid with stale tobacco and the stench of untrimmed paper.

I linger for a second on the threshold. Sr. Balaguer is sitting at the back table, which is piled high with documents, books, and copies of *La Gaceta de Madrid*—a genuinely judicial hotchpotch. Behind him, on a hanger, are the broad-collared cape and bowler that I have often seen Sr. Guardiola, the court clerk, wearing in the street. Complete silence reigns—the silence that comes from the staff being half asleep. I can hear the pen of Sr. Balaguer scrape the paper as he scrawls in his solemn, pompous handwriting.

I take a step back. The bailiff, hat on, sits behind the door eating with his fingers: fried fish on a slice of bread. His mouth and mustache drip with oil. He eats obsessively, wholly engrossed in his crispy red sea bream.

Finally Sr. Balaguer finally notices me. He leaves his table, comes over, and escorts me to Sr. Guardiola at the back of the room. Sr. Guardiola greets me warmly, stands up straight, his mouth puckering like a hen's behind, as he swoops his arm forward to stroke my cheek in mannered fashion.

"Oh, esteemed sir!" he says, excessively politely. "Welcome to this establishment . . . Balaguer, you see to him. We can talk later. I am rather busy at the moment. I do apologize, my dear Pla. Please make yourself at home."

Tripping along like a young lady, body sashaying, holding his paperwork pertly between two fingers, Sr. Guardiola crosses the room and shuts himself in the magistrate's office.

Sr. Balaguer, in the meantime, sits me down at his table, facing him. He shows me how to fold wax-sealed documents, offers me a pen and invites me to copy a death certificate from a very thick tome of the civil register. Burning with enthusiasm, I start to write.

After scraping away for ten minutes, the task becomes mechanical. Meanwhile, I think about Sr. Guardiola. A strange man! He must be in his fifties; he is tall, flabby, gaunt, pink-faced, with bluish eyes. Bald on top, he backcombs a greased sheet of hair flat over his head, like a thin wig. His whole body gives an impression of softness, of lack of consistency. A confirmed bachelor, he lives with his sister—a pious lady who puts on airs. With her at his side, his career has been one long pilgrimage across the shabby offices of the judiciary. His appearance, his way of walking, talking, and dressing, his gestures have contributed to a widely held hypothesis about the equivocal nature of his sex. He's become a laughingstock to many, and in this sense, his life must have been very hard. His attire is distinguished by three distinct items: a bowler hat shiny with overuse, a white waistcoat with pink mother-of-pearl buttons, and a short cloak with a red velvet lining. His feminine, playfully coquettish way of walking recalls some ridiculous, superannuated, crazy music-hall singer.

As I'm thinking about this, in walks the Kid, Paguina by name, bell ringer at the church and messenger boy for the rectory. He is a small, lean, stooping hunchback, with a twisting posture and sidelong walk, always sucking on a cheap cheroot. He heads towards Sr. Balaguer's table, and without removing his hat inquires in a high, piping voice that makes my skin crawl, "Has that idiot finished the job?"

"What do you mean, 'that idiot'?" ripostes Sr. Balaguer, hardly concealing his indignation.

"I mean Sr. Guardiola. He promised the birth certificate five days ago and it's still not ready. The vicar needs to see it."

"Will you please watch your language?" Sr. Balaguer replies edgily. "Be careful with the words you use."

At this point in the conversation the door to the magistrate's office flies open and Sr. Guardiola—who has probably heard every word they were shouting—twists half his body around the door and with a cheerful, most affectionate look on his face says, "Please, Paguina, come back this afternoon, after six, and you will have it. Please give my best regards to the vicar."

Paguina's response is dry and lugubrious: "If you say so!"

The door shuts. The bell ringer puffs on his cigar and moves away from the table. Sr. Balaguer observes his sad, silent departure, shrugs his shoulders to show his lack of interest, and goes back to work. The bailiff, having long since finished his breakfast, greets Paguina warmly at the front door. He then sits down in his corner chair, voluptuously inhaling the smoke from a cheap black cigar. It could be a stick of licorice.

I take a break, light a cigarette, and examine the office at length. The day has clouded over and the light from the yard is now an even duller, darker gray. In the corner opposite the bailiff, the darkest corner in the office, next to a bookcase with one end tilting forward under the weight of papers and volumes that I think must be the Alcubilla legal compendium, a man is sitting on a chair, absolutely motionless and in handcuffs. I am slightly taken aback. He is an old man, dressed in velvet, with an open shirtfront, bare head, and unkempt hair. He's grimy and must be a charcoal burner. He is so still and so deeply withdrawn that I assume he is asleep.

"Who is that, Sr. Balaguer?" I ask as quietly as I can manage.

"The civil guard brought him in this morning. A real yokel. I've never seen him before.

"And what did he do?"

"Apparently he stole two pesetas from a workmate."

"What will you do with him?"

"We're waiting for the magistrate."

"Is he out?"

"He told us he was going for lunch in Calella. I imagine he'll be back this afternoon."

"But what will you do with this fellow during lunch?"

"What do you think? We'll have to lock him up downstairs. There's no other option."

At a quarter to one on the dot, Sr. Guardiola emerges from his office, walks over to the hat stand, puts on his bowler and cape, bellows "Good day, everyone!," and heads towards the front door. As he walks past the desk, he glances lingeringly at his nails. When he has gone, a sweet, rancid trace of perfume hangs in the air.

A few seconds later, Sr. Balaguer opens a desk drawer, takes out a huge key, summons the bailiff, and hands him the key. He says, "Take this man downstairs."

"Shouldn't we give him some lunch?"

"You talk to him. You decide ... His Honor the magistrate should be here in the afternoon. We can't do a thing until then."

"Yes, sir. Very good."

I put on my cap and coat. Sr. Balaguer follows suit. We go to lunch, slowly, not saying a word.

In the evening I go to the café at the Fraternal Center. Almost all my friends are there. These include Tomàs Gallart, Joan B. Coromina, Enric Frigola, Josep Bofill de Carreres (known to everybody as Gori), Lluís Medir, Casabó the chemist, Josep Ganiquer. Deep in a long conversation about women, the usual conversation. Then someone introduces the subject of justice. I mean justice as a general principle.

One of the most marked differences between conversations in the Ampurdan and in Barcelona—when the participants are of equal social status—is, for example, that in the city they keep to empirical terrain: details, odd facts, anecdotes. But, in the Ampurdan, someone is always hell-bent on progressing from a confused bunch of details to a more general overview. When the word *justice* comes up, everyone automatically chuckles.

Tomàs Gallart remembers that when Josep Ferrer was a justice of the peace he always said that justice is very important, but no one should be in a hurry to administer it. Gori, who has been the town magistrate and wants to be so again because he believes the post is tailor-made for him, praises his insight to the skies. Bofill says, "Justice, when applied strictly, like a chemical agent, can be devastating and lead to a huge number of victims. In a world that is essentially unjust, theoretical, absolute justice can provoke violent revulsion. Justice must be handled judiciously, applied in small doses."

"The latest from the Russian Revolution suggests you are right," says Sr. Enric Frigola.

"Could be!" says Bofill. "The Russians are imposing justice on their country. They will suffer greatly and go through a wretched time of it. They'll be forced to create a cold, sinister police state. There will be great hunger and thirst, prisons will expand, and everything that brings pleasure to life will be abolished. And even so they won't have imposed justice. The way I see it there can be no sustaining collective life, not even at a minimal level, without a degree of injustice. Why must there be ugly women and *beautiful* women? Intelligent men and *stupid* men? Isn't that unjust? To apply justice, we'd have no choice but to kill those *beautiful* women and *intelligent* men."

Confusion escalates around the table. Nobody can think what to say. Coromina nervously bites a nail. The others act as if their minds are elsewhere: nose in the air, smoking. From pure fatigue, the gathering breaks up earlier than usual.

18 March. This morning I saw the first swallow of the year on the water tank in the garden. The bird had perched on the stone rim of the cistern, very close to the water's edge. With great difficulty it was attempting to drink.

In the afternoon, when I walked past the church, the swallows were mewling as they flew in large circles around the belfry. They circled, beaks open, chasing mosquitoes, flies, and insects.

Don Josep Gich, the pharmacist on carrer de Cavallers, was the magistrate in Palafrugell for years. I remember him as an old man and a shadow of himself: small, with a drooping mustache singed by chain-smoking, and tired red and yellow eyes floating in pools of lymph. At home, he wore a white—dazzlingly white—silk scarf around his neck. He was a politician with liberal inclinations, and in the animated conversations that took place at the pharmacy he apparently made and unmade reputations. He could lay claim to many incisive observations about the people of the Ampurdan and said we had such lively imaginations we mistook flies for eagles. Very true.

Despite such observations, Sr. Gich himself was a fine representative of the Ampurdan with a highly imaginative temperament. But there is an episode that shows he was also a man with great common sense.

One day the bailiff went to him and whispered mysteriously in his ear that he'd caught a man on top of a woman by the windmill outside town—or a woman on top of a man, I don't remember which way around.

"Forget it!" Sr. Gich retorted, with a very serious look. "That's nothing out of the ordinary. Please don't mention it again. Can't you understand that one simply stumbled over the other. Very funny things do happen."

The people of the Ampurdan are probably the most enthusiastic and elemental in all of Catalonia—provided their enthusiasm doesn't have to last too long.

One of the graces of the place is that it hardly ever produces the kind of man I, for my part, find especially irritating. The kind who likes to hear his own voice, who stares at his toe caps as he walks along, who jangles his coins and keys in his trouser pocket to show off, who talks endlessly about his trivial concerns and summons you to his side to speak in a hushed tone, and so on.

In the Ampurdan—and probably everywhere—it is the picturesque that fascinates. In this country, a man who knows how to milk that vein can literally do whatever he wants. Perhaps the picturesque brings its own kind of morality—significantly different from the conventional sort. Sometimes it is remarkable how quickly morality collapses before a boutade, a joke, a particular tone of voice, a piece of silliness, or even an adjective.

Our Lord God has given us poor folk a sense of the dignity of our own poverty. The poor man who doubts the dignity of his own poverty has more than one screw loose.

19 March. Saint Joseph. Grandma Marieta has sent us one of her special sponge cakes. My mother has made the cream. But just as my saint's day cream sponge cake followed tradition, so did today's desserts: custom and nothing more.

My father is a very methodical man.
    At ten on the dot, he locks the front door—after surveying the

house to make sure that everything open has been closed—and goes to Cafè Pallot. In the winter, whatever the weather, his coat is slung over his shoulder. He only really puts it on one day of the week: Sundays. He converses in the café with Sr. Balaguer, from the magistrate's court; Sr. Mascort, the clerk to the town hall; Emeri Gironés, a coal and timber merchant; Sr. Jordi, known as Quica, a first-rate, sophisticated confectioner; and if he happens to be in town, Sr. Rossend Girbal, known also as Girbal Jau, and, in the Rosselló, as the Fat Trader.

Sr. Rossend is a hefty member of the species, weighing in at more than two hundred and sixty pounds. He is a horse trader, and although he comes from a hundred percent Catholic bourgeois family, he has adopted Gypsy airs so wholeheartedly that his every mannerism derives from local Romany. Not only does he talk like a Gypsy but he is also vaguely unreliable, in a wistful, confused, absentminded fashion. He has the run of the café—in fact of countless cafés in the country—and is a highly valued conversation partner. He makes himself comfortable by occupying two chairs. Only he is automatically served a chaser when ordering coffee: a glass of anisette.

The conversation is pleasant enough, if a tad humdrum, proceeding in a permanent atmosphere of speculation and hypothesis. When the opening half hour of local gossip is done, talk turns to the inevitable question of what ought to be done: We'll do this, do that; should do this, should do that; what if we did this, did that. It isn't as if all participants are imbued with the same futurist frenzy. They differ by degrees. Sr. Mascort is the only one to remain stubbornly unmoved by this way of understanding the world. He is the relentlessly efficient bureaucrat, the fearsome clerk at the town hall.

Still, when Sr. Mascort starts speaking about his fondness for fishing—a sport he has been practicing for years, every Sunday, in Tamariu—he becomes, quite unawares, a raving, hallucinating prophet. One day we'll catch a red grouper, the next the perch will bite.

Sr. Girbal, half asleep, listens to this banal, wishful thinking with a hint of mute irritation. But sometimes he decides to restore a proper hierarchy to things. He demonstrates his own superiority by launching into a tirade with a supercilious twist. "Those among us who have tasted life in Perpignan," he says, "those who are familiar with life in Figueres..."

When the church clock strikes midnight, my father gets up: It is time for bed. If something out of the ordinary takes place in town or in the conversation, his timetable will change. A fire must be burning somewhere or an additional agricultural engineer must have chanced to join their circle. Otherwise twelve o'clock is the cutoff point.

Everybody wends his own way home from the café entrance.

Then Sr. Jordi, known as Quica, goes back to his sweetshop, selects the best, makes a delicious little parcel, and returns to the street. Well wrapped up, clutching his parcel, he walks along the darkest back streets and spends a while at one or another of the establishments with young ladies.

Read *The Planets of the Greenfinch* by Josep Carner.

When he writes in prose or verse, Carner is surely one of the most splendid stylists of the day. His tremendous control over the Catalan language and its mysteries triggers genuine envy. The dangers from such virtuosity: descent into provincialism, literary games for their own sake, and relinquishing content for form. Generally speaking, Carner is graceful—formally, that is always the case. Even though he is from Barcelona, he's never inelegant. The inelegance of Barcelona writers is sometimes visible even in society columns: like the pedantic, precious rural tics of writers from outside the city.

In Josep Carner's work, the literary fireworks exceed any genuine human feeling. A mountain gives birth to a mouse. Carner seems like a man who has imposed frontiers on his mental life out of tact—or timidity, perhaps—or even, perhaps, out of a sense of the absurd.

21 March. We practice a very peculiar custom in this part of the world. When two of us meet face-to-face in the street, we can hardly think of a thing to say. However, after we have said goodbye and walked on seven or eight paces, a whole series of items spring to mind that we must urgently communicate to the individual we left only a moment ago. We shout out, summon them, raise our voices, and wave our arms wildly. Naturally, the other person replies, shouts, and waves equally energetically. As we stroll along and the distance from our interlocutor increases, the conversation turns into a horrendous shouting match. In the end, the distance is so great it is almost impossible to hear anything. Then one of us will say, with a great effort, "All right, let's talk some other time."

The other replies, like a man possessed, "Yes, indeed, another time."

And when we do finally meet again, we find nothing to say.

Out of the blue, some of father's friends decided to create a place to go to drink their coffee and converse without too much bother. They asked him to come up with a name in the spirit of the locality that reflects the purpose they have in mind. He suggested calling the place Porxo d'En Massot with the secondary title of Traditionalist Republican Center.

Porxo d'En Massot was a throwback to Mont-ras and my father's youth. The Massot family were liberal republicans from this village and wielded huge influence, especially Massot senior. On Sundays fellow believers from the neighborhood met under the porch at the Massots' house, and everyone wore a red beret. It was both a political meeting and a chance to relax: They drank local wine, played cards, and insulted the government. Grandma Marieta, a close friend of the old gentleman, would say, "Grandfather Massot never went to mass, but he was the best man in Mont-ras, the most sensible and perceptive of men. He spoke his mind when people carried on like fools."

My father often went to Porxo d'En Massot as a child; he also has fond memories of this man.

On the other hand, the addition—I mean the Traditionalist Republican Center—is a splendid idea. At first sight the name looks like a contradiction and probably would be anywhere apart from the Ampurdan. Here, however, republicanism is one of the few real, living traditions with the advantage that it is relatively recent. Other traditions disappear into obscurity with the passage of time and now serve practically no purpose.

Moreover, it is just like my father to come up with this name. For a man with a rather stiff, insecure, whimsical temperament, quick to slide from anguish into depression, the name represents an attempt to overcome the quandary by aligning the conflicting elements in the dilemma.

"It's a good name," I told him one day, "but Hegel would have reached a synthesis."

"Don't talk to me about syntheses!" he responded in horror.

"No, no. It *is* a handsome name …"

After several years of heated conversations, Porxo d'En Massot dissolved and Club 3 x 4 was established in the same house on carrer de Cavallers. The slightly Kabbalistic name meant simply that the club was restricted to twelve members. Its founders, nearly all exporters of bottle corks to central Europe, always fancied the most childish, Germanic buffoonery. Later they decided that anyone could join the club provided he was an orthodox believer in capitalism, and the group came to be called Club 3 x 4 *Plus*.

My mother subscribes to *El Pan de los Pobres*, a pious biweekly from Bilbao that promotes charity in every imaginable shape and offers tips on how to perform all sorts of easy, unobtrusive, unfussy, homespun miracles. One miracle allows students who have fallen hopelessly behind in their studies to pass their school certificate exams.

"Maybe," I tell my mother with a chuckle, "it would make more sense just to be charitable instead of subscribing to magazines about it."

Eyes wide open, she stares rooted to the spot. She seems deeply shocked.

Joan B. Coromina says that in the café he overheard a young, excited nineteen-year-old ask his seventeen-year-old fiancée: "Carmeta, can you imagine what we will be like when we're an old, old couple?"

24 March. When Gori returns from hunting or an outing, he heads straight to his haberdashery on carrer de Cavallers, makes himself comfortable in his small study, and reads until it's time for supper.

Pauleta, a relative of his, sees to the customers' needs in a pleasant, friendly manner.

As a reader, Gori is a singular specimen. It would be an exaggeration to say he likes his literature heroic, full of swords and sabers, but he *is* fascinated by the ethereal and precious, books charged with emotional affectation, featuring extraordinary feats and characters with only a tenuous grip on reality.

He is scathing about Rousseau's *Confessions* but has the highest praise for *Julie, or the New Heloise* and in particular *Reveries of a Solitary Walker*. He finds positive satisfaction in the sort of thing now considered dull, insipid, and rarefied, particularly if it is furnished with fake landscapes, bogus idylls, and cardboard sentiments. I'm amazed that such a tall, burly man—and Gori is *very* tall and *very* burly—who drinks two pints of 16 percent wine and stuffs himself with tasty fish, hare, rabbit, and partridge, should like such faded, evanescent whimsy.

Today, in his office, he told me that if anyone is mistaken, confused, and clueless when it comes to literature, it's me.

"Literature," he said, "should be idealistic, delicate, out of the ordinary. It should come from here"—and he placed his hand over his heart.

"And why must literature be like that?" I asked.

"Because literature is for moments when there is nothing to do, when nothing is pressing, the only time there's a vague possibility that people might want to curl up with a book. Man wasn't brought into this world to read books. Make no mistake . . . the single serious problem we face in this world is how to get by, that is, how to earn or spend money. Men and women devote ninety-eight percent of their conscious life to that. And that's probably an understatement. So, literature will always be a Sunday-afternoon activity, a moment on the day in the week when maybe—and this was truer years ago, since nowadays people go to the movies—*maybe* they'll feel like some distraction from their abiding obsessions. And you expect them to pine for your raw, spare, realist fiction? Why? They've already had more than their fill of your real life. Your kind of literature is redundant, flat-footed, commonplace, blindingly obvious."

"I see what you mean."

"It would be a great pity if you didn't!" he responds triumphantly, then paused to allow his loud guffaws to evaporate in the air of his small office. "To sum up!" he says. "You like literature for every day and so you overrate your craft. That is why literature written today is full of trivia. It would do you good to remember that until very recently, your trade only gained you admission via the tradesman's entrance. No, what I like is *good* literature, extraordinary scenes, and exceptional feelings, perfect literature for a pleasant Sunday afternoon."

We go on discussing his recent visit to Barcelona. In the course of these business trips to the capital, he insists on going to the best "performances" at the theater. Now he remembers the last one he saw and waxes indignant, yells, flies off the handle.

"They expect you to pay to see reality, things that happen every day, things you can see by simply looking out of the window! This is intolerable! This is unacceptable! I'm never going to the theater again." He makes the sign of the cross.

According to the papers, though the Germans are still winning on all fronts, they have lost the war—it is in its death throes. Arguments between the pro-French camp and the pro-German one are more infrequent by the day. They've lost whatever interest they had. The pro-Germans have grown quieter, more and more of them can be seen wearing badges in their lapels that say: *Don't talk to me about the war.* A piece of absurd escapism.

"The Ampurdan," I hear people say, "is a country of whimsy lovers, rakes, wastrels, and fly-by-nights." That's true enough.

But it is also true that in this region people abound who spend their lives raising objections, putting spokes in the wheels of anyone keen enough to take initiative or try somehow to break with routine. Objections proliferate from all sides until people learn to hold their tongues. If you want to kill fruit parasites or the mole crickets that devastate the potato crop or to exterminate the common fly or challenge the stinginess of small farmers, all you will hear is constant carping: "You want to do that? And why on earth? You say we don't have any get-up-and-go? These things aren't going to happen. You fool! You don't know what you're talking about."

In this country, a love of whimsy may just be the sign of a listless fellow who is exhausted from being put down publicly and treated as a buffoon and simpleton all the time.

Then there are the constitutionally fanciful, the rakes who are driven by inner energy, and the professional wastrels. However, they are quite different.

25 March. I entered the church. That nasty, indefinable stench—the stench of air that has been breathed time and again, that is stale and ravaged, deprived of oxygen and reduced to an ancient, dense concentrate of microbes, a sweetish, insipid, sticky, unpleasant air that gives you goose bumps.

I apologize, but I'm sensitive to those, let us say, petty details. Two things have forged my sensibility which requires fresh air and cleanliness: the cold I have to endure in the house on carrer del Sol (the house where we live) and my mother's almost frenzied addiction to domestic chores. My mother—forgive me for saying so—is wedded to cleaning up tirelessly, constantly, and can never rest. Voltaire, in *The Century of Louis XIV*, relates how Minister Colbert, on entering his office and seeing a table heaped with papers to be dispatched, will rub his hands in delight. My mother likes nothing more than to have a big clean-out, a long, interminable Saturday, overseeing the painters doing a thorough whitewash and moving furniture endlessly.

The land on which my father built the house on carrer del Sol was called the Field of Eggs. This was the road from the town to the station after the "small" train had been opened. This house is situated differently from the one where I spent my childhood on carrer Nou. That house faced north, so the back rooms were very comfortable. I still remember conversations in the sunny dining room with plump, petite Srta. Enriqueta, who was so good-natured and so expertly squeezed into her corset, though slightly herpetic. The house on carrer del Sol, on the other hand, faces south, making its north-facing living rooms cold and gloomy. It wouldn't be so bad if a gallery had been built over the ground-floor rooms, but no gallery was, and from the moment we stepped into that house, we had to get used to the cold.

It was a distilled, filtered, chemically concentrated pure cold. And that was the least of it. There was a fire in the dining room on the harshest, most unforgiving days, it is true, yet even that wasn't straightforward. My mother was against it always: She said that fire brings disorder and dirt. And she was right to an extent. Only sometimes when the wind blew from a particular direction—I don't remember which—would the chimney draw normally. Nobody knew how to build a chimney back then, and if you had one that worked, well that was pure chance, a gift of providence.

It was bitingly cold. The floor tiles were icy, the air chilling. My mother had to admit—her manic cleanliness didn't prevent her from being objective—that to live in that house was like going naked all winter. But the only thing anybody ever did was to put on more clothes while my mother frantically opened windows and doors, no matter that it was freezing. Half a minute out of bed and all the balcony doors were open wide. The tiles were wiped clean every two days, and week in week out, Saturdays were for cleaning.

This meant that the air inside the house was extremely pure—as pure as the outdoor air. I became used to intensely fresh, odorless air. I remember those days with horror—I must confess—and yet that Spartan temperature endowed me with me a hyperactive pituitary gland. Ever since I've been repelled by stuffy rooms and other closed-off spaces, where people are or have been, leaving behind the stale smell that people do. I also can't stand individuals drenched in sticky sweet perfumes. The smell of stale cigarette smoke—smoked smoke—of food gone cold, of wine that has been drunk, provokes a somatic crisis, my whole metabolism protests. The smell of air that has been breathed, ravaged, looted, decomposed, the smell of secondhand air that you find in a church, this always forces me to make a quick exit.

You might think that a watchmaker's shop would be the most gleaming, precise, orderly, and agreeable shop in the world. Quite the reverse is true.

You go in and not a single watch or clock marks the same beat or rhythm. Some maintain a stately, solemn pace. Others proceed at an anxious, agitated rate, as if they are in a hurry and want to catch up and pass all the rest. In a watchmaker's shop the awful superimposed layers of tick-tocks, confused rhythms, stressing out-of-sync pulsations create a din that provokes an absurd sensation of anguish. This is no place for anyone with a nervous condition: It is *not* a good place at all. On the other hand, I can imagine a watchmaker's shop where watches and clocks have all stopped and . . . have even been turned to face the wall, because nothing induces calm like a clock that has come to a halt—a watch that has fallen asleep.

Fortunately, it is physically impossible to simulate sincerity, so whenever I come across a person—and they are rife here—who proclaims his sincerity or invites me, whether or not it's opportune, to act in a fantastically (as they usually put it) sincere way, I feel I am dealing with the most childish, vulgar form of hypocrisy. Hypocrisy has this advantage: The slightest excess and it sticks out a mile.

During the morning, I try yet again to read Jacint Verdaguer. So far I have been unable to finish a single canto from *L'Atlàntida* or *Canigó.* I am almost ashamed to admit to this . . . I make another effort. I will try once more. I sink my teeth in . . . but I can't swallow the cake. The colossal scale of the geology, all those extraordinary stories don't appeal in the slightest. I understand that these pages represent something grand and imposing and that literature must contain such hulks just as great palaces require vast, ornate fireplaces that don't give off any heat, along with tapestries on their walls. I also understand that my sensibility is sorely at fault. But I can do no more. What a feeling of emptiness! What a flood of rhetoric completely disconnected from genuine, human life! These grandiose, sonorous stanzas kill my interest and curiosity dead.

I once heard someone say with a sigh: "Oh, the mysticism, the mystical poetry of Verdaguer!"

But please tell me what connection there is between mysticism and this country of small farmers, greenhorn merchants, and industrialists. And please tell me what Verdaguer was up to when he linked us, through mysticism, to what is an intrinsically alien way of writing.

People don't seem to grasp, though one day they'll have no choice, that the way today's writers relate to reality, the curiosity that inspires them, the passion that drives them, reflect a sensibility that is completely different from the academicism of previous eras and society. What came before was the exception: Realism is now the rule.

2 April. "I've always been poor," says Joan B. Coromina in the café, "so I've spent a lot of time listening to people."

"Are you boasting about being poor?" asks Gori, starting indignantly.

"Naturally. I don't think I've wasted my time—"

"I'll make you eat your own words. Do you think there is *any* reason to think poverty interesting? If you say so, you are a pathetic bore!" says Gori, flaring up, thumping the table, his eyes bloodshot, visibly affected by the wine at dinner.

He pays up and leaves without even a good night. Those of us still around the table are slightly taken aback. Coromina has turned as white as a sheet.

"Coromina is right!" says Enric Frigola, with his customary mix of timidity and coldness. Frigola is a landowner who has lived in the United States. He is the languages teacher at the town school. He adds: "Poverty brings few advantages, evidently, but it does bring one: the need to listen to people. I don't mean you must listen to everybody. You have to listen to the right person. And you better listen carefully or at least look like you are. You must appear to be genuinely fascinated by the person who is speaking. Your thoughts may be elsewhere but you must look like you are being attentive and hanging on every word. That's easy enough: Keep an alert eye, and wear a warm and friendly expression, nod your head in time to the ideas your interlocutor is formulating. And from time to time add: 'Would you be so good as to repeat what you said a moment ago? Would you be so kind as to clarify that concept you elaborated a second ago?' Men like being listened to. They like it more than money, women, good food, and wine. A man with an audience becomes a total show-off. It's also true that when men realize they have an audience, they weaken. These moments of frailty are cracks in human granite from which shards of generosity may fall. A poor man may be in luck. If he doesn't know how to create such moments or benefit from them, then he really is in a bad way indeed. Men and women have naturally established a system of parasitic existence based on flattery—on the sheer physical pleasure of being flattered—and the most common, most surreptitious (hence, most enduring) form of flattery is knowing how to listen discreetly but actively. Act natural, which is easier to do if you aren't so stupid as to let on about anything you might know. You have to hide your own knowledge on the matter in hand—presuming you have any—but without going so far as to highlight your stupidity." Frigola speaks very quickly, and his hands shake slightly, though he never actually gesticulates. He is embarrassed to speak, so he blushes and then grins sarcastically.

"You see," he continues, "the art of listening is incredibly exhausting and it is worth having an income to spare yourself having to practice it. To my mind, the most tangible, pleasant form of independence is being able to live without being forced to listen to anyone. The strongest men, with robust biological resources, usually don't listen to anyone. They make a big impact. They hurl themselves into projects blindly, unthinkingly, relying on their instincts, or on highly idiosyncratic, very obscure calculations of their own. They never heed other people. In the Old Testament, the strong, powerful, dominant characters act without a trace of forethought, without caution, swept along by the impetuous ebb and flow of their temperaments. It is astonishing, the lack of awareness and sheer lunacy that spurs humans into actions that are then deemed to be important."

A pause—a long one. A deep silence descends on the table—silence amid the din from other tables. Frigola glances up at the ceiling, wrinkles his forehead and frowns as if the effort hurts, takes two or three drags on his cigarette, and suddenly says, anxiously, "I can't remember what I was going to say."

We all felt immensely relieved, as if a great burden had been lifted from our minds.

When we leave the café we hear a fire alarm and go to see what is wrong. It is a small, insignificant fire: a cork seller's tiny shop on carrer de la Rajola that is burning, flaring like a sulfur match.

Years ago, whenever there was a fire, half the town would come out to watch. I am surprised to see only a handful of people watching this fire: two night watchmen, a couple of civil guards, neighbors hoping that the flames won't spread, and two or three idlers from the local tavern. In recent years, with the difficulties brought by the war, there have been so many fires that people have lost interest. The small shop is burning amid general indifference and without the sound of a single bucket.

"This is already old news," says Tomàs Gallart. "Good night, sleep well, tomorrow is another day."

We walk off, heading to bed.

6 April. If ever I decide to pen portraits of my family, perhaps the following details might come in handy.

By virtue of that curious principle, vigorously upheld in our country, that makes us believe we are different from the way we really are, my father has always been taken to be a practical man, a man of action. This involved him in a series of adventures that have left him bruised all over and, finally, bankrupt. He should have performed admirably in any task he was assigned to do because he is an intelligent, conscientious man. Naturally enthusiastic, he is convinced that, with the country in such a backward state, there is everything to do and he should have been a first-rate team player in new endeavors. However, his positive qualities were undermined by his inability to master the economic side of life. Many of his friends tell him that if he'd limited himself to going to the café and reading the paper, he'd have doubled his fortune and led a life of luxury.

He finds criticism of his lack of practicality galling. He defends himself by recalling how little in the way of conscience exists in a world that cannot stomach honest individuals. And that is true enough: There is little morality in this world. But if you possess such a finicky moral sense you should perhaps enter a monastery or stay at home. It is easy to hold forth on what it means to be moral when you are outside the world of business. Doing so on the inside is dangerous. This is an unpleasant truth, but once you've gone to the dance you must dance.

What does a proper upbringing—something people are always talking about—entail? I've never managed to work it out. Sometimes I concluded that a proper upbringing is all about instilling respect—a blind respect of authority, respect that is imposed, not freely given. Parents are figures on pedestals that children must obey. In my family's case, obedience is achieved not by using coercion but by maintaining distance between children and parents. This was how it was done in my country—the only method apart from the cane. Children were vulnerable, parents provided a natural shelter, and respect grew. But in late adolescence there was a moment when a meltdown began: Respect became a form of irony and bonds grew brittle. Some children are mere stumps, part of the vegetation; others can be almost unpleasantly ironic and are best kept well out of sight. It is a small, very complex world.

In truth, a so-called proper upbringing meant leaving it up to the school. Today I suspect that our parents lacked the ability or means to resolve the crux. Their only choice was to pass the "parcel" on to the school. I don't recall a single conversation with my parents, before or immediately after I reached the age of reason, about anything other than everyday family life—the administrative side, as it were. At school—at least the one I went to—I never saw anyone take the slightest interest in a proper family upbringing. At the time, pedagogy didn't include elements of affection, any activity that wasn't strictly instructional. I suppose that must always have been the case. Pedagogy has never involved affection—or if it has, affection was kept well hidden, barely visible. At school, respect for parents was enforced as an immortal principle. The issue was never providing a proper upbringing. Discipline was at stake. Discipline overrode everything else. In religious schools, this was even clearer since the staff was bereft of emotional sophistication. Discipline, pedagogy (grammar, arithmetic, etcetera), and a religion that was part pedagogy and part discipline was what was on offer there.

Consequently, I don't know what kind of upbringing our family provided. Respect existed, that's for sure, but I don't know that any upbringing was ever involved. That's why I find it impossible to say how I might have turned out had it existed. I can only imagine I would have been very different. Perhaps I wouldn't have been so shy, sarcastic, or dreamy. I was naturally respectful, though that has diminished over the years. Otherwise things were very vague and unstable. I lived in the family terrain without feeling at all responsible for it, or even knowing what I was doing.

Grandmother Marieta.

I suspect Grandmother Marieta has firm, precise convictions. One of her most enduring, deeply rooted convictions is that she must never be still, that she must be up and doing at any given moment. Every afternoon she walks to our farmhouse—always wearing black, with a head scarf and basket. She is a little old lady with blue eyes and pink cheeks. She potters nonstop for two or three hours, goes in and out of the garden, goes up and down the flower beds, fills a big bag with weeds, pulls up an herb, sweeps for a while, eats a walnut or almond—scurries like an ant. She talks in a monotonous drawl, quietly, never shouts, apparently interested in everything that is being said, while giving the impression that she is without a care in the world. Eventually she walks back to town with a full basket: It holds a succulent cabbage heart, a couple of potatoes, four onions, a carrot, and a sprig of parsley.

Lluïseta.

When Aunt Lluïsa (Lluïseta) talks about religion—her forte—she always underlines what she calls its "little sides."

"Religion has little sides to it!" she says, with a tiny, luminous chuckle.

I saw a lad from the Ampurdan approaching in the distance when I was strolling along carrer de Cavallers. He is short, fair-haired, nervy, a live wire. We chat for a time. With disconcerting ease, irrepressible verbal diarrhea, and great energy, my acquaintance jumps from one issue to another like a grasshopper over stubble. His range is exhausting—as it would be for a dancer breaking into an impromptu performance. He will meet the same fate as a good number of individuals in our country: Chattering away he will lose his voice, and when he tries to say something, it will be pure hot air.

In two and a half minutes of conversation, he has mentioned Bergson, "chaste Susana" from the church in Castelló d'Empúries, and Garreta's latest sardana. He told me that everyone is daydreaming, that nobody has his feet on the ground, that everything is hopeless. Suddenly he dries up before rushing off to see a young lady—or so he said.

Such behavior in our country is all too common and thoroughly unpleasant, or so I conclude. But, after a moment's reflection and summary soul-searching I wonder if I have any reason to believe that I am any different from this typical young man. I won't go into detail. Rather, I will go to the heart of the matter.

Deep down, of course, I am interested in women, but I don't recall ever making any effort to meet one, so that here and now I can say with the poet: *"Fiamma d'amor nel cor non m'è rimasa."*

I'd like to be everywhere and never leave home. I'd like to encompass everything and in fact feel indifferent about everything. I'd like, I'd like…what would I like?

What can I ever achieve in life with this kind of temperament? Will I ever do anything more than chat, pass the time of day, gawp, ponder, or flit around? I'm like that tinsmith from Palafrugell who once told me, "Do you know what I do when I'm buried by work, when they're crying out for me everywhere? I'll tell you what I do: I take myself off to bed."

11 April. Almost all our neighbors on carrer del Sol are at odds and at each other's throats. They hate and squabble at every turn. The smaller a town is, the more people live cheek by jowl, the fiercer the rows.

The feelings provoked by overly close human contact can become so tangibly objective that they could be studied with the precision that is brought to the scrutiny of spiders or ants. Contemplated from a cloud, these quarrels would seem trivial, if they were even visible. Observed at close quarters they irritate and annoy because they are generally so incomprehensible. One day when I was telling Gori how they were beyond my comprehension, he responded, "You think everything is strange. I would urge you not to waste your time on the ridiculous exercise of opening open doors. You'll soon be making the same mistake the federalists made in Sant Feliu de Guíxols and that Christ made when he said that man is redeemable."

Tall Roseta lives on the corner of our street. True to her name, she is a well-built, lofty lady. She was widowed young, saw her children die young, and is fond of poking her head out of her door and windows to talk to passersby and has been much criticized for so doing. We reckon she is adept—like in the Middle Ages—at facilitating secret, exceedingly complicated, difficult liaisons. It would be hard to prove. In any case, these things don't matter in Palafrugell, where everything is open for all to see and the benefits from such archaic skills are not as esteemed as they should be. Roseta treats everyone well. Perhaps being a go-between is calming.

And these are my neighbors—in this year of grace that is slipping by.

12 April. My father, who watches me scrutinizing my textbooks, suggests I go up to the attic.

"You'll be better there," he says. "If you want to work for a while, nobody will bother you."

And so that afternoon, after idling around the house, I went right to the top. As I walk up the steps, my books under my arm, a gentle, warm light from the skylight catches me. Quite charming.

The attic is a large, low-ceilinged room with exposed rafters, and is full of junk, all in order. My mother's presence is palpable throughout the house. I suspect she would order our feelings if she could. The windows open onto a south-facing terrace. This terrace looks over the marvelous landscape surrounding the town and between the humps of distant hills to patches of sea. This terrace is one of the best things about the house. That said, it's years since I've been up there.

Like many children from a good Catholic family, more or less of our era, as a child I played at saying mass and being priest. I played that here in this same attic on rainy days. I remember how skilled a little friend of mine was at cutting out paper chasubles from the broadsheets of *Las Noticias*. I search the neat pile of lumber under the roof for traces of those old games and find nothing. What can have happened to that small gilt altar, with white string bags, that the Wise Men brought us one year? Certainly everything up here is very tidy, but I know I will search in vain for any particular object. That's the problem with tidiness. It paralyzes, overawes, and suggests that it is better not to touch. Postpone everything until tomorrow. But to postpone something until tomorrow is to postpone it forever.

The attics I like are the topsy-turvy ones full of battered junk and faded melancholy. The attic in my house is too cold.

I don't remember if we enjoyed those old clerical games. But they did make an impression, and one day I heard a housemaid tell a friend: "These kids always get their own way. They want a drum, they get a drum. They want a trumpet, they get a trumpet. They want to say mass, they say mass."

I spent the afternoon thinking about all that. One more irremediably wasted afternoon.

When reading Víctor Català I often wonder if the countryside really harbors all the drama she finds there. Money is the main drama in her world, but I don't think that's restricted to rural parts. It is everywhere. Are there so many dramas in the mountains? I'm sure there are fewer on the plains. I don't know the mountains. Víctor Català certainly does. She is familiar with many mountains, particularly the Montgrí range—a Montgrí that might be on the stage, with special effects à la Maeterlinck.

In the end one might say this about Víctor Català: Take away the stage set, quaint customs, naturalism, and entertainingly artful sociology, and what is left? A crime writer of some note.

16 April. Sometimes I walk with the sole purpose of observing the passing faces of the men and women in the street. The faces of men and women over thirty are especially striking! What pint-size cauldrons of obscure human mysteries! Poisonous, impotent sadness, cadaverous expectations dashed year after year; fleeting robotic courtesies; despondency and resignation before the Great Beast that is nature and life!

There are days when I'll come up with any excuse to speak to the people I encounter. I look into their eyes. It isn't easy. It's the last place people want you to look. I'm horrified by the few eyes there are that retain any trace of expectation and poetry—the expectation and poetry of a seventeen-year-old. From most eyes the glint has gone for things intangible, gracious, gratuitous, fascinating, uncertain, or enthralling. Those eyes are hard, sickly, or completely flattened. They belong to robots, impossible to surprise, indifferent to adventure and the ineffable.

Yesterday the cork furnaces broke down and the workers had to go home early. Much to his surprise, one worker found a man in his underpants sitting in a rocking chair in the passageway of his house, cheerful and jolly, without a care in the world. Next to him was a small table with cookies and a glass of pungent wine.

"What, sir, are you doing here?" asks the husband, taken aback.

"I came to do a job for your wife ... and it was getting hot ... you know," drawled the man without a care in the world.

The husband was dumbstruck!

My friend R. Medir (an authority on matters of local history) likes to say that the men of Palafrugell are particularly skilled at getting down to our underpants quickly, anywhere, whatever the weather.

There are countless people in Palafrugell—maybe it's the same everywhere—who can only think about their next meal. Breakfast, lunch, afternoon snack, dinner—sometimes afternoon snack-cum-dinner. Their ideal is the next meal. You could say it's their *only* ideal. This must be why not a single eyebrow was raised when it came out that Sr. Vergés, Esquire, on carrer de Sant Martí, had Borell the tailor make him some bespoke eating trousers. Everyone thought it made perfect sense.

I'm not familiar with the trousers, but a person who has inspected them closely assures me they are practical, comfortable, adaptable, and elegantly "conceived."

A few days ago, Don Narcís Miquel appeared to be on his deathbed. Don Narcís, a gentleman from Palafrugell's glory days, the era of French champagne, Scottish whiskey, and Munich beer, weighs more than two hundred and sixty pounds. He pleaded with his family: "Save me! Do whatever you can! If I make it through, I promise I'll never eat so much."

But that promise was, to put it scientifically, only a working hypothesis for the testing that later developments proved to be false. Don Narcís is healthy again, eats as much, or even more, than ever.

There are three local dishes that people are particularly crazy about. They create expectations so great that people will travel hours to eat them. Without grousing, as they say. The dishes are: black rice with shellfish in a succulent sauce; cod steak and pork-belly stew with stockfish, cod tripe, pigeon, and aioli; and lobster with chicken.

For my group of friends food is no less important. If, for some reason, we have to forego the second supper Marieta serves us in the early hours, we conclude that life is without meaning, absurd, and cruel.

Today Enric Frigola said that he knows a big fat man with a sensitive soul who feels immediately relieved of all material needs and worries, in a state of grace, whenever he loosens his belt a notch.

Coromina laughs when he hears this piece of information, and Frigola launches into him with feigned indignation, half ironic, half annoyed. "You mock everything!" he says. "I give you physical proof of states of mind that are purely spiritual and you laugh. What more do you want? You're never satisfied."

I think about it coldly, and the one moment in life when it must be impossible to deny that Providence exists has to be the moment you die.

21 April. My incursion into our attic, on my father's advice, bore fruit, even if it didn't ease my way into those hardcover textbooks. I found a bunch of family papers in a drawer—all having to do with my mother's side, and specifically, Sr. Esteve Casadevall. I'd understood that before Sr. Casadevall went to Cuba, some of his distant uncles had gone there and returned with little to show, because not one came back with the airs of an *americano*, a rich émigré from South America. One of them would visit us every once in a while and he wrote a few lines on Palamós, fascinated, naturally, by the extraordinary beauty of its bay.

A serious individual, concerned about serious things, starts out to write with the sole desire of delving into the memories of his nearest and dearest in order to discover such substantial matters as will impress and give the writer renown. I have searched every corner of the family, have scrutinized my family tree, interrogated the elderly, and found nothing. I never imagined any of my forebears might be a hero or a great man and it wouldn't be at all odd if I was as lacking in enterprise as my grandparents. I'd have felt fulfilled if I'd simply found a red beret or brocade breeches. That would help me win over the critics.

However, I have turned up one scrap of renown, though it was hardly worth the candle.

The other day, rummaging through papers, I discovered the set of an old Spanish daily, *El Eco Bisbalense*, that often sank so low as to slander that good citizen, Benet Mercader the painter. According to *El Eco*: "Benet lived with a concubine in Barcelona; as if the Ten Commandments had been demolished as devastatingly as the deadline for valuing country estates." This is how they once spoke about painting. Then again, Bisbal people have always been rather legalistic. Among the papers I found an article, written by a twice-removed uncle of mine, a quaint fellow and an actor, who fathered various natural children with various refined ladies, emigrated to South America, established an important tanning business, and died poor and mad in a hospital in the free port of Hamburg. In 1880 this worthy ancestor left here for Hamburg and wrote a fluent, clear article portraying the town of Palamós as he'd left it in 1855 that contrasts with the affectation, pedantry, and dryness of descriptions that were typical of his time.

I have often wondered why this great-uncle of mine, no literary man, who must have written these few lines because God willed it, why the one and only time he faced a blank page, did he speak of Palamós, a place that was foreign to him? Why didn't he describe his town Calella de Palafrugell? Answering this question hasn't been a sterile pursuit, but it has deepened my knowledge of the family and that's always useful, if unpleasant.

In the course of his travels, my relative, a notorious wastrel, found himself stranded again and again without a penny. His wallet, you could say, suffered from malingering anemia. He'd escaped from Palamós before the usual bills were presented. But years passed—not that many—and one day our cowboy contacted his creditors anew. Most had to make an effort to remember who he was. Memory tends to be an opportunist, clinging to what is possible. Memory, Goethe said, extends as far as our self-interest. After writing off a debt, it is laughable how quickly memory of it dissolves into thin air. The pile of paper they faced was much thicker than normal. It came from Chile. First they found a check payable at any bank for the amount of unpaid debt that brought a cheerful glow to their cheeks. Sr. Maragall has described the Ampurdan as a windy palace, and the inhabitants of this palace are notoriously keen on being paid. A visiting card was also enclosed, which depicted above my relative's full name a triangle surrounded by a glowering human eye. Across the card a pen had scrawled a delightful phrase that conjures up a taste of bananas and Creole colonialism. It is a phrase that deserves to find a home in a lyric sung by some languid South American. The phrase went: *Paying makes you happy.* Finally, they found a long, elaborate manuscript, on untrimmed paper, with a rather insipid, overwrought ballad.

One of the fortunate creditors, feeling duty-bound to express gratitude, called on friends he had in the incipient world of local journalism and published the manuscript in the aforementioned Bisbal newssheet. It is a piece that oozes nostalgia. I think the payment of a long-overdue debt says a lot in favor of an individual. To accompany payment with a piece of writing that recalls and praises the town where one's creditors live must be extraordinary. Such an expression of exquisite feeling must say, in my view: "Friends, let's forget this! We can all find ourselves in a tight corner from one day to the next. What's past is past."

The piece I refer to is what follows. It is very objective and not at all badly written. It has extra value for me because it is the only known piece of writing by my relative and the only slightly sophisticated thing I found in the public history of the long line of my ancestors. It goes like this:

In the year of 1855, Palamós was a charming town. It has now begun to lose some of its character. Over time, factories and port developments, yet to be built, will erase it entirely.

In those times, it was a wealthy, attractive town of sailors and shippers, of small manufacturers and shopkeepers. It was like any town on the sea of Genoa. It smelled of peppermint if you turned landward and shellfish if you faced seaward. When I lived there, two or three expeditions would sail to fish the coral reefs of the Azores and Cape Verde every year, and that brought great prosperity. Today this industry is in the hands of Greek divers who sail in rickety three-masters, plunder, and play dirty tricks.

I have always thought the bay of Palamós, at the heart of which lies the town, was extremely elegant. Some friends have disputed this and I let them have their say. The town was small and it was crammed onto an expanse of rock. There were ramps down to the sea. From the beach one could see a thousand windows, small windows and skylights suspended like nests from the white walls.

The houses faced a kind of rocky esplanade that jutted out into the sea, prolonged by a battered, barnacled jetty, beaten by the waves. Brigs were always anchoring on that jetty. A tall post rose up at the very end, topped by a ring where a miner's lamp had been attached. At night the lantern was lit and its weak, red light was crisscrossed by cobwebs. On winter nights, the wind sometimes swung the lantern and it seared and flashed like lightning.

There were five or six filthy, smoke-filled, dubious taverns on the esplanade. They sold dreadful chufa milk and undiluted rotgut. From the outside they looked gross and wretched, but inside I enjoyed myself. I particularly liked a tiny brig that hung from the reddish ceiling in one tavern: Painted black and white, every detail was true to life. The most influential person in that neighborhood was the Hag, a tall, square-built, deathly pale woman, who drank rotgut as if it were water. The Hag hunted for scraps of food along the jetty, smoked half a thin cigar behind the barrels, and saw to the needs of sailors. The Hag wore red-striped stockings, knew three or four songs from her heyday, but couldn't sing because her mouth was always parched. Nobody had ever seen the Hag drunk, and the notary from Palamós, who wore a cape full of tiny holes and was reputed to be a sorcerer, used to say that the woman's liver must be pickled in alcohol.

The streets in the town were extremely narrow and paved with pebbles from the bed of the gully. Houses were large, on the gloomy side, and had terraces. On summer evenings people sat on their terraces and enjoyed the cool air. One would see young women in light-colored dresses and hear children making a hullabaloo. At such magical, blissful moments, it was great fun to glimpse the pigeons of Sr. Marquès in full flight. The pigeon loft and the belfry were the highest points in town. Sometimes seagulls and the occasional late swallow flew by Sr. Marquès's triangle-shaped loft. A gull often flew from the triangle, plunged, and glided over the port's still waters.

At that time of day, Palamós possessed a distant, colonial air and a complex, warped sensuality. On such evenings I always felt I might engineer a rendezvous with the apothecary's wife, whose eyes smoldered, or with the customs officer's daughter. At night, one could hear the weary, voluptuous gasps of the sea and, when it was calm, the creaking of the brigs' moorings. On moonlit nights, Palamós seemed unreal and fantastic suspended over the sea.

I went to the square most afternoons. The town wall facing

the sea looked like a line of teeth, and the square, like a gap between two teeth. I spent many hours there in a state of enchantment observing the bay from the square. On the western
horizon, between trails of smoke, you could see the vinegary-
colored cape by Tossa, and within the sweep of the bay, the Aro
beach like a saffron brushstroke across the soft, dark green of
the pine trees. There was also a rocky outcrop where foam
hissed, and the ancient Valentina watch tower. The land beyond
sank into a pine-filled valley that extended as far as the northern boundary of Palamós. Between the pine trees and the first
houses lay market gardens with vegetables and a fig tree with a
statuesque, golden oriole.

I loved to watch the comings and goings in the small port.
There was always a boat upside down on the flat, ribs exposed.
You could hear the master carpenters striking their adzes and
see them maneuvering a pot of smoking tar. I also loved to
watch the stevedores, carts, horses, and carabineers. When a
brig or smack came or went, it was an event. A crowd would
huddle on the square and assess the maneuver with a running
commentary. I was very young at the time and thought that in-
terplay of sails, ropes, and flags was a miracle of intricacy.

When roaming the world, I have often recalled Palamós
and the tranquil, placid lives of its inhabitants. Alone and de-
spairing because of the bad turn my business affairs have taken,
I frequently tear my hair out and think of the folk here, who
only seem to labor in order to work up an appetite, hunger in
order to eat, eat to make love lingeringly with their wives, and
make love to clear their heads and insides. I tear my hair out,
understand what an idiot, simpleton, and ignoramus I am, but
the years pass and I've not been cured, nor have I returned.

The article by my ancestor finishes thus. It is the weightiest item I
have found in my gray, uninteresting family tree.

24 April. When someone in a household is an out-and-out lunatic, usually the whole family is at least slightly touched.

Miracles, inasmuch as they imply the breaking of the most general laws imaginable, raise the question of whether they are a good idea. If, for the purpose of argument, I had a private income, I might say no. But a poor man ... a poor man who doesn't believe in miracles is not only a hundred times poorer than he really is but is a poor man who's got it wrong to boot. The only treasure the poor can hoard is the prospect of a miracle.

Even so, it is very difficult to be rich and independent. To make it in this world you must suffer long bouts of unpleasant wheeling and dealing. But, in the end, it is conceivable. What is literally inconceivable is to be at once poor and independent.

There can be—in my view—only two ways of exercising free will: strength or guile.

The renowned Trica, my friend Trica from Llançà, must have been one of the most active precursors of communism in the Ampurdan. No longer.

After the revolution in 1909, one of Ferrer Guàrdia's brothers came to live in Llançà. He was an easygoing character with a long white beard—a bucolic anarchist, a gardener with a green thumb, and a horticulturalist who grew wonderful roses. He made many friends. His wholesome, idyllic anarchism, based on generosity and universal brotherhood, appealed particularly to that Ampurdan species of individualist, solitary cultivator of orchards, olive groves, and vineyards, who is fond of far-flung, poor terrains situated between heaven and earth. They would visit him and listen in awe. He was a discreet man, not bent on making trouble, and his disciples were equally discreet. Not that boisterous loudmouths didn't filter into his society. One of them was Trica, who spent his entire youth proclaiming to anybody prepared to listen: "Things must be shared among all, in equal portions."

It just so happened that Trica's wife inherited a small house, a slice of a vineyard, and a market garden. And people in the village were quick to say, "Trica, things must be shared among all, in equal portions."

And poor Trica had to spend the second half of his life exclaiming in high dudgeon, "Go to hell with your equal portions, to hell with them!"

Clearly as good a way to pass the time as any other, but in the end it becomes wearisome and encourages you to find some other form of entertainment. In small villages, it is better to have no ideas than to change your opinions. Not even your friends will forgive you.

In our café, Enric Frigola says, "I am in favor of having only a few books. I've noticed that the more people have, the less they read."

Life in these villages is awful, asphyxiating, and horrific.

I don't know if it's the same everywhere, but in this part of the world only personal foibles, interests, and affairs carry any grist, flavor, or importance. This country, as an amalgam of citizens with certain aspirations in common, has yet to be built. Common interests exist only when it appears they might have an impact on one's individual livelihood. In subdued tones, we talk for hours and hours about the grief of others, we bemoan and berate to our hearts' content the abandoned, poverty-stricken, backward state of our country. But it is all quite trivial and comes up just as casually as when we talk about the weather, with the proviso, of course, that the weather isn't going to affect our wheat or vines.

In the café I hear Gori say, "Music, music! Why don't we talk about it with a little more respect and sincerity? I heard the best music I've ever heard at Sr. Cumané the notary's, when this gentleman read out the will, and it turned out I was an heir. The voice of the notary Cumané isn't at all musical. It's gruff, for the most part. Sometimes it cracks slightly. Often it grates and makes your hair stand on end. I can assure you, on that occasion Sr. Cumané's voice sounded infinitely melodious, enchanting, and endearing."

I go out for a breath of fresh air.

I never tire of reading Montaigne's *Essays*. I spend hours and hours with them at night in bed. They have a calming, sedative effect and usher in a delightful rest. Montaigne's wit almost never runs dry; he is endlessly full of surprises. One source of surprise derives, I think, from Montaigne's precise estimation of the insignificant position man occupies on earth.

26 April. At certain times of the day, at twilight, for example, the scent from the acacias that are now beginning to blossom on carrer del Sol is intoxicatingly sweet, almost sickeningly so, an excessively sticky, gummy, sad aroma, as stale as a nineteenth-century print. Acacia comes from *acanthus*, which means "thorn" in Greek. But more extraordinary than the powerful perfume of the acacias is the etymology of its name—a wintry etymology that sounds very strange in these days of spring.

For some days I have been trying to crystallize in a few lines the impression made on me by a recent reading of Santiago Rusiñol's *The Gray Village*.

The book ought to be precise, excellent, perfect, but it isn't. The idea, reality, subject addressed in each chapter couldn't be more exact and concrete. All of us who live in a village—even if it is a touch more appealing, and less Aragonese (say), less of a caricature than *The Gray Village*—can tell that each chapter responds directly to a reality that is unobjectionably true and observed. But Rusiñol takes the facts, exaggerates them, inflates or shrinks them, imposes his monotonous comic twists on them, and transforms what is alive and kicking into a toy, a commonplace, a derisory mechanical device. Faced by the wonders of reality, Rusiñol lacks tact; he fights shy of the slightest subtlety. He performs mechanically, with the coldness of a cog, a predictable wheel producing sentences and slotting in adjectives that are equally Rusiñolesque. Once you have read a number of his books, you can guess every next sentence.

Page after page of such writing is positively exhausting, especially when the author attempts poetry. Nothing could be more disastrous in poetry than being able to guess automatically the line that will follow the last one.

Rusiñol clearly demonstrates that affectation is the worst defect a writer can have.

Rusiñol, who is always making fun of machines—he has just published a cartoon of a machine for sweetening strawberries—is the most mechanical author in modern Catalan literature.

Rusiñol—an amazing, unprecedented case of talent squandered.

I meet Hermós on the street. He's wearing a black squid skipper's cap, tilted slightly over one ear. The face under the cap has an astonishing gorilla look: He hasn't shaved for three days and his white hair sticks up over the black leather like the teeth of a comb. Bloody filaments float in the yellow lymph of his eyes. He caught malaria in Algiers and is taking quinine. He looks rather the worse for wear.

We go to Gervasi's tavern for a glass of wine. Hermós seems unhappy. He wants to go and live by himself in Aigua Xal·lida. He is tired of taking orders. "Anyone who wants it, can have my share," he says. He is sure he can earn a living in Aigua Xal·lida with a small boat and four fishing lines. "I will be the Baron of Cabres Cove. Nobody will order me about. I won't eat very much, but I'll do what *I* want. Besides, it's been a terrible year. We've caught hardly any squid. The weather is always bad. When I come home empty-handed I wonder what Donya Rosa is going to say and I suffer."

His declarations warm my heart. If I admire anything in men it is their longing for freedom.

All of a sudden, he looks me in the eye and tells me how a few days ago there was a stranger in Can Batlle, the tavern in Calella, who said that once upon a time people believed that the sun circled the earth, and subsequently it was discovered the reverse was the case, the earth went around the sun.

"You must know about all that," he said with a grin that could have been respectful or mocking. "I expect I'll find the truth out when I read you."

"What that gentleman said is beyond dispute."

"Really?"

"Of course, for heaven's sake!"

"All right, all right ... so what?" he retorted brusquely, slightly annoyed. "So what? All this silliness is like water off a duck's back."

In the café Tomàs Gallart says, "Bankers are gentlemen who lend you an umbrella when the sun shines. When it rains, don't count on their help."

Coromina has been closely following the news from the Russian Revolution in the dailies and the incessant journalistic commentary on the nature of socialism. He declares that Gallart is right, that the capitalist system is simultaneously chaotic, disorderly, irrational, capricious, wasteful, and stingy. Anyone who needs a loan from the banks to pursue an opportunity, however good it may be, is going to be tortured dreadfully.

"What Coromina just said," Gori excitedly remarks, "is literally, axiomatically, and undeniably true. The capitalist system is disorderly, irrational, and chaotic. Irrational is the exact word. And because it is entirely capricious, it is painful, cruel, and sad. Yes, Coromina is absolutely right. The capitalist system is everything he said and a lot worse at that. We could spend all night listing its drawbacks. But if you don't mind, I want to ask one question: Do you, after everything we've said and everything we could go on to say, do you argue that we need to replace this system with another system that is developed a priori?"

"Sometimes I think so, yes."

"You do? Good God! I beg to disagree. You really think the conclusion to draw from all the failings of capitalism we've just run through—failings that are undeniable—is that the system ought to be replaced? I think, on the contrary, what we've demonstrated is that it is absolutely necessary to defend and sustain it on every front. Capitalism is irrational, chaotic, incomprehensible, disorderly, capricious, unjust, painful, sad, and ridiculous ... just like nature and life. A banker will only listen to you, an intelligent, energetic, respectable man, if you are going to earn him money. Then he goes and opens his vaults to the gentleman who lives three doors up the street and is a total idiot. Nature has given me this awful nose when it could have given me a perfect specimen. The fellow who lives like a beggar and never washes is now rich, having inherited a fortune he doesn't know how to handle. We could have all been endowed with strong, resistant, perfect spleens but instead have to make do with spleens that are worn out already."

"So what do *you* conclude from all this?"

"I conclude that nature, life, and capitalism all flow from the same source. Capitalism was born from human life for the same reasons that grass grows from the earth in springtime. That it is born and flourishes naturally doesn't make it moral or immoral. There's nothing intrinsically good or bad about nature. Nature is pure cosmography, total indifference. Nothing has a transcendent purpose. At most, this natural drive and growth are symptoms of undoubted biological vitality, a natural power drive."

"A vitality that creates such injustice, that is so repulsive, loathsome, intolerable—"

"Entirely agreed. But then I've never seen nature attempt to be just. Has anyone? It would have been perfectly just for nature to endow me with an elegant, graceful, enticing nose, given my romantic disposition, yet look at the deplorable schnozzle I was landed with. Wouldn't you think it ridiculous if I tried to replace the nature we have with one that was more just, a nature that supplied perfect Greek noses and strong, sturdy spleens impervious to alcohol? You'd think it plain crazy. You are up in arms at the wickedness of capitalism and want to replace it, want to kill its biological character, its spontaneous growth and inner drive. You want to replace it with a regime that is rational, just, orderly, and satisfactory from the perspective of routine everyday morality. You believe that by simply replacing a real regime, however cruel, with an artificial, albeit hypothetically perfect one, you will improve the lot of mankind. I doubt it! I don't believe it! The French like to say the best is the enemy of the good. My opinion is that exchanging a real, albeit irrational system for this other one, in spite of the proposed system's theoretical perfection, will lead to something infinitely worse, much more painful and intractable and with many fewer opportunities."

"You are a hardened conservative," says Coromina, on edge, "with no imagination."

"And you are a child in diapers," Gori retorts, tipping two shots of firewater into his coffee.

29 April. Strolling along the road to our farmhouse in Llofriu, I see a young boy flying a kite—*un estel,* as they say in Barcelona. The boy stands tall on Les Torretes, those little humps of hills that overlook Palafrugell from the north. These hillocks describe a long, gentle curve that brings to mind the horizontal body of an adolescent. The string of the kite stretches, a pure arc lengthening across a bright static sky. The kite alternates nervous nods with a stiff stillness. Its tail, with its red pennants, swings like a pendulum. The light gentle breeze stirs, squeezes, and caresses the lengthening arc of the kite string, as if a living form floated upon the air.

A magnificent spring afternoon. Getting on. Swallows whistle by the eaves of the houses. An almost deserted street. Three or four people carrying aluminum cans, on their way to buy milk. The small white acacia blossom gives off a rather sad, morbid smell. Up the street, the blacksmith hammers on his anvil. Three or four doors down from our house, the electrician's son, his window open, practices the violin painfully, endlessly, monotonously. Nothing grates more than an out-of-tune violin. Daylight hangs on. The western sky is intensely pale orange—like the sound of the electrician's son's violin—a color I almost recognize as the essence of affectation, of background color in pious prints.

At this time of the year I wonder where my emotional and spiritual languor and emptiness come from.

On these springtime evenings one of the few things that lifts me—that distracts me, I mean—is the sight of the allotments on the outskirts of town. They are wonderfully kept and exquisitely cultivated. I hear the measured steps of an old animal turning a creaking waterwheel in need of oil, the sad music of poverty dazzled by fresh vegetables. A man, grappling with a well rope, fills a water tank. A boy, hoe in hand, reworks a furrow. These little plots are full of the coolness of the earth. The soft green leaves, coursing with sap, bring calm and repose to the mind. This plentiful harvest combats the painful light of the declining day.

To look at the sky, listen to the swallows, daydream, and contemplate the hazy life of things calms my nerves. Youth is a time of sadness—I think—because it is the only age when we respond to the intangible, that is, to what doesn't exist at all.

In this country, when it heats up, we smell of sheep's wool, while in winter we smell of green pinewood smoke. These must be the odors of the Latin race.

2 May. In the café, Coromina asks for the newspapers. For Gori's benefit we remark on the news from the First of May. Despite conscription, despite the war, there have been large workers' demonstrations in all the main cities of Europe. In Barcelona, all the trade unions are growing, as everyone can see. In Palafrugell, the only body that has real worker support is the anarcho-syndicalist Confederació.

Gori glances at the dailies, but soon tires of them.

"Nothing could be clearer," he says, making the classic café noise, the *drring* of a spoon against a wineglass. "It's a fact. People want the stick, Coromina. I hate to repeat the words of Salat the rag-and-bone man, but I can't help it, they are spot-on. People want their bread and wine and meat and fish doled out. They are tired of being free. They want to go back to begging for charity from here or there. Now they want charity from the state and will line up all day outside the bakeries and coal merchants, if necessary. They want to return to the good old days, to the Middle Ages, to the era of guilds and brotherhoods, that is, I mean, to the era of unions, to the poverty, hunger, and plagues of yesteryear. Nothing to worry us. We will see *all* this, if we live long enough."

"I'm not so sure we will," responds Frigola, hesitantly. "I find that hard to believe."

"What is so difficult to believe?" asks Gori, dropping all the newspapers on the floor in dismay.

"What are you saying? Don't fool yourself. They've lost their spirit. It has flown elsewhere. The cage is empty—"

"What spirit has flown?"

"The secular spirit, if you like, the scientific spirit."

"Don't raise your hopes, my dear Enric. That spirit is very important but the men embodying it are usually garbage. If this spirit, for some reason, doesn't suit the leaders of the lines and demonstrations and isn't the way they want it—"

"The people in the lines will turn it to their own purpose, or those who don't join will decide," rejoins Frigola quickly.

"Yes, that is also a possibility."

Future generations will find it strange that the initial success in our country of *Glosari* by Eugeni d'Ors stemmed from the fact that in the popular press Xènius was the first writer of our Catalan renaissance (a pretentious word I use for want of a better one) to handle fluently, or relatively fluently, the occasional gratuitous idea—that is, an idea stripped of any immediate practical use. It was a revelation.

5 May. Gervasi's on plaça Nova is one of the most pleasant taverns in town to drop by. The wine is usually good and the company is agreeable.

In the Ampurdan life has always been centered on its taverns. There are ancient taverns that are transformed into clubs during elections, especially if the voting happens to coincide with the arrival of a new wine. Then organized drinking sessions lubricate the arguments government eternally provokes. In the taverns all sorts of Oriental buffoonery take place on the benches between wooden casks while the most austere, chilly political doctrines are debated, even if these are expressed in simplified, elementary fashion. It is a strange combination.

These taverns never change. They used to alternate "La Marseillaise" and the "Waltz of the Waves." Nowadays they sing "The Internationale" and music-hall songs. The people remain the same. The songs come and go.

Gervasi's is very important; though its political renown may have fluctuated over the years, no other tavern serves better drinks.

To write the history of Gervasi's tavern would be to write the history of my beloved birthplace. It would be a peculiar history because, apart from being very short, all that would stand out would be the absence of glorious deeds or famous people. Many people, I suspect, would find this lack of brilliance depressing. Personally, I am delighted to have been born in a town that has produced no redeemer, no connoisseur of exotic sensations, no stentorian preacher. It makes me feel light and free.

In ancient times Palafrugell was a tiny, walled town. People depended on agriculture. The tavern was next to the tower at the southeast corner of the wall. An olive grove extended in front of the tavern. The regulars were mainly people who lived on the outskirts of town. On market days and Sunday afternoons the tavern would be packed with people drinking and doing deals and, when the occasion demanded, songs were sung between slices of sea perch and chicken wings.

Then the people from the outskirts of town and even farther afield invaded, and Palafrugell's tiny walls burst like a ripe pomegranate. The town spread out on all sides and Gervasi's was left in the center. This made it even more famous. People came from far and wide on Sundays, while the locals were there all week, and Mondays in particular. Snails, sea bream, stew, and herrings were on the menu. Herrings—a poor man's fare—were served on a thick slice of toast with olive oil and vinegar. The tavern was filled with smoke, the herrings shone like gold on the toast, and wine spurted pink and bubbly from the wineskins. The tavern bustled until evening fell and the light faded and died over the land toward the sea.

Urban planning arrived, and with it a mania for straight streets and a town of uniform rectangles. The tower on the southeast corner of the street was the only remnant of the ancient walls, and it was tall, round, and slender like a happily married woman. But the tower was demolished to make a street straighter, which spelt the death of the old watering hole. One of the busiest corners in town disappeared, especially in winter, since the concave space created by the tower and the adjacent stretch of town wall had served as a shelter. When the north wind blew, town idlers gathered and gossiped there. A council of slackers and cynics who might be joined by the occasional tinker traveling from town to town or an itinerant umbrella mender, the kind who carry a wooden box and a pot that leaks black juice along the road. These characters would spend the little they had in the tavern and undoubtedly held Gervasi in high esteem.

Gervasi was in his fifties when the tower was demolished. He was tall and strong, with bushy eyebrows, a healthy color, and a strikingly noble face. The disappearance of the ancient tavern with its familiar benches and tables, huge casks standing by the walls, and bell-shaped roof, its bar with a tap, bottles, and dubious wine jars, and the great open fireplace at the back filled him with a sadness that alternated with moments of seething indignation and rage. He never recovered. He watched his establishment adapt to the new era with ill-concealed displeasure and total antagonism. They furnished the new tavern with an imitation marble bar, chairs, a showy spiral tap, and a fish tank. Gervasi despaired. To make matters worse, his old customers stopped coming and were replaced by artisans who wore a collar and tie on Sundays.

"Between them, they have killed off the tavern," Gervasi told his wife, a small woman with a nose like a hazelnut and weepy eyes.

"You have to change with the times," said an eavesdropper.

"Change? Change what? What is it we must change?" And in a moment of frenzied traditionalism, Gervasi exclaimed, "You'll never go anywhere, you asses! What is it we must change? I'm leaving, they've smashed my guitar and I'm dying of sadness."

The family owned a shack on a piece of stony ground above one of the coastal ridges. It had been planted with vines, which had been devastated by phylloxera. The shack was falling down and the well was full of stones, but Gervasi went to live there.

He refurbished the shack, cleaned out the well, and began to till the land in order to plant new vines. He made drystone walls from the rocks and little outcroppings on the slopes and started to plant. He bought an old hunting gun. A half-dead dog that nobody wanted appeared, and to keep it amused he occasionally went shooting. He put four or five beehives behind the shack. When it rained, Gervasi grabbed a tin lantern and a large umbrella and wandered down gullies looking for snails.

One of the local tramps helped him plant the vines. This stranger slept in the shack, ate what he could, and worked when he felt like it. The vines gradually gained ground and after a few years the wine from Gervasi's vineyard became locally famous. The vines, in fact, produced little wine, the land being difficult to till, but what they did give was of high quality.

The vines were a pleasure to behold. On summer evenings, Gervasi sat near his doorstep on a stone that he used to mash garlic. His ancient dog sat at his feet wagging its tail as Gervasi surveyed his handiwork and the landscape. From the ridge you could see an expanse of sea where boats bobbed like walnut shells. On the landside, you could see the Pyrenees and El Canigó, and, much closer, the belfry and the houses in town and a wide stretch of cultivated land. There were vines, other crops, and fields of alfalfa. The pine and olive groves gave a little style to and somehow lightened the landscape where man had made such a heavy mark.

As the sun went down, Gervasi hoisted a huge pink conch shell and blew into it from the four corners of his little plot. He made quite a din. His cheeks puffed out. He did this at sunrise, midday, and sunset. Gervasi established this custom from the day he arrived and the habit created a tradition. At first people thought his horn-blowing was simply a joke. Then they began to take notice of it, and today Gervasi's horn is an established institution that people follow, especially when they're working. Its gruff, somber sounds are the chronometer for those parts.

However, *chronometer* might be a bit of an exaggeration given the precision the word suggests. It's not the moment when the sun actually comes up over the sea that the conch heralds but the moment Gervasi sees it rise, and the same goes for the sunset. And when an overcast, hazy, or very cloudy sky blocks Gervasi's perception of the exact moment of the sunrise or sunset, he uses his judgment, delaying or advancing his announcement as he thinks fit.

One day, the hermit in Sant Sebastià told him, "You got ahead of yourself on Wednesday."

"Don't be fussy," Gervasi retorted. "When I blow a fanfare at the sunsets, you can be sure the sun won't reappear."

He's also had to fend off criticism from finicky owners of watches. They complain that he never blows at twelve on the dot and that sometimes he is very late, and he answers, "Let's get this straight! I don't blow at twelve on the dot? What do you mean by twelve on the dot? You sound like a lot of accountants! I blow at lunchtime and when do I have lunch? At twelve! Got it? Your newfangled ways of doing things are going to put my head in a spin."

The truth is that by now people couldn't survive without Gervasi's horn; his lowing is part of the rhythm of the land, and the day Gervasi dies and the conch stays quiet, everyone will realize something is missing from that solitude.

The ships out sailing are also familiar with the blasts of Gervasi's horn and there are three-masters and brigs that always hoist their flags to greet him when they sail level with his vineyard. The first time that happened, Gervasi's heart brimmed over with happiness and his head was full of dreams. That day Gervasi kept the conch on his lips for more than two hours and played a veritable symphony, until the brig disappeared over the horizon. He blew so much he was forced to go to bed with collapsed lungs and a head that was throbbing like a drum.

That day the people who live inland thought Gervasi must have been announcing the end of the world.

6 May. López-Picó's journal, *La Revista*, has just published a long essay by Joan Estelrich on Kierkegaard, a Danish Protestant chaplain. This essay introduces a completely new way of thinking into our country, an absolutely original perspective. Accustomed as we are to the philosophical small change that circulates here—a stale Thomism on the right, positivism on the left—the novelty of these reflections both surprises and dazzles. Given the way things are going these days, and in the light of the romantic frenzy taking hold everywhere—a surface romanticism that only seeks to arrive at a more complex conception of reality, and then apply itself indiscriminately in every sphere, including poetry—Kierkegaard's reflections open a vast and mysterious terra incognita. People are increasingly fed up with word games in philosophy. The only way to restore authenticity to it is to make it spend a season in the purgatory of the personal confession, subjective understanding, or the private diary.

Josep Carner.

Last winter in Barcelona Joan Climent reminded me how refined and delightful Carner's writing is. It is more than that: Carner is a great poet. He is one in the technical sense, I would say, of the school exercise. At this level, he is a huge writer, probably one of the greatest now writing. This last claim of mine can only be understood by taking into account that Carner works with a Catalan language that lacks literary form, that is poor, inflexible, ossified, lexically restricted, riddled with corruptions, bone-dry, and marked by an orthographical anarchy that the country's intellectual elite continues to defend, a language developing in a sprawling, chaotic city, to the indifference of a large swath of the population, and at the heart of a human mass that possesses not so much a diamond edge as a purely biological power of absorption—the aspirations of a gigantic sponge. In this sense, the Catalan language is a permanent tragedy. We should be forever grateful to Carner for the technical endeavor he has undertaken.

But then there is this: Carner's work doesn't grip, has no human depth, and though it is never frivolous, it remains aloof from the lives and obsessions of people today. It occasionally has the effect of a shop-window Provençal, always graceful and elegant, but without any gut feeling.

Obviously Carner will have his followers. (Something perhaps we could do without.) But those who adopt his verbal polish and filigrees will soon fade away while those who accommodate their own mental array to Carner's rhetoric will sound like English or Scandinavian poets in translation. Carner is a poetic fountain that will soon run dry.

On the other hand, it is difficult not to appreciate Mossèn Verdaguer. It's surprising how in countries where literary ambitions quickly run out of steam instances of great vitality and genuine biological strength still appear. Verdaguer was a strong, violent, proud man who stood his ground. He had no other choice: He took a Catalan that had been thoughtlessly preserved by country folk, as if he were shaping clay in his hands, and turned it into a new form of poetic expression. This is no mean feat…which is easily said! In light of this success, all that one can say in praise of Verdaguer is nothing compared to what he deserves.

But our generation wants to use the language that Verdaguer restored only yesterday to express everything more developed languages say as a matter of course. Perhaps we aim too high. Then again, you can't live without aiming high. In that sense, the problem lies as much in having something to say as in how to say it. This is what distinguishes our moment from Verdaguer's.

L'Atlàntida and *Canigó* are genuine literary phenomena. They display features of great interest but they don't have the slightest appeal. Their theatricality is simply exasperating. And they look like a sad waste of time from the perspective of modern literature. Modern literature attempts to grasp truth and life, indifferent to practically all else. These poems commemorate a grand rhetoric that is defunct.

How to explain Verdaguer's mysticism? Mysticism is a literary genre that springs out of a specific social situation. It represents a reaction against certain outpourings of sensuality and amorality that finally disgust. Mysticism occurs when the usual level of animality is exceeded—when there is too much of it per square yard. Then a cadaverous spiritualism shows up and launches a predictable counterattack—a longing for heaven. Castilian mysticism makes it clear that Castile, in terms of its people, is no mystical country. Can Verdaguer's mysticism be explained by its period? Is it a reaction against the surfeit of hypocrisy that characterized the generations produced by Catalonia's first industrial revolution?

As for Verdaguer's prose, it is unrivaled and magnificent.

7 May. The last few days have been really hot, but early this morning it rained for several hours. The afternoon earthy sultriness mixes delightfully with the freshness in the air.

I take the road past the cemetery to our farm. There is a splendid vista from Morena: the white Pyrenees against an immense sky; the mountains of Montgrí in the mid-distance and between the two mountains a huge hollow extends under a swath of pink mist the color of seashells, the mist off the sea in the Gulf of Roses; Lower Ampurdan, in the foreground, like a perfectly painted miniature.

The rain has refreshed the green of the pine groves and the fields of alfalfa. Everything is bronzed and gleaming. The wheat is about to shift from green to the white, golden foam of ripeness. The small hills undulating on both sides of the landscape—parallel to the sea—are gently luminous, alive, and graceful, like a sleeping, breathing nude. The colors are strong and glowing and the outlines, clearly cut incisions, sharp folds. The landscape is like the primitive paintings I sometimes see reproduced. Someday will I see this painting?

At three o'clock it is extremely hot and the light is harsh. When I walk into the main living room of our farmhouse it is like plunging into delicious shadows. I experience the tranquility I have longed for. I open the balcony door a crack and the wind billows in the curtain. From the balcony I can see a broody hen on the threshing floor—a red, yellow, and black hen, ruffling her feathers on a pile of rusty silver straw like a reflection of the moon. Under its vaulted ceiling, the room is vast and empty. The rooms leading on to it have been shut up for days and are cool and slightly humid in the half-light from the sun. The grandfather clock ticks slowly. Outside, sparrows chatter in the nearby acacias. That the birds are there somehow deepens the silence, a silence that always astonishes me as something extraordinary, even mysterious. I sit for a while in a chair, at a loss. The wind swells and spreads out the curtain.

11 May. Good music appeals to men more than women! Perhaps because of a difference in sensual drive. At every stage in life we men probably have less drive. So music may be the imaginative sensual pleasure of the frail and the poor—of the poor in every sense of the word! The music of women—like that of Don Juan—is surely regimental.

Time spans in the Ampurdan.

When the Cork-Lid was founded in Palafrugell, that is, the choir of yore, our glorious choir of yore, it was agreed that its banner should be made of cork. After a year and a half of deliberation over what a choir's cork banner should look like, it was further decided that the cork banner should be as magnificent as possible, a subtle, consummate work of art. A citizen by the name of Martí, the father of Dr. Martí, was commissioned to do the job. He devoted all his talents to the task and created an extraordinary cork altarpiece, a work that has been much admired by everybody. It took him several years to finish the banner. By the time he had completed the banner, the choir had been disbanded.

"Nearly all the really orderly or apparently orderly people I have known," says Coromina in the café, "learned to write neatly by placing a piece of lined paper—a guide sheet—under the page in their exercise book."

This may seem like a joke. It may be beside the point. Maybe not. The fact is that as a small child I could never discipline myself to write with a guide sheet under my page.

With goodwill and patience one can shake off a bore, what people usually call a bore. It is impossible to shake off an apparently cheerful, intelligent, and attractive bore.

In fact, there is never time for anything: whether to give serious praise or to seriously slander. When you are in the mood to do so, with the best of will, patiently and systematically, a lady or gentleman will be sure to interrupt to ask the time.

Walking the streets, I think about my conversations with my friend Joan Climent last winter in Barcelona.

Josep Maria Capdevila and Joan Climent (first-rank disciples of d'Ors) want to stand up for a kind of open neo-Catholicism, without cobwebs or darkness, with clean clothes, clean teeth, antirural and anti-Carlist, no muskets or snuff, and jettisoning the old-fashioned *canaris*, *tutis*, and *manilles* card games. They are for spruce soutanes, pious dears who practice tolerance and normal haircuts. "One must not place too many obstacles in the way of human hopes and aspirations," Climent would say. People should discover the good and the bad directly, through their own experiences. Prompted by Xènius, whom they consider to be their leader, these young men are devouring the writings of Joseph Joubert.

"The direction our spirit takes is more important than the actual progress it makes." "I prefer all that makes vice agreeable to all that degrades virtue," etcetera. These are some of the thoughts of Joseph Joubert. They are splendid.

Climent broke with two or three friends because he heard them blaspheming indecently. If they had told even the dirtiest stories in a refined, polite manner, in choice words, employing a select diction and sophisticated tone, he would have listened without flinching. I can't imagine what he would have thought of the stories—that's materially impossible. But I am sure he *would* have listened and not flinched. The young men I'm describing defend the confessional as a source of psychological hygiene and communion as an exercise in discipline and self-improvement. This is Belgian-style Catholicism. It lives in comfort in a two-hundred-and-fifty-peseta-apartment with running water and a bathroom, with chaplains and monks who ride bicycles, etcetera.

I like refinement myself. Particularly when it is a minority taste, before it becomes popular. When it spreads, it can become witless and dehumanized.

I suspect my friends' ideas will make little headway with people in this country. Here, we prefer the devil we know to the devil we don't. This is a land of suspicion, of ancestral suspicion, of twisted minds, of people who are convinced you can do everything by assuming the stance of the bell ringer when he knocks on the door to collect the fee for renting chairs in church.

In the café Dr. Reixach says that while eating an orange, his mother-in-law once said, "This orange is bitter, but the bitterness is so intense I find it sweet."

When standing in front of the window display at a photographic studio and contemplating the way people pose for photographs, we grasp the fact that most human happiness is routine and unconscious. However, having our photo taken in a studio is a rare, blissful, conscious moment of happiness.

It is exactly two miles from Palafrugell to the Calella beaches. Last year a friend of mine went to live in Calella with his family. This year they have decided to curtail their stay. "I imagine you weren't very happy there," I observe. "On the contrary," my friend replies. "We were very happy there, but felt inexplicably homesick for here." I am shocked by his response. Is it possible to feel homesick two miles from one's birthplace? Or maybe Catalans are naturally homesick animals?

15 May. A fierce north wind. From my bed I can hear it whistling. In fact, I can always find out what kind of wind is blowing without leaving the house. I only have to listen to the church bells. If they ring crisp, clean, and pure, it is the north wind; if the chimes are blurred, cracked, and frayed, it's a southwesterly.

When this invasive hurricane (something I hate) is blowing, I feel queasy. I prefer nature to be static and calm rather than delirious, agitated, and violent. The beauty of the tempest provokes a physical repugnance in me. But every year it is the same. These frenzied, pointless gales blast away on the threshold of summer. If this happens as the grain is ripening in the ears of wheat, the damage can be beyond repair. Years ago, my father watched helplessly while a fierce north wind blew the whole of his harvest away. The wind swept up the grain like thin, white dust.

In the afternoon a funeral cortege passes along carrer de Cavallers chased by the north wind. The wind makes the wreaths rattle. It sounds like a cat's claws scraping tin. It gives me goose bumps. The ribbons flew up over the hearse like the legs of an octopus or, to put it more elegantly, like Salomé's veils. High in his seat the coachman looked battered and crushed—like a doll flattened by a heavy hammer blow to his leather-capped head. In the empty street's raw, sharp, bright afternoon light, under the sky's immense, metallic void, the bleakly clad cortege looks absurdly grotesque. Swollen surplice billowing in the wind, the priest seems about to float away. With the coffin lifted high in front of him, the sexton struggles to keep walking. The mourners, fighting with both hands to hold down their hats, show no sorrow. The bells toll and the wind blusters away their solemnity: the chimes fly pell-mell through the air like parakeets. The funeral procession mounts carrer Estret: a fabulous animal locked in combat with a sinister power.

17 May. The wind has dried out the countryside. In a few hours we have gone from gentle, warm greens to glinting, bleached yellows. An unpleasant change. Everything is now covered in dirt and filth. Nothing can be more irritating than dust. It depresses me to see a farmer chased by the small cloud of dust his plow throws up. We'll have to wait for rain to see a splash of green, and that may mean waiting until September. The summer here tends to be Saharan, with everything parched and shriveled.

At dusk I go to Llafranc with Gallart and Coromina. After the recent gales, the earth, the sea, and nature seem exhausted, as if emerging from a state of convalescence. The sea is placid, swooning in lethargy the opal glow of twilight imbues with gentle melancholy. Nobody is on the beach. The pale, late-afternoon light dies away on the white walls of the shacks to the east. Then a dense, opaque gray drifts down from the pines on the hillside and invades the sea and the land.

Sprawled on the beach, I survey the bay and all that surrounds me. I hear the water gurgling through the fine sand, the only sound there is. The broad beams from the lighthouse turn slowly through the dying light of dusk. There's a sad, greasy glimmer over the tavern door. The solitude, the languor, the silence, reinforced by the empty, shut-up houses, accelerates dreams of escape to faraway places. The atmosphere is exactly right for contemplating the sea. The only way to give the sea serious consideration is to divide your consciousness in two. The dull murmur we carry within, throwing our mind into confusion when our heart is moved, can prevent us from seeing anything and it doesn't help when you're distracted by nearby noise. But if you ever break free from inner obsession and outer commotion, the sea will slowly penetrate and enrapture you with insidious force, dissolving the senses in a deliquescent haze.

We have dinner in Mata's tavern. Conxita bring us a huge plate of grilled sardines: fat, fresh, silvery. The olive oil gleams on the scales where they have been singed by the fire. The flame from the gas jet scatters sharp little points of light over the bluish scales in a swarm of sparkles. We stuff ourselves on sardines. Eating grilled sardines sets my whole body atingle with unprecedented feelings. As if the sardines free up my feelings, weakening my reason and firing my imagination with the most graceful shapes. The phenomenon is so marked that I sometimes wonder whether the sentimental, poetic raptures of the Celts might not derive from their fondness for sardines.

After endless speechifying about the human condition, we head home in the early morning—a delicate, subdued, silken dawn with an absinthe-colored sky that makes things stand out with the artificial clarity of a print. The cool, invigorating breeze from inland clears our heads. Perhaps it's the right moment to strike up a conversation with a friendly, good-looking woman who is unhappily married.

19 May. The first night of summer was a delight. We drank coffee under the spindly trees on plaça Nova. The lovely sound of water from the fountain in the square when taps are turned and pitchers filled. It is a still, warm, windless night. The stars twinkle above the roofs. I think of Dante's music:

> *... sì dolcemente*
> *che la dolcezza ancor dentro mi suona!*

A long conversation with Gallart, Coromina, and Frigola. The next-to-eternal topic: women. The first two finally come around to saying that nothing in the world can compare to a woman. Both are prone to falling in love and melting at the sight of female underwear. Passionate love would seem to be connected to a certain arrogance of temperament.

Frigola looks on with icy indifference as they talk. He declares that he observes the spectacle of the world with a complete and serene lack of concern. He pretends to be an out-and-out fatalist. "Spendthrifts," he declares, "can't stop spending money; misers can't help clinging to it. That's how it is when it comes to women and making love. There is an exact percentage, statistically speaking, of available women per year; the rest are out of reach, untouchable. And with the latter, appearances always deceive."

Coromina asks Frigola if he thinks it should somehow be possible to increase the statistical quota of available women.

"Perhaps," says Frigola. "A special diet, systematically pursued, especially if accompanied by a course of congenial psychological persuasion, might slightly increase the number we mentioned—"

"What do you mean by 'a course of congenial psychological persuasion'?"

"Releasing women from material concerns. Poverty is incompatible with any kind of sensuality, though freedom from such concerns may in the long run turn a human being into a vegetable. The most visible difference between Adam and Eve before eating the apple and Adam and Eve after eating the apple may be that before, the couple had no worries. They led an easy, comfortable, abundant life of luxury.

Afterward, they had nothing but worries and notoriously everything started to close down. To that extent, I'm sure that original sin describes a profound human truth, the significance of which can hardly be understated."

When we break up, the town seems strangely sad and forlorn. Nothing is obviously tiresome, or trying; nothing at all. But there is something mysterious and indefinable in the air that makes it seem that nothing matters. Days and nights when you feel like this, time drags bitterly and insomnia is guaranteed. It strikes two, and I'm full of anxiety but it is going to take me hours to fall asleep. I try to make up lyrics to a lullaby for twenty-one-year-olds.

23 May. After its long winter hibernation, our garden tortoise has shown signs of life. It may already have been making its rounds for a few days without my noticing. Under its yellow-striped shell it walks out of the shade under the hydrangea pots. It pokes out its good-natured reptilian head, its absurd tail, and waddles along with grotesque, foolish slowness.

I can't think what parasitic drive leads a tortoise to live close to human beings. The dog is man's companion in every latitude and clime. The mouse feeds off of us. The cat feeds on mice. We surround ourselves with animals we then consume at the table with knife and fork, amid the peace and tranquility of family life. What does a tortoise find in the proximity of men and women to make it feel so much at home?

This tortoise is very old. We are as accustomed to its presence in summer as we are to its absence in winter. We take no heed of what it does. Like the orange trees, palm trees, and woodshed it is part of the garden. It is one of life's accidents, without meaning.

We've had a number of different dogs during the time the tortoise has lived in the garden. Relations between the dogs and the tortoise have always been bad. The tortoise has the nasty habit, no doubt nothing but a conditioned reflex, of pissing on the dog's bed. This deplorable deed enrages the dog. When the dog catches sight of the tortoise, it throws itself on it, flips it over with its paw, and spins it around like a dinner plate. The tortoise lies there with its belly facing the sun. It wiggles its legs, head, and tail wildly trying to right itself. To no avail. It can't. It would stay belly-side up for the rest of its life if no one came to turn it over. When the dog sees one of us do that, it barks furiously in protest. It seems that if the survival of tortoises depended on dogs, the species would probably have long since disappeared. An upside-down tortoise, unable to right itself and without any other animal to come to its rescue, couldn't help but die eventually. But human beings, men and women, boys and girls, and especially children, can't bear to see a tortoise upside down and so we put them right. I don't know if it's because we're sentimental. Perhaps it's because a tortoise with its belly up—its whitish, mud-colored belly—strikes us as even more horrible than a tortoise with its feet on the ground. In any case, dogs are bad luck for tortoises; men and women represent the charming side of a benign providence.

At the barber's I read Santiago Rusiñol's pieces in *L'Esquella*. Generally unintelligible, he writes in what he likes to call colloquial Catalan. The liberties he takes once he picks up his pen make his writings seem like a rambling, messy, thoughtless monologue. Do literature and thoughtlessness have something in common by any chance?

Still, every so often what he writes makes patchy sense, and if the piece isn't completely trivial, it can be compelling. Rusiñol writes in a way that has nothing in common, for example, with what the French understand by writing. Rusiñol's writing simply talks, with all the dead wood of the most garbled colloquial speech, with all the disorder of a gushing monologue, a writing that, in spite of everything, gives occasional pleasure and leads you to think that when he talks Rusiñol must be literally fascinating.

By the same token his humor at its most spontaneous is unfailingly mechanical and monotonous. Read at length, such writing lacks surprises. Its greatest impact comes in tiny, intermittent doses. There are always unmistakably witty moments.

Who were the humorists Rusiñol read as a young man in Paris? That might shed some light on things. It's hardly worthwhile trying to pinpoint the influence of the great masters on him. Writers who subject themselves to the great masters tend to reveal their own lack of personalities. But for certain individuals the carefully considered influence of a minor work, of a more restricted range, can be just the thing.

Why do I make these literary judgments? What right do I have to make literary judgments when I know next to nothing about anything? I have to wonder why some things endure and others, seemingly so much better, fade and disappear. It's a complete mystery.

For example, it's not as if Rusiñol has completely lost it. He may be a laid-back, leisurely writer, disorderly and chaotic, a let's-see-if-I-guess-correctly kind of fellow, a sleepwalker with a pen, incapable of surviving a single haircut, but he did create the character of Sr. Esteve and that is in his favor. To be able to commit a bright idea to paper, or a colorful character, to devise a melody, to create a form—these can secure the renown and happiness of a family, provided, of course, that the family is susceptible to such happiness.

24 May. Family memories.

When we were children, my father played desperately unfunny practical jokes. He'd summon one of us and say in all seriousness, "Go to my desk and see if you can find my..."

We'd go to it like obedient robots and when we returned to the dining room gawping like empty-handed dolts, the fine fellow would chuckle: "What a big ass you are, my son!"

He did it to keep us on our toes. All the same, I do feel that being a paterfamilias must be a difficult vocation.

Aunt Marieta, a great-aunt, my maternal grandmother's sister, sometimes paid us a surprise visit. We'd get up and find her sitting in the dining room, chewing bread and dried figs with her few remaining teeth. Occasionally she'd already had breakfast and would just sit there, hands clasped on her lap.

Aunt Marieta Llach lived in Calonge and always walked to Palafrugell to see us. She didn't take the main roads; she preferred shortcuts. In her basket she carried two walnuts, four almonds, a handful of dried figs, and a slice of brown bread. A tall, sinuous, gray-haired, rosy-cheeked woman, she dressed in black. She walked for hours and hours and really knew that countryside. She was deeply rural and the member of the Llach clan who kept most loyally to the traditions of Cavorca and Fitor. All her brothers and sisters had married and lived by the sea. Some were in France. At heart, she pitied them. She loved Sa Bardissa de Calonge. Her skirts brought into our home the scents of rockrose, gorse, and heather blossom.

Though she is our most rustic, solitary relative, she is the one who gathers news of my mother's side. She flits from house to house and investigates the situation of every single member of our extended family. She reports back on a stream of relatives we haven't a clue about: Aunt Llúcia and Aunt Roseta, male and female cousins, exotic uncles and unknown nephews. We children thought someone who knew so many people must possess magic powers. The fact she's a childless widow may explain Aunt Marieta's concern for the family. We didn't see her for a long, long time after her marriage at a ripe age to Radó, a small property owner from Calonge. When widowed for a second time, she reappeared in no time. Besides, auntie is poor, and unlike the rich, the poor cannot dissipate their mental energies: The poor wear blinkers, like horses.

The affinities that bind people together are peculiar. My mother is her flesh-and-blood niece but they don't see eye to eye at all. Their tastes, ideas, and way of seeing things are different. The meaning of reality for them—that is, the meaning of words—never coincides. However, Grandmother Marieta and Aunt Marieta's arguments are lively and never-ending. As she has nothing to do at home and soon tires of children and local gossip, in the afternoon Aunt Marieta slips off without saying a word and accompanies Grandmother Marieta to our farmhouse in Llofriu. There they talk about the things of the earth. They savor the taste of an apple or a pear for five whole minutes.

When Grandmother says the haricots or tomatoes have got black spot, our aunt from Calonge feels it in her bones, because these are things she knows about. Both know when it's time to graft, whether the moon is waxing or waning, why the cork will take or not, when it's being peeled. So does my father. We youngsters don't. The two old women toil away on the farm like a couple of ants. One day I caught them—both at the same time—sticking their hands into a bag of millet. They liked to feel the tiny lukewarm grains on their fingers.

On recent visits Aunt Marieta seemed obsessed by one idea: the desire to own a niche in Calonge cemetery. She repeatedly mentioned this strange business. Time and again she said the prospect of being buried underground horrified her. Apparently Sr. Rosselló is one fine upstanding man in Calonge she trusts completely. Every week she takes him two pesetas. When there are enough pesetas in the pot, they'll start on the niche. Niches cost the earth nowadays. And she wants a good south-facing one, sunny, dry, and well built. Not a single cracked tile to be home to a lizard or a salamander. Everything must be solid. Aunt Marieta talks about possessing one with such passion that when she *does* possess a niche, apart from feeling contented, she apparently believes she'll see everything more clearly, in particular what will happen to her when she dies.

Suddenly Aunt Marieta has upped and gone. She has done what she always does: made a last-minute decision. She's enjoyed her day... and since we were asleep, she didn't want to wake us up. Which path did she take? Who knows. She left on foot, as always, in black rope sandals, carrying her basket, with a scarf around her head.

There is an ancient custom on the Pla farmstead: The names of Sant Antoni and Sant Josep are used as Christian names for successive heirs. That's why I'm Josep. My father, Antoni. My grandfather, Josep. My great-grandfather, Antoni. My great-great-grandfather, Josep. Etcetera, etcetera. If I have a son and keep to tradition, he will necessarily be an Antoni.

When the time came to baptize me, this tradition led to conflict. My paternal grandfather would have been my godfather, if he'd been alive when I was taken to the font. But he was dead, and only Grand-mother Marieta could be a godmother. The role of godfather fell to the maternal side and, there being no Casadevall present, it was rightly the responsibility of a Llach. To be precise, the husband of the oldest Llach great-aunt. This gentleman had the bright idea of calling me Ernest and wouldn't relent, thus sparking an entertaining, ani-mated squabble.

I never had the pleasure of meeting the uncle who held me at the font, who was only ever a potential godfather, because of the row I mentioned. I only have the vaguest idea about him. I know he was a fine old man, a lifelong federalist, fond of his wine and of the heaviest, most solemn tomes in the republican libraries of his day.

If we place him in the Ampurdan liberal tradition, there are grounds for believing that he intended to name the baby "Ernest" af-ter Renan. "Impious" Renan, to be exact.

Tampering with the Ampurdan first-name tradition began in the era of General Espartero. The Baldomeros we have met in the Ampur-dan—and we know a number—were named after the general. The Emilis, after Castelar. The Nicolauses, after Salmerón. Etcetera. Then came classical names, always alternating with scientific names: Ulisses, Arquímedes, Darwin, Hermògenes, Edison. Girls were Salomé, Llib-ertat, Harmonia. This curious revolution in the realm of first names ended in boisterous laughter prompted by an excess of zeal when an upstanding citizen of Begur decided to call his son Comas i Solà after he'd been gazing at the moon with ineffable enthusiasm through the telescope in the Fabra observatory that Comas directed. Our little Begurian would thus have been Comas-Solà Pi i Romaní.

My godfather suggested the name of Ernest, but all the shades in the Pla household tradition moaned and groaned. People negotiated endlessly. The old fellow stuck to his guns in the name of a godfather's rights. The baptism had to be adjourned. The split in the family wid-ened and hostilities were so fierce, the pressure from the magistrate and rector so powerful, that the godfather had to beat a retreat as sick and angry as a Royalist corporal. From that day on the two families have led separate lives and have never again greeted each other. People are *always* bumping into each other in villages and small towns. That refusal to say hello implies the existence of rancor that silently smolders on.

That's a succinct account of blurred scenes from bygone days.

"All that gets my goat!" I hear my sister Rosa comment.

29 May. Our dear friend Pere Poch reappears in our circle at the café and we're very pleased to see him. He's back from Santiago de Compostela where he had been at the university—studying to be an apothecary. He must have sat his examinations on 20 May and is now going to spend the summer here. However, I'm only guessing.

"So, Pere, happy with what you've seen so far?" I ask.

"I've not noticed any big changes. The same as it ever was!" he replies in his modest, deadpan tone.

"Quite, I see," Gori agrees, feigning a stiff, solemn tone. "It seems only yesterday—"

"Exactly!" says Poch, as if waving an arm at a murky horizon.

Our friend must be thirty-five by now. He's been studying pharmacology for nigh on twenty years. He initially stumbled on a subject that went by the name of "technology in physics and pharmacology." A devil of a subject that apparently involves describing from memory the apparatus pharmaceutical science makes use of in its procedures: stills, retorts, and all important tubes. Complicated devices: not the kind of knowledge you'd pick up from *conversazione* at the back of a pharmacist's shop. It is the apparatus one glimpses in the shadows of Goethe's *Faust, Part One*. Whose memory could ever retain the exact, scientific description of a tube? The very thought is terrifying. A tube is the thing most unlike a Venus man ever created—and who could ever describe a Venus? These contraptions become insidious and evil once transmuted into examination topics.

Lo and behold, these descriptions dogged Poch's path through life. After repeatedly failing technology at the University of Barcelona—a technology that the most unlettered mechanics master spontaneously, intuitively—Poch tried elsewhere, making pilgrimages to every center of learning on the Peninsula. A pointless pilgrim! He has shown repeatedly that he can run a first-class pharmacy but has never managed to pass the infamous technology examination, and that has burdened him with an inferiority complex, making him feel shy and resentful. As a result, Poch, never an early riser, finds it impossible to jump out of bed when examination day comes around. Intense pressure from the cosmos traps him between the sheets. The mere thought of the word *technology* jams the springs that should trigger verticality. The years drifting like vague hopes have passed him by, bringing neither fish nor fowl.

Some people reckon that Poch lacks willpower and is a real barfly. True enough, from one point of view. Generally speaking, though, I find him to be extremely tenacious. Right now he looks tired and drawn. You must have a true calling to travel from Santiago de Compostela by train, probably in third class. The oppression that traveling by rail causes seems to hang heavily over him.

Physically, his nose doesn't do him any favors. It's flat on one side and sticks out on the other—like a cork that doesn't fit a bottle's neck properly. However, his botched caricature of a nose is what everybody likes about him. The ugliest men are often thought to be the most likeable. It seems fairer that way. Yet his Sunday habit of wearing a green hat jauntily on the tilt and almost red shoes spoils all that. Such garish petulance jars with the gray-brown, earthy, humble, off-putting hue of his skin. This fellow, who has spent so many years in the great centers of advanced learning, acts like an unrepentant rake on his holidays. He loses the plot on Sundays. In a nutshell, he is a weekday man.

He is very susceptible, like most people beset by shyness. The mere likelihood of innuendo alarms him, however unfounded it may be. Flatter him—even insincerely—and he is extremely happy. He can't resist praise. He relishes the tiniest hint of sweetness from the pastry shop of compliments—even if they are empty words and plastic pastries. In the café today he said, "My family is such a pleasure. They are so thoughtful and polite they never asked me if I've sat an examination, or whether Santiago de Compostela is a pretty place. They welcomed me as if I'd only left this morning."

Poch spoke in a spirit of self-satisfaction. All will be forgiven him forever because of the technology business. Perhaps the division between poets and taxi drivers is in fact useful. At any rate, the upshot is to make us irremediably sad.

When conversation dried up earlier than usual, we said goodbye in the café entrance and watched our friend head up carrer del Clos, on his way, no doubt, to the brothel. We watched him cross the light cast by a streetlamp: shuffling along, looking unimaginably somber and depressed, hands in his pockets, hat brim pulled down.

3 June. After supper at the end of a sultry day, heavy thunder and lightning, a summer storm complete with celestial fireworks. In this country rain is always delightful. Now, with this downpour, it's easy to imagine the physical pleasure trees must feel. When water hits our dusty, Saharan countryside, any vegetation must wallow in the wetness. You could chart the intensity of pleasure a level of moisture and rain brings to the tissues of trees, grass, and soil with a line that ascends from the burden of death through decomposition to renewal and the flourishing of precise, vigorous forms. That line represents our entire adventure in the cosmos.

It rained cats and dogs for almost two hours. When the thick cloud broke, the wind swept away the yellow-and-purple-tinged clouds, and a bright half-moon and glittering, enameled stars appeared. The stars shone bright and iridescent on the wet eaves, turned potholes dark and tinny, while moonbeams plashed off misty, distant roofs. I could have spent the night listening to the water splash down drainpipes, pour out of gutters onto the wet roads. But the downpour stopped and that delightful sound with it. The town was plunged into empty silence.

While it was raining, in the café a wan J. B. Coromina said, "I've got a pain here!"—pointing to his heart.

Perhaps that led me to predict, with real relish—sad to say—that I might be about to enjoy a deep, restful sleep.

5 June. I struggle hard to overcome a Pernod-driven hangover. At home I act as if I am ill. My mother—who misses nothing—turns a blind eye. I suffer for hours and hours from a head like a lead balloon, a mouth as dry as leather, and intermittent hot flashes, as if the skin on my face and body were on fire. I get up just before seven. I feel like cardboard. My God! Vice leaves a bitter taste. Virtue brings sweet consolation. Alcohol does me untold damage...but I am always so thirsty! Besides, I turn to alcohol with the kind of expectation I find irresistible, driven by a longing for strong, stunning experiences. The full, taut, lucid feeling of a body and mind that have been limitlessly expanded! My mind cherishes such high hopes and I'm convinced that such vehemence is wholesome and necessary.

For a single duro (five pesetas, twenty miserable rals) you can buy four genuine Pernods (from Pernod Fils), icy, delicious, and exquisite...and be gripped in a Dionysian whirl for seven or eight hours. This brings ease of response and brilliant flashes of insight in conversation. Alcohol stirs the mental reflexes of the cynic. You watch how people listen, laugh, and even court you with their eyes. As far as human vanity or your own vanity is concerned, nothing pleases or exhilarates like knowing you're being heard and having an audience that is apparently, or even genuinely, attentive. As your vanity is massaged, you feel your thirst mount. You enter a horribly twisted round of swagger and thirst. This alternating of desires lasts as long as it lasts. But in the end it snaps, and you collapse, felled by tremendous physical exhaustion. After the rainbow euphoria of swollen veins and galloping heartbeats you feel a huge emptiness in your gut, your bones crack, your body rends its fibers and you sink into uncanny, immense, horrific despair.

Many are the drunkards I have known in the Ampurdan, and almost all are unable to resist the rhetorical flourishes of their own vanity. I don't know a single one with a tendency to become tranquil and pensive. They are all tenacious talkers: They drink to talk and talk to drink.

In Palafrugell alcohol changes my rhythm of life. In Barcelona, I get up early to go to the university and attend my lectures. I come here and inevitably start getting up at twelve on the dot. Alcoholic tachycardia and a restless heart made an insomniac of me. I find it impossible to sleep at night and have to sleep in the morning: It's the only solution. In recent months this has happened so often it has driven deep inroads into my life. Sometimes I feel . . . how shall I put it?

Sometimes I feel I will never be a man for the morning. My interest in this time of day diminishes by the day. When I get up and leave the house, I feel I am in people's way, simply a nuisance. In the morning people are working, rushing off, going about their business and don't want to be disturbed. I myself, in the morning, have nothing to do—nothing, that is, like what other people do in the morning. My presence annoys and irritates, an unnecessary imposition. That's why I think these must be the most futile moments in the day, the most devoid of meaning and purpose, the most dispensable. It is highly likely that I will get up late throughout my life as a matter of tact, to avoid putting a spoke in the wheels of others, to let them get on with being busy.

(On rereading this last paragraph I can see it is prompted by a casuist's guile rather than by objectivity and reason. What I wrote stands in the face of objective reality. The human intellect! Our intellect, naturally, always conspires on behalf of our likes and desires. It's a more or less sophisticated device that supplies the arguments, all manner of argument, to prop up our most absurd whims. I'd love to know if this kind of intellect serves any other purpose.)

6 June. Alcohol.

I found this curious paragraph in "Snapshot" by Josep Ferrer:

Alcoholic intoxication makes misers prodigal, gives wit to the ignorant, turns egotists into altruists, transforms skinflints into wastrels and good into bad. The most tight-fisted, foolish, out-and-out bore is capable of generosity when under the influence of alcohol—capable of a gesture that would be literally impossible to expect in their normal state. Alcoholic intoxication fosters the most excellent of traits—from the perspective of moral frankness. Each and every one of us has an *alter ego*—a better ego, given that alcohol improves man.

All in all, perhaps one other influence can replicate the effects Ferrer attributes to alcohol: the flattering of personal vanity. The man (or woman) who cannot satisfy the mysterious cravings driven by vanity soon becomes dismal, hard, devious, and spiteful—and this will happen whatever the level of vanity in play. When a man (or woman) feels their vanity is satisfied, the diamantine crystals of potential resentment we carry within us liquefy—only slightly, of course, enough to point up a sense of the ridiculous.

It is plausible to imagine a society of boasters; a society of the meek would be uninhabitable and extremely dangerous.

The sea.

One always feels disappointed by sight of the sea. The sea cannot be portrayed, described, grasped, or understood, and remains totally indifferent.

The Oriental theory—that I have heard so many praise—according to which you attain deeper knowledge through a state of grace rather than patient study, must be based on the ability to delude and mystify that some irresistibly appealing individuals often display.

A poor man passes through Palafrugell every now and then, a man who, when he's out begging, says he is a tax collector.

Thyme, at first, smells sharp and pungent, then softens; rosemary, now in flower, begins gently, then hangs heavy.

Nobody would deny, I believe, that mountains are well made. If anyone dissents . . . that is their problem. Some people are never happy.

7 June. Family memories.

Aunt Lluïsa recounts how her grandmother—my great-grandmother—who was another Lluïsa, felt the need to test the honesty of her servants from time to time. She would put two-cent coins in different corners of the farmhouse. When the time seemed right, she revisited the coins, then whispered, looking askance—as disappointed as she was pleased: "The coins are still there, but it's too early to draw conclusions . . . we'll see soon enough."

Grandmother Marieta and Aunt Marieta from Calonge are walking along the road to our farmhouse in Llofriu. The usual telegraph posts line the road. The wires vibrate in the wind, a persistent growl that sometimes dwindles to a shrill whistle. Aunt Marieta nods in their direction and says, "The wires are making a fuss because they're talking to each other."

"I wonder what they're saying?" asks Grandmother, intrigued.

"You can guess! In the morning they talk about what to do in the evening."

"Naturally, and in the evening about what to do in the morning!" declares Grandmother, chuckling at this parallel confirmation of what is self-evident.

The passage across this earth of infinite generations of obscure country folk may give rise to a man—in this case, myself—who serves no distinct purpose and suffers all the misery in the world when forced to write one of those stupid items known as a local news piece. The end product is always trivial, in my view.

A genuine self-portrait as promised to Srta. Lola S., never sent for fear I'd seem just too ludicrous.

Height: five feet eight and a half inches. If we go by Retzius's classification, my skull decidedly verges on the brachycephalic. I have a short head but a big one. I have thick, abundant hair. I wouldn't have worried if I'd had none, but as a barber on carrer de Cavallers prophesied to my mother when I was a child, I'm predestined never to lose my hair. I'll have hair until the day I die, something that must have made my parents feel intensely proud and contented. It doesn't amount to much, you might say, but it's just as well to be happy with what one has. I don't possess a huge, expansive, mercurial forehead, one that houses (hypothetically) a powerful intellect, that commonplace of novelists. I have a normal forehead that's at a right angle in relation to the earth. My hair is neither blond nor jet-black. It's somewhere in between.

My nose was once a decent, elegantly arranged piece of cartilage. However, I myself destroyed the shape of my nose during the annual fiestas in a village on the east coast where we went on summer vacation one year. During a slippery pole contest I grabbed the trophy from the top of the pole and won first prize (a couple of chickens) after performing acrobatic feats on a greasy, slippery, very tall tree. When I was up there, I grasped the flag but had the bad luck to smash my head against the competition pole. There was a horrible, terrifyingly loud crack. I was dragged from the water more dead than alive, unconscious, blood spurting from my nose and mouth—the sight of blood is always frightening. A numb, purple, and terribly swollen nose. Broken bones in my nose and mashed-up cartilage. Three weeks in bed.

"And what are we supposed to do with these chickens?" asked my family.

It was the most wretched of the few prizes I have won in life. Slightly flattened at one corner, my nose lost its pristine elegance and has been entirely uninteresting ever since.

Beneath eyebrows and lashes bereft of any romantic sweep or intriguing slant, my small eyes, enclosed within piggy-bank slits, are reasonably bright and lively, and are—so I'm told—highly impressionable, responding in equal measure to external prompts and inner reflections. They are untrained, unhypocritical eyes that apparently betray me at every turn. This defect is typical of my facial features, which are so full of movement that whenever an artist friend starts painting my portrait he has to rush to finish the job. What a pity I don't have static, fixed, impassive features, or a textbook arrangement of features. But what's the point of the traits I *do* have? What do they imply? I don't think they suggest sublime sensibility—no more than a broad forehead implies real intellect, whatever novelists like to say. If your face is this active, better to stay at home and avoid all contact with others. If you can't hide the feelings others provoke in you— can't conceal your disappointments in young ladies—you'd better beat a swift retreat from the madding crowd. That would be my good advice to anyone unfortunate enough to be landed with features like mine. On the other hand, I can't tell you the exact color of my eyes. Maybe they're too small for me ever to get a proper look. I sometimes think they're grayish black with an occasional glint or sparkle.

My face is awfully flat with broad, jutting cheeks. Some of my friends in Barcelona have said that I look like a Russian from the Mediterranean—Màrius Aguilar later elaborated the idea in a daily newspaper. I found that highly amusing and was inspired to chart an imaginary family tree. According to this pedigree, I'm descended from the Slavs, if not the Mongols, captured by Algerian pirates, and freed within sight of these beaches by a Christian vessel. Disembarked and baptized, my forebears found life to be so good in this country they decided they'd stay. Friends—and enemies—have invented so much detail and burdened my family tree with so many items ranging from the absurd to the plausible that I sometimes think they believe what they say when they start to discuss it.

In any case, I'm not so boorish as to believe that I am a hundred percent "Latin." My paternal surname is Roman. When Xènius first saw the two words *Josep Pla* in print he said most categorically that my name was earthbound, with its feet on the ground. However, what does the Casadevall from my mother's side imply? In Barcelona, Girona, and the Ampurdan this surname is considered Hebraic, palpably Israelite. One repeatedly finds Casadevalls in the lists of people burnt alive in Castelló d'Empúries in the Middle Ages in the successive pogroms against the Jewish ghetto. In any case, the name is perhaps purer than my mongrel blood, because I don't think I possess the three typical physical traits of the Jews. Sephardic and Ashkenazi Jews have the sad-eyed, baleful look of beaten dogs, and rather than curved and aquiline noses, theirs are flabby and flat at the bottom where small drops of sweat tend to gather; thirdly, the napes of their necks are squat, not well-defined. So then, I don't have sad eyes, a damp nose, or a squat neck. My eyes are bright, sometimes very bright, as you, Lola, have seen for yourself; my nose is dry and the nape of my neck has the lines of a well-written melody. No denying these observations!

It's true, on the other hand, that paternal forebears on my mother's side have always been interested and skilled in commerce: Objectivity compels me to state I've never been blessed with any such flair. I'm absolutely unfit to trade, an acknowledged anticommercial being, perhaps because my surname is Jewish and my race rather mixed. I suspect I'm more Jewish in name than in deed. Conversely, from the perspective of the principles established by Houston Stewart Chamberlain and the dogmas of the purists of Aryanism, in whose direction I was steered by Alexandre Plana, I'm a typical Mediterranean sewer rat. And I don't regret that one bit. I find an excess of blond or whitish blond quite wearisome.

I have a large mouth, full fleshy lips, and excellent teeth. My ears are ordinary and very close to my skull. A strong jaw—though one devoid of excessive or hypothetical willfulness. The putative connection between a person's jaw and his will is another cliché novelists peddle. A beauty spot on my left cheek—decidedly southern and disturbing—adds to the constant movement of my features . . . and we're back to where we were a moment ago! Yes, my unstable features were and are a lifelong obsession. I speak about myself, senyora, as a person completely detached from my existence—a character out of a novel. It's a real misfortune to have such compromising features. My expression can change from grim introspection to childish sentimentality, from icy indifference to burning anguish all in a flash. In this way, my features conspire against consistency of feeling, and lead people I deal with to imagine that my affections and taste are insecure and ever shifting. They conclude I'm superficial and devious, unstable and fickle, drifting and fitful. A theory has even emerged about my supposed cynical frivolity. Others don't trust me. I don't inspire confidence. People think I'm a two-faced, three-faced man, to be relied on as a last resort. I'm sure this distrust has kept many away from my small circle of friends—though that's quite unimportant—and meant others have done all they can to keep me from theirs. And all down to my malleable features, the disturbing beauty spot on my left cheek and a face that shifts and changes so—none my own choosing, that's for sure! If I could have selected my physiognomy, I'd have opted for the stiff, stony features of an English butler. Senyora, this is very sad, but what can I do? My features are a given—and you do what you can with what you have, and no more should be expected.

To this day I have never sported a beard or mustache. From the time hair started to grow on my face when I was at a religious school, I've preferred to be clean-shaven. Apart from some mornings when I suffer an attack of acute misanthropy, I shave daily. From early on I've worn my hair flat, shaped like a brush—*à la parisienne*, as they said then. I've alternated with hair combed back or parted on the left. I have never used pomades or perfumes. Clean water, that's all. I've never worn it long or tried to make it wavy, whether in public or behind closed doors. The women of my day adored wavy hair on men. I spurned such trivia, probably because I never had the time. Forgive my vanity, senyora: My hair has always been visibly understated. I've never believed that a man with long or short hair, combed this way or that, was any different from someone who styled or combed it another way. My naïveté, a consequence of my inner life, is astonishing.

Some young ladies say I have beautiful hands. I'm glad I don't have stubby, misshapen fingers and puffy hands—the kind attributed to butchers, but I must say I wouldn't have lost any sleep if nature *had* endowed me with other tactile extremities. I've seen many a butcher's hand in the most aristocratic circles that still retain their old-style respectability—at least on the surface. I wear a 38–39 shoe. My feet are small and dainty and, unlike my big head, my legs are rather slender. Ladies should have neat, elegant feet, not chubby, flat, dead lumps. That's not so vital for men though it's preferable—providing one avoids miniaturist affectation that is inseparable from extreme vulgarity. I don't deny I have a big head. In fact, I have a big head, a small stomach, an average-size mouth, and an irregular body. Sometimes tears come easily and inexplicably: the uncontrollable reflex action of heart tissue on tear ducts. My lachrymose talents, particularly in the first phase of moistening, are considerable and have ushered in displays of female attachment I'd have done well to avoid. At other times such secretions are nearly impossible and no dialectal reasoning will activate my ducts. So when it comes to the emotions, I'm not a man for the happy mean, conventional, controlled, or balanced. I'm an all-or-nothing man: *Aut Caesar aut nihil*...

I am more sensitive to the poverty of others than to my own. I like bad music and can do nothing about it; I've noticed that people who like only good music do so for the same reasons I like bad music. I'd be able to flatter anyone intelligent in any branch of learning if he teaches me something, but I'd be unable to praise anyone else unless I was extremely poor. I prefer pleasant ladies to beautiful ones; I cultivate rationalism informed by irony; I like well-dressed company, but personally have never thought what I wear at all important; the clothes others wear are fine by me, provided the fabric is good. I've never felt titillated by the bespoke. I like comfortable shoes, even old ones. I'm not ambitious, and could never wheel and deal to guarantee myself a place in the limelight. I'd like to have money—money brings freedom, especially in our country—but not for its own sake, managing money wastes too much time and generates sterile anguish. I'd rather converse with a trader, industrialist, farmer, or veterinarian than with a colleague.

I tend to assume that others are right—to see their point of view—rather than insist I'm right, even if it may harm my own interests. I don't expect you to believe this and you'll think I'm a common hypocrite. But it's true! I mistrust myself more than anyone. I feel horror verging on nausea and disgust at the very idea of fretting about the motives behind the actions of others. The motives behind my own actions, on the other hand, have led me to die of shame a thousand times. I've never attempted to cultivate my powers of memory in order to demonstrate humanity's lack of dignity. In this respect I believe amnesiacs are on the right track in life. While we're on the subject of memory, I'm quite skilled in retaining the contents of what I read generally and from books and have always had a keen interest in detail, in small, insignificant things. I feel as passionately about the dead as the living. Historical memory is as real to me as present time.

You'll say you can't travel the world holding such beliefs, that failure is guaranteed, inexorable, fated. Most likely! But I did promise to speak candidly. Later, if you wish, we'll debate these matters further and see if we can shed more light on them.

I am much more drawn to science than to metaphysics and theology.

In terms of health and hygiene I've always thought sleep extremely important. Indeed, I think it's more important than eating or indulging other physical needs. Of course, one shouldn't say this to a lady, because ladies occasionally like their men to be awake. But what do we do if the desire to sleep conquers all, even the strongest longings that seem hard as granite? When I sleep the hours I need to sleep, I feel myself to be in fine fettle, more energetic. If my sleep is fretful and broken, exhaustion, enervation, physical discomfort, and swollen veins may lead me to act foolishly, to use radical language and make judgments that are more off the cuff than usual.

You see, senyora, this *is* interminable. So far I've told you what I am like, skimming the surface, which is the only way I can approach the task. Everything I've said is true. But it's not the whole story. Truth, in the end, depends on means of expression and my means are limited. Very limited! If I said it was impossible to venture further, I'd be lying. But I personally can't continue right now and remain intelligible. Perhaps I can add something another day—and it won't be as puerile as what I've written so far. I'll complete the self-portrait now by telling you how I'd like to be.

You'll have noticed how I judge things from a generous, tolerant perspective, taking pleasure in hearing and understanding others. The mere existence of one man on earth creates sufficient unease and protest, let alone others, so no need to want to add insult to injury with one's own, unsolicited deliberations. Better to go unnoticed or if you like, senyora, to slip through the net. This is particularly vital in countries like ours that harbor so much envy, where so many people unable to live by their own lights thus prefer to ravage others. Sometimes, being fat is the best way to go unnoticed: Fatness forges character and creates a distinct tone. Thin men are usually precise, tireless, and finicky; fat men are vague, aimless, and amusing. The former usually perform fanatically, using a compass and ruler; the latter operate with rough guesses and inexact, appealing gestures. If I were fat, I'd probably spend my time on the small pleasures of food and drink and go to the café every evening to snooze for a while, and when appropriate, between naps I'd talk to my friends. I'd be tentative, discreet, leave things half unsaid, hint, use a light touch, and, as fat men do, I'd crack frivolous jokes about the dead and those keeping vigil, and spare the dead on their way elsewhere the solemn obituaries while the living enjoy and witness the depths of my goodness and my frailty. If someone made fun of me, I wouldn't even get up from my chair, because nothing discomforts a fat man more than being forced to make the effort to rise from the chair or chairs he occupies on this earth. Yes, senyora, it is true. Quantity molds character, and quantity cannot be judged by our usual sense of what is ridiculous.

I'm implying that a fat man personally carries a tremendous burden of the irrevocable and undeniable absurdity of life. By the same token, a fat man is exceptionally placed to be good, almost averse to vanity, to see the world as a fatally unjust spectacle, and to be hostile to ideas of precision and impossible perfectibility.

I'd like to aspire to occupy such a place in this world. I find it sad to have to say that morality in practice is based on glandular levels of lethargy, diminished lust for life, and severe erosion of the senses. When blood's coursing through your veins, it's time to tie a knot in your tail. Any other form of morality is bookish debate and treatises such as bookshops sell. I said that's the place I'd *like* to occupy; I doubt I'll ever make it, in any substantial way.

When future historians examine my family tree, they may decide that I've been quite unlucky with my forebears. Men judge things by their surface, and though it's an attitude in decline, it's hard to deny that we humans are easily dazzled. True enough, my forebears are obscure, but I've surely inherited their traditional hospitality and openness. I'm not fond of fanatics and don't believe fanaticism has ever influenced me in personal matters. My grandfather Josep took such a stance to its final consequence. At the time of the Second Carlist War, he billeted Royalist officers and ardent Carlists in his spacious home. He never shut anyone out and served everybody the same beef, peas, and stew. If those crazed fools had dared, they could have sat at the same table and my commonsense grandfather would have acted as the usual friendly host. But the roles they were bent on performing never allowed them, and the maids of the house often had their work cut out serving four suppers in a row in different parts of the house as a result of this civil strife. If a man with Count Gobineau's gift for fantasy had deigned to study my case, he might have concluded I carry in my blood too few seeds of violence and dogmatism to be thought a dummy of the first order. In short, I am a man of these climes, a maritime fellow from this corner of Europe, an adept of halftones, of rain and gray mists, ironic rather than confrontational, contemplative rather than manic. In any case, I believe there are more important forms of lunacy.

Doing what he did with those men, my grandfather perhaps wanted to suggest that he was humble yet enlightened, a man who wanted to be at peace with himself and the world around him. I think such a gesture was linked to reason and reality rather than any combination of weakness and cynicism. In this respect I don't think I have followed in his footsteps. My most typical trait is lack of resistance and a lack of resistance is dangerous because it can contain the seeds of a great deal that is unjust. I feel like the chrysalis that never makes it to a butterfly. I am swayed by one implausible or unpleasant thing after another that I can't cast off. That's why I'm bad in business, make so many wrong moves, yet never reform. I fall in love with women the day before disillusion sets in. Quite unintentionally I insult people I love and cherish hidden affection for out-and-out enemies. Oh, senyora, what a comedy of errors!

I've written ever since I was a child, but writing for me is an artificial, superfluous activity. I have no clear idea—as is often the case—about what I ought to have done in life, especially what I *could* have done. Nonetheless, this hobby has disfigured me, has spawned a strange person within my inner, spontaneous self, and even I haven't a clue how we came to be related given that we are so different. As a result of this split personality, I seem naturally frail and low-spirited, and when I pick up my pen I become aggressively Dionysian, enter a state of silent exultation, and can defend a position to the last. How can one make any sense of this? What does it mean? Has the cultural

milieu that contaminates us all to a varying degree damaged me beyond repair? While civilized man is gentler, more compassionate and
tolerant, I still rile and flail. Perhaps I'd have been better served by a
massive injection of good grace instead of a coating in that cultural
dross.

In the end, I'd have no worries if the metamorphosis was complete
and I could carry on as normal. The world wants be rounded and
craves a bit of everything. But it's not easy. I search, test the waters, try
every angle, and find nothing and nobody. Everyone goes about their
own business with enough from daily routines to occupy them. The
terrain is deserted. Nobody wants to argue or is in the mood for any
nonsense. People simply get on with their lives.

So I'd like to be fat but am lean; I'd like to learn but find no colleagues; I'd like to debate but find closed minds. It is at once pitiful
and comic. This wretched situation gives me the air of a man at a loss,
searching for work but not finding any. And so, senyora, I feel I fit in
nowhere and roam the world like a lost soul.

13 June. I accompany Bofill de Carreras (Gori) to Tamariu. We walk
along the wonderful coastal road Linares built during the war to give
work to the unemployed. Bofill is a hunting man, and a keen walker.
If you want to live well in a small town, he says, you must know how
to hike.

We meet our friends in Tamariu, the usual suspects, the marooned,
scabby hoboes from Palafrugell and thereabouts. The usual rabble.
Foreigners too. A Russian has made an appearance, a taciturn misan-
thropist who never says a word, despite being, so they reckon, a poly-
glot, and nobody knows where he's from. The pedestrian postman is
an old Spaniard. When they gave him the job, they supplied him with
a new cap with a silvery metal band. Acidic sweat from his brow has
transformed the band into a kind of black plastic leather. In the summer, men trawl with a dragnet; in winter, they turn to art. When it's
cold, they seem to shrivel and wither, and when the warm weather

comes, they expand and revive. They live in a state of intermittent intoxication and compete for the favors of two or three women whose combined ages add up to a good two centuries. The sea is sad and humiliating, but they react to this humiliation as if it were some abject, almighty drug.

"These men," I say to Gori, "have got a screw loose."

"And so have I . . . and so have you!" he retorts, with a cackling grin.

"You live better than these guys."

"You're kidding! Happiness starts at a decent level of unawareness."

Bofill secretly envies these people their appalling freedom. They are his friends. They amuse him. He probably uses them to stage Olympic rounds of laughter. He's the kind that finds poverty picturesque.

A rather cold, unappealing walk back. We massage our egos all the way.

15 June. "How do you expect me to paint angels," Gustave Courbet asked a group of friends, "when I've yet to see one?"

When the old critic Alfred Opisso heard this anecdote, he wittily dubbed Courbet "the Royalist corporal of all realists."

Goethe's famous serenity, if it did ever transcend his style and constitute an aspect of his life, is frankly repellent, if you ask me.

I've been reading *Saint Francis* by the Dane Jörgensen. It's a pleasant, uncluttered book, a delicate tracery of lines and forms within the lightest mist. A Saint Francis out of sentimental fiction coupled with the ambience of a week in England. The terrible, harsh world we live in tends to convert the "Poverello" into a mere decorative detail in prints or scenes for the dining-room wall: the fate of Millet's *Angelus*.

I've never seen tragedy performed, but I imagine an audience should stand for tragedy. Strictly speaking, only comedies can be performed to a seated audience.

The most important, chemically pure daydreamers are those who gawp at the ground.

Romain Rolland's position on the war was what led most visibly to the collapse of his popularity, which had been huge here, especially among music buffs, when I arrived in Barcelona in 1913. Rolland's following here was avant-garde and pro-French. Today there's no point trying to justify his stand by invoking the moral unity of Europe and claiming the noble high ground by placing oneself *au-dessus de la mêlée*. A waste of time. Passion is all and passion is contagious. People say he is unpatriotic, a deserter, and think they've shut the case. Something similar happens with Xènius. He's on the decline on every front. You might say you can't pull the wool over people's eyes now.

The shrillness and biological idiocy of a woman's laughter requires a swift counterattack: Stop it once and for all and move on. When appearances don't deceive (and that's quite unusual), the result is highly positive. When the laughter subsides, you feel you've been relieved of a great burden.

Sitting at my desk, pen in hand, faced by an immaculately blank quarto sheet, I often think hope is a most overrated virtue.

19 June. My obsession with the university, though faltering, still persists. I sometimes dream of the place. I'll wake up in a panic, thinking I must go to this or that class in the morning and haven't memorized the set texts. Or an examinations panel suddenly appears in a flow of hallucinating images: three crotchety bores sitting on a high podium at a table behind a lottery drum for selecting numbered balls, bathed in the grayish light that filters through the massive bars over the Law

Faculty lecture theater windows. Books, ideas, benches, courtyards, lecture theaters, beadles, conversations, flagstones, columns, fellow students—the whole caboodle leaves me adrift in a morass of cold anguish, feeling it's all contrived, incomprehensible, and devoid of interest. So far I've found nothing there to spark the slightest curiosity, and certainly not the people whose business it should be to do the sparking. Most students who walk through the doors of that immense edifice are convinced there's nothing doing.

I sometimes think that if workers, traders, industrialists, small farmers, and bankers behaved in their work, industry, fields, and banks like my university lecturers, we'd have ground to a halt long ago. The country would be at a standstill.

Dreams of the university! How grotesque! A world that should inspire such beautiful dreams, yet conjures up images of gentlemen nodding off in front of a table mounted on a podium.

I have read the eighty-five sentences in the French translation of Plato directed by Victor Cousin (translated by Saisset) that are grouped under the general title of *Définitions*. The majority are filled with such obvious banalities they seem like fake pensées contrived by an illustrious representative of French *sagesse*. In any case, if they were written two and half millennia ago by the man held to be the most adroit writer of our era, they should perhaps have turned out to be longer and meatier.

I also read that a line had been recovered from a lost poem attributed to Homer, the contemporary relevance of which is undeniable—at least insofar as I'm concerned: "He knew lots, but poorly."

In Catalonia, cordiality lasts two or three days—at most, even between people who are closely connected or have a real interest in making a connection.

In Gervasi's tavern on plaça Nova I hear one man say to another, holding a glass of white wine:

In Campmany they grow turnips;
in Cabanes, gourds;
in Vilabertran, peppers,
aubergines, and tomatoes.

The still life invoked by these lines gives me a delicious feeling of the end of spring and the start of summer.

A delicious combination in this month of June: cheese and cherries for dessert. As I see it, the taste of cheese and cherries complement each other. A pity the cheeses in this country are so bland and uninspired. The best cherries aren't the first crop, that is, the whitish ones, but the hard, luscious, fleshy red cherries they call pigeon-heart or kill-stone. Those pecked by a sparrow are particularly delicious.

20 June. Dinner with Ramon Casabó.

He's come to conclude the sale of the pharmacy he owned here. He discovered that being a small-town pharmacist is a dismal business that permanently pins a man to his desk. He's gone back to his part of the world (Olot) and begun to study dentistry. In the years he lived here, we became very good friends—in fair weather and foul.

He hasn't changed a bit. He's a rather round-shouldered young man with the whitest skin, an almost hairless face, and blue eyes, and he's distinguished by being a nervous chain smoker, leg-puller, and caustic wit. He reckons people have always thought what he wanted them to think about him. He's astonished by how psychologically straightforward people in the Ampurdan are. Despite his markedly shy, retiring appearance, he's the only one of us in recent years to attempt cold, calculated acts of daring.

Casabó wants to make the most of life. Everything's fine as long as no one bothers him too much. He's intelligent but makes unimaginable efforts to ensure people don't realize it. He's always trying to act up as the poor wretch, the nincompoop. Of course, one must work—though as little as possible. He thinks it's vital to marry a rich woman to prosper in life. "When I have achieved that," he says, "I'll devote my life to painting." He is eagle-eyed and not in thrall to any ideology or prejudice. Words don't begin to express him. What really holds him back is his fear of seeming ridiculous. However, I don't know what he'd do if he were pulled in different directions by his self-interest and this fear. React like anyone else, I suppose.

"The difference," he affirms, "between earning one's crust in Olot or Palafrugell is that you need to be more two-faced in Olot." Then he pauses and adds: "But you do realize that doesn't bother me one bit? I couldn't care less."

In the club where we go for coffee, we resurrect past habits as a gambling duo and play baccarat for a while. We each win thirteen duros. Thirteen duros is a fabulous amount: sixty-five pesetas, in other words, two hundred and sixty magnificent cups of aromatic coffee.

"Gambling does more damage than alcohol," I tell Casabó, trying to think of something to say.

"That depends!" he retorts timidly. "Gambling on a winning streak is one of the healthiest exercises ever invented. When your head aches and you gamble and win, the impact's more immediate than any aspirin. Losing is what gets a man down."

In the early hours a second supper with Gallart, Coromina, and friends at Cal Tinyoi. Round after round of drink. Crazy nonsense. The owner of the establishment presides over the repast: larger than life, abrupt, hoarse, ruddy-cheeked, and dead tired. He's spent the whole day chasing quail and now faces a dish of the birds succulently roasted and awash in fat. He eats like clockwork, eyes half closed, cap tilted over the back of his neck. His teeth crunch the bones and set mine on edge. Casabó orders cold sausage, red wine, and an onion omelet. Huge amounts are imbibed. The conversation turns into a shouting match. Ominous tachycardia; growing discomfort. It's cool in the barroom, but drops of sweat trickle down cheeks, comically.

At four in the morning, Coromina notices that Casabó has disappeared. We search high and low. Not a trace. A dinner that ends with one's guest disappearing is an unusual event.

"It only happens in this neck of the woods," says fatty Girbal, looking embarrassed, as if he's not partial to such practices.

"He must have run to catch the last train," says an incoherent Coromina.

"Of course, the first train . . . he must have taken fright and fled," says a glum Gallart.

The night was dreadful. Despite his strange disappearance, we will surely miss Ramon over the next few days.

23 June. Nighttime. Saint John's Eve festivities.

By the evening people are sweeping and washing down the streets. The acacias give off a strong sweet scent. Children bring all kinds of junk to the bonfires. As melancholy as ever, the town livens up— nearly. People sit on café terraces. Streetlights don't seem their usual dull yellow. Girls walk by, dolled up and off to a big party. They leave a trail of cheap sickly perfume in the air. If I went to one, I wonder what I'd do. When night falls, the sky is dark blue and immense: a dismally oppressive emptiness.

I went out late. By now everything's gone up in flames. A smell in the air of burnt cork that's cooled down. People are sending their children to bed. There's always the odd one with a sooty black smear on his brow or cheek who keeps skipping over the extinguished fire. Embers glow under the ash on street corners. It is a warm, peaceful night and, as the smoky smell fades, the air seems silken. People sit outside their front doors half asleep, motionless, silent, and stunned by the fresh air, as if the flames had sucked all feeling from their lives and left only wax dummies.

25 June. Second day of the main fiestas in Palamós. I went for a while in the early evening. Inspected the marquee, went in and out of cafés, wandered the streets like a lost soul. People in their Sunday best wearily drank beer and fizzy lemonade. The hullaballoo, stalls, pushing and shoving, merry-go-rounds, music, children, and families took me out of myself. One year, late at night, I spotted Don Pau Matas, long white beard, dress shirt with winged collar, lowering the English flag on the balcony of his consular office.

It was a rather bittersweet holiday, dampened by the downpours that the summer solstice brings. At other times it could be swept by the cooler, wetter southwesterlies of our climate.

The sea, bay, and small port of Palamós are so wonderfully animated you couldn't ask for a better backdrop for a fiesta than its color and contours on a calm day, and its gentle warmth, dazzling brightness, and freedom on a windswept one. The whole party took place on the beach, thirty yards from the water, beneath the great heavenly vault over the bay, above the twilight blue and purple streaks of the distant Gavarres sierra. Together with the festive red and green illuminations, the glint of ships' lights flickering on still water and the high rigging silhouetted against the stars, the silent, sleeping port offered next to the crowd bustling in the white, acetylene glare an atmosphere of mystery and solitude that was ripe, if underexploited, for affairs of the heart and vagaries of the mind. In the early hours, the stars twinkled in the murky green glow and one's thoughts and will drifted in random reveries.

Because I started going to the big fiestas during the black-silk stocking era, I don't remember the earlier farmhouse celebrations, long lunches with six or seven main courses, dancing in the main living room and violins playing mournfully to the rustle of crinolines.

I do recall a childhood image from a day when there was a big party at the Pla farmhouse: A young man—his back to the window, silhouetted against an orange-juice sunset, wearing a black, thin-lapelled jacket, stiff collar, and tie, his blond beard magnified by the light inside—was deep in conversation with a sad-eyed, sallow young lady, the toes of whose leather shoes peeped out from her long skirt like the heads of tiny mice, and whose blouse languished in ribbons and bows beneath a hairdo at once lofty and solemn in its architectural design. Every now and then, my uncle Martí knocked ash from his cigarette rolled in 0.45 paper with a long, ivory finger. The young lady's back was half turned, as she gazed into the dusk with that rapture people—at the time—feigned, when in fact they felt completely unmoved. Everyone would say they'd felt a frisson, and it was always the same people who quivered with the same frisson. She suddenly tipped her head back, flashed her teeth sadly, and said, "There's an awful draft here."

He replied, "You're quite right. We'd better not take any chances."

The young lady walked in first and both slowly faded away.

26 June. My father has coupled up the cart and will go to Aigua Xaŀlida this afternoon with my brother and me, along the old track to Begur. It is a glorious, dazzling summer afternoon, with none of the sultry stickiness of the dog days.

The path we take is so wonderful and I shudder to think how all my efforts to describe it have failed completely. This track was one of my early literary exercises like the scenery along the road to Sant Sebastià. So many paltry attempts!

When you reach the Can Marquès del Puig saddle, a unique coastal landscape comes into sight: solitary, silent, deep purple highlands shot through with gullies and crags. I can feel a stifling air of mystery floating over the sullen rocks, as if there'd been a pirate raid, and I can hear a female prisoner's distant wailing. Ric and Moncal are on the right, the Falugues in the center, Aigua Xaŀlida and Tamariu in the background, Cala Pedrosa and Sant Sebastià (a rear view) on the right.

I have often gazed at this landscape with Joan B. Coromina, who finds it equally resonant and evocative. You can imagine yourself in an isolated, comfortable house in the company of a young lady with a morose, primitive temperament, who is nonetheless slim and dressed elegantly and simply: sturdy shoes, sheer nylons, a red scarf around her neck, hair loose, perfumed by the wind, and ready to strip off at a timely moment. And good tobacco, books, etcetera. Coromina's theory is that one's interest in a woman doesn't depend on beauty, style of dress, or accent, or even on the physical or mental qualities her presence may suggest: In the end, at every moment, it is shaped by the suitability of the landscape in which she moves. There are women for many landscapes, some women are right for only one, and some women for none at all. When the fit is right, infatuation is guaranteed, automatic, inevitable.

After reaching the well at En Callol, we make our way down through sandy pine groves to Aigua Xal·lida. The blossoming trees give off a dry scent. Clumps of heather and scrub bring a dull glow to the shady woods. The crickets' song crackles loudly—and sometimes vanishes as if they've fled far away. Patches of bright bluish, warm, luminous sky through gaps between branches. The shadows seem to be slumbering in the stillness of the air.

My father is deeply in love with Aigua Xal·lida. Sentimentally and tenderly so. Sitting on the tiny sandy beach, listening to the water flow from the fountain, opposite a calm sea, in that remote, isolated spot, he tells us, rather sententiously, that the coast—and Aigua Xal·lida in particular—awaits a future we can barely imagine. The sun falls on the basalt of the Bufadors mountains and burns, smolders, and bewitches.

My brother takes off his shoes and collects sea urchins from the nearby rocks—sea urchins we crack open with a stone and eat with a slice of bread and a drop of wine. Delicious.

As the sun goes down, the afternoon seems to clear, colors deepen, and outlines sharpen. Reefs and cliffs stand out purple against the pearl-white motionless sea. Crimson basalt turns bright red. Sad, gloomy shadows thicken under the gleaming crests of the pines.

On our way back, we see a brig out at sea between the teeth of the Falugues Islands: still, as if etched on porcelain, the sun dying on its limp sails. Many ships sail by. The sea asks for nothing more.

From the Can Marquès del Puig saddle we watch the pale pink twilight, a rather tawdry postcard affair. The humidity in the air is intense, and woods and plants exhale soft, densely velvet puffs of scent.

30 June. Gori went to Calella yesterday—it was Saint Peter's Day, their big fiesta—and one might invoke of him (Gori, that is) these lines by Pitarra, "a great man for stuffing himself / and searching out what he wants," because he came back irritated by the second supper he'd been served. It seems, all in all, that the lobster and chicken he was offered for starters were tasty enough. Conversely, the goose (or duck, I don't remember which) and turnips that were dished up immediately afterward were leathery, inedible, and unremittingly tough.

By virtue of this sad business he launches into a disquisition on the feeding of ducks and geese in this country. "When I think of their diet," he says, "I become quite livid. Local farmers tend more and more to fatten their animals on the small gray snails we call 'joanets.' The ducks and geese swallow them whole: shell and snail together. Digesting this mainly calcareous mix must be very laborious, literally an athletic feat. The animals' stomachs are pointlessly tired. And exhaustion prompts a general drying out of their entire body and an inability to produce white, tender, juicy flesh—such flesh as God created to melt in our mouths, if indeed this universe has any meaning!" he exclaims, carried away by his own eloquence. "These animals thus come to death cheerless, skinny, and desiccated, deprived of that minimal joie de vivre that food should bring. Distraught ducks and mad, hysterical geese! Hence these dismal second suppers, the leathery meat, the monotonous, mechanical masticating, impregnated with pessimism and melancholy."

When Gori speaks of things that don't interest him, he is clever, witty, and sharp in the way he argues. When, on the other hand, he refers to personal matters, he tends, unconsciously of course, to become exceedingly pompous and long-winded. And this is perhaps a trait we people from the Ampurdan often display. Self-interest and rhetoric are two things we combine. Consequently, although the issue of these diets is very topical, especially now, if he'd continued his speech in this vein we'd have been lulled to sleep by the waves of words, cradled by the music of the spheres.

So I am led to think that rapture and Dionysian transports here tend to be sparked by urgent self-interest. Their impetus is expressed in pompous rhetoric. If such impulses meet a whiff of alcohol, the swagger escalates. That must be why drunkards in the Ampurdan—

few but a fine crew—are usually fearful, quarrelsome, strong orators. And dreadful bores. I flee them as the devil flees the cross.

2 July. The excursion to Aigua Xal·lida made me think of Begur. Now that's a town I like. Popularly, Begur is the supreme essence of Palafrugell, the perfect fulfillment of Palafrugell—a town of free, easygoing, spontaneous folk. My old friend Brincs is one of them, a real character. His story is simple enough.

Pere Brincs reaches the hut on his vineyard after sunrise. He throws the door wide open, and after hanging his shepherd's pouch on a nail and putting his stick behind the door, he claps his hands. Four hens rush noisily out, excitedly fluttering their wings in the sun and leaving a fluffy feather dangling from his mustache.

"Cluck, cluck, cluck . . ."

Pere Brincs keeps four hens to bring a spot of color to his vineyard.

As the mornings are cool, he lights a fire in the hearth. In the summer he does so in the shadows by the doorstep. He lights a cigarette, toasts his bread, and singes his herrings. Then he sits on the big stone by the entrance to eat his toast dressed with oil and vinegar and rubbed with a clove of garlic. The slice of bread has a luxurious sheen, like a piece of a cardinal's chasuble touched by the dying sun. There are many handsome chasubles. The rather salty toast makes him thirsty. Once he's eaten it, he fills up on wine.

After a good smoke, he walks around the vineyard with his hoe. Every day at this time, he asks the same question: "Where should I start?" He walks around his plot slowly, like a dog around its bowl. He sometimes looks at the vines askance, as if to say "You make me laugh."

His vines are on the southern slope of Cape Begur, overlooking Fornells. Right at the top, in the thinnest soil, there are old, patched-up olive trees, a fig tree that's a challenge to keep upright, and six or seven pines that cast shade. A garishly golden oriole sometimes settles on the fig tree. It's a plot of land tailor-made for petulant partridges that prefer to hop. There is a well halfway down, with two columns supporting a pine-branch arch and a blue sink for preparing sulfate. At the bottom end, the vineyard joins the carabineers' path, a white ribbon that twists and turns gently along the rocky outcrop over the sea. If you walk along it, a strong smell of seaweed and marine fennel hits you. In foul weather sea spray splatters the front row of vines.

The vineyard receives the sun the whole year. In the autumn it turns the color of toast, and when you walk between the vines you expect the earth to crunch as if you were treading on bread crumbs. From the sea it looks like a crucible spitting fire and ash when the sulfur flames up in the pit and sink. From the hut you can see the sea and the old-fashioned elegance of ships sailing across the entire Fornells bay, with the Falugues antlers to the right and Cape Begur to the left. The Falugues are mountains the color of a dove's neck where the rocks seemed to have rusted and blossomed. You can also see the houses of Fornells, a dazzling white, yellow, and pink, the graceful shadows of Aiguablava beach, foam spiraling up the rocks, and other vineyards, pine and olive groves on the warm, sunny slope.

And, finally, after all that, he much prefers to hoe and weed. Spreading sulfate requires too much walking. Pruning and grafting make you drowsy, and it's hardly fun waking up with a rock against your back and a vine tendril up your nostril. From a distance, ruddy, long-faced Pere Brincs looks like a partridge pecking at its tray.

Who knows how long he works at a stretch. Perhaps he can't last for more than an hour. When he reckons he's done his stint, he straightens his back, wipes his brow, glances at the sun, and declares, "Lads, now for a drop of the wet stuff."

He walks back to his hut, takes the gourd from its hook, presses the neck, and a spurt of wine hits his tongue. Then he slowly returns to his tilling. As he does so, he stoops here, stops there, pulls up weeds or bracken, picks fennel, throws a stone away, straightens a vine shoot, dusts a green bug from a vine leaf.

Suddenly it's midday. He draws a bucket of water to keep his wine cool and in winter spends half an hour coaxing a log to burn on the embers in his hearth. He blows on the red cinders and the fire glows on his cheeks. He spreads out his tablecloth, toasts bread, eats his fish tail or gnaws a cutlet. Then he chooses a bunch of grapes, savors their sweetness, or cracks a few nuts.

"The best thing for now," he then says, "would be a snooze."

If it's hot, he lies under the soft, caressing rustle of the tall pines. From the shade he watches the white, lathering, languid sea. The horizon is blue and cool. A seagull glides by flapping its wings. The landscape has an antique stillness, at once benign and paternal. If someone shouts, the wind carries the cry gently away. Time passes, like a trickle of olive oil.

If the sun is mild, he beds down under a blanket in a hollow full of graybeard leaves that the breeze blows there from the vines. Sometimes he can still feel the warmth of a hare. He curls up like a bug. The serene sky glazes his eyes and he looks up into the air as if a wondrous swarm of golden bees were drifting by, closes his eyes slowly, still savoring the bitter aftertaste of walnut on his lips and the warmth of the earth in his bones. He is lulled to sleep by a lilting refrain:

The people from Banyols and la Roca
one year did go to the fair . . .

If he dreams, he dreams of his youth, particularly of the Sundays when he and his friends came to the vineyard to feast and frolic. In the morning, the hunters would gather and go out to shoot, making a huge racket with their dogs. They'd bring back three-quarters of a rabbit or a partridge. The fishermen would collect a bag of mussels or a net full of sprats. Then they'd cook succulent rice fit for a king—rice soaked in silvery shellfish juices. Sauces sizzled in the pan sparking a festive fervor, and stomachs tingled anticipating the final bubbles. They sang to their hearts' content and returned home hands numb, mouths thick and doughy, heads hazy and aching, flesh soft and sweet. The scent of rosemary was refreshing to a point, but inspired thoughts of female thighs and downy cheeks.

One day Pere Brincs appeared in his vineyard with a rifle over his shoulder. A skinny, lugubrious old dog trailed after him. When the dog saw a butterfly or a locust, it stopped dead and looked askance at his master. Then it sniffed, shook the dust from its ears, and leapt at the insect. However, its legs wouldn't obey. It often fell on its back and started whimpering. Then, as its eyes moistened, it followed the flight of the butterfly and limped on, crestfallen.

Apparently Pere Brincs armed himself and kept a dog in order to go hunting; in fact, he bought the gun to scare off the carabineers who were stealing his grapes. The dog simply gave him cover. He wasn't a hunting man: He preferred to keep out of harm's way and the smell of gunpowder did nothing for him.

When the carabineers found out, they stopped visiting his vineyard. That saddened him.

"What shall I do with my gun now?" he wondered and worried.

He hung it up high in a corner of his hut, clean, next to a full cartridge belt. He soon tired of seeing it there and let it be known that it was for sale; meanwhile he faced up to his dog and decided to get rid of it too. However, as he felt attached to the animal, it was a case of having to, though it hurt. He found it prone beneath the fig tree, drowsy and dozing, eyeing a passing fly.

"This dog," he muttered, "acts as if it's owed and nobody is paying up."

"Such a poor, old, miserable sod!" he thought, on the other hand.

"What are we going to do with you, Lleó?" he asked woefully, reflecting his indecisive, hesitant state of mind.

Lleó looked him up and down, without flinching, curled its lip, and dozed off again and when the time came followed the master.

Along the way Brincs was torn between selfishness and compassion. First he squinted at the dog, then eyed it tenderly. Exclaimed "You don't like this dog one bit," then muttered a sorrowful "Poor old Lleó!" The dog walked on, oblivious, resigned, and aloof. He suddenly felt a rush of spite, gritted his teeth, blushed in shame, and hissed, "Lleó, you're an evil bastard. If I chucked a few stones at you, you'd soon clear off."

When they reached the spot where the tracks crossed, the dog came to a halt a few feet from its master. It looked at him, stared, bowed in his direction, and took the path on the left. Brincs had to go right. His heart missed a beat. He watched it pad into the distance, flip-flap, flip-flap. He screamed: "Lleó!" The dog went on, never turned around, and that was the last he saw of it.

This episode knocked the stuffing out of him.

"Where the hell are you, poor Lleó?" he'd say, rubbing the back of his neck.

These wretched scenes tried him sorely. What with this, the filched grapes, his purchase of the shotgun, and everything else, he raged furiously against the carabineers. He never could stand the sight of them; now they threw him into a fury. He loathed them even more when a joker at the barbershop said there'd be no smuggled goods if it weren't for the carabineers. He'd sometimes stand in the entrance to his hut and watch them climbing up a slope, with their hardware and capes, looking for snails and asparagus. It was too much for him. He made a trumpet with his hands and bawled, "Bloody bastards!"

His cry slowly faded out to sea and through the pines. He was still bawling when fear gripped him. Then he felt another wave of anger surge and shouted again, walking backwards, feeling weak around the knees. Bawling and walking backwards, he finally shut himself up in his hut.

"Try not to lose your temper!" he'd say, standing by the window to see what happened.

God knows where the carabineer was.

On rainy days he stayed undercover. He lit a good fire from dry branches and played a soporific game of solitaire with a pack of thick cards. Now and then he ventured out with his umbrella. Studied the weather and shuffled back inside, muttering. His chimney billowed smoke. He was taken aback by the swirling, gray-black clouds, where raindrops glittered like shards of glass.

Later, in the early evening, he'd put on his clogs, lock his hut—the hens were already roosting—and hike along the coast under a huge umbrella battered noisily by the big cascading drops.

As he walked uphill, his imagination often ran riot. It was a time to dwell on what he'd like to do and say. He drew castles in the air; his vineyard seemed broader and longer. Or he'd feel resentful and like nothing he saw around him. The wet pines were a somber green, the gorse dripped rain, and the soil reeked of death.

He'd sit and rest on a rock at the top of the saddle. From there one could take in the twilit countryside and Brincs sitting there like a shadow. Then he would resume his forced march. One day, as he rose from the rock, he let out a great sigh seeing the moon rise over the sea like a wheel of cheese.

3 July. I overhear Maria, an old maid who now works for us after being in service in Girona for many years, telling my sisters: "When I was on plaça del Vi, I preferred funerals best of all, especially when they were burying an officer or soldier and the regimental band played. Because you know, my dearies, the band always strikes up at these funerals. When I heard it in the distance, I couldn't resist going out on the balcony. I'd sometimes rush downstairs quick as lightning to watch the cortege pass by. On the other hand, marriages left me cold. When I saw another married couple going into Unal the photographer's to get their marriage photos taken, I thought they looked so sad, worried, and tongue-tied, they didn't set me dreaming at all."

"So Maria," I would say, "you must like the Day of the Dead and the cemetery."

"That's right, master Josep, I do indeed, but I'd like it even more if I could hear the regimental band playing, and playing the tunes they play at funerals, if you see what I mean."

In the evening, I catch Sr. Balaguer in his shirtsleeves enjoying the cool on the terrace of the Pallot café.

"You've not been back to the magistrate's court," he said with a laugh. "You obviously don't like watching justice in action."

"Yes, sir, I do. A lot, though frankly I think that justice loses its shine, when seen close up. On the other hand, at a distance—"

"I get you! You're the choosy sort who wants everything in the garden to be rosy."

"Sr. Balaguer, please don't think I'm a wretched—"

"You listen to me! If you go on being so stuck up and don't come down a peg or two, you'll have lots of upsets in life. Justice, close up, is like almost anything close up. It's like men, women, food, this horrible heat, this coffee they've just served me. Justice, close up, like almost anything close up, is pure shi—"

6 July. The war is about to end. Germany is reacting like a cornered animal. The Americans are landing in Bordeaux by the thousands. All the arrogance of the early years of the war has evaporated like a puff of smoke. The pro-Germans have shut up. The Kaiser's swagger now begins to look absurd and grotesquely flamboyant. The war will end in a matter of weeks.

Mossèn Cosí bumps into Grandmother Marieta in the street. Mossèn Cosí, the parish sacristan, cultivates a plot of land he rents from Grandmother Marieta. He says, "Just you see, Sra. Marieta, just you see! England will win again! We had such high hopes, all dashed to the ground! The Protestants are going to win again, the simpletons who believe in freedom of conscience. What will become of us, Sra. Marieta? The future looks very bleak, very bleak indeed. We'd have been so happy under the order established by the Germans! Now, to be frank, I'm not sure I'll be able to pay you your rent."

"What was that?" Grandmother Marieta retorts energetically. "Are you saying you won't pay me my rent because England is going to win the war? What kind of excuse is that, Mossèn Emili? Have you gone mad? If you don't pay the rent by Michaelmas, you'll be out on your ear. Whatever *has* gotten into you?"

Reactionaries in our country always have been and always will be pro-German. Their bête noire will forever be England. And that is because of what Mossèn Cosí was saying a moment ago, because England embodies the spirit of freedom of conscience. It's the perennial complaint. Those who reckon this stand is inconsistent because Germany is as Protestant as England are quite wrong. These people aren't at all inconsistent, quite the contrary: They have a perfect grasp of the problem. They know that Protestantism in Germany is quite harmless. We should be clear about that: German Protestantism counts for nothing compared to the German military spirit of authoritarianism and subordination. And this is the spirit of Germany they find fascinating. They know that German Protestantism has no punch and literally counts for zero in comparison to this military spirit. And they are right. Germany is a country where authority is all-important, even though it is Protestant. England is *the* country of freedom of conscience, whatever its army is like. Mossèn Cosí knows what he's talking about.

8 July. In a small town everybody knows everybody up to a point, so apart from your personal irritations in life, you must also put up with the presence of others and their endless speculation.

You suddenly see members of a family walking down the street in single file, dressed in raven-black cloth. These apparitions come as a nasty shock especially in the blistering sunlight of summer. The pallid children in their black tunics look straight out of an orphanage. Wrapped in the same sooty cloth, the fat, deformed females seem even fatter and more deformed: Their skin turns a sickly sallow. The skinny variety looks like dressed-up reeds. Worn and dusty in the sunlight, the men's black clothes and hats suggest sinister shiftiness, emanating fake, rehearsed resignation. It is unbelievable how adept people are at taking advantage of the slightest opportunity to linger on the horrible, unpleasant aspects of life. One might assume the deceased left for the other side to avoid the spectacle of their family in mourning.

I also firmly believe that dignified mourning requires lots of money.

In the café this evening, Gori, who's been reading a modern poet— Juan Ramón Jiménez, I suspect—didn't seem at all enthused by what he calls the modern sensibility.

"Just imagine," he was saying, "they want to thrill you with any fool thing, any meaningless trivia. They hope something so dull will move people who are unmoved by a dead body, by the family keeping vigil, or by the greatest catastrophes. These poets are so sensitive that if they walk down a street and see a cracked windowpane, they immediately become overwrought and out of control." A brief pause and then: "Perhaps they're not as overwrought as they say. God only knows!"

9 July. Countless people think they will never die and are certain that they will remain on this earth forever—by virtue of irrational conviction, the strongest kind imaginable. Almost everybody; perhaps everybody. Man isn't made to think about death. Not only does he think he will never die, but if perchance the thought does occur, he finds it inconceivable.

Day in, day out, one funeral or another passes by. We find it natural. I mean, we find it natural others should die and absurd that death might strike us down. This curious self-defense mechanism means that man's capacity for rational thought is permanently undermined by such amnesia. Life displays a limited capacity for rational thought. Removed from the presence of death, human reasoning becomes exactly what it is: a pedantic game. Conversely, reason plays a key role in everything that is untouched by the long reach of death—the system of mathematical propositions, for example—and the theories it builds seem eternal and etched on tablets of stone.

I've always preferred the company of people baptized long before me. Young men of my age send me to sleep. A student who is my contemporary has never caught my attention. All my friends are at least fifteen years older than I am. This has led me to experience some things close at hand. Nearly all the mistakes my friends have made come from their belief that they will never die. On the other hand, nearly all their successes spring from the same delusion, the identical fantasy.

Belief in physical permanence on earth is the engine that drives men and women to act. The idea that these actions may end in success *or* failure is rarely contemplated. Our organism thrives on blind belief in the illusion of physical permanence. What moralists and naturalists advance as the motives behind human actions—money, sensuality, hunger—are external forms of a more powerful kind of vanity: the expectation of permanence.

Idealists postulate that our spirit's thirst for immortality is a tangible reality. In practice, hardly anyone can grasp such a sentiment, let alone be guided by it. And that could hardly be any different, given we believe so blindly in the illusion of personal indestructibility. In other words, the illusion of spiritual immortality is generally much harder to grasp than the illusory immortality of our tangible material being. At every turn what we see in the world leads us to contemplate our own destruction. But we can't believe it. Nature doesn't hide it from our sight: It's our eyes that shut before the spectacle offered by nature. We hide from it—like children.

All the same, what would the world be like if we didn't believe that we were never going to die? Life would become empty, passive, and uncertain. That illusion leads man to tackle the most challenging feats of endurance. Misers, for example, lead a dog's life on the assumption that they will live forever. Whichever way you look at it, it is a mirage that is hugely positive. The fact that we can apply thought to our many trivial acts but not to our profound follies is a great boon, generally speaking.

When Tolstoy's literary creativity was waning, he wrote his *Diary*, a document haunted by the presence of death. Apparently he wrote it at night. After recording the day's events, he'd sign off with the next day's date and the three Russian letters that correspond to S.D.V.— namely, God willing. After what I've just written, I can't say that such an obsession is incomprehensible. I can say, however, that it is a futile, intolerable, and dreadful thing.

15 July. I've not written anything for some days. It's been very hot. A rabid heat. (I think this adjective, from Horace apparently, is magnificent.) The rabid heat ended with the inevitable tempest, thunder, lightning, and hailstones . . . yes, hailstones on cue to destroy the grape harvest. The foibles of Mother Nature! The spectacle of lightning so close, phosphorescent, purple and violet, streaked with yellow and dark red through a thick, ghostly curtain of gray sleet is a sight no stage could rival, however splendid and startling the set might be. No silhouette of a smoldering Salomé can compare to the zigzag of snake lightning serrating the earth, no veils of Salomé's could be more bewitching than a hailstorm's translucent, azure, filigree mists.

The chill was short-lived.

I took advantage of the cool brought by the final claps of thunder to walk to our farmhouse. I spent two or three hours looking at papers and tidying drawers. I confirmed what I'd imagined: my ancestors' aversion to the printed word. I found three old books: Aesop's *Fables* in an edition with crude melodramatic woodcuts, the 1814 edition of Ballot's *Catalan Grammar*, and copies of the *Dialogues* by Lluís Vives.

I also discovered secondary-school and university textbooks that had belonged to my father and to Uncle Martí, and some eighty pounds of missals that were the property of Sr. Esteve Casadevall. Modesty aside, at the age of twenty I have purchased more books than the previous dozen generations of my family. I am not sure this augurs well for the sane, sensible progress of our family as an institution. Perhaps Aunt Lluïsa is right when she sees me coming with "another book" and rasps, "More money wasted!"

17 July. Friends.

Tomàs Gallart returns from Barcelona with a swollen cheek. I can't hide my surprise. He is someone I only ever imagine in the best of health—independent of life's ups and downs. I appreciate his loud, gritty sense of humor and ability to pinpoint the grotesque. He is tall and muscular with energetic eyebrows. He makes me think of a man who responds to Montaigne's ideal, "living in a lodging house, laughing with our friends, dying among strangers."

At night I often go for an hour or two's stroll with him under the acacias on carrer del Sol. He is one of the few manufacturers in Palafrugell able to converse "gratuitously," I mean, about issues completely unconnected to immediate economic concerns. I particularly like hearing him recount his student days in France and England. His memories of London are most entertaining and delightful, if rather idealized. Perhaps we wouldn't be such close friends if we were the same age. Constant interchange with people whose memories are the same isn't exactly fun.

Enric Frigola has strange habits. He's always reading the Bible, especially the Old Testament, and his party trick in the café is to relate verbatim, in a stern, icy-cold manner, the monstrosities he keeps unearthing. The different reactions Hebrew madness provokes in the minds of people today are surprising, even shocking. However, his performance becomes monotonous after the guffaws unleashed by the first such absurdity. Though no one would dare try and stop him, since *he* finds it all so entertaining.

"Frigola," a priest told him one day, "you're a solemn soul."

"That's to be expected," he retorted. "It's because I've read the Bible more than you."

"I've never read the Bible. Who do you take me for? I'm a man for the Gospels."

"Well, there you go," replied Frigola, with a grin.

As a language-school teacher of French, he uses Flaubert's *Madame Bovary* as a reading text. Gori once asked him why.

"Don't you think Flaubert is a great writer?" came the reply.

"Yes, of course."

"Ah!"

Casabó's pharmacy has been bought by Almeda, a distinguished apothecary from Girona who joins our group now and then. He is thin and extremely shortsighted, with a bulbous red nose and large, gold-rimmed spectacles that give him a serious, attentive, meticulous look. He slicks his hair with grease, is a dapper dresser, and keeps his pants creases firm and straight. I expect he places them daintily under his mattress at night so as to press them. He sports a little brush of a mustache.

Almeda constantly deploys diminutives especially, when speaking to women. "You must dab a little spot of ointment on that tiny pimple," he tells female customers, or "You should sip a little spoonful of this thin syrup." His delivery is soft, persuasive, and smarmy. Unfortunately, his voice is a touch too nasal and he tries hard to hide the true nature of his sarcastic patter. He usually manages to conceal his agenda and many people, impressed by his warmth, think him an innocent abroad, some young ladies even imagining him in a young boy's short pants and sailor top.

He is icily cynical in his dealings with friends and, as he is from Girona—and belongs to the old school—he seems even colder. He is a systematic, lucid cultivator of adulterous love: His basic premise in life is that the application of accountability to emotions betrays a lack of charm. "A feeling," he maintains, "though paid for only with grilled cutlets, ceases to be a feeling." And he is in his element when embroiled in adulterous affairs, which are always fortuitous, often problematic, infinitely complex, and even highly unpleasant—like the caning he received, which never came to light because he'd bribed night watchmen and police to be discreet. Deep down he is a pure idealist. It's almost a fact that he is more interested in irritating husbands than in possessing their wives. One day when people in the café were discussing his tenacity and patience in the field, he interjected, his usual nasal, slightly querulous self, "Can you tell me anything half as nice as my little doings?"

18 July. In the late afternoon I went to our farmhouse. They were threshing with the mares. The sun has scorched everyone. The mix of dust, chaff, and sweat adds a claylike crust to eyes, already a ghostly white, that now turn the hue of a fly's wing at twilight. The animals shine with sweat and froth white at the mouth. The laborers unyoke them and sit on the ground, exhausted.

I walk home in a luminously white, pale pink twilight under the arching sky's deep, sterile blue.

A young woman walks past the café terrace, that disturbing, constrained, opaque allure of adolescence, her short skirt ballooning out over taut flesh, rear, thighs, and full legs. A man at the next table winks at me.

If I remember correctly, his hair fell messily over his forehead and his eyes were large, blank, and deep-set—adrift in a haze—his pink cheek tinged with crimson.

The girl has gone and what remains hanging in the air is my neighbor's sinister wink.

If our souls represent our capacity for hope—our hopes—that has to be why so many of us are such empty vessels.

I wouldn't know how to choose between those who never say no and those who never say yes. They are the two most frequent stances adopted by our country's extremists.

Money.

Born in La Pera like General Savalls, timber merchant Ciset Vilà loves to tell how one day when Savalls was marauding during the Second Carlist War, he rode into the village of his birth on his renowned white steed that figures in all the prints, surrounded by the leading characters on his side. The general's mother, who lived poverty-stricken in La Pera, stuck her head out of the window the moment she heard the galloping horses, and once she'd recovered the first wave of fright and shock prompted by her son's presence, she reacted in a vigorous, indignant manner.

"Hey, is that you, you good-for-nothing?" she shouted, staring at him scornfully. "We can put that wall straight now, I suppose! Aren't you ashamed you're causing so much trouble? All our land is barren . . . and all you do is ride from one end of the country to the other, fighting a savage war, you good-for-nothing."

Savalls listened to the farm woman bellowing angrily from her window, blowing off steam. He chuckled but didn't dismount.

"Mother, skirts at the ready?" he replied, as he felt her onslaught slacken.

"Are you out of your mind, you rapscallion!"

"I said, 'Skirts at the ready!'" shouted the general, beaming like a blissfully happy animal.

And while she bawled, he threw a handful of gold coins through her open window.

The old woman vanished momentarily from the window, the time it took to retrieve the coins he'd scattered over the ground. Then she reemerged, looking sweet and changing her tune: "Come in! Time for an afternoon snack. It's been so long! Our cold sausage is first-rate this year."

The general dismounted, and mother and son tenderly embraced. He not only snacked but dined and slept in his parents' house. In fact he stayed as long as his own personal safety allowed. His mother's contentment lasted all that time and a little longer—until the gold coins of war ran out.

20 July. Saint Margaret's, Palafrugell's annual fiestas.

The experts predict they will be meager now that industrial exports have collapsed after the end of the war. Unemployment and anarchist propaganda is spreading, along with poverty. A soup kitchen has been set up at the hospital where many workers and the poor line up.

Even so, it was a shock to come out of church into the glare of summer. As people left through the main door, they looked as if they'd been pumped up by Mercadante's pompous music, which played during the service. The light shimmered on the faces of the stiff and stout corseted ladies under their red umbrellas. Lugubriously dressed and generally bearded, the men seemed mere cardboard silhouettes in that gassy, effervescent light. The squeak of the bourgeoisie's new shoes was noteworthy. Year after year, local shoes moan the most. Some leathers creak in a denser, dreamier way so each step their owners take sounds like they're trampling on eggshells. Sardanas before lunch in plaça Nova. A crowd under the casinos' extended awnings. Aperitifs with olives. Scorching heat, searing light. The polemic provoked by Juli Garreta's sardanas is livelier than ever. The usual sardana dancers decry the musician from Sant Feliu. The most active bourgeois group in town defends Garreta. Garreta is splendid and the orchestra from Peralada plays a sardana by him, but the dancers refuse to dance, saying his music is a mess and unintelligible (sardanas for the concert hall, according to them) and the square seems even more luminous than usual for July in this country. The sardanas, the tenora... what a performance! Cloying music and childish melodies played in a nasally boisterous, impish fashion. To that extent, it must be the supreme expression of our country's unsophisticated spirit. After the sardanas I make my way home down various streets. Intoxicating smells from a range of sauces waft towards me from open windows. From near and far, I hear the sharp, lively clatter of knives, forks, and spoons. We are rather scatterbrained in the Ampurdan— no point denying that!—but our sauces are unrivaled, indisputably the country's best. The locals have an infallible touch when it comes to that kind of flair.

I bump into a hesitant, disoriented Gori during an interval in the afternoon sardanas.

"These grand fiestas," he tells me, "disrupt my way of life. I don't like them at all. I have to say I prefer our normal, everyday routines. I like to eat on time and keep to my side of the road. I like our conversations in the café. I can absolutely do without the strange faces that are a pure mystery. What have you done today, my afternoon friends? I saw Frigola separated from Gallart by a crowd of strangers. You want a coffee but don't know which café to go to. Please spare me these frenzied, modern ways."

So many people crowd into the square I see how, even as Gori talks to me, the bustling, shoving throng gradually comes between us. Eventually we must raise our voices to make ourselves heard. His temper worsens. I shout from afar: "Keep calm... I understand why you prefer monotony."

"Exactly, absolutely right!" he shouts like a wild man, flailing his arm in an inevitable, irreversible farewell.

21 July. Second day of the fiestas. By afternoon people start to look slightly exhausted. The festivities unfold in an uproar interspersed with moments of sad, silent calm. At such times, one hears the pop of a cork from a bottle of frothy lemonade dancing impetuously before the eager face of a child who's rooted to the spot. People's eyes glint in the din. When there is a lull, they look incredibly glum. Happiness is being dead to the world.

Bourgeois life.

Suddenly I find a sensational item of gossip is circulating in town: Dr. Martí, Don Francisco Martí, has made his mind up to install a bathroom in his house. "Did you know Sr. Francisco is going to have a bathroom installed?" three or four people of very different social status ask me within a short space of time.

Sr. Francisco is a pillar of the local community and tied, in my mind, to the old bourgeois way of life. He is our family doctor—and, consequently, an excellent doctor. A short, stout, apoplectic man, he puffs like a dolphin when he climbs stairs. A thin cord around his fleshy ear covered in golden down connects to his spectacles, which tremble over his eyes that always seem too big for their sockets. His diagnoses are forceful and categorically imperative. A man of his time—he must be in his sixties—his knowledge is based on his clinical eye. If that eye were matched by a morbid, languorous temperament, it probably would have been quite unproductive. However, driven by his pugnacious spirit it has been a source of boundless trust. Those who pay for his services are convinced he is a man who battles sickness with his bare hands. It's all rather farcical, but can a middle class exist without a touch of farce?

Once he has paid his visit, which he makes in a brougham pulled by a sweaty horse and driven by the loyal Molines, Sra. Carolina (his wife) is by then quite anxious. Sra. Carolina is deaf as a post, but her difficulty in communicating has forced her to refine the art of finding out the news. Sra. Carolina is one of the biggest gossipers locally. She knows everything. Nothing escapes her. She is a sponge that soaks up everything around her. She likes to stir things up. Her usual communication with people proceeds like this: She always has a press cutting in hand. When she finds herself in someone's company, she fashions the newsprint into a cornet, pokes it in their faces, looking intrigued and saying, "Go on, tell me . . ."

Sra. Carolina is tall, black, bony, and slovenly. At the same time, she is the most good-natured person around. She is of mixed race, with some Cuban qualities. In her presence—or so they say—Sr. Francisco has to trim his sails and curb his excitable temperament in order to maintain order in the family. That was particularly the case when they lost their only daughter. This little girl died of a very strange disease. She already had black hair. When she fell ill she started to turn black, black as can be, and then she finally died and made the usual gasp, the kind of gasp people make when they are slightly hungry. (That's the version from the servant who saw her die.) When they laid her out, her natural color seemed to return, one that had been forgotten, put behind her. Her cheeks were firm and prominent, her nose flattened, and her lips fleshy. She was the color of a real little black girl.

In Sr. Francisco's house they eat stew on weekdays and rice on Sunday. Six days of broth, meat stew, and a small plate of meat or fish. And rice on Sundays, for a change. I suspect this has been the menu in well-off households for many years. It represents the backbone of the family diet, which is why it is now fascinating to observe the first signs of resistance to a tradition that once seemed fully secure. In town one detects certain elements that are hostile to meat stew. These elements are passionate and I feel they will be victorious. Such profound changes in the culture are the consequence of war. That is self-evident. At the moment the winds of revolution are blowing across the world, winds that oppose monotony, and meat stew is thought to be monotonous, lacking variety, simply repetitious. At the same time, it is an expensive dish and housewives are short on cash. It is natural that in houses with unsteady convictions meat stew should be under threat.

After lunch, Sr. Francisco lights up a cigar from the tobacconist's and heads for the house of his brother-in-law Sr. Maspera. This gentleman is tall, skinny, rather elderly, and always stooping, with a yellow beard and hair combed and parted. He is married to Sra. Irene. Sra. Irene is Sra. Carolina's sister. Sr. Maspera is a person of independent means. He enjoys an income that allows him to eat broth and meat stew every day without batting an eye. He is extremely polite, always joking, unable to cause offense or utter a word that hasn't been repeated time and again. Bourgeois life is repetition.

Just before or after Sr. Francisco puts in an appearance, two or three other gentlemen—Sr. Puig, Sr. Ferrer, etcetera—come to the house, having eaten their respective plates of meat stew. When they are all gathered there, they sit around a table, Sra. Irene produces a pack of cards, and they start a game of ombre. They begin at a specific time: when the workers walk past on their way back to the factory. However, the length of the game is open-ended. It depends on whether Sr. Francisco's coachman arrives with bad news—bad news, that is, for the sick person whom it concerns. In that case, the doctor abandons the game, clambers into his brougham, and goes off to pay a call.

The Masperas live life in their doorway from the first swallows to the advent of cold weather. They spend their whole time in the entrance to their house, when they aren't eating or sleeping, that is. A glass-paneled door, always open in summer, is the only thing separating them from the street. In winter, they reluctantly withdraw to their dining room and converse around the brazier.

Sra. Irene suffers most from this momentary eclipse. She keeps a comfortable woven-reed rocking chair by the doorway, near the step, one that fits the rather spare lines of her body. Sra. Irene has spent a large part of her life in this chair. And her favorite time for sitting there is when her husband and his friends—Sr. Puig, Sr. Ferrer, etcetera—play cards. Smoke fills the room. One can't breathe in that smog. The game develops—like most games—amid persistent bad temper. They've all eaten the same meat stew, but there is no way they can see eye to eye. Like diets don't guarantee like minds. One or the other of the players bangs his fists on the table—violently—and scatters the seeds or whatever they use to score all over the floor. It is a strikingly theatrical scene. Bourgeois life is a perpetual repeat performance.

You would think such an act would greatly annoy the players and family. Not for one minute. In that household, all the potential side effects of ombre are accepted and anticipated a priori. When the grains of maize are dispersed on the floor, Sra. Irene abandons her rocking chair and picks up each scattered seed, one by one, taking the utmost care.

While doing so, she will make the same remarks she always does, remarks which are now part of a hallowed ritual.

"That's what I like to see!" she says. "Men must show their character! That's what you call playing cards."

When I reflect on all this, I understand why people are so eager to gossip about Sr. Francisco's up-and-coming bathroom.

25 July. Saint James's Day. The main fiestas in Mont-ras, the neighboring village. Gori suggests we go, and it turns out that he hates the fiestas in his own town but goes to those held in villages all around and, while he is fond of the regular routine for himself, he is always keen to disturb the routines of his neighbors.

"What do you expect?" he says, anticipating my possible objections. "If it weren't for our contradictions, what point would there be to our wretched lives?"

We go. It is barely a mile and a quarter. The village is very pretty, set against the first row of the Fitor mountains. We walk up to the church. There is a cemetery next to the church. From the walls of the cemetery strewn with dry leaves, there is a beautiful vista of the plain of Palafrugell, dotted with farmhouses and small huts, and the sea in Calella. The reaped fields are a mass of light golden shocks. Clumps of red poppies stand out against the earth. The pine groves of Ermedàs seem dark, shadowy, and melodramatic. The afternoon sun gilds the old stones. The sea surges in the distance. A smell of apple stuffing floats over the village. As we walk down the streets, this smell sometimes mingles—on a bend—with the scent of dry fennel.

The fiesta is held in the square. Years ago there would have been a huge crowd. Now the throng seems smaller. The musicians are playing against the wall of Can Rocas, a large house with an extended balcony that runs along its whole façade. Gori is shocked when he sees how empty the balcony is and how nearly lifeless the house is.

"This is the house," he says, "that a few years ago hosted the most visitors during the Saint James fiestas. The wealthiest local landowners with their wives and daughters would drape themselves over that balcony rail when it was time for sardanas. You'd see the great and the good from hereabouts. I still remember many of their faces. That balcony was like a Goya painting . . . now there's nobody. They must be in bad shape."

"What do you mean by 'a few years ago'?"

"I mean in the days of Don Baldomer, Don Baldomer Roca. Don Baldomer was a great gentleman. He had huge mustache like President Castelar's. He was prudent, moderate, and even-tempered. From his Christian name we can assume that his parents were supporters of Espartero. He was a conservative. And a politician. He had a circle of friends and maintained the group's cohesion by keeping a pot on the boil: The Catalan beret was always ready for a cup of coffee. As if that weren't enough, Don Baldomer would take his friends to a café in Palafrugell. The cry would go up in the street: 'Here come the people from Mont-ras!' Nonetheless, my impression is that politics dealt him more than one bad hand. I don't think he ever managed a clear victory or got to be boss. It gets rather unpleasant and unseemly, especially if you've paid for so many coffees, by the end of the year. Here the master was always old Massot, a beret-wearing republican. Your forbears, dear friend, were aligned with him."

"Of course."

"Ah, you know for sure?"

"Grandmother Marieta has very vivid memories of old Massot. She admires him. According to her, if Don Baldomer was respectable and a gentleman, Massot was a good man and on the side of justice."

"Possibly . . . at any rate, Don Baldomer was an imposing figure. I can still see him coming from his orchard, Sra. Clareta, his wife, on one arm and a basket of strawberries on the other. They made a big impact on people—especially on the poor, who regarded them with a mixture of admiration and envy that was very primitive, with deep biological roots. They'd give them the same tender looks members of the canine species give their masters—the sweet, velvety eyes of calves swooning at the sight of juicy grass. Respectability there was, too, you know."

"My dear Gori, your grandiose descriptions sadden me."

"Sadden you? Well, let's not say another word."

A muted return home under hazy stars, to the sound of a small, humble—ironic—concert performed by crickets.

26 July. There are days—some more than others—when I can't tolerate solitude. It's quite impossible. If I try to analyze the situation I find:

a) One could tolerate solitude if one were built (as so many people are) to cope with an intense feeling of loathing and horror at life and reality (narcissism). One might if one's heart had literally withered away. Hardening of the heart isn't congenital. It is an acquired condition. It depends on experience of life. What poets and novelists call narcissism is generally congenital and *is* symptomatic of genuine abnormality. The level of loathing reality brings clearly can increase in ratio to one's experience of life.

b) When the latter is short, confused, and contradictory, it would be pretentious, however painful the experience has been, to act like someone who has overcome everything and is completely coldhearted. I look on in horror as everything drives me into a state of callow indifference, but I'd be a clown to act as if I've touched rock bottom. Perhaps, even in the worst cases, a feeling of genuine tenderness always remains. In this country, it is mostly education that hardens our feelings—that is, the sense of the ridiculous that education forces on us at every point.

c) When one's heart hasn't turned to stone, one cannot kill off vanity, the painful longing to be heard, flattered, loved, cherished, etcetera. Our vain heart leads us to do the most absurd things and embark on lunatic initiatives: to interfere in other people's lives, to catechize them in one way or the other—in a word, to invade their solitude. Perhaps, indeed, vain hearts make it impossible for us to tolerate solitude. Thus, as any rift in our own solitude implies the violation of the solitude of others, we make our greatest mistakes when we take that path.

Human solitude is a fact consecrated by biology. Man is a self-enclosed animal, impenetrable, inexplicable, who cannot be explained from inside out or outside in. Perhaps we tend to show our real selves—just possibly!—when money or commodities are at stake. But our vanity, our self-love, drives us to invade the sacred solitude of others in the hope that they will surrender themselves for free. Self-love deludes us into thinking we might obtain something from others without paying—gratis and for nothing—the illusion that they will abolish their own sense of self-preservation and ineluctable solitude to please us. It's not surprising that such exaggerated expectations create insoluble problems and bitter rancor.

In one respect, it isn't a good idea to withdraw completely because that leads to total silence. I have seen people start off in life as quite reasonable human beings yet it's been ages since they spoke to me. The ideal must be to reach the right level of withdrawal—enough to ensure you don't forget that the only important act in life is the act of paying and that the most convenient formula to guarantee coexistence is banality—banal conversation, as banal as you can make it. Banal interactions are positively relaxing and help preserve the level of mental haze indispensable for a continuous healthy life. Banality can be expanded or curtailed at will. What more could one want?

Enric Frigola has often told me that the philosophy behind social life in England is banality. What causes violent displeasure in the English is any attempt to probe excessively, to explore indiscreetly to any depth. The English will only tolerate depth in poets they never read. Intellectuals with any kind of ambition have no status whatsoever in English society. Thus banality is not aristocracy's only invention. It must simply be a reflection of the English way of life.

In any case, if solitude is irresistible, at least we can't deny that it comes cheaply. All misers are solitary and all are equally miserly with their feelings and words.

There are people who tend to be governed by self-love—sometimes blindly so—just as others are more or less in thrall to a sense of the absurd.

When I think of the married couples I know, I believe the best matched are those who straddle both camps. Couples who are really well suited (a rarity) combine a temperament expanded by self-love and a temperament bound by a sense of the absurd. One half huffs and puffs theatrically—it could just as well be the man as the woman—and the other concedes with a mysterious, rabbity grin.

The combination of similar temperaments in a single couple does not bode well. Two temperaments based on self-love make life intolerably argumentative. Two temperaments bound by a sense of the absurd inevitably leads to unpaid rent, unpaid utilities, and unpaid servants.

In this Ampurdan of ours it's common to find the kind of man who describes himself as emancipated—from conventional ways, that is—and enumerates happily in the café all the fraud, extortion, and embezzlement (*pruning*, to use a word favored around here) that he has suffered throughout his life.

"It's true!" he says. "They skin me alive time and again."

An advocate of the most childish kind of vanity, the braggart wants, above all, to be pitied.

29 July. It is time to go to Calella.

When I was a child, the prospect thrilled me. Less so now. Everything happens in such a routine way: First the cart leaves with our mattresses and clothes, and then the family in the horse and trap. When I walk on the beach, my first contact with the sea is slightly enervating—it triggers stress without purpose. You sometimes feel the cold between your clothes and your body. Today has been typical in terms of such feelings. A southerly wind is blowing, wet and cold. The waves pound the sand with a muffled thud. Driven frantic by this wind, mother throws herself into tireless activity, her face blanched by a migraine or a headache. She never stops. Nobody can do anything right. She has to do it all with her own hands. It's the same every year. This is our summer excitement.

The small house, centered on El Canadell beach, is clean and pleasant but makes me uneasy when I enter. It takes me three or four days to acclimatize. Initially I feel as if I'm living in the street. Its construction, with a central passageway running from south to north, creates a draft that makes the place even colder. There is a little front garden with a wrought-iron fence and a small orchard in the back. The orchard has two or three trees laden with the tastiest greengage plums. The water from the well is cool and abundant. The front garden has two acacias with round clusters of branches that give good shade, and a sour green wisteria climbs along the fence, a riot of bitter-scented red flowers.

At the end of the afternoon, we launch *Nuestra Señora del Carmen*, our small nineteen-hand boat, which has taken us on so many outings along this coast. It is quite an effort to slide it down to the water on poles that are barely greased. It is an old, heavy craft. Collar unbuttoned, my brother gets into a lather and sweats like a carter. Unaccustomed to exercising my arms, I feel so exhausted it shocks me. Finally we launch it into the water and suddenly it seems different: suppler and lighter. Once the oars are in place, we row to the beach under Can Joubert and it feels as light as a feather. Strangely enough the only physical effort I've been able to make so far without exhausting myself is rowing a boat. Sitting aboard with a couple of oars in my hands, I've rowed for hours and hours and not felt the least discomfort. The mechanical rhythm of rowing seems, in my case, to generate its own energy and to be quite inexhaustible. My brother experiences something similar, though perhaps not to the same degree.

When a cloud of steam rises from the haricot beans and boiled potatoes, summer for our family has begun. But this welcome moment seems to increase the fatigue that accompanies so much rapid change. When it is time for dessert, my mother falls asleep. The maid nodded off some time ago. When we shut the door—well before ten o'clock—the small acetylene gas lamps flicker over the childlike architecture of the small houses in El Canadell and the dying southerly wind seems to extinguish the lamps and then to revive them, casting large, tremulous blue shadows on the washed-out crimson walls.

2 August. Summery weather: northeasterly breeze in the morning; slight sirocco at midday; light southerly in the afternoon; an inland breeze at night. By day, cicadas sing; in the evening, crickets.

One of the greatest joys of El Canadell is to spend a couple of hours after lunch lying in the shadow of the belly of a boat. At two o'clock, the toast-colored shadow is a foot wide and the sand the sun has just deserted is still warm. But as it gets later in the afternoon, the shadow spreads and the sand cools. At first you can stretch out on your side; then there's enough to lie on your back. The light is a hazy, effervescent, dazzling white. It melds with the air, white walls, and pinkish sand to create misty vapors that glide, twist, and turn. The pale, bluish void of sky seems to shimmer with light. The herd of foaming white horses gallops monotonously over the azure of the sea. Everything happens so quickly and spontaneously and in the red-hot frenzy the shade is so cooling that a drowsy stupor spreads through your body releasing and relaxing your entrails. If you are in conversation, a moment comes when one or the other doesn't answer. Your eyelids descend over the image in your pupils of the boats anchored at sea level. A moment later the colored stripes from the painted boats shimmering on the sea glaze your eyes. Twinkling lights float over the line of the horizon, dotted by tufts of foam, like shapeless objects adrift at sea. The southern coast—the Forcats, Cape Roig, and Cape Planes—fades into nothingness, an image your inner epiphany unravels and blurs. A moment comes when you can no longer see the Formigues Islands. Nonetheless, this slow descent into blindness never attains complete unconsciousness. However sleepy you may be, two or three specific sensations keep you lucid: the wind caressing your skin, the smell from the cigarette you've just smoked—or if you aren't smoking, the aroma of sun-scorched seashells and seaweed.

Two or three hours later, when you open your eyes and lift your head, you are shivering with cold. The afternoon has moved on, the shade has spread, and the wind, now blowing strongly, has made it wet and chilly. You touch the sand and it feels like you are touching a wet cloth. After all that incandescence, the colors are now still and more precise; the vista, colder and static.

3 August. Summer in El Canadell is a twilight, family affair. It is a beach made by a *riera* that, as on all beaches, is lined by small houses with tiny front gardens and iron-barred gates. As if drawn by children. These houses belong to the wealthy of Palafrugell. Everyone knows everyone. Josepet Batlle's canvas-covered cart rides up and down with his clients and baskets of goods. Price for the longest trip, twenty-five cents. Mossèn Narcís, who was born in Calonge—Narcís Mallart, priest—presides over the small parish church. He is a good man. He carries a walking stick with a crook and, at once unambitious and self-effacing, he looks like a small rural landowner. He pays the families a visit and sits in the acacia-canopy shade of their small gardens. He is an elderly arthritic and moves slowly and silently. If he sits in a rocking chair, he does so stiffly, never allowing himself to lean back, remains as straight-backed as a martyr. He has a slow way of speaking and a wonderfully infantile mind. Calonge has this tendency to produce chaplains and anarchists! First a few words of greeting and then he asks after the family. After that, he launches into his thoughts on the immorality one encounters on beaches and the diabolical turn the world has taken, which will inevitably lead to disaster. Then he shuts up and assumes the stance of someone caring for an invalid. Once he has put in a good visit, he bids farewell and returns to the rectory, briskly tapping his steel stick.

Summer is monotonous. In the morning, the young ladies go to Sr. Ferriol's pine grove to crochet or embroider. At twelve o'clock, high-minded people go quickly in and out of the water. When the sea makes contact with female thighs, the women scream like holy innocents beheaded. In the afternoon, people go for a bite to eat. When dusk falls and the bell rings, people go to church to tell their rosary beads. In the evening, behind wrought-iron fences, under the light from oil lamps, two or three halfhearted conversations get under way. If by chance a man with a hurdy-gurdy turns up, then he is hired for "a bit of a dance." Young people enjoy themselves. Young masters and misses dance in the illumined area, maids and fishermen in the dark shadows. Gas lamps splutter gloomily. Their small flames flicker and glow yellow. When the light goes out, there is the small recourse to sleep—that never fails.

4 August. The woes of Pardal.

The story of Pardal, a true story, has moved me whenever I've heard it told.

Pardal lived as happily as a fish in water. He had a wife and two sons. His wife worked in one of those ramshackle fish-salting factories in Calella and always smelled of salted anchovies. His boys played at pirates on the rocks, fished with the silliest of rods, and toasted pine nuts among the pine trees in summer. They spent the day in the small black boats used for transporting fish, completely naked, their dark bodies covered in scales, sailing around the port creating havoc and diving in the sun.

Pardal was a good fisherman who knew how to cook and could steer a boat well. He would get drunk at the two or three big fiestas during the year and when drunk would inevitably beat his wife. After beating her black and blue, he would go to the tavern, pleased as punch, to sing "Song of the Year of Hunger," his favorite song. The rest of the year, Pardal was a good family man, a sensible, prudent man who'd never hurt a soul.

As he liked talking and was never at a loss for words, he often chatted to the people on their summer holidays. One day, a man with a straw hat, the kind who thinks it's clever to humiliate other people, asked Pardal, "Do you know how to read, Pardal?"

"Yes, sir, I do, unfortunately."

"Pardal, what you just said was simply idiotic," said the gentleman, his hackles rising.

"Idiotic?" said Pardal scornfully. "Not at all. I know exactly what I mean."

"Well, since you can read, pray tell me," continued the gentleman on his holiday, mellowing. "Which books have you read?"

"Books? I've never read one. Don't we have enough woes?" replied long, sad-faced Pardal, his velvety, doggy eyes beset by life's troubles.

"You're a real idiot, Pardal!" retorted the gentleman, flushed, angry, and embarrassed. "You're real idiot, Pardal!"

This exchange was much debated by the summer colony and all agreed there wasn't a scrap of culture in the village. Pardal's primitive state became something newcomers had to hear about. There was so much talk about Pardal being an idiot that the comment entered the archives of resources at the disposal of café conversations. When people talked about Pardal, about whether he'd played a good hand of *tuti* or fished a red grouper with trawl lines off the island, you knew what was coming by way of introduction: "Pardal, who is an idiot..." Etcetera.

When this epithet was in full swing, Pardal's household began to suffer a series of misfortunes. Within two years his wife ran off with a carabineer from Murcia, a melancholy, bilious type who resembled a dried ship's biscuit. The carabineer was very powerful and sailed in the customs boat. Pardal's eldest son died serving the king in the hammock on a gunboat and the other was confined to bed with syphilis and had to be taken to the hospital in Girona.

Pardal was alone. He grew feeble and felt his world was collapsing around him. He ate anything, didn't dare enter his deserted house, and slept under fishing boats on the beach. He was too downcast to go to the café or drink a glass of wine in the shelter of the tavern.

Suffering so, he finally made up his mind. He went into his house and saw the walls were flaking like the bark from eucalyptus trees in winter. He gathered a bundle of clothes, left the door wide open, and went in search of the priest.

"I want to leave," he told him, "and I've come to sell the corner of the cemetery that belongs to me."

The priest was taken aback. "But these things aren't for sale, for heaven's sake!"

"I couldn't care less. I want to go to sea and don't want to leave anything here on land."

"What an idiot you are, Pardal! What an idiot you are!" said the priest shaking his head, with the expression of someone beholding a totally lost cause.

Pardal returned his gaze, like a cocky child. The priest gave him a few pesetas. He took them, went back to his house, picked up his bundle of clothes, gave the arcades and square one last look, drank from the fountain, walked across the village, and disappeared into the pine grove.

It was late evening and the boats were beginning to steer again with the westerly. There were blotches of greasy light in the doorways. Women bent busily over their stoves. Bluish smoke spiraled above garden plots and the first star was twinkling.

5 August. Families.

There is a degree of promiscuity among families in El Canadell. The same families have been coming for years. That means that there are few secrets.

Some families are characterized by their punctuality. They open and shut their doors at the same time, follow a strict timetable, program their lives, and cease all activity to preserve punctuality, and God forbid anyone should sit down at anytime but the appointed hour! They wouldn't enjoy their food and they'd never hear the last of it.

When it is time to swim, the same individuals always scream. These screamers could very easily be grouped according to family. On the other hand, there are others—including, naturally, children in diapers—who enter the water fearlessly, without a whimper. Some families feel an atavistic panic before the sea and wouldn't embark on a trip to Portbò from La Torre Point, even on the calmest of days. Others leap aboard and could spend a lifetime at sea—like the pregnant ladies.

Some seem unable not to take the same stroll every day, come what may, and others couldn't live without engaging in a more relaxed, spontaneous freedom of movement.

One family is entirely absorbed by constipation. Obsessed. They keep a pot in the dining room that houses a substance made from a mixture of flower of sulfate powder and mashed garlic which they use to season almost everything they eat, as if it were mustard or mayonnaise. They are a family one inevitably smells from afar. Then, there is a more frivolous kind of family—comprised of middle-aged spinsters—that usually provides the grand finale by singing "*Si a tu ventana llega*" from Gaztambide's operetta, etcetera.

The level of promiscuity you find during an El Canadell summer is much greater that anything that might develop in winter in any village, no matter how small. It is something people enjoy immensely. I remember how Srta. Tereseta's gloomy face lit up when she could tell her friends that Sr. and Sra. So-and-so from La Bisbal spent six or seven pesetas a day going to the square.

The family is an institution that does exist. And it is a hallowed, mysterious piece of junk.

6 August. In El Canadell there is a young lady who is so distinguished and posh that she calls a barometer a "baarometah." On the other hand, fishermen call a thermometer a "tharmarmeta."

After reading Carles Riba's wonderful translation of the *Odyssey*, what one most misses in the air along this coast is the smell of grilled meat, hecatombs of oxen and calves spread on these pagan strands in the era of Homer. This scent makes you daydream. The smell of pinecones is very pleasant. The smell of shellfish is more intense than persistent. The southwesterly brings a briny smell. What we lack is the strong, virile smell of grilling legs of beef. With this added aroma, this country would be complete, sensational.

I observe three or four fourteen- or fifteen-year-olds making holes with their catapults in the walls of the wooden beach huts so they can watch the ladies undressing when it is time for a swim. It is always amusing to see perennial schoolboy themes come up against the touchstone of reality.

In my adolescent days we too made holes in beach-hut walls. However, it is evident that these lads work in a much more discreet, coordinated fashion. While one is twisting his catapult, two or three others provide a screen so nobody can suspect what he is about to do. In my day we were much more blasé. We made our holes out in the open with no attempt to camouflage or keep secret what we were doing. No doubt about it: On this front, progress has been made.

Because of the war there are a number of families in El Canadell who would normally live in France and Germany. They've taken refuge here while they wait for the war to end. These families have spent their lives doing business together. They've always been acquainted and are related, in one way or another, either closely or distantly. Now war has come between them. They've quarreled and spend their time scowling or grimacing at each other. When they meet on the beach or anywhere else, they create a spectacle, the type of amusing spectacle a head-on meeting of Marshal Hindenburg and General Foch might generate. They become rigid and defiant and are only stopped from trading insults or coming to blows by the presence of too many people.

Xènius, in his *Glosari*, brandishes from one day to the next the idea of the moral unity of Europe. It is an admirable, sublime idea, but the situation in El Canadell shows that any such moral unity has splintered. It is sad to acknowledge that the most sublime principles are subject to the pull of the moment. Man is no rational animal. He is a sensual beast.

After an afternoon spent at sea, buffeted by a cool southwesterly, I step back on land feeling that my stomach is exhausted—the usual exhaustion I experience after a long time on the water. It isn't a feeling of hunger or thirst—or even of being empty or full. It is an indefinable fatigue of the stomach—as if this organ had been working hard and is now drained and flattened.

Ever since I can remember, the sea has had this same effect on me. My memories are clear and perfectly distinct in this respect. Perhaps the head is the key organ for the reception of external sensations on land, whereas at sea the most sensitive organ is the stomach. I don't know if other people have shared this experience. I have no doubts in my case: Every external stimulus brings the cruelest repercussion to my stomach.

None of this is connected to seasickness. I feel next to no queasiness at sea. I have rarely been seasick. The simple fact remains that, in these circumstances, everything my body encounters inevitably provokes a reaction in my stomach.

This leads me to suspect that the first indispensable attribute a good sailor must possess is a stomach that can adapt to the sea, that is, a stomach tirelessly resistant to the sea.

8 August. The sea.

These green, blue, white waves passing by blunt our minds like a file, depersonalize us, flattening the distinguishing features of our human presence. We gape at them, are bewitched and captivated. Perhaps this is why man can only be contemplative before the sea.

The ever-changing, infinite sea drains our imagination. And when we feel ourselves being drained we find the sea is smooth, monotonous, identical, and similar. At first the sea bewilders and gives pleasure. Then it fills us with anguish and creates unease.

To break this spell we need to find an exact, all-embracing word for the sea … but the moment we think we've found it, it escapes us as if it were a gust of wind or the voluptuous curve of a fleeting wave.

Late in the afternoon, the wind blew from inland and the waves galloped across the beach into the sea.

The sea at the sand's edge was the color of unripe wheat. The wind whipped up the sea into amusingly errant spirals, dark then light— evanescent liquid, shivering tremors.

The line of the horizon was deep and long. A dark sash of cloud ran above it. A hazy glare, a yellow rose potpourri lay between this sash and the horizon. Waves crashed and raced over the distant sea; boiling foam splattered the horizon; a wave surged momentarily above the rest like the back of a whale. In the west, embers smoldered. An impression of solitude reinforced by the sea's silence—as the sound shifted to the far horizon. When dusk fell, this watery silence along the edge of the strand plunged us into an atmosphere of mystery.

Early in the morning, it is sometimes so hot that grayish mist settles on the water. These summer mists over the becalmed, soapy sea sometimes linger for long periods and conjure strange mirages. However, if a wind blows in, the mist frays and fades into the vagaries of sky and sea.

The instant the mist shrinks you see a sail pass, like a phantom, like a seagull flapping its wings over the sea. It is a shock. As if the sea were giving birth to these things.

Seagulls circle and wheel, and touch the water with the tips of their beaks. They screech past, wings beating. They must shiver with pleasure when the saltwater trickles from their ruffled feathers to the hot skin beneath.

By the time the northeasterly starts to blow, the sky is bright and the morning radiant. It is a gentle breeze and the small waves—like undulating jewels—trace beautiful, flat tracks across the ocean. As the day advances, everything is marooned in a dazzling light. The sand on the beach is a fine paste of pale crimson glass. The sea flows like dark, molten glass. Outlines of objects shimmer and blur. The infinite sky is an abyss. A moment comes when there is so much light nothing is clear. Even the faces of your family look different.

10 August. In the morning I read Francesc Rierola's *Diary* in the pine grove in Ferriol.

Situated to the east, overlooking El Canadell, the pine grove is cool and refreshing. The northwesterly gusts are voluptuous and playful. Your body feels good. Girls seated in a circle sew and knit under the gentle shade of the pine trees. A patch of light-blue sun settles on a tree now and then. Maria Sagrera asks from afar if the book I am reading is by Paul Bourget. The summer visitors read only Paul Bourget. As I have no wish to appear pompous, I tell her that it is indeed Paul Bourget.

Rierola is a real character! A man from Vic. A reactionary romantic to the marrow of his bones. It is the same mixture you find in Chateaubriand—keeping a due sense of proportion. But the result is the opposite, quite different. I have heard Josep Ferrer say occasionally that Chateaubriand is one of the greatest writers of all time. The man from Vic bellows rather than writes. He shouts and rants. It is so much easier. Shouting requires no effort. It leads nowhere.

Perhaps we'd have been better served if he'd described rather than opined. If he'd used his diary to describe his times, we would now have a document of the first order. But Rierola wanted to opine and never considered that his opinions might be worthless. It was quite enough to have the bishop's and the governor's opinions from that time. That makes his rants seem futile, unnecessary, repetitious.

The drama of literature never changes: It is much more difficult to describe than to opine. In view of which, everyone prefers to opine.

Jewels.

At the turn of the century, women wore and displayed great quantities of jewels. Now that fortunes have been made from the war, jewels have reappeared. In this respect, attendance at mass in Calella is an eye-opener. Current fashion transforms ladies into voluminous creatures. Jewels increase the volume. Beside their wives, husbands seem even more derisory in their drill suits and minimal lapels. When a bourgeois couple passes by in the street, the wife seems to carry a jug, namely her husband.

At the turn of the century, these displays of jewelry were so comic that, when the Cork-Lid choir went to a competition in Béziers, the gentleman from Palafrugell known as Jaumet d'Arenys who carried the Catalan flag did something quite extraordinary. As it would get chilly in Béziers, Sr. Jaumet d'Arenys slipped on leather gloves in order to carry the flag more comfortably and wore heavily bejeweled rings over his gloved fingers. Everybody thought he cut a splendid figure.

Apart from this new profusion of jewels, the war has also led to the emergence of a new profession: dentistry. Dentists are more important by the day. One sees huge gold and silver dentures in people's mouths. What with their jewels and flashy dentures, the spectacle of the middle class with its swank and swagger is quite appalling.

The perfumes they use are sweet and unsubtle.

It all makes me think of J. B. Coromina's comment on the decadent writer Jean Lorrain: "If it weren't for the real or fake jewels, the hardware and shitty perfumes ... he might be a half-decent writer!"

There is a lot of criticism now of those who've made money, and with good reason. Throughout Europe there is almost an obsession with the nouveaux riches. But I disagree with one aspect of this criticism. The iron structures being put up everywhere to support windmills are horrendous. They look awful beside the old, run-down houses belonging to small farmers. They don't fit the landscape at all. But that is the extent of it. In Saharan territory, water—a drop of water—is a blessing from God. Even if the machinery mars the view, a well-watered orchard and cool, refreshing vegetation is a joy; an exhausted orchard and dusty, parched vegetation is a disaster.

14 August. The Vayreda family from Olot has arrived and will spend a few days in the mansion in Calella that belongs to Sra. Puig de la Bellacasa. They are related. The Vayredas include Sra. Casabó, the widow of the great painter, and their children: Francesc, a frightening hunchback, and Montserrat, one of the prettiest, most elegant girls around. We have spent the last few afternoons with this family, sailing along the coast in our craft *Nuestra Señora del Carmen*. This girl is wonderfully, strikingly beautiful! It is a delight to transport such a young blond goddess, albeit in our small vessel. The monstrous geology of basalt and granite, arid limestone and dark slate vanishes at the sight of a well-made human form.

We went on long trips. We made it to Cape Begur in one direction and as far as Castell in the other. With my brother's help, we sailed great distances and kept on task. Everything has gone perfectly. People from inland usually experience the sea with silent awe. We spent these afternoons speaking only when it was strictly necessary and listening to the wind.

We had very good weather: calm seas and fair winds. No one has felt unduly upset. Naturally, in choppy water near the coast, by reefs and rocks, the boat occasionally dipped and produced that familiar emptiness in the stomach, a moment of anguish, a slight pallor on the faces and lips and cold sweat on the brow. But apart from that, nothing else remarkable happened. It is good to watch a goddess in a state of permanent physical well-being. It ensures one doesn't yield to excesses of Senecan aloofness.

One can admire Goethe for many reasons. I admire him for his private as much as for his public life. Goethe has been slandered and dubbed an egotist because he avoided his female friends in childbirth and the death agonies and burials of his friends. Personally, such attitudes don't turn me against him. An ability not to resist the temptations of more or less absolute indifference—always a little equivocal —of glacial detachment and Senecan stoicism need not necessarily be a failing. Overfamiliarity, on the other hand, is onerous, from every point of view.

15 August. The Virgin Mary's August fiesta. The saint's day of the lady of the house: Mummy's. Family gathering in El Canadell.

It has been a dazzlingly bright and blisteringly sunny day. Cool northwesterly in the morning. Lively, cool southwesterly in the afternoon.

The excursion to mass was a stupendous theatrical performance. The ladies donned their corsets; the gentlemen their Sunday best. The ladies wore elegant stockings and gilded shoes—shoes that irradiate an artificial violet hue that seems to climb up the leg—and floppy hats with feathers that fall to the shoulder.

Mossèn Narcís said mass slowly, amid a deep silence; the only sound was the coughing and shuffling of recalcitrant bronchitics. The quantity of cheap jewelry exhibited seemed excessive. Jewels create heat in summer. A curious fact.

The men wore dark, winter clothes. It was a thoroughly domesticated, ultra-conventional and tawdry menagerie—a menagerie that didn't in any way forego truly frightful detail and outright greed. The small walking sticks the men carried painfully emphasized the conventionality of their garb. These shiny metal sticks with curved handles seem so unnecessary that the mere sight of them curdles your blood. At any moment, you think they'll poke them between your legs and trip you.

The church in Calella—my uncle Esteve Casadevall played a decisive role in its construction—has a watery blue ceiling. Small stars are dotted across this blue like pasta in a bowl of soup, creating a sentimental postcard mood. It is all part of a system of religious feelings I can't explain because it is overfamiliar. A smell of rice powder and concentrated violet lotion floats across the small church's starry vault. But that only describes the smell inside: In the entrance, the northwesterly breeze, saturated with pine, gorse, fennel, graybeard, and shellfish, whisks away the feathery front of fake perfume. As if the congregation were stripped naked.

Grandmother Marieta, a habitué of the seven o'clock evening mass, attended the morning service slightly ruffled. She was sheathed in black: black head scarf, black dress—three or four underskirts— and low-heeled black shoes. I felt her outfit—half popular, half antique—was one of the most elegant in church.

When the churchgoers leave, they mainly disperse. But the *hopefuls* step into the shadow of the rectory's façade to watch the ladies parade slowly by. How many adulteries are there? Perhaps none. It's a law-abiding country, with a surfeit of exemplary virtue.

When the church and small square had emptied out, Mossèn Narcís grabbed his gleaming heather-wood cane, put on his skullcap, and went off to congratulate the Marias. There are many in El Canadell. Mossèn Narcís visited the homes celebrating the big day. He conversed in tiny gardens, in the shade of blossoming acacias, bordered by a pool of light. He was offered shade as if it were a box of snuff. Mossèn Narcís speaks slowly. His eyes are sad, his cheeks ruddy, and his ears the color of a dried apricot. He seems on the verge of an apoplectic attack. He is always short on time. He can never say everything he would like to. While he offers congratulations and predicts great happiness, Josepet Batlle's cart trundles from house to house, laden with baskets and orders: desserts, honeydew melons and watermelons, and muscatel grapes. Permeating it all is the odor of the Latin race given off by a Josepet who hasn't had a bath in at least twenty years. Incoherent exchanges ensue: "Please do go on, Mossèn Narcís, do go on . . . These melons are ours…Mossèn Narcís is too nice…We shall all meet up in heaven, of course, God willing…Now the cream rolls are missing…Those are for Can Quica…Yes, yes, the ones on order…If we didn't have the Virgin Mary, who could we ever turn to?…Not another word, Mossèn Narcís, one takes that for granted…The melons must be put in the well immediately…Fruit gets hot quickly…Do enjoy yourself, Mossèn Narcís…Stay for lunch…Would you like to stay for lunch?"

Mossèn Narcís bids farewell and the cart pursues him, auguring inevitable disruption. In each house where a Maria lives, the same incoherent, blundering conversations, the same mix of rural and religious confections.

Swimming in the sea is wonderful. The best swimming of the season takes place around the Virgin Mary's day in August. But, as in all such things, everyone has an opinion. Each person is a world unto himself. To my mind, a swim in the sea is a delightful surprise: the strange feeling prompted by immersion in a different, unusual medium. Beach huts in El Canadell are never completely private or completely single. There's always a touch of promiscuity. No one undresses completely naturally in these huts, which gives everyone a peculiar feeling. We've been wearing clothes for so long! As a child I often went barefoot and enjoyed it, and now I still welcome a barefoot walk on sand, rocks, and land; on the other hand, I get goose bumps walking on the floor tiles—particularly a room with mosaic tiles—or if I see someone else walk there barefoot.

It is lovely to go for a swim, but plunging into the sea always makes my chest feel tight. Others move in the sea more easily, perhaps more naturally. Perhaps *nobody* is entirely natural. Man belongs more to the air than to any liquid element. Generally speaking, he is not built to live in water. Fishermen and sailors learn how to swim and swim as young children. They never swim as adults. They feel terror at the mere thought of immersion in the sea. I expect because the pressure from the wind is enough for them…often too much so.

At one o'clock the clatter of plates, forks, spoons, glasses, and knives in every house. Tables are being set. By five past one the beach is empty and everyone is in place, cold and hungry after their swim: hollow cheeks, quivering noses, and sparkling eyes.

Lunch for Holy Mary's Day: fish rice with a rich tomato sauce, stewed lobster, roast chicken. After fifteen or twenty days of eating fish, chicken is a delicious novelty. Pastries, melon, coffee. The cake shops of Palafrugell—and generally in the country—are first-rate. Calella water makes excellent coffee. Father lights up a twenty-five-cent cigar, delicious smoke that is a perfect compliment to the coffee.

I digest and relax in the shade of the boats. No foreseeable problems. This must be bliss. Could it be otherwise? Sr. Narcís, the watchmaker, is rod fishing off the Barret Rock in a canary-yellow suit and a straw boater.

In the evening a few groups of farmers invade the beach. They have come to wash their feet. The water terrifies them. One yokel, cap pulled down over his ears, squeals the moment he feels water reach his ankles. They let their animals swim. Just a little. They leave them for a while on the beach with the water touching their bellies. Horses and shaggy mares exhausted from threshing stand still for an hour, their vacant eyes taking in the horizon.

In the evening, dancing to a hurdy-gurdy under acetylene lights. A sad, tame wind. The sky is murky, an opaque white. In the distance the sound of the undertow on the coast. Everything seems slightly exhausted. The sheets are slightly damp and stick to the skin in step with one's own sweat. One cold cheek, one warm.

17 August. A cloudy, sullen day; sultry sky and oppressive air. Mist floats over the sea's horizon, which now and then looks hazily like land—a vague mirage. A light southwesterly. Lots of humidity. The chaos from Holy Mary's Day still seems to reign.

In the evening, there was an unexpected event in El Canadell: Sr. Joanola set up his telescope in his small garden.

Originally from Palafrugell, Sr. Joanola is a gentleman who owns a pharmacy in Barcelona. He is absolutely ruled by the clock. In his household, the schedule is strict and immutable. At the same time he frantically tries to impose order and precision on everything else in the world. He has countless little drawers in his house where everything is wonderfully organized and labeled: corks, tacks, tools, screws, keys, twine, etcetera. You couldn't ask for more. At first glance, you imagine that a man like him wouldn't be at all curious—because if the purpose of order isn't to control the torment curiosity unleashes, what is it? Nevertheless, Sr. Joanola is an extremely curious man. When a vessel he doesn't recognize sails by, he produces his telescope, investigates, and finds out what it's doing there. It doesn't happen very often because Sr. Joanola is a great fan of the sea and acquainted with almost all the ships that sail along the coast. Consequently, when he brings out his telescope, it's because there is something new—and that amounts to an event in El Canadell.

He keeps the device in two polished wooden boxes, which are a delight to handle. He keeps the cylinder of the telescope in one box, on green velvet, like a small bed, the tripod in the other. He gingerly opens the two boxes with his fingertips. He extends the tripod and places it on the ground, in the shade of the acacia, as if performing a kind of ritual. With anticipation he lifts the cylinder from its bed and wipes the lens with a cloth. Then calmly and expertly screws the cylinder into the tripod.

Once he's set up his telescope, Sr. Joanola leaves the garden and goes into his house. He crosses the dining room. Sra. Joanola is almost always sitting there on a rocking chair, her head against a pillow, complaining of persistent headaches and painful migraines. Sr. Joanola, having entered the house bareheaded, now emerges wearing a magnificent Japanese peaked leather cap. It resembles a naval officer's cap—but Sr. Joanola doesn't belong to the merchant navy, so he wears this Japanese cap.

With his signature cap tilted and his body bent like a discus thrower, he puts his eye to the viewer and adjusts the sight to focus on the vessel he's just glimpsed, or thought he has, on the horizon. It must be a strange, completely unknown vessel for him to have set up his telescope.

News of the instrument's appearance immediately spread through El Canadell and people, especially youngsters and children, rushed to the wrought-iron fence. Sr. Joanola has brought out his telescope! Mummy, Sr. Joanola has brought out his telescope! A huge, very peculiar steamship is sailing by! The telescope! The telescope! There was a flurry of activity and countless individuals now stood in the street gaping at Sr. Joanola and his telescope.

All of a sudden, a young lady piped up: "Why not let *us* have a look?"

As he smiled tentatively, a loud throng quickly invaded his garden. Noisy kids encircled his gadget.

"Let me have a look! Let me have a look! I want a look, too!"

And the shoving and pushing started around his telescope—the uproar got louder and louder until the unforgivable happened. A hand appeared on the shiny, yellow brass of the telescope. Sr. Joanola lost his temper. He shouted: "If anyone touches my telescope, I'll smash their face in! Who do you think you are, you louts! Please have a little respect!"

To a stunned silence, he wiped away the marks left by that sacrilegious hand. When he had calmed down, he said, "Let's have a little order, please. Everybody in line. That's right. You can start..."

We lined up and one at time put our eye to the viewer for a moment.

"Is that focused?"

"Yes, sir, excellent."

But as the line proceeded, disappointment showed on people's faces. When we looked through the viewer, there seemed to be a hazy shape bobbing on the distant horizon. But it was impossible to focus it. In fact, nobody saw a thing.

"Did you see anything?"

"No, did you?"

"To be frank, I saw nothing at all."

Finally, one daredevil asked Sr. Joanola, "Did you see anything, Sr. Joanola?"

"Initially I thought I could see smoke coming out of a steamer's funnel. Then I thought it was something smaller. In fact, I saw nothing. Nothing whatsoever."

"So what was it? Because I think yours is a good telescope."

"You can say that again. It is magnificent! Should I be candid with you? To be honest, it was a false alarm!" said a diffident, rather embarrassed Sr. Joanola.

A line of long faces left the garden, then slowly dispersed. Sr. Joanola unscrewed the device with liturgical solemnity, put the pieces in their boxes and carried them inside. He hung his Japanese cap in his wardrobe. And that is how we innocently spend our summers in El Canadell.

19 August. In the afternoon, local boys and girls in El Canadell usually go to picnic elsewhere: to the En Roques or En Xeco wells, the pine groves of Cape Roig, to Pinell. Rides out to sea are only for calm days, and as a southwesterly tends to blow in the afternoon, such excursions are the exception at the moment. Besides, the young ladies are so pale, so dressed up, so fragile that they are usually seasick, because seasickness is prized as a badge of refined sensibility and rarified sentiment. Normal good health and out-and-out vitality is held to be vulgar, something considered the preserve of ordinary people, the plebs. If you enter their dining rooms, you will find the huge quantities of medications, preparations, powders, pills, and potions currently being swallowed by the middle classes. "Have you taken your drops?" "Bring me a spoon for the cod-liver oil." "You ready for your dose of lime salts?" These are the exchanges one hears at mealtime in the homes of El Canadell. They believe the ingestion of these childish placebos is a mark of distinction. So the sea, thought to be an aberration of nature in itself, is now simply seen as a pretext for summertime displays of plebeian vulgarity.

Excursions over land inevitably include the presence of one, if not two stern spinsters, and sometimes a mother or two. It is the mission of these mature females, tacitly appointed to the task by the society on the beach, to chaperone, thereby ensuring the excursion's high moral standards, and to report, whenever they deem fit, any perceived or anticipated breach of boundaries to the relevant family. Nothing...

The excursion starts with preparations for the picnic, usually a slice of bread or a roll containing two pieces of chocolate, or if the family is wealthier, slices of pork or cold sausage. These ingredients are wrapped in the thinnest possible paper that is in turn wrapped in a page from *La Vanguardia*. Then people gather at one house or another and set out on their walk with that hint of lethargic languor—*languore*, as the Italians say—that currently characterizes social, particularly female, life. Along with the picnic parcel everyone takes a garment—sometimes a shawl—to ward off the cool of evening. They never take any kind of drink. That would be considered infra dig, most vulgar.

And this is how the excursion develops. When the path narrows, the group spreads into a lengthy single file. When it broadens, it splits into pairs. If there is a wood of cork oak or pine to be crossed, they walk in a group or extended line. They do their best to spend the whole afternoon mouthing as many clichés and platitudes as is humanly possible. In fact, gloom descends the moment they move off.

Perhaps now and then one catches a knowing look, an impatient gesture immediately suppressed, a blatant attempt to break out of the shell, an effort to underscore the absurdity of it all. In general, however, everything is obtuse, trite, trivial, and dull. Sometimes a young man will pick a wildflower and shyly offer it to a young lady with a tentative shrug of the shoulders and a hint of pink in his cheeks. I have no experience of these things, but I imagine that this kind of love must end up being the costliest.

When the strollers reach their goal, they sit in a semicircle opposite the vista on offer. They slowly unpack their picnics. The sea is in full view, a great expanse of sea glimpsed between branches of pine trees. The young ladies nibble their rolls and chocolate most elegantly with the tips of their teeth. The sky is a wan, almost white blue, and the wind is hauling a yellowish cloud over the horizon. The young ladies' teeth are like those of mice. The pine needles, moistened by the southwest wind, give off a strong smell, sometimes mixed with scents of purple gorse, ferns, and sea fennel. When the young ladies are midway through their rolls, their teeth suddenly stop nibbling, thus subtly signaling their indifference to food. They aren't at all suggesting that they are full. They are longing to show that they are creatures untainted by greed and, hence, prone to detachment. The wind blows impassively over the sea, the cicadas perform hysterically, screeching from the pine trees; the setting sun's crimson light, streaked with gold and greenish gray, glows over the mountains in the west. When they have finished their picnic, the young ladies wipe their bloodless lips on thin napkins and dust off a crumb that has fallen onto a skirt pleat. At that, the old spinster says in hushed tones, "Your legs, Maria Lluïsa, your legs, for the love of God!"

"Oh, dear!" says Srta. Maria Lluïsa, blushing a deep red.

Then they start the return journey. They put on the clothes they've been carrying the whole afternoon to ward off the damp and cold. The return tends to be more subdued than the outward trip. Some young ladies walk in silence, self-engrossed, staring at the ground—like allegorical representations of philosophy. What *are* they thinking? What images can be floating through *their* minds? Sometimes a young man surveys the scene, realizes that nobody will see him, and plucks up the courage to clasp his partner's hand. Her body tenses; a strange look of shame spreads over her face. It is all quite distressing.

They leave behind the groves of pine and cork, the agaves, heather, and gorse. They start to drag their feet—a sign of fatigue—striking a pathetic note in the silent countryside. The wind doesn't abate: It blusters blindly in the darkness of twilight. Everything is slightly damp and feels as if it has gone cold: grass, tree trunks, clothes, and hair. The grass moistens espadrilles. When the lights of Calella appear on the last bend in the path, everyone sighs with relief inside. Eyes sparkle with the last glimmer of twilight.

22 August. Yesterday was a bad day. A light easterly wind (or wind from the eastern plains). Intermittent downpours. Summer visitors at a loss. Their houses are too small to withstand a cloudburst. Fishermen keep their clogs on all day. The novel sight and sound of clogs echoing along streets. Today people have returned to their espadrilles. Everything has dried out. A lively north wind and blue sky, and it's as if everything has been resurrected anew. The chill in the air has gone. At any rate, the air is lighter, less dense, and the dog days have ended.

The gentle wind is so pleasant, like a splash of cool water on one's cheek.

Hermós is fixing a trawl line in the shadow of a boat hauled up on the sand. I go over when he calls. He takes off his skipper's cap and reveals a sizable whitish-yellow bald patch. Small, distinct drops of sweat run down his pate. His face is ferocious and hairy with a primate's flared nostrils and flabby lips.

"So he says the war is coming to an end?" he comments, knocking a fishhook on the rim of the boat.

"Who does?"

"A gentleman wearing shoes, in the café."

"Good heavens!"

After a long pause he declares, "Anyway, it is bad news."

"It's bad news to say the war is coming to an end?"

"Yes, wars produce fish."

"Hey, come on!"

"I'm telling you! The voice of experience. I've had a new net made for catching argentines. I'm about to dye it. If the war ends, you can say goodbye to the argentines. You won't see one for love or money. Fish like noise, buzz, cannon fire, flotsam."

Sometimes, contact with humanity can be depressing.

Hermós said this with eyes that saddened as he spoke: His eyes believed what he was saying. My depression deepened. I never know what to say in such circumstances.

Fishermen like to sing—particularly songs with lyrics the mouth can savor to a tune provided by the roll of the waves.

A Calella fisherman who is fond of singing says to me, "I'd much rather be able to play the guitar than have a fancy mausoleum."

When he speaks of his companion whom he thinks sings out of tune, he says, "He sings and it's like a fire crackling."

I spend a long time that evening talking fish with fishermen.

At ten o'clock, one gets up from his chair and I hear him say, "Well, lads, up early tomorrow. I'm off to bed. Good night."

As soon as he's said "Good night," he grabs the first chair within reach, sits down and says, "Pepet, bring me a nip!" Then lights a thin cigar.

As I walk home I gaze at the moon sailing across the sky draped in a fine mist. It hangs there seamlessly in the softest down. Light and mist melt in a silent, passive ecstasy.

23 August. Scenes of first love.

The Roca and Pujades families from Barcelona spend the summer in Calella. They are the oldest—the first—families in the colony. Both had put down roots there. Their houses were in town, fishermen's cottages they'd refurbished—probably for the worse—in order to create tame, twilight petit bourgeois summer residences. The houses were adjacent but completely unalike. The Roca family's was a one-story house with a small garden. The Pujades family's was a two-story, but without a garden and just one cramped exit.

Sra. Roca, who took her home very seriously, was a flower lover, and as her garden had a well-watered well, her flowerpots were a joy to behold and admired by many. That summer she'd managed to nurture eighteen varieties of roses, roses that were much appreciated by everyone.

Srta. Concepció Pujades often went to pick a bouquet from Sra. Roca's garden. Not only neighbors, the two families were also good friends. Sra. Roca, childless after her twenty years of marriage, seemed to find real pleasure in talking to Concepció Pujades. The tender inflections that layered her sentences weren't in the least affected. She was often surprised at how spontaneous she was in conversation with young Srta. Pujades.

That afternoon—dusk was falling and the swallows were crying over Calella— Sra. Roca asked Srta. Pujades if what she'd heard was true: namely, if she really was courting.

"Yes, of course!" Srta. Pujades quickly replied with a radiant smile. "My fiancé is Martí Valet i Cases."

Srta. Pujades was very young and, consequently, rather forward and prone to gushing. Besides, she really trusted Sra. Roca.

"Did you say his name is Martí Valet i Cases?" asked Sra. Roca.

"Yes, senyora, Martí Valet i Cases."

"And, Concepció, who might this Martí Valet i Cases be?"

"What do you expect little me to say? He's a very polite young man."

"He isn't the son of Don Narcís Valet i Roig the notary?"

"No, senyora. Theirs is a knitwear family."

"Why, yes, of course! My dear, I do congratulate you! You have been lucky. It's an excellent family."

"He is now studying for a law degree."

"How far has he progressed?"

"He's in his fourth year. Modesty apart, he's a really able—"

"Oh, that doesn't surprise me. The Valets have always been very bright."

"His mama says we are very young."

"How old is Joan?"

"No, he's Martí. He's just nineteen. I'll soon be eighteen."

"Concepció, take it slowly!"

"Yes, senyora. My birthday is in May."

"That's eight months away. What a hurry you are in, by the Holy Virgin!"

"Time simply flies."

"True enough . . . no need to tell me! And does he write poetry like his father?"

"Don't you read the newspapers?"

"I do, my dear, but we have been so very busy! We've not been in a fit state to do anything this winter, what with my poor father-in-law passing away."

"Well, you know, he published his book of poetry to great praise."

"Is it inspired, as people say?"

"Inspired? Don't make me laugh! If Martí could hear you! Nobody is after inspired poetry nowadays."

"Concepció, are you suggesting we belong to a bygone era?"

"Oh, not at all, Sra. Roca!"

"You think we are ignoramuses, if you are truthful. We only pass this way once, you know."

"Sra. Roca, please don't go on so! All I can say is that I like the poetry he writes."

"And I have *always* liked poetry. But what they write today is so peculiar! When it comes to poetry, there's nobody like Mossèn Cinto, we must be clear about that!"

"What am I supposed to say? Martí never talks about anyone but Baudelaire."

"Baudelaire is very anticlerical."

"On the surface, but it's not true. He is much more respectful than people think."

"I don't know, I . . . I think I heard someone say that last summer."

"But people say such silly things! I've read *Les fleurs du mal* and didn't find anything to upset me."

"Pleased to hear that, Concepció, pleased to. Critics do so much harm."

"How pretty your flowers are today, Sra. Roca! Can I make up a bouquet?"

"A bouquet? As many as you want, Concepció. You don't need to ask."

"Thank you so much! Will you go to rosary this evening?"

But Sra. Roca didn't catch her question. She'd gone to the well for a bucket of water. It was time to water her flowers with a peppermint-green watering can that looked freshly painted when it was wet and shiny.

For one of the groups in the colony that first love was *the* love of that summer—and it was a very hot summer, I might add. The couple was the focus of general admiration. They seemed made for each other. He was sturdy, angular, and pasty; tufts of hair dotted his skin and his features complimented his somewhat gauche manner. He spoke through his nose. Conxita was a rather shapeless, spindly girl, pale pink complexion, vacant eyes, a tooth poised graciously on her lip, and a nose that nature had overdosed. She was an inquisitive, sneaky butterfly, and her attitude of wanting to seem older and more sensible than her age gave her an unpleasant demeanor that enraptured everyone. After dinner, they'd sit on two swings and court, facing the sea, their backs to the house, on terrain that was neither the promenade nor the beach—the maritime zone, in a nutshell. It was the beginning of their idyll.

That was when I would go for a stroll around the town. I'd often reach as far as Els Canyars. Sometimes a friend accompanied me, though my promenade was often solitary. When I passed the idyll on the swings, I often felt perplexed and halted. I was distracted by that first love—a love that was ripening.

"Concepció!"

"Yes, Martí?"

"Don't you find this simply divine?"

"I never want to be anywhere else."

"Look at the sea."

"It is so lovely."

"It is slightly moist."

"What do you mean?"

"You can't imagine who *I* met today."

"I have no idea."

"Guess."

"Don't be so tedious!"

"Go on, have a guess!"

"You are such a jester!"

"Well, I met Lluïseta."

"Just as I thought."

"She was so elegant."

"That's what you always say. Why don't you marry her?"

"I can't tell you a thing, Conxita!"

"Quite frankly, you are always whistling the same tune."

"You are so self-centered!"

"What are those sheets of paper poking out of your pocket?"

"Dalmau's sonnets."

"Dalmau's sonnets?"

"Yes, he sent them to me today."

"That chump writes sonnets as well?"

"The poor fellow! Why do you speak ill of him?"

"Given that's what he is."

"Will you remember Calella when we're back in Barcelona?"

"What a question!"

"I'll remember it forever more."

"That's what they all say."

"You really think so?"

"Well, look who's talking."

"I tell you, that white dress really suits you."

"Do you *really* think so?"

"Yes, it looks super."

"Well, you won't believe this but it's the worst garment in my wardrobe."

"To tell the truth, anything looks good on you."

"The Manegats are off to bed."

"How do you know?"

"Look."

"Is the light on in their bedroom?"

"That's right. You know, the old dear has just had a wisdom tooth out."

"No, she's still downstairs. The light's on in the newlyweds' bedroom."

"If you start on that, I'll go."

"Ho, ho, aren't we so very touchy!"

"You must understand that I'm not like the others."

"You don't need to tell *me* that, Concepció!"

"Even worse, if you know."

"Are you trying to annoy me?"

"That's up to you."

"What shall we do tomorrow?"

"I've got *Baby Jesus* in the afternoon."

"And in the morning?"

"In the morning we're going to the pine woods."

"Can't we go up to Sant Sebastià?"

"If you want, we can go later on, if you like, just for a while."

Those familiar with my customary modesty may perhaps be shocked by my audacious attempt at describing first love. As soon as they see I have failed miserably, they can sit back and relax.

It's true: Like the great and much admired masters of romantic literature, I have felt the desire to write a piece in this vein. To be more precise, I wanted to write about a first love that was at least half local. The topic is engaging and cries out for a little embroidery. But so far every effort I've made to write a decent text has failed. I think I can account for the impossible nature of the task. I have concluded that only writers with great imaginations can write on this subject and I've never been at all imaginative. If I were to be frank, I would say, moreover, that the clichés circulating on the subject of first love ring untrue. One sees throughout this curious phenomenon whole-scale vagueness, rapture, and infatuation, which could not be more genuine. But I think such states are *not* inspired by the causes that are generally said to be necessary. It is evident, I believe, that the ingredients of first love—excitement and warmth—are not driven by any particular obsession or focus. I think, in fact, they are provoked by a state of martyrdom. Someone who has fallen in love for the first time is probably closer to a figure from the annals of martyrdom. Their struggle is typically heroic: It is the struggle to say something waged by a person who has nothing to say. These struggles are most unpleasant and the men and women that see them through to the end usually cheat. Shyness conceals a failure to find the appropriate words. Their rapture makes one forget the banal thoughts of first-time lovers. Tenderness hides an almost total inability to confide and to speak. That silence is triggered and sustained by mental states that are concerned with the repression of instinct. Moreover, these states are battered by the wildest forces imaginable. This is so obvious that, although a first love is an essay in amorous rapture, one can take it for granted that if those concerned *could* carry it through to a conclusion, they would prefer not to. An individual smitten for the first time is an unprepossessing figure: someone who spends the whole day fighting off what he most wants, what comes most naturally. This kind of problem for authors who have no imagination, for authors who always need to work with the truth, is entirely unproductive. I don't regret the time I've spent tearing my hair out over first love, but I do believe I would have found it more fruitful if I'd dedicated myself to later, more autumnal love.

Furthermore, life's situations of mutual silence are decided by happenstance. First conversations are the most difficult. The inability to communicate creates moments that are so unpleasant that if the individuals concerned dared and if it were acceptable they'd spend part of their courtship throwing the occasional flurry of tender, loving punches. After letting off steam in that way, not from any hatred or animosity but driven by an overwhelming need to create a different atmosphere, words would flow more fluently, more powerfully.

Nonetheless, a moment comes when something strange, arbitrary, and unpremeditated happens between the loving couple. It is unpredictable and its timing can never be orchestrated. In consequence, the amorous couple feels their respective images have penetrated the inner being of the other and lodged there. There is still a long way to go, but the ice has been broken and a terrain of trust has opened up.

In my experience this highly dramatic development in first love is linked to the discovery of weakness. When chance allows us to uncover a weakness and this discovery generates an increase in tenderness, compassion, or wonder, rather than repelling the person before you, the creation of the objective conditions for love has finally begun. In personal relationships, acquaintance with the weaknesses of the other is an active, integrating element. It creates a secret bond between two people, a shadowy space of complicity that unites their souls.

This mechanism doesn't have great poetic potential, but it would be unforgivable to discard it. It is so important in love stories that I, for one, could never ignore it. Discarding this aspect would, to my mind, place oneself in the camp of the favorite writers of the least demanding readership that exists: the fans of sentimental fiction.

Concepció and Martí were sitting on a ridge in the higher reaches of Els Canyars. It was ten o'clock and the craggy cliffs loomed hazily before them. Beyond them, the sea. They were looking eastwards and watching the moonrise. The brightest ingot of light branded the sea. A sailing boat rocked to and fro in the liquid silver and gold; a soft frothy light spread over the rushing waves. Blue phosphorescence danced on the edges of the ingot. It was a splendid night and the stars shone with diamantine purity. The walls of Calella were like a castle in a dream and the lighthouse hung over the sea like a huge lightbulb. A swarm of drunken insects floated in the thick glow from the pale green glass. There was no wind, no tears, and no mystery: the only sound the weary breathing of the sea. The murky light from the small town was a mere intuition behind the cliffs. Beyond that, the moon silvered the white caps of the waves along the beach and splashed pine trees and rocky outcrops with patches of ocher. Another intuition: the lofty, grandiose coastline within that consummate light. Seated on their ridge, microscopic specks in the night, the couple's minds had been in abeyance for ages—searching for a half-decent word to enable them to abandon the silence sealing their lips. The silence seemed purified. The moment was sublime, the place ideal, and such warmth and such a gentle breeze floated over the land that everything pointed to a moment when something must happen, sooner rather than later. Concepció was waiting for a word from Martí, a quivering, excited, never-to-be-forgotten word; Martí was hoping for something similar from Concepció. Time went endlessly by. Martí spoke up at last—in what sounded like an exceptionally deep lament.

"Concepció . . ."

"Martí . . ."

"I've got a really bad toothache."

It was light—though not bright enough to see the exact expression on Concepció's face. You could see her look down, disappointed. She stared at him for a while and then passed from disillusionment to pity, her face aglow with love.

"I'm sorry, Concepció, I've got a toothache. On a night like this, it is totally ridiculous for me to be telling you that I've got a toothache—"

"But it's the most natural thing in the world," she said, taking his hand.

"Do you really think so?" asked Martí, giving her an anguished glance.

"Doesn't this landscape make you think of Beethoven?"

"What can I say? More like Brahms."

"Yes, you may be right: Brahms."

"What a night for love!"

"Listen, Martí."

"What is it?"

"Why don't you tell me some of the things you wrote last winter?"

"What can I tell you? I wouldn't dare."

"Oh . . . are you afraid?"

"You do like to make fun."

"You sometimes say things—"

"All right, forget that. Perhaps it's not the moment, no matter."

"Your letters were so beautiful."

"Please, let's not exaggerate."

"Well, what do you expect me to say? I really liked them."

"Haven't you heard? Mummy must have an operation."

"What's that?"

"She isn't at all well and needs an operation."

"When did you find out?"

"Oh, months ago."

"Why didn't you tell me before?"

"I didn't think we were close enough."

"What a way to act, Martí! I find that quite frightening. You are most peculiar."

"Why do you say that?"

"You tell me."

"Hey, please don't get like that."

"Do you hold me in such low regard?"

"Well, you know, I don't like to make anyone suffer."

"What can I say? I do think I have a right to know certain things."

"Naturally, Conxita! You must tell me . . ."

As the reader can see, the change was almost instantaneous. The impact of happenstance is swift and fulminating. Sometimes a specific cause produces a similar effect, sometimes the strangest, most unexpected effect. Martí's toothache, that small inflammation starting in the root of a molar, the first twinges of which he was already suffering, that would soon make his cheek swell grotesquely, created between the two a first moment of normal, human conversation in a relationship hitherto vitiated by awkwardness.

The tissue of human relationships is governed by such a lack of reason or naturalness that if one stops and scrutinizes the latest episode from real life, one is shocked by the number of situations and impulses that are paradoxical, unexpected, unpremeditated, and entirely unheralded.

Nonetheless, in our specific example the change was instantaneous. I am at an advantage given that I can vouchsafe it happened like that and I can do so for the following reasons. Once my dearth of imagination had demonstrated to me that I was incapable of writing about first love, I decided to spare myself the effort by reducing my task to the painstaking transcription of real events. My first love—and I would like to emphasize this—is an entirely *true* story of first love. I have re-created the feelings, situations and words on paper, aiming above all for fidelity. That's why it probably seems banal. What can *I* do if things are really like that? Men and women receive a thorough enough education at school, don't they? They are taught history and grammar, arithmetic and physics, gymnastics and French. I can't understand why they don't receive lessons in idealism, warmth, and love. School curricula are sufficiently impractical for these subjects to be added without lowering moral standards. As long as *Romeo and Juliet* isn't included in the school curriculum, men and women will leave school with some learning but little self-knowledge. And novelists who devote themselves to investigating these mysteries will have no choice but to tell lies or seem banal.

They went rowing that day during the most delightful hours of summer: six to eight in the evening. It was lovely to see them together in the poop of their boat. The gentle to-and-fro of the waves blurred the line of the horizon behind them. The sun had set and everything followed in sequence. The sea was still. The last gust of wind had blown and nightfall was beginning to spread its dark purple mantle over the land. In the oblique light from the brightness in the west, the town looked like an antique print. The enraptured couple held hands. The sailor, rowing from the hip, was whistling and humming, spellbound.

"Tell me now, Martí!"

"I can't find the words, Concepció!"

"You are a poet and can't find the words?"

"So it would seem."

"So will we never progress?"

"You never tell me anything."

"What else is there for me to tell? I've told you a thousand times."

"Why do you grimace like that?"

"A mosquito just bit me on the shoulder."

"And what will it be like when we're back in Barcelona?"

"Don't even mention it. You'll make me so sad."

"If you give up your piano lessons, we'll see very little of each other."

"We must try and arrange something."

"Oh, didn't I tell you? Yesterday Father said, 'I think you like Concepció.'"

"And what did you say?"

"What do you think?"

"Come on, don't be so selfish! Tell me."

"What would *you* have replied?"

"If Mummy asked me, I'd . . . but, Daddy!"

"Well, I said, 'Yes, I like Concepció.'"

"And what did your daddy say?"

"He seemed to take it in his stride."

"Is that all?"

"Well, you know we are awfully young."

"What do you mean?"

"I am only in my fourth year."

"So what?"

"Hasn't your family ever mentioned that?"

"What do you expect them to say? It's obvious enough."

"Do you think they are happy at the prospect?"

"You know nobody likes this kind of thing."

"But when two people are in love—"

"So what?"

"Well, they love each other, and that's that!"

"Oh, you have the strangest ideas!"

"That's reality for you."

"I must have told you a thousand times that I don't like reality."

"I don't either, you know that."

"All right, go on."

"Will we see a lot of each other in Barcelona?"

"Look, Daddy is on the balcony."

"So what?"

"It's strange that he is wearing a jacket. He never does usually."

"Your daddy is very nice."

"Daddy!"

To avoid adding to the effort required to read about this first love I have deliberately suppressed all the explanations, interjections, and descriptions practitioners of the genre put around the dialogues to make them sound genuine. As these dialogues aren't imagined but transcribed from reality—the author of this book typed up the originals after their respective circumstances—I thought any complementary padding would be superfluous. But one shouldn't conclude that the dialogue flowed with the same facility with which it can be read. These dialogues are the result of efforts that only people who've suffered in the same way can acknowledge. I was an onlooker and lost my patience several times but my sacred duty to give my readers the wherewithal to while away their time made me persist in my attempt. I paused endlessly, the writing was painful and words often emerged framed by rage. Even if they are only inchoate, one can imagine states of mind. Fear, alienation, the feeling you don't really know what is being said, the fear of appearing ridiculous, the worry you can't really engage, tormented because you can't intuit their exchanges. The truth of the matter is that the author was the one *most* damaged by the poverty of his material. It is always more uplifting to show friends how well you can write in the elevated mode.

Perhaps the occasional reader will complain about my characters' lack of malice. However, that complaint is unfounded. My characters are as good or as malicious as those who tend to be that way: except they don't allow those qualities to surface. My characters belonged to a time when passion was unusual. In other eras passions reached similar levels, but if they seemed stronger, it was because individuals were better educated and words flowed more easily. The first requisite in order to feel passion is to be able to express it. The extent to which we have all become inarticulate, inept, and ignorant is unimaginable. We are total asses. However, that doesn't mean passions have never led ordinary people to experience loss of appetite or sleepless nights. Martí and Concepció ate, drank, slept, and dreamed normally as their first love climaxed. The fact of their love was revealed in that process of creating an image in common and focusing almost all their most vivid memories on a specific moment. They were as malicious as anyone could be, who can doubt that? When memory focuses on a specific image then it is usually imbued with sensuality. However, as they were fortunate in having good companions, they'd never been corroded by cynicism, and their physical drive was simply at a normal level; they didn't know, one might say, what to do with their desires. That apart, they were individuals like any others, exactly as we all are. They were generally sensitive, and if they had no choice but to act foolishly or spitefully, they did so and then called it quits.

After lunch, they sat in the passageway. A refreshingly cool sea breeze was blowing. Patches of sun danced on the white walls. The glaring light shone iridescent in cracks on the doors. Conxita sat in her rocking chair, dripping with sweat and fanning herself. Martí, in his shirtsleeves, collar open, hadn't buttoned up the top of his trousers.

"Conxita, I've written another song."

"You work too hard."

"One must make the most of life's happy moments."

"You are right: One only falls in love once."

"Don't you think it is lovely to be in love?"

"Don't start on that again."

"Do you love me, Conxita?"

"Don't start, I said!"

"What do you mean?"

"I don't want a repeat of what happened yesterday."

"Hey, I only kissed you a couple of times!"

"Then people start talking and I don't like that."

"Ignore them."

"Look at who's being shameless."

"I dreamed about you today, Conxita."

"Do you remember what you wrote in that letter to me?"

"Well, what exactly *did* I say?"

"That it's immoral to dream. Who said that? López-Picó?"

"No, Esclasans. And what are you suggesting?"

"I think the rice has made me sick."

"It was too heavy."

"I only like rice with strips of salted cod."

"Why didn't you say so, Conxita? Nobody at home likes fish rice. We cooked it like that because we thought that's how you liked it!"

"Not to worry."

"When we're married, we shall always eat rice with cod."

"Please don't be so forward."

"Why not? I like to talk about these things."

"Where would you prefer to live, in Sant Gervasi or Sarrià?"

"They both have their pros and cons."

"No need to tell me."

"Why don't you read your song to me? What's the title?"

"I gave it one that doesn't go with the song, but I like it all the same."

"What is it?"

"'Song of an Epigrammatic Elegy.'"

"That's really nice."

"It sounds a bit like Maragall."

"Aren't you happy with it?"

"It might seem rather daring, don't you think?"

"Do you always intend to write in verse?"

"Yes, if I can. Why do you ask?"

"You'll be forever in the clouds."

"Doesn't that appeal to you?"

"It does and it doesn't."

"Are you very jealous, Conxita?"

"Much more than you might think."

"I like that."

"And aren't you ever jealous?"

"We'd be in a bad state if I weren't. Sometimes, when I see you speaking to a particular person, I don't know how I might react."

"You are so strange, Martí!"

"What do you expect, Conxita?"

"I've got a touch of heartburn. Give me a glass of water."

Their stamina was remarkable. Suffering every minute, they talked and talked for hours, tirelessly. Each sentence was torture, each word, a drama. In the evening, when they went to bed, they were worn out. Naturally they grew accustomed to their martyrdom. Everything tends to become routine, even the most loving conversations. It wasn't at all exceptional when, over time, their dialogues became mere repetitions of words and phrases. Men and women can act with boundless monotony. In some countries people find monotony more necessary than bread and potatoes. Our country is in first place in this respect.

I must confess that when I began planning a first love I did so with the intention of writing a page full of romantic excitement and idealism. As I am a writer so bereft of ability, with such meager resources, I imagined that if I chose the subject of tender love and affection, I might at least grow small wings. If my literary culture is quite insubstantial, that doesn't mean it hasn't developed a certain sense of direction by dint of trying. In fact, I wanted to show I had developed along those lines by writing a page of bubbling emotion and loving candor. If I couldn't carry it through it was because my imagination didn't rise to the task of transforming a heavy concentration of opaque, ashen gray into a mother-of-pearl rainbow glow. It is not easy to triumph over the pressure of a passive life. The only recourse we possess to introduce a little variety into our humdrum intellectual lives is to argue with our neighbors. How can we fight such pettiness? Our age-old gravitas doesn't tolerate the tiniest mental game, the slightest criticism, or most reasonable of comments. There is no spirit of adventure and we are numbed by a sense of order; we are not any better when it comes to obeying or giving orders. This is a terrible burden borne by the psychology of my characters. These are the ingredients for a long, gray novel. In such a state of mind, it is impossible to write the story of a first love that is at once ardent and tender.

There was a full moon. The sea was becalmed. The only sound along the beach was the plash-plash of water lapping on sand. A yellowish light floated above Calella, muted by the dying days of August. A bluish haze over the hills and mountains melded into the pale yellow of the spectral moon. They walked out to the sea. The town was slumbering in the heavy, oppressive stillness. As ever. The lights from the trawlers flickered wearily over the sea. The strident growl of a gramophone spread out from the town. It was very, very humid. The sea smelled strongly of sea.

The boat was moored in a southwesterly corner. They jumped aboard. They pushed the anchor ropes to one side. Concepció sat in the poop. Martí fitted the oars into the oarlocks. They splashed in the silence of the night. Concepció's face looked rather tired and her body seemed slack and languid. Martí rowed clumsily, but rather like an excited schoolboy. They said nothing for a while. The boat was going nowhere, simply moving away from the beach. Concepció was looking up—apparently staring at the stars blurred by a misty haze. As he rowed, Martí looked at the bilge that was taking in water—nothing out of the ordinary there. The moonlight endowed the external world with an air of motionless mystery and everything seemed stylized. The breeze had stilled. The strident music had receded into the distance. The magnificent moon sailed gently across the sky.

Concepció suddenly opened her eyes, leaned forward, and exclaimed, palpably annoyed, "Martí, row harder!"

"I'd say '*voga*,' not '*rema*.' It's more Catalan, less Spanish!" the young man retorted, with a self-satisfied titter.

"I couldn't care less, Martí, just row harder!"

"And why do you want me to row harder! Look how far we've moved away from—"

"Not at all! You can still see the houses. I want you to take me to infinity tonight, Martí. Row harder!"

"Where do you want to go? One must be careful out at sea, Conxita. Believe me. Otherwise one will pay a high price."

"So what? You never change. Sometimes I think you're so slow, so wooden...how can I put it, so droopy, I don't think you could be more so. You really don't understand me, Martí, do you?"

"No, I don't, Conxita!"

"Are all men as droopy as you are?"

"The things you ask...I find you upsetting! What am I supposed to say?"

"Come and sit next to me!"

"You can't be serious? You can't just drop the oars. You know I'm not very expert."

"No, really."

"It's such a pleasant night," the young man piped up after a moment's pause.

"Don't talk to me about it! It *is* a pleasant night, but one that does nothing for me."

"What *do* you mean?"

"It's very humid."

"More so on the beach. I don't think it's that bad now."

"Why do you act like this, Martí?" retorted Concepció.

"How do you expect me to act? I think I've always been like this."

"True enough," said Concepció, dispiritedly.

Time passed suspended in silence. The only sound came from the oars splashing in the sea and the squeaking oarlocks. Martí was a poor rower. He sent up the occasional shower of water.

"Martí!" Concepció continued.

"Go on."

"Why are you *always* like this? Why are you *always* so droopy and wooden? Why can you never understand me?"

He was depressed and speechless. He kept rowing and kept his head down.

"I don't like you one bit when you are—"

"Don't say that, Concepció! I find that hurtful."

"I wish you were different."

"How would you prefer me?"

"Won't you come and sit next to me? I'll row with one oar and you with the other."

"Don't do anything so silly! What if the boat capsizes and we fall into the water? We are a long way from the beach."

"Don't you see *why* I don't like you? You are unbearably dense, an idiot. You don't understand me, and you never will!"

"That's enough of that, Conxita, quite enough! You say that to me far too often."

"You can go on repeating it is a pleasant night . . . I feel stifled, hot, I don't know what's wrong with me."

"Take off your sweater."

"Sweater? What do you mean 'sweater'? I'm not wearing one! Haven't you even noticed what I'm wearing? You're so witless. My sweater! You mean the sweater *another* girl was wearing."

"Like you wore the other day."

"It's hopeless. I don't like you."

"Would you be so good as to tell me what I must do for you to like me?"

"You are an empty vessel."

"Thank you very much."

"You should be naughtier. Come and sit next to me!"

"I've already told you what I think about all *that*."

"You're afraid of what people might say."

"And of what you said about being naughty, thank you very much!"

"Yes, my kind sir. I tell you, there's more where that came from. You've not heard the half of it. I'd like you to be naughty now, and you're being doltish."

"Conxita. Please! Stop being so vulgar!"

"And you think everything is fine and dandy because all this is out in the open. How wrong can you be!"

"But what's wrong, Conxita. I think you've changed."

"One day or the next you'd have found out." And then her manner changed brusquely. "Well, will you or won't you come and sit next to me?"

"Not that again! Do you want us both to fall into the water?"

"My God, you are so tedious! Will you or won't you? You won't? Well, turn the boat around and let's head home."

"Don't be like that, Conxita!"

"I said let's head home, immediately! I can't stand any more of this. I've got a headache."

"I usually carry aspirins with me but I left them behind today."

"You are so pathetic!"

"Do forgive me."

"But I wasn't referring to the aspirins."

"I never forget them but today I did."

"That's enough, Martí! Let's go back!"

Concepció looked down. The boat sailed noiselessly through the silent night towards the beach. From time to time the blade of the oar threw up a shower of water. The lights of Calella flickered wanly. The glow from the moon gave the town's white walls an air of unreal stillness. Two tall, slender palm trees were silhouetted against its enchanted walls. A dog suddenly barked. When it stopped, they heard the noise from that gravel-toned gramophone.

"The Fiols still have their gramophone switched on!" said Martí, intrigued.

Concepció didn't respond.

Back in the southwesterly corner of the beach, they anchored the boat as best they could and disembarked with difficulty. Martí almost fell into the water. One of his trouser legs was sopping wet. Everything was dripping with damp. There was a steamy, frothy light over the sand on the beach, like woolly fluff. The trawler lights glinted on the sea like fireflies. The inland breeze that was now picking up brought with it a dry, hot smell of stubble, cork oaks, and cicadas.

They followed the walls of the houses that looked over the beach. They walked in silence. They saw nobody. As usual. Martí seemed to be limping in his soaked trousers. Concepció looked down at the ground. A sad smile occasionally came to her lips. When they reached her front door, they said good night and went their different ways.

In the end, of course, they married. And today he is a much-loved teacher. They married after the requisite seven years. The process leading to this outcome is quite uninteresting. By the time the image of Martí Valet i Cases was etched deep on Conxita's heart, observers realized she would take it with her to the grave. She was so confident she never once faltered. The process took longer for Martí. His interest would wane and then wax incredibly strong. He managed to construct arguments both in favor of and against marriage. His arguments were so subtle, so genuine, and so apposite that when he spoke of these matters he was like an apothecary weighing the most minute doses on perfectly balanced scales. It's hardly worth recalling now: One day they jumped into a trap drawn by two horses and were married. Afterwards, their heads wracked by such arguments, they went from city to city on a tour of the Continent.

They were happy, who can doubt that? The enduring strength of marriages, in the case of normal individuals, depends on the range of subjects they have to debate. I speak, naturally, of childless marriages, as was their case. While there is dialogue, there is marriage. Of course, to ensure a range of possible conversations one only requires a little ill health and bad luck. Concepció's health, which was never robust, worsened after they married and henceforth remained fragile. For his part, once he had reached the status to which he had aspired, Martí became rather a bighead. Not just *slightly*—he occupied precisely the region implied by "rather." A similar mental outlook can also be beneficial for matrimony. It is a conservative position, because a bighead, however gross he may be, never goes back on what he's done. He is never wrong. And, as we know all too well, the speech of a man who is never wrong has three qualities: It is confident, fluent, and interminable. These three qualities distinguish that which is never in short supply: mediocrity, downright mediocrity.

24 August. Drawbacks of Calella.

Cape Roig is very pretty. The coast from Forcats Point to Els Canyars is planted with cork oaks. The cork oak is a rather doleful tree, the color of a fly's wing, a dusty, austere, impoverished affair. The cork-oak plantations seem to be saying: What do you expect if that's the way we are? This tree has a moment when it livens up—in winter when it rains and in spring when it blossoms. Green momentarily vanquishes the sallow gray. Although I don't share other people's enthusiasm for pine trees, I do accept that this tree is considerably enhanced when it grows by the sea. The parabolas made by the crests of the Three Pines in La Torre are the most beautiful curves in the geometry of Calella. The fishermen's village—the arches, the apricot-tinged roofs, the way the houses tease the rugged coastline—is pure delight. The town's color is beautiful too. El Canadell—the *barri* where the wealthy reside—is less so. That line of chalets, front gardens surrounded by wrought-iron fences, look more like plots in a zoo—except instead of a tiger or a giraffe stepping out, a small investor emerges with his wife and daughter. El Canadell squats over a set of tunnels that lead to the beach and corral it within the town. It is the best possible arrangement if one wants a swim in the sea. It is excellent. But in my view, Calella has one big defect: That whole expanse of sloping land that acts as a backdrop—the area known as "the long haul"—is almost bereft of trees, meager, and stunted. It is poor, thin, sparse land with a little wheat and a few vines that turn a dirty, dusty monotone yellow in summer. The day when its hinterland possesses the vegetation it cries out for—olives, cypresses, and pines—Calella will be one of the most beautiful towns along this coast. However, I doubt we shall see that wondrous transformation in our lifetime—unless there is a change in ownership. Besides, if Calella had a greater density of plants and trees, its winter temperatures would be much gentler. Trees are the best defense against the wind. The coastal path from Calella to Llafranc is fascinating—despite the barren desert around La Torre. Cape Sant Sebastià, the beach, and the pine trees are the three Graces of Llafranc. A real delight. Two delicious things in Calella: the fish, which is really tasty, and the cool, light water. The church (which belongs to its bourgeois era) is freezing cold and irredeemably third-rate.

25 August. We launch *Nuestra Señora del Carmen* in the afternoon. My brother and I hoist the three-cornered mainsail and, with the help of a light southwesterly, head towards Aiguablava. We find dolphins beyond the bay of Tamariu, playful, powerful dolphins that surge and leap. The dolphin is a beautiful fish to watch as it swims through water: even more so than tuna. Their strong surges as they speed along arrest the eye. If they cut across whitish, cloudy water and the sun is shining bright, the colloidal veneer covering them adds a glassy sheen and they are like glass fish snaking through the sea in zigzag streaks of lightning; if the water is deep and dark blue, they weave and wend, a vertiginous escape like mysterious, phantom shadows. On a whim, they decide to race under our boat and almost hit the keel as they rush on with that blind, voracious enthusiasm of theirs. My brother, who wants to see them move even more quickly, bangs the tiller against the boat's side and we watch them dive and disappear vertically into the watery abyss.

Every year we make a number of trips to Aiguablava. The lords and masters of the cove are the Forgas family from Begur. Sra. Lola is very welcoming. Sr. Francisco is an excellent person: They own the best wine made in these parts. They have four daughters, Teresita, Isabel, Matildeta, and Lolita who are dark or fair and incomparably beautiful. We always enjoy ourselves in their house. We have a bite to eat on the terrace.

Aiguablava is a cove sheltered from the southwesterly. The sea is calm, which seems to deepen the solitude and remoteness of the land. There is a strong scent of the pines. This aroma seems to heighten the flavors of the white bread, cold sausage, and dry white wine. The afternoon light enters a slow death agony over the fine sand on the small beach. Still blue-green waters in the small bay, inner reflections of sand and fish, pink to crimson granite along the coast shimmering like an expanse of flesh over the sea: like a wondrous dream.

In the bright midday sun, Aiguablava is an incandescent, clear, transparent cove of pinkish sand. But there is an equally beautiful spot in the Fornells basin: the dark blue and faded blue sand of the Platja Fonda.

The southwesterly whistles at sunset. Our return journey is difficult against the head wind. We have no choice but to row. It is a real effort to round Es Mut Point. The boat is too small and too light. The waves constantly bring it to a halt. We sail close to the coast, taking advantage of sheltered spots as much as we can. But as dusk falls, the wind quickens and the drag tightens. The gusts and spray soak us. At

Blanc Point, my brother breaks two strops in succession and I break one oarlock. In the time we need to repair the tackle, the wind and current force us back. We decide to return to Aiguablava and appeal for hospitality there. We arrive sopping wet. Sra. Lola gives us a change of clothes. We walk into the dining room just as the haricot beans appear in a comforting white cloud of steam that augurs well. The girls look beautiful in the light of their home. Dr. Arruga, who has spent the late afternoon trekking along the coastal cliffs with his camera, saw the efforts we made to round Blanc Point and says we were rash to attempt the impossible. I think that we'd have made it past the danger point if our tackle hadn't snapped.

Arruga is a great character. He looks like an Arab, not the kind whose skin is greasy, oily, but the handsome, muscular, sturdy, strong kind. He is slim and young, with wavy black hair, deep-set eyes, olive skin, admirable teeth, and long, gnarled fingers that bring to mind the tentacles of an insect. His gaze seems capable of intense concentration. He speaks slowly—too smoothly at times—and explains things with great clarity, stressing precise detail. He describes the mechanisms at work in our conversation with genuine voluptuous relish. At the same time he is the least conventional man I know, the bluntest in his use of words and the most resistant to banal gossip. At any rate, he is a man I like. I think he is an unusual phenomenon in this country, almost a *new* man, with great physical and moral strength. His curiosity and capacity for work are quite extraordinary and his fingers, lithe and dexterous. He has a small black mustache and when he finds something of interest he twirls the end of his mustache as if he were winding a pocket watch. His hair is so wavy that anyone near him can hear the silken, spiraling rustle when he runs his hand through it.

26 August. Return to Calella as the scent of pines from Cabres Cove and the Musclera suffuses the chill morning. Even without a wind, the swell crashes against the coast. When we are about to set sail, Dr. Arruga, an early riser, waves a farewell handkerchief from their terrace. We reach Calella at eight, quite exhausted.

In the midafternoon, my friend Rossend Girbal, the horse dealer, known as Jan hereabouts and as the Fat Trader in the Rosselló, arrives in El Canadell in his windowed carriage. He weighs a good two hundred and sixty pounds. Today a couple of skinny, weedy, laughable ponies drag him along as best they can. In order to alight from his carriage he must ease his paunch sideways through the door in a well-rehearsed maneuver. He'd otherwise find it impossible to make an exit. Feet firmly on the ground, he unhitches the horses and I greet him cheerily as he starts to lead them by the halters to the beach.

"I'm sick of these horses," he says. "Their legs are so feeble. I told Clotes the blacksmith: 'Give them a lick of Maré Red.' He gave them a lick of Maré Red. It made no difference! I want to see if the sea will toughen them up. I don't have much faith in these things: The drawback with water is that it's water. But sometimes a spot of lunacy works wonders, you know? Besides I have things to do. I have to go to Figueres and Perpignan. A lady is waiting on me in Figueres. That's today's world, right? You know, I'm buried under work, and that's the truth."

Despite being so stout, Sr. Girbal speaks in a studied, affected way, with the swaggering, impertinent tone Gypsies sometimes adopt.

Sr. Girbal is a man who suffers. That was my first impression on meeting him. His voluminous Roman emperor's neck is crammed into an ironed collar with a tie knotted as small and round as an olive stone. He also sports a waistcoat embroidered with an exquisite floral pattern. He is very hot. He wilts in the heat. His collar feels tight and he occasionally gives it a wrench in a violent attempt to free his sweating flesh from that starched collar. He's quite a spectacle—so fat, so rotund, yet so dapper—dragging his two nags behind him on his way to the beach. Released from their headgear, the horses seem more laughable than ever: an expanse of horsehide stretched over four poles. Their hide looks as if it might tear on their bony haunches at any moment. The skinniness of their legs is due to the fact Sr. Girbal starves them. He is a glib, smooth talker but never in a hurry to feed his horses.

By the water's edge he encourages them to go in: He holds the halters, cracks his whip, and flicks its tip over their rumps. The horses don't budge. They stand and gawp at the sea—as if seeing it for the first time. He has no option but to crack his whip and back up his actions with the choicest of words. All to no avail. The horses remain absolutely unmoved. They don't flinch even when flogged.

"They're shocked by the sight of so much water," says Sr. Girbal calmly, not concealing his annoyance. "They don't fancy a swim in the briny. They don't realize saltwater will strengthen their shanks. They must be inland animals, from deep in the sticks . . . animals that can't adapt."

One last attempt: He beats them with the whip handle. The noise makes them prick up their ears—ever so slightly. They don't budge one inch.

In the wake of these repeated failures, Sr. Girbal twists and contorts his neck and turns red with rage. I fear there will be an outbreak of violence any moment now—the violence fat men sometimes resort to. But Sr. Girbal restrains himself and his temper. He turns the horses around and, gripping the halters, walks them back up the El Canadell ramp. He strides towards his carriage in lordly fashion, attaches the horses, and climbs in sideways. Then says from on high "Let's try to dine on pigeon one of these days!" before disappearing up the slope, straight as a rod behind the windows of his carriage.

The reference to pigeon makes me think of the diet this friend of mine prefers. No other acquaintance has eaten so many pigeons in his lifetime. I would exaggerate if I claimed that's all he eats but he *has* devoured huge quantities of the birds. The first thing he asks upon entering an inn, lodging house, or restaurant is whether they have a pigeon or two. He eats them roasted—or stewed with onions. If he ever comes across an establishment that has run out of pigeons, he ranks it a failure, a hostelry that's beyond the pale, that doesn't really exist.

I linger for a second and reflect on the infinite number of pigeons whose inexorable destiny it has been to drop, sooner or later, onto his plate. So pretty on the wing, yet their final fate was the fork of this fat, ferocious man! As he has splendid teeth—his mouth is much better shod than his horses'—he eats them whole and never leaves a scrap. He crunches their small heads—the most savory part of the pigeon, which leaves a slightly bitter aftertaste—and the bones of their wings, legs, and carcasses, creating an impressive racket as he devours them, his head erect, chest protruding, triangular napkin over the embroidered waistcoat, baring his white, voracious teeth.

28 August. Uncle Esteve Casadevall built our small house in Calella. The house is full of reminders of the man. There is a diploma in my bedroom granting him the title of "Sponsoring Member" of the "Spanish Lifeboat Society for the Rescue of the Shipwrecked" signed by the Queen Regent. It is an elegant diploma written in a calligrapher's ornate hand and embellished with flowers and animals in the style of the period. A drawer in the wardrobe contains a book with the "List of Members of the Spanish Lifeboat Society for the Rescue of the Shipwrecked." The volume has a very loose binding because we read and handled it carelessly when we were children with tonsillitis. Six polished lithographs, surely from Munich, Germany, hang on the dining-room walls: a still life of shellfish, oysters, and lobsters, another of fish, and four frostbitten wintry landscapes in gloomy Alpine style.

Relatively well-heeled people from Palafrugell have owned houses near the beaches here for years. Those keen on fishing or eating fish had always owned houses they'd constructed themselves. But they were never strictly summer people: Their time at the beach lasted a couple days at most—generally during public holidays. They had work in town that they couldn't leave for much longer. I suspect the first genuine holidaymakers were the *americanos*. They were people of leisure, who possessed fortunes and fragile health. The *americanos* introduced the idea of the hot seawater bath—which at one time was believed to be a panacea. One still finds elderly people who like to take them. They were also thrifty folk and their stay cost them next to nothing.

They must have led twilight lives of absolute moderation. In the morning they sat in the shade from the acacias and haggled with fishmongers over the catch of the day. Batlle's cart brought their provisions from town and the latest news. They lunched well—as always: vegetable stew, meat stew, and a little plate of fish. They spent their afternoons playing ombre. A person who was free to play ombre in the afternoon seemed to enjoy all the necessary trappings of wealth. Later on, they'd pick up their walking sticks and go for a stroll to see the "views" of Llafranc and return in time for the rosary, that is, after they'd had the church built. Then dinner and bed, for the next day they had matins.

This is how the *americanos* from Begur created Sa Tuna. Those from Palafrugell built a great number of houses in Llafranc and Calella.

Although they were mostly people who'd retired from the fishing industry, they continued to own a small boat and fishing tackle and employed local fisherman to fish for them. The latter were usually men who'd been sailors in their youth and plied the route to North America. The one we employed, named Fidel, was tall, gaunt, and rheumatic. These fishermen also looked after the houses in winter and used the small boats to fish for squid. Sometimes the gentlemen—the "gents"—would accompany them for some line fishing. On days when the sea was calm, the fisherman would bring his wife and children for a sail. The lady wrapped a shawl around her shoulders and crocheted scarves around the children's necks. Everyone came back exhausted. In truth, the sea pleased and suited no one: It was too cold and too wet. The best summer nights were thought to be those when you could sleep under a light blanket; nights requiring an eiderdown were less appealing. These holidaymakers felt the cold and liked to bundle up. When it was time to go home, they felt relieved of a great burden and were in much better spirits.

Music plays an important part in my memories of childhood in El Canadell.

At the time the hurdy-gurdy was the instrument people thought most serviceable to get people on their feet and dancing. But that mechanical round of grinding, metallic jingles left no imprint on my memory: The only lingering trace is the unpleasant smell from the gas lamps that lit up the open-air dances.

However, there was *one* high-quality instrument in El Canadell:

the piano that belonged to the Genover family. The older brother and sister used to play it, usually performing as a duet: Maria and Xico. When the sea was perfectly still—under a blistering morning sun or in the gentle warmth of twilight—one would hear the piano in the distance as it cast a kind of spell over El Canadell and people walking by Can Genover would automatically tend to tiptoe.

Maria and Xico sat at the piano. Seen from afar—playing in a long, ground-floor room with a large window looking over the street—they performed like two robots. As they played, they held themselves stiff and corseted. They preferred fine music. As well as playing the piano, Maria sang cloying, wistful songs. Xico would tirelessly accompany her. Bad music is usually pleasant enough, which is surely why those who enjoy it like to wallow in it. Those fond of fine music are more constrained, hard to please, and fussy. Xico and Maria—or Maria and Xico—weren't inclined that way, however, and made just the right demands on the notes they played. When an acquaintance approached them in a pleasant, courteous manner and said, "Oh, Xico (or Maria), do play the Rhapsody! It is so lovely!," one relished the comforting sight of them—however little time they might have—walking to the piano, sitting opposite the keys, opening the score, and playing Liszt's Hungarian Rhapsody no. 2. Before beginning they exchanged glances to confirm their intentions: a pensive pause, which ended in a serious smile. A deep silence fell over the room. Everyone was concentrating. Everyone would simulate that pained expression one must adopt when listening to high-flown music. And Liszt's Hungarian Rhapsody no. 2 would emerge from the piano, its brilliance only slightly dimmed by the petit bourgeois ambience.

The piece required absolute concentration and was extremely demanding. The most rapturous moments gave people goose bumps—or so they said. During quieter, more reflective soirees—occasions perhaps with a more select audience, who no longer pretended to suffer but simply looked glum—another great morceau suggested itself: Beethoven's *Moonlight* Sonata. If the Rhapsody was hard on the fingers and required lots of bounce, the *Moonlight* Sonata was about feeling. Together they comprised an entire musical microcosm.

My adolescence in El Canadell was thus literally saturated by the

Rhapsody and *Moonlight* Sonata. And now I have no choice: That is the fine music that will accompany my memories of those days for as long as I live. It is the music that will always bind me to El Canadell—as I am also bound to it by the sugary scent of rice powder and patchouli, the taste of grilled red mullet dressed in vinaigrette oil, the novels of Paul Bourget, and the rare glimpse of the calves of the indistinct forms of young ladies of that era.

30 August. Saint Rose. My sister's saint's day. Llafranc's main fiesta.

When I arrive in the afternoon, the *riera* and a large part of the beach are packed with countrymen's carts complete with canvas tops. They have come to wash their feet, give their animals a bath, and eat outdoors. The sun shines down on this superb spectacle as the southwesterly wind blows things around. It is like a nomad encampment by the sea, between the honey-colored sand and the green pine trees.

The moist breeze makes the sardana band sound gruff. The loud, harsh music flowing from the wooden and metal instruments has a puff pastry quality. The volume of music produced by the band bears no relation to the performers' swollen cheeks. They blow like men gone crazy, but the insidiously moist breeze deflates the sardanas, which soon sag.

At dusk, the countrymen remove the large pot and big six-pound loaf of brown bread from their carts. They carry the pot down to the beach and sit around it in a circle. When they remove the lid a rich, comforting smell of cold roast chicken fills the air. They tie big napkins around their necks; it lends to the scene a true fiesta touch. The young women wear gaudy red or yellow dresses and the young men, long white shirts. When the chickens have been distributed, a deep silence descends around the pot. Brandishing chicken legs in the right hand and big slices of bread in the left, these folk devour their food hungrily, chew and chomp, gawp occasionally, eyes bulging. Sitting on their voluminous skirts, with belted midriffs and buxom bosoms, the country wives look like pumpkins and state the obvious as rural folk do.

"Take care!" I hear one say. "Take care you don't get sand on your roast, it could chip your teeth!"

In the dusk, one can see the passacaglia pass by the beach. In the circles of light cast by the gas lamps one sees it progress on the promenade raising a cloud of dust. The first band walks along playing "*L'airet, l'airet, l'airet de matinada.*" A throng of local youngsters, in rows of four to six, arm in arm, jump and hop behind in step with the clockwork rhythm. The dust is reddish. First, they wend through the shadows of the pines over the houses streaked with bluish light, then the music moves on to darker, more propitious paths. Now and then someone falls to the ground, those behind trip, and so on. A grisly way to amuse oneself. Scholars assert that the passacaglia might be a throwback to ancient Bacchanalian celebrations. If that's the case, it's been badly watered down. Celebrants today are nourished on lemonade and chufa milk—at most a small alcoholic aperitif with olives. At any rate, the strolling show seems more of an invention to allow shy young fellows to clasp tightly any willing young senyoreta who is so predisposed.

When the bustle leaves the secrecy of the shadows and returns to the familiar flickering lights, one sees amid the dust hazy young faces, girls' flushed cheeks, sparkling eyes, trembling bodies; the young men can't decide where to put their sweaty hands and their mouths are parched. It all ends with a round of shandy beer.

How gratifying to learn that the country's moral standards grow sterner by the day—an increase in what bank employees call solid respectability.

Afterwards, a great calm descends on Llafranc. It is dinnertime. The clatter of plates, knives, and forks reaches as far as the street. The southwesterly wind continues to blow damp and indifferent over everything. The smell of pine resin melds with the aroma of roast chicken. Stretched out on the beach next to their empty pot, half asleep, the country folk gaze up at misty stars, which passing clouds hide for a moment.

The dance begins late. People stare at a young farmer with thick wavy hair—a rural romantic attempting to dance an Argentine tango (that is all the rage) with a young lady in a canary-yellow dress. This is Llafranc's last word in modernity.

In the early hours, for no reason at all, I feel extremely weary. I stagger back to Calella.

1st September. Return to Palafrugell.

The summer holidays are inexorably coming to an end. The cart from our farmhouse is loaded up with mattresses and other objects. Those who will stay on—a matter of two or three days—seem more spent than those immediately departing. Midafternoon I start to walk along the road. A light—no longer summery—bathes the delightful plain of Santa Margarida in a warm, vaguely peach color.

When I return home, I find that putting my shoes back on is quite unpleasant—they are a bit small now—and my tie is irritating. I go out when the streetlights come on. I feel I've been squeezed into a constricting corset. Even so, I like being in a sheltered place where the sea and the wind are not so much in evidence. The electric light is bright, warm, and soothing. People—fewer in shirtsleeves or barechested—seem more polite, less aggressive.

2 September. It's been a hot day. In the evening, one feels the cold in the street. In spring, we wanted the heat, and people were quick to shed their clothes. Now we are bundled up and wish the wind would blow harder. It is the same year in, year out. People have been playing this childish, alternating game for centuries. How unbearably monotonous!

Almeda the pharmacist is walking up and down outside his shop on carrer de Cavallers wearing his straw-colored laboratory coat. As he wipes his spectacle lenses with a white handkerchief, he says in his nasal tone, "Just imagine, the other day a young girl came into the shop. I asked her, 'What do you want, little girl?' 'Mummy asked me to buy ten cents' worth of cold cream.' 'Ten cents' worth of cold cream?' 'That's right, sir, ten cents' worth of cold cream.' 'Ten cents' worth!

Should I put it in two small boxes, my lovely?' 'Yes, please, sir, of course!' I put the cold cream in two small boxes and wrapped them in a thin sheet of paper. 'Mummy said,' says the girl holding out her hand for the boxes, 'that she'll pop by tomorrow and pay.' 'All right, dear, all right.'"

Sr. Almeda stands there thoughtfully for a moment and then says, half resigned, half grumbling, "This is the kind of life we apothecaries must put up with in these villages, you see?"

That night, in the café, I'm shocked by the tremendous din, the uproar created by men playing dominoes, *manilles*, *tuti*, *canari*, etcetera. It is horrific, unbearably rude, and objectionable. I've been used to this noise for years, but every September when I return from the subtle silence of the sea, I think I can't possibly adapt once more to this deafening, pointless barrage.

In Palafrugell—and generally in the whole area—there are a certain number of fellows who feel duty-bound to sing after lunch or dinner. This country permanently hankers after a *grande bouffe* that will end with a song. The obsession is such that people break into song even if lunch or dinner is nothing out of the ordinary. If one abstains, it is reluctantly—one simply doesn't want to be thought of as crazy.

There was once such a fellow in Barcelona. He was staying at the Fonda del Padre or the Fonda de l'Univers—I don't remember which. They served him the usual fare dished out in these third-rate establishments. He must have reckoned it was excellent because the minute he'd finished eating, he announced to the waiter at the top of his voice, rubbing his hands with pleasure, clearly quite instinctively: "I will now give you a song…"

His fellow diners halted their forks for a second between plate and mouth and stared in amazement. After a while, when they'd given him a good look, they gestured, as if to say "He must be crazy," and went back to their chewing. The poor man from Palafrugell caught the look on their faces and flushed bright red. Then he left the room, shamefaced and dejected.

A lengthy café conversation with Joan B. Coromina. He is pale and fretful. I am probably more agitated than he is, but it is less obvious because I've just returned from Calella with a healthy tan.

3 September. The war.

It has lasted more than four years—four years and one month to be precise. The number of dead, the amount of suffering, the volume of destruction and devastation the war has produced is beyond words. The polemics between the pro-French and pro-Germans have dissipated. It's not possible to sustain such tension for four years. People are now simply thinking about making money... and tomorrow is another day. If war wasn't imbued with the arrant idiocy of cosmic phenomena, if the organization of war depended on the convergence of forthright, determined wills, it would delineate and expose human pettiness more clearly than any other act or argument—more than if a million tons of rocks were to crash on our backs. Human pettiness is indescribable. It makes absolutely no difference what people think—or don't think—whether they believe or not.

Watching how war influences certain individuals is like observing lunacy. A large number of nouveaux riches have had gold, silver, or porcelain teeth and molars fitted—complete sets of teeth. Some have naturally horsey faces. Others tend to create a similar effect by having huge teeth or dentures fitted that are quite out of proportion to their mouths—veritable equine items of dentistry. In years to come, when these characters hear the name of Verdun, they will think, "Ah, Verdun, Verdun, oh right, that was when they fitted me with those teeth that proved to be so heavy I had to have them removed."

Only a few days ago Sr. C. was telling me with candid glee, "Well, surely you wouldn't want to deny it? We made a nice little pile out of this war. And you'll never guess what I told my good lady. You know, I told her, 'Emília, we should have a water closet installed.' 'Are you really sure, Artur, are you sure?' my wife replied. I felt she was being overcautious. A few words did the trick: I summoned the plumber, and he installed the WC in next to no time. You realize we couldn't go on as before, not for a single day. Life's not been the same since, you know?"

4 September. I bump into Marian Vinyas from Sant Feliu de Guíxols on carrer de Cavallers. He is perhaps the best performer of Chopin in these parts. Tall, elegant, urbane, smart, and incisive, he stills bears traces of the era of modernism—the modern style. Like his close friend Cambó, he wears his collar too high and too stiff. He tends to hold himself straight-backed. Nonetheless, Vinyas is extremely witty and contemporary ways haven't changed this excellent quality of his.

We talk about Juli Garreta, the composer of sardanas.

"You know, we are good friends. A delightful man. We began playing together. He is a man who knows nothing much with any precision or detail but fresh, dynamic music pours endlessly from him. He is a miracle of infallible spontaneity and the best musician we have at the moment, and I think his best is yet to come. He is very fond of rain. When it rains, he carries on like a madman. So do I! He was telling me yesterday that what he would really like would be a house in some barren wasteland, an isolated farmstead, so he could repair there on rainy days—simply to see and hear the rain."

Vinyas pauses, then goes on. "Last week he went to Roses on some business or other. He saw a local girl, probably a fishwife, beautiful, buxom, and brimming with energy. He thought he'd seen a Greek marble statue and wrote a sardana. Back in Sant Feliu he asked Rafael Pitxot to give it a Greek name, a dedication to a young woman. Pitxot laughed and said, 'Call it "Nydia."' Take note, I believe 'Nydia' is the best sardana ever written in this country. It is truly wondrous."

I reluctantly bid farewell to Vinyas. We friends in the Ampurdan live within a stone's throw of each other but never meet. It is inexplicable, most peculiar. If we had more frequent contact, perhaps we'd waste less time.

In the café, Joan B. Coromina says, "The perennial, if not the only, problem with easel painting is this: Is it or isn't it a good likeness? A painting is either realism or trash."

Coromina makes this judgment as a result of his very understandable fascination for the paintings by the old artist Gimeno, who continues to paint—in a famished, feverish state—in the solitary spaces of Fornells. His opinion is possibly too judgmental. I think there is much more one could say.

The pro-French are all smiles. At last we are beginning to throw off our obsession with Germany and this makes us think we feel more lighthearted. It is like being weaned off margarine.

I take my temperature day in, day out. Despite all the pressures and pitfalls, I realize that I tend to be rather passive and don't feel a genuine yearning to possess the things of this life. Perhaps it's more than timidity; it's probably a fundamental, constitutional, somatic predisposition. I am totally convinced I will always be what they call unhappy.

5 September. I often wonder if this diary is sincere, if it is a bona fide record of my innermost state.

The first question one must ask oneself is: Is it possible to express what is innermost? I mean, to achieve a clear, coherent, intelligible description of our innermost being. What is really innermost, in essence, must be spontaneity pure and simple, that is, a visceral, untrammeled flow. If we had the language and vocabulary to encapsulate this flow, there would be no problem. But the fact is that no style exists that can give voice to that authenticity, never mind find the right lexicon. However, even if we were to imagine for a moment that it was possible to express our innermost state, who would grasp or understand it? If it weren't unique, highly individual, very personal, and totally elemental, what would it look like, how could one imagine its presence? When we are unable to see through our inner fog, we usually say "I know what I mean." Drunks say as much. I suspect young children think the same when they manage to communicate. My sense of the matter, then, is that our innermost feelings cannot be expressed:

We lack the necessary tools to describe them so that it remains almost impossible to fashion a way to project them outwards. One has only to reflect on the distortions and falsifications of the traditional style, spelling, and syntax in the least attempt to express the seemingly most simple of thoughts or to describe the most insignificant object.

And if that weren't enough, there are all those invincible gremlins: vanity, hypocrisy, status, egotism, convention, envy, resentment, humiliation, the influence of money or lack of money, impotence ... in other words, the detritus of passions and feelings one drags behind one from the moment of waking until bedtime. Pulled by this undertow of dark but weighty forces, our innermost contradictions are never resolved. For example: In public, I endeavor to fight sentimentality as something pornographic or unhealthy, but the fact is I myself readily act like a simpering, whimpering calf. When alone, I'll sometimes laugh or sometimes a tear will fall that has no rational justification and goes against all the demands of reason I defend elsewhere. I have even walked into a church and begun crying, likewise while reading a book, watching a play, or leafing through the newspaper. Leafing through a newspaper! But it is true. Another angle to this: I have a modest reputation as a strong man and I pose—to echo Stendhal—as a *tête brulée*. But the reality is very different. I am incredibly feeble in most situations. A drop of blood, a twitch of physical pain, the presence of a dead body, the sight of injustice, a friend's misfortune, the sorrow of sad, cowering eyes and I'm plunged into such a morose, miserably enfeebled state that it affects me physically. I am *only* strong at appearing to possess a lively sense of what's ridiculous—in public.

You could be sincere if you were consistent: When in public you—any normal human being, that is—act so differently from when you are by yourself. As long as the visible, permanent discontinuity exists between these two states, it will be impossible to communicate sincerity.

So then, what are we to make of our innermost self? Etcetera, etcetera.

6 September. The family.

Me and myself. In the café I repeatedly claim I'm not in the least bit vain. Perhaps my friends are inclined to believe me. Back home I stand in front of the mirror. I've returned from Calella with a fine tan—a splendid glow. My teeth gleam. I feel myself to be a handsome fellow.

My sister Maria goes for a stroll with my mother along carrer de Cavallers and stops to look at the photographs in the display case the town photographer has set up in the street.

My mother tugs on her blouse sleeve and exclaims quite spontaneously, perhaps sourly, "They are horrid! It's incredible how people dare to have their photo taken! Unbelievable…"

I constantly argue with my father. There is no way I can agree with him on hardly anything. Generations move on and points of view and ideas must diverge. It is all relative: Socially speaking, what is true in Figueres is a lie in Perpignan; what was dogma in 1900 is up for discussion in 1918.

Perhaps that is too objective, too cold. The differences between generations are unavoidable: We know that to be true, but even so, these conflicts continue to arise. It is ingenuous to help them along but we do so all the same.

It is almost a kind of fate that living in close proximity finally becomes an insoluble problem. The more distant and separate people's lives become, the more they like each other. The greater the contact, the greater the contempt.

What's more, there is upbringing. Our upbringing demands we adapt wonderfully well to newcomers and behave like cats and dogs in our family. While he remains a stranger, I can harmoniously coexist with a fellow opposed to my way of thinking. On the other hand, the slightest silliness is a pretext for me to argue with my father bitterly, if not angrily. It is a situation that feeds on the smallest excuse. To an extent, disputes take off like clockwork, as if responding to some incontrollable, unconscious force.

Old people—the previous generation—defend what is. Youngsters—the present generation—defend what ought to be. My father thinks the world cannot change from what it is now. I think it could. Young people think the old hypocritical and too inclined to take the easy option. The old think youngsters are rash, unruly, and superficial. I imagine the criteria of young people are more easily expressed in countries where structures are not as ossified or crystallized or furred up. Ours is one of the latter. Popular language is saturated with sayings from bygone times. "No change for change's sake," "Every wash, you lose a sock," etcetera. These expressions that people repeat endlessly drive me around the bend.

However, in the end, all this grousing, when analyzed coldly, is rather childish. My father and I sometimes go three or four days without saying a word to each other, exchanging glances, waiting for that unconscious mechanism to click into place. Our reconciliations have a thin veneer of cordiality; they solve nothing. Sometimes I think my father hates and despises me. When I scrutinize my own feelings, I recognize that, in my heart of hearts, I love him.

Naturally, all this is refracted through the opinions of others. In their eyes, I seem unhappy, a lazy good-for-nothing. The first extreme is far from being the truth. The second is probably accurate: I find it difficult to stir myself, lack the ability to do anything practical, and feel distant from the world of money. I can understand why my family suffers on my behalf.

Grandmother Marieta eats bread with everything.

She eats figs, apricots, and peaches with bread. She eats grapes with bread. If she's nibbling a handful of hazels, a walnut, an almond, a chestnut, or a raisin, she also has some bread. She will munch a crust with jam, nougat, with any kind of tidbit. If she is drinking a glass of rancid wine, she'll dunk in a biscuit. When we were children and in her house on carrer Estret for lunch, she'd offer us the excellent sponge cake she'd just baked and say, "Take a little bread, just a crumb."

This longing for bread reminds me of the olden days in the farmhouses, when bread was the basic, almost the only, nourishment.

My father doesn't enjoy good health. When he speaks angrily or heatedly, his voice turns hoarse and he gets a sore throat. If he goes to the café and there's too much smoke in the air, he feels queasy and has to leave. The doctors say he has acute arthritis and very high blood pressure. I think a path has been irremediably beaten for me.

9 September. A day spent in Girona—mostly at loose ends. The return train fare costs three pesetas and sixty cents. Everyone says it's expensive. I'm not sure: I have no point of comparison. So far in life I haven't earned a cent. Money is extraordinarily important. That's only too clear. On the one hand, I feel my provisional immunity from its impact makes me seem an incomplete man; on the other, it keeps me in a state of almost angelic innocence. I am a kind of cuddly, infantile, foolish thing.

It is drizzling. Fine mist. A steamy vapor of light rain hangs over the fields. The distant countryside drifts in bluish fog. Smoke rises languidly from farmhouse chimneys. The landscape seems to have dozed off in indifferent silence.

Girona is at its most striking when it rains. Wet windows. The gutters along the old streets. The inner iron splendor the moisture brings to the golden stone of the massive old houses. The weeds sprouting on walls drip. The murk turns the cathedral's white stone pale green tinged with crimson. Shapes seem to meld and mellow. The green of the Devesa becomes vaguely purplish. Ensconced in decrepit houses, the women all seem enticing. Archaeology as an aphrodisiac. Sant Pere de Galligants assumes a rustic, timorous, peasant air, with its Romanesque lilt. Romanesqu-ish, Romanesqu-ish! Umbrellas hop and skip along the narrow streets. The precipitous slopes make the walkers look smaller. The cathedral interior is fierce and forbidding, a sternness that scares. It feels cold and numbingly harsh. This atmosphere seems to say: Take it or leave it. Chilling, fanatical convictions! I walk out into the cloisters. A blast of damp, cool air—most refreshing. The cloisters seem liberating despite the buttress walls that overwhelm them. Through the exit they provide, beyond the Galligants, I can see the red clay mountain of Montjuïc and rocks the color of dry thyme spring from the earth. I'm back on the streets. Muddy slime underfoot. Cafés under arches. I drink two delicious Pernods that depress me. Dim provincial city lights. Jaundiced electricity. You can see raindrops falling through the light from the bulbs. People stroll up and down the arcades, enjoying the cool breeze on their faces. A velvet smell wafts from the clothes shops—a smell that takes me by surprise. The odor of winter...

Return journey in a slow, sad train. People seem frightened. Sitting silently on third-class compartment benches, they cling to their belongings on their laps with both hands, as if someone might steal them. A sleepless night. Exhausted.

11 September. We are approaching the autumn equinox and in the afternoon I hear the sea growling. It is a dull, distant, diffuse roar. The usual squall from the east is about to break. It rains, rather heavily, throughout the day. Gusts of wind batter and soak, bang and then whimper. The spring equinox brings storms for broad beans; this one sluices down the boats. It's time to prepare for the grape harvest. The mere fact that barrels and vats are littering the streets fills the town with a strong, if illusory, smell of grape must.

The houses in Palafrugell peter out miserably. Ineffable melancholy and loneliness descend where the city walls end in the first fields— particularly if one is walking out late in the first gloom of nightfall. As darkness blots out the landscape, the dwellings on the outskirts cast patches of light over the darkening urban panorama. The heath around Tren, the garden walls of Can Barris, Els Forns, La Garriga, Les Torretes, Vila-seca, El Pedró, and El Molí de Vent, have the same miserable tone, the particular pale shades found in paintings by Urgell. If you feel like hardening your heart and resisting the attractions of town life, best to take a stroll in the outskirts when the lights come on—especially now, when the onset of autumn hits you in the gut.

Years ago, when this time of the year came around, as night fell, I secretly envied people going I wasn't sure where, the couple vanishing into the shadows on the street, the blurred figures catching the evening train, people I saw entering a house that wasn't theirs after they'd glanced up and down the street to make sure no one was on their trail.

12 September. The squall continues, on a minor scale. Sheets of rain fall now and then. The weather clears in the afternoon and the growling sea quiets down. Slivers of warm blue sky appear amid the errant mists.

The way some women's faces resemble men's is quite alarming—you only need a single glance. Between the feminine and the masculine, there's often nothing more than an imperceptible difference—a hair.

A Castilian word I find difficult to digest: *pájaro*—bird. It's as if you had a rod stuck in your mouth that was choking you. Another word in the same category: *trigo*—corn. The worst of all: *mugir*—to low.

In the lexicon of the Catalan Floral Games there are words that make you wince. Three of the many: *xamosa*—ducky; *joliua*—lovely; *aimia*—me mate. It seems incredible that this poverty-stricken language has progressed from the Floral Games to the perfect pages penned by Joaquim Ruyra. The fact of this transfiguration implies potential—perhaps.

14 September. Girona.

My last visit has refreshed my memories of that city. I find the place so fascinating I have devoted countless hours to my attempts to commit to paper something intelligible about the years I spent there.

Nothing of worth, as yet. Perhaps this story is the only one that could be spared from the bonfire.

I spent my secondary-school years boarding at a private religious school in Girona. I don't want to describe my vita from the time, I'd simply like to relate a curious story of something that happened then—one of the first incidents of interest I ever experienced and one that left an indelible mark.

The religious establishment I mentioned allowed its pupils to leave the premises one day in a month. That day was my day of freedom, of wonderful freedom, and I'd like to describe it because, although it will be an effort, I'd be thrilled to transport myself, in my imagination, back to those pleasant, lovely days when I made an escape from boarding school. But now I want to relate something else, the story I alluded to, and by so doing I hope to get out it of my system. Memories of being seventeen are never exact and coherent, but they can surface obsessively.

In my first years as a boarder, my free day never failed me once. We always had the good fortune, whatever the weather, to see a relative or someone turn up to take us out on the first Sunday of the month, although it was a real sacrifice to make the journey from our hometown to Girona. After the service at school—our second mass of the morning—we'd be ordered to go to the reception area. Having spent two or three days wondering whether anyone would actually come, we headed to reception on edge, fit to faint. Sometimes Grandmother Marieta was there, or Father, or Aunt Lluïsa—Father's pious, prematurely graying spinster sister. She was extremely absentminded and a touch simple and, thus, agreeable and kindly in her manner, though not as predictable as she might have seemed at first sight. After the requisite greetings, it took only a moment to fetch cap and coat. We felt so happy to walk through that door.

When it was Grandmother Marieta, we'd go first to hear mass in the cathedral—our third of the day. It was a mass characterized by a grandiloquent sermon—sonorous rhetoric that boomed across the huge nave of that terrible cathedral. Then we went to Hotel dels Italians for lunch, displaying an air of great savoir faire. You had to be on your best behavior, because the general and his adjutant were dining two tables away, and at the back of the dining room, next to a languishing palm tree, the civil governor and his family were also lunching. It was all so provincial! Grandmother Marieta dressed in black and had the whitest of white hair: If she glanced at you, it filled you with respect. We'd spend a rather chilly, solemn, slow Sunday with her, but it was very useful in terms of learning what she called "having a proper attitude" and "knowing how to keep one's distance."

My father was more bucolic and never came to Girona without taking us for a walk in the Devesa and admiring the broad avenues of the tallest plane trees—the height and grandeur of which always amazed him. I could never understand this recurrent amazement. Perhaps he was simply perplexed by the sight of such fertile land, able to support such aristocratic, striking trees, and fated to be simply decorative. But that's only a guess and it's not based on anything more tangible. After our morning stroll, we'd go for lunch at Hotel del Comerç, where my father was an old and much revered customer. In the afternoon he took us on visits, very quick visits ("In and out," he would say) that merely gave him an excuse to take a long walk. He was a strong walker, no doubt about that. When it was time to return to school—half an hour before his train left—his tiredness was negligible compared to our exhaustion. Having a father who likes a good walk is a very good thing for a family, though such a virtue can be a pain for those forced to accompany him.

Aunt Lluïsa took us first to the Jesuit church—which she found "quite lovely," and then we'd go window-shopping in the old part of the city. That good lady no doubt intended to buy something or other when she set out. However, the more windows she saw the more she dithered, so much so that I never saw her buy anything, no matter how long we lingered in the shops. The way she'd stand and gawp for a while, fluttering between shops, surely intent on purchasing but never making up her mind, frankly exhausted me—though perhaps the fact I had to pretend all the time was what I found most tiring. Finally she would realize that it was two o'clock and, with the excuse that it was late, we'd enter the first place we could find to have lunch. Once seated, we listened with rapt attention as the waiter or waitress ran through the menu. But, curiously, once the dishes had been listed, our aunt unfailingly requested a dish that had never—even re-motely—been mentioned. When she looked at me unenthusiastically and said, "What we'd really like is cannelloni," you could be sure the restaurant had everything but cannelloni. She ordered squid the moment they said there was only hake, and hake when the seafood of the day was octopus. Her peculiar conception of lunch based on yester-day's or tomorrow's menu caused confusion and delay, and worst of all meant we ended up eating stale, oily omelet and leathery steaks with potatoes that had seen better days. But that was what she was like: She was an out-of-the-ordinary character when it came to the immediate things in life. Sundays in Girona with Aunt Lluïsa were Sundays of dashed expectations and treats left hanging in the air.

However, the years passed by, pitilessly as ever, and things changed. Poor Grandmother Marieta died at the age of seventy-four. Father had a mild attack of apoplexy—at least his doctors said it was mild, though it left him good for nothing ever after. Aunt Lluïsa's persistent bronchitis took a horrific turn for the worse and it was decided she shouldn't budge from home. We thus reached my final year at second-ary school and I faced the dreaded possibility that my day out would end. Our family situation was so precarious they couldn't contem-plate sending anyone to see me, and it looked as if I would have to re-sign myself to receiving no more visits. However, my father, who must have understood what that day meant for us, did all he could to ensure things continued in the same vein and that our day out would be guaranteed.

My father had a childhood friend in Girona who'd left our town as an adolescent and made his mark with a small business in the immortal city. He was Sr. Ramon Colomines. Sr. Colomines owned a little shop well stocked with stationery and writing materials on carrer de les Ballesteries.

I had met him because he'd been one of the rapid visits—those "in-and-out" visits—that father made in our company. The visit to Sr. Co-lomines was part of our long, boring ramble down the city streets. On the course of one such visit I had the pleasure of finding out about the distinguished shopkeeper. And I say "distinguished" because he was introduced to me as a gentleman of merit and shining virtue—an example of remarkable tenacity and strong will. These adjectives were trotted out emphatically, with the intention of presenting him as an example for us. In fact, Sr. Colomines was introduced to us as a man worthy of imitation in every way.

In the course of that first introduction—to make a long story short—we learned he had entered the shop at an extremely young age, that years later he'd married his employer's daughter when she was widowed, and that, finally, when his father-in-law died, he became a partner in the business, received a small fortune, and was endowed with respectability. I couldn't say—all these years later—whether we listened attentively to his life story. We probably didn't. What's certain is that the figure of Sr. Colomines as a gentleman who deserved to be emulated was duly engraved on our minds, soft and impressionable as clay, back then.

When we met him, he was small and stocky, well past fifty, with a sallow complexion and the flabbiest features. He was blue-eyed, fair, and thin on top. As it was early autumn and the weather was still fine, Sr. Colomines wore his jacket open and loose, and as he liked to gesticulate, we could contemplate his first-class accessories, his buckled belt and splendid suspenders. He was a shopkeeper, not so much in his physical appearance—shopkeepers, after all, come in all shapes and sizes—but in his conversation and mind-set. The mind-set of a shopkeeper—I was to learn much later—is a severe case of tunnel vision: It consists of believing that the very center of the world, the axis of the earth, is one's shop and of being unable to keep that belief to oneself. Now I'm not about to embark on a critique of such an important, honorable estate. Clearly the estate must exist, even if we individuals who are born with vaguely poetic leanings think it, quite frankly, a wholly incomprehensible, lackluster condition.

As our day in the city that first Sunday in October had been ruled out for the reasons I've mentioned, we were astounded to see Sr. Colomines in the reception area and almost at a loss to find the words to greet him. The reception door was glass-paneled, so we saw him before we went in, positioned under a photo of our Holy Father, seated on a black wooden bench upholstered in red velvet. My first hunch was that Sr. Colomines had come to bring regards from his family and to offer to help in any way. That intuition was not quite accurate. When we were opposite him, speechless, our hands outstretched, we watched him as he stood up, shook our hands, and said, "Colomines, at your service. When you are ready, we could perhaps go for lunch."

No doubt about it, he was guaranteeing our day out!

That man unleashed a surge of gratitude I couldn't repress. Although his appearance did him no favors, I felt well-disposed toward him. That a wealthy man, the owner of an important business, should worry about an insignificant boarding-school runt said it all! I thought him generous and remarkable. The effort Sr. Colomines had had to expend to reach my school contributed to my positive feelings. He'd had to climb old Girona's narrow streets to get there. He'd exhausted himself. He was gasping. And six or seven minutes later he was still gasping. He'd stood up for a moment to greet me, but sat down again immediately. As he did so, he said resignedly, "My bellows."

I heard a voice, very nearby, repeat with a certain reticence, "Yes, sir, it's your bellows, it's your bellows!"

Someone else was sitting in the armchair next to Sr. Colomines. I hadn't noticed him because I didn't think he was connected with the shopkeeper from carrer de les Ballesteries. Coming into the reception area, all you could see of this gentleman were his extremities because he was holding a huge broadsheet over the top of which jutted a head of blue-black hair (possibly dyed). I believe the newspaper was *El Correo Catalán*. During our first exchanges, this gentleman had continued reading his daily. Afterward, when the peculiar allusion to bellows had been made, I realized they'd come together.

"Is this gentleman a relative of yours, Sr. Colomines?" I asked.

As soon as he heard my question, the man in the adjacent armchair put his newspaper down, got up, and shook my hand. Sr. Colomines was quite taken aback by his colleague's rapid reaction and gasped even more breathlessly.

"No, sir, we are not related," said his neighbor. "Allow me to introduce myself: Roca, Public Attorney."

"Sr. Roca is a neighbor," added Sr. Colomines. "He accompanied me. These narrow, uphill streets make me gasp. He loves them."

"Yes, sir," said Sr. Roca swiftly. "I love them: 'Love' is the right word. I love old Girona. Young man, for your information: Girona is a fantastic cluster of archaeological sites!"

"Of course it is, Roca, of course!" said Sr. Colomines, flapping wearily. "Of course it is! But you know I suffer from asthma, and these sloping streets and diabolical steps will be the death of me. I prefer my archaeological clusters, as you call them, on the level—"

"Heresy, Sr. Colomines, heresy!" retorted Roca with a vehemence I felt was out of place. "Don't you understand that the supreme charm of our city resides in these deep, dark, shadowy vistas that loom so mysteriously and solitary from every steep incline! For God's sake, Colomines, don't be so prosaic!"

"My bellows, Roca, my bellows!" the shopkeeper objected, smiling sourly and revealing the poor state of his teeth.

"Bah!" replied Roca halfheartedly, almost sarcastically. "Why won't you admit you have no feeling for art. That's the truth."

"Say what you like, Roca, whatever you like, but please don't provoke my asthma."

"I don't want to hurt you, naturally, but your lack of understanding is more than I can stomach. There comes a moment when I feel that I have had my fill of shopkeepers. You know..."

They wrangled on for a while. As Sr. Roca's forceful tones filled the icy atmosphere in the reception area, Sr. Colomines's sense of oppression deepened. He finally seemed to lose interest in his companion's harangue—despite the undoubtedly rude verbal battering Sr. Roca was dispensing.

As you would imagine, I'd remained totally unmoved by Sr. Roca's artistic flights of imagination and used the time to look him over. He was a small, slightly hunchbacked, sharp-featured gentleman dressed in black, with a black cravat and a face that looked as if it was about to pounce and gobble you up. His forehead, eyes, mouth, teeth, lips, and ears were large and out of proportion, all underscored by his swarthy skin. His cheeks were long and sunken above a protruding chin and flat gravestone of a beard. He looked most odd standing in front of Sr. Colomines: He was one of those hunchbacks who, when they stand up, have one haunch that sticks farther out than the other, an intriguingly prominent, stiff bone, like the stump left on a branch that's been pruned. He wore rimless glasses on his nose, glasses his nervous state constantly shifted though never to the point at which they actually fell off. A black cord attached to the glasses dangled down his face before disappearing into a hidden waistcoat pocket. His long, narrow head was thickly populated by lank hair so worn down by the sophisticated treatments it suffered that it looked more like a wig, though it was natural enough. That helped give Sr. Roca a stubbornly fanatical mien: His dyed hair transmuted his head into one worthy of the stage. But perhaps his hat was what was most alarming. He had placed it on a puffy red velvet chair beside him: a dramatic black blotch on the red velvet, a small, shapeless hat, tapering to a sharp point, and made from such soft, thin felt you could easily imagine its brim either pulled up or down over his ears. While Sr. Roca lambasted shopkeepers and praised the beauties of Girona's archaeological clusters, I became intrigued with what slant the hat would eventually take on his head. Unfortunately—and anticipating the end of my tale—I never had the chance to see. When we went out, Sr. Roca folded his hat into a cylindrical shape and tucked it under his arm as if it were an ordinary piece of cloth.

At the same time Sr. Roca's vehemence lessened and he gradually calmed down. From an objective viewpoint, his harangue seemed to have done Sr. Colomines a power of good: Sr. Colomines had gradually stopped gasping for air. In the meantime I fetched my cap with the school's insignia stamped on its peak. As soon as the shopkeeper gave the signal, we set off.

Once we were out of the school, Sr. Roca felt the need to launch into another artistic-archaeological speech.

"As we are up here," he said, "we might as well go to the Lledoners' fountain . . . I am certain you will like it!"

"Roca, my dear friend, don't make me climb any higher. Or are you trying to kill me?"

"Colominas, my dear friend, is that an ultimatum or yet more evidence of your lack of curiosity?" asked Roca sarcastically.

"It's an ultimatum! Sr. Roca! It is an ultimatum, and let that be the last word. Young man," he added, addressing me, "we will now go for lunch."

"What a country!" Sr. Roca hissed, looking down his nose in irritation.

We walked slowly down carrer de Cervantes. When we reached carrer de la Força, Sr. Roca said farewell after agreeing to join us later for coffee. We immediately headed toward the stationery and writing materials shop Sr. Colomines owned on Ballesteries. Reunited with a level Girona, the shopkeeper's spirits visibly lifted.

The shop was open and a young lad, dressed far too flashily, was standing behind the counter: Sr. Colomines introduced Albert Fargues, his shop assistant. Fargues was also from my town and seemed fated to experience the same twists and turns in life as his boss. Like Sr. Colomines, several years earlier Fargues had left the town when very young; he had studied to become a priest but decided his sense of the vocation was weak and abandoned the seminary. When introducing us, Sr. Colomines took it for granted that we knew each other because we were from the same small town. I looked at Fargues, he looked at me, and the fact was we'd never seen each other before. He must have been twenty or twenty-one, and I was seventeen. When you are young, this small age gap represents almost another generation. It sounds strange, but it's undeniably true.

Fargues was a likable lad. It was obvious straightaway that he was from a humble background, poorly educated, with unerring bad taste, yet he was saved by his own good grace and the successes life kept showering on him, practically of their own accord. He was the darling of the neighborhood, the fascinating country boy, the lad most loved in that thousand square yards of apartments and houses, the young man at the center of gossip whether in the salted-cod shop, at the seamstresses', in the haberdashery or the local barbershop. He was tall, dark, and healthy with bushy eyebrows, glistening teeth, and a glint in his eye.

I thought the shop magnificent: small, narrow, and deep, its walls literally covered by countless tiny drawers. Everything was admirably classified in these drawers according to a complex system invented by Sr. Colomines's deceased father-in-law—a system of rational classification I would have liked to describe if I hadn't unfortunately let it slip from my mind. Each drawer had a yellow brass lip you pulled to slide out the drawer; inside one always found what one wanted. I was most impressed.

Everything was clean, polished, and shiny in that splendid shop. The table was varnished chestnut. The cupboards on the wall were pinewood painted dark mahogany: a wonder to behold. Toward the back, a standard lamp stood next to a table, its bulb enclosed in a highly unusual parchment shade. A shiny brass chandelier hung from the ceiling. The window frontage was small—in Girona trade is conducted in ridiculously constrained spaces—but displayed everything from boxes of compasses, fountain pens, pencils of every kind and quality to innumerable varieties of paper for business or personal use or deluxe stationery. Notably, some cardboard boxes with blue silk bows at their corners that presumably housed the much sought after pale violet paper for writing love letters to inaccessible, recalcitrant widows.

"In Barcelona," said Sr. Colomines as he showed me around, "this would be a shop like any other, but in Girona it is quite a different matter!"

After mouthing this platitude, a smiling Sr. Colomines rubbed his hands nervously together.

Overlooking the shop, from the top of the back wall, was a tiny niche with a small image of Our Mother of God of the Seven Sorrows. Our Mother of God was seated, her face deeply anguished, her heart skewered by seven white, oversize sabers. The image jarred somewhat with the icy cold, intense, highly organized veneer of that emporium. The small dark red glass light, lit every first Friday of the month in front of the image, was probably even more out of character. Although it involves disrupting the chronological flow, I will now relate what I was to learn later: namely that Sr. Colomines's wife was called Doloretes (Little Sorrows), that she was an extremely pious lady with many virtues, and that she had insisted on the presence of Our Mother of God of the Seven Sorrows. And, as far as Sr. Colomines was concerned, an order from his wife, indeed a mere suggestion from his wife, was a categorical imperative, and so the image was enthroned.

A tiny, austere door beneath Our Mother of God led to the shop extension that was part store, part office. Completely starved of natural light, this area of the premises was lit by the dim, yellowish, ghostly glow emanating from a bulb in the ceiling. One could easily imagine Sr. Colomines's sallow skin deepening through the endless hours spent in this gloomy, depressing spot. The narrowest of stairways led to the first floor of Sr. Colomines's private residence.

When I entered, I was introduced to Sra. Doloretes, a small, dark, thin woman with grayish hair who seemed friendly enough. She welcomed me effusively and asked after my well-being. I thanked her for her kindness and generosity and for ensuring my monthly Sunday outing. Sra. Doloretes interrupted me to say there was no need to stand on ceremony. She then spoke about the "disastrous" state of lunch: It was highly regrettable but she (Sra. Dolores) had expected to have cuttlefish to add to the rice ("Cuttlefish," she affirmed, "makes for excellent rice"), cuttlefish that she'd been promised...which hadn't materialized. She'd been obliged to use squid instead.

"It's most upsetting!" said Sra. Doloretes. "You won't believe this, but my husband is a real gourmet and likes his food to be just so! I keep wondering: 'By the Most Holy Virgin, what is he going say?' On the other hand, I wanted to cook a little chicken dish for the second course, and can you believe it? I couldn't find a single chicken in the market that didn't seem too fat. You'll have to make do with steak and chips."

"Please, senyora, don't worry on my account."

"I must confess my custard has turned out rather watery. Alas! What a disaster! And to top it off, the tavern where I buy our wine changed their special offer today. My husband always says, 'Bread fresh from the oven and always the same wine from the cellar.' And today they brought us a new one. Now, isn't that just one misfortune after another?"

While Sra. Doloretes rattled off these excuses—and more—she showed me around the house. The dining room was at the front and overlooked the street. A small kitchen as big as your fist was behind it. The Colomineses' matrimonial bedroom was at the back of the apartment, sumptuous and solemn, with family portraits and prints with holy images on the walls.

The overall impression was extraordinary. If a shopkeeper's mentality was evident in the routine, commercially efficient way the shop was organized, the apartment was the expression of quite a different, astonishing orderliness. It was a small apartment, not to say tiny, yet it housed a prodigious array of objects. There were so many they filled the space; one dared not move for fear of breaking something, for fear of knocking something over. The location of every object had been coldly calculated, taking into account position and distance, access, people's potential movements, and the arrangement of chairs. It was a bewildering sight! And most curious of all, this endless display was of objects that were of no use at all, purely decorative, mere whims of Sr. Colomines or his wife, generally unfashionable, horrendous items, which one long-forgotten day had helped to fill an empty space and there they had stayed because the place they occupied was predestined. Only order, a ruthless, rigid conception of order can perform such miracles. I was surprised to see there wasn't a single book in the place—apart from the senyora's missal I found on the dining-room sideboard. Probably because nothing else could fit under those ceilings—perhaps the family had its fill of paper with the receipt books they sold in the shop below.

Despite the proliferation of objects packed within those walls in such exquisite order, the apartment seemed so little lived in, so cold and unfriendly, and things were so bereft of the milk of human kindness, that it seemed more like a bazaar for the sale of ghastly baubles than a space for human beings to inhabit. In that house any act of human frailty—a simple, polite yawn, say—seemed subject to a preset pattern of movements. It was mind-numbing. A vase of artificial flowers stood on the sideboard.

We had completed the tour of the house when Sr. Colomines joined us—he had just been, as he told us, "to run a little water over his hands." He was exuberantly cheerful. He obviously loved his little apartment.

"Well then, young man," he addressed me, "what do think of all this? I shouldn't be the one to say this, but I think it is quite spellbinding, for a provincial capital, naturally... I must tell you it's none of my doing. It is all the work of my wife, over the years. Although you are here with us, Doloretes, I'd like to tell the young man the whole story.

My wife feels truly passionate about our house, about the things in our house. It is remarkable how she hasn't budged from here in thirty years, apart, that is, from the brief interlude every morning when she goes to mass and the market. She likes it that way, you know? She only feels at ease in her own home."

"Oh, you do exaggerate, you really do!" exclaimed Sra. Doloretes, blushing red as a poppy, quite beside herself.

"Please don't take any notice of her at all!" retorted Sr. Colomines, with a laugh. "This is all her doing, and that cannot be overstated. My wife is a homebody, she couldn't be more so."

"Of course I am," said Sra. Doloretes, fighting off her embarrassment. "It's what I always say: How would I spend my time if I didn't like my house? The cinema does nothing for me and the theater even less. I've never liked visiting other people's homes and gossiping. Where could I go? I believe the time has long since past when I could stroll along the Rambla. The fact is I only like being at home. That's the truth of the matter!"

"Senyora, your house is magnificent. One feels your presence throughout."

While I uttered these polite banalities I felt myself going red. I wished I'd had a mirror to see myself. I had flushed as I'd registered the extraordinary—albeit unconscious—ease of my lie. However, my lack of sincerity had been as unconscious and spontaneous as my blushing. When you are seventeen, your feelings are like that: They surprise you.

As a result, I sank momentarily into a state of embarrassment and gave those fine folk the impression I was a hapless, callow youth. Fortunately we'd reached the dining room where we sat down straightaway. I had my first sighting of a small, thin old maid. Although there were so many highly visible objects in that house, some were evidently not for show. The maid brought in a platter of sardines in oil, strips of cold sausage, and radishes. The hors d'oeuvres.

The lunch was little more than mediocre, but my judgment was clouded by the fact that I was forced to join in a conversation to which I had nothing to contribute. Lunch consisted of home-cooked rice and rabbit as in so many households: sticky rice, raw rabbit, and a sauce cobbled together at the last minute. Shreds of tomato that hadn't been absorbed in the cooking floated over the rice and rabbit. This gave way to distinctly provincial steak and chips. And immediately afterward cake accompanied by what they called a dessert wine: I feebly succumbed. The last thing I should have done! That sweet adulterated concoction reduced my stomach to a melancholy mess.

Sra. Doloretes ate with what was known in the 1912–13 period as *istil*—*istil* as adopted by lower-middle-class milieus, especially in the company of strangers. It was an exaggerated simulation of good manners. One kept one's body stiff and straight-backed. One transported food from plate to mouth, with a spoon or a fork, in a majestic arc these implements described with the help of one's arm. When the food reached one's mouth, one absorbed it with the edge of one's lips, with great refinement, while adopting an expression of bored indifference. The task of chewing was more visible at cheek than at jaw level. Liquids were imbibed in a series of sips that were so tiny, so insignificant, and so inadequate that glasses seemed to contain more liquid after rather than before the act of drinking. It was horrific.

Sr. Colomines acted much more naturally. His behavior was quite different from his wife's. At the time two kinds of people existed in these matters: those who sat at the table for the purpose of eating and those who ate to show off their *istil*. When the latter left the table, they usually went to the kitchen in search of additional nourishment after ingesting next to nothing during the meal. Sr. Colomines ate with relish and went at the rice with gusto.

"We—and this young man will endorse me in this," he reiterated, while gorging heartily, "we come from a town where people have always eaten well. We may not possess other virtues, but this is one we do have. Isn't that right, young man? You did know that, didn't you, Doloretes?"

That gentleman was convinced his rice was delicious. He thought so because of an experience culled in some way ab ovo in the maternal cloister of his birthplace. Because of the same experience, I felt the rice to be inedible. How is it possible—I wondered in the rare moments the conversation left me free to think—that one can be so wrong about so many things in such a short space of time?

When the coffeepot appeared with the sugar bowl and tiny coffee cups, the bell rang. Sr. Colomines raised his head slightly and chuckled. Sra. Doloretes gazed at him in rapture. The figure of Sr. Roca loomed in the doorway and was greeted effusively. In the dining-room gloom, he didn't seem such a strange—almost sinister—person as by the light of day. After greeting us enthusiastically, the acceptably courteous Sr. Roca sat down and was poured a coffee that was frankly excellent. I was thus released from the annoyance of constantly having to converse. Sr. Roca became the focus of attention in that small area—small, that is, only in the spatial sense, naturally.

When it came time to fill our glasses with another liquid, I can't exactly remember whether it was a digestif or Calisay, Sr. Roca had indeed become the center of attention. Seated comfortably on his chair, though his height enabled him to emerge (barely) a foot above table level, all eyes were on him. After rummaging through his pockets for a moment, he extracted a case from which he took one of those cigars that were then called *senyoretes* and lit up. When the columns of smoke began to curl through the air, he gave them an affectionate, self-satisfied look.

"Are you the bringer of good tidings, Sr. Roca?" asked Sr. Colomines, struggling to contain his impatience.

"I have investigated the matter and will duly speak thereof."

Such an enigmatic statement led me to suggest that I was in the way and should simply remove myself. But none of those gentlefolk thought it necessary. Sra. Doloretes was absolutely forthright: "It has to do with the shop, a trivial business involving the shop assistant," she declared persuasively enough.

"Sra. Doloretes is quite right in what she says," Sr. Roca concurred. "It *is* a trivial matter. But let us be clear: It is a matter that is trivial, at this precise moment in time. We will see what happens shortly. Remember the wise adage: 'In for a peck, in for a bushel.' I think it would be rash not to bear it in mind."

The Public Attorney paused, puffed on his small cigar, and continued to speak to a growing circle of interest. "As I was saying, I have studied the case. You know the depths of my friendship with you. I will speak frankly and bluntly."

"I am grateful, Roca, my friend, thank you," responded an excited Sr. Colomines, bowing his head slightly, his voice trembling.

"To begin with, I must say," the attorney went on, rising to the occasion, "that my investigations in respect of Fargues's period in the seminary have borne little fruit. I went to see Reverend Pastells, who was involved with the seminary years ago, and he confirmed he had known the student. Pastells is an unpleasant man. He received me very rudely, in a vile temper. After I'd explained the reason for my visit, he didn't pause a second to reflect and replied that he knew nothing, that times had changed and he didn't feel compelled, on the small allowance he received, to keep abreast of all the fashions and tomfooleries of the day. Priests are extremely poor. The allowance they are paid is pitiful. It is a feat of heroism to exercise their ministry on such a pittance.

"'We earn nothing, Sr. Roca, nothing at all...they don't even give us enough to eat!' Sr. Pastells squeaked repeatedly, his eyes half shut. However, you will understand that my visit to Sr. Pastells was not prompted by any need to discuss the budget of the minister for grace and justice. Everybody is aware of what *that* good man said—so aware it has practically been forgotten. All the same I tried to pacify him, indeed, to console him. Don't think that that was an easy task. Quite the contrary. Fortunately, it was my lucky day and I finally succeeded after innumerable attempts."

"Sr. Roca, Sr. Pastells is famed for his bad temper, and only you could reach his good side," remarked Sra. Doloretes, also rising excitedly to the occasion.

"Senyora, you are too kind!" answered the attorney, putting on a show of humility. "In this world, as you know, everything is a question of will. My visit to Sr. Pastells had a precise objective and it would have reflected poorly if I hadn't achieved it one way or another. Once we'd got over his frosty welcome, we were finally able to talk. However, the conversation was disappointing. Sr. Pastells knew Fargues years ago.

"He was a lad, so he told me, who was completely hopeless, despite his extreme poverty. He showed no vocation whatsoever in the seminary. Harebrained. Quite vain, though in a superficial manner, so this defect, which can sometimes become a virtue, in his case did not. He had such a lack of attention, lack of interest in his studies and school discipline that his exclusion from the establishment took place as naturally as his admission."

"So, no leads there," commented Sra. Doloretes, visibly downcast.

"Indeed, senyora, that's the sad truth: no leads, apart from a few tiny scraps of what amounts to insignificant evidence. For example: One day, the photo of a young country girl was found among his scant clothing, which led people to assume she was meeting the student secretly during the holidays. This created a level of concern. In the end it turned out to be a photo of his sister. On another occasion, some of his companions stated that Fargues had received a mysterious letter described as 'unmentionable.' However, Sr. Pastells was instructed to see what it was all about in person. He came to the conclusion that said letter had never existed and that it was simply children, seminary brats, plotting in a reasonably poisonous manner."

"Sr. Roca, a drop more of coffee?" asked Sr. Colomines, stooping over the table, coffeepot at the ready.

"Yes, sir, a couple of drops will do. Thank you! Senyora, your coffee is first-rate, as ever. Many thanks. In fact, Fargues's real life begins when he left the seminary and, quite unheralded, entered your shop, that is, the shop downstairs. Then he started to change in a big way. The young man fell upon your shop like a man diving into cold water at the height of summer. He landed on his feet from day one. He found everything fascinating and extraordinary. I've talked to many people in the neighborhood who know Fargues. A few days after joining your business, he told the barber he regretted all the years he'd wasted. Fargues's life was like a tree beginning to bud. Until he found his new occupation, he'd felt invisible tongs were squeezing and pressurizing his brain from the outside in. He'd no doubt thought earlier on it would be too risky to test the waters. His fear must have been too great—or at least sufficient for him not to try what people vulgarly refer to as 'letting your hair down.' The change in his life made him feel that those invisible tongs were now exercising quite a different part of him. He sensed his muscles flexing, the blood coursing through his veins: He was coming to after a fainting fit. The bittersweet breeze on the street hit his face, the sap rose to his cheeks and his hands tingled. Life, for Fargues, brought fresh delights daily—"

"You are right enough there, Sr. Roca," interjected Sr. Colomines clearly impressed by the attorney's description. "Personally I was often struck by the change in him."

"Of course! The lad was discovering a new world, seeing many things for the first time. He was galloping, one might say, mounted on the steed of his childish, if bewildering, expectations. He was anticipating the next new pleasures in life. Perhaps he didn't know exactly what he wanted. It was something vague, a mirage, an impulse titillating his senses. This vagueness sapped his memory. It is sad to see how energetic, avid folk so easily forget what might be irksome, how they literally wipe the slate clean. Perhaps sickly individuals like me are the only people blessed with a good memory, if you reflect for a moment. If Fargues was at all aware, he'd have been appalled by the ease with which he'd forgotten his previous life and those enlightening steps he'd taken towards a religious life. To justify this forgetfulness he was obliged to tell his first big lies. He lied so expertly, with such aplomb and sangfroid, that he gave the impression he was a professional—I mean a man of mature years. Once inside the shop, he'd occasionally realize that he might bump into one of his old teachers. He was surprised by how easily and swiftly he could avoid one approaching from afar. As soon he turned a quick corner, he forgot his teacher's face— but if the latter's censorious expression *had* lodged in his eyes, before he'd melted away, he quickly erased it with a phrase from clerical patter or an ironic or sarcastic jibe. I suspect that, in this process of self-invention, the realization that one could stare women in the face was a decisive turning point. Glances on the sly, out of the corner of an eye, are the most intense and make the greatest impact. However, others are more effective. An askance look requires too much imagination and falls short, like a hypothesis. People aren't usually very imaginative. They prefer long, possessive, rounded stares. But this is irrelevant to my present brief. These are things *I* worry about. I have spoken to many people who know your assistant and could reconstruct his life in minute detail."

"Do continue, Sr. Roca, I pray," cooed Sr. Colomines. "If I had your silver tongue, I'd have explained everything exactly as you have just done."

"Thank you. Let's get down to the nitty-gritty. As Fargues gradually considered himself, he realized he'd go nowhere fast wearing that short, threadbare suit, the darned shirt and collar, and down-at-heel shoes. Those clothes clearly did him no favors. I recognize that as an objective truth. One only has to compare his scruffy appearance in that suit and those shoes with the undeniably pleasant, comely appearance he now has. He seems taller, has lost the red pimples on his face, and his eyes, which seemed so small, and his eyelashes, which seemed so short, have clearly much improved. All this is easy to grasp. Fargues is an individual whose ideas, feelings, and general aspect are inseparable from the clothes he wears. There is no shortage of such people. No need to belabor the point. The truth is he began to focus on this issue very visibly. He spoke at length to his friends about the need to dress up and be smart. He discovered that shopkeepers have rather vulgar tastes. A shop shapes character and you, Sr. Colomines, must forgive me if I speak so candidly. Like a true shopkeeper, though he was only a beginner, Fargues surfaced with his taste ready-made. He dreamed of buying a checkered suit, ankle-level, white-lyre-patterned purple socks, a red polka-dot shirt, orange shoes, a gleaming, shiny tie, a hat, and a pipe. He wasn't entirely to blame for this range of items, or any of those he dreamt singly of possessing. They entered his dreams, following the whims of the day. At that particular time, shop assistants had started smoking pipes, and obviously Fargues decided it was essential to own a pipe. As he hadn't any money, he wrote to his family asking them to send some."

"Yes, sir, that is so true! I saw the letter!" Sra. Doloretes confirmed.

"Absolutely, senyora! My dear Colomines, a drop more coffee, if you don't mind. Coffee is my weakness. As I was saying, he wrote to his family, but received no reply. It wasn't that they were turning a blind eye; I think in fact they were in no position to help. Time passed and when it seemed that Fargues was becoming resigned to his fate, disaster struck. At any rate, Sr. Colomines, you registered the disappearance of the first twenty-five-peseta note from the cash drawer, and that coincided with your assistant's purchase of his new suit. Am I right?"

"Yes, sir, absolutely."

"I will refrain, as you will understand, from detailing the circumstances of the deed done by Fargues. I wasn't there and would be hardput to describe what happened. This kind of decision usually requires a long period of premeditation; however, once the decision was taken, he went straight into action. I imagine him a few seconds before the shop closed looking at that note as a cat watches a frightened bird. You'd already gone upstairs. He wanted to take it and was scared. The things he wanted were dancing before his eyes, yet at the same time he understood the seriousness of what he was about to do. What swayed the scales was perhaps the thought he turned over in his mind: 'Sr. Colomines won't find out. He's not counted the money in the drawer for days. And if he does notice, he will forgive me my peccadillo.' His self-confidence and optimism blinded him. I am sure he put his hand in firmly, coldly, with eyes wide open. His head must have been on fire, naturally. The fresh air outside calmed his brow. The fact is, Sr. Colomines, the moment you discovered a note had gone missing, Fargues was walking toward his lodgings, clutching a box that contained the orange shoes he'd so dreamed about."

Sr. and Sra. Colomines thought this last twist sounded particularly plausible. While Sr. Roca told his tale, Sra. Doloretes looked repeatedly at her husband, and Sr. Colomines looked repeatedly at his wife. They were looks of accord and admiration—the admiration people experience before statements of the obvious.

"And now, if you agree, Sr. Colomines," resumed the attorney, "we will examine what we might call *your* tactics after that first deed—tactics you have sustained over a series of such acts. I shall begin by saying I support them one hundred percent. I think it is exactly what had to be done if one wants to reach a full and final conclusion. Faced by the first misdeed, you, Sr. Colomines, had two options: summon him, make him see the enormity of the felony he had committed, spell out some moral considerations, and forgive him. If you'd done that, what would have been the end result? Nothing. Nothing whatsoever. Fine words have never delivered results. When it comes to rash, foolish youngsters, fine words are a waste of time, water down the drain. It was necessary to take a different course of action, and that, Sr. Colomines, is what you did. It was necessary to be patient and wait, with the sole aim of catching him in flagrante and making an example of him. Half measures are useless with this kind of fellow. I think one can take that for granted. One must wait until a blatant act is committed, one that merits a swift riposte, and once it's done, go for the jugular. Recall another wise adage: 'Make hay while the sun shines.' However impatient one may become, this always works, especially if one plays one's cards right, if you know what I mean. Petty felonies are only important as symptoms of something else. They are the first signs of a temperament that is inevitably going to resurface. It is a mistake, in my view, to be swayed by an excess of sentiment and to obstruct the natural course of things, to prevent an individual from showing his true character. This is the only way to ensure an evildoer gets his comeuppance. Sr. Colomines, you have pursued this path, and I give you my wholehearted support. Now if I am to find my bearings in this matter, I need you, Sr. Colomines, to tell me what happened on the day after that first felony. I think it is highly important."

"Well, it was like this: My shop assistant arrived in the morning, at the usual time. I thought he looked pale, though much more talkative and animated than previously. Indeed, he was quite garrulous. When he was pulling a drawer out, it slipped and fell on the floor. The customer—a young lady, to be precise—wanted to buy some writing paper and Fargues burst out laughing. It was perhaps a reaction to some inner turmoil. Perhaps he'd had a sleepless night. Perhaps fear he might be caught out was making him anxious and he was attempting to hide it with excited behavior and nervous chatter. I possibly made an error of judgment. That morning I decided to act more affectionately toward him. Until then I'd treated him the way one treats young shop assistants: rather curtly, if not brusquely. That morning I decided it was my duty to soften, to be more open with him. I put on a smile and even laughed at one of his, shall we say, pearls of wisdom. I am sure he noticed my change of attitude, and that made him more suspicious."

"Don't doubt that for one minute, Sr. Colomines!" exclaimed the attorney, beaming contentedly.

"When he saw how well-disposed I was toward him," continued the shopkeeper, "he simply became more and more agitated. That morning, Fargues joked in an exaggerated, spontaneous manner with every customer who came into the shop. Whenever he opened the drawer and put inside the money he'd been given, he glanced in my direction with a mixture of dread, fear, and nervousness. Believe it or not, I soon started to feel sorry for him, concluding my change of attitude had confirmed him in his worst suspicions. He was evidently convinced I'd found him out. 'This man is onto me, I'm done for!' he must have been telling himself, in the intervals between his excited outbursts. Perhaps, in a moment of weakness, he may have thought about getting it all off his chest and begging me for forgiveness. The poor wretch must have been wondering: 'If this fellow *has* figured it out, why is he holding back? Why doesn't he confront me and demand an explanation? Why doesn't he come straight out with it now that he's being so nice and ask me to confess all and go down on my knees in shame, or why doesn't he hit me?' The very thought he *was* in such a quandary was precisely what made me feel sorry for him. However, I'd made my decision to say nothing and wait. I couldn't deviate from that. And then it was time to shut up shop and go for lunch. Subsequently, things seemed to calm down. Given my lack of reaction, Fargues must have decided the whole business was forgotten—"

"Allow me for a moment, Sr. Colomines!" interjected Sr. Roca. "One cannot assume, dear friend, that this business was over and done with at that point. With your permission I will flesh out your own explanation. I have told you time and again how I questioned some of Fargues's acquaintances, quite surreptitiously, naturally. I am a good friend of Srta. Tereseta, the owner of the lodging house where your assistant lives. It was that Sunday two or three days after the first felony. Fargues felt ill and spent the entire day in bed. Srta. Tereseta entered his bedroom and found him pale, out of sorts, and quite exhausted. She asked him what was wrong, and Fargues said he was very tired. He begged her to leave him alone and in darkness, not to disturb him, because he felt on his last legs. Srta. Tereseta couldn't understand how a strong young man like Fargues could have gone from his cheerfulness on Saturday to that depressed state and yet not suffer from any sickness in particular. At lunchtime, she took him a bowl of broth he could barely hold; his arms were limp; he had the shakes. You will remember, Sr. Colomines, how your assistant never came to the shop the Monday after. He sent a message saying he was ill. Well then, in my opinion, in my humble opinion, all that has a very obvious explanation. Human resistance has its limits. No man can in the end resist his abiding obsessions. Fargues had resisted three very long days—very long, that is, for him—but then could stand it no more: He had, as they say, snapped. He was a physical wreck and had to stay in bed, more dead than alive, drained and exhausted. Could one wish for a clearer demonstration of the power of moral conscience?"

"So right, so right," chorused Sr. and Sra. Colomines.

"Well then, on the Tuesday he got up and came to the shop as fresh as a daisy, as if nothing was amiss, I am sure he'd been forced to make an enormous effort to decide to get up. But he had no choice. To accept he was really sick would have been tantamount to recognizing his felony. At least that is what he must have been thinking—though that is hardly our concern. He had to put in an appearance at the shop, whatever happened, he had to see if anything had changed in terms of his status. Srta. Tereseta told me how surprised she was by way the lad had transformed overnight. Although he'd taken no medication and eaten very little, he seemed a changed boy. He was ravenous at breakfast. He surprised the other shop assistants by talking persistently about a girl from the neighborhood. He spoke about her as if she were standing in front of him, as if he were talking to her and touching her. 'He could see nothing but that girl.' In other words, his senses were entering a convalescent phase after the exhaustion generated by his inner obsession. They were stimulating him. Yet again an energetic, greedy individual's ability to forget the past was making itself felt. Fargues now set out fatally on the road that was to lead him to commit his second felony. Does this ring true, Sr. Colomines?"

"Yes, sir, you couldn't have put it more clearly."

"I simply wish to demonstrate how, once the first deed was done, the consequences were inevitable. Fargues was on a slippery slope and had no choice but to slide right down. I hope, dear friend, you will now confirm this was the case. What did he do after his first misdemeanor?"

"There have been others over the last two or three months."

"How many?"

"Three or four."

"This is most promising! The matter is following its proper course. At this juncture I would make one observation, a kind of presentiment I cannot keep to myself. I am sure he has committed later misdemeanors more cynically and brazenly than the first. Nothing unusual in that: Once he felt he'd been found out and was done for, he concluded that any self-justification was otiose. 'If they catch me,' he must have thought, 'what can happen that's not happened already?' That's the state of mind you need to be in to snaffle one banknote after another. A moment ago I said that the matter, in my view, is following its normal course. I must reiterate that. At the same time I think it has entered its final phase. One must be patient while awaiting this outcome and bring one's diplomatic skills into play. Events should—how should I put it?—be facilitated inasmuch as they can be, if you get my drift. Always leave a high-denomination note in the drawer. Allow the young man to spread his wings, you know? He needs an opportunity to show his true self in a relaxed, spontaneous fashion. I have set everything in motion, and can you imagine what a figure this vigorous young man will cut, between two civil guards, when the moment of truth comes? He will see how the folks in the neighborhood will have a good laugh at his expense."

"So, Sr. Roca," asked Sra. Doloretes, "your advice would be . . . ?"

"I've just told you: Simply wait, don't lose heart, be patient!"

The attorney took a few more sips of coffee and a shot of the liqueur that was on the table. Then he lit up a small cigar and bid farewell as affably as ever.

Once he'd departed, I was in a way rediscovered by the Colomineses. I'd enjoyed a lovely afternoon, in my view: Nobody had spoken to me. I'd been able to listen to their conversation and weigh every word.

"Poor lad!" said Sra. Doloretes, suddenly remembering I was there. "How we must have bored you!"

"Not at all, senyora! I've really enjoyed my afternoon. It has been a pleasure to listen to Sr. Roca—"

"My wife is quite right, young man," said a rather shamefaced Sr.

Colomines. "We simply forgot all about you. We completely neglected you. That was hardly what we agreed to with your father."

He glanced at his watch and saw it was half past four.

"Good heavens!" he exclaimed, bewildered. "How time flies! Hurry up, do. We'll go for a walk. There's still time before you have to be back at school. All the same, you must believe me when I say that what happened today was quite exceptional."

Sra. Doloretes said goodbye almost maternally. We went out into the languid, morose light of Sunday afternoon. We meandered. We had coffee at the dairy under the arches on plaça del Vi. When the time came—six o'clock—I walked up to my school, feeling very anxious. Sr. Colomines said very little. I said goodbye and kept polite banalities to a minimum.

I continued to feel anxious and extraordinarily confused over the next few hours. Adolescence may be the time in life when things seem to appear at their messiest and most confused, but the situation in which I found myself was even more complex. I didn't know Fargues at all. I had caught sight of him for a moment in Sr. Colomines's shop. He seemed both nice enough and a nuisance, a neighborhood braggart of limited appeal. Ostensibly, Fargues had committed a gross blunder, an inexcusable faux pas. But I thought the way they were planning to handle it—my first response, a gut reaction, if you will— was abominable and iniquitous. I anguished over the case hour after hour. I went to sleep very late. And the more I ruminated, the more naïve the boy seemed and the more disgusting the outcome those self-important gentlemen were planning to manufacture. The cynical, icy meanness of the outcome Sr. Roca had suggested, which the shopkeepers fully accepted, seemed more poisonous than Fargues's childish exploits. I felt it was reprehensible to destroy a young man like that, coldly, taking advantage of a situation that could have been used to give him moral insight if approached with a grain of common sense.

The following day I wrote to my father. At the time, whenever I was in a quandary, the first thing I did was write to my father. In principle, I think it was the best thing to do. It was hellishly difficult to describe the case in a nutshell. But, in the end, I succeeded, with greater or lesser clarity. The letter was rather confused. After informing him of the facts of the case, I said it was most urgent to contact the Fargues family in order to get their son out of that shop on any pretext and bring him back to our town. The security and peace of mind of the shop assistant's family depended on that. For the first time in my life I tried to adopt an imploring, pathetic tone in my letter. Until then I had only written letters that were . . . well, strictly ordinary. Afterward, when I reread those lines, I saw that an imploring, pathetic register wasn't necessarily my forte. It was uninspired and lachrymose. In the afternoon I gave the letter to a day student who mailed it from the main post office situated at the time at the top of carrer de la Força—I remember these details very precisely. I handed the letter over to be posted fully convinced that my father, supposing he managed to read between the lines of my narrative, would think it an entirely perfunctory, trivial matter.

Days passed and I heard nothing about the Fargues affair. I alluded to it several times in my everyday correspondence with my family but received no response. That exasperated me to no end: I was at an age when one is easily exasperated. I had to learn to be patient, and patience is a state one certainly must acquire over time.

The first Sunday in November was approaching and the issue of the monthly outing was again on the agenda. I received a letter from Sr. Colomines who said they were expecting me for lunch that day. I hastily replied that I couldn't accept his generous invitation because I was sick. The invitation was repeated for the first Sunday in December and elicited an identical reaction from me. It was no white lie that I'd used for an excuse. It was genuine and real. The very thought I might see those people again made me feel pain throughout my body.

I finally had the opportunity to discover the outcome during the Christmas holidays.

Influenced by my letter and against all my expectations, father had decided he ought to take an interest in the case of the shop assistant. He quickly tracked down the Fargues family, and they turned out to be tenant farmers who looked after a rather down-at-heel farmstead on the outskirts of town. He interceded skillfully on their behalf. He spoke to the justice of the peace, a close friend of his, a retired doctor and a good-hearted man who was part of his social-cum-agricultural circle. The judge had plenty of time on his hands and attacked the issue with a spirit prompted by local interest, a spirit that always works in these parts. When the judge found he had a chance to do townsfolk a favor, he acted swiftly. The Fargues family was summoned to the court. They went there in a state of shock and terror. In this country, a priori, authority always provokes panic. Then time passes, things become drawn out, passions cool, and everything ends in platitudes. Fargues's father listened to the judge's suggestions with curiosity but rarely intervened. He probably didn't really understand what it was all about. He was a single-minded fellow, a small farmer who concentrated purely on his poor land, his bread, wine, and ancestral poverty. His wife reacted quite differently. She listened to the judge in intense, sad silence and was extraordinarily attentive.

In mid-November—it was crisp and cold under a silvery sky—that woman went to Girona carrying a basket under her arm, a willow basket with a lid. She was dressed in black with a scarf around her head—a scarf that hung down in a sharp point over her forehead. She was a small, rotund woman with pink cheeks and white hair. She went straight from the station to her son's lodging house, but Fargues was already in the shop by the time his mother arrived. She hadn't foreseen this possibility but *had* anticipated that three or four minutes' conversation with her son would be enough to sort things out. So now she headed to the shop, which made her hesitate momentarily.

"Senyora, what can I do for you?" asked Sr. Colomines pleasantly enough, rubbing his hands together (it was quite cold in the shop), when he saw her standing in front of the counter, looking extremely intent.

"I would like to speak to my son, a lad who works here, by the name of Fargues."

"He went out a minute ago. He'll be back very soon. How can I help you, senyora? How can I help? It would give me great pleasure to—"

"It would me as well, Sr. Colomines! I have come for my boy. We need him at home. We have to sow the fields and his father isn't really well enough."

"But, senyora, what are you saying! I find this astonishing."

"Sr. Colomines, sowing is not something we can delay. On the other hand, it seems my boy isn't up to much good."

"And, senyora, *who* pray tell has told you he isn't up to much good?" asked Sr. Colomines, absolutely taken aback.

"It's just an idea of mine, you know? These are children with empty heads. They are soon led astray, you do understand, don't you? They are poor souls who have forgotten what side their bread's buttered on."

"Well, now that you mention it, I must say you are quite right. Your son has not been up to much good."

The old countrywoman's white teeth and pink cheeks broke into quiet laughter.

"Nothing I wasn't expecting, Sr. Colomines. This comes as no surprise to me! Tell me what I owe you and we'll soon be straight. Let every man get his just due, I say, and not a word more on the subject. Don't you agree?"

"But, senyora, no need to take it so far, immediately—"

"What you mean by 'immediately'?" retorted the woman, highly irritated. "But do you think these things should continue? I assure you they won't for a minute more. What can you have been thinking? I've come to get my boy and I will take him home, even if I'm forced to drag him. And you, Sr. Colomines, will be so good as to tell me what I owe you and we can settle for good."

"Senyora, you don't owe me a thing!" answered the shopkeeper, shifting from a tone of surprise to one that was icy and withering.

"Sr. Colomines, don't start being all hoity-toity with me. You should realize that whatever we can settle with hard cash will be a good deal for you. It is the tail this business might have wagged that would have cost us dear. The figure buzzing in my head tells me I owe you some two hundred and fifty pesetas. Now you tell me if that tallies with your own calculations."

"But, senyora, you need this—"

"Of course I need this money, Sr. Colomines! You have no idea *how much* I need it. But what do you expect me to do? I am used to it. Here you are!"

She opened the basket she'd been holding tightly under her arm the entire time and placed some carefully folded banknotes on the counter.

"Here you are! Count them! And please tell me if we can consider this a done deal."

At that very moment Fargues walked through the door, his hat on the slant, smoking a pipe—the monstrous short-stem kind, singed by fire, which shop assistants like to smoke. As soon as he saw his mother, he stopped in his tracks and the look on his face changed. The old woman stared at him with a touch of warmth that lasted a second. Then she took three or four steps in his direction and spoke to him in a hard, brusque voice that wasn't, however, completely without affection.

"What's the matter, lad?" she began. "I've come to fetch you. You will be better off at home. You won't need to play the fool any more. If you need to collect anything from the shop, get it now. We'll go for lunch. On plaça de Sant Agustí. I expect you there right away, without fail. Sr. Colomines, excuse me, I must say goodbye. I hope you have a good day."

She held out a dry, calloused hand that Sr. Colomines shook in his warm, flaccid paw.

Fargues went into action immediately, like a robot, mute and head down. Sr. Colomines was left flummoxed and completely at a loss for words.

The old lady left the shop visibly proud and pleased. All the same, things hadn't turned out as she'd imagined. She was expecting to find resistance from her son but, conversely, support from Sr. Colomines. She had thought Sr. Colomines would be in a rush to rid himself of such an undesirable assistant. The exact opposite had occurred. This was proof that the justice of the peace had managed to engineer the right effect without being forced to tell the whole story—he had kept the worst to himself.

Mother and son had lunch on a bench on plaça de Sant Agustí, in front of the statue of General Álvarez de Castro and a monument to the heroes of 1808. First from the basket were two omelets inside two slices of bread, followed by two figs, four walnuts, and some hazelnuts. It was cold. There was a silvery, snow-filled sky—a motionless, icy sky. The old woman had brought a small bottle of rosé wine. Then they drank a cup of hot coffee in the café on the square and waited until it was time to go home.

They took the mail train. As they had nothing to say to each other, few words were exchanged. In the coach, with the train in motion, the old lady looked out the window while it was still light. Farmers were sowing their plowed fields. Fargues had put a bundle on the seat opposite him. He was wearing his red polka-dot shirt and orange shoes. The mere sight of him chilled the blood.

17 September. When I scrutinize people from the point of view of the rituals of conversation, I note the following:

The poor, the really poor, are sullen, and their talk is often brief and curt. The poor, the really poor, are interested in nothing, are difficult to engage in conversation. The poor, the really poor, are obsessed by their own poverty.

The rich are equally elusive: They are the only beings in the country who can allow themselves the luxury of living in harmony with the weather. They do this or that, use this or that cliché, depending on the humidity or the wind: whether it's a northerly wind or a southwesterly.

People of modest means—the middle class—are usually polite and on their best behavior. In fact, it is with the people of this class that one engages in conversation.

Nonetheless, the rituals of conversation with such people can bring their own surprises. One can start conversing with an outburst of conventional verbal diarrhea, with much head-bowing and reiterated deference, with cries of admiration for the clichés and truisms one imagines close to the heart of one's interlocutor, but as the conversation unfolds the stream of words dries up, the initial impetus grinds to a halt, and at a certain point the platitudes end abruptly in a blind alley.

Well, at that moment, you can be sure of one thing. You can be quite sure you are in the presence of a desperately poor person, who for a second aspired to be taken for someone else—for a member of the middle class.

18 September. A long stroll through the outskirts of Palafrugell—going nowhere in particular—with Joan B. Coromina. A most splendid, in fact, a glorious temperature. Early evening, in this country, is pure bliss.

The pine woods mean that this landscape can never be mistaken for anywhere else. The basic shape is nearly always a straightforward geometrical figure: a triangle, a rectangle, and sometimes a perfect square. Pinkish white ribbons run alongside the pines—crumbled granite sand paths—this being the local geological makeup.

The straight rows of pines—drawn with a plumb line—suggest geometrical projections. If they are pink in summer—D'Annunzio's *pini biondi*—they are now reverting to their genuine green. A light, bright, airy green floats under the treetops. If seen singly the tops look like parabolas, observed all together from above the woods they are like the gentle waves of an unbroken verdant sea. A breath of wind and the pines make music—as do eastern cottonwood or black poplar, though it's a very different kind of music. Not long ago I read a poem by the Majorcan Miquel Ferrà that spoke of "high eddies in the pines." The chiming of black poplar is playful and graceful and brings to mind the free flowing music of Mozart. Pines make organ music for a requiem.

Vines are elements that bring color to the landscape—a changing, diverse melody. Now they are an elegant golden gray. They are planted on undulating hills as firm as the breasts of an adolescent girl from these parts. Next to each vineyard one finds a sulfate pit and a hut. Such urban elements scattered across the land humanize the scene and make it companionable. Everything is small, ordered, tidy, and pleasant—to such an extent that we sometimes feel like agreeing with the ladies when they say "How lovely!," though that isn't quite right.

A late-afternoon stroll in early autumn is delightful—a truly physical pleasure.

Back in plaça Nova, we meet Mossèn Renart, who is striding toward his rectory. He looks worried. Coromina, a friend of his—no ardent anticlerical in these parts doesn't have a priest for a friend—asks in a roundabout way if anything is the matter. Mossèn Renart is famed for always being in dispute with his bishop.

"No, nothing really," said the rector forcing a laugh. "More of the same. I've often told you how it's harder to be the rector of a village like Mont-ras than the Bishop of Girona. The lord bishop gets a considerable slice of income, more than fourteen million pesetas, and I must make do with a few coppers. But there is nothing one can do about that."

Village priests make one sad. They are indescribably poor.

Coromina looks thunderous.

"Mossèn Renart," he says, "has spoiled the landscape and our stroll. It seems incredible that such pretty countryside can contain so much wretchedness."

20 September. My family.

Grandmother Marieta was widowed very young. Her husband—my grandfather—was buried in the cemetery in Llofriu. This cemetery was next to the church at the time, by the main entrance, as is the case in many country villages. Because of this proximity—and no doubt for many other reasons—Grandmother Marieta pledged never to go to mass in Llofriu ever again and she has kept her pledge. It is years and years since she visited the cemetery in Llofriu. Grandmother Marieta adored her husband.

Of course this is because of the fear of the dead and of cemeteries that exists in the countryside. The panic created is beyond words. Some people are obsessed throughout their lives by the friends and families they have lost yet would never return to the cemetery where they are buried. If they do so—a big if!—on the Day of the Dead, it is because so many pay their respects. The accompanying hubbub transforms their visit into a promenade. Cemeteries are usually empty places, without a living soul in sight, particularly rural cemeteries. Sometimes, out of curiosity, I've tried to visit a rural cemetery and been unable to locate a key anywhere—as if someone had stolen it.

A certain vogue for necrophilia has popularized skulls and crossbones, undermining the mysterious aura of cemeteries and playing havoc with memories of the deceased. It must be horrible—unbearable, beyond physical endurance—to imagine a person one has loved in the form of a skeleton. One only remembers people one's memory can resurrect.

"*Fratelli a un tempo stesso amore è morte,*" says Leopardi, "*ingenerò la sorte…*" Yes, that happens a lot. People disappear when we most need them. Nonetheless, the living cannot conceive of the fatal bond that exists between love and death.

My mother tends not to believe in miracles, and as she is quite unconventional, we can say that openly. Aunt Lluïsa, on the contrary, reads all the little magazines that recount every miracle, and always has two or three fantastic cures at hand and holds forth on the entire range of wonders wrought by strange supernatural interventions. When she tries to palm these captivating fantasies off on my mother, my mother cuts her off.

"Come on, Lluïsa," mother says, "please don't start on that nonsense! I am too busy."

Today, when Aunt Lluïsa was about to inform her of a heavenly intercession involving the economic salvation of a bankrupt—a news article in one of her little magazines—my mother shouted, "Please! I can only take so much!"

Sra. Maria—everyone knows my mother by this name—is a fervent Catholic: She always does her duty and goes to mass in any weather. She has to be extremely sick not to go to church. In the winter, when it is raining, cold, or snowing, or simply if the north wind blows too fiercely, Aunt Lluïsa may decide it's too dangerous to risk an excursion. She will stay close to her brazier or bed, and complain endlessly, has tremendous flair for playing *le malade imaginaire*. She always finds an excuse not to do her duty.

Autumn.

The time of year when very few people are seen walking the streets of Palafrugell at night is early autumn. When you hear young men serenading, down a dark street, one window or another, you can be sure that spring is here. You never hear songs beneath these windows—however enrapturing and compelling the beauty enclosed within. When you walk down three or four streets at any hour of the night and don't meet a living soul, you can be sure it's autumn. People's lives adapt to the reduction or increase in light. In autumn, they lead wintry lives. When the almond trees blossom—in the freezing cold—it's already beginning to look like spring.

23 September. This country is passionate about gambling. Of course, I don't detect any fondness for lotteries, whether national or not, or any other game of that kind. People prefer to stake their money individually, on real tables, in real places, opposite real human beings they know. There is gambling in which the individual is the protagonist, the immediate protagonist, with the necessary tools in his hand, and these are the games preferred by genuine gamblers (betting games rather than any other sort of wagering), and then there is more indirect gambling, when money is at stake via a mechanism controlled by others. These are games with a banker—roulette, dice, seven and a half, or monte, etcetera.

Dice is the game that fascinates most men here—for better or for worse. In Palafrugell, we call the dice "bones." The noise—click-clack—that the bones make when they are thrown and hit the wooden board in front of the croupier, a somber, cemetery sound, tinkles pleasantly in local people's ears.

I've often wondered whether vanity and swagger aren't behind this passion for gambling—games in which an individual is pitted against an individual or a banker; those about winning tricks is held in much lower esteem. In this country, a gambler is not considered an outlaw from polite society. I don't think any woman has ever refused to marry a man simply because he was a passionate gambler. A gambler always has a mysterious, intriguing allure. Naturally there are Saturday-night gamblers ready to lose their weekly wage at a tavern table. The wives of these fanatics come to the town hall or barracks every Monday, child in arms, to complain of their poverty-stricken situation. But that doesn't cause a ripple socially and is viewed as everyday business that must settled, a routine event in life. Then one finds normal gamblers, professional or otherwise, who lead exemplary family lives, according to the strictest bourgeois canons, and bankrupt themselves or win, yet never involve the law. The admiration an orderly life prompts is enhanced by the additional halo of mystery surrounding a man who goes to bed late, eats a second supper, and occasionally stakes five hundred pesetas.

Nobody considers gambling to be a scandalous vice. A man with a vice is one who drinks, visits brothels, or inhabits a run-down mansion, or the man who lives a lazy, self-indulgent life and has nothing in the bank. The gambler fond of that modest second supper in the early hours, with his white napkin and glass of white wine and soda, is considered a citizen who helps the wheels of commerce turn. This is probably ample proof that the passion for gambling in these parts—I mean the sympathy in society towards this passion—is age-old and predates the act of walking.

The bragging, anger, and visible vanity that *are* part and parcel of the passion of gamblers may derive from the fact that gambling is how these people escape life's humiliations. To sit down at a gaming table, extract a hundred and fifty or two hundred pesetas from one's wallet, and stake them, come what may, in front of friends, enemies, and a range of the local citizenry—including the stolid bourgeois—is to assert one's sense of vital freedom. As if to say "I'm gambling all my money...so what?"

Such a gesture, thought, and decision must be morally uplifting and physically pleasing for the man who wants to wreak revenge on life's humiliations. High society or the bourgeoisie, a friend, foe, or complete stranger have humiliated or are humiliating me—thinks the gambler—but at this very moment when I'm gambling my own money I am proving that I am alive and affirming that I exist. Not everyone can say "I think, therefore I am." For gamblers, "I gamble, therefore I am" is the apt saying.

Almost all the gamblers I know are mavericks: fiercely individualistic and distinctive—whether rich or poor, from high estate or the glebe, literary or unlettered. A gambler is never gray, is never subservient nor timid, never neither fish nor fowl. In a uniformly mediocre world, a gambler is always *his own* man, one way or another.

When a game is over, winners don't usually boast. Rather they chalk it up to luck and try to go unnoticed—apologizing for their good fortune, in essence.

Losers are usually more strident and boastful. They can be a bit trying and sentimental. It is not that they want to provoke pity—although sometimes it appears that way. Nevertheless, when a gambler says "I lost five hundred pesetas yesterday" and sees his friends pitying him in his misfortune, his satisfaction is self-evident. Misfortune—and losing when gambling *is* a misfortune—creates turmoil, and all turmoil creates great inner pleasure that people try to conceal behind a display of indignation. If misfortunes weren't accompanied by the pleasures of turmoil, they would be quite unbearable.

I have no vocation as a gambler. It is an ability that providence hasn't granted me. I'm not familiar with the fabled strategies of cardsharps (I don't know how to play *tresillo* or *manilles*) or crazy about individual or casino-style games. I can see how gambling—any kind of gambling when money is at stake—enables one to forget the twilight miseries of life, and it is a fascinating pastime (judging by what I see), perhaps even more so than the opposite sex. I feel, however, that I wasn't born for such intense amusements. My thoughts soon wander elsewhere, I'm easily distracted, and my selfishness is perhaps too ingrained and domineering to let me embark on such strong commitments. (The only commitment I like is prompted by the presence of a fountain pen in my hand.) Besides, I don't fanatically seek out humiliation, turmoil, or insults. I'd rather sidestep resentful bores. I believe the cultivation of amnesia is a fine activity that encourages you to get on with life.

Thus, when I'm next to gaming tables—and they seem to have

multiplied with the war—the most I will agree to be is a sleeping partner, always provided the other person will handle my money. (This detail shows what a hopeless gambler I am.) If I win, I spend the money immediately and hardly give it a second thought. If I lose, I couldn't care less.

28 September. I don't know which political party my father belongs to. Probably none. I am sure he would like to, but I don't think he ever has. He is then a man who must have spent a lifetime looking for the party that best suited him, and as he has yet to find it, he keeps looking. The position he represents is more widespread in the country than it might seem at first.

My father would have preferred politics that drive society forward, galvanize sources of wealth—especially agricultural wealth—and put an end to neglect, ignorance, pettiness, and inertia in private life. I am sure he has read and studied all the political programs launched since 1888 and has registered how inane they all are. As he has never found an organization that practices what he requires, he has remained on the fringes of all political movements.

Ten or twelve years ago, when I started high school, I heard him say, "Everything has yet to be done in this country."

Now I often hear him say, "It's impossible to do anything in this country."

In the interval between, he suffered a curious, regrettable setback: the infamous Pals affair, or conversion of a large number of acres of barren, unproductive land into wonderful, fertile terrain. My father played a crucial role in this huge operation—the most important around here for centuries in the agricultural sector. He lost his fortune and dreams in that adventure and only God's will ensured he didn't lose his skin as well. In other words, he knows what politics are about and the huge power wielded by political influence in these latitudes. A mere caprice of the Marquis de Robert, abetted by his ignorant backwoods friends in Torroella de Montgrí, sufficed to trigger a stupid, futile, incomprehensible struggle that changed an excellent initiative, beneficial to the general interests of the country, into a complete disaster. In the end, rice was grown, but the damage inflicted by what was supposed to be a positive initiative was irreparable and enduring.

Sometimes we talk about all that and I say, "You were up against reactionaries and the extreme right."

"Of course," he replies. "They are the people who own the land. But I think if I'd been up against people on the left, the situation would have been no different."

"What do you mean?"

"Well, you should understand that in this country the person who most resembles a man of the left is a man of the right. They are identical, interchangeable, and no doubt weaned on the same milk. And how could it be any different? You must understand it is a meaningless opposition."

"But perhaps a different one could exist?"

"Yes, I think so. In my view much deeper, more precise kinds of opposition exist: between intelligent people and idiots, between good and bad."

"If that's really true," I asked after a pause, "what's your advice?"

"I have none!"

"How can you possibly have none?"

"I don't!"

"Would you advise me to be cunning or trusting?"

My father is silent for a moment. He stares at me. Then stares at the floor. Then finally says, with intense concentration, "Don't spread it around, but I'd advise you to be cunning, and now not one word more."

The aftermath of the Pals rice episode was a huge, distressing, complicated sequence of bills of exchange that poisoned our family life for years and years.

That flow of bills accompanied my entry into politics and was my first schooling in politics. I don't regret having to say that.

30 September. Pagans the butcher is older than a mountain path. His lower lip droops under a thick, bushy Republican Federal mustache.

He was born in La Pera. As a youngster, he studied to enter the priesthood and had a good grasp of Latin. He later abandoned the cloth and discovered his vocation as a butcher. Once he'd entered this trade he engaged in an orgy of republicanism—to repeat the phrase coined by Don Joan Manyé i Flaquer. As a child of La Pera, Pagans must have known several members of the Savalls family: Sr. Josep, the heir; Xico Savalls, the Carlist leader; and other representatives of their stock.

When he talks about this general he likes to recount an incident that would enlighten students of politics in this country.

At the time of the negotiations with Martínez Campos, in the Hostal de la Corda, a man from La Pera bumped into his famous fellow countryman and asked, "Well, Xico, how's it going in the Hostal? What news do you have?"

"Good news. The war is over. You can start spreading the word."

"What do you mean the war is over? Are you in cloud-cuckoo land?"

"I said the war is over! Listen: Martínez Campos has given his word that priests will start being paid again. That's been agreed."

"I understand. But—"

"But what? Who's going to want to wage war after what I've just told you, you fool? Who's going to want to wage war now? Please start spreading the word that it's all over."

I find Pere Poch idling in the café—I mean not busy playing cards. He is the abstract purist kind of a gambler: He is as excited staking grains of wheat as ten-cent coins. We talk about various things. The conversation drifts to Madrid, and he says in his usual monotone drawl, "You hear the word *señor* so often, everywhere you go, in Madrid—it's a word that maids, coachmen, porters, taxi drivers, waiters, stall owners, shop assistants, and everyone in service constantly repeats—'You tell me, *señor*'; 'At your orders, *señor*'; 'Excuse me, *señor*'; 'What do you want, *señor*?'; 'At your disposition, *señor*'; 'Good night, *señor*!'; etcetera—and you end up feeling that you live not simply close to but on the most intimate terms with our *Señor Eterno*. It's very odd and takes a lot of getting used to."

"Well, it is very different here, my dear Poch; it's that situation in reverse. It is a word that is never used, not even with doctors. The last time I heard it was in Llafranc. In Llafranc there is a bohemian by the name of Canadell, with whom you are probably acquainted, and when he hears a five-peseta silver coin ring on a marble tabletop he will automatically say, very sarcastically, 'What can I do for you, *senyor?*'"

1 October. In the café with sudden candor, shyness, and braggadocio, Coromina announces, "The ladies are after me."

"I think her name is Amparo," says Frigola after a pause, looking at the floor and tapping the steel tip of his cane in an abrupt, irritated manner.

"Indeed, I think that's true," replies Coromina.

"Then it must be in honor of her name and signature. Your aspirations are purely based on names. Imagine where you'd be if, instead of an Amparo offering shelter, she was a Consuelo offering consolation."

I've often thought about the phrase one hears so often in these parts: "tangling with a woman." It is a phrase with frankly contemptuous connotations—a blatant invitation to anyone who may be tangled up to disentangle quickly, the sooner the better. At least that's how I'd feel as one who'd be delighted to entangle himself at any time of day!

After recovering from Frigola's barbed comment with the help of one or two shots of rum, Coromina says to Gori, "If we took our time to examine the phenomenon case by case, we'd be forced to wonder, with Proudhon, if theft wasn't the origin of property. Look at the fortunes that have been made from the war. It is literally indecent."

"I can see that," replies Gori, looking at the ceiling as if he is yawning. "But would you want to deprive anyone of the opportunity of becoming a thief?"

"Absolutely not!"

"So what's your point? Becoming a member of the property-owning class is simply a matter of patience."

The current surge against the nouveaux riches is growing

everywhere. The foreign press is in full swing. It is a vociferous campaign that could seemingly turn the world upside down. Naturally it will do nothing of the sort because it involves so much envy—and, conversely, so much flattery. If the roles were reversed, the campaign wouldn't change one iota.

Sleeping when you aren't sleepy is the hardest thing ever.

3 October. In this weather café conversations strike up again. Heat scatters people; cold huddles them back together. I sometimes spend my evenings with my father's group at Cafè Pallot only to resurface later as if I'd been for a swim in a boundless ocean of trivia and pusillanimous detail. I couldn't stand it as part of my daily diet; I'd choke. Nonetheless, I recognize that pettiness of vision makes for a good schooling in modesty and stoicism—a schooling for real life.

At the moment, conversations in Cafè Pallot are packed.

The gatherings appear highly serious, but there's a strong, facetious undercurrent. Human relationships are strong on facetiousness. One may occasionally discern a sense of positive admiration and respect when strangers are present. In any event, the only people who are really respected are the dead—especially when memories have been purged of the deceased's major or minor lapses. When people know each other and are in frequent contact, they tend to indulge in confessions, which implies the revelation of countless frailties, dreadful errors, pathetic misdemeanors, and innumerable absurdities. Friends —it is often said—are all forgiving. Not true. They never forgive you your trespasses. Among friends, irony always has the last word.

A café conversation is comprised of people who've been seeing each other for years and know each other intimately. It's a long-established exchange that holds no secrets. All present have confessed so often, have been repeatedly indiscreet and engaged in so much gossip that the ice was broken years ago. One more revelation makes no odds. And, as everyone carries a thorn in their side—that the others must necessarily accept because they too have occasionally fallen by the wayside—these gatherings serve to sluice away the dregs of personal obsession. This thorn is almost always linked to self-interest. The spelling out of any kind of self-interest triggers an entire set of contrary preoccupations. This is a poor country, people are interconnected, and everything is interdependent. When one tile shifts, they all shift. These men are all friends, but insofar as they embody self-interests in conflict with each other, by the mere fact of existing, regarding the self-interests of others, they are at loggerheads. So although these café conversations have a civilized veneer, beneath is a permanent free-for-all: They fight like cats and dogs.

Conversely, the participants all have the biggest, most stubborn egos. They are hardheaded. When they speak of their own corner, of their likes and inclinations, they're like sleepwalkers driven by some internal force; they're unable to bring the slightest critical acumen or strategic thinking to bear on what they say and feel. One can't imagine a force that might shift their personal stances one iota. A café conversation is a most authentic, marvelous phenomenon: a convergence of troglodytes.

As I reflect on these observations, I begin thinking how any group over time, becomes a biological phenomenon of considerable power. One's first reaction might be: If these men manage to make life so impossible for each other by constantly reconvening, why don't they split up and go their separate ways? The truth is that despite the bickering, they converge every day. A blind force compels them to. They go there to suffer. But they go all the same. They don't miss a day. A fondness for infighting binds them together, self-inflicted suffering—as yet unvisited by any tragedy—that can be devastating.

4 October. Continuing the previous entry.

The thorns we carry in our sides usually derive from moments in life when we've been afraid we might lose something. Fear, in my view, is behind the mechanism of memory. Memory seems especially destined to keep fear alive—the moments of fear that the body refuses to digest and eliminate. These moments of terror that are never erased are what drives the human organism, what makes it progress from adolescence to its definitive crystallization. Fear is a character-defining force. It assumes an element in our organism that functions to keep memories alive—in a permanent state of tension and anguish. When we are young, we tend to have little in the way of memories—apart from the sexual sort, which are dispersed and interchangeable—even though the occasional child can recite a page from a book or play the piano with great talent. Moral memory—the only memory that matters—is born at a specific moment in the development of our organism. Fear of losing what we have, or fear of failing to achieve what we've set our sights on, is what makes an impact on life and shapes it. Fear is born from injustices wrought by biology, from the potential or real threat to the notion of justice every organism possesses simply by virtue of existing.

These café conversations are affected by such elemental human mechanisms, by a continual reiteration of old obsessions that bubble away, though they seem nonexistent and opaque to the passing spectator. Everyone is paranoid when his own self-interest is at stake—what idealist writers call egotism.

Sr. Mascort, the town hall secretary—that is, Secretary Mascort—was hounded from office years ago by a joint cabal of republicans and the mayor. A deft alliance. When he thinks about it—and there is every sign he does and often—when he thinks how one day he was forced to abandon his position, he reacts in such a panicky way he suddenly becomes domineering, frenzied, and horribly agitated. Everyone has forgotten the intrigue—which nobody apart from him knew about anyway—no matter their earlier curiosity. But *he* remembers and is obsessed by every tiny detail as if it were yesterday.

Sr. Joanet Granés is small, dark, and potbellied, with extremely long arms, hairy eyebrows, a singed, drooping mustache, and untidy stubble. Glib, slimy, and servile, he is quite a character. A notary clerk—though his niece married the notary and family squabbles lost him his post. Good God! How he has bemoaned this injustice night and day for five years! He's lined up forces he thinks might support him against the official notary. He has set up an office in Granota, a district of Palafrugell within the boundaries of Mont-ras, so that the notary of Palamós can go there and sign papers pretending to be the one from Palafrugell. A nasty business...

Sr. Balaguer is the most active, intelligent, upstanding member of the local judiciary. When the magistrate, his deputy, the prosecutor, his assistants, the secretary need to write a report, they must have recourse to him. His is the most out-of-the-way desk in the office. Imagine what Sr. Balaguer's idea of justice must be like!

Sr. Pons is a doctor and a Carlist with deeply rooted convictions who finds it intolerable that all man and womankind don't share his convictions. "The world is doomed!" he says widening the whites of his lugubrious, receding eyes. "The end is nigh!" he adds. "Where will it all end?" For heaven's sake! If Sr. Pons had concentrated more on his medical books than on attending to the pages of *El Correo Catalán*, he might have made his mark as a doctor. But who will bell the cat, given that these fellows are all such upright, serious, and respectable citizens? His position in the group: a man who is barely tolerated!

Trader in timber and forestry that he is, Sr. Gironès has the most minimal conception of polite form but gasps like a dolphin when recounting his woes as a victim—of injustice in general and bureaucratic arbitrariness in particular. A glass house.

Don Rossend Girbal often stumbles over such devious maneuvers to ensure that he doesn't buy or sell his nags that he must leave town to get rid of these headaches by devouring roast or stewed pigeon in the first inn on the road.

Etcetera, etcetera.

This isn't simply a list. It's an unbelievably complex and intricate world.

My father finds these conversations more entertaining than life at home. He's respected because he is a victim and has always lost money. He speaks up for himself—when in the mood—and tries, in his usual timid way, to get his café colleagues to say their piece. Then the debate takes a frenzied, lunatic turn as everyone finds grist for his own particular mill and won't accept that there might be a more interesting, more enthralling perspective than the one each is speaking from.

That's the high point of the day every day. It is, in essence, what people mean when they say they are getting along. Alas!

Gori speaks as forcefully as ever in the café. Red-cheeked and apoplectic, he says, "If this war did anything, it brought about one big change: It introduced short underpants. After centuries of wearing long underpants mankind today can finally breathe. We used to wear wool in winter and cotton in summer, tied around the ankle with ribbons. We wore a warrior's underpants. Now things have shortened and fresh air circulates in spaces that were traditionally closed. This is a huge revolution in the way we dress, an ineffable revolution."

A countryman drinking coffee at the adjacent table whispers in my ear, "This gentleman speaks of revolution. Is he perhaps aware of new developments?"

"No, sir, not at all! Sr. Gori is simply talking about short underpants."

"Oh! So I was right, nothing really new has happened."

10 October. Eugeni d'Ors began his literary career, which was initially in philosophy, by attacking Balmes. Balmes was the country's most important philosopher and it was quite normal for one philosopher to make his mark at the expense of a predecessor. The mechanical round of one generation succeeding another required this to happen. Ors was twenty and stated in a lecture in the Catalan University Congress in the early years of the century that nobody would ever reach the South Pole holding a copy Balmes's *El Criteri*. Ors's boutade won him instant renown and opened a series of doors that have never shut on him—nor is it likely that they ever will.

Although Balmes as a man has his fascinating side, as a philosopher he is of scant interest (his ability to spin out words leads him to write such sentences that by the time you reach the final full stop you have forgotten how they began). He was skilled at combining his studies with the practical interests of his family, who owned a very successful and famous shop for clerical headwear in Vic. I can no more stand visionaries than I can mean merchants with one-track minds. A joint dose of the two constitutes the norm in this country. In the course of his journeys to Paris and Brussels to research philosophy there wasn't a single day when Balmes didn't express an interest in the state of the market for clerical goods, in matters of the style of such hats, their manufacture and price.

I'm not trying—nor will I ever try—to present a vulgar, shopkeeping Balmes: It's simply a rounded portrait.

Catalan literature today has a very attractive quality: It is a literature completely devoid of mannerism. Mannerism palls immediately. Its style is so difficult, so hard, so stiff, and so rigidly written and hedged with obstacles, that everybody writes as best he can ... and make of it what you will! Carner is the man most in control of his trade. Wonderful control. He sometimes tends to be precious and mannered. However, it would be difficult for anyone to imitate him, unless it was superficially. I mean that others will imitate his adjectives and external forms; his extremely complex mental games are out of reach.

Sensuality makes young people miserable. It's a bad business.

I sometimes think of the number of hours I've wasted thinking about fornicating with dreamy, imaginary young women. Nevertheless, you might perhaps draw a single conclusion in this respect: Those hours would probably have been even more wasted if I'd actually spent them fornicating with real, tangible young women.

When one is young, sensuality is inhuman, insoluble, and unbelievably grotesque.

Gori likes to say, "Marriage teaches one a lot. It's a very instructive state of being—an institution at the root of man's evolution. There's nothing like marriage to create chaste, orderly behavior. But there's nothing like leading a chaste, orderly life to help one see the vast quantities of women with positive, outstanding qualities that are quite different from those displayed by one's own wife."

"So nothing one can do about that either, you mean?"

Gori guffaws, scornfully flexes a shoulder, and fails to reply.

For a lazy man to earn his bread in this country (without resorting to a servile trade or being incredibly parasitic) he must be very intelligent.

Machines have progressed in leaps and bounds, and are capable of astonishing movements one never could have imagined. Nonetheless, I don't think that machines, for all their sophistication, will ever imitate the very peculiar, very funny, very endearing way that cats' (especially kittens') ears wriggle.

11 October. I'm sure that people my age, and even slightly older, who have read M. Joseph Joubert, have obtained great insights and experienced even greater pleasure. We should be grateful to Eugeni d'Ors, who urged us and urges us still to read him.

"When we isolate our ability to reason from all other abilities," writes Joubert, "we succeed in making abstract, in the mind's eye, what is most real and even most concrete in the world, for the senses and the heart, everything is then thrown into doubt and can be challenged. What can we say about order and beauty? As far as our ability to reason is concerned, there is only yes or no, or existence or absence, things or non-things."

This too...

"True metaphysics," continues Joubert, "doesn't consist in making what is sensuous abstract, but in making what is abstract sensuous, making apparent what is hidden, imaginable—and if it's possible— what is non-intelligible; rendering intelligible, in a word, what is concealed from our attention."

These texts are crucial for individuals like myself who feel an almost biological incapacity for metaphysics and the keenest sense of the absurd in respect to words, those who believe that attempts to enclose the human spirit within the strictures of formal logic or any other system is grotesque effrontery. I think I shall never forget these texts, however many years go by. My reading of them hit the nail on the head.

What should we do? What is most appropriate and most plausible: *Vox populi vox Dei*, or *vox populi vox stultorum*?

Who could ever know beyond what empiricism tells us? It's one of those problems we imagine we'll have to reflect on throughout life with the expectation that we will never be any the wiser. After a lifetime's meditation, one dies and the waters are as murky as ever.

The prime virtue one needs in order to devote oneself to literature—to the novel, for example—is candor, naïveté. Writers are interested in other people's business and attempt to understand people and inquire after others. Could anything be more childish or puerile?

A café conversation.

"What do you mean by an important funeral—in Palafrugell?" I hear a man ask, looking a tad sarcastic.

"An important funeral is one with seventy people in attendance in order to give the cortege weight and significance."

"And who might these seventy people be whose presence lends importance to a funeral?"

"They are the seventy individuals who own clothes fit for attending a funeral."

12 October. I sometimes reflect on the city of Figueres. It is a place where I would like to live—or at least one where I think I could live comfortably.

I got to know the town several years ago. I first went there at the age of ten to take a high-school entrance examination. I returned the year after for the first-year examinations. This examination nightmare didn't succeed in stifling the pleasant impact the city had on me. The old Franciscan monastery refurbished into the General and Technical High School didn't tarnish the bright, cheerful impression it made.

In recent years, I have occasionally returned and my first impression has held firm.

Figueres was the reason for my first discovery of the world; my entry into its dynamic flow happened there. To reach the city I had to take my first real train, the "big" train, as it was then called. It was the first urban center I'd ever seen. The Rambla was the first constructed road I ever laid my eyes on. Hotel París, the first hotel life offered me. The Red Restaurant on the Rambla was the first restaurant I ate in. They served me grilled red mullet with a touch of garlic and parsley that I thought magnificent. I sipped my first non-homebrewed coffee in the cafés of Figueres—hardly a trivial matter for a man who subsequently has been such a habitué of cafés. The first bookshop I ever entered was the Canet Bookshop in Figueres. At the time it was located at the top of the Rambla, on the corner of Castle Hill. It was a small place, tucked away, but I was so happy there. Before going to Figueres I'd seen the occasional solitary soldier at a loose end, and there I saw a whole battalion march past; I'd never before seen the military in its full glory and I must say, en passant, that it didn't have the impact on me I thought it would. Before going to Figueres, I knew what a sardana was, but until I heard one played on the Rambla I didn't realize how delightful they were. Before going to Figueres, I knew what grammar was, more or less—perhaps less rather than more—but there I discovered how painful grammar could be after being questioned by a trio of solemn dolts at the General and Technical High School. All this is extremely significant as far as I'm concerned, because it forms part of the deep mesh of my life—of the skein of dreams and realities constituting my inner life.

Until my first trip to Figueres, I had a single idea about life; afterward, the world seemed infinitely more complex. Life comprises a succession of panoramas viewed from different perspectives. The succession is sometimes on the ascendant: Each new panorama is viewed from a much higher level that allows one to see even farther. My first slightly vaster vision of life came from the vantage point of the Rambla in Figueres. It's not anything one would call profound or serious, but it has a certain distinction. At least I think so.

I've heard it said that one is born lucky or unlucky. I'm not sure.

Anyway, this business of luck seems curious and intangible. I think our minds are formed by the milieus we experience in the decisive years of our adolescence. It is possible that the admiration I feel for everything bourgeois, clean, and free, that the belief I hold in some kind of justice, well-being, and civilized dialogue is partly because of the way I entered life along the Rambla in Figueres.

Bright and cheerful Figueres is a flourishing center of agriculture and commerce, human activities of the first order. It is a typical city with a weekly market; but just as this class of city tends to be sordid and run-down, Figueres is open, clean, and pleasant. The closeness of the frontier imparts a spirit of tolerance to the city. The frontier isn't a boundary; it is a large, open window.

I personally enjoy city milieus that have the spirit Figueres embodies. I feel at ease there. I think this is a city, properly speaking, what one should call a city. Denser, more extensive concentrations of humans may exist . . . but without the same degree of urbanity. Figueres is a small, yet fully rounded city. And if it is enchanting because it is fully rounded, it is all the more so because it is small. Large cities are tiring, stressful, uncomfortable, pretentious, and grandiose; they tend to give a false idea of life. Small cities seem more made-to-measure for ordinary mortals, more advantageous for work and leisure, and offer a life that is more direct. One doesn't waste so much time, though naturally one doesn't earn so much money.

When I go to Figueres, I stroll along the Rambla and the streets. The city is clean and hospitable. I go to see the plain of the High Ampurdan from Castle Hill. A magnificent sight: an incomparable, entrancing, beautiful landscape. What wondrous sky, sea, and land! Gray days perfect that panorama to an exquisite, ineffable degree. The breeze from the north brings bright diamantine precision. It is a landscape that makes you proud to be a part of this country. Afterwards, back in the city center, I talk to people. The inhabitants of Figueres speak naturally. They don't raise their voices, or pose, or give themselves airs; they are friendly, warm, and relaxed. Courteous people. Time there passes slowly and peacefully. What else could one ask for?

14 October. Our generation—in Catalonia—avidly read the work of Pío Baroja. When I was seventeen, I devoured it and I can say I know every word. It influenced all of us—and most visibly the prose of Josep Maria de Sagarra. This writer, whose poetry has such a distinct, individual voice, writes a prose that is Barojan to its marrow. The careless, unkempt feel of Baroja's style fits perfectly with Sagarra's nonchalance.

Baroja has surely written the best character portraits and, no doubt, the best landscapes in the Castilian language. He is a highly sensitive realist, acutely so when it comes to shades of gray. His novels have very little in the way of plot, and people who read for the shock and high emotion of melodrama will be disappointed. However, Spanish contemporary life is wonderfully portrayed in his novels. In this sense, his work characterizes the human comedy caught at a particular moment. His style, which is so negligent, adheres wonderfully to reality—much more than Galdós's that is plastered with artistic and literary stucco. Baroja writes badly, his style is slack, say the neoclassicists. Of course he does! All writers who attend more to form than content, who falsify reality, who believe literature is a formalistic, rhetorical art, who focus entirely on the construction of their sentences say the same. These ideas of elegant literature ruled for centuries. Today they aren't valued even in France, the most academy-ruled country in the world. In this sense, Baroja follows the literary tendency of our time, a writer in tune with European literary sensibility.

Baroja's defect derives from his careless use of adjectives. He apportions and places them at random—throws them out like a donkey farts.

The vision of Spanish life Baroja has created is a depressing one: bitterness, pessimism, and permanent (often justifiably so) dissatisfaction, a tone of ascetic transcendence. He triggers huge revulsion in his young readers—to my mind, a healthy, sane revulsion. Baroja never placates one with affectations, fictions, window dressing, or half measures. Everything is as it is—bitter, cutting, and actual.

In the course of his work, Baroja has expounded many ideas and points of view. He has been much maligned, insulted, and socially marginalized. If we are to be honest, Baroja has the ideas of the average European. In terms of religion, science, art, social life, and human relations he professes ideas defended by millions and millions. The revulsion prompted by his vision of Spain derives precisely from the fact that Baroja looks at Spain through the eyes of an average European. There are people who like Baroja's work but don't grasp this aspect of it clearly. They will in time. Rather, it will become crystal clear in a number of years. Baroja is a liberal, tolerant, civilized man.

My sense is that when a Basque displays intolerance and force he becomes quintessentially Castilian. When, conversely, his temperament and education incline him to be tolerant and friendly, he becomes absolutely Central European.

Those of us who constitute the young generation of Catalans really appreciate these qualities in Baroja.

15 October. Today I went to the funeral of old Trill the locksmith, a lifelong neighbor of ours. He was a small, nervy man, with black to iron-dark skin always covered in oil, a man fond of backwoods behavior. He drank huge amounts of wine and his liver must have been pickled in alcohol. For sixty-seven years, as soon as spring arrived and the carnations flowered, with a nervous spring in his step, out of sight of his wife, he'd present young women with carnations. He was tarred by the brush of life's madness; he enjoyed pure chaos: taverns, frantic dancing, carnival, disguises, gossiping, ridiculing Carlists, always at the ready to kill one neighbor or another. He behaved well towards others, not—I suspect—because he liked to but because he craved an audience. He sometimes played very annoying pranks. He was grotesque.

With Trill's death, the Palafrugell carnival has lost an important element.

His eldest, downcast son, Telm, presided over the funeral, his hat slung over the back of his neck. Lots of people came.

As I walked back from the cemetery I thought how people change in these parts, according to whether they wear a hat or not. They seem different.

16 October. Rain. Three o'clock and it's still raining. The Ampurdan in the rain is a delight. I couldn't wish for anything more: I love to watch the rain falling, particularly a fine rain, which seems to fall absent-mindedly—a drizzle that doesn't force you to stay inside. This kind of rain—not common in this country, which tends more often toward violent, sudden downpours—often encourages me to go for a walk outside town. In dry, ossified, parched countries like ours you begin to glimpse—when it rains—the voluptuous way in which soil, trees, and plants celebrate. On days like this I prefer to take the road to Sant Sebastià, one of the most solitary and beautiful in these parts. Past En Casaca bridge you start smelling the strong, bewitching perfume of pine.

Four or five years ago I would walk up as far as Pasteres carrying my pencil and pad. I'd sit on a rock and try to describe a tree or the colors in the sky. I was in such a state of astonishment that if I bumped into someone on my way back without having written a word—which was usually the case—I would turn a bright red. It was like the ridiculous return of a hunter who hasn't made a single kill.

In the evening I join the café conversation at the Fraternal Center with my friends. I meet up with Coromina, Lluís Medir, Enric Frigola, Tomàs Gallart, Gori, Almeda, Ganiguer. They are talking about Palafrugell. In other words, it is time yet again to speak ill of Palafrugell. In turn we bemoan how the place has no social life, nobody is trying to excel; on the contrary, people strive to be bland, to vanish into complete anonymity and irresponsibility.

Coromina, who isn't from Palafrugell (he's from La Bisbal), listens in silence, and as his boredom at our unanimity escalates, he says, "That is all very well…but what about Don Joan Miquel? I don't think he is at all ordinary or commonplace. And he's hardly irresponsible. And as for anonymity…"

Nobody says a word. Everyone looks surprised and hugely shame-faced.

Unamuno gave a (political) lecture on the soul in the Madrid Athenaeum. What a crazy, nonsensical man and country!

18 October, Friday. Influenza is causing terrible devastation. Our family has had to split up to attend all the funerals. Marian de Linares's was held in La Bisbal. In Palafrugell, an eighteen-year-old girl's (a lovely child) in the S. family. I went to La Bisbal.

The crying could be heard from the street. Sobbing in houses and on stairways. A striking spectacle that contrasts with people's silent mood—a mood that dips and sinks the second they hear that sobbing. These expressions of grief transform everything, even the countryside. When people hear sobbing, they adopt the expressions of people who are unfailingly good. Suddenly a man who had remained still, stiff, and dry-eyed shifts nervously and begins shedding tears. Which is preferable: to barricade oneself in icy indifference and fatalism, or to lapse into lachrymose ululations? When people cry, do they suffer? Those who don't cry, suffer less.

The funeral of Sr. Linares was a highly emotional affair.

The small train takes us home in the evening, in the dim, murky carriage light. The engine sputters despairingly and sparks fly up from the chimney. The train is full. People sit in subdued silence. Those coming from market imitate those who've been to the funeral. If one imagines a train full of thinkers, this would be it. The brims of our hats cast shadows over our faces. What are we thinking? Nothing at all, I expect. The drama derives from the fact that there is so much here we cannot understand—so much that it renders the mechanics of our minds quite useless.

20 October, Sunday. A wonderfully radiant morning. Long, monumental Roman columns of clouds against a crisp, blue sky. The whiteness of the houses has a childish tone and the whitewash seems equally innocent. People walk along the sunny carrer de Cavallers in their Sunday best, stiff-backed and close-shaven, a humorous glint in their eyes.

I go to eleven o'clock mass. Most of the people listening seem rather aloof. It is the mass for the rich. The man who's not smirking at his shiny shoes glances at the ceiling, the face of the lady next to him, his fingernails, or the rays the color of crystallized fruit beaming down from the rose window. Showing off is part of our Sunday agenda—like rice and fish followed by cream-filled puff pastry for Sunday lunch. Mossèn Bosch, the parish priest, a wily peasant, cuts a Romanesque figure in the pulpit. He delivers a tedious sermon, devoid of rhetoric or frantic gestures, in the sad, limp style of someone paying a dutiful visit. He speaks so quietly, in such gray, dense prose, that nobody understands a word, but this is also part of our Sunday agenda.

I spent most of the afternoon in Calella with Tomàs Gallart and Joan B. Coromina. We walk back in the dark, in the moonlight, with little appetite for argument. It is a deeply silent night. Not a leaf rustles. There is an intense aroma of fennel in the air. The moonlight turns honey yellow against the deep green of the pines. Our steps boom strangely on the empty road. We hear the town's church bells solemnly strike eight in the distance. The stillness of things among the patches of moonlight invites meditation; all is quiet, dreamlike, and eerie.

Later I go to the cinema. Suddenly—when I'm half asleep—I hear the pianist playing a Bach aria followed by a Mendelssohn drinking song, Schumann's Rêverie and Beethoven's Romance in F Major. I wait for people to react: None do. Perhaps everybody is asleep—I wonder. I'm surprised there hasn't been a single reaction. I ask the usher about the pianist and he says Sr. Recolons (the cinema's owner) has hired a new pianist, who apparently comes from Argentina; his name is Roldós and he was in fact born locally. On my way out, I introduce myself. My initial impression is that Roldós is a poor, shy, vaguely bohemian character and down on his luck.

Second supper in the early hours. Sundays like today, when one performs every cartoon cameo in the book, are more exhausting than felling trees from dawn to dusk.

21 October. J. B. Coromina returns from Girona in the late afternoon and tells us about Massó the architect who sports a beard, Palol the

poet, and other friends from there. Coromina has a soft spot for
Massó, who is renowned for his intellect, though I've always wondered why he has such poor taste as an architect. Can you imagine the
farmhouse Massó would build if he were asked to design one? I don't
deny that intelligence and good taste can't coexist in the same person.
One experiences that day in and day out, and to an extent, it must be
a characteristic of modern man. Insofar as I understand these things,
I think (intuitively, of course) that man in ancient times, to judge
from his works, didn't suffer so violently from such dislocations. I
mean that he was more at one with himself.

Coromina shows me various reproductions of antique sculpture in
the School of Arts. I can think of nothing in the world that fascinates
me more than the Venus of Cyrene. I am sorry, but it's the truth. Our
friend tells us about Maillol, who recently visited Girona. In his view,
Maillol's work can stand close comparison with some of those antique
stones. I'm not so sure... Maillol sculpts small figures because he's
imitating beauty in real life. The Greeks stylized, lengthened, and idealized. To convince when blurring the contours of reality one must
know how to draw really well. That doesn't mean I don't agree that
Maillol isn't one of the greatest—living—geniuses in these parts.

Nighttime—which is often short on advice—leads us toward the residence of the young ladies in town, to Maison Tellier. As we are important people—Sr. Girbal is accompanying us—we enter through a
secret back door. We go into the dining room with a table in the center, six or seven chairs against the walls, and an electric bulb in the
ceiling emitting a dim, flickering light. A portrait photograph of the
proprietor hangs on the wall—a small, fat man, mustache protected
by a nighttime sheath, hair neatly combed, glittering with jewels, extremely constrained in his suit, and beneath the cuffs of his baggy
trousers are shoes with mother-of-pearl buttons that have been re-
touched by the photographer and look ghastly. The fine fellow is leaning his elbow on a chipped, pseudo-classical column contemplating
the outside world with an energetic and rather paternally benign air.

As the establishment was without customers, we went straight into the drawing room. The drawing room! The girls were huddled around the brazier, which was almost out. One coughed; another had lost her voice; the third had a sinister, alcoholic rasp. I can't imagine anything sadder, more wretched, colder, more gross, gaunt, gutless, shabby, crude, cruel, and unappetizing than one of these small-town dives for vice and pleasure. Good heavens! There is no place more likely to induce complete, absolute frigidity. Perhaps the images these establishments spawn are what contribute most directly to the fact that people in this country never get beyond the most violent, spectacularly base displays of sensuality and never aspire to any form of human tenderness. One day or another, all men have had to pass through legs like sticks or hams stuffed in laddered or loose black stockings, through anatomical forms the memory of which produces dread or terror, remorse or shame, involving us in all kinds of hypocrisy. These astonishing establishments keep the tradition of Senecan stoicism alive and strong across the Peninsula.

22 October. A misty day. I walk up as far as Sant Sebastià. In the deep silence, everything is dripping. I reach the Ermitans fountain hanging over the sea. A choppy sea—*fair she blows*. The sea churns and growls. Pine trees drip. A sticky sheen coats the granite coast. Great black-backed gulls glide drowsily on the heavy air. Cliff-climbing mists swirl wondrously up from the sea. The occasional eddy surges, rolls over; others flatten out on the vertical rock face as if driven by a desire to assume a fixed shape. After a while, however, I find such close contact with the pitiless weather exhausting and the overbearing geology enervating. The solitudes of Sant Sebastià almost seem like a sickness. On my return, the golden (so soft) hue of the vines is the marvelous plum color of slightly watery wine (it glows!).

Implacable, influenza continues to kill people. I have had to attend several funerals over the last few days, which naturally begins to harden one's emotional responses to death—real, genuine feelings turn into a kind of administrative routine. Our feelings are always affected by too little or too much—and shift indecently. If only for this reason it would be better if this shocking pathology ended—and the flu stopped killing people.

23 October. A stroll with Coromina along the old road to Begur, reading Francesc Pujols. (His *General Concept...* is just out). When I read the book it had a strange, almost revelatory impact I now find impossible to pin down. Coromina underlines aspects that strike me as highly original and interest me greatly. However, is Pujols an author to read when out for a stroll? I think not—even though the book is printed in such miniscule letters that they require natural light.

We also speak, at length, about Josep Ferrer. My friend thinks Ferrer's writing is that of a rationalist. I think quite the contrary. I've never known anyone who was deeply sensual—as Ferrer was—to be a rationalist. Rationalists tend to be vegetarian, abstemious, moderate in their habits, and poor in their health. But I am alarmed by our lack of agreement. How is it possible for two men from this country, who have read almost the same books and had an identical education, who have seen the same things and ingested the same food, to think so differently about a man and a recent book?

At one point in our dialogue, Coromina says that I have a primitivist vein and perhaps see things simplistically, in a very one-sided, unsubtle manner. With the natural diplomacy of a timid man, he adds that my powers of expression are confused and ineffective, that they lack the means to disentangle an issue and give it its necessary profile and relief—and that this is most visible when I try to abandon my natural tendency to be simple and schematic. I completely agree with what Coromina says—and not for the sake of being agreeable but genuinely, without resentment. But so what? My passion for writing is intense. In truth, it's the *only* thing I think about.

Once we are past Esclanyà, it's time to retrace our steps. It starts raining. We take shelter in a country laborer's cottage inhabited by people we don't know. A dirty-faced little boy stands and stares at us, a finger stuck up a nostril; a little girl, whose face is even dirtier, stands still, lifting her skirt slightly. The adults give us a frosty, silent reception. We soon sense that we are annoying the good folk. We arrive back in town, soaked and half asleep.

In the evening, a café conversation in the Fraternal Center. Clouds of smoke, a stench of uric acid, the smell of the Latin race, stale and damp. A feeling of unease. Something isn't quite right. Then suddenly someone recalls—I can't remember whom—the epitaph to Mazzini that Carducci wrote. I copied it down. It says: *L'uomo che tutto sacrificò, che amò tanto e molto compatì, e non odiò mai.* When I hear these words, I regain my patience. The café doesn't seem quite so sordid or the people so dour. At certain times—and this is one of them—such a style of writing does make an impact. One could say that this kind of literature—and thus this epitaph—is gratuitous. So what? At certain specific times, it makes a huge, undeniable impact.

It has been raining for days. I enjoy lying in bed and listening to the water stream off the roof into the tank in the garden—it's as soporific as a sleeping aid.

26 October. A noisy—regrettable—row with my mother because I went to bed too late. As a result of this miserable episode I decide it is a categorical error not to earn one's living at the age of twenty-one. How else to avoid these emotional crises that are so damaging? I decide to reflect seriously, day and night, and to try to resolve the issue of my independence as quickly as I can.

To clear my head, I walk up to Sant Sebastià in the early afternoon with Roldós the pianist. In this country, autumn is a real joy. It is the best, and by far the most delightful, season of the year. It is a time to go out and walk, awestruck by the country's magnificent landscape. It is neither cold nor hot. The air feels alive. Objects are light and airy.

The landscape is serene and calm. Within that calm, everything has a genuine presence and makes its mark. Dreamy, languid smoke spirals from the chimneys of farmers' cottages. When one looks down from Pasteres, the sea at twilight is like a transparent pane of glass brushed by a remote inner light: blue, an evanescent blue with a subtle, inspired grace. As evening descends, the hermitage radiates peace and solitude. The subdued breeze blows in concert with that building's quiet pulse. The lighthouse switches on, a moment of dazzling illumination that turns into a blank, steady spin. The diffuse light transforms the glass into viscous tissue—like the eyes of an octopus. Illumined by the gyrating light, the sea swells, remote and dreamy—a mystery one will never solve. In the distance, the tiny lights of Palafrugell burn like minute will-o'-the-wisps, languidly but enough to save them from being snuffed out.

In the course of our stroll, I get the impression that Roldós is an affable, easygoing individual. It must be the Buenos Aires character that he maintains despite the exhaustion of life. He refuses to take anything seriously and jokes about everything—even his own impoverished state. It is a stance that palls in the end, but clearly it is a stance as valid as any other.

All the same I am grateful to him. I think it shows real courage for a cinema pianist to play two or three Bach fugues or several pages of Beethoven, braving his audience's yawns. This act itself is a healthy jolt to sterile, small-town life.

27 October. Excursion to the farmhouse that Enric and Octavi, the Frigola brothers, own in the Calonge mountains. We leave in a trap before nine. What bliss! Everything is serene and bright, clean, crisp, and pure in the radiant air. The late-risers among us always run the same risk, the risk that our discovery of the morning will make us seem foolish. Coromina is part of the outing.

The young horse canters along at a lively rate. Nothing seen through the arch of a trap is ugly. The very act of traveling in a trap constantly invites you—if you're simply asleep—to sense the beauty of things. I wonder, why is the arch the architectural form most likely to magnify the human instinct for beauty? Does this phenomenon derive from the limitations the arch imposes?

We cross Palamós: a gust of southwesterly wind perfumed by stripped cork. The fragrance of hereabouts.

Calonge. The town is self-absorbed, secluded, silent, and apparently secretive. I feel as if I am at home. This is the homeland of one side of my family. Sa Bardissa. I remember Srta. Ponjoan, a girl I met in the Calonge fiestas of my adolescence: wonderfully young, firm, svelte, fair flesh.

The Frigolas' farmstead occupies an elevated position. From the threshing floor one enjoys a great vista to the east and the large expanse of the sea. The farmstead is surrounded by cork oaks and olive trees and, most immediately, by faded grainy-colored terraces—like blotches made on a sheet of paper by a young child. Goats and cows. Southern smells, dry, strongly scented herbs. From this vantage point, Palamós is a geometrically perfect projection of a town. A thing of beauty. The geometry of towns, which generally strikes one as horrendous up close, profits when seen panoramically.

Lunch is abundant, succulent, far too heavy for my taste, and endless. With his pale brow, aquiline nose, beady partridge eyes, and skinny neck, Coromina never shuts up. He rattles off a stream of facetious jokes, including one about a Girona carpenter who is convinced of the importance of his trade and—revealing its secrets—likes to repeat: "With four scraps of timber I could make you a right royal bed."

We spend almost all afternoon seated around the table, watching daylight slowly fade from the windows, like an eyelid closing.

We start our return journey, half sunk in a state of unconsciousness. Our hands are shaking slightly. As usual, in this country at this time of day, one feels the lack of generous, pleasant female company. It is wearying to be surrounded solely by men. The result is that it all goes badly wrong and tails off into obscene songs and gross behavior. The songs sound terrible. The rendering of "The Monk's Cord" is tuneless and dreary. Enric Frigola, who is the steadiest of us all, keeps the trap on the right path. We make rapid progress. We cross with the train on the Vall-llobrega plain. Burning wood, the engine throws out sparks like an angry dragon. A sickle moon emerges and bathes the ground in a cold, metallic green. The beams of the lighthouse appear in the arch of the trap. By day, the whiteness of the hermitage, by night this light: I find both beautiful.

It all ends well—in bed.

29 October. In Calonge the other day, the blood rushed to my cheeks as I remembered the girls from the previous year. This was during their main fiestas. We walked from Palafrugell to Calonge (thirteen to fourteen kilometers). Ganiguer was with us. Early in the night we stumbled across a group of splendid girls—particularly Srta. Ponjoan. A marvelous creature, with a crimson seashell tone to her firm flesh! I felt a ravaging frenzy. Fortunately I met dry, toothless, humble Aunt Marieta washing glasses in the kitchen of a café, a cold shower for my heady emotions. We walked back in the early hours, grim-faced. Occasionally I had to carry Ganiguer whose skinful was making him totter.

Coromina is shy. He looks at a girl . . . and that's the end of it! Really, nine and a half out of ten times, he will never make a move. But perhaps he isn't as shy as I am. I've never noticed anyone looking at me. The advantage of having a deadpan face is that it stops you from acting the fool, thus sparing a lot of heartache.

I'm reading *General Concept* . . . by Francesc Pujols. It is quite brilliant and much of it is very new, as far as I am concerned. It casts me into a sea of confusion. I find out things I didn't know. "Southerners," writes Pujols, "are legendary; northerners, hypothetical." I find many of the assertions too bewildering and the book itself too fascinating for me to come to any tangible conclusions.

His style is less impressive—which doesn't mean it isn't absorbing—but all those long, flowing, interminable, clause-laden sentences! I've heard it said that Pujols takes his form of expression from the music of Wagner. I think its precedents are more to be found in the style of what is called sacred oratory. *The Catalan Tradition*, by Bishop Torras i Bages, is written in the same style, though with less affectation. Pujols prefers things that are anachronistic, slightly dog-eared, and weary. Resolution: to get to know and become acquainted with Pujols, come what may.

I owe T. G. twenty-five pesetas. That's too much.

1 November. All Saints'. Friday. Bofill (Gori), Mata (a bartender in Llafranc), Nuts (a beachcomber), and I take our guns up to Can Vidal de Sant Climent, via Can Torró. We catch the early-morning train and alight in Sant Climent station. There is frost on the ground and blue puffs of breath precede us. Nuts is very striking: He is small, fat, and hairy, with a black sash over his belly and a huge cap, now on a slant, like a cloud seen from the side. He looks like a throwback to the villains of the civil war.

Sr. Torró comes out and gives us a warm, noisy welcome. He is followed by his dogs that ferret in the clumps of wet grass. He is carrying two guns. We go hunting along the gully in front of his house.

It is the first time I've ever been hunting. At most I've fired a pistol once or twice in my life. Sr. Torró hands me his spare rifle, a single-barrel, and a couple of cartridges. They tell me to wait at the ready on a small track. The hunters disperse. The dogs bark. After a while I see a rabbit running along the track towards me. I hurriedly put the gun to my cheek, shut an eye to get a better aim, and shoot. The bang is horrendous and, for a moment, I see stars. The butt rebounding against my shoulder throws me into a terrible dither. Not really knowing what I am doing, I fling the gun away. The weapon makes a strange noise as it falls into a clump of brambles—as if something has cracked. I hear loud guffaws go up from different parts of the gully. Bofill, Torró, Mata, and Nuts are laughing and holding their bellies in a display of wild, primitive glee. I am a dismal failure as a hunter. I retrieve the gun, which I respectfully return to its owner. No, I don't think I am a man fated to fire bullets.

We go into Can Torró. It is a very secluded farmhouse. From the front, one can see the gully stretching out, covered in brambles and undergrowth. Inside, we find a young lady, an older lady, a phonograph with a trumpet, and tomes from the era of the University of Cervera. I think Sr. Torró looks as rustic as any tenant farmer. He is a man for fairs and markets, pro-German out of a wish to revenge 1808, and seemingly not without money. His ideal is spending summer in Llafranc. He is the kind of person who, when introduced to someone, asks "So where do you like to spend your summer?" in order to place that individual properly.

Sr. Torró gives a detailed analysis, from every possible perspective, of why I failed as a hunter. We enjoy ourselves for a while, aided and abetted by several glasses of rather sharp wine.

Then we set out for the Vidal farmhouse, which we reach after a very long hike. It is a solitary place halfway up a mountain. We are welcomed on the doorstep by Sra. Bofill (Donya Carme), a sickly, sallow, exhausted woman with sunken eyes, and her mother, Donya Consuelo, who is small, fat, garrulous, and rather affected. After the usual pleasantries, we go into the dining room and sit down around the table. Gori solemnly asks the usual question, rather vehemently, "What's for lunch?"

It turns out that there are snails à la vinaigrette and roast wild rabbit with aioli. It is a prospect that couldn't be bettered. A big fire is burning in the dining-room hearth, enormously welcome after our walk through the wet woods. Gori shows Nuts the way to the kitchen and the cellar—the final touch.

Vast quantities of snails, in spicy sauce, with hot capsicum, whet our appetites. We swallow three at a time with sprigs of heather. We eat like wolves. We drink wine from wineskins. Nuts makes frequent visits to the cellar. The dogs prowl hungrily around the table. "What's the matter, Secretary?" asks Mata, stroking a dog's head. We get incredibly sodden. The least gesture, the slightest word reveals what narrow personalities these men have, how completely closed and limited they are. At a certain moment the ladies decide it would be wise to withdraw. Everyone finds that quite natural. It seems to be the old local custom: the men in one corner and the women in another. "That way everything is much simpler," remarks Bofill, a string of snails across his palm. After they withdraw, everything reaches a predictable pitch. The consumption of aioli increases and the wine simply flows.

Bofill is beaming, in his element. He is tall, red-faced, noisy, larger-than-life, incredibly obvious, self-satisfied, invulnerable to red wine, and inured to all that is unpleasant in life. He is a clear-eyed individualist, a complete fatalist, and reacts to things with great bursts of laughter. "Make the most of the moment," he likes to say, "all else is unsure, hypothetical, unpredictable."

Everything encourages us to stay put and not budge from the dining room. The fire glows brightly on our faces. The farmhouse nurtures meditative moments; it's rather smothered by the mountains. It has few views. It is a farmhouse in the forest—built for people who inhabit gullies and streambeds. The bedrooms—which we visited on our arrival—contain huge, very high double beds, with mattresses stuffed with maize and covered in thick bedclothes. This guarantees a dignified exit from the dining room—a comfortable retreat.

On the surface, Mata seems to be a cynic, but the more I deal with him, the more I see that his deepest convictions are related to the claims of his family and clan interests. He is a notorious good-for-nothing, all forelock and side-whiskers, a toothpick behind his ear, a tireless player of truco—a card game he introduced locally—and a rabbit hunter who melts like a lump of sugar in the presence of his wife.

Mata tells us about the lives of the permanent residents of Llafranc. Canadell has two women who desire him; Joan de Sant Feliu likes the sound of his own bombastic voice and has children by three different women as if he were a millionaire. Despite this torrent of family feelings, when he can't decide where to bed down, he stretches out in a niche in the old cemetery. Pinyana is a former cork cutter, lazy, lying, and penniless; he is manic about wearing ironed shirts, celluloid collars, and starched cuffs. To earn people's trust—he will often say—one must dress well. Tinyola is a very elemental anarchist intellectual and was a friend of Ferrer Guàrdia; he has a vicious temper soon calmed by a wineskin. One-armed Serviano belongs to the smart Majorcan smuggler set. Martí, the Sant Sebastià hermit, is a secretive, mysterious fellow, an enigma. Gori finds this whole world—

out of Gorki—amusing, justified, and in the end, necessary. I find it gross, superfluous, and distinctly unappealing.

Midafternoon, Sr. Barceló, the Bisbal schoolteacher, appears with a group of his pupils of both sexes in a most welcome, unexpected visit. I've drunk one glass too many and prudence tells me to keep a strategic silence. The innocent boys and girls take fright when they see the red glow on our cheeks. Fortunately, the ladies of the Vidal farmstead find an easy solution to the problem. At nine o'clock, Nuts gets his orders: No more visits to the cellar.

2 November. In the afternoon Mata, Nuts, and I walk down from Can Vidal along the path to Can Janoher. As we walk along, Nuts, who is wearing magnificent beribboned espadrilles, velvet trousers, a loose black sash, a red-lined waistcoat, and a huge cap above his stubbly face, tells us he will feel deeply nostalgic for these hours spent in Can Vidal. Yesterday was one of the happiest days of his life. His enthusiasm for wine is so keen and lively he doesn't want to die before quaffing at least two gallons of young wine in a single drinking session. It can't be said he did that today; he almost made it, fifteen pints. On the other hand, lunch was just right: Nuts would have ordered exactly the same from the kitchen if he'd had the opportunity.

Snails play a big role in his conception of the world. They are the touchstone by which he judges people. Pau is a fifty snailer. Pere, a hundred-and-fiftier. Berenguer, two hundreder. His friendships oscillate around the fifty-snail mark. Those who don't make that benchmark belong to a world of weaklings—a kind of limbo without fire or light, embers or smoke.

"How many did you eat yesterday, Nuts?" I ask.

"Three hundred. I am a three-hundreder, though far be it from me to say so."

"Who is the most important man you have ever met?"

"Granddad Rovira, the man who hires out horse and traps, nicknamed En Berruga, is a one-hundred-and-fiftier."

"Have you seen him eat that number?"

"Naturally."

When we reach the made-up road, Nuts bids us farewell. This comes as a surprise. He looks pale and exhausted.

"So you're leaving us?" Mata asks him, gravely.

"Yes. I am. I'm beginning to feel nostalgic. You make me think about what I've missed out on in life and I could do without that. I feel sad."

"And where do you think you'll go?"

"I don't know... I'll have to look around."

We watch him walk up the road as if he's wandering at random, with no firm goal in mind. After walking for a time he suddenly swings around and bellows, "I am a three-hundred snailer, I hope you got that!"

Three hundred yards on the road straightens and his body resembles a black beetle. Then we lose sight of him.

3 November, Sunday. Spent with friends. Piera the tailor, Bonany, etcetera. I walk up to Sant Sebastià. A beautiful afternoon. The sinuous ribbon of road draws the loveliest afternoon light. I hear someone chopping wood in the distance. A donkey brays in a remote spot. A black-and-white magpie jumps over the green alfalfa. When I walk past Ros, I think, as I always do: I wish I owned Ros, the vineyard and the pinewood. By the hermitage, total solitude. Opposite Calella, boats—bobbing like walnuts—fish for squid. Two brigs appear on the Italian horizon, driven by a northeasterly wind. The sea is purple-edged beneath the hermitage terrace. Far out at sea, opposite Tamariu, another sailing ship is returning. A crabbing boat sails slowly by Cape Begur. An empty steamer passes arrogantly by, very close to land, spitting large mouthfuls of water overboard in fits and starts—like a dog barking. The water on the horizon turns deep violet; the water by the strip of land darkens. We circle the hermitage, marveling, awestruck. The afternoon seems in limbo, abstracted from time—a creation of the mind. If I could imagine or create another world, it would be a world like this.

We return at dusk. The road is thronged by the shadows of hunters and mushroom pickers; we hear the hum of invisible people conversing. As I stand on En Casaca bridge, I remember the frog that sang there in summer. The evening dissolves into a delicate gauze, a misty haze floating and shimmering above the land. The sky is very clear and the starlight cold and metallic.

A night at the cinema. *Frou-Frou*, with Francesca Bertini, Gustavo Serena, and the usual Italian suspects. A very ordinary plot played by people who spend hours and hours posing for their portraits—who would like to pose, night and day, indefinitely. Bewildering, enthusiastic cries of admiration go up from the audience when a luxurious set or an elegant dress puts in an appearance.

As we leave the cinema, Roldós plays a Schumann score for Coromina, Lluís Medir, and me. Schumann never got a note wrong. He is as round as an apple. Or an almond. Though slightly sweet, with a circumference that's ever so, ever so slightly too perfect. Schumann seems two-dimensional. Chopin, three.

4 November. Feeling idle, unable to devote a moment to my textbooks, rather bored by café conversation, I go for an afternoon stroll. I walk along the road to Llafranc. At this time of year, the plain of Santa Margarida is simply beautiful. I can't walk by the fence around Can Vehí without remembering the scent of the roses of Sant Ponç. Llafranc is so deserted it seems skeletal. You sometimes see a gaunt figure taking a stroll, or a hesitant cat or dog, on the other side of the beach. Everything reinforces the effect. Seagulls flap their wings near the beach, above the green sea. They emit cries now and then that sound almost human. As dusk approaches, the contours of the mountains in the west glow with an archaic light. I wrote: an archaic light. What *is* an archaic light? I mean a light from an antique painting, the luminosity that remains on a painting when it's engrained with centuries-old layers of dust and grime. Like a light that passes through thick, yellow glass. To the west—Maragall's warm, gentle west—the vineyards in the foreground are blood-red. The crab fishers returning to Portbò in Calella, helped by a blustery tailwind. When I gaze at the pine trees by the side of the sea it makes me think of the curves, the idiosyncratic, unmistakable arabesques painted by Joaquim Sunyer. A Gypsy woman stands under a streetlamp by the entrance to town cradling a half-naked child: The child opens her eyes wide, too wide—perhaps from the cold. These eyes also make me think of eyes painted by Joaquim Sunyer.

At night in bed, I return to Plato's *Dialogues*. How wonderful! In the early hours, fifty gross, crazy roosters are screeching, but I can't switch off the light. The power of suggestion is so strong, so fascinating I sometimes think that it's inevitable I will encounter Socrates in the street one day. I don't think this could happen with any other figure in the history of culture. How is it possible to suggest so many things with so few words, in such an apparently simple fashion?

5 November. Coromina has purchased a motorcycle—one of the first to be ridden in the country. He is beaming and—as one would expect—has become an ardent champion of motorcycles. He has bought a helmet, goggles, and some flashy gloves. He is almost scary.

Today he made me try out the attractions of his new toy, so I straddled the rear seat—if it can be called a seat. We sped along the Bisbal-Pals-Begur-Palafrugell circuit. Hellish roads that Coromina climbed cheerfully.

The machine flies and that sensation of flying would feel even more real if it weren't for the hugely uncomfortable seat. The ridges in the road resonate on my posterior through a merciless iron mesh separated from my flesh by a single, stupid cushion that has no substance or guts. But I act bravehearted. I have no choice.

Now and then, he turns around slightly and says, "Are you all right? We're going seventy an hour."

"I am fine. My backside's hurting a lot, I'm not sure I can stand much more, but I think it's a wonderful experience."

"You'll soon get used to it."

"Many years from now maybe. We'll see!"

We stop in Begur and drink a glass of cognac. It's the drink of choice for those who deal in iron engines and tools. I reflect on our trip for a moment. I realize that I wasn't at all frightened. If it had been any different, I would say so. I found the speed fascinating though never what you might call rapturous. They are unique moments when you forget almost everything else. Though not entirely. The machine always made me feel safe—for example. And something else was always mentally present—an awareness that my butt was slowly becoming a misshapen, painful lump of dough.

"Forget it!" Coromina exclaims, sternly.

"If you say so."

Just then Lola Fargas crosses the square, dressed for winter. She is a pure delight. I find it incredible that women who can be so shapeless and off-putting can furnish such distinct, tangible beauty. What an apparition! I try to interest Coromina in my thoughts. But it's hopeless. He is obsessed by his machine. He has become the perfect motorcyclist and dodges the issue with a platitude worthy of the village wit. He says, "Yes, you can say what you like, but her beauty is as fleeting as the road my bike leaves behind it."

The old road from Begur is hellish and on our way back we have to do without gears. Nevertheless, my nether parts continue to suffer. I reach home a sore, battered, mutilated man, as if I'd been given a real caning. But all in all the worst of the journey was Coromina's wisecrack. His sentence is a sure sign that machines will create literature, and horrible literature at that.

The newspapers are full of grim news. Half of Europe is collapsing, like a battered building that's subsided and falling apart. Russia, Austria, Germany... my feelings sway me toward the side that's collapsing. My reason doesn't!

At night I read Pompeu Fabra's *Catalan Grammar*. It brings to mind a standard European grammar—Augier's *French Grammar*, for example—and above all it makes me forget those grisly texts that made high school such a torture. How beautiful a grammar that is clear, simple, precise, and understandable! As I read, I wonder how I could make so many spelling mistakes. I can't seem to impose any discipline on myself. This feeling of insecurity I have when I discover I'm a slovenly bohemian is extremely unpleasant. However, there's nothing at all I can do about it . . .

6 November. In the afternoon, I walk up to Can Calç de Sant Climent along the path by the cemetery and the Morena spring. It's a farmhouse that belongs to my mother: three hundred square yards of cork oaks, a shadowy kitchen garden, a small patch of thin wheat-growing earth, and an old family house on the ridge. All in the parish boundaries of Fitor.

It's a luminously white afternoon with a cream-cake glow in the sky. The snow on the peak of El Canigó is opaque and dull. Its lower, snowless buttresses are gray, soft, and doughy. Water whines down irrigation channels. Everything is damp and slimy.

The woods are full of voices. Woodcutters are chopping everywhere. You occasionally hear the sound of a tree falling. The owners make charcoal or sell the logs. It will soon all be bare. It's an astonishing sight. The number of trees that must have been felled in these war years is crazy, too many to count.

At three o'clock I reach the Teula spring. The water flows impassively in that dark, solitary spot. The remnants of a banquet of snails litter the stone table. The surrounding shabby eucalyptus trees secrete sadness. Country springs are so cheerful in summer, so dismal in winter. When I reach the Fitor saddle, past the dead vines, the vista opens up and out: I see the dull, tinny sea by Estartit and the Medes Islands.

The farmhouse is a rural drama. I'm almost afraid to go in. When they see me coming, they give me strange, suspicious glances out of the corner of their eyes. It's hard to start a conversation. Luckily, two hungry hounds, ears drooping, pad over and sniff my shoes. That provides an excuse to talk. The forlorn, squalid house is home to the tenant farmer, his wife—a twisted, squint-eyed, filthy woman with unkempt hair—a coal-black charcoal burner, and a son of theirs who looks like a complete moron.

Naturalism—I believe—has just one defect: telling it as it is. Carner's quip about reading naturalist books with a bouquet of roses at your side is rather trite, but it *is* sensible advice. Naturalism will never be popular because it implies the description or recognition of that sewer—large or small—where we all slog. We mount our mean, miserable convictions over that sewer. Gori is right: Idealistic literature will always be what readers like—even if it is a fairy tale, as long as it is idealized.

I walk back at dusk, through the damp cork-oak woods. Owls fly across the low, gray sky.

Before supper, a long conversation with my father about the new map of Europe and the massive upsurge of socialism. My father, who'd clung to the idea that Germany would win the war as long as possible because—in his view—it was best for the onward march of progress, is shaken. Nonetheless, curiously enough, we speak perfectly calmly. Personally this sudden advance by the poor impresses me: an inextricable mixture of satisfaction and fear.

At night, at the club, my friends and I pitch in to play baccarat. When it is time to add up it turns out we have won four pesetas per head, that is, sixteen coffees each.

Afterwards, Coromina and my brother—a chemical sciences student—get embroiled in an endless argument about science. To my great surprise, Coromina attacks my brother's deeply rooted belief in the absolute priority of science in any system of human knowledge. Like all antirationalists, Coromina fashions brilliant, beautiful turns of phrase: He says, for example, that the discovery of Hertzian waves was more the fruit of poetic intuition than of any systematic observation. My brother is indignant. It has always been a mystery to me that some people seem fated to be rationalists and others antirationalists. Why? Is it prompted by the branch of studies or the body of knowledge pursued? I think not. There are very sensitive individuals with artistic temperaments who are rationalists, and individuals obsessed by particularly technological inclinations who are antirationalists. Is a difference in temperament the root cause? Or a difference in curiosity? There are rationalists with extreme tunnel vision. Generally antirationalists are not interested and are indeed irritated by any tangible scrap of knowledge. Why?

The smallest, most fundamental problem hurls me into an abyss of ignorance and sadness.

A long, solitary stroll in the early hours, along the town's deserted streets. I see the light from the Sant Sebastià lighthouse burning from different positions. The beam shines ineluctably, with perfect precision. At four o'clock, it is still burning. Faced by the relentless tenacity of machines I can't help but think about the extent to which man has been diminished. One sometimes feels like taking a bucket of water and putting out that light.

7 November. A very loud, noisy family row. They heard me come home too late. I've still not been able to solve the problem of entering the house without making noise. I can't report any progress on my old pledge to become economically independent. I serve no purpose. I am totally useless.

I spend the afternoon reading. Zola is considered a naturalist, but I see in the *Mercure de Paris* that in fact he documents himself very little on real humans. So just as you eat slices of melon in the summer, naturalists devour slices of life. However, Zola generally improvised, invented. That explains one thing that had baffled me until now: the one-sided, rather simplistic, rarely contradictory psychology of the characters in his novels. They are characters—with different clothing, in a different era—of a piece, hewn from a single kind of stone, like Racine's.

I am rereading *Shadows on the Peaks*, by Ramón Pérez de Ayala, which impressed me when it was published. Now the book drops from my hands. It is a brilliant first novel, no doubt. Ayala has real, natural control over the spiraling sentences of Castilian prose—something Baroja and Azorín don't have.

It was a bright day and a warm afternoon that waned as I watched through my window. Twilight clusters of dark clouds against the off-white vault of the sky, a touch of pink and streaks of purple in the west.

Before dinner, I pop into the Arts School for a moment. I find Lluís Medir, Coromina's assistant, tidying away materials with a passion for order, cleanliness, and efficiency I find admirable. Lluís Medir is one of the most estimable youngsters of my generation, with a striking understanding of concrete things. I think I am drawn to him largely because of my own—often frenzied—longing to learn. Deep down I am only interested in people who can teach me something. I feel Medir is well aware of this.

Aperitifs unravel the final part of my day. Countless cafés after supper. I lose my hat and coat playing baccarat. A second supper, late at night, with my friends. I never have money but there is always somebody who does. Besides, people are trusting. Gori eats solemnly, like a priest. Someone decides to order manzanilla. The Spanish drink gives me a splitting headache. Pain at the top of my head—between the encephalic mass and my skull. We spend the last hours of the night in the brothel. Paquita.

8 November. A stroll along the road to Sant Sebastià. A beautiful, colorful day. The sky is a bright gray, a swarm of light. The pale whites are wonderfully subtle. On the house walls certain whites seem alive. Trees pose elegantly in the gray mist. A gentle breeze blows, like a rose petal caressing one's skin, and makes the bamboo hum. The mountain is full of mushroom hunters. I climb Cape Frares via Ros. A magnificent spectacle. From the side of Sant Sebastià, the raw, vertical geology is oppressive. The scene is more appealing to the north: a pale leaden Cape Begur, pinkish Cabres Cove, and Aigua Xal·lida. Tamariu, above the dark green of the pinewoods. The sea is a grayish blue. Banks of great cottony clouds on the horizon drenched in the light of sunset. The land in repose. The red vines are a ripe, creamy, oily red. A cypress dreams. The west dissolves into orange juice.

At dusk, from one window I can see a flock of sheep munching grass in the old cemetery. I can make out a bunch of white flowers—little white heads—as if some child were buried beneath. Beyond, the grass fields seem to be shivering from the cold.

A bright, animated night under a vitreous vault.

At two in the morning a fire alarm sounds. The sinister bells underline how peaceful the town is—peace that can strike terror. Tomorrow people will be saying: First, they store; then they burn. I don't think there is a community in the world more insensitive to fires.

8 November. Walk to Aigua Xal·lida from Pals with the Bofills (father and son) and my father and brother. A murky day, the color of watered-down milk.

Old Bofill is never silent; he chatters away impressively about anything under the sun. His son, Miquel, listens attentively, ready to join in, but sometimes his eyes and ears can't keep pace. A relentless republican, with an anticlerical vein—he subscribes to Nakens's "Free-thinking Sundays"—he comes out with sentences that throw my father into deep confusion. Today he came out with this: In Spain they've managed to transform Jesus Christ into a folkloric commodity.

Despite the contact with fresh air, my thinking is lethargic and my senses seem wrapped in cotton wool. This is due partly to old Bofill's verbal outpourings and partly to the distillation of all the alcohol I have foolishly imbibed these last few days.

We lunch under the pines. Grilled mushrooms. Ineffable shades of green, a riot of color. The microbes flowering on Roquefort cheese cannot compete. However, the colors are too much for my physical state. A tapioca broth would have been better: the broth—alas!—of this country's libertines.

The sea looks as if it is walking; a northeasterly wind blusters away. On our way back, Sr. Bofill's facility with words rises in a crescendo. While crossing the solitary lengths of the Llor farmstead I feel a great desire to stay put. The day is petering out, like eyes slowly dimming.

All in all we've walked for six hours. It has been years since I've longed for bed so.

9 November. Autumn in Calella.

This year, the shift from summer to autumn came suddenly and unexpectedly. One windy, rainy night changed the appearance and color of land and sea. It also changed the smell. Autumn is the season of fine aromas. On these damp, misty, starry nights, fields and trees exude a strong scent of sweet almonds and mint.

Now it is a real delight to walk through the fields in the early evening. The vines are turning gold, the pinewoods wear a thick layer of dark green and the olive trees an airy silver-gray. The stubble in the fields takes on a granulated, reddish tone. The whole landscape could fit nicely between a pot of honey and a bottle of rum.

Walking along, every now and then you hear a gang of lads bawling and a cart clattering slowly along a gully, a dog barking, loud bangs followed by a spiral of bluish-white smoke from a hunter's gun. As darkness falls the last crickets sing sadly, as if saying we are on our last legs, and night birds swoop though the silent, languid, laden air.

In the Ampurdan, autumn doesn't have the Dionysian sensuality it has in many other climes and centers of civilization. Gazing at this landscape, one couldn't create an autumnal allegory in the classical style: opulent garlands, cornucopias, and a warm Venus with a dainty head and huge buttocks strolling through a meadow surrounded by trees wreathed in mist. Autumn here is rather serene, linear, and never harsh but somewhat languorous, inducing a vague, bitter melancholy. Things attain their maximum meaning by dint of concentration, finding the requisite angle and filtering through to human awareness.

Here it would be equally impossible to imagine a clichéd autumn, the deeply sad autumn of the romantics. The absurd despair certain individuals feel at the sight of falling leaves and bare trees, the inspiration of so much poetry, which verges on the ridiculous. A falling leaf is part of the mechanics of life and has no transcendence. As for those other items, autumn's sexual myths—pink bedrooms, near-naked small women in a dying light, the gloom of exhausted virility—they are like so many dreary, and sepia-tinted postcards.

Autumn is the season most suited to the work of men today. At this time of year city dwellers discover that streets and squares are clean and luminous, the air is light and cool, and people walk with a spring in their step. Since this has to do with temperament, I think I am a man of the sea and working at sea is what I find most congenial, agreeable, and easy to grasp. I cannot disassociate the sea from autumn.

Obviously the circumstances of life at times force a man to depend on something that may not be in line with his temperament and instinct. But this kind of disharmony, shaped by the ups and downs of Providence, explains why the greater the need to work in the bustling city, the more intense the pleasure of gazing at the sea from a cliff or boat.

The sea is a changing, varied song, delightfully subtle and unpredictable. The sun rarely annoys. The African nature of our landscape, the monotonous sky, white walls, parched fields, and unbending bodies soften in a swirl of light smoke. I take the time to speak to priests and women. Priests seem to have abandoned their muskets and cartridge belts momentarily in a corner of the rectory, and women aren't fussing and squeaking as much and, although they gambol friskily as if they'd just eaten roast kid, can be agreeably indolent.

I'm in my element during this time of the year. I have a boat and triangular sail that I love. Solving problems of wind and sail is easy and straightforward, a spare, precise task. Sailing is a mix of caution and risk and the rudder gives one a beady partridge's eye.

Canvas hoisted, I sail close to the coves and the villages encrusted in the geological grandeur of the coast. I always have a friend at hand ready to eat a hundred snails or stewed fish or wild rabbit; a cross word is never exchanged with these wise friends. The wine from sea-facing vines is delicious with a sharp taste that kicks and bites the tongue. And sometimes, as a starter, you eat grilled mill-cap or penny bun mushrooms, and it's like nibbling a young lady's ear saturated with pine.

And if you have all this, what else could you want? Can you really long for life today, a life so sophisticated on the one hand and so arid and regimented on the other—a whiff of acetylene and dog-eared paper? If you make any concessions to appearance, they harness you up more firmly to their cardboard calashes, claptrap, ribbons, and bows. Who today is excited by nature? Who is uplifted by truth? Almost everything is fictive, mere façade, and every day moves us further from reality. I wouldn't swap the life of the people in these towns without churches or clocks for the life our clever, hard-nosed optimists lead. What does life mean? Here you can find the meaning of life. Everyone should take up his shepherd's pouch and shotgun and go hunt the melodies in this world that soar higher and higher...

At the end of the afternoon we launched the boat and raised the sail, which the wind from inland swelled like a heart. The wind streaked and striped the sea black, hissed around pulleys and halyards. A brig sailed across the deserted, purple, scarlet horizon. A boat shrouded in shadows passed hard by, its crew rowing strongly. Gradually we left the town lights behind us. The lighthouse lit up and dazzling beams began to turn mechanically, forbidding and paternal.

Will this landscape and its random ways ever give us a feeling of peace and tranquillity?

Autumn is more delightful by the day. The weather is rainy and a fine drizzle falls, foreshortening the mountains in a bluish, almost mauve mist.

Sometimes it clears by midafternoon and you can go for a walk. I almost always stroll along the seashore. When it rains, everything is calm. The water seems to slumber. You hear it softly eddying over rocks and lapping on the sand. The sea is a yellowish-pearly white. An inner light seems to rise up from its depths. For three days a large brig hasn't budged opposite the town. Drowsy, motionless, becalmed, its deflated sails droop, like an injured bird...

The other afternoon some sailors were curious and launched a boat and went out to the vessel. A crowd was waiting when they returned.

They said its hull was covered in peculiar letters, which suggested it was a Greek vessel. As they drew nearer, they heard singing accompanied by accordions and timber being pounded. From a few yards away, they saw seven or eight men seated around the prow. Opposite them a near-naked black man was contorting his body and stamping his heels. He went over to the side of the brig and asked the sailors in Castilian—which isn't at all strange because all blacks understand Castilian, even if they don't speak it—what the women in town were like, and he added that if the lull continued, he would dive into the water and swim to town. The local people weren't at all keen on that *negrito*.

I'm sure that last night many people dreamed of the spectacle of a black man arriving on their beach. This morning, however, we noticed with some regret that the vessel had disappeared. We were told an inland wind had started to blow and the brig had sailed eastwards as swift as a deer. Night owls had watched the brig's red light head out to sea, glow, then fade into the distant mists.

Midmorning we had to shut ourselves indoors once again. The rain started to pour down. People say this rain is good and will make mushrooms. The best mushroom is the Caesar, which grows in the cork-oak woods. Its flesh is tender, rich, and sticky and tastes excellent grilled. The dense watery air that makes body and mind so slothful encourages these mushrooms to spring up and germinate rapidly.

This weather doesn't do much for sailors. All the same, they like to have an excuse to spend the day playing cards in a café or semi-supine under the arches gazing at the rain bubbles pattering over the sea. For a sailor, idleness brings a warm, sweet glow. In fact, sleep induced by well-managed drowsiness is their ideal.

I believe the mariner state of mind about life is a higher mental state. When a man comes to a small town like this, the lack of things to do rapidly creates a state of exasperation, a nervous tension that may seem grotesque to the observer. Then, one soon enters a stage of morbid melancholy, which attacks the muscles that activate movement and creates intense lethargy and a desire to live life horizontally. However, one can overreact—I'm familiar with the delights of this state—and find diversion in the tiniest thing. Tiredness caused by wiling away time on trifles is a joy, paradise. Tedium, if accepted with grace, is ineffable.

I begin to find pleasure in everything. Watching how it rains, lighting a fire by the side of a field, following the maneuvers of a boat, chewing a sprig of thyme, breathing air heavy with pine resin, and searching for mushrooms, asparagus, or snails are occupations that honor an honest person of humble means.

If I ever succeed in achieving the state of inertia that characterizes this country, I'll consider myself a man who is on the right track. Every symptom indicates I'm hovering near the edge, that I am hot, rather than cold. A good sign is the fact that I no longer rate women, novels, adventure, or money. In any case, it *is* a struggle to free oneself from vanity, swagger, from the tendency to think you are always right and blindly so. It's as if vanity is secreted from our very tissues. It is a force that's never stilled, that acts relentlessly, like our heart, like our vital organs.

I have more than enough tasks to get on with. The small, damp garden in front of our house is overgrown with grass and weeds, and I spend a while cleaning and tidying it with the hoe. Now and then I go the café and at night to the tavern where the parishioners have created a choir. People sing, drink, show off, and stumble their way home, ears on fire, skin taut, and hearts pumping.

There are a lot of cats in town. There are frisky cats, deadpan cats, and large sleepy Pharaonic cats. You wouldn't believe the number of stories old people tell about cats they've known. Old women tell me lots of interesting facts, complete with spicy details, and if they so desire, they can recount their lives around a central thread of four or five generations of cats. I've noticed that old women secretly admire devilish, thieving cats and hide their subtly emphatic pleasure behind a veil of shocked expressions.

I sometimes read, but not much. A friend often writes to say I am a lazybones and should write, but I feel I am such a negligible writer it would be better not to mention the subject.

On Sundays I go to the dance. The musicians arrive—flugelhorn, cornet, violin, bass—and climb the narrow steps to a stage that's propped against the wall. A room that is used to store salted cod during the week reeks on Sunday with a smell that hits you in the face. There are four gas lamps on the wall. Sturdy, fair-haired town girls come with their black-clad mothers in tow and sit on the benches around the room. They spend hours like this, hands clasped over their bellies, yawning occasionally. The young men form a circle under the brass chandelier hanging from the ceiling. It is raining outside and you can hear the gruff song of the sea.

The musicians play fitfully: brassy sounds, snatches of out-of-fashion dance tunes. And I sometimes dance a mazurka from twenty years ago with a fresh-cheeked, spirited young lady or dive into a bygone, jerky polka.

10 November, Sunday. I meet Sra. Carme Girbal (Sr. Esteve Casadevall's sister-in-law) on carrer de Cavallers coming from mass. She seems like a little old lady preserved in a glass case. She is exquisitely dressed. Her pale pink face and whitest of white hair are like out of a miniature. Her arresting presence catches me opposite the beautiful oranges on her trees that gleam in the pools of sunlight in her bright, orderly, beautiful kitchen garden. She speaks with a bygone grace. She says, "I am on my way to a meeting of the Daughters of Mary. I am in such a hurry. We must discuss the triduum of the Puríssima. We are still without a preacher. We have never been in such a situation! What a world, by the Most Holy Virgin! What a responsibility!"

In Germany, everyone is abdicating.

It has been a dreary day—a dangerous, hurtful day to justify any youthful prank. A day when you feel your insides have spilled out. I've made a real effort not to put a foot wrong in any household. But the moment comes when you wonder: An effort to what end? What is the point?

Nietzsche's dictum "beauty is risk" means what exactly? Does it perhaps mean that beauty is the opposite of the spirit that rules things in this country?

11 November. To Cala de Gents, with Roldós the pianist. As we don't feel like conversing, we walk silently along. Roldós sometimes whistles for a while, then suddenly goes quiet and turns red, as if he were embarrassed.

Dirty, rough foam batters the coast. In any case, I find the games that geology plays oppressive. There is a flat fishing boat out at sea— solitary, futile, and superfluous. When we walk through the pinewoods, the rustling in the trees sounds as if someone is watching us—out of sight. In the bay of Palamós, the sea is a blue that seems artificial, a sweet sugary blue and the water is paler… (I can't find the right adjective). It's a blue against the light, the blue of revelation, a blue… (finding the right adjective is impossible). It's an annoyingly physiological, non-marine blue, a blue you can only see through greenish waters… (I'm a total failure). Roldós behaves as if he is miles away. It's almost dark by the time we reach the hermitage and someone shuts the door from the inside. A cricket is still singing. The silence cradled by the wind swaying the pinewoods is so great that you could hear a feather hit the ground. The sonorous silence seems to express the immensely voluptuous nature of the earth. We walk back in silence. Roldós—who is wearing an overcoat, a chocolate-colored overcoat—seems to shiver now and then from the cold.

Friends.

Puig Grasetes came to our club tonight; he went to Palafrugell to work as a journalist when he was young and now resides in Seville. He is his usual self: edgy, edgier than ever, overwhelmed, overworked, unkempt, and anxious. He is dressed in black and, being thin and sallow (you'd think he'd been coated in sulfur), he looks like a high-court judge. We celebrate his presence with copious libations and in his honor play a session of baccarat that sends a shudder through the spheres. At root, people always know they will lose. He is the only one who won't accept that fact.

Carles Serra (Carlitos) always assumes a stern stance. If he is unlucky enough to burst out laughing, it will be followed by the most painful, protracted, endless hiccups. The doctors have told him that if he laughs, he will fall apart. Apparently when he laughs and starts to hiccup, it's a real spectacle. After one or two hours everyone disappears because his death seems a foregone conclusion.

Gori is always too selfish and preoccupied to be at peace with his friends.

Linares is always eagle-eyed, on the lookout for a quick deal, and that's why he attracts merchants. They only complain when he provides the invoice.

Mundet, the small-building contractor, tells me he is so busy he can never concentrate for half a minute on a single idea. Poor fellow, how I pity him!

One of the few people capable of any irony towards his relationships is the gloomiest man about town: Enric Frigola.

When people decide Puig Grasetes has lost too much for his first day, we go off together for a second supper. That's the height of happiness in this little town.

In the early hours a rumor that an armistice has been signed.

12 November. The news of the armistice is confirmed when the newspapers arrive in the early morning. A demonstration is organized complete with an orchestra, and a great song and dance. Superficial, frivolous enthusiasm—and all quite gratuitous. What have we done to deserve this outcome, if not sit and chatter away for four and a half years in our cafés? The day begins to look like a civic, republican fiesta. Sardanas and dancing give way to the occasional short, alcohol-driven speech.

As I walk through the streets, I bump into Paquina the bell ringer who is walking around smoking a small, thin cigar. He tells me, "The rectory is the place in Palafrugell that has reacted most dismally to Germany's defeat. Today they've been fearful, nervous, ill at ease."

I go to sleep early. Once they have won, I find the winners less interesting than before. History, what people call history, is best read in bed as far I'm concerned.

13 November, Wednesday. The war is over. We had become so accustomed to the war it beggars belief. Now war will break out here. The populace has jumped and danced. Federalists have had a fine time. Pro-French liberals have contained themselves—just. Fear of the poor grows by the day. At any rate, such an important, historical event as the armistice, for a small town seventy kilometers from the French frontier, is of little consequence.

A letter from Isern Dalmau, who sent me a book of his prose writings. Isern is ill but has a will of iron. He is at daggers drawn with the poets in Barcelona. He practically disregarded my soothing words when I told him years ago that those apartment-bound poets have never seen a bird, a tree, or a blade of grass. Isern is from the Ampurdan and knows this countryside very well. I eagerly read his book, which is quite romantic and melancholy, though it contains many visual, subtle pages. Perhaps he should have worked more on the outlines—drafted more. It is an excellent first book.

My brother is a young man of strong convictions, slow but stubborn. I was pleased to discover his instinctive fear regarding the culture of countries in which dogmatism rules. He finds this culture contains a form of systematic falsification—a sort of vicious hatred of free inquiry, namely of genuine scientific attitudes. My brother is perhaps more willful than insightful. In this country, I think that is a positive quality. Conversely, I don't think it's easy to change his mind.

I stroll along carrer Ample and out of town. This street is home to a black-haired girl, as fresh as the plains of Ermedàs that spread out in the distance. Dark golden eyes, brazen red lips, wet glistening teeth. Crowned by morning freshness, the fields are strong in color. The color is so solid and dense you feel you could slice it like ham. I see the sea far off: green, wrinkled, and pale.

15 November. It's raining. I go to Sra. G.'s funeral. The trees, roofs, and streets sparkle. Big drops of rain stream down noisily and hang from small branches above the umbrellas carried by the cortege. Priests' voices are hoarse and shaky. Sra. G. died of cancer. Her cheeks were fresh and pink like wax apples, and she was plump. Next to me, one gentleman says to another, "She was such a chatterbox! She enjoyed life so much!"

Gabriele D'Annunzio, the Italian poet, has become the great star of international politics. He has set himself up in Fiume with four adventurers and cries out night and day like a specter: "*La fiamma è bella ... la fiamma è bella ...*" Absolutely!

I am not an expert when it comes to politics. I suspect that international politics can only be understood by the people involved—and even then one can never be sure. Domestic politics is the tamest, most humdrum thing imaginable. I've never understood why people are so interested in politicians, in what people call the human value of politicians. There are people of greater value in any other estate. Public meetings, political rallies bore me. I flee the madding crowds. I find gatherings that are an exercise in collective flattery exasperating.

The subtlest commentary on politics I have ever read is to be found in the *Conversations* between Goethe and Eckermann. Eckermann: "Napoleon must have possessed exceptional powers of seduction, because everyone lined up enthusiastically behind him and let him take the lead." Goethe: "There is no doubt that Napoleon had a superior personality. But the main reason for his power of attraction was this: Men were convinced they would attain *their* goals if they were guided by him. That is why they supported him, why people support anyone who inspires a similar belief. Actors back a new director when they think he will give them good roles. It is an old, old story that is perennially repeated—human nature was ever so. No man serves another simply for the sake of it; however, if he thinks that by serving him he will serve himself, he does so willingly. Napoleon had a good knowledge of men and knew how to exploit their weaknesses."

Now to return to D'Annunzio's syncopated gripes, I can think of a sentence from Goethe on religion that goes: "Religion that reasons, religion that is dead." Strident politics, dead politics. The most recent shocking example of Goethe's dictum in the field of religion is Renan. The most recent illustration of his phrase as applied to politics is the Italian poet. One day or other someone will pay dearly for his griping.

At midnight I accompany several friends to eat stewed butifarra in Enric Frigola's garden. Octavi (Enric's brother), Gori, etcetera come along.

The streets are very muddy. The moon is high in the sky. A wind blows. In the moonlight, from the garden porch, you can see the geometrical lines of cultivated terraces: the land's orderly patterns. The broccoli heads are a delightful pink. At the entrance, a good set of agricultural tools; the handles of the hoes have a polished glint. The electric light shines on the strings of garlic and onions hanging from the ceiling and gives their skins an iridescent glow. All around one senses a perfect, most pleasant, unforced cleanliness.

Enric Frigola is good at making toast. He claims he learned to do it in New York, on gas cookers. After the butifarras he offers us winter pears and grapes as cold as snow. Nothing could be more enjoyable than eating cold food while a hot fire warms one's back. Gori eats and drinks as gravely as ever and refuses to discuss anything connected with matters of the moment.

"It's fine now," he says. "Everything that exists is fine. I have absolutely nothing to say. On with the smoking!"

In his usual brusque, monotonous, ironic style, Frigola speaks for an hour nonstop about the Old Testament, while puffing frantically away. Always in search of some ideal victory, Gori becomes increasingly irritated and finally declares that the Old Testament is essentially a book for horses, mules, and she-mules. I think that's a horrific, vivid image of life itself.

We go our different ways very late and irreconcilably at odds.

17 November. I spend a good part of the afternoon with Mossèn Vicenç Piera. He is a very distinguished priest, the son of Piera the tailor. They are not without money.

Mossèn Vicenç always looks perplexed and perpetually astonished: He never seems to know what he should be doing or saying. This gives him the air of a spiritual, gracious, obedient, submissive man. He is turned in on himself. When someone tells a joke, Mossèn Vicenç says nothing, just sits there, blue eyes wide open, obviously enjoying it inwardly. For him, everything happens within.

Once when telling us about his literary tastes, he said that as a very young man he wrote a poem whose central theme was the existence of only one source of beauty, its own demise. This is a completely orthodox idea—although it might seem romantic—and a hundred percent Catholic. However, I have never glorified this kind of sensibility, and I regret it because I do hold Mossèn Vicenç in high esteem.

After dinner at the club, I drink four cups of very strong coffee. How silly and stupid of me! What drives my tendency to get drunk? In the state of unease triggered by my thumping heart I make a list of abhorrent things in order of their iniquity: a) a gambling table; b) a house of prostitution; c) a drinking session; d) a local university; e) the city suburbs of . . . etcetera.

19 November. A northerly breeze in the morning that gusts wildly in the evening. The wind and the moonlight seem to broaden the street. Not a person in sight. The north wind is wearing, unpleasant, and horrific by day. Palafrugell is an ice-cold town, unremittingly mediocre without a single saving grace. At night, if the moon shines, it improves things a little. The whites of the walls—particularly outside town, by a row of cypresses—are pretty. But the wind steals the night away.

In the café conversation Coromina says he talked four hours nonstop to the same young lady. Gori, sarcastically: "And got nowhere?" Coromina, bewildered: "Well, you know, she is a very intelligent young lady!" Gori, flushed and vicious: "An intelligent young lady who must be studying to become a midwife, like all the young ladies in this country. You are shy and the culture of these ladies overawes you. You'll never get anywhere."

On Coromina's lips, a passing comment expands. On Gori's, everything becomes more precise.

Barren, wasted, irrevocably wasted days, spent idling in endless whimsy. I can't concentrate and it makes me feel hot and bothered. If all life resembles what people call youth, then it is a sad business. I watch my mother and sister climb the stairs to bed. I think how tomorrow they might be dead. My mind can think of nothing else. I can't drive this obsession out of my mind. Life is unbearable!

21 November. Lunch at the farmhouse with the whole family. A luminous, blissful morning. Fields, pine groves, woods have a character and presence that almost makes your head spin. The vines still display their dark, golden sheen.

The landscape around Palafrugell is dotted with small houses and cottages. It is a well-furnished, lively landscape. I sometimes long for the untrammeled lives of the men who live in these whitewashed cottages, set between vineyards and pine groves. But, alas, I don't even know how to light a fire, what would I do there? Vanity pure and simple!

They are sowing on the plain. The farmworkers do so, moving naturally and humbly, so unlike those depicted by sculptors and artists.

The arty ones, with their inflated, grandiloquent gestures, seem spreaders of ideas not of seeds.

I sunbathe while waiting for my lunch of rice and pigeon. How delightful! I must be feeling exactly what a lizard feels. Or a cat. The cats are sunbathing by the haystacks. Pigeons circle above the house. Pigeons live as they choose in the farmhouse attics. Dogs sleep cheek on ear. Roosters mount hens with a naturalness only available to creatures untouched by original sin. If a hen offers any resistance at all, the rooster sinks his beak into her crest and flattens her head. Seconds later they separate feathers flying everywhere. Sparrows fly in short bursts, land, peck, and fornicate endlessly. This is peace.

Francisca, the farmer's wife, appears on the threshing floor with a basket of grain. She calls "Henny, henny" and the hens run to her from the fields. She calls "Chicky chicks" and the broody hens come at a more leisurely pace, with their greedy chicks. She goes "Quack, quack" and ducks and geese patter over in a tizzy like animals that are disjointed and lame but highly respectable. Then she goes "Shoo, shoo" to frighten off the sparrows, though the sparrows largely ignore her and don't obey.

The young farmhand's clerically purple sash is a garish gash. In this world of pure, vital freedom it seems like the symbol of a constituted society that isn't well constituted. What they call a necessary evil, as the cliché goes.

In the meantime, my mother, who is always affected by the weather, is pointing up the southern wind. She is impossibly stressed, touchy, and nervous. The rice and pigeon—which is excellent—fresh endives and light wine don't relax her. She finds fresh air lethal. We have to go home.

We pass a poor woman on the road carrying a huge bundle of wood on her back. Dutch painters—from the reproductions I've seen—have painted numerous figures carrying bundles of wood. In their paintings, however, the bundles are usually smaller. Here they are huge. It is upsetting and depressing to see a woman carrying one this size.

Farther on, we meet a herd of goats. They sprinkle the road with little turds under the small cloud of dust they throw up in their wake. To see a herd of goats and think how poor the country is, is one and the same thing to me. These herds do more evil than good, but the more evil they do, the more we have.

As the afternoon drifts by, objects are magnified in presence and profile for the briefest moment. Suddenly the light breaks, shadows descend, quickly shrink and are saturated in chilly moisture from the southwesterly wind. Grayness impregnates everything. Close to town we see the iron windmills they are installing almost everywhere for irrigation. They aren't exactly pretty, but they are useful. In a country with such a dearth of useful things, this has to be a prime consideration. If the money made from the war were invested in useful things, then perhaps the bundles of wood people carry wouldn't be so heavy...

The locals tend—that is, *we* tend—towards the verbose and garrulous. Some even lose their hides playing this kind of word game. Palafrugell has an alderman who can't utter a word without saying "aesthetics." It's awful—he is so embarrassing. We have tried to tell him that aesthetics isn't an alderman's concern, that he should be focusing on real, small, concrete items, on the details, that the best way to operate is to keep level. All quite pointless. In the town hall everyone is holding forth about aesthetics and right now there's not a single local road you can walk down.

After a long illness and large funeral (in social terms), the family of the deceased enters a state of peace and calm, a kind of vegetative, neutral, most pleasant tranquility. "I feel for you in your sorrow." "Oh, you do, thank you!" Perhaps it would be better to say "I do hope you sleep soundly. Sweet dreams!"

21 November, continued.

That night, news comes of the death of my friend Gervasi.

He died on his vineyard and was found stiff and prostrate under his vines. After he was certified dead, they buried him. The day people didn't hear his conch shell they said he must be in Girona or perhaps seeing to business at the notary's. It was a very bright autumn after-noon, a month of Mary kind of blue, and dazzlingly still. His dog started barking after lunch in the vineyard. It was still barking at dusk. The neighbors were curious and paid a visit. Secretary, poor Gervasi's dog, was making all the noise. When it saw people coming, its barks turned into guttural laments. They shouted "Secretary!," but it didn't budge. They went towards it, more intrigued than ever. And found Gervasi a couple of feet away, lying on his side, as cold as marble.

His bright ruddy face had turned pale pink. Bluebottles and faded moths were already hovering over him.

His funeral was like any other.

The decisive events in Gervasi's recent life were nothing out of the ordinary. The first dog he owned, when he'd built the house and planted his vines, died of old age, nothing new. Recent years were good years. His wine had fetched a better price. He made such good wine that when people hinted at its quality in Palafrugell he would wink. What's more, he had Secretary. One day, late in the afternoon, he was walking by a row of vines haphazardly pulling up weeds. All of a sudden he heard a noise under the vine leaves and saw the face of a mongrel. It was a dog like thousands of others in our country, spotted, without a distinctive shape, without a tail, and thin as a rake. When he was closer, he asked, "What does this secretary want?"

The dog waved the stump of its tail, raised its front legs, and reared up against Gervasi. They exchanged mutually friendly grins. When he'd tired of weeding, he went back into his shack. The dog, an optimist, followed him, remarkably self-confident. Gervasi gave it the name he'd first called it: Secretary. For Gervasi the word *secretary* suggested, as it does to all free countrymen, the image of a kind of hungry, worn-out, cunning individual. The name fit perfectly.

The dog liked thieving, though it behaved well towards its master. It went on expeditions to find fodder and ambled back, stuffed. It went into farmworkers' houses, opened day laborers' baskets, and snatched items from under the noses of hunters. It was considerate toward Ger-vasi, and if he only gave it a raw snail to eat, it ate that too. It did that but offered little else in the way of companionship: In effect, it disappeared elsewhere to find its livelihood. In time when it felt perkier, it adopted another attitude. It stopped barking at passersby as furiously as before. It watched them approaching, whether priests or tramps, in carts or traps, with absolute indifference. It also lost its lively animal inclinations and viewed the miseries of the flesh with aristocratic disdain. However, it couldn't stop stealing. One neighbor, a member of the militia, tired of finding his pantry empty and said he'd tell the corporal. At heart, everyone likes his dog to be a petty thief. It's proof of a vitality and canine intelligence that are as useful as a bank account is to a human. All that secretly pleased Gervasi.

"Just watch your step, Secretary!" he'd say with a laugh. "You've got a sharp tooth and the government will act."

Gervasi was never a big hunter. When guns were single-barreled he would still try his hand. When they became two-barreled, his fingers got entangled on the triggers, his throat went dry, and his prey scampered happily away. One day a friend sighted a limping rabbit and shouted at him, through gritted teeth, "Fire the second barrel, Gervasi!," but he lost it completely, aimed blindly, and killed his friend's dog, which was a darling. This death was the source of dreadful upsets. The two families fell out, the heads of both households insulted each other, and if it didn't end in a fistfight it was because they both were too annoyed when the moment came. Whenever he thought about that incident or saw a two-barreled gun he'd look pensive and snarl, "You're a donkey, Gervasi! A real donkey!"

In the end Secretary decided it didn't want to hunt anymore and Gervasi hung up his rifle without any regrets. In the meantime, he developed a deep, smoldering passion for good food and became obsessed with cooking. He'd happily walk three-quarters of an hour to put fresh fish on his table. When he was cooking, he didn't notice the time go by. He could spend forty-five minutes pounding garlic or whatever. It came out tasting delicious and refined. His onion, tomato, and garlic sauce traced calligraphic spirals over the plate. His mouth melted over his stove. In the pantry, by a jar of anchovies or a pot of caramelized peppers, his imagination soared into the hazy, melodious ether. However, snails were his tour de force. On rainy nights he went out with his torch and, if he saw one, he tiptoed over to catch it by its horns. From the day he caught it to the day he ate it, the snail furnished him with an excuse to indulge in pleasurable sensations on the palate. This was the enjoyable stage. He was gifted when it came to intuiting the moment a snail's tastiness reached perfection, not to mention the vinaigrettes he made with such care and effort. Moreover, the wine from his vineyard was good and abundant. Many a day when the time came to blow his conch, he'd tilt his hat, hold his paunch with both hands, and raise a leg slightly.. He grinned like a Buddha, became light-headed and bubbly…

Few remained of the many friends who came and spent a while in his wooden hut. However, a quite new acquaintance had recently appeared, a man people called El Guenyo, though his real name was Meliton Rovira. El Guenyo had one eye as white as the white of a fried egg and was a thin, fair man of average height with light-colored hair. He wore the black suit he was married in, with absurdly small lapels, which had gone shiny from wear. His clothes were small on him, his collar oversize. He knew how to handle women, could soft-soap, and everyone said he never tired of blowing his own horn. It was true: El Guenyo was the local conquistador and had never worked. His ideas were reactionary, and he liked to stroll with a sprig of fennel in his ear and drop in on people for a bite to eat. He was amazingly adept at getting invitations to eat at other people's houses. Gervasi didn't like him. When he saw him approaching through the pine trees, he acted the innocent, looked over his shoulder, and said bad-temperedly, "Secretary, El Guenyo will be the death of us!"

He couldn't get rid of him. El Guenyo strode into his kitchen and, talking nonstop, lifted the saucepan lid and stuck his nose inside.

"The snails are just right, Gervasi!" he'd say matter-of-factly. "Don't let them cook a second longer. You'll regret it."

Gervasi sliced the bread, put the saucepan on the table, and fed him. From the first morsel, El Guenyo took charge, acted as host, started to hand out advice, felt completely free to carp.

"Gervasi, one thing has led to your downfall," he would say. "Shouting. You shout too much and speak too loud. When you ask your wife for your underpants you sound like a sergeant major. And what does that mean, you idiot? It means you have to fetch them yourself."

"Guenyo, eat and shut up. You're one to say that!"

"You're wrong, Gervasi, I tell you, you're wrong. In this world it's best to make no racket, tread softly, and work on the sly."

Gervasi was at a loss for words and felt disarmed. He stared for a while, said nothing, half intrigued, half indignant. He gazed at El Guenyo's lazy eye, rubber collar, fair skin, and shiny black suit. He felt like flattening him. Halfway through the meal, to round things off, Ei Guenyo would start to go back on what he'd praised. He had heartburn or really wasn't well, he didn't like this year's wine. El Guenyo always wanted last year's. When he saw his fellow diner produce a bottle after half an hour of unsubtle hints, he'd chuckle and laugh. But he'd always find something to quibble about.

"You listening, Gervasi? There's something about this wine I don't like. It has a strange taste."

"You wretch, I bet you'd like to get drunk on a dozen bottles a year!"

"I wouldn't want it even if you gave it me. What's got into you now?"

"What's got into me? I've got it into me that you are a lazy good-for-nothing."

"Don't change the subject, Gervasi. This wine has a strange edge to it. I don't like it. It tastes odd. Be careful! Or you'll lose the lot. And you deserve to because you are a complete idiot."

They generally ended up at each other's throat. After they'd eaten, while he used a toothpick, El Guenyo unleashed his poisonous tongue and called Gervasi everything under the sun. He tore into his honor and his ancestors. Gervasi labored to shut him up and see him out the door. El Guenyo would stalk off, his face livid and body rigid. And then he'd be back after a couple of days as if everything was fine.

El Guenyo gave Gervasi an awful time and was constantly upsetting him. Gervasi's tolerance toward this rude waster showed how he had changed. Gervasi had once been a stalwart individualist who pleased only himself. None of this would have happened two years ago. He was getting old and simple-minded. A potential source of consolation, his dog had become hugely disdainful. In the early days, its hunger made it attentive and servile. Like all farm dogs, it took things as they came and jumped to do its master's bidding. If Gervasi was on his way from the vineyard, felt like a cigarette, and said, "Blast,

I've left my cigarette case," the dog quickly ran to fetch it. All that was a pleasant thing of the past. The dog led a completely separate life and whatever it was told went in one ear and out the other. It was a free, liberated, idle dog.

So Gervasi was growing old and, by way of consolation, turned to cooking and two-year-old wine. In the end he died and his conch shell was silenced. Those on land missed the conch for a few days, then did without it with an indifference that was quite natural. Some of the sailing ships that pass by still signal by raising a flag. To no avail: nobody answers and they lower their flags to the silence of the sea. Ships that signal become rarer by the day...

22 November, Friday. Xènius now writes articles for La Veu de Catalunya under the heading of "The Valley of Josaphat." He pours into them everything he knows, everything he has read and heard. And that is how it should be. His articles are very good, instructive, and useful.

Today he wrote: "If you took the genius and personality away from Benvenuto Cellini, he'd be a picaresque Gil Blas de Santillana." In my view, this is a good way to approach the idea of the Renaissance or of the complete man, with his vices and virtues, warts and all.

Of course, it would be wonderful if the history of culture didn't harbor scoundrels. It would be ideal, splendid. But the fact remains that humanity's efforts to eliminate and do without this kind of person have been unsuccessful, nearly futile. The portraits of artists, literati, and characters from the Renaissance, which De Santis draws in his unforgettable History of Italian Literature, are horrendous.

Sometimes these men are very talented. Herein lies the drama. The love of truth can coexist with the most repulsive personal greed. Freedom of thought and broad-mindedness can prosper in a cruel temperament; the basest form of hypocrisy in the most gifted individual; the most prized social graces in a highly dangerous individual; poetic intuition or the art of objectivity in a monster of perversity. The concept of the whole personality is inseparable from our very idea of the Renaissance.

In leaner times—like the present, with the exception of scientific research—criteria are very different. Everything is external. Appearances rule tyrannically. The adoration of cardboard is universal. If we want to feel we are alive and kicking, we must have recourse to reading about the virtues, sores, and lesions of others. The only thing we value is what other people think of us. The street is the universal touchstone. An era of masks.

I never tire of Nietzsche, whom I read in the translations published by Mercure de France. One can see why he had such an influence on the previous generation that had grown tired of professorial posing and staid mediocrity. Aphorism 240 of *Human, All Too Human* states: "The more cultured a man, the less open he is to mockery and satire." When Taine wrote that Nietzsche is the true heir to the great French moralists, he was absolutely right. How true!

Last year I loaned G. *The Birth of Tragedy*. When he returned it, he asked, "If you think you've understood something by Nietzsche, does that mean you have taken a step backwards or forwards?" I immediately saw what a huge mistake I'd made in lending him the book. His question will remain scored on my brain, however many years go by.

If you believe in your own talent but are incapable of irony, it can be very harmful. But the damage is entirely relative. More serious is the hurt one can do to others.

If the practice of love's passions weren't hedged in by all those complications, prejudices, obstacles, and confusions, it would become a touch monotonous. Women's sensitive spots are always in the same places and many carry that sensitivity in the palms of their hands. Fortunately, this practice induces sleep and the outcome is invaluable.

23 November. Five o'clock. Sweet tedium by the fireside.

At night, I go for a solitary stroll around town. There's nobody in sight. A night watchman's torch shines around a distant street corner.

As I walk, I hear clocks ticking inside houses. Almost all are fast. In industrial areas, clocks usually run ahead of themselves; in the country, they lag behind. I sometimes hear water gushing from a tap. Lots of people—particularly the poor—sleep with their shutters open; some, very few, with their window half open. Those who want to sleep in, sleep with their shutters down. When I was an adolescent, a flash of light in a window would be like an aphrodisiac, now it induces asceticism. I sometimes hear a person dreaming. In single-story houses, you can even hear people turning over in their beds. Somewhere or other, a lady is saying "Ay, Lord!"

25 November, Monday. I am hungover. Life is opaque. A strange sensation; fear of dying.

At night, I go to the cinema. Roldós is very muted. The place is almost empty. Everything is banal, lackluster, and routine.

I think about yesterday. I went for a walk along carrer de Cavallers. My pre-supper stroll. So many girls! They all looked well turned out in their winter clothes and some seemed very beautiful. The woman who doesn't look like herself is the same woman at a different time of the day. Perhaps men are less subject to change; we seem more constant. Then I went to the dance at the Casino. I actually went down to dance! The hall was like an oven. It was crammed full. All the smells of the Latin race blended with cheap perfumes. The walls trickled from the smelly sweat and breathing. I danced with Ll., the plumber's daughter. I had to scale a wall of timidity, embarrassment, and smallmindedness. Ll. seems rather misty-eyed. She's pleasant, too deferential, and is—probably—very obedient. But perhaps that isn't quite right. When I finish dancing, I feel a great burden has been lifted from my shoulders. My lack of naturalness is real enough and most unpleasant.

If I had to choose between Unamuno's confusion and lack of definition and Eugeni d'Ors's tendency to define, I'd prefer the latter. Hunger makes me say such a thing.

26 November. Sr. Torras Jonama.

He emigrated from our country as a very young man and made a fortune from cork in the United States and Cuba. Afterwards he gambled on Wall Street and won. And now he is back here in a new guise as a philanthropist. We have named a street after him, and when he comes we welcome him with an orchestra and the full works.

He suffered from nostalgia despite his riches, and remarkably so, given that he was poverty-stricken when he emigrated. This country provokes nostalgia, and that's the truth. He wanted to buy the small railway and bring life to the country. He then suggested he could pay for the work necessary to finish the church belfry. Apparently he has now decided to pay for schools in Palafrugell and the surrounding villages and to subsidize children who want to continue studying. However, it seems the subsidy idea hasn't gone down as well as he expected.

He is tall and stout, robust and ruddy-cheeked, elegantly dressed and shod, a white mustache and hair, and full of energy. His blue suits, red complexion, white hair, and vigorous neck give him the looks of an American senator. He has clearly eaten very well in life. His wife is an Italian, originally from Florence and rather cold and distant.

Like all those from this country who have crossed "the pond," Sr. Torras seems at first glance rather unhinged. It is a question of proportions. His world, the world in which he became a rich self-made man, is one with hundreds and thousands of people; the contrast with the smallness and poverty here must be immediate and distressing. Here, as a philanthropist, all is forgiven him. Everybody seems sleepy and rather dozy, so Sr. Torras, possessed with such vitality, treats everybody like donkeys, old crocks, and farm animals and doesn't spare a soul, not even the parish priest. Perhaps he rather overdoes it. However, I am inclined to think that if a philanthropist can't allow himself to take these liberties with people he has favored with largesse, heaven knows who can.

Today he was telling me how, when he was young and poor and driven by a longing for adventure, he joined the Carlist troops as a volunteer (during the Second Carlist War) and finished up in Estella (Navarra) at the court of the pretender. They assigned him to the royal band as a flutist. Lots of the musicians were Catalan. Things weren't going well. There was no money. Nobody was being paid. Soldiers were poorer than church mice. It was all protests and bad blood. One day, starving Catalan soldiers demonstrated along the streets of Estella with a pennant that bore this inscription:

If we're not paid today
or even tomorrow,
when we meet the enemy
we won't open fire!

"They must have executed the lot," I replied.

"No, siree. They executed nobody. Those days there were many fewer laws than there are now. Such an act was never legislated for. Now everything is. If something novel happened then, people were forced to invent a response and at that time they preferred to sleep rather than rack their brains. The demonstration brought results. They paid us a pittance and I continued playing the flute in the band."

28 November. Today in "The Valley of Josaphat," Xènius writes about Shakespeare. He says that he is "Might and Law." "What does he mean by that?" asks Gori, intrigued. "It's his synthesis, his definition," replies Coromina, wiping the back of his neck. "Yes, of course," says Gori, "I can see it's a synthesis. But it's a bad sign when people use these big words with capital letters, don't you think? They are facile devices; ways of speaking about things that people haven't a clue about. Never trust vague words with capital letters. They are snares set for the simpleminded."

Stendhal, Stendhal—his is the right way to go. There is a single aspect of Stendhal's work that will always be of extreme contemporary relevance in this country: his analysis of hypocrisy.

I draw up a balance sheet. I owe T. G. money, various second suppers, a big bill at the club, and Lavinya the bookseller for a large number of books. I acknowledge these debts with complete humility and declare that they are real and true. I would like to be a good payer, but I'm still not poor enough to be forced to pay cash up front. All in due time...

Aimless exhaustion is the only defense against that sinister place of encounter that horrifies me and never entirely sends me to sleep.

I've been out walking all afternoon. I return from Sant Sebastià with sore feet. It was very gray. The sunless heath in Ros is distinctly gloomy. A dark purple field between two green strips of land: a velvet eye. Listless sails out at sea. Meandering dogs chase a rabbit through solitary pine trees. A tree's shape sometimes suggests a human form. I even imagine I can hear a human voice in the peaceful woods. The frozen basin of the Portalada fountain was like a sliver of moonlight...

Sometimes a surfeit of physical exhaustion puts your nerves on edge, and you end up in the very place you hoped to avoid when you set out.

29 November. Against the green background of his bookshop, Lavinya talks to me about the future of anarchism, in that shrill hermaphrodite's voice of his. He is wearing a cream-colored overall—one of those garments that can be scary because, depending on the wearer, there may be nothing else underneath.

He, personally, is not interested in any kind of book—apart from those written by members of his sect. They have solved everything. Everything is planned out for the day after their victory. Nothing can go wrong. We will do this, that, and the other. What is the source of the arrogance, envy, brazen swagger of these primary folk? There must be a source and it's probably quite ancient. I understand all the social utopias, all the ideas behind them, whatever they may be. Anarchism, however, always makes me feel physically uneasy, unpleasantly disturbed—like going to bed and finding it still unmade.

Tomorrow is Saint Andrew's Day. For Saint Andrew, rain or snow down the flue or frost. There will be a fair in Torroella—colorful as a patchwork quilt—against the rosemary and lavender backdrop of Montgrí. When I was a child I used to go with my father—with our trap and mare.

In the café today, Enric Frigola was speaking to Josep M. Avellí, a friend of his generation, who possesses a magnificent pink, broad, and round baldpate: "Europe is unlike America. Our appearance is too solemn and dull. We wear too much black and never use color to make ourselves look more attractive. In this respect, Americans are smarter and more entertaining. They constantly use color and sometimes highly imaginatively. You have a striking, nay, unforgettable baldpate. You ought to have a face or landscape painted on it now and then, or just a few colorful brushstrokes. Do you see what I mean? Imagine the uproar you'd create one day if you had the Gioconda painted on your pate. The whole world, literally the whole world, would talk about nothing else."

1 December, Sunday. A damp, cold, rainy day. Bodily and spiritually calm. Sluggishness.

I really like Maurice Barrès. He is a most elegant, magnificent stylist. I think the national-materialist doctrine he professes closely reflects reality and seems appealing. He is the master of incisive foreshortening in his descriptions. *Le jardin de Bérénice* has paragraphs that literally smell of violets and female lingerie, slightly ruffled, silky, and pleasant to touch.

At home, family life is almost nonexistent. There is a rigid external order, but in practice everybody does what he feels like doing. That may constitute a good bringing up or a bad one. We shall soon see. Time will tell in the end. In any case, that's what there is. A Catholic upbringing in this country—pleasant and chaotic.

At night, feeling shy and sorry for myself, I dance for a while at the Mercantile Circle and am completely taken aback by my decision to do so. It's ghastly. I think everyone must be looking at me. I always feel I am being spied on, watched, pursued by cold, mocking, inquisitorial eyes. I can never enjoy a moment of pure, genuine spontaneity, freedom, and complete abandon. As I dance, I find this obsession irritating. So what? Isn't the essence of bourgeois life precisely that physical sensation of feeling you're being constantly watched, of living in a glass display case? Yes, I have no doubts about it: I am a bourgeois, and a fully fledged bourgeois at that.

2 December, Monday. Sr. Bofill (Gori) invites me to go hunting in the Llafranc gully. I turn down his offer of a gun. After my disastrous failure in Sant Climent, I have a very clear sense of my ability with guns.

We leave straight after lunch. It is a delightfully bright and sunny afternoon. A damp smell of mushrooms lingers in shadowy arbors. We don't meet a living soul. While Bofill and his dogs explore the gully, I wander by myself through the pinewoods, smoking cigarettes. I walk along as if in a perpetual daydream. At times like this I'm often searching for a plot for a novel. And I come up with nothing. I've never had sufficient imagination to see life in the shape of a novel. It's probably because I am totally ignorant and inexperienced when it comes to life itself.

I suddenly hear two shots in a row close by, huge bangs that resound down the empty gully. Four or five minutes later I hear another shot. A quarter of an hour later, another, the last one. I think how tasty local rabbits must be.

When Gori comes along, I see he is carrying an empty bag. He has missed three rabbits. He embarks on a long explanation, but the fact remains that he missed three rabbits. "They would have been so good stewed or roasted," he tells me angrily, positively ashamed.

"Gori," I tell him, "you are a wonderful fellow. However, it has to be said you are much less wonderful as a hunter."

During our—silent—return to town, I notice his back stooping more and more. He adopts the hunchbacked stance of hunters who've killed nothing. He goes into his house and doesn't even wish me good night.

When Preses the pharmacist reminisces in the club about his time in the Amazon—where he lived for many years selling pharmaceutical products to the natives—it is an astonishing performance. He is a shy, discreet man who suddenly bolts like a wild horse. He starts to embroider things, to exaggerate. His megalomania expands, bolstered by his wondrous, unbounded optimism.

"One day," he was telling us, "we rented a house on the edge of the jungle, by the riverbank. But we were soon driven out. Snakes came in by the back door and went out through the front. Some were so long they filled half the passageway. They were huge and thick as a thigh."

His audience listened in awe, transported perhaps by his overblown yarn, perhaps because snakes always send a shiver down the spine. Who can say?

When Sr. Preses enters these realms of inflated hyperbole, he turns pale and takes on the air of a visionary.

The Fraternal Center sent me a very official invitation card to the Victory Party. It is one of the first invitations of this kind I have ever received. The invitation and the party leave me rather cold.

5 December. Roldós the pianist loves walking and today he and I went for a long stroll. It was a mild afternoon, a light southwesterly was blowing, tinged with a hint of deep pink the color of quince jam—one of the most delicious jams. A most pleasant temperature.

First we went to Calella. Cape Roig is Calella's colored pearl with its warm colors and, as its name suggests, a sumptuously dark red. As dusk fell it turned the primary color of burning hot coals. Everything else around seemed more evanescent in contrast. Roldós's response to the slumbering splendor of land and sea was a hazardous, literary aside. "It's a Titian show," he said.

To ward off further hazards, I invite him to have a bite to eat in Llafranc. After our meal we find it difficult to go back to our walk. Who could ever leave Llafranc? A clean table—not disgusting lino-leum—fresh fish, toasted white bread, fragrant oil, good wine, coffee, tobacco, and endless glasses. Who could ever leave Llafranc? In the delicate twilight, the beach gleams like glass streaked with crimson. There are two brigs on the horizon, still and tranquil, as if they had stopped to enjoy the view. The sea is utterly placid.

We take a shortcut up to Sant Sebastià. The pines and damp brush give off an intoxicating perfume. Adela, a young girl from the light-house, sees us climbing and welcomes us from on high with a seagull's hoarse cry. Adela is twelve: lively, full of energy, with big round black eyes. She slips from my hands . . .

In the hermitage we come across Joan Linares who's had the strange idea of settling down there for a few days' peace and quiet. More glasses of wine. Too many. Roldós turns pale. He can see I'm going red and begins to get very agitated. Linares is very superficial—in fact, he is all surface. To make an impression he thinks he must beg for forgiveness all the time and constantly proclaim that he has no moral principles. His gratuitous lack of shame, which is all show, is as annoying as it would be if it were genuine.

When we make it back to town, Roldós say he feels like playing the piano. We go to the cinema. The dark, empty space is like a huge cavern where all you can see is the piano light illuminating the score and Roldós's blotchy face. He plays Bach and Beethoven. Beethoven sounds like music that is walking, slipping away, bidding farewell . . . Roldós doesn't have the right tempo. He suddenly stops mid-phrase and closes the piano, looking exhausted. Alcohol is to blame.

In the early hours Coromina presents me with a small gold coin from Ampurias, the emperor Diocletian.

6 December. In the afternoon I set out for our farmhouse. On the way, I feel chilled, uncomfortable, and my freezing back shivers with cold. I beat a retreat. I am frightened for a moment. I think it must be influenza; if it is, death is inevitable. When I swing around, I gaze at the town of Pals, perched on a hill, always so beautiful, its antique golden stone crowned by a light bluish haze seemingly streaked by watery purple and mauve fingers. Once home I drink a big bowl of hot milk with a dash of cognac. I feel it as soon as I am in bed.

Sleeplessness. I think how unadventurous people are here, particularly the most intelligent: They tend toward self-restraint, have no ambition, and shirk responsibility. When one is young, almost everyone has an attack of vanity which is generally short-lived. If it persists, it is considered to be a sign of undeniable stupidity. People here want: a) to live well; b) to live well at home or lead a completely private life; c) to see the world exclusively in the light of their own self-interest; d) to never worry about things that don't impinge on them directly. I like this individualistic focus. Obviously it has one big drawback: It makes it impossible for people to connect, and social life becomes practically impossible. Conversation, that healthy lubricant of social relationships, is what is most lacking in this country. However, if I were forced to choose between conversation and freedom—solitary freedom—I would always opt for freedom.

Convictions.

Last year, the likable wife of one of my childhood friends went into labor. It was a very difficult business. I felt duty-bound to ask my friend for news about how she had fared. I'd find him in his dining room in a state of collapse staring at a plate of biscuits and a glass of strong wine, trying to recover his spirits. As we talked, I heard his wife's strident voice wail.

"Never again! Never again!" she'd shout.

"What does your wife mean when she says 'never again'?" I asked.

"I suppose she means she will never sleep with me again," he replied, in a resigned tone.

Within weeks, the good lady was pregnant again.

Ah, my dear, old Montaigne! Life is *ondoyante*...

I am embarrassed when I think of the fuss I often make in public praising the way the people cook. In fact, I find their cooking horrible and irritating.

7 December. It is a fine day. I wander along the streets in the sun, staring. Through one window I see a sallow, weary man in loose-fitting clothes, a white kerchief around his neck. He is watching people walk by as if his thoughts were perhaps colored by persistent envy. He is a sick man.

The sight of him makes me recall something I heard Dr. Reixach say a few days ago in the café. Dr. Reixach is a fat, plain-speaking man, whose thoughts rush over things quickly. "Pus," he was saying, "is, definitively, only a concentration of white globules." The word *definitively* is the jewel in his sentence.

Strolling along I come to the station. I find people waiting for the three o'clock train, although it always leaves at a quarter to. It's the train that connects with the express in Flaçà. At this time of day, towards the end of the year, the great and the good of Palafrugell are to be seen in the station. Srta. V. is standing next to me with a young man from town. Srta. V. has big black eyes. She is waiting for the train. She is going to Barcelona. She dresses elegantly and always has a pretty expression on her face. Perhaps she is feeling nervous. Perhaps she wants to underline how important her journey is. The young man gazes at her, his surprise growing by the minute. Finally he blurts out, tartly, "I can see you putting on all those airs. It isn't such a big deal, you know. We're all the same in Palafrugell: fried fish and grilled gurnard."

The young lady stiffens, slightly shaken—and cut to the quick.

Sr. Torras Jonama.

This gentleman is the talk of the town. Apparently he was going to give a good five thousand pesetas toward the building of schools in the town and surrounding villages. He is our local philanthropist. However, there have been varied reactions to his generosity. Very few people take him seriously. Others say: Who does this gentleman think he is with his schools? Does he think we're such asses? Is he mad or does he simply act mad? An even more biting comment, if that's possible, overheard in the street: "This rich fellow wants to pay for our schools? He must be doing it for a reason. He's got something in mind."

It's unfair, but people are both incurably curious and increasingly touchy. But I don't think one can do anything about that. If he doesn't quickly return to the United States, this will descend into a small-town farce à la Molière. The time will come when the people around him will struggle, will labor terribly to hide what is being said about him—and that will be at the center of the farce.

When I occasionally bump into him and he isn't too busy, he tells me more about the Second Carlist War and his stay in Navarra. He remembers it vividly. Today he was saying, "Oh, if you'd only seen the king, the pretender, with his long beard, scapulars, and insignia. He was quite a sight. He was a man held in high esteem by the local ladies and had an entrée into all the homes. He was a real stallion, a genuine old-fashioned king! He only had to raise his hand . . . though I'm not sure he ever had much of a grip on things. He listened to the band as if he were praying his rosary and prayed his rosary as if he were listening to the band. But he *was* an old-fashioned monarch, a good old king."

Coromina relates how one day, in Girona, a very respectable citizen of that city said to Rusiñol, "Don Santiago, how can you and your friends, such upright, good, popular people, possibly tarry with these horrible local women, these three-peseta tarts—"

"Hey, not so fast!" interjected Rusiñol brusquely. "Mine cost four!"

8 December. The Immaculate Conception. Sunday. Very festive. People parade by in their new winter garb. The streets are full of the fine smell of new clothing. At the dance that night I speak to several young ladies. Although Srta V. is so dark, she is very romantic. I never know what to do in the company of romantic individuals: whether to laugh or cry. But I always encounter the same problem of how to bring it to fruition: The young ladies are impenetrable, insoluble, impossible, unattainable, unapproachable, untouchable, intangible, and irreducible. Exhaustion kills enchantment and the time comes when you doubt whether they really exist.

I have dinner, in the early hours, with various friends: Enric Saüch, Josep M. Vehí, Enric Vergés, Roldós, and the usual crowd. Saüch talks about his life, reminisces, like a man who views sin with bored disdain. When he is about to admit to something indiscreet, he whispers, lowers his eyelids, and waves his hand irritably. He is really a man of his time, a huge presence—like a stagecoach from a bygone era.

We are all rather surprised by the presence of J. M. Vehí. He is a considerable heir, the son of a family that finds itself in a rather sad state, and he looks somewhat worn out and impoverished. He goes for long periods without leaving his house—reading by the fireside or in bed. Because of this, almost everybody feels duty-bound to rant about his lack of will, the dull pessimism that seems to overwhelm him. Vehí—who is much more intelligent than he allows—apologizes for his forebears and the rather dubious inheritance he has been forced to take on. However, as the drinks are downed, everybody continues with a questionable lack of tact. The heavy moralizing and self-righteous advice handed out begin to pall. Vehí finally reacts and says, quite beside himself, waving his arms as if he were swatting flies, "If you keep on and turn this into a question of principle, I will commit suicide here and now."

Later Roldós tells me, in that wheezy voice of his, how he entered the choir school of Montserrat when he was a young boy, intending to become a Benedictine monk. He learned music in Montserrat but outside the monastery he was inclined to be frivolous and cynical. Roldós is so deadpan when he talks about himself, it's as if he's talking about a distant acquaintance. Our after-dinner chat peters out as a result of that surfeit of impersonality.

9 December. After-lunch conversation with friends in the Fraternal Center.

"The amount of space in the human imagination given over to women is huge," declares Coromina.

"This is true for some men at a particular stage in life," retorts Frigola. "I don't think it's accurate in terms of most men once they have moved on. The space you mention is hypothetical and arbitrary."

"And is the actual contact made equally hypothetical?"

"There's a lot of swagger and impertinent chatter about it, but considerably more chastity than you imagine—and a lot of quite normal people."

"Going against the tide, as ever."

"I don't accept that. When a man is driven by sex, he becomes purely unconscious, a being driven by blind, unknown forces. An out-and-out moron. A man in that state stands out a mile because his lack of balance has repercussions on everything else he does. If the male mind devoted as much space to women as you imagine, society would cease to function. Trains would never make it to Flaçà."

"Well, we'd face that scenario if marriage hadn't been imposed with an iron hand."

"I don't believe marriage is the only reason for the existence of restraint and a certain normality. I believe moderation in terms of sensuality has undeniably concrete, physical causes. They are the same levers that lead to frugality, hygiene, caution, and measure in life. Our need to feel comfortable is the root cause."

The conversation trails off. After a while, Coromina redirects our dialogue toward another, if different, issue. "Frigola," he asks, "would you advise me to get married?"

"I have no advice to give. Marriage has one advantage: It is voluntary. I have never married. I am a confirmed bachelor. People who marry very young enter the matrimonial state for reasons of money, blindness, or ignorance. Nature is a powerful force. Later on, things become clearer. Many people marry; however, if they had the chance to divorce one day, most would be scandalized. But I meant to discuss something else. The lack of awareness I just mentioned, that moment of unawareness and emotional union shapes character traits that then last a lifetime. I have never met a bachelor who was intrinsically stupid. Manic perhaps, but not stupid. Marriage should be the roundabout way to attain two other forms of love: the love between parents and children and the love between brother and sister, which is where marriages finish up when the fire goes out. The male ideal—in terms of feeling—should be an imaginary sister."

As he uttered this last sentence, he got up from the table and snuffed out his cigarette, his hands trembling. Then put on his hat and coat and left.

After that, Gallart recounts an incident. A few days ago the navy corporal in Calella fined a fisherman five pesetas. The latter got angry and said, rashly, "I'll give you one too, and we'll be quits!" Coromina nods approvingly. Gori gets up indignantly—and turns a bright red, his eyes possessed. Everyone is expecting him to make a dramatic statement. However, to everyone's surprise, he simply clenches his fists and glances furiously around. Then, without saying a word, goes out the door and down the street.

The café conversation breaks up from exhaustion. A northerly breeze.

In midafternoon, the funeral of the butcher and Gypsy (by race) Bastons, alias Xeix. He was a tall, dry, silent, self-absorbed, aloof, dark-skinned man. Lots of Gypsies came to the ceremony. In church, in the yellow candlelight, they formed a group, a world apart, with a very distinctive character—particularly because they seemed so confused and frightened. Their faces were tense. None came to the cemetery. They'd fled before it reached that point.

11 December. When I get up, I see that light from a yellowish—vaguely reddish—straw-colored sun is shining on the world. A wintry sun. Every day at this time I see the same things when I open my window:

a tiled roof covered in green vegetation; a bare white wall at the bottom of the garden; small terraces, which are muddy throughout winter, with tiled borders and in the foreground, two glittering palms that make me feel cold. I think the palms are too statuesque and symmetrical. The landscape always has that same structure. Every day, however, is different—just as the color of one's tongue and state of mind is different every day at this time.

It's been a bright, sunny afternoon—all in high relief. At dusk, a soft, fine mist settled over the ground and transformed the trees into faint, elegant silhouettes.

Perhaps humiliation is the most dynamic impulse driving humans to act—or else the desire to shrug it off. In small-town life, everything is small-scale and thus easily observed. However, everything (whether big or small) is always essentially the same. People who've never felt humiliated generally have a spring in their step. Those who have met with too much humiliation seemed muted and dull. They are like travelers waiting for a long-delayed night train . . .

L'avi Munné, a weekly from Sant Feliu de Guíxols, publishes peevish articles about me in almost every issue. It finds my articles in *Baix Empordà*—written simply as mere space-fillers—pedantic and over-intricate. They are certainly that—I might add—but a lot more besides. Infinitely more—if one is unpleasant, the next is even more so. On this point, we shall soon agree.

13 December. Saint Llúcia. A traditional gathering at the hermitage in Sant Sebastià. I go in the afternoon. Lots of people. Farmers' traps and carts—with awnings. Hustle and bustle on the mountain. I see a loving couple holding hands under a pine tree. With his other hand he tapers the tip of his mustache. She looks at the ground.

Earlier the weather was bright and mild. El Canigó soared overhead, icy and metallic. The plain of Palafrugell lay still and quiet. The foreground drawn as in a miniature painting. The vault of the sky soaks up the sardanas being played at full blast. A protracted, blood-orange twilight begins in midafternoon. The sky is soft and watery—patches of pale green and wan, innocent blue. The west glows like an incandescent oven. The crosslight seeps through the windows of the hermitage. Through the bars, this light creates the atmosphere of a melancholy, abandoned monastery. From the terrace one can see the becalmed, bluish sea—calm brought on by futile fatigue. Lots of ships in irons; no wind. If I embarked now, what a delight that wouldn't be . . .

I try to make off from the kitchen with a butifarra—they are delicious here—between two slices of bread. Hopeless: It's too crowded. I return to the party with Gich, a medical student and young, optimistic, unsubtle soul. I find lack of subtlety annoying. I accompany Srta. V. for a while. In the gray twilight I see her large, glinting black eyes—with slightly red-rimmed eyelids. Several aperitifs. The void deepens. Total indifference—a kind of vegetative melancholy. Years ago I'd have expected so much from today!

"No misfortunes await the weak body; grief requires a robust heart." (Dostoyevsky). This possibly means that the first requirement for suffering is iron health.

16 December, Monday. Small-town life.

Lluís Matas, the pharmacist, is so extroverted that if he dared, he'd put a pane of glass over his stomach so people would stop and see how it was built and worked. Roldós is the other extreme; in his old-fashioned threadbare green overcoat, with its two shoulder pads and slits in the back, he looks depressed and demoralized. His only worry seems to be how to give the impression he doesn't exist.

"If he was eighteen and she was fifteen, it wouldn't be so difficult to understand," remarks Coromina in the café. He says that with a laugh, convinced he'll meet with unanimous agreement.

"What do you expect me to say?" retorts Frigola, unmovable and icy. "I don't feel a need for any more headaches than I already have."

I imagine that the cinema must reduce people to imbecility everywhere. It is a feeling that turns to exasperation in small towns. Films are too long and slow, take too much time to get going. Actors and actresses perform so immodestly that if they were members of your family, you'd be red with embarrassment.

The *General Concept . . .* by Francesc Pujol is a splendid book, but too patriotic.

One of my dreams I'd like to see come true would be to own the learned publications published by the Institute for Catalan Studies. I never owned a single one because I never had the money. All the efforts I have made in town to persuade someone to buy them—so I could have at least indirect access—have come to nothing. This is a barren wasteland—much more barren than the university.

18 December. Lunch in Cala Pedrosa, in the wooden house that belongs to the Vergés family. I meet up with Enric Vergés, Mata, Hermós, Xico Pla (the club concierge), Jaumet from Cafè Pallot, and three or four other devotees. We light a fire on the stones on the beach. Hermós is chef and bawls like a wild man. Rice cooked by Hermós is not what you'd call out of this world: His best dish is meat stew. Vergés prepares a cocktail—a drink that has finally reached this country—and before lunch most people are tipsy. We lunch in the shade, surrounded by the stupid disorder that erupts at such times. When it comes to the dessert I watch one fellow set fire to a chair; another starts smashing plates; another dives into the water in his overcoat; the fellow farthest away hurls the coffeepot into the cistern. It is a kind of frenzied, grotesque lunacy. I take advantage of a moment of confusion to make my escape, heart thudding, up an unexpected track. I feel a sense of release as the cove disappears out of sight. On the road, I meet Adela, the girl from the lighthouse. She is more fun and more scrumptious than ever. She walks towards me hoping for a good laugh. I try to caress her, but suddenly she sees something peculiar in my expression, turns pale, struggles nervously, and takes off like a rocket. Then I feel depressed by the alcohol and remorseful because of all the violence. One of the most unpleasant days I've ever experienced.

Old people always talk about conscience—the burden of conscience or the burdens of conscience. I wonder if conscience can turn into a sickness. Perhaps it can if a person isn't normal. With well-balanced individuals, enjoying good health and normal reflexes—*reflexes* being a new word I've learned—I don't think it could. "Normal" consists precisely in having a conscience that contributes to the proper functioning of one's general health.

Space is like a woman: obtuse and impenetrable. Time, the passage of time, is painful. If we imagine that total optimists and pessimists exist—absolute things only exist in the realm of thought—the former must feel and thrive best in space; the latter, in time. The former's (illusory) bliss must be the odometer and the latter's (palpable) sadness must be a watch.

Everything in this country is caustic, corrosive, and slightly mediocre, but Gori affirms—confidently—that life here is good.

20 December. A long stroll on the outskirts of town, with a volume by Barrès for company. In the places I mention you find delightful shelter from the wind, shady spots for dodging the sun, and superb stratagems for combating winter. The earth is pinkish. The afternoon's smoke and vapors paint a brushstroke of light blue over the pink landscape. I get as far as Pasteres. A large liner gleaming in the sun sails very close to the Formigues Islands. A fantastic sight! How I wish I could travel! I see Adela, the young girl from the lighthouse, in the distance. For one moment I see her against the blue sky, like a sculpted figure. This girl has such a mysterious aura! She's exuberant, strong, playful, artful, and wriggles from your hands like a warm, slippery bird. I find I am strangely fascinated by her wiles—the wiles of a thirteen-year-old.

In the evening, a few drops of rain fall and the icy north wind persists. I feel the cold from previous years in my bones, remember the interminable winters of my childhood—the whistling wind, the deep blue sky, the sound of sand on windowpanes, my parched mouth, stuffed-up nose, the wind beating on my back and cheeks, nerves on edge, the wind blowing under every door, through unsuspected crevices in balconies and windows. A wind drilling through any obstacle. When it's like this, one of the most uncomfortable houses, of the many in town, is ours. The north-facing rooms that overlook the garden are freezing. They have a mosaic-tile floor that feels like a bar of ice under the soles of your feet. The badly built fireplaces leak smoke. Bed is the only good place to be—provided you don't hang your arms out and aren't tempted to read. If you poke your nose or arms out of the folds you freeze. My mother's incredible mania for doing a Saturday cleaning on almost every day of the week, and mopping the floor, make it unbearably cold. It's like living out in the street. Mine is a Spartan upbringing.

21 December. We have reached the shortest day of the year. Following the strictest social ritual—imitating government bureaucracy—they light the stove in the club. Officially, up to this point in time nobody has felt the cold.

To try and banish the cold, Roldós and I go for a long walk. He doesn't feel like conversing, nor do I. We walk in silence. What a pleasure it is to be with people who don't feel the constant need to chatter endlessly to prove their friendship. A brown gray wintry pall hangs over the fields in contrast with the bright green of the pine trees. The colder it gets, the greener the trees. Little Adela, coming from school, satchel on her back, draws close to us for a moment. Her features are somewhat blurred, as if she were already traversing adolescence...

In the course of our stroll we meet a relative of Medir just back from Germany. He has lived abroad for many years and has returned to see the country. He is wandering across the fields. After the usual pleasantries he joins us, but seems not to want to talk, either. He stares at the ground, eyes bulging, obsessive, a touch paranoid.

On our way back it starts to rain in Palau's orchard. Roldós breaks into a run—cursing nature. I stand under a tree. The man who has attached himself to us keeps walking as if nothing had changed—obsessed by the landscape.

Home, before supper. I hear a noise when they open the kitchen door: They are frying potatoes. Maria is cooking. Rosa is ironing. I can hear rain falling outside.

23 December. Now the atmosphere is so full of that ineffable, humanly tender, and loving event known as Christmas, I'm obsessed by my emotional coldness and sterility of feeling. I find this sterility alarming given it must form part of my inner nature. I don't feel the least desire to adore anything. My fondness for social occasions is scant, negligible. I hear my family talking enthusiastically about midnight mass. I can't generate the tiniest spark of interest. Objectively speaking, it's highly unpleasant to feel one has nothing much to look forward to—in respect to women, money, or ever making a mark in life—beyond this secret, devilish, manic need to write (with so little to show), to which I sacrifice everything and will probably continue to sacrifice everything in life. I wonder: What's better—a halfhearted, resigned, mediocre passage, or living with this passionate, tense, relentless obsession?

25 December. Christmas. Wednesday. The moment comes when you've been in your party clothes a long time, everything has been said that can be said about the said garments, and you begin to tire of it all. A normal human body can't stomach the combination of roast chicken and local champagnes. The French champagnes—that I drank years ago with Josep Sagrera—are past history, have been destroyed. The local kind is worthless: That which is barely drinkable leaves an earthy aftertaste and is horribly sweet. Perhaps the soil here is too rich, too loamy to create a light, effervescent wine. The combination of cakes, tidbits, and sweet wine is eternally cloying. After a light supper, I go to bed. I read Stendhal—a good, crisp antidote.

26 December. Saint Stephen's Day. Solemn mass in the parish church for the soul of Sr. Esteve Casadevall. I arrive very late. When my mother sees me, she is so surprised she manages a quick smile in my direction. She was certain I wouldn't bother.

At night, dances everywhere. I'm drawn to dances. I like the awful music. I'm seduced by the dancing: It depresses and bewitches, makes me feel shy, and triggers a kind of physical pain. I fail to cut a dash for a single second! Finally I abandon these wearisome contradictions and wander through the noisy, excited throng.

Joan Linares, whom I meet in the café, behaves as if he's taking my pulse and shouts at me, as the deaf do, "Behaving badly isn't easy, right?"

A cold north wind in the street—a northerly gust that immediately gives me a headache.

27 December, Friday. I accompany Roldós to Palamós. It is a clear, sharp morning, with a cold, bright sun. We eat lunch in the home of a friend of his: Castelló, a cultured, educated worker. Broth and meat stew, cod with peppers and tomato, toast, sugared almonds, good wine and excellent coffee. Castelló lives modestly with his wife and two children. It is a spotless but freezing house. His wife seems extremely hardworking, energetic, tireless.

We talk about Beethoven for almost all lunch. Sra. Castelló didn't say a word. What can she have been thinking? The glances she cast in our direction—astonished, suspicious, or frankly ironic—seemed to beg the questions: Who can these fellows be? What do they want from my husband? What are they after with their rudeness? Perhaps this lady would enjoy a quieter life if her husband weren't so cultured.

Afterward we go for a walk along the quayside. Palamós is now a very busy cosmopolitan port of call for many ships and the dens for drinking and sinning are packed with large numbers of motley sailors. I heard sweet, nostalgic accordions being played on sailing ships bound for France. The "tramps," the large-tonnage vessels, don't seem to bring any kind of traditional sailor sentimentality in tow. These vessels are usually manned by scary-looking sailors. It doesn't seem possible that men who live this outdoor life, which is apparently so healthy, could have such drawn faces, pus-colored skin, and alcohol-ravaged eyes. They look like escaped convicts with their tattoos and the kerchiefs around their necks.

Palamós is a delightful town. Its worst feature is the Swiss chalets and modernist houses. Perhaps there are not as many as I imagine, but they are so visible I can't stop thinking about them. Traditional Palamós, with its rows of whitewashed houses around the bay, is enchanting. The light in Palamós is literally ineffable. The town's gentlemen take the sun on the promenade and look highly self-satisfied. This town—the one place in my country where I'd choose to live, if I had the choice—has three unique attractions: the light, the bay, and the sunsets as seen from the lighthouse or the casino square.

We walk back. It is very cold. I ask Roldós, "What did you think of your friend's wife?"

"Scary!" is his quick response.

The clothes Roldós is wearing, the beret pushed down over his ears, and his wan face make him look like a convalescent Pierrot under that pale sky.

I read in the newspaper that the university is going to reopen on 2 January. So it will soon be time for me to return to Barcelona. The thought makes me anxious and rapidly quite indifferent.

29 December. Today's *Glosari*, on Gluck, like almost all the glosses in "The Valley of Josaphat," is a pleasure to read. Eugeni d'Ors's fascination with finding definitions has found exactly the right home.

Strange, unexceptional days that are empty and barren. I think the single cause must be the fact that it's the time of the year when unpaid bills are re-sent. The little power of concentration I have, my ability to think things through now must focus on solving my own financial problems—which can only be resolved, like all real problems, by being postponed.

A magnificent, clear, radiant night under the luminous vault of the sky. I hear a cat meow in the street, under the bare trees, though it's not the month for cats yet. It must be a precocious, impatient cat.

30 December, Monday. The daily newspapers.

In the course of the war, people read two journalists in particular: Agustí Calvet, "Gaziel," who was *La Vanguardia*'s Paris correspondent, and Domínguez Rodiño, sent by the same paper, on the suggestion of Don Àngel Guimerà, to Berlin. These two men became immensely popular and their custom-made shirts from the tailor were always on the house. Calvet was a Frenchified man from the Ampurdan, clever, thoughtful, with an academic's sarcasm, who wrote magnificent chronicles. When there is a war, the ideal journalist is not bellicose.

Now the war is over, the writers of ideologically inspired articles have reappeared and the articles by Jaume Brossa in *La Publicidad* are popular. Brossa—from the photos I have seen—is a man with a beard, from the days of modernism. He has a "mug" destined for the police archives. He is an ultraliberal: that is, an anarchist.

Always sensitive to what Xènius calls "the pulse of our times," Gori was talking about this kind of writing today: "It is a real pity there have to be two kinds of liberals: conservative liberals and anarchist liberals. It demonstrates, nevertheless, that they are separated by a different degree of tension in temperament rather than by their ideas. Brossa belongs to the second category. In barbershops he is thought to be a difficult author. In fact he is infantile. To everyone's great surprise, he has come out emphatically against the Russian Revolution and against the German Revolution that is now in full swing. A revolution is but a sudden change of leaders. In Russia the revolution is far-reaching: The change of personnel is one hundred percent. In Germany the revolution is simply a process that will return to the same starting point exactly. Every rapid change in personnel implies the establishment of a new conception of the world—implying revolution. The shifting of power from the aristocracy to the bourgeoisie implies a revolution. The shifting of power from the bourgeoisie to the workers is a revolution. The shifting of power from one bourgeois group to another is not a revolution. In such situations, shades of political freedom are at stake. In the previous case, political freedom will count for little; the establishing of economic equality will be the decisive factor.

"Brossa's problems have to do with political freedom. He is as radical as you like, but he is a man who stopped at the French Revolution. For him, there can only be freedom with democracy, namely human equality before the law. For socialists, on the contrary, there can only be freedom if there is equality before the bread cupboard, and that cupboard lays down the law. Brossa is, then, an anachronism. In Russia he'd be thought a trite sniveler, always close to tears.

"As far as I'm concerned, Brossa's position is extremely powerful and irrefutable. How is it possible to establish economic equality without an iron dictatorship? At this point socialists equivocate and deceive people. Why don't they come out and say they are going to establish a dictatorship, and then we will all know where we stand.

"Besides, Brossa's position is human. He experienced the great era of the bourgeoisie, of expansion, of doors opening to human aspirations. He is terrified by the destruction of commerce, the origin of economic inequality, or the destruction of everything that makes life comfortable. He thinks life isn't worth living if you have to spend your day queuing outside the bakery. I quite agree. The mere thought horrifies me."

"The man who has money and does business," says Coromina in the café, "is like the individual who sweats from every pore and stands next to the fireplace."

"That was before, in the heyday of the rentiers," retorts Frigola. "Those of us who now live on our income receive less and less and one reduction follows another. The process of capital evaporation is very swift. I have calculated that if you want to maintain the rate of return on your accumulated capital, you must add in half the income you earn every three months."

Not a day passes when I don't think about the room in the farmhouse attic that faces the rising sun and the south. I often ask myself: "When can I go and live there?" But at the same time I am ashamed and horrified to see that I am just twenty-one, a pathetic coward and conservative and already so old.

They are giving last rites to Teresita Bordas, daughter of Xico Bordas, the vermicelli maker on carrer Estret. Grandmother Marieta is a next-door neighbor. Teresita is sixteen, a lovely, beautiful girl. It strikes midnight. A group of indistinct figures casts a dark shadow on her front door. They are shivering with cold and whispering silently. One man can't stop himself from yawning. The candles bring a yellow glow to the damp walls above the muddy street. The priest pursues the little bell that moves off into the emptiness of the night. The poor child dying behind that wall . . .

In the early hours Roldós plays the first three English Suites by Bach. The first is in a virtuoso style—too much so, for my taste. The other two are splendid: the gently seductive, distant contours of Bach's musical mountains.

It is raining. From my bed I can hear rain pattering on the ground, on the roofs of neighboring houses—I hear water gurgling down the channel along the side of the balcony. Sometimes—for a long or short while—water splashes monotonously on the porch tiles.

31 December. Rain and damp. In the café a white-and-blue disgusting smog is steaming up the windows. I play billiards with friends. I'm a hopeless, dreadful player. I see I need a cannon but can't do it. Everything I do is rough and clumsy: I always hit the ball too hard. I move on to the piano in the cinema, which is as empty as a dark, cavernous grotto. I am wearing my overcoat with the collar turned up. The cold there chills the bones. I feel I'm wasting away. Roldós plays Bach for a while. Gavottes, which are a delight. I go to bed early. Rain makes a civilized man of me, and a sleepy one. The pleasures of a warm bed and slow, hesitant rain.

1919

1 January. I must draw up a proper balance sheet. "Proper" doesn't imply any hypocritical intent. I mean that I'm prepared to write frankly, inasmuch as I can.

I have no talent for friendship. I only like people who can teach me something—and, for a little while, those who help the time go by. I find effusive expressions of interest from others simply annoying. Praise makes my blood boil. The sweet-scented—cheap-scented—pleasantries from Roldós make me want to vomit. If I were rich and could employ a pianist, I'd have fired Roldós long ago. My selfishness is nauseating and contemptible.

On the other hand, I've noticed that, as the months go by, I become increasingly tongue in cheek. I love to play games, throw up smoke screens that, by the cold light of day, I find distasteful. I have a tendency—even an ability—to invent and manipulate things to suit myself. I sometimes silence an interlocutor with an observation I know to be a complete lie that I just invented. These games often surface spontaneously, pure fun for fun's sake. It's quite inexplicable how such impulses, which seem so deliberate and premeditated, surge forth so readily. How unpleasant to think I might mystify someone unknowingly!

Man is permanently in a state of sin. (Reader, please don't rush to any hasty conclusions.) One either accepts this as a fact—in my opinion—or pretends to be pure. Nonetheless, it is impossible to throw off sin. Likewise injustice, which perhaps can be equally dangerous. If one attempts to throw off sin, two things can happen: Either one fails due to a huge burden of sin or because one thinks one has thrown off sin, when one hasn't, so it's a lie, or one becomes a fake, a hypocrite, capable of doing the direst deed in the name of simulated purity. If one thinks of oneself as an assiduous, dastardly sinner, one can at least aspire to a level of humility and discretion. I hope I never abandon this belief in the course of my life. It's my only hope.

Last Sunday the cinema showed *La Passaggera* with Pina Menichelli, a thin, tense, dark, tempting woman, like the reproduction I've seen of the Capitoline Venus. On the way out, I asked a lady, who is always in and out of church, if she'd liked her.

"She goes too far, far too far," she tittered, most cheerfully.

2 January. It's cold. It is the same every year: longer days, colder days.

Grandmother Marieta was honored with a visit from our relative Joan Prats, lawyer and property-owner, a very rich, greedy, sordid fellow who is unbelievably stingy. She wished him a happy New Year as she does every year.

"Marieta, it's very cold," said Sr. Joan Prats.

"Yes, Joan, very cold," answered Grandmother Marieta.

"I'll tell you something: I'm still not wearing my underpants. It's true, I tell you! These days one cannot be too careful."

And while he confided in this way, he rubbed his hands nervously together, out of pure delight, which is what misers do when they're thinking of the savings they are making.

Roldós comes with me to bid farewell to Sant Sebastià. An almost anguished silence on the mountain. A wet southwesterly. The pine trees drip. I'm nervous and upset. I don't see the petite Adela anywhere. She must be in the lighthouse kitchen—I think—which must be cold and functional, like all lighthouse kitchens. The sea is rough, swollen, and full of itself. Soft, spongy clouds roll over the horizon, frayed at the edges. We walk down to Llafranc where we will have a bite to eat. Back in town, I invite three or four girls to drink aperitifs

with us. I fail to find the slightest shaft of wit—only the usual platitudes. We are all stiff and on ceremony around the table. The girls are
so prudent they already act as if they were married with children. I go
to bed immediately after. A long, long, interminable night spent planning—and, above all, concluding miserably that I find it impossible to
focus on anything.

2 January, continued. Calella, winter.

The weather is fine. The January moon is the brightest of the year.
It's a real pleasure to go for a walk, whatever the time of day. My
thoughts are expansive, youthful, and vague. Everything has a purpose, yearns for infinity, and fervor and desire count for more than
possession. At night the moon casts a thick, soft glow on the garden
walls; at night the eucalyptus trees possess an Oriental stillness, orange blossom perfumes the warm air. When the sun shines, the beach
shimmers with small pink flames like tiny tongues of fire. In the afternoon, white cloudlets cross the sky, go this way and that, then dissolve
into the blue—a wonderful way to die.

Nonetheless, reactions in small towns are violent, perhaps because
people live so close to life and reality. Vagueness always runs in tan-
dem with an austere vein. The indifference of nature, the melancholy
of things, the sensual naturalness of the landscape release pure dis-
enchantment once the power of the imagination runs dry. However,
one should reflect on this decline and not be swept away by slow,
elegiac resignation when human pettiness takes its place within the
immense frame of life.

All things are not equally beautiful. The sun brings to the sea an
anxious stillness that, in the end, is exhausting. A child with bare
feet—delicate pink and dark skin—is stirring a pot of steaming tar
with a stick and the air is filled with a warm, sticky, chemical smell. As
I walk along the road, elemental cooking smells—often appealing—
waft before me and make me look away. A basketful of live fish, fresh
off a boat, in the gentle, late-afternoon light seems like a huge, sickly,

festering human ulcer, flecked with mineral jewels. You need to feel strong to go to the end of the beach in that sun and smell the water in a large rock pool—a mixture of sea and rainwater—and breathe in the putrefying mix of rotting seaweed and clay, the spicy stench saturating the air...

Small-town life has a single rhythm that shifts from desire to tedium and back again. If one adapts too impulsively to this rhythm, in the end the swing of the pendulum triggers a dull headache as sweet as honey.

In the morning, a northerly wind. I'm brought coffee in bed and when they throw open the shutters, the glaring African light we always get in this country floods the room. A wintry light, with a raw, sour, sterilized, metallic purity. My bedroom is white and bare. The wood of the rafters is unpainted. There is a red flowery mattress on the heavy, old-fashioned bed. Under the bed, a large chamber pot. The iron washbasin in the corner shivers, naked and cold. There is a Valencia-style calendar on the wall. A linen mat, the sort they use in cheap boardinghouses, thin as a cat's ear, lies half under the bed. My open suitcase yawns endlessly on the pretentiously shaped chair.

If I look up from my pillow, I can see the sky and the sea. Masts stand firm opposite my window. The sky is a rinsed-out, shiny blue. The horizon is turning a raw purple. I watch the wind gust fiercely over the sea. The greenish water seems to be in flight from the land. By the coast the water ripples. About twenty fathoms out, however, its flight becomes more frenzied. The waves break, push, and leap with the lunatic energy of a school of deluded dolphins. The horizon is too small for the spreading sea and seems to complain. The wind whistles around street corners, scratches roofs with cat's claws, blasts furiously in and out of porches, pounces on the sea, swirls and eddies impetuously. In the cloudless sky, the sun is like a young lion. It tinges the dark green bellies of the waves, the gleaming whitecaps, the diamond sparkle of the spray. The silhouette of a large steamer looms—it is trying to round Cape Sant Sebastià, straining its neck, battling stubbornly against a thousand currents of sunny water. A brig sails by, swift as a deer, a drifting snowflake, sails furled, on its way from Italy.

The half-submerged Formigues Islands stick out—a tooth of bleeding red rock. From my bed I watch nature unleash itself on the serene, bright air.

I drink coffee. I can't take my eyes off the window. I'm fascinated by the savagery of the wind over the sea. The water's shimmering scales dazzle me. I bundle up well and walk over to the window. The beach is deserted. Not a soul walking down the street. The boats painted apple green or red with a tar-colored stripe look sad, shabby, and forlorn on the tawny gold of the sand. I shiver back to bed and slowly warm up. I think it must be fun to be in the sun and out of the wind. It is the season when oranges turn golden and almond trees splash their first coral pinks. Awnings are full of cats sunning their bellies, legs stretched out, one eye half shut. A kitten is always playing with the shadow from its tail or a wandering feather. I also think how on days like this anglerfish soup tastes its best, with toast, a spoonful of aioli, and wine from Llançà. I think about so many other things. Not for long, however. The window draws me close, bewitches me.

The sunlight is like a sheet of glass. Wind and sea battle in a futile, delirious fury. Everything stays the same, impassive and still—the coral of the almond trees, the playful kitten, the aioli, and the anglerfish soup. The things of this world pass by the light in my window—wind, water, and diamond spray racing toward the raw purple of the horizon. The brightness turns daylight into haze and my eyelids droop after that sudden shimmering, dazzling illumination.

I walk nowhere in particular, my head a mass of roaming thoughts, my senses pulled this way and that. Wherever I go, I see the Sant Sebastià hermitage in front of me, sometimes closer, sometimes more distant. The hermitage is the essence of our spirit, the perennial bastion of our territory. Its four walls make me feel my roots: This is my land, I was born here; generations of the family of which I am but a passing dream lie at rest in the nearby two or three tiny cemeteries. If all goes well, I too will be buried here.

The hermitage is the high point in our lives: It is our first vista, the landscape of our youth and our loves, the vantage point from which the stars seem nearer and we shape our idea of the world's extended stage. It represents our life as mortals: We all cherish the memory en-graved on our hearts of a tomato-and-garlic sauce at the hermitage and rosé wine sparkling in our eyes. And the last thing we shall see when we die, what our dead always see, is the prow of the hermit-age, hanging between the sea and the sky in a void of fabulous ob-livion.

The songs, the country's serene light, the small avenue of cypress trees opposite the sea, over the hill, the scent of thyme and rosemary beneath rustling pines, the land to be tilled, the anxious chameleon sea ... in harmony with these elemental traits, the pleasures and sor-rows of past generations created a tradition, a law that inexorably gov-erned our dead, that guides us, and that will guide those who follow us. It is pure folly to try to escape this stubborn spirit. Tradition has shaped our hearts, the childish joys of the hermitage have shaped our language, and our thoughts are fashioned by the melody of the sky, the hill, and the branch that descends on the craggy outcrops of basalt and granite.

I return home. I amuse myself by the fireside, silently burning rub-bish, remembering, or reading. I also look back over the year. What happened in Calella? There have been four deaths (three elderly peo-ple past sixty, and a twenty-year-old girl), four weddings, five births, four misfortunes, four great expectations, and five mysteries. The fish-ing has gone as badly as ever and people are living on credit. The par-ish priest has aged tremendously. The big event of the year was—I remember now—the pillaging of a steamer.

The steamer, I don't know its name, was sailing from Gibraltar to Liorna, following the obvious route. It ran into bad weather and drew closer to land to await milder weather. It was Christmas. The galley slaves on board wanted to celebrate. They roped up the helm. They were exhausted after the recent storm. They ate, drank, sang, and got drunk. The steamer sailed for hour after hour without anyone at the helm, and as night closed in, it hit the Formigues Islands. The hull was breached and it was marooned on rocks by small reefs. The crew, amid an infernal racket, lowered a boat and headed for the lights on the land that seemed nearest. The men arrived half dead and couldn't handle what had happened. They created a stir in the tavern. After they'd gotten over their scare, drunkenness finished them off and they slept like animals.

It was a dark but very still night. The sea was silent. Far off a green light was still visible: It was a light on the steamer that for some chance reason had remained lit—a forlorn light that was a real temptation. People peered at the glow with a glint in their eye. Shadows ran down to the beach and boats were launched. Rowing silently—their oars attracting fireflies—they drew near to the vessel. Its carcass looked like the shadow of a dead ghost. They clawed their way up, then slid the booty into their boats along ropes they lowered down. Not a word was uttered during the looting. It is great fun to loot a steamer. It was all over by early morning and everybody was soon peacefully asleep in bed.

The vessel stays marooned on the rocks. Waves whipped up by the north wind crash against the black hull and streamers of white foam glint in the sunlight. At dusk, the dying sun gives the hulk a sinister, mysterious air. Darkness falls. The wind whistles around street corners, a child's cries rent the air, the yellow light in a window dims. The Sant Sebastià light switches on and its beams swirl, majestic and solitary.

4 January. I spend the (cold) afternoon copying out the articles from Josep Ferrer's *Lenten Suite* for the projected book. When will it come out? They are good articles.

Life here (politically speaking) is developing in unexpected ways and is much more interesting. Until now it looked as if all the conflict in society was about the desire for a better administration. Now it has become highly emotional. It's very likely that a few months ago people would have been satisfied by administrative reform. We've gone quite beyond that point and the speed at which we're moving is visible to all.

Artists.

I bump into Marian Vinyas, who has come on some pretext or other, and who tells me an anecdote about Maurice Ravel the musician. When the great composer came to Barcelona, L'Orfeó paid homage with a big concert. Vinyas accompanied him in the presidential box. The first part of the program comprised Catalan songs; the second part, songs he had written himself; and the third part, large, imposing choral works—one of which was *La mort de l'escolà*, by Nicolau. At the end of *La mort de l'escolà*, there are two small, very beautiful dissonances.

"Well, maestro, what did you think?" asked Vinyas.

"The two small dissonances at the end are a delight," answered Ravel with his boulevardier air, moving his Adam's apple in that absolutely French manner.

Artists today are like that: Their only touchstone is their own highly personal taste, the drift of their own work, their own manias. Ravel has created many dissonances. If he hadn't found a couple in *La mort de l'escolà*, the work wouldn't have existed as far as he was concerned.

5 January, Sunday. A day with a very southwesterly wind, temperatures on the rise, extreme humidity, a sticky humidity you can touch with your hand. This weather is unbearable by the sea; inland the degree of misery evens out slightly. When you leave the heavy fog in the café, the first blast of fresh air seems intriguing. The wind forces you to slow your pace and to speak allusively. As contact continues you feel your ears droop. By the time you reach home you are incoherent and at a loss for words, as if your joints had softened and your bones become more brittle.

In his curious and amusing *Life of Don Quixote and Sancho Panza*, which I have just read, Unamuno describes Cervantes as a picaresque character. In "The Valley of Josaphat" Xènius now says that Cervantes is picaresque in the first part of his work and ironic in the second part, an irony shot through with sentimentality. I have always thought of Unamuno as the great spreader of confusion: He is a liberal saturated with English ideas who must navigate the almost feudal milieu of Castile. This could be his justification—up to a point. On this occasion, however, Xènius has gotten the better hand and has done so out of a desire to be à la page, to show he is aware of the latest trends. I wonder why nobody ever speaks of Cervantes as he really was: a man who starved, who was weary and sad. That's the impression he always gives to any normal person who reads him.

During the last war, there was a revolution in men's clothing: the appearance of short underpants. There has also been a revolution in women's clothing: the abolition of stays. And there has been a revolution in literary taste: People have started to read thrillers. This is something new in our country. After the war, people's sensibilities seem much coarser.

In my view, if the detectives in these novels were to act ridiculously now and then, they'd be more appealing. But they never err and always get it right. Scotland Yard is becoming so renowned! I also suspect these novels would become even more popular if they were occasionally written from the perspective of the thieves instead of the inevitably triumphant police. You shouldn't always kill off the goose —I reckon!

7 January. I begin to box things up to leave for Barcelona. I find my textbooks where they were—looking rather dowdy. They seem dogeared, futile, lifeless objects. Most things can seem commonplace, can become incredibly banal. But nothing, in this regard, can rival textbooks. When they are so battered and shabby, you begin to take pity on them.

Reading about the situation in Europe literally makes one's head spin. Russia is in a state of total chaos. Convulsion follows convulsion without end in Germany. The social situation in that country worsens by the day. Violence is spilling out into the streets. One must have real nerve to be part of a system that claims a monopoly on the creation of such madness. Frankly, it requires absurd levels of arrogance.

When it is time for aperitifs I indulge in a gloomy Amer Picon with P. G.—a chubby-cheeked joker of a clerk who is fair-haired, lively, ready for anything, and an optimist. He thinks everything is first-rate, that if things weren't so good last year, this year they should go wonderfully well. I think my friend is splendid. The minute I decide to leave, I suddenly feel depressed—as if I'd had more aperitifs than I have.

9 January. Almost the entire family will depart for Barcelona in the morning: my mother, my sisters, my brother, and the maid—Angeleta. The weather is sharp, clear, and bright. From the small train's platform I can see the white lighthouse in the distance, the green pinewoods, Les Torretes, and Palafrugell beach. Then, inside the icy carriage, smoke-filled with misted windows, I fall prey to an insipid daydream. I think endlessly about this pointless notebook. I could easily have ditched nearly almost everything I've written here.

A windowed carriage pulled by a skinny nag transports the whole family from estació de França to the apartment on carrer de Mallorca—Mallorca, 244, 2°, 1ª. The glass panes rattle with the cobbles in the streets. Barcelona advances with such shaking and vibrating. Obviously everything is very different, in terms of life's immediate claims, bigger and more important, but I find little that appeals to me. After climbing the dark stairs, the apartment seems colorless, odorless, and dull. And surprisingly small. The reduced space means we fall over one another. If we'd nothing else to do, we would feel miserable—with the exception of Angeleta who, perhaps because she is more countrified than we are, is full of enthusiasm and doesn't stop toiling for a second.

In the midafternoon I go along rambla de Catalunya—our apartment is very close to rambla de Catalunya—and Gran Via—to the university and Law Faculty courtyard. Straightaway I meet my old friend Salvador Eures and fellow students: Xavier Güell, Martí Esteve, Plaja, Albiol, Escursell, Gener, Rebull, etcetera. We greet one another with the usual noisy glee but keep our distance, as ever—a distance that seems so small, yet is perhaps quite considerable. The courtyard is bare, cold, and damp, its stone the color of stew. Thousands upon thousands of students have passed this way and it seems nobody has ever lived there. Hands in my pockets, a cigarette between my lips, I then go to the College of Lawyers library in the Casa de l'Ardiaca, opposite the cathedral. The crowded streets seem anodyne and terribly lonely. People hurry along when hooted at by irritated car drivers. However, the women are beautiful. They walk by. The shopwindows gleam. I've never felt the need to stop and look into a shopwindow. How strange! The College of Lawyers is dark and solitary. The small, badly lit garden in the entrance is a delight. You feel a gentle peace there. You feel relaxed under the green partitions around the library tables and the shelves of dark, solemn tomes. But life is far away. Life is a remote hum—like the sound of the sea—that reaches me through the closed balcony windows.

10 January. I thought I caught sight of Tomàs Gallart in the distance walking past the Cine Catalunya. He was dressed in mourning clothes and wore black gloves. His mother must have died—I reflect—she had breast cancer and was in the clinic. Gallart was walking along, shoulders hunched, looking pale and haggard. I don't dare go after him, simply for my own comfort. My selfishness and cowardice are unerring.

I roam through Barcelona. I meet a hot and bothered Narcís Coromina and Josep M. Pi i Sunyer on carrer de Pelai. They have been friends from their first years at the university, from the days of chaos, the conversations we once enjoyed in that memorable mezzanine Salvador Eures owned between Universitat and València. They say they are in a rush to get to Poblenou to contract a medium for a séance. A tall, gangly, grotesque figure, with a pasty complexion and a flat nose, Josep M. Pi is as amusing and buffoonish as a character out of Dickens: A man of considerable intellectual subtlety, he tells me that all Barcelona is now keen on spiritualism and that the mediums in

Poblenou are unrivaled when it comes to making a table dance or talking to Nebuchadnezzar.

I open—rather anxiously—my bedroom table's drawers. I find they are full of old papers, newspaper cuttings, notes, and drafts—countless drafts. It is a struggle to start tearing up papers because vanity blinds. But once I start I could tear everything up—even my birth certificate if it fell into my hands.

The Rambla before supper. Women in the bright light. Bewitching, breathtaking. It must be easy to give up things of the mind and everyday duties—but I doubt there exists another place like this, that makes renunciation so easy.

11 January. Now that I am nearing the end of my degree, as they say, I think I have not really lived as a proper student does. I've never experienced the traditional dissipation of student life or lived in sordid lodging houses, because my family wanted to make sure I didn't get shipwrecked on the reefs of youth or the temptations of the day, and so we moved to an apartment in Barcelona, where we have lived up to this point as orderly as the offspring of a well-behaved family. Though I've never experienced student lodgings, I have become acquainted with cafés with billiard tables and tables for playing seven and a half.

12 January. I become a temporary member of the Barcelona Athenaeum: seven and a half pesetas a month. I like the building. The pleasant feeling of having a safe haven. The first desire you must satisfy in a big city is being alone. This is a very useful desire, and if you can satisfy it, the city can be a very productive place where you can work to great profit. What would be the point of big cities if it weren't for the impulse toward solitude that a life lived among so many people generates?

Even so, I'm not sure the Athenaeum is the ideal place to be alone. A short while after I sit down—rather at a loss—at a small table in the library, the young librarian who admitted me so pleasantly, comes over and introduces me to a young man dressed like a shop assistant.

"This is So-and-so the poet," he tells me. "I am sure you will become friends."

I get up, hold out my hand, and say, "Delighted to meet you. Are you a poet?"

"Yes, sir. A *noucentista* poet."

"Splendid! Tell me more."

He is a tiny, pale, skinny fellow with a timid, piping voice and a huge forehead that seems illuminated from within. He waves his hands energetically.

He pulls a chair over. There's hardly anyone in the library. The librarian stands and stares at us. The poet gabbles and I find him difficult to follow.

"I have heard you write too," he tells me.

"No, senyor...vaguely...nothing much really."

From what he recounts at great speed—if I've understood him correctly—it seems there is going to be a poetry festival in some distant town or other. There are money prizes. Accordingly, he says, one should do something to win these prizes. The only point of a poetry festival—he stresses at some point—is to win all the prizes, and he meant *all* the prizes. Festivals have no other purpose. To this end, one must have a team of friends and act—he says—organically. He will be the prime mover. He is hand in glove with the festival director. He knows a most influential priest. He has wealthy uncles in the town where the festival will be held. He was born in a neighboring town, although he has lived in Barcelona for many a year. He ostentatiously emphasizes the fact that he resides in Barcelona—pronouncing *Barcelona* with a very open *o*. In a nutshell, it appears that the municipality in question is home to two literary groups that are at each other's throats like cats and dogs. He—the *noucentiste* poet—is a leading member of his group, and his faction prefers to align itself with outside elements rather than witness the unpleasant spectacle of prizes going to the opposing faction. His group wants to go for the whole caboodle, to sweep the board with the prizes. Sweeping the board is one of the ideals of this country: The thinner and paler the hopeful individual, the greater the urge to sweep the board.

"My dear poet," I say, feeling my patience running out, "all this is quite beyond me—"

"I am simply proposing a deal, a little deal that is quite feasible."

"I'm not interested in deals."

"So what are you interested in? I have heard that you write."

"Oh, it's a marginal activity. I'd prefer for you to leave me in peace."

The poet gets up from his seat as if a spring has been sprung. The seat makes a lot of noise. The librarian looks at me for a moment wide-eyed, then is very pleasant. A gentleman reading at the next table comes over, grinning. The poet disappears in a temper, though he doesn't blow his top.

"No need to get upset, no need at all!" says the gentleman with the smile.

The librarian, who seems quite appalled—and who is fated to introduce me to people today—says, "Sr. Alexandre Plana."

"Delighted to make your acquaintance."

"Don't take things so to heart, I beg you!" he adds, broadening his smile.

And then he returns to his table and to what he was reading. I can tell he is reading the *Mercure de France* from the purple covers.

I feel somewhat depressed. My entry into the Athenaeum has won me another enemy. I cannot control myself. It is hopeless. I believe what I think and do what I believe. How childish! It's not a good route to take. Socially it is quite the wrong route and totally negative. I tell myself I must correct my ways. You must immediately apologize to the poet the next time you see him, I tell myself. I imagine that being a good *noucentiste* poet, following the norms laid down by the Master, he must be married—like so many poets in this country—and blessed with strong, splendid children.

14 January. Whenever I walk through the entrance to the university I think of the many hours I've wasted there, the wretched things I've endured there, the good it could have done me and didn't. This horrible building is an indescribably dead, futile, alarming pile of stone!

I only remember two activities with pleasure from the whole of my degree program: a melancholy, almost tearful evocation of the Parthenon by Don Antoni Rubió i Lluch when he was talking about literary classicism and an analysis of Bismarck's politics given by Don Josep M. Trias de Bes from his chair in international public law.

When I attended Don Antoni Rubió's course on the history of literature in 1913–14, he was a small, stocky, plump gentleman, who wore a bowler hat and an overcoat with a velvet collar. He was very old by then but still held himself upright and steady; he was red-cheeked, a congealed, rather inflamed shade of red that contrasted with the whitest mustache and hair. His hair was always combed very tidily, with a part, a small forelock à la française beautifully shaped by the thick, broad teeth of his comb. He carried a small cane. He walked rather hesitantly across the faculty courtyard in his ironed, neatly hung gown, beneath a red-tasseled cap. Because he was very shortsighted and his eyes were weak, weary, and bloodshot behind thick, mournful spectacle lenses that obliged him to walk with a stiff gait, staring ahead like a blind man, he gave the impression he was a distinguished, determined, entirely serious gentleman. He was patient and generous as a teacher and listened to the puerile—at best—comments we parroted from the manuals, as he wiped his lenses with a snow-white handkerchief. His bloodshot eyes stared at us and I imagine he saw us as if we were shadows in a misty haze.

17 January. Yesterday I went to the Palace of Catalan Music. Bach and the *Kreutzer* Sonata on the program. It is a horrendous, wretched venue that defies description. I find it quite impossible to concentrate on music when faced by that frenzied panorama of plaster and majolica. Besides, I was in pain: My shoes had just been mended and squeaked noisily. I admitted defeat halfway though the concert and left. How is it possible that the venue for one of the few decent things we have can be so off-putting? Obviously the Orfeó is decent and can hold its own anywhere. Could it be true that in this country things that aren't inflicted with bad taste suffer a stunted life?

The Rambla is wonderful. It is one of the few streets in Barcelona where I feel completely at ease. There are always enough people to guarantee that one will meet an acquaintance or two, but there are also enough that one can lose oneself, if one feels like it. Taking a morning walk along the Rambla, between forensic practice and mercantile law, is like passing from death into life. So many fascinating sights! Today I saw cigars from Havana in the tobacconist on carrer de Sant Pau that sported this sublime name: Flor del Senado.

Before dinner, a group of young artists who tell me they belong to the Courbet Group make a big song and dance. They are bubbly, entertaining, and fiendishly energetic. There are two small fellows—Serra and Viladomat—who are mad as hatters: One is tall, shortsighted, and pitted by smallpox and looks like a ghost, while the other, whom I find wittier, is profoundly serious and always seems to trail behind. Everything people might do to keep the Rambla from turning into a stiff, cold place is highly welcome. If large cities don't have a degree of naturalness and spontaneity, their gravitas is intolerably monotonous.

There are three delicious things in Barcelona: bread, kidney beans, and cod. Cod cooked in any manner: baked, stewed, with potatoes ... etcetera. There are also excellent pastries—but as I don't have a sweet tooth, I rarely partake—and coffee and tobacco. Barcelona's damp climate preserves tobacco leaves in an ideal state. Moneyed people can smoke phenomenally well in this city. The Continental and Suís cafés are perfect down to the last detail.

18 January. I like to spend my afternoons wandering along the streets of old Barcelona. Today I saw a magnificent girl on carrer de Ferran and carrer de la Llibreteria: sultry, fleshy lips and mouth; gleaming wet teeth; bright alert eyes, like a gazelle's; round, firm buttocks; long, firm legs under thin stockings. Long legs and full calves. As they say in French, "*Les mollets bien fournis!*" A magnificent specimen! Glorious Astarté!

I was enjoying the view when Salvi Balmanya's face popped up in front of me—from La Bisbal. I immediately recognized his noisy, affected, invasive rural accent. Balmanya does a perfect imitation of the way Coromina talks and gesticulates, and when I see it isn't him, I'm doubly upset that I lost sight of that sultry girl. When I realize she's gone for good, Balmanya bids me farewell and disappears into the crowd.

As I walked through the throng I realized how difficult it is to see people's faces with any precision. Physical traits are elusive and constantly hiding. The faces of men and women, who are so close, approach, pass, and disappear into the labyrinth of old streets as if they were flying two yards above the ground. That fact has surprised me more than once: I've sometimes tried to describe the face of a person with whom I have consorted for a length of time and have been unable to recall a single feature—not one. Conversely, I do retain, obsessively, elements I've glimpsed for a moment, a fleeting detail, a particular eye, a very specific movement of the mouth . . .

As dusk falls, I often pop into the College of Lawyers library. It's a magnificent building. The library is dark and severe, and the atmosphere solemn, monotonous, and gloomy—so morose as to be laughable. I have spent very many long, long hours there in the course of my degree despite the place's unhelpful catalogue. The chiming cathedral bells rescue me from my torpor, my chemically pure—legalistic—torpor. I've experienced moments of such deep silence that when the vibration of the bells fades, I often hear the worms at work in the wood, in a parchment, in the paneling . . .

The only approachable, pleasant individual in the building is one of the few who is not a member of the guild: Sr. Venanci, the librarian. You ask him for a book. He takes fifteen or twenty minutes to bring it, but hands it over with a smile that momentarily lights up his long dark overalls and sad, yellow teeth. He is the only person with whom people allow themselves to relax. The other day I heard a gentleman ask, "Sr. Venanci, would you believe that the Madrid *Gazette* also comes out in Galician?"

19 January. However, since I've been a member of the Athenaeum I don't visit the library in the Casa de l'Ardiaca nearly as often. Carrer de Canuda is now my final port of call.

In that learned institution, Costa the barman serves good, if weak, coffee. He is a pleasant, restrained fellow, even-tempered, unlike Ramon the waiter, who is a brutish, rude oaf. The library holdings are extensive, entertaining, and for my tastes almost inexhaustible, but I find the atmosphere too distracting. I've made friends with Alexandre Plana, and we grow closer by the day. He looks shy but is in fact quite a gossip. He promised to take me one day to the club he belongs to, which is the Athenaeum club par excellence. Plana writes with a great facility he lacks when speaking. He is extremely knowledgeable, but his tendency to extrapolate and complicate rather than simplify leaves me cold. Mentally, I find him rather domineering.

When I sit in my corner of the library, I sometimes think about what I've left behind. My memories of Sant Sebastià are fading. Those of Palafrugell endure more energetically. All in all, I recognize that the sudden surges of sensuality that have made me suffer so are starting to yield slightly—thank God. I can now read for three or four hours without being distracted. This must be a consequence of the poor quality of food in Barcelona that cannot rival the cooking in the countryside—especially the meat and fish.

After dinner, I go to Cafè Suís with Xavier Güell and my brother. It's a wonderfully luminous café, the color of fresh butter, and it's a great pleasure to be there. A waiter walks past our table carrying a splendid plate of oysters. I am twenty-one and have yet to eat oysters. I am such an unlucky man!

When the revolving door turns, it is as if the whole tumult on the Rambla sweeps into the café. This illusory intrusion of the street constantly changes the shapes and colors inside, but this blurring of things is a short-lived mirage. It's like reading an inspiring book—a great novel, for example. Such a book rushes through your mind and body like a surging wave of life. But there *is* a difference: The book changes you—more or less—leaving its mark, injecting a substance that one day, sooner or later, will come to the surface and flower.

The humanity of the Rambla! It's an inscrutably human street! So many stories come and go every day from these cafés, shops, and stairways! The air is saturated with their human feel. You sometimes see strange people, men and women, standing and staring at you for a second in rather absurd stances, as if they are bewildered or stunned. These gazes, that are quite empty, impact me as if I were looking at myself.

On my way back, in Canaletes, a couple of Civil Guards—several pairs, in fact—are frisking people. Passersby stand with their hands in the air. What a performance! Those arrested are taken to plaça de Catalunya, under the palm trees, where you can see a large group of people. We try to pass by unnoticed and do so. Barcelona is under military occupation. Social unrest is on the rise. Everyone is talking about revolution—in a faintly intrigued tone. But isn't government not about wanting to avoid revolution but about avoiding the very use of the word? I have little interest in such matters. They are for idle folk. The only revolutions I like—and that's saying something!—are those that are over and done with, those that are useful to teachers and historians who want to keep their pot on the boil and see their pupils through high school on a strict diet of literary exercises.

19 January. Professors.

I read this phrase in Xènius today: "The problem with professors is neither the system nor their ideas nor their temperament; it is the podium." And it brings me right back to my latent obsession with my university.

When I think how I've now spent more than five years in this establishment, I cannot avoid harping on the enormous sacrifices my family has had to make to enable me to study at a university. I see red. The professoriat professors . . . is there anything else like it in this life?

There are, for example, professors one cannot hear. There were two in my day: Sr. Joan Permanyer and Sr. Planes i Casals. No doubt they were fine, upstanding citizens with distinguished reputations as lawyers. They were very old gentlemen, having attained a respectable old age. Sr. Planes i Casals was a great expert on civil law. Don Joan Permanyer was a legal expert reputed to have an admirably perfect knowledge of Catalan law. He was, moreover, a legendary person: In the days of the Renaixença, he rode leisurely to Madrid in a trap drawn by a country mare. What's more, he or his brother had been a minister. However, time forgives no one: They'd reached a state in which, from their professorial chairs, they were absolutely unable to communicate their thoughts to their students. Their voices were so weak that unless you sat a foot from their lips you couldn't possibly catch what they said. But that was unimaginable because there was a podium and tiered seats in between. The result: I never managed to hear what they said or ever succeeded in getting them to hear me—because they were both hard of hearing. From a pedagogical perspective it was like having two deaf-mute teachers. They represented the failure of the podium theory of university education.

20 January. I play truant from forensic practices. I haven't been to class for three or four days. I spend the morning strolling along the Rambla. I spend hours in the afternoon in the Athenaeum library. Apart from this scribbling, I have managed to write a couple of quartos in one week that are vaguely intelligible. How can one be so patient?

The day that began so gloriously in the morning ended at three in the afternoon under a low, blanched sky.

When I read that Beau Brummell's luxurious shirts and gaudy ties gave Lord Byron violent nightmares, I think about the turn life has taken today, a turn that is more pronounced by the day. I would no longer dare to wear even a modestly fancy waistcoat. But that is quite understandable, given my temperament. It's much harder to say why even exhibitionists don't dare wear such things. Encouraging men to cultivate their most personal, individual, idiosyncratic taste is a thing of the past. One is now encouraged to cultivate general, imitable mediocrity. It may not be so picturesque, but I imagine it is much pleasanter to live in this gray world than in a world teeming with stiflingly ostentatious characters.

At night fog, a misty fog, turns the glow from streetlamps pink. Damp. Sticky, wet curbs. The damp cold makes silhouettes take refuge in shadowy doorways. The gloomy atmosphere brings an ocher tinge.

Shadows shine and shiver; lights drip. The dampness is quite oppressive, makes you shiver with cold. You need a haven. I think: If only we had a fireplace at home! All we have is icy floor tiling and yellowing, funereal wallpaper.

22 January. Early in the morning, when I am going to the university, I sometimes pass spinsters with a mantilla, prayer book, rosary beads, and purple circles around their eyes—one has dark eyes and smooth hair. These apparitions make me think of Girona, prompting that city's sanctimonious, early-morning life to dance before my eyes. By virtue of a mechanism that remains a mystery, my mind always links what I would have liked to do and didn't dare do—that is, clandestinely—with Girona. Its old stones always acted like an aphrodisiac. I'm thinking of the cups of hot chocolate with long, thin biscuits that ladies indulge in on their way back from mass and of the many other things in the possibly permanently unfulfilled desires of these devout women, who look so gentle and dull, though all that may be very practical.

There are streets in the old quarter of Barcelona whose narrow, enclosed space seems to diminish and muffle the hubbub from the city, in fact, all noise, generally speaking: a carpenter's plane, a locksmith's file, a baker's kneading. Even the light seems to fade. I remember seeing a cavalryman's glinting gilt buttons line up next to the white blotch of an apron at the back of a dark entrance to such street. When you walk, as if dead to the world, through that vast labyrinth and feel the fog lifting you get the sensation of people on the move—scattering as they emerge from the cinema.

Barcelona migraine: headache, a feeling of distant pain, sharp, intermittent twinges and violent cold shivers—which finally drain your whole body, as if total exhaustion has struck you down. I haven't heard of anyone noticing how these states are linked to the southwesterly wind. My mother withstands these migraines by stiffening her nervous system between attacks of pain.

I am also quite prone but my defenses are different: I defend myself by entering a state of soporific apathy.

If I analyze a migraine, I feel it has two ways of operating: sometimes a deep, dull pain, like the pain caries causes in the jaw, in gums, when it starts destroying a tooth. At other times, we could say the feeling is linear, as if a small mosquito had taken possession of a nerve end and has started to fly: The mosquito pulls and the nerve unravels like a ball of thread . . . and finally you feel—when the thread runs out—that there is a great void in your head, a void that can be so insidious, so immediately perceptible anywhere on your body it gives you a temperature.

24 *January.* Joan Linares approaches me this morning as I walk past the Nouvel Hotel on carrer de Santa Anna. He is always so excitable, small, and friendly. I think Linares perhaps seems so polite on the surface because he is deaf. Afterward, in an aside during our lively conversation, he informs me that Roldós died on the eighteenth.

When I arrive home I find a letter from the deceased's sister that is tragically simple in its account. The pianist's poverty was relentless. Any bricklayer's mate earned more than that sensitive but hapless individual. Who could ever account for the powerful illusion art deploys to create such resistance to granite-hard reality? The news takes me back to the last few weeks spent with Roldós in Palafrugell: at the San Sebastià hermitage, amid the scent from the pines; our picnics in Llafranc, by the misty sea; the hours spent listening to him play the piano in the empty cinema; the girls, the aperitifs, the light-headed early hours fired by cognac. Poor Roldós! I'd like to find someone else to whom I could speak about him at length and remember him. There is nobody. And yet there are so many people bustling around me! His sister writes in her letter: "Perhaps Our Lord God has given him what he needed most." The word *perhaps* is redundant here.

It's raining. The Athenaeum. I am quite overwhelmed by the library with its green lightshades in the darkness at four in the afternoon. Weepy palm trees languish in the courtyard. The books smell of damp because they've been shut inside so long; the paper has a damp quality. I go out into the street. Rain shoots off the balcony guttering onto people's umbrellas—umbrellas that hop along the streets. Soft, trodden mud—like mush. I go into the cathedral. Inside, with the low sky and light filtered by rain, it's a pale purple, like lilac. Immersion in nonmaterial raptures that lasts a long while—until they close. I trudge home on foot. Arrive wet and tired.

25 January. Athenaeum, from four to seven o'clock.

As I don't have anything I can send Roldós's sister, I write an article dedicated to his memory, for *Baix Empordà*, which I send to Linares. While I write I realize I can't recall his first name at all. Roldós, then. I haven't the slightest idea what his first name was. Perhaps I never knew what it was, or perhaps I've simply forgotten. It is curious how we all tend to cultivate forgetfulness. Roldós seems particularly apposite in that sense. Many people who knew him and will read my article will have to make an effort to remember him, to focus on the vague, evanescent image he has become in their memory. Perhaps Roldós's anguished suffering was simply about his need to return, and the sooner the better, to total darkness, to eternal peace.

As I'm leaving I bump into Josep Codolà, a fellow student, by the door to our apartment. We walk together up Passeig de Gràcia. Though only a youngster, Codolà displays a good knowledge of the wheeling and dealing of local politicians. He tries to fill me in but I struggle to pay attention. I don't succeed, because I notice, as we walk, that my friend becomes more and more resigned, as if to say: This young fellow's going nowhere, hasn't much of a future. By the second or third street corner, he says goodbye—he must have decided it wasn't worth wasting any more of his time on me.

26 January. I spent the morning strolling along the quay with my friend Xavier Güell. Apart from being a law student, Güell is a designer of so-called decadent fashions and trivia. Even so, direct contact with reality, our stroll along the quayside, was pleasant enough.

We saw the battleship *Pelayo*, the captive German submarine and the Spanish submarine anchored next to it. The latter seems to be made of tin. It has seen little of the sea. The German specimen is draped in slag from the sea and looks like a slumbering monster covered in algae.

A cool southwesterly wind. The gusts chase over the harbor waters and darken them for a moment. Two sloops maneuver in the wind, lying on their sides, like two winged arrows. We watched a passenger ship come into port. The passengers waved their handkerchiefs. Who were they greeting from so far away, unable to see anyone? They must be greeting their own arrival on dry land. The sea horrifies everybody and it is only natural that people are delighted to reach port. A tugboat, with an absurdly tall, thin chimney, gasps as it pulls barges along. The Barcelona quay is cold and artificial, a routine geometrical display of stone, but some areas are sooty, aging and seem warmer. Things of the sea can be so pretty!

We walk up the Rambla. The light is harsh and underlines the earthy stewpot gray of Barcelona. The brightness emphasizes people's ravaged, weathered features. So much drama on their fleeting, ineffable faces! Then we continue up Passeig de Gràcia. The morning gets even brighter and seems to expand. The Rambla is full of what artists thirty years ago called model heads. Passeig de Gràcia is full of perfect, stiff, shaven heads.

I try to write in the Athenaeum library but nothing happens. I sometimes think my recurrent writer's block is peculiar in a literary milieu that is home to so many poets. In the first place, I have never written a single poem. My lack of ability, on this front, is so acute I have never even tried. Many people write poetry from their tenderest childhood, almost unconsciously. A tune catches their ear and they feel the need to elaborate. The moment comes, however, when the tune—for whatever reason—abandons them. I assume that explains why there are so many twenty-five-year-old ex-poets—poets who've retired from poetry. In a country so abundantly musical, writing in prose, describing any object—a tree, a mustache, a rabbit—is more taxing.

The problem of literature is hugely complex. If one sits, pen in hand, before reality, the first challenge is making oneself understood. Initially, this is far from easy. Reality is dense, chaotic, and impenetrable. One might formulate the problem of pinning dense reality down to this: Given that reality presents itself as if every detail was determined by the purest chance, to what extent can we understand things? The movements made by men and women are so various and so entangled that they are as dense as any jungle foliage. (Knowledge of a person's inner being isn't even on the agenda because it is beyond reach.) In his infinite smallness, and using only intuition, a writer has to focus on a specific piece of land, on a particular face, features he finds characteristic, generic, and permanent within the shapeless stream of what life secretes. To reach that point, he must select, identify the vital traits, and find the perfect signs to create life, matching the right adjective with the right noun. How do you do that? How do you proceed? That is the question—and the task is hugely difficult.

At night, in the apartment, I spend two or three hours tearing up sheets of paper. On a slightly yellowing square page I come across a sentence I think particularly clumsy. It says: "Almost unawares I raise my arms, hands, and head in the air, and open my fists to snatch a scrap of blue." The description of this inchoate desire for blue and heaven that Maragall created so effectively in poetry is simply grotesque in prose. But this sentence reminds me that I was sixteen once—with a sixteen-year-old's sensibility. The fact that writing reflects one's sensibility at sixteen, twenty, or forty-five doesn't increase its worth. Writing that endures gives the impression of a sensibility that is both intelligible and generic.

31 January. Alexandre Plana introduces me to the poet Marià Manent, a Catholic poet to be precise, as I later learn. We talk at length. He seems to be a highly intelligent young man: perfectly discriminating and perfectly able to control his impetuosity and manage his irony. He is a young man who is very organized at home and at the office—one of those people whose desk is always clean and tidy with everything where it ought to be. It is natural, given these parameters, that Manent is fascinated by English neo-pagan poets—Shelley, Keats, etcetera—who lived dreaming of the adorable nudes of Greece and Italy stretched out under a Mediterranean sun.

Manent asks me for financial help to publish the writing of Giral, a young man of good standing, who wrote like an angel. I can give him nothing because my own poverty is beyond doubt.

It's raining. I can hear water falling on the other side of the windows. I always like water, wherever it is. The streetlights create an astonishing play of light against the soaked, battered horse carriages and automobiles. Cities in the rain—if it doesn't rain too hard—seem sumptuous, with a pleasant, welcoming air. One feels pleased to be indoors, working under a lampshade. At night, I hear the rain splashing monotonously on the skylight. The gutters drip. I wake up when the weather is clearing. I open a balcony door slightly. The sky has a vaguely phosphorescent glow and the air, a purple and mauve hue. A stunning silence. Barcelona is like one endless cemetery.

1 February, Sunday.

Candlemas. So many memories! When I was a youngster, I used to take red, green, and yellow spiraled candles to the exuberantly baroque high altar, glowing so deeply golden it was like a pastry oozing its filling. The light from the rose window gave the choirboys' rochets and priests' chasubles a rainbow hue. The wax crackled and spat out golden sparks, like a shower of tiny stars. As the wax was greasy, people gripped their candles in small folded white handkerchiefs. The offertory was conducted with appealing solemnity. How many years ago was all that? Who knows! The glow and the red, green, and yellow candles are no more. The chasm is absolute. Does that mean I'm perhaps edging closer to something else? I don't know. We can hardly lift our heads above water: That is our malaise today.

I go into Can Parés. Paintings by Tamburini. A bad start to the day. When you think how the critics say this artist was trained on the banks of the Thames in contact with English painting, you feel you're going crazy. Is this the English Pre-Raphaelites? I suspect Tamburini's eyes were elsewhere. The effect is horrific.

In the afternoon, at the library, I feel despondent, momentarily downcast—a kind of nostalgia for the simple life. How can you shut yourself up in this book-lined tomb, under these green lampshades, in this stale, dusty atmosphere, when the whole of life is out there waiting to be lived! Those divine Sunday afternoons that shop assistants, soldiers, members of the Lliga, dancers, film and football fans, etcetera must enjoy. Sunday afternoons impart a mighty dose of free-afternoon poison, which is extremely difficult to turn down. Fully in its thrall I wonder if those of us who come to the Athenaeum library on a Sunday afternoon aren't the crème de la crème of the city's idiots.

At dusk, the sky over the Tibidabo was wondrous: a mandarin-orange sheen.

2 *February*. Uncle Martí, my father's brother, has come to visit from La Bisbal. He is a lawyer in that small town. He is rather reserved, seemingly shy, with a fair beard that's beginning to turn gray. He sometimes seems on the sickly side. He has a melancholy, depressed manner and reacts lethargically. I've only seen a glint come to his eyes when there is talk of hunting, dogs, rabbits, or partridges.

After supper, he insists we go to the theater. I had never thought of doing such a thing. I think it's an astonishing idea. My sister Maria and I accompany him to the Poliorama. They're performing *Marrying My Husband*. When we come out, he smiles at us enigmatically and says nothing. Then he takes out his cigarette case and lights up while we walk to Canaletes. We take a tram home.

The play's stupidity upset me. I don't feel sleepy and stay in my study. By chance I look at the calendar and see it is Saint Blas's Day. I automatically think of Brother Blas in the Marist school in Palafrugell. I wallow in a swamp of sentimentality. He was a small, vigorous man, with an unforgettably tough physique. He taught me to read and write and to think clearly—in truth, he taught me all I know. I feel duty-bound to proclaim that I am infinitely grateful to him. Likewise I feel duty-bound to say I am grateful to my parents for everything they did for me and to my forebears who perhaps toiled away darkly—who can tell?—on our behalf, and the friends who have taught me so much. A strange business! It lasted a few seconds. Why didn't it last longer? Outpourings of sentiment should bring happiness. It makes me suspect that every pantheistic pose conceals a dream of happiness, rather than a concern for truth.

As a result of this to-and-fro I recall that it is only a year since I first heard Beethoven's Sixth Symphony—the *Pastoral*. The description of a landscape and man's fusion with nature has possibly never been evoked so clearly. Some foolish scholars have compared the score's molten emotion to Bernini's *Saint Teresa*. (I've seen reproductions of this torrent of sickly sentimentality.) Beethoven is infinitely superior: He is virile, noble, uncluttered, and clear. The baroque irritates and disgusts me. Baroque verism is literally pornographic.

I could succinctly sum up what I wrote (26 January) on the approach to the problem of literature. It is about restraint, focus, and precision. What carpenters call working on the detail. Extracting from the shapeless mass of life the graceful or dramatic line of a melody, the vivid profile of a human life, a form. In short, it is a struggle against excess and the infinite. A struggle that makes you sweat.

Perhaps this is the problem posed by the big city: Tackling its diversity means enduring its tedium.

Sentences of that sort are the best paid in today's newspapers. They open every door. They are sentences penned by all-conquering *noucentisme*.

3 February. Don José Ortega y Gasset writes like an angel. He has extremely felicitous moments. He says, for example, in yesterday's *El Sol*: "I would say that the sign of a great poet is the ability to tell us something that nobody had told us before but that isn't new to ourselves. Every great poet plagiarizes us." To attain this level of dynamic synthesis implies a huge general culture and a lively wit. I have been reading Ortega from the publication of the first issue of the magazine *España*. I don't know what impact the magazine might have on me now. It was considerable at that time. However, I have recently read that "the encephalic mass of the nation has emulsified" around Don José Ortega y Gasset in Madrid. That is quite another matter.

Phrases. There are fancy phrases. For example: the irreproachable silence; gastronomic bliss; the soothing spring...

In the daily newspapers one often reads about sentences that are pregnant with meaning. The idea that there are sentences that are pregnant with meaning has passed, thanks to inertia, from novels and plays into journalism. Nonetheless, it is a fact that this kind of sentence exists. It wouldn't be the first time "Tomorrow is another day" has halted me in my tracks. It is relatively easy to create such sentences. Throwing them off afterward is the real headache. They are useless, artificial dead weight one carries in one's head for years.

A weedy young lady, a pharmacy student, stands in front of the statue of Ramon Llull in the university lobby and tells me she would like to accompany some of her friends to plaça de Catalunya to see if there are "still soldiers on guard there."

"If only you could go and watch it on a big, noisy motorbike that runs like the wind, know what I mean?"

"Oh, wouldn't that be perfect."

"And if they fired a few canons in the meanwhile...wouldn't that be even more interesting!"

The young lady gives me a would-be shameless glance, smiles hopefully, and walks off without giving me an answer.

I'm drinking much less than in Palafrugell. I wouldn't resist even slightly more than my usual intake.

4 February. Uncle Martí returns to La Bisbal with his suitcase in its yellow cover and a sealed roll of paper under his arm. He went to the theater every night. He belongs to the generation that goes to the theater. When Gori comes to Barcelona, he does exactly the same. When he's in the mood, he will tell us what he's seen over the last few nights.

Uncle Martí brought a kind of drowsy calm to the apartment in the time he spent with us. It probably isn't what he intended, and he must have been the first (involuntary) victim of the situation his presence engineered. However, it's true that family habits are indestructible. When he walked through our door I expect he thought, "These nephews and niece of mine are unbearably solemn."

Now everyone will go back to doing what he wants. At any rate, I must confess that this year I haven't felt the need to escape from the apartment in the early hours—and to tiptoe back holding my shoes.

Joan Climent, whom I met at the university—he was two or three years my senior—and whom I have just seen in the Athenaeum library, is preparing for the entrance examinations for the consular service and now returns my "Story of Raincoat Number 33404." He tells me this story wasn't quite right for *D'Ací i d'Allà*. Fine. I immediately blush. This was something I struggled to put together two years ago and in fact had quite forgotten. But I reacted by blushing. I tell myself I must never go red again even if the ground gives way beneath me. Then I pull myself together. I accept that Climent's decision isn't at all unfair. It is a fair decision. I regret all the hours I wasted writing the piece and not receiving any good advice earlier. But good advice is so difficult to find! Even if I had been lucky enough to receive any, however, I'd have probably rejected it for reasons of pride, vanity, pedantry...

It is absurd to write the story of a raincoat. That's plain. It requires no effort to see that. What interest could such a story have? Joan Climent is older than I am. He's very cultured and very generous, and has exquisite taste. Why didn't he say something at the time?

As I walk home up Passeig de Gràcia depression reasserts itself. I walk slowly, head down, thinking that I shall never write well and will have to devote myself to the legal profession. Then I mentally review the anodyne, insipid group of my fellow students. They are pleasant, intelligent young men without substance. Most will never achieve anything. I will have to devote myself to the legal profession. When I think about this, I feel powerless, and go cold.

5 February. My generation. When I speak of my generation, it is laughable. What do I know about my generation? I mean the literary generation. The rest—my time at the university—is barely of any interest to me.

However, when I speak of my generation, I am speaking for myself. I am my generation—because I am sure there *is* a group dotted around, people I don't know and can't pinpoint, who see things and think as I do.

It is when I talk to people twenty years older that I clearly grasp the characteristics of the generation to which I belong. We come from books. We have read books and more books. We think we have lived because we have read books. Books have given us hope. Books have brought us hope in something. We have waited years and years for that something to happen. And what has happened? Absolutely nothing. At all. This has led us to conclude that books say one thing and life says another. Books tell us that the world, that men and women are made in a certain way. Life tells us that the world, that men and women are made in quite a different way. Books tell us that love, glory, goodness, and greatness exist. Life tells us that none of this exists. What do poets talk about? What meaning do the words of poets have? Why do they speak as they do? What makes them speak as they do?

I was born in a tiny, tiny place. My life's horizons have been very restricted. My circumstances have led me to be particularly sensitive to the dazzling flame of the printed word. Books were placed in my hands and I read them. What beautiful things one finds in books! Life is this and that and more besides—so books say. But then it turns out that nobody is any wiser, that nobody makes any effort to create what books affirm. One discovers that what books say serves to hide, to *camouflage*—to use a word in vogue—life that is mediocre and unprincipled. Nothing one finds in books exists. One person differs very slightly from another: a little cleaner, better educated, with varying levels of hypocrisy. Books don't contain what they contain in order to deceive us deliberately! Their authors simply never thought we would take them so seriously. Every era has been the same and the so-called great eras only existed in the imaginations of those who have written the books about the so-called . . .

6 February. Montjuïc.

In my first years as a student in Barcelona, barely out of adolescence, I was very fond of taking walks on the mountain of Montjuïc. I knew all the streets and backstreets in Poble-sec that cover the sides of the mountain. Poble-sec was a teeming mass of humanity like those I've been told exist in southern Italy. There is so much washing hanging out to dry from windows and on balconies, so many children shouting in the streets, so many groups of men and women sitting in doorways, so many hurdy-gurdies, so much singing and such a racket from balcony to balcony that passing through this world was like being pummeled and bashed on your back. In the month of May, daylight was white and impish, and the humility and privacy of life seemed to evaporate: Everything became vulgar, coarse, and ragamuffinish. I remember, nevertheless, that whenever I walked that way, I saw a twelve- or thirteen-year-old girl, with large, still, dark eyes, tousled hair, in rags, sitting on the curb in a daydream and indifferent to all around her. She ate peanuts and hummed sentimental songs about the poverty of the district.

Beyond the urban congestion, deep silence descended on the boundary the mountain carved for itself. I took a path flanked by oil drums. On each side were tiny, miserly plots of red clay, which had been added to the slope. I never saw anybody in these plots. The path was stony: Rubble from city demolitions was deposited here, and dusty, sour green prickly pears were everywhere. However, the mountain wasteland began past that huddle of sad little plots. A great panorama came into view. I sought out a patch of dry grass to sit on under the bright shade from a fig tree. There was a strong smell of thyme and lavender. The delightful peace and quiet above the faint hubbub from Barcelona was quite wonderful. These remote spaces were so intriguing, and their lyrical presence, which I soaked up, gave more substance to immediate sounds: the wind in the pine trees, the tremulous breeze in the shade of the fig tree, the barking of a distant, invisible dog.

The castle stood out at the top. Like any anachronistic fortress, Montjuïc seemed highly romantic. It made me think of eighteenth-century Spanish lithographs and French serial fiction—two things I have always liked. The castle and surrounding bare mountain composed a single oblong print. You could only see the cowed, receding rim of the structures jutting out above the long, horizontal lines of the glacis. I imagined General Espartero—a mug from a matchbox—putting his French omelet of a beard on the parapet to better direct the bombing of Barcelona and to put down the republican uprising of the Jamància. You could also see a large expanse of sea and black steamers and sailing ships heading out of port or landward like abandoned toys. Then the spectacle of the great city appeared between your knees, gently sloping down from Collserola to the harbor's gleaming white, blotched by the turtledove gray of its old stone. Seen from the outside, Barcelona is a white city. From the inside, it is yellowish gray—an earthy stew-like color. In the sun, a bright, lively flame rises above the white city that flickers westward and eastwards with the wind, and sometimes carries into the far distance . . .

I climbed a little farther. I've spent hours among the rocks on the far southern and western sides of the castle. From these vantage points you can see the plain of Llobregat evaporating over the Garraf mountains, a spongy haze behind a transparent mist, streaked bluish, mauve, and pearl. In the foreground, the scrub-covered slope hurtled precipitously down. The altitude brought a fragile breeze scented by dry fennel and flowering gorse. The wind whistled sharp and faraway through telegraph aerials. Black semaphore spheres went up and down on the small castle turret. The plain of Llobregat was spread out like an imaginary map. A train was progressing cross-country, a tiny, serious, professorial train. Shots from a hunter's gun rang out in the distance: The small white puff from the powder rose, then evaporated in the still air after a moment of delightful indecision. Children were flying their kites on the mountainside. The reddish tails fluttered nervously in the air; the cords described full, ripe curves. One kite slowly drifted away and seemed to draw a gaggle of children behind it through the scrub. In the cemetery the tips of the cypress trees burned with a yellow glow in the setting sun.

I started the walk back at dusk, my stomach churning acids, my mouth parched, and I perhaps glimpsed a dubious couple or threesome searching for a hiding place. The path ran alongside the glacis and the silhouettes of sentinels were blurred against the gray-red sky. Green gusts of wind set off a distant cry, the screech of the iron water-wheel among the cultivated plots. And suddenly, in the pearl-colored sky, a sharp bugle blast from the castle seemed to bring the day to a close on a strident, petulant note. Its piercing falsetto made the first stars tremble.

I reached the highway proper as the lights of Barcelona came on. They began coming on in fits and starts, but sometimes they lit up in a flood—describing a long line. The small, moribund lights in the port entrance stole my heart. The atmosphere in most of the city was luminous rather than dotted with light, a glowing haze that seemed prompted by the spread of invisible rain. There were tense lights, morbid lights, sad lights, lights one could describe as possessing a fictitious zest: so many kinds of light drifting uncertain and diluted in my memories of days that are dead and gone.

I began to descend feeling exhausted; it was all too much for my legs. I felt unjustifiably oppressed. The soldiers on patrol often shouted "Halt," and their stern cries sapped my spirits. They were a few feet away but I could see only shadows. I gradually left the castle's dramatic silhouette behind and suddenly heard the notes of a hurdy-gurdy coming from somewhere. The music seemed nearby but never within grasp, and the notes buzzed around my head. From then on, every step I took ineluctably led me back to the hustle and bustle of the city. That morass of people, lights, and sounds made me lose sight of the world for a moment. My body felt as if it was turning into rubber. I blinked and I could see the poverty dripping from balconies in the bright, clear night air. I reached the Paral·lel in a sweat, my hands cold and dry. I saw the reflection of my pale, drawn face in shopwindows. I walked slowly for fear my rubbery body might bounce up onto the balcony of some lodging house for absurd, peroxide blond artists.

The tragic death of my friend Ramon, a denizen of the northern skirts of Montjuïc—the one that touches Poble-sec—saddened me and reminded me of that past era in my life. Deceased Ramon owned a tiny, ramshackle amusement park consisting of a carousel and a booth with a shooting range. The park opened in the summer and in the winter the owner used his magical powers to transform the park into an afternoon dance hall.

The whole lot occupied the shadowy depths of an orchard on one of the Poble-sec streets that went up to the mountain. You had to cross a sprawling, noisy, boisterous neighborhood to reach it.

Ramon was a Sunday friend. In the winter, by this time, I'd almost always go to his place after Sunday lunch. After six days of university constraint, we were light-headed for a few hours: It was a true escape. At that time of day the Poble-sec was bathed in large expanses of warm, sunny silence perfumed by the bittersweet smell of oranges past their prime. This intense, still tranquility was constantly under assault from the distant screams of a gang of squabbling kids and the dull buzz from taverns full of guitars twanging monotonously. As you walked by, you'd spot the musician by a marble-topped table, twisted around, one leg crossed over another, displaying a red sock, a cigarette behind his ear, a forelock of hair twirled like a rolled wafer over his forehead, surrounded by a large circle of moist, gaping mouths.

I remember, as if it were today, the precentor's voice of an old, very tall, bearded blind man who walked around Poble-sec singing the ballad of the shipwreck of the *Valbanera*. Locals crowded onto their balconies to listen to him: the women in their petticoats, the men in their yellow overalls. When the blind man walked past taverns, he tramped on peanut shells, and as he clearly hated the noise, he'd hop quickly over them like a clumsy bird. In tavern doorways there was always a young worker, an oblique figure, in an ironed blue suit, the band of his peaked cap on the tilt, a butt end on his lips, a carnation in his ear, haughty and silent, with a hint of roosterish cruelty on his lips. Girls from Castile and Aragon also walked arm in arm, a mother-of-pearl pink-apple glow on their cheeks, their black hair wet, wavy, and combed flat. These girls sometimes gave a helping hand to small, weary, snub-nosed soldiers chomping on orange peels and peanut shells.

There were a lot of the war-wounded, crippled, maimed, and poor, and occasionally they formed a kind of barricade with their walking sticks, twisted limbs, wooden legs, crutches, and other tools of the trade that belonged to this hapless crew.

After crossing this neighborhood, I took the road to the castle. I turned down a track that followed the glacis, sat for a while to gaze at the sky, the Barcelona sky in winter, which is beautiful, especially on windy days—a sky where white clumps of cloud scudded over warm blues, faded greens, and a crimson haze—and later, with a sprig of thyme on my lips, hands in pockets, my feelings and thoughts wandering vaguely, I'd amble down the path to the rudimentary park where a pompous municipal building stood among foliage and reach the skirts of the mountain and go and take a look at the late-lamented Ramon's afternoon dance.

I did so with trepidation because the heavy haze inside made me feel dizzy and the dim lights kept flickering. When my eyes got used to it, in the center of the threadbare marquee I could discern a kiosk made from four staves supporting a platform surrounded by chicken wire. Perched inside that cage, in a sea of smoke and dust, were the murky figures of three musicians clinging to their instruments as if they were life buoys. The gaslight reflected in dull, vaguely melancholy fashion on the gilded metal of a flugelhorn. Towards the back, you could see the merry-go-round under wraps in the late-evening gloom. Between that grandiose hulk and the marquee's canvas walls a large slit allowed you a glimpse of the starry night.

When the musicians weren't playing there was a muffled hubbub of noise in the marquee. Occasionally a girl screamed in that Spanish chocolate-colored circle of hustle and bustle as if she'd just lost a tooth. Children played chase between the legs of the dancers and sometimes three or four rolled in a ball across the floor. There was always a mother sitting on a chair suckling a child. The wan, lined complexions of these mothers, in that light, made me think of Sisley's paintings, though I'm not sure why.

Ramon always carried a stick he used to adjust the gas lamps and remove grease. He slithered around like an eel, was everywhere, shouted at the musicians, kept an eye on the ticket office, sorted out problems, moved on people jamming the entrance, threw out bad payers and troublemakers.

Rather than simply sound out, the music groaned and roared. It was bodily-driven music, pure explosions from the lungs that hit you in the guts. When it started up, a huge, rowdy, brightly colored mass of humanity encircled the cage, swelling, changing shape. On main holidays the plume on some soldier's tin helmet would stick out above people's heads, a hussar's helmet floating over the polkas and mazurkas. Dust turned the gaslights red, the haze was granulated, speckled with droplets of grayish pus.

Ramon was a small, lean, bald man with thick, bushy eyebrows. He wore an ironed rubber collar and celluloid cuffs; his voice was gravelly and he drawled like a superannuated comedian. It was obvious he longed to be a bohemian artist because he let the nail on his little finger grow, made outlandish statements, and had a tendency to dress like a dandy: He wore, for example, a pale turtledove-colored fancy waistcoat and wielded a gnarled, wooden walking stick. This vein in Ramon's spiritual life found an expression in his passion for rod fishing on the breakwater, a thing he loved to do, even though he was a third-rate fisherman.

Ramon was a human beanpole who concealed an enormous sloth behind a façade of decency. Basically he was what good writers call a misunderstood man. He took an interest in anything out of the ordinary. He felt that working, that is, organizing a dance, on a day when everybody else had a day off was proof of his superiority.

Ramon lived on the merry-go-round. His kitchen was at the top. His pantry was in the belly of one of the papier-mâché horses that pranced up and down. He hung his clothes on the trumpets played by the carousel organ's nymphs. He welcomed people sitting on his rose-garlanded portable chair—the chair children's mothers used on the merry-go-round. In the circular hollow between the central column and revolving roundabout he kept a stack of four shabby, brown-painted small boxes, four old shoes, faded clothes, and long, extravagant fishing rods. When he walked through the Barceloneta with his rods, he was out to create a big stir.

The most original touch was his bedroom. Ramon would hoist himself into the bellows of his carousel's organ. The bellows were connected to the carousel by a mesh and a pulley. When the carousel went around, the bellows swelled and deflated. When it was full of wind, the bellows looked like a truncated pyramid, a kind of frog's mouth with a leather-covered iron frame that folded when it deflated. The

bellows were set horizontally behind the frieze of nymphs and dancers who lifted gilded trumpets to their lips and whose swollen cheeks
pretended to puff when the nasal-toned organ played.

I remember telling Ramon one day that it was dangerous to sleep
in that lair.

"One day, the carousel will start up for some reason and the bellows will compress and you will be mashed to death. Luckily, however," I added with a laugh, "while you're being ironed as flat as a pair
of trousers the nymphs' trumpets will blast out a fanfare and the
dancers will raise a leg."

"It will be a death with a charm of its own," he retorted in that
childishly vain tone artists adopt when recounting their peculiar ec-
centricities, and scratched his wrinkled forehead and bushy eyebrows
with the long yellow nail of his little finger.

When I heard that Ramon had died I went to the amusement
park. I entered the orchard. Not a living soul to be seen. The shooting
range was closed up and the carousel covered over. I was about to leave
when I saw a woman with a sack of paper over her shoulder and an
orange in one hand.

"They buried him yesterday," she said. "They found him dead inside the bellows."

"Why did he die?"

"Nobody knows. The day before yesterday he went to the breakwater with his rods and today he's pushing up the daisies."

"Do you live in the neighborhood?" I asked.

"Yes, why? You're not a policeman, are you?"

"Did the neighbors hear the trumpets blast a fanfare the night he
died?"

"I think I heard someone say something of the sort. You *are* a
policeman, aren't you?"

A slight pause. Then: "Did Sr. Ramon have many enemies?"

"I don't know, who would?"

"Perhaps someone from the breakwater, you know?" I reacted, just
to spin out the conversation.

"He was a good man, but a dead loss," she muttered incoherently.
"You know, they didn't find a scrap of paper in his trunks."

350 · THE GRAY NOTEBOOK

"You collect paper in the street, right?" I asked, without looking up.

"Yes, sir, why?"

Another short pause. I poked the ground with my thin, gnarled stick, using its point to dig out a clean white pebble.

"Did anyone go to his funeral?" I asked, blankly.

The woman stared at me, her face shook and she couldn't stifle her laughter. Then she began to peel her orange.

I looked at her, rather perplexed. I realized I had committed a gaffe. What a peculiar question! I thought of the last funeral I'd heard about, which had been packed out. I said, "I'm sorry. Enjoy your orange."

"Thank you!" replied the woman, keeping her eyes on her orange.

Then I went out into the street and slowly walked away.

I have become good friends with Alexandre Plana at the library. I see him there at one time or another every day. He is a man who tries to give friendship a paternal twist. He likes to provide guidance and useful advice. He sometimes stands and stares at me, looking rather enraptured. I don't know what he sees in me; perhaps it is my extreme youthfulness. Like Josep Maria Junoy—to whom Plana introduced me—he likes (I suspect) to test out literary virgins. I prefer to have contact with older people and Plana with younger ones. We are on course to be as thick as thieves.

He is tall, very tall—so tall you feel if he looked at the ground he'd be dizzy. His whole manner is hieratic, slow, and spare. He enjoys stasis. This isn't the result of any deliberate decision on his part; it is a consequence of his height. He is so lanky it can be annoying. There's always a part of his body that doesn't know where to put itself—and he has to take care not to stumble. That's why he keeps looking ahead. His face is slightly pitted from smallpox. His gray-blue eyes are the eyes not of a dreamer but of a man who has grown tired of dreaming.

I sometimes think he seems slightly Oriental. He likes stasis, contemplation, and I can imagine him without his cane and top hat, which give him such a Western air. I can imagine him dressed like Tagore, with a tunic down to his feet, long hair, an iodine yellow face, sandals, pockets stuffed with birds and butterflies, gazing at the sea through a film of melancholy ecstasy.

Plana's culture is very Western. He reads from beginning to end *the* magazine of the intellectual world at large: *La Nouvelle Revue Française*. He has the major defect I detect in all those who take this magazine too seriously: He confuses first-order and second-order notions. However, that doesn't mean his inner complexion isn't Oriental. He has the warmth of a sage, the patience of a wise man, the gift of friendship, and he is an infinite fount of goodness and understanding. You don't have to be a friend of Plana for him to take you seriously! Would you like to hear something from on high, from a dizzy height? Even if you aren't on close terms with him, tell him about your work. Act fearlessly, speak, and don't hide a thing. Plana will listen, will listen endlessly, as long as is necessary. His silences are stubborn, persistent, radical, and final. Faced by his appealing unresponsiveness, you might perfectly well think you could say, "This fellow agrees with me." Or else: "I know as much as or more than this fellow."

Tell yourself whatever you want. The more favorably you speak of yourself, the more genuinely happy Alexandre Plana will feel. Talk to him, charm him, marvel over yourself and your work. Plana will help you. He is constituted to give you help, to make you feel happy, and to love your little insights. In this sense, his role is priceless, quite invaluable.

Now if I had to say what lies at the heart of this strained, enraptured, Oriental wonder, I wouldn't know where to begin. I sometimes think it's pure candor; sometimes I see a hint of sloth. It's almost as if Plana's acquiescence, his tendency to keep nodding, responds to a kind of profound lethargy that prevents him from formulating any kind of value judgment that would endanger the preservation of his contemplative, entranced quietism.

In this sense Plana is pure mystery—a man impossible to see at all clearly. Superficially, everyone thinks of him as clear and straightforward; the more I deal with him, the more elusive he becomes. This game he involves me in has done me a world of good because it has cured me of my abrupt, summary syntheses. Perhaps he will provide me with a way to probe his mystery. He immediately tells me that he'd really like to own a house in the Ampurdan, by the sea, to live there with me and lead the quiet life of a sage. I could be the one fishing with a rod, gazing into space, nose stuck in the air, while dreamy-eyed Plana followed the flight of the birds through the sky from under a pine tree. I'd have to respect his stubborn silences—this would be our deal—and he, my sorties into the real heat of life. In this way, according to him, we will die as we have lived: our feet touching the ground and our heads adrift and iridescent. If this kind of coexistence didn't succeed in providing the key to his mystery, I can't think what would.

8 February, Saturday. The Industrial University of the Mancomunitat. Philosophy seminary. A lecture by Eugeni d'Ors on Cournot. As a lecturer à la française, Xènius scales voluptuous heights. He is magnificent. I suspect it is many, many years since Catalan has been spoken so correctly, ambitiously, and incisively.

Joan Climent accompanies me on a tour of the building. Intelligent leadership and refined taste are evident down the smallest detail. From a spiritual point of view, the seminary must now be the most august edifice in Barcelona. For a student at the official university as I am, accustomed to that sordid place, the seminary's external appearance—curtains, flowers, lights, seats, tables, books, and cleanliness—is like a dream. The tone of people there reveals a world I couldn't even have imagined existed.

As he is saying goodbye, Climent gives me Joubert's book to read. I open it in the tram. I read: "Simplicity has never corrupted taste."

When I reach home, I continue reading Joubert. I find him infinitely agreeable. Joubert is a very reasonable man, never sour or pedantic, and he has admirable taste. It is inconceivable that such a writer could be from these parts. Teachers here become pedants and their pupils, anarchists.

By virtue of an almost unconscious insight, I attempt to establish a parallel between Joubert's book and another I have just read: Baroja's *Momentum Catastrophicum*. Although Baroja is one of the most European writers in the country and the least localist in his outlook, he was pro-German during the last war. As he can't publish in newspapers or anywhere else, he is now bringing out a book every two or three months, commenting on the situation today. It is rampant, unbridled lunacy. All Baroja's misanthropy, savagery, and grotesquerie are unleashed. He is subversive, bitter, stunning as a cosh, strident, spontaneous, disrespectful, sentimental, confused, bilious, chaotic, mutely ironic, apocalyptic. From time to time a splendidly real observation appears amid the turmoil—which is, nonetheless, never strong enough, however impressive, to compensate for the general deluge. When these matters gush from an open spout, they lose their qualities and can't be taken seriously; the violence fizzles out from pure excess. In the end, Baroja's pamphlet sounds like an outburst from a good-natured father who has lost his temper over something trivial and vague.

I'm not acquainted with France. Joubert's book is inconceivable without a society behind it. Baroja's book is attached to nothing; at best it is literary freewheeling, a verbal game.

9 February, Sunday. A morning that spat icy rain. A polished sky. An unpleasant, insidious cold. I should have gone to the Military Academy in Drassanes to start my training. I didn't.

In the afternoon, I accompany Xavier Güell to his home—a solid, luxurious apartment on Passeig de Gràcia. It has a fireplace. The sight of a proper fire in Barcelona is inspiring. What a delight! There are houses here with cardboard made to imitate wood in the fireplaces. They place a red electric bulb on top. And that's that. Then I walk in the gentle rain down to the monument to Columbus.

At the Catalan Students Association I listen to chapters from a novel by Vidal Jover. A romantic writer: lots of setting suns, the moon, copious references to Chopin, but nobody has a clue what his characters live on. Daddy and Mummy must be paying. In this country, it's very difficult for pathos to be convincing. It has to be very good and completely genuine not to be considered a scam. Maragall's pathos is considered acceptable. Who else's?

Afterward we go to the Refectòrium with Elies the cartoonist (a sarcastic spirit behind the *Anem* cartoons), Arús the poet, fellow student Vidal, and two or three other youngsters. Stabs in the back are various and in good supply. Boredom from excess. Everything is gratuitous and off-the-cuff. However, objective observations of reality rarely amuse people in Barcelona. They prefer grisly incisions in the vein—presented, naturally, in a good-hearted fashion.

In the first phase of intoxication, absinthe makes you feel tired and exhausted and at the same time induces a real lightness of being.

11 February. The concierges of Barcelona, when they talk to people, can never keep a straight-faced expression: They can't pretend. However long they've been on the job, they still carry on with a gossip's curious expression on their faces, as on the day they started.

One could argue that differences of opinion in daily newspapers are really the result of differences in the organic constitutions of their clientele and not of differences in political attitude: There are dailies for the bilious, for hypochondriacs, for the neurotic, for the erotic . . .

When we were children, if we didn't go to school we said we were playing hooky. Now if we don't go to our university classes, we say we're playing truant. It means exactly the same. Life's childish phase lasts a good long time. I've just played truant quite inopportunely. They performed "La Marseillaise" and "Els Segadors" at the university. I made myself miss the show.

While meandering along the city streets I met a lad from Palafrugell who sings baritone.

"Calvet," he introduced himself. "Don't you remember when I used to sing in church?"

Of course I do, as if it was yesterday. I try to get him to tell me what he's done since, but I see that he hasn't much to say for himself. Like so many who have left Palafrugell, he seems to have lost his center of gravity.

"Singing's a joy," he replies absentmindedly, "but the toasted bread is what I miss!"

The Athenaeum library until two o'clock. A stroll down the Rambla. Lots of hustle and bustle. The erotic marketplace in front of the Comèdies theater is striking. Many tall, buxom, majestic young ladies from the south of France. Their buttocks pass by and gyrate like spheres seemingly controlled by mechanical springs. The concentration of people here is quite cosmopolitan. Facial features are shaped by greed—by a sad tough veneer or fake joy. There are carts of greens by the Boquería, plump cabbages sprinkled by drops of water, and pinkish broccoli. Workers begin to emerge in the streets that crisscross the Rambla; they carry their lunch tins, white silk scarves around their necks.

12 February. It has rained a lot over the last few days. Everyone has a cough and a cold. Freezing cold permeates these apartments. The smelly oil stoves become unpleasant. The weather finally improves: It is a benign evening and a starry night.

Latest news: Fiume, D'Annunzio. Europe is a madhouse. The Peace Conference is soon discredited.

I think about Roldós. He was a cloying, clinging fellow, who liked to posture, swagger, and dispense things that were like scraps of colored paper. For my taste, he'd have been more agreeable if he'd been more straightforward, even if he'd have preferred the full, rounded sort of straightforwardness. But the ways of the clergy leave their mark on some individuals. Apart from that, Roldós was a hundred percent good; he was remarkably ingenuous.

As I see it, a genuine literary challenge would be an attempt to attain the most complete ordinariness.

14 February, Friday. The burial of a distant uncle—Uncle Pepet Colomer. I use the diminutive form of Pepet, not because I knew him well, because I didn't; I do so, because that was how he was always referred to at home. He had married an aunt from Mont-ras on Grandmother Marieta's side. He was tall, pale, haggard, feeble, methodical, and fastidious and seemed afraid of debate: the template for the average clerk. Whenever I saw him he appeared to be recovering from life's hard knocks.

When I reach the apartment on Avinguda de la República Argentina, I hear weeping as I climb the stairs. An almighty anguish. Grandmother Marieta—who has come to the funeral—is beside herself trying to console everyone, and above all trying to comfort Aunt Carolina, who is devastated.

The priests arrive. Vague chanting. It is a radiant, sunny morning. The burial party organizes itself, those attending greet one another amid the trams, cars, and passersby. Long ride to the old cemetery in the windowed carriage. Halt at the level-crossing to let the boat train pass. An aging cemetery, well preserved: a handyman who still hasn't finished the niche, tips to give, not knowing what to say. Afterward we go back to the apartment with Quimet—a relative of my uncle's who is a jeweler by trade—his son, and Bosch, the son-in-law of the house. Grandmother Marieta consoles everybody, as indefatigable as ever. Uncle was goodness itself; he'd been much abused.

When I return to the university after the funeral I find the place is on strike. The Civil Guard is in the entrance; the only access is through the half-shut lobby. Nobody can tell me why there is a strike. I suspect it is an offshoot from the general situation. There is much working-class agitation in the city. Everyone says we are moving toward a general strike. The vigilante militia is recruiting and openly arming people.

The newspapers report the death of Jaume Brossa. At the Athenaeum, Plana tells me that whenever there was the slightest disturbance in Barcelona, Brossa was one of the first the police arrested. It seems his file was never closed. When they went for him today, he was on his last legs.

Before dinner I go to the Military Academy in Drassanes for training. I simply have to turn up for drill; my military service is postponed because I'm exempted as a student. The academy is next to the military pharmacy. As I walk through the entrance, I smell the odor exhaled by this kind of establishment. The Drassanes antique book stalls are on the other side of the road.

I am sent to a long corridor, poorly lit by yellow bulbs, where forty or fifty strapping youths, practically all strangers, are creating quite a din. A sergeant reads the roll call and people calm down a little. We put on cartridge belts under our jackets and they give us Mausers. Then we go out into the street and are put through our paces in the customs area, under arc lights. There are so many idlers in Barcelona that, despite the cold, inopportune weather, we always have an audience. When it rains or the weather is bad—so the sergeant said—we will stay inside and read theoretical articles.

Bolt and chamber. We have to buy the manual. "You must learn the manual by heart!" the nervy, bad-tempered sergeant often tells us in Spanish. As far as I'm concerned the description of the gun in the manual is unintelligible. A practical lesson would make much more sense. It isn't at all easy to understand the description of a mechanical device. This is all completely new to me and very peculiar.

That night, at home, I read *Aurora* by Nietzsche. I vaguely feel that I'm coming to grasp life in the ancient world by reading Nietzsche. I say it's a vague feeling—evidently. I can't say more than that, unfortunately. No other scholar has influenced me like Nietzsche.

16 February, Sunday. The upheavals in the university continued until yesterday, Saturday. The workers' disturbances are spreading. People are waiting on what will happen tomorrow, Monday. There is a very real fear that Barcelona could be left at any moment without light or power.

I spent part of the evening with Salvador Eures in his apartment on carrer de la Universitat. He's been jotting in notebooks from long before the chaos group existed—I gather it is a very intellectual diary. His apartment hasn't changed: It is dark and fusty. His idols remain unchanged: Nietzsche and Wagner. In fact, Eures is a conservative whom Nietzsche has thrown into disarray. He is still actively anti-democratic. He loves German declarations about vital superiority and the slave ethic.

The notebooks Eures reads me in snippets have one common element: an obsession with women. There is an endless stream of comments against women. "I am a feminophobe," Eures tells me, and the word amuses me, "but that doesn't make me effeminate.

"To perform woman's only worthy function, the most essential act they do, a purifying mass is necessary." I find his tone revolting and rather sinister. He writes elsewhere: "If a man in an amorous relationship acts with the reserve the woman usually adopts—for, if men are open, women hold back—then the woman, with most calculating cheek, will broadcast the terms of their relationship."

I think: "And so what?"

But are strategies of love as important as Eures thinks? I think the problem is of a different order. I remind him of the Wagner-Nietzsche anecdote.

Wagner to Nietzsche: "Get hold of a woman, Herr Nietzsche, get hold of a woman!"

Nietzsche: "How can one get hold of a woman?"

Wagner: "Steal one! Drag one off! Smash all obstacles!"

Like so many young men who are supposed to be the product of a serious, careful education, Eures may mistakenly believe that man is a rational rather than a sensual animal.

Grandmother Marieta is still here; she says she doesn't feel at home.

Deprived of her carrer Estret and the opportunity to go out with her shopping basket every day, she doesn't know what to do with herself.

"There are so many people here in Barcelona!" she tells me. "Too many for my liking. When I was a child, fifty or more years ago, we thought Barcelona was a large city. But it was nothing to what it is now. Moreover, everything is so different from what it was in my day! When we lived in plaça del Palau, everybody ate stewed meat every day. Now hardly anyone cooks that. And have you seen all the dairies? In my day, only the sick drank milk."

18 February. As the situation in Barcelona is still very tense and you can't go anywhere without putting your arms in the air, I stay in and work at home. I sometimes start to become obsessive about the years I've spent at the university. Why do people always talk about the carefree student life? I've never been able to understand the meaning of such words, at least as they might have applied to me personally. I sometimes recall episodes from my life as a student.

My father was forced to have recourse to the normal processes of the law, first to put an end to the disastrous rice business in Pals and then to set in motion the rice-field venture in the province of Huesca (in Ariestolas-Montsó): what is vulgarly known as the snowballing of letters of exchange. This one lasted a long time. It soured my youth. I was forced to experience hard times.

My father wrote me from Palafrugell: "On the fourth a letter for 1,800 pesetas runs out. It will have to be paid at the Magí Valls Bank on plaça Urquinaona. Don't leave the house on the fourth. I'll send you the money by messenger. When you receive it, go to the bank and cancel the letter. You must give this priority over everything else: It is important. It has to be done to avoid all the other costs."

When the fourth came, I stayed in the apartment and waited for the messenger. I waited anxiously. Three things could happen: The messenger and the money might come on time. In this case, it was simply a question of going to the bank, queuing for a long time, and canceling the letter with an unhelpful, rude clerk who's just made a profit and acts as if he's done you a great favor. Unfortunately, however, this likelihood was the exception. Generally, things followed a different pattern.

The messenger usually came to the apartment at half past twelve. He had to follow a preset itinerary and couldn't have arrived earlier. With the money now in my possession, I raced downstairs, caught the tram to plaça de Catalunya, then ran along the Ronda to Urquinaona and galloped up the stairs to the bank—because the bank was on the first floor. I joined the remnant of a line in front of the window. I was generally last. At that point it would strike one o'clock. The cashier would glance at the people waiting. If he spotted a regular customer or a well-dressed gentleman he would deign to carry on working a little longer. Then one might hope to achieve a transaction. But generally, when the clock struck, the door to his little window shut immediately. We were left glowering with disappointment. We looked silently at one another. People tended to leave, crestfallen. You could hear them walk slowly downstairs.

I once dared to rap on the polished glass with my knuckles. The cashier, taken aback, opened up a crack.

"I had to pay off a letter," I would say shyly, almost shaking.

"It's too late! Letters of exchange must be paid before twelve."

"That's right. But it's not my fault. It was out of my control. The messenger came late."

"What am I supposed to say? Notice of nonpayment has been sent. If you hurry—"

"Where must I go?"

"To the College of Notaries. If you hurry you'll get there before their usual time for dispatch."

That would be the case if the cashier was in a good mood or even took pity on me. He'd usually have much more important matters on his mind and would shut the window after our first exchange.

Then I ran to the College of Notaries. I had to go so often the concierge came to treat me quite affably. He accompanied me to an office where a gentleman in a yellow overall sat: a clerk who wrote on sheets of paper that each carried a seal. The concierge whispered in his ear. The clerk disappeared for a time and then returned with a bundle of letters of exchange. We looked for our letter. They never let me look for it. I'd place the money on the table and he'd hand me the document.

"That's eighteen pesetas!" he'd say angrily, as he handed it over.

One day, after rummaging nervously in my pockets, I still didn't manage to find the money for the charges the college made. I clearly remember that now. Eighteen pesetas isn't very much money. It is an absurd, pathetic amount. It is a pathetic amount, particularly, when you have it. When you don't, it humiliates you and makes you look ridiculous. The porter had a surge of compassion and advanced me the four or five pesetas I was short. I walked back to the apartment and arrived at a quarter to four, feeling harassed, pitiful, and unbearable.

But there was a third possibility: that my father hadn't been able get the money together for the fourth and the messenger thus brought it on the fifth. Then there'd be no point going to the bank. I'd go straight to the College of Notaries and explain things to the relevant clerk in a yellow overall.

"The letter," he would say, "has been sent."

"Yes, yes, of course. To which notary?"

The clerk would leisurely open his desk drawer and take out a typewritten list. He'd glance over it slowly and carefully like a genuine notary until he found it.

"Notary So-and-so has got it, on carrer de Casp," he told me, puffing on his yellowing cigarette. "That's where you'll find it."

I ran to notary So-and-so on carrer de Casp. Notaries live in central locations, usually impressive, spacious apartments with high ceilings. A pleasant sense of calm and well-being usually reigns. It was disheartening to have to enter these places looking like a poor debtor, with an almost criminal air, to cancel a referred letter. A referred letter! It was horrible, intolerable! I'd have much rather walked into one of these apartments to lunch with the notary and his wife and children!

The suspicious, inquisitive hack would receive me, the clerk usually sitting in the small pre-pre-office space at the notaries—hacks who have usually aged prematurely with pale, ravaged faces and elbow pads.

"What are you after, young man?" you heard him say.

"I've come to pay a referred letter of exchange."

Some took advantage of the opportunity to trot out all the relevant legal rigmarole.

"A letter of exchange, young man, is a document that bears a degree of compulsion."

"That's why I have come to pay it. Please take note—"

"Very good, so be it. Wait a moment."

The scribe would disappear through a door that was concealed behind a curtain, because notary offices have a secret, artificial air about them. After a prudent interlude, the clerk would reappear along with another gentleman who didn't wear elbow pads. This gentleman carried a piece of paper: It was the letter.

"Tell me what I owe you, please," I'd say after putting the amount to cancel the letter on the table.

"That will be thirty-eight pesetas."

The amount differed according to the amount owed and the time that had elapsed since its referral, but thirty-eight pesetas was the standard payment.

I'd walk downstairs with the letter in my pocket feeling relieved, as if a great weight had been lifted from my shoulders, but exhausted: Two days of dreadful tension had played havoc with my nerves. Back on the street, it would have cheered me up to see everything in a prettier light, but generally I could only see black circles on a yellow background going up and down before my eyes. I often sat on a bench, let time go by, and held my hat in my hand. I felt faint. As soon as I grew stronger, I'd recall that next month I'd have to repeat the routine.

Brought up to obey the strictest bourgeois orthodoxy, to be sensitive to the horror of being in debt, and taught to earn and pay up promptly, I could never adapt to that wretched, peremptory, stifling situation. I'd have preferred total poverty to the monthly humiliation of accumulating letters of exchange. If only I could have let my hair down. But how, and with whom? All this happened when I was between seventeen and nineteen—at an age when I still couldn't formulate a coherent, plausible critical judgment. On the other hand, my loyalty to my family was absolute: I believed my father had done all he possibly could and that if he'd made any errors they were more a consequence of the way he'd been trained in his day than of any intrinsic failing on his part. The only thing I began to grasp was how ridiculous it was to go into business if you didn't have the right temperament. The whole sorry mess led me to meditate on the right strategies to adopt in life. I began to see that taking responsibility for one's own shortcomings was a matter of survival. If one's awareness of one's shortcomings were obscured by the glow of one's positive features—or virtues, if you prefer—the result could be lethal. I've always believed that the marrow in the bone of Socratic wisdom—"Know yourself"—is "Know your own failings."

These are some episodes from my life as a student. They've influenced my development infinitely more than the university itself. If I were to say that letters of exchange, till windows, and the whole cycle of referral and cancellation have horrified me ever since, that would make it seem a mere picturesque detail. They horrify me so that if I ever disappear, you're much more likely to find me digging roads than going in and out of banks or standing in line at a till window. They've left me with much more than a sense of repulsion; they have left me with a bitter taste in my mouth—a taste of ashes.

20 February, Thursday. Life as usual. I'm working—more or less. I go to the university, attend my military training exercises—chamber, bolt, short barrel, etcetera—and go to the Athenaeum. Long conversations with Joan Climent and Alexandre Plana. The former is a Catholic who respects atheists. The latter is an atheist who respects Catholics. Climent, who knows his side well, trusts atheists. Plana, who knows his too, trusts Catholics. The social unrest remains threatening and tense.

Salvador Eures, who lives on the fringes of everything and is surprised that the world isn't what he says it is in his notebooks, invites me to spend carnival day in his town: in El Vendrell.

I went to the funeral of Professor Boix's young child.

Grandmother Marieta left on the evening mail train. She didn't need to put on mourning dress for Uncle Pepet. She told me she's been wearing it for more than thirty years. She departed with her whitest of white hair under a scarf and a basket on her arm.

21 February, Friday. Alexandre Plana advises me to become involved in proper literary activity: He suggests translating a really tough French book. He proposes *L'Écornifleur* by Jules Renard. The title of Renard's novel plunges us into an endless discussion. What does it mean? Can one translate *L'Écornifleur* (*The Sponger*) by *El tastaolletes* (*The Dilettante*)? Of course, that isn't quite the same thing. Translating is a devilishly difficult occupation but I see how useful it is. Especially useful for getting to know one's own language.

In the Athenaeum I met Miquel Ferrà, who seems a very genuine sort. He is a poet and librarian at the Clinical Hospital. I was predisposed against him because when he was a librarian at the university he never brought me any of the books I ordered. Soon after I had handed him my chit he'd search me out, book in hand, and say, "This novel by Pérez Galdós will do to while your time away, won't it?"

I'd look astonished and he'd grin. Today he said, "There are a lot of very good books in the university library. You asked me for a number. I always saw you leafing through the catalogue. I never brought you any of them. I always followed the same criteria as Sr. Aguiló in this matter. Good books should never be taken to the library reading room. It's a place for reading Blasco Ibáñez or Pérez Galdós, you know?"

Ferrà is a polite, energetic, neat man. His nose is rather Murcian, a waif's, a nose from a skull belonging to Argar Bronze Age culture. I like him, above all, for his independent judgment—even though he hales from Majorca.

Barcelona is remarkable tonight. Everything has been plunged into darkness. It is so astonishing it is literally beyond words. The silence is what's most striking—the deep, deep silence. You can hear neither the distant wail of vessels setting sail nor distant trains. Nothing at all. It's like living under the heaviest slab of lead.

22 February. The weather is very good—inexplicably good, almost hot. Clothes are annoying. The leather on your hat sticks to your forehead; the breeze out on the street is too gentle and warm. I bump into Gich, a medical student, on my way to the Athenaeum. He says he's going to Palafrugell for carnival. He doesn't tempt me to go. I don't have the time. Even idlers like me have to miss out on so much for lack of time!

I work on the Renard translation in the library. It is tough. I would never have thought it. I'm embarrassed to see myself surrounded by so many dictionaries. It is quite beyond the pale. Nonetheless it allows me to understand why people who devote themselves to learning are so happy. What bliss it must be to rummage among papers and be surrounded by tons of books! The life of the scholar is so enjoyable!

After lunch I stay in the apartment for a while. The girls have gone to school. It's very peaceful. The noise from the street is quite subdued. I prepare coffee at my desk—a pleasant task—and read. My mother sits next to me, darning. Now and then she pushes her spectacles over her forehead and looks at me for a moment—how shall I put it?—objectively. What can she be thinking? When she notices that I know she's looking at me, she puts her spectacles back in place and goes on with her darning.

Late in the afternoon I go to the Lyon d'Or with Xavier Güell. People are arguing heatedly at a couple of tables. Those raising their voices argue about the general situation and present wave of strikes. Those talking in more muted tones are debating the resurgence of the influenza epidemic. There is a fresh outbreak of the flu. Güell tells me it's nothing to worry about and that you only die once. Individuals who are in love—and Güell has fallen in love with a most elegant, willowy young lady—are courageous.

We leave the café and walk up carrer de Sant Pau. We want to see the situation in the city for ourselves. As we progress, the bustle in the street mounts. The cinema exit seems to vomit people. They're roasting chestnuts on street corners; people eating chestnuts and peanuts prop up the walls. Small shopwindows display dishes of boiled haricots. Billiard balls click in bars and cafés. I can see a group of men's heads poking out above the corner of a screen. They must be playing seven and a half. Bullfight posters on the walls—leftovers from the summer. Couples disappear through doors and up stairways. Orange peel on the street. Lights flicker sadly in apartments. The white blotch of a dress is draped over a balcony. We turn up carrer de la Cadena. There is less bustle and light than on Sant Pau. People are poorer, the street gloomier, the stairways darker and dirtier. The women on the sidewalks are old. Unrelentingly oppressive—that is, lugubrious. A girl with a pitcher of water—her skirt like a cowbell. When I walk past a particular house where I stayed a few years ago, I think of the dining room, that fat lady who always sat in her rocking chair—who'd have her hair combed after supper by an old hairdresser. The walls were covered in a purplish paper dotted with family portraits. I think of the faces on those portraits—of the sitters' anonymous, enigmatic expressions.

24 February, Monday. I spent the whole of yesterday and part of today in bed with the flu. Sweated like a horse. For thirty-six hours on the trot. I get up looking pale and out of sorts. On the other hand, I think how I might have died, something I've only just avoided. When I can get up despite feeling exhausted, I conclude it must have been a benign strain. Mossèn Clascar and the poet Joaquim Folguera have died within the last few days. Like so many others! The number of death notices is enormous. It scares you stiff! People say the infectious microbes attack particularly strong, robust organisms. However, if that's the case, how can you explain Joaquim Folguera's death? I knew him by sight. He was hunchbacked and dramatically deformed. When I walked past the Continental, I'd see him through the window, the top of his cane sometimes resting on the bar counter, while he sat at a table with López-Picó, Carles Riba, and Obiols. He was the man behind *La Revista*—its inspiration and guiding spirit. I admired him immensely and would liked to have been on sociable terms with him. I especially took to him because I thought he was occasionally short-tempered in this pressure cooker that is Barcelona.

Through the window.

It is a bright, sunny afternoon, frighteningly fragile and delicate. White clouds. The sun gives them a pink lining. The sun glistens, the afternoon is blue and the shadows are almost as light as in springtime. A very gentle breeze blows. And death on my doorstep! I decide I'd like to go to the quayside and watch those ridiculous little steamers with their tall, thin funnels, as if they'd been drawn by children, sail over the thick, oily, oyster shell–green water. Driven no doubt by terrible thirst, I want to go into a tavern and drink a glass of cold dry white wine. Twilight and a pale orange sky in the month when cats are in heat again. I feel my high temperature returning.

I own very few books. I wish I'd been born into a house full of them. There are fellow students who grew up surrounded by piles of books. It would give me so much pleasure to own Flaubert's complete works. Twelve volumes of Flaubert cost thirty-eight pesetas and a few cents. Where can I ever find such an amount? I have trouble enough paying the Athenaeum.

25 February. I stay at home all day. Plana has been so kind as to send me *The Life of Friedrich Nietzsche* by Daniel Halévy. I spend two or three hours leafing through the book. I think it's well written and interesting.

In the end Nietzsche becomes a bad habit. His writing comes in staccato bursts. His probing keeps your intellectual curiosity on high alert. I look for the Greeks throughout his work. His wit and humanity make the speculation of his contemporary German Hellenists seem like sludge in comparison—one, Erwin Rohde, is particularly boring and intolerable.

Nietzsche has a side I'm finding more and more surprising: his secret, hidden passion for France and everything French. One detects that he feels a constant, though secret fatigue at the chaos in German scholarship, a lack of faith, a kind of lingering hunger for release, wit, and levity.

My father, who has just arrived from Palafrugell, thinking he will find me on my sickbed, is shocked to see me reading when he walks into my bedroom. We talk at length. He tells me about things back home. Apparently there are lots of fires in the bottle-cork factories. The alarm bells are constantly ringing. The general feeling seems to be that there's a citizen specializing in this line of work—and available for hire. They keep spotting him in the cafés, talkative, optimistic, and in high spirits—always ready to eat and drink. He is very able and, so far, it's all been fine for him. At the moment in Palafrugell there is general mirth surrounding the issue of insurance companies.

When we were children, our sense of moral restraint stopped functioning almost the second we spotted a pot of jam or basket of greengages. But it isn't merely a childhood phenomenon. Later on in life, it stops functioning in relation to a host of much more important matters.

Young people have noble ambitions because they have no ulterior motives.

One of the most disconcerting, unpleasant, and sordid aspects of life is the awareness that nearly all of us find an evil deed more exciting than a good one.

Shyness can lead as easily to inner turmoil as to a sense of accomplishment. A permanent state of attenuated, if genuine, shyness leaves one permanently sidelined. It's a state that is difficult to throw off. When shyness becomes this stifling and intolerable, one always hopes boldness will inevitably (suddenly) erupt. And it does.

It would be most interesting to see to what extent good physical health and physical contentment create good people. The possession of a well-stocked wallet helps in terms of producing physical satisfaction. I have brief, negligible experience in the matter. In specific cases I have, however, seen a definite willingness to forgive and forget on the part of people in good health—to forgive and forget rancor, malevolence, revenge, and cruelty. If you don't have an active, deranged, sick memory, acts of gratuitous, capricious cruelty are inconceivable. Civilized man's greatest virtue is his real or apparent ability to forget. A peaceful, solid society is based on the concealment of passive feelings of mutual contempt.

Those of us from outside come to Barcelona anticipating the worst. Generally for no good reason.

26 February. My sense of smell is coming back and I am quite delighted by the aroma of good tobacco, of tobacco from Havana, which one finds in many places in Barcelona. Sometimes, when you are walking down the street, you are stopped in your tracks by a sweet scent of tobacco wafting through the air. I am an inveterate smoker, but my economic state doesn't allow me to smoke good-quality tobacco. I am a very humble contributor to the nation's taxes in that sense, but precisely because I see these things with the eye of the imagination I appreciate them much more.

Good tobacco-leaf cigars especially require a certain level of humidity. The winds that frequent this country, and Barcelona in particular, are warm, sticky winds from the south. The humidity of these winds can harm people who suffer from rheumatism or migraine, but keep the aroma and taste of tobacco in a wonderful state of preservation. Humidity prevents the leaf from drying like parchment, developing hard patches, turning brittle, and breaking up. When the wind from Montseny—the local north wind—blows, the tobacco is not as good, by a long shot, as when a southwesterly is blowing.

The climate in this part of the Mediterranean allows one to enjoy some wonderful smokes. On the other hand, this doesn't mean the climate can transform bad tobacco into good. That would be claiming too much. What it does is to bring out the best of the good qualities of particular kinds of tobacco. The leaf retains its density, fleshy nature, and oily texture as if it were impregnated by a light, very subtle oleaginous substance. The aromatic depths of Havana tobacco contain a hint of decomposition, of vegetal fiber fermenting in a damp place—almost of putrefaction. You catch a taste of rich loam saturated with bacteria in the fiber.

Some people enjoy the aroma of tobacco, especially out in the open. I find it is quite delightful in a sitting room. The sight of a woman or a group of pleasant women across a perfumed haze of Havana tobacco helps life go by.

27 February. Back to normal. I go to the university and then to the Athenaeum. I am translating Renard. Harder by the day. I'm done with all the dictionaries at home. Renard reckoned that La Bruyère was the best French writer of all time. La Bruyère, whom I knew only superficially and am now reading more closely, writes clearly but is complex beneath that apparent simplicity. I suspect La Bruyère would be even more difficult to translate than Renard.

A gloss by Xènius on Mossèn Clascar, who has just died, describes him as the most important priest of his time in Catalonia. He makes me regret never meeting him. All the same, I can think of so many other priests. The church is so powerful! It can digest everything. It is humanity at its purest. It is when one sees that the "excursions into history" of present-day preachers can rival men of the fiber of Mossèn Clascar that one becomes very aware of the granite—human—substance of this amazing bulwark.

When people leave a library, they usually look tired and drained. I've noticed that when you walk out the door to the street, the concierges deign to greet you. Some do so by tipping their caps—maybe to avoid looking into your pitiful face. Others acknowledge you with a quick nod—even perhaps with the faintest of smiles. By the time the smile broadens and is visible, you are out the door. If you turn around now, how will you respond to the concierge's ironic stare? I have—so far—

never dared to turn around. If I do so one day, I don't know what will happen: I will either hug him or punch him.

The university. My fellow students. It is a strange world that reflects our society.

We have an important fellow student: Martí Esteve. He is part of the group that brings out *La Revista* and acts very Catalan in a rather pedantic way. He speaks about intellectual things as if he were attacking them furiously. I'm not criticizing him for that. On the contrary, it's proof he has a strong personality. Is there another young man in our year interested in anything beyond getting a pass? They are much less interested in learning than in achieving a pass. What are these fellows made of? What makes them tick? As there's nothing there, we must assume they are conservative. I sometimes hear them talking about their "daddy" and "mummy." Are they interested in anything in the world at large? Have they ever been moved by a book, an idea, or a feeling? Could we at least say that they are interested in women? I doubt it. I have no proof in that direction, either. Without financial backing from their family, which must be why they are studying, where would most of them be now? Without such money, come to think of it, where would I be?

The boldest and most confident in what they say in the faculty courtyard are the least equipped to act; they are the most insecure, the most vacuous, those who've shown the least firmness before the least adversity.

The class on mercantile law was conducted in the Catalan language today. I was expecting some protests. I recalled previous declarations I had thought were inflammatory. Everyone was delighted and thought it was wonderful. This is a flaky-pastry world. No energy to acquiesce; no energy to protest.

Today Dr. Cuello Calón, the chair in penal law, a pleasant man, one of the few teachers in the faculty with a proper university outlook, made reference to the death in Salamanca of Professor Dorado Montero. He was Dr. Cuello's teacher and a man of distinction. Dr. Cuello's words were clear, simple, and expressed with feeling. Professor Montero was too good a man—he said—to be a professional point-scorer.

When I got home I found everything turned upside down. We are afraid my brother has caught the flu. I feel very panicky.

28 February. Widespread anxiety. Everyone is convinced that a huge strike is about to erupt in Barcelona in the electricity, water, transport, and bakery industries. The Confederació acts like a giant. Salvador Seguí is the boss. Pestaña is his deputy. I know them both by sight. Seguí is a fat, rather apoplectic, slightly squint-eyed Catalan with an open manner. Pestaña is a thin, priestly, pale, suspicious-looking Spaniard. Two complementary elements united via very emphatic bilingualism. Romanones has closed the Catalan parliament and a declaration of a state of war is expected at any moment. In his *Glosari*, Xènius praises the grain of sand—the obscure life of the man who works quietly and contributes to the foundations of society. His tone has a strange ring to it.

Joan Climent.

He is a rather feminine spirit, well organized, aware, and receptive. He suggests cuts, changes, and revisions to the work of others for their benefit. He thinks I'm not yet fully formed because I lack a bit of good-natured skepticism.

"Clever thinking is not what thinking is about!" I tell him.

"I don't agree," he replies. "Wit is more important than thought."

"Why are you reading Nietzsche?" he asked me one day. "He is a savage. Voltaire is wittier. Though we must find ways to put Voltaire behind us."

"I don't think the distinction you make between Nietzsche and Voltaire is so clear. They are very similar, except for their respective eras, countries, and level of wit."

"Possibly, but the different level of wit is very important. It's the tone that makes the song. However, that's a secondary issue. I was saying we should put Voltaire behind us. Monsieur Joubert is the ideal author for today."

"Joubert is an invitation to skepticism. Do you really think invitations to skepticism are what's needed? When life has lashed us sufficiently, we'll all get there, God willing."

"You are too stiff, too tense."

"Do you know a cure?"

"Put a drop of wine in your water."

"Wouldn't it be better to pour a *lot* of wine into my water?"

When Professor Dorado Montero was buried, the university bell didn't toll. According to the newspapers, it was a civil burial.

It is drizzling. My brother seems to be on the mend.

1 March. The family's economic situation has worsened dramatically in recent months and we'll have to give up the apartment on carrer de Mallorca. It is a decision we've perhaps taken rather late in the day—as all unpleasant things tend to be left until the last minute—but in the end, we couldn't delay any longer. My mother and sisters went to Palafrugell today. The furniture will follow immediately. My brother and I will continue to live in Barcelona. We will find another home, and tomorrow is another day.

Our last night in the apartment on Mallorca. These four cold, icy walls make me feel neither sad nor happy; they make no impact at all. I have spent the most vital—the saddest—years of my youth here. I remember how, when making my escape from the apartment at night, years ago, to go to the Paral·lel or the Rambla, I would grope my way along and open the doors on the stairs, shutting my eyes and shrugging my shoulders. I suppose I thought I'd make less noise that way. It was completely absurd, a grotesque farce.

I don't know why but I was suddenly reminded of Aunt Marieta from Calonge. A very clear, sharp image! I think of that poor, extremely poor woman's life, but a life without doubts: rising early, working on the land, feeding her sweet animals, stewing a little meat with streaky bacon, two potatoes, and a cabbage leaf; spending her evenings by the fireside, reading stories in the *Urchin*, completely entranced; going to Calonge on Sundays to earn a few pesetas washing glasses in the café and watching the dance for a moment through a crack in the door. I can see her small farmhouse, lost in a barren waste, the end of its roof jutting over the edge of the wood, the stream in front, the owl on the tiles, the cat on the stone floor, and the four hens adding a touch of color. Perhaps—perhaps!—that is what constitutes a wise and peaceful life.

2 March, Sunday. Carnival.

Angeleta, a country girl fascinated by the city—a tall, dark, awkward lass, with very plain features but extremely likable—immediately found a position in another household. She says goodbye to us with tears in her eyes. I don't think she will ever go back to the countryside.

My brother and I go to live in a lodging house on carrer de Pelai, number 12. We bump into a few fellow students from our schooldays in Girona and many strangers. It is student lodging—impoverished, noisy, and chaotic.

Carnival afternoon. I spend hours in the Athenaeum's lugubrious library. Hardly anyone there. In my heart of hearts I envy the people who are having a good time—even if it's only for show. Progress on the Renard translation is painstakingly wearisome. López-Picó writes a letter to say that he will publish a prose piece by me in *La Revista*. When I hear that, any doubts disappear: It's a terrible piece of prose.

I hear Miquel Ferrà at the adjacent table lightheartedly tell Mossèn Riber he has never had any financial worries. Mossèn Riber glances at him benignly, unctuously. I could have hung, drawn, and quartered him.

4 March. Joan Climent.

His irony is barely perceptible—and in this respect I think he is supremely Barcelonan. His taste is excellent and his classical (Latin) culture well placed in relation to life. One day he told me—and I thought it very odd—that his knowledge of Latin was what gave him the most security and confidence in life. A Catholic who hardly believes in hell, he thinks of heaven as a haven of spiritual life. That life finds its meaning in the pursuit of individual perfection. He writes the cleverest epigrams, which he refuses to publish. He thinks passions can be salutary. He translates Latin poets, Villiers de l'Isle-Adam and Gautier. He fell out with two or three old friends because he heard them blaspheme. The afterlife doesn't bother him. He defends rituals of worship, confession, and communion as steps toward perfectibility. He says that it's necessary to defend any kind of aspiration: The first thing people relinquish are their aspirations, if they can't overcome the unexpected obstacles blocking their path. He is a delightful conversationalist—rather tortured by shyness—and a great friend. His favorite classical figure is Saint Francis de Sales, the most insipid, saccharine saint of them all.

He was telling me today that I am too geometrical. I didn't entirely grasp what he was suggesting. If he means my prose is hard, spare, devoid of languor and drooping eyelids, then he is right. If he means that my—insatiable—quest for clarity detracts, then he's right there too.

Writing. You often hear it said that blank sheets lose their virginity to writing. However, the sheets' virginity is unimportant. And the virginity of the "sleet"—the word suggested by Carner to describe this kind of paper—is even less so. What really loses its virginity when we start to write is the hypothetical thought in our minds and the means of expression we delude ourselves into believing we have at our fingertips. These are irrevocable losses of virginity. Before we put pen to paper, we all think we are great writers. Literary subject: Sketch the flight of a bird in a line and a half.

5 March. Ash Wednesday. I meander down the city streets, feeling drowsy and morose.

From the top of carrer de Claris, at the end of Via Laietana, I catch a glimpse of the sea. The sea seems to be resting peacefully on the horizon.

Catalan commonsense is a positive, commercial form of skepticism.

These graceful, willowy, long-legged young ladies and their bright, hopeful eyes passing by now are destined—generally speaking—to weigh eighty-five kilos and wear dressing gowns with tasseled belts for most of their lives.

There are times when I am obsessed by the landscape of the Ampurdan. Although it is vaguely elegant, it is never wan, weak or watery.

Joubert's observation comes to mind: "When a friend of mine is one-eyed, I look at him in profile."

Angeleta. She has already visited us twice in our new lodgings and today—she must have had a day off—she left a note that was moving in its simplicity. She says she misses us a lot and that if we have a pair of shoes in need of half soles, she will take them to the cobbler's for us. Apparently she knows one who is wonderful. Angeleta remembers us. We'd almost forgotten her!

At night, on carrer de Mallorca we never heard any bells pealing—or at least I don't remember hearing any. On carrer de Pelai several peal, a solemn, sonorous splendor that hangs in the air for a while.

6 March. My lodgings.

Although I've been here only a few days, I am beginning to discern the tragic atmosphere of the place. A mother, her two daughters, and a maid, Maria, run the show. The mother cooks and rarely sticks her head out into the passage. She is a human being ravaged by the heat in the kitchen and by poverty: a pale, dour woman, buffeted by life, her hair turned a faded gray by distress. Her eldest daughter—a tall, dark, black-haired girl—is courting. She'd like to marry in order to leave this house and lead a quiet life. Anxiety about her marriage keeps her in a constant state of nervous excitement and makes her tetchy. At the least excuse she loses control and her face—and body—start to shudder and convulse. The first thing she then says is that she is going commit suicide one of these days by jumping out the window. The youngest daughter is ten years old. She is chubby with the face of a simpleton. They occasionally send her out to buy things and she can be gone for two hours. They ask her what she's been doing, where she went, why it took so long, and she gapes and says nothing. Maria, the maid—a short, skinny girl who likes to flirt halfheartedly in a lethargic manner—speaks with an accent from Lleida and has had to deal with the frenzied attentions of nearly all the lodgers. One Don Eligio is the lodger who pursues her most assiduously. I sometimes wonder: Whenever these fools get anywhere with the girl, what on earth do they do?

One lodger is called Lluch. He is a swarthy South American–like Catalan and is tall, smartly dressed, amazingly pedantic, and full of himself and of wind. He speaks with an accent, with the self-restraint of a man who is listening to himself and holding back—even if he is only asking the time of day—and swaggers incredibly in dark, velvet-trim jackets of the type Lloyd George made fashionable.

Another lodger, Mateu, has a mania for shoes. He exudes the typical smell given off by new, particularly cheap shoes—the nasty smell of fresh leather. He keeps several pairs under his bed and almost all are a shiny color verging on red. This young man's ideal would be to walk out in new shoes every day. It is an odd, amusing ideal fully in keeping with our times: In recent years, shoes have become more important than I can ever remember them being.

Disorder is rampant in the place. At six in the evening the beds are usually still unmade and chamber pots are still by their night tables waiting to be emptied.

8 March.

Balzac is an extremely boring, turgid writer. One never finds a precise, exact adjective in his novels—an adjective that rings true. Balzac's scientific insights—care of Mesmer and Gall—are laughable.

I am working. I have a lot on my plate. But I do everything poorly. I'm finding it very difficult to learn what I'm forced to learn for my military service. I can never concentrate. I have even reached the point of tying a piece of string around my leg to remind myself which is my right and which is my left, so I can obey orders and not march off on the wrong leg.

The military men in the academy where I am receiving instruction seem peaceful and good-natured. Their uniforms hang loosely on them, and you can see they aren't used to wearing them. Their faces bear the gray expressions of men unused to handling firearms. They obviously find life healthier by the fireside.

Common sense.

According to Bishop Torras i Bages, who must have lived during the most placid period of the Restoration, Catalans are practical, moderate, tenacious, not prone to flights of fancy. In my view, Balmes, who lived in a period of ceaseless outcry, would have disagreed. If you read *La Sociedad* and other political writings of his, it is obvious Balmes didn't trust the common sense of the Catalans. The external, material conditions present in different eras change and this variation modifies even fundamental criteria.

Balmes constantly gives you the impression of a man who can judge things objectively (except, naturally, in the religious sphere) and is rarely stirred by patriotic prejudices. A pity about his style: It is unimaginably stodgy.

A family can show off a son at university. But what most enhances a family is a son who is living abroad.

A good number of people live on their private income, which is something palpable and solid. Writing is higher octane: It makes one live on fresh air—on presentiments, whims, hypotheses, and prophecies.

If I have to thrust a sword one day, and everything points that way, may God ensure it isn't too mannered a thrust.

From Nietzsche's *Twilight of the Idols*: "When a woman has masculine virtues, no one can resist her; when she doesn't have masculine virtues, she is the one who can never resist."

9 March, Sunday. I have spent most of today in the port. I went this morning and came back midafternoon.

From the day I arrived in Barcelona, I've loved meandering in the port. I've spent hours there. I've become fairly familiar with the area. So far I have tried to sustain three literary exercises: jotting down notes on the sea; writing about Girona; continuing this diary. I have failed in the first two. I don't know whether I can keep up the third.

I have written lots of short pieces on the sea. I have published some in different local publications. They are too lyrical, and at the same time pedantic, and often incomprehensible. I find the sea fascinating, but the topic has proved to be dry and sterile.

Today was a typical March day.

Fishermen say that in the winter the sea and wind act as if they are constrained. They mean the tension, pent-up force, point of eruption are much more intense. A cool summer wind is infinitely milder and more manageable than a cool winter wind. And when the month of March comes around, it begins almost imperceptibly, gently. One starts to grasp Aeschylus's words: the sea, an elusive smile.

The sea, ever elusive, has been at its most diverse. It has been sunny, windy, foggy, rainy, and under a waning moon. Radiant in the sun, graceful and light with wind, silent in fog, childishly sulky in the rain; the moon created on the water finely curved snails and horns of abundance—pale reflections—on the water.

In the sun, everything seems dazzled. Dramatic clouds over a cool blue sea. Pure, shimmering shades of white, a dense Oriental white.

Then a strong northeasterly made its appearance, swelling the waves. From afar, the long sweep of the beach at dusk seemed like one more delicate wave, the color of toast, glinting in the sun. On the horizon, clouds crisscross a mauve-streaked sky.

The sea has brought fog. The wind has dropped. The sea's swirling whitish foam has turned pine-colored, streaked with purple. Everything is dreamily phantasmagorical—like the imaginings of a dying child lost in a haze of hallucinations.

A gentle drizzle started. Seagulls' wings flap. The shore of Can Tunis, as far as Llobregat, looked beautiful under a haze of white spray. Small bubbles of rain pop on the water.

The clouds have parted to reveal a moon over the deserted harbor that tints the billowing clouds yellow and violet. The March wind strikes fresh and sharp and makes the hawsers whine.

10 March. My lodgings.

Sra. Emília, one of the landlady's sisters, has just arrived. She is a fat, well-preserved lady of mature years, with a pink face as round as an apple, white hair, and a slow gait. Her temperament—from what one has seen—is quite the opposite of her poor sister's. She's impassive, gifted with an inability to react to her senses. It's all the same to her: the usual horrendous noise in the household or silence; disorder or order; white or black; sorrow or joy. She simply lives. She isn't interested in giving orders. She presides over the table of lodgers as if she were an additional piece of furniture. The saucy remarks she is forced to hear leave her absolutely unmoved.

Roseta, the landlady's eldest daughter, gets thinner and more anxious by the day: She is as nervy as a swallow.

Apart from the students and young Lluch, the South American dandy, whose swagger increases by the day, there is a very peculiar fellow in the house: Don Eligio. He enjoys quite a reputation among the students and is a fine example of the lodging-house parasite.

Don Eligio is a boastful, wearisome Andalusian with the gift of the gab. He specializes in the business of theaters, cinemas, drugstores, and taverns. He is a small, dark, prickly character whose old clothes are in a fine state of repair, and whose few strands of hair are combed over his gleaming pate. His face bears an astonishing resemblance to a *cave man*; his nose looks as if it has been gnawed by rats, two orifices like twin keyholes on the wall of his face.

Don Eligio is a man with a single principle: pay the least possible and, "given the chance," as he says, simply pay nothing at all. Whenever the landlady suggests he should settle accounts and pay his arrears, he flies into a violent rage. He rants and raves and says he can't stand being surrounded by second-rate, incomprehensible inhuman beings, by "Catalan Jews" is what he actually says. It is an age-old ploy, and these scenes would hardly matter if it weren't for the fact that the students always side with this loathsome parasite. When Don Eligio starts to shout and act the fool, the students join in the fun, and the landlady has no option but to shut herself in the kitchen, embarrassed and at a loss as to what to do. The involvement of this band of petty-criminal gents in the affairs of this poor woman is simply repugnant. Meanwhile, Sra. Emília sits in her corner, completely indifferent. Roseta writes letters to her fiancé and licks her dry lips.

The atmosphere in the household is tense and unpredictable.

Guardiola, the student from Esparreguera, is a villain from the mountains of Monserrat. He is an intelligent, sharp lad but he is also manic, unruly, falsely modest, and driven by strange whims that make him seem unpleasant, brittle, and mercurial. Money is the only thing that interests him. When the postman comes presumably carrying a postal order for someone, Guardiola silently opens his bedroom door and looks nervously and impatiently through the crack in the door. If the money is for him, he stands there knavishly, head down, glancing right and left suspiciously, and collects the notes with a vain, self-satisfied grin.

Finestres, the medical student from Girona, is a typical handsome young man, well-dressed in the worst taste. He is young, a supporter of Maura, and a daddy's boy; he is a great parasite and tries to hide his incredible indolence. He is interested only in things that impinge upon him, very private, personal matters, and he spends the whole day saying, "That's of no interest to me . . . that isn't either . . ."

They are twenty-year-old lads riding the crest of the wave. Every day that passes, however, they become more childish. They are elemental beings with only one possible outcome in life, if that: marriage to a wealthy woman. A loaded lady—as they like to put it.

It is a cheap lodging house: one hundred and twenty-five pesetas a month. The menu is organized around fried eggs and fried hake and steak and potatoes, a steak that is leathery, gristly, thin as a cat's ear, and extremely tough. In this country they really know how to slice meat thin. Followed by an orange or a banana—this increasingly popular fruit, which I find tasteless, uninteresting, and miserable. What with this meager diet and all the coffee one drinks on the street, one's constitution tends to remain in a state of high tension.

The lodging house is very close to the brand-new Damians Department Store. You can see the globe that crowns the store from the balcony over the street. How irredeemably trite!

The railway station to Sarrià is on the other side of the road, with the rails and faded yellow carriages that pass up and down carrer de Balmes, whistling at each street corner. Beyond the station, there are many houses and sheds, with monotonous, repulsively hard roofs.

11 March. After lunch, I meet Alexandre Plana in the library. He takes my arm and leads me to the grand circle in the Athenaeum. It is also known as Dr. Borralleras's club. We go down the stairs from the first floor, walk through the room with the foreign papers and into the low-ceilinged room where the renowned circle gathers.

Plana introduces me to Dr. Borralleras, who is sitting at the back. He welcomes me most cordially, which demonstrates that Planas has smoothed my entry. Then Borralleras introduces me to the others there. I recall Dr. Dalí, Don Enric Jardí, Don Eugeni d'Ors, Francesc Pujols, Camps Margarit, Josep M. de Sagarra, Don Pere Rahola, Don Antoni Homar, Sr. Andreu Barber, Dr. Mainou, Lluís Valeri, Lluís Llimona, Estanislau Duran, Teodor Saló, Màrius Aguilar, Labarta the painter, Professor Tayà, Solé de Sojo, Miró i Folguera, Magí Sandiumenge, Maestro Pahissa, Joan Crexells, Josep Barbey... there may be others I've forgotten for the moment.

Naturally I am given a rather cold, reserved welcome. I am quite embarrassed. Plana seems happy. When I sit down by the door, Dr. Borralleras smiles pleasantly in my direction and looks receptive and interested.

12 March. University.

After you have spent five years at a university, people usually say it's a waste of time and when you leave, you must start work and above all you must forget what you learned there. However, that is absolutely secondary.

In my view, the worst impact of this kind of establishment is the way it falsifies one's sensibility, intellect, and character. You tend to see things not as they really are but through a layer of cardboard. The university doesn't strive to move from the simple to the complex—which is what life requires—so as to develop a vision of the essence of human life. It strives to simplify though systematic sleight of hand. It makes you see things in miniature, as if you were myopic, and favors the hunch, the trick, guile; it excuses bad behavior as a fact of life. Knowledge is what's least valued; passing examinations is all. I have spent five years in the Law Faculty: I have never once heard anyone speak of justice, not even for medicinal purposes. I have never once heard the word mentioned. It would probably have been out of place in an atmosphere that fosters rogues rather than people with a degree of human equanimity. In this way, the pedagogical institution provides heavy-duty ammunition to the weak-minded and morally maimed, to petty social climbers, hardened hypocrites, fanatics, and pedants. There they learn the arts of pretense and one-upmanship, of flattery and sharp practice. Nobility and frankness are never encountered. The university stifles and corrupts strong temperaments.

13 March. The Mancomunitat has created an Institute of Education and Joan Climent keeps encouraging me to enroll. The classes will be given in the Industrial University. I really think that business—being a schoolmaster, a teacher—is rather peculiar. Will I end up teaching some subject or other in Canet de Mar, Puigcerdà, or Valls? But Climent insists and I find that rather disturbing. Why is he so insistent? Does it mean he is sure I will never become a writer? This upsets me and makes me shiver. I have so far sacrificed everything—absolutely everything—to reaching that goal. Did I take a wrong turn?

Nonetheless, I sometimes think Climent is right and that one of these days the two hundred pesetas a month from my family is going to dry up.

It's raining. Through the windows of the club's meeting room one can see dripping wet trees gleaming through the tobacco smoke—a delicious scent of Havana tobacco. It is a delightful afternoon and the atmosphere inside is pleasant. Domènec Carles explains how on one of the most dramatic days during the course of the last round of influenza—that is still rife—he bumped into a friend with a financial interest in the funeral business.

"A lot of people are ill," Carles told him. "It is horrific."

"Yes, lots and lots of people are ill . . . however," the man from the undertaker replied, "now it's a benign strain of flu, a flu that people survive."

In the library I reach the hundredth quarto sheet of my translation of Renard.

The Rambla, by night. The rain has created a damp sultriness in the air that at times is oppressive and at other times seems like an early sign of spring. The ladies of the street walk along under their umbrellas, swaying their wonderful, country-mare butts. It is a purely mechanical act of extreme provocation. The noise of coins rolling on gambling tables can be heard under the trees on the Rambla though you couldn't say from precisely where. Some establishments have their doors and windows wide open. I go into the Excelsior. They still have pennants from the armistice days up on the walls and the shelves behind the bar. It is crowded. Full of foreigners. Young women wearing diamonds. Everyone is sweating and seems to have a cold, though when drunks are well-dressed, they never seem as drunk. I go back to the Rambla. It is easier to breathe there. The butts of the young ladies continue to make those impressive rotating movements as they walk up and down under their umbrellas. A large raindrop sometimes falls on an umbrella and, on impact, the liquid flashes iridescent in the glow from the streetlamps.

14 March. Working-class agitation is surfacing again. Everyone says that the looming conflicts will be bigger than ever. It is impossible to find out from the newspapers what exactly is in dispute. Information is confused, diffuse, and censured. One is completely in the dark. Many of the trams are being driven by soldiers. People are stocking up on candles. It is sad how there has to be a revolution every week to create the smallest stir in this country

A strange contradiction. Everyone says life is short, brief, that it lasts a moment, but then everyone says they are bored, that they don't know what to do or how to pass the time and are tired of having to read every episode of the latest cartoon in order to kill time.

Man's tendency to forget is a law of history. If this tendency to suffer memory fatigue weren't so common, it would be impossible to imagine the intermittent appearance of great adventurers, those who are considered historical figures. Historians want to make us believe that history is grand. The history we have lived and are now living isn't at all; in fact, it is quite the contrary.

It is hardly edifying to think things will turn out fine if the north-westerly wind blows and poorly if it is a southwesterly.

15 March. The club's routines. Enric Jardí is usually the first person to arrive after lunch. He walks at a leisurely pace with two newspapers under his arm: *L'Action Française* and *L'Humanité*. He is a man who lucidly follows, with a sharp dialectical mind, the movements of extremist ideas—the only ones that matter at the end of the day. In the center, one may find truth but hardly ideas. Truth is an idea that has been accepted, an idea that has gone cold. Jardí orders a coffee, sits down, and lights a cigar, which he smokes in a short cigar holder. Costa brings the tray in, the flaps of his morning coat flying. The imposing mass of Dr. Rafael Dalí, a municipal doctor, enters breathlessly right after. Although I am barely acquainted with him, I have been led to understand that Dr. Dalí is a first-rate gourmet and a real connoisseur of menus.

Dr. Joaquim Borralleras is usually the third to arrive. He is the animating spirit behind the conversations, their backbone, the one who guarantees their continuity. He is a doctor, a bachelor, a small rentier, and a man of leisure. But he is the strangest man of leisure: He always has a task at hand, is always immersed in work. There are two things in his life that he considers his duties: the club and music; and another two that he approaches as a dilettante: painting and literature. Dr. Borralleras sits at the back of the room, opposite the entrance. There are two parallel rows of ordinary cane chairs on either side of where he sits and a line of marble tables down the center. The room overlooks the garden, which is on the same level and accessible through the French doors. The walls in the room are bare and white.

Since the day he finished his degree, one could say that Dr. Borralleras conducted himself as a man of leisure—he has risen at half past one in the afternoon ever since. He has a light lunch and then he heads from his house on carrer del Bisbe—with balconies overlooking plaça de Sant Jaume—to the Athenaeum. Once ensconced in his club, he engages in conversation until half past seven in the evening. Then he visits one or two exhibitions, goes into a couple of bookshops, and finally orders an absinthe in a café in the city center, in the Colón or Continental. He returns home for supper. Later on, if there is a concert, he will go to it accompanied by his close friend, Josep M. Albinyana. If there isn't a concert, he goes back to his circle and stays there until it breaks up in the early hours. On the other hand, if he does go to a concert, he will drop in at the club when it's over. When that breaks up, Dr. Borralleras will walk down the Rambla with a cigarette on his lip, a cigarette he never gives up. He is always with someone; generally, Josep M. de Sagarra accompanies him. After strolling down the Rambla, they enter the Gambrinus and, as if by magic, another conversation will strike up around him—this usually lasts until five or six in the morning. He has a gift for welding human beings together in conversations that are usually cordial. But those in the Gambrinus are not conversations he directs. Those are unofficial, an extra helping, an encore, as it were. When the light of dawn reaches the shadows on carrer del Pi, Dr. Borralleras abandons the Gambrinus, walks slowly up carrer del Bisbe, and goes home after a routine—generally lengthy—exchange with the night watchman.

In the early afternoon Dr. Borralleras presides over a conversation with people who more or less work. The first shift of club members usually lasts until five or half past. When these gentlemen disperse another group arrives—those who work in the early afternoon. Pompeu Fabra is usually there. Naturally this is not an absolute rule: There are individuals who on certain days, even over a number of days, find it possible to spend the whole afternoon in conversation.

Nighttime meetings are a mixture of the afternoon crowd and strictly nocturnal adepts. There are still a lot of people in Barcelona who go out at night, who believe, for example, that it is more congenial or simply more practical to join in conversations at night rather than in the afternoon. Consequently Dr. Borralleras is busy during the day and most of the night presiding over conversations that are in a ceaseless process of constant renewal. The waves of humanity this man provokes—whom they call in conversation Quim—generates continuous metamorphosis. Without moving from his chair, he sees and speaks to more than two hundred different people each day, at the very least, variously seated in various places.

I don't know Quim very well, but he has been quite a revelation. I have hardly heard him speak in the many hours I have now spent in his company. He sits in his seat in a morose, twilight state—lethargic and indifferent—and sometimes I feel he is completely absent from everything around him. It's true, with his broad, pallid Buddhist mask of a face, clean-shaven with a melancholy pout that sadness sometimes deepens, and small, beady, almost invisible eyes that miss nothing, Quim has directed at most a rather forced laugh at one individual or a mute, obscure comment at someone else. He has sat there, silent, lighting up and smoking cigarettes for hours. Plana assures me this is unusual and that it would be rash to take it too far. I will only add, like the nineteenth-century writers of serial fiction when the cliff-hanging moment of climax arrives: "And here my pen will halt..."

17 March, Monday. Everybody knows everybody in Palafrugell, which means that the passions, the motives behind things, the reasons for certain actions related to town business, and the day-to-day life of its citizens are always visible and, of course, are usually quite ridiculous. I see nothing in Barcelona. I am completely in the dark. It's probably because my sight has yet to adapt to other levels of vision. I am like a mole at the moment.

If one has a philosophical bent, there are two things one can do when faced with an obstacle, for example, a literary obstacle: turn around and bite one's tail or break into song. If singing were allowed in the public libraries frequented by writers, a frightful uproar would inevitably erupt.

When spring is in the air, and a lover adopts a passive, pensive, melancholy pose before the object of his love, it suggests that he has worked out his vein of verbal persuasion. It is a moment of great delicacy, because at this time of year what women hate the most are pauses.

Situation of the poor admirer, low on resources, who finally manages to invite his hero—of any stripe—to a coffee. "Would you be so kind..." The object of admiration thinks: "Ah, hah..."

The proper function of the intellect should not consist—as people generally think on this peninsula—of recognizing the difference between a hypothesis and a fantasy. Its proper function consists in being able to distinguish what is from what isn't.

Mediocrity has the same taste and color as café au lait.

18 March. Night. I stay in my bedroom at the lodging house. It is the eve of my saint's day. I remember how years ago, in Palafrugell, on a night like this bands of men would go from house to house singing songs of joy.

"Josep, be our advocate in this our mortal life," they would sing. Absolutely. You gave them a dozen eggs and begged them to stop singing. I remember the thin, out-of-tune voice of a man with a gleaming baldpate, who looked rather like a horse and sang while clinging to the small lapels of his jacket with his huge hands as if he were clinging to the bars over a window. But all that is so distant and long ago!

I find, among other papers, these lines I wrote three years ago:

> I have always lagged behind somewhat and when I was a child I was notoriously slow. I was particularly insensitive and poorly equipped when it came to understanding anything about religion. I grasped nearly nothing about the creed: I learned it by heart as if it were grammar. I would say prayers quickly, as a pure memory exercise, never thinking about what the words meant. Once in bed, I could remember nothing. I remember the strangest things about church: I was more attracted by the glinting particles of dust floating in the rays of polychrome light than by the service itself; more by the garments worn by the clergy and their voices than the sermons from the pulpit; more by the hair of the mustache and beard of the poor, rickety lady who always sat in the front row than in any thoughts of transcendence.

I'm wondering now if this fragment bore any relation to reality. From a literary point of view it is very poor, but I think it describes the reality of those times.

I have moments when I feel tired. I have occasional moments of depression—generally with no clear cause. Naturally it is laughable to feel old at the age of twenty-one. The truth is that I often want to escape, to shut myself up in our farmhouse and go to bed with the hens—or to go to sunny, remote Aigua Xal·lida, with that radiant sea and sky, and sleep on the ground amid rustling pines. I am exasperated by the precise physical sensation—when I am not in bed—of feeling that I am walking this world yoked to the back of a cart.

19 March. My sister Rosa writes to tell me that the swallows have arrived. Now—I reflect—the spring symphony must be in full swing on the farm: frogs, crickets, the owl that breeds in the roof, behind the chimney, the cuckoo, and the mewling swallows . . .

20 March. The beginning of spring. The library.

While translating Renard I think it's more important to feel at home in any trade than to have a vast, far-ranging curiosity. One can improvise curiosity but not a trade. Curiosity is superficially pleasant but leaves a certain sour emptiness within. A trade is monotonous and boring but there are moments of voluptuous fascination that compensate for the monotony.

A well-balanced man must, from one perspective, be full of good qualities and, from the other, full of defects.

Of all the advertisements I have seen in Barcelona—and there are some beautiful ones—the one that has struck me most because of its vagueness is the following: "First Communions—from 6 to 8."

Another magnificent advertisement: "The Loved Ones." Barcelona has such wonderful sides to it!

Alfred de Vigny's *Journal d'un poète* has one sentence in italics: *L'ésperance est la plus grande de nos folies.* On the surface, it seems an awful sentence and yet it may be quite plausible and apposite in terms of life itself. If one can succeed in living on the margins of what Vigny calls the greatest madness, anything pleasant that happens, however small, will bring dazzling happiness. Conversely, for those who live dreaming of great things, whatever they experience, however enthralling, will seem petty, miserable, absurd, and trifling. To live in hope is to live a life of continuous, irremediable disappointment.

22 March. High culture.

Naturally things could have been very different. When I finished at high school, I didn't intend studying to become a lawyer. I'd have liked to study chemistry and pursue what I thought was my vocation, so I enrolled in the introductory course to the sciences. Enrolled! Take note of that little word! The truth is that when the year started I was immersed in a human torrent of more than three hundred students, a genuine human throng comprising the best and the worst from every household in Catalonia, Majorca, and Valencia. The introduction to the sciences was a general course for all students who then went on to study medicine, pharmacy, and sciences. It was a herd of young men who created a terrific din and kerfuffle.

When I was part of that young, frantic hubbub I felt bewildered and bereft, and I think that was how all of us who set out on that adventure with a minimum of seriousness reacted. I don't mean a sense of responsibility because the offspring of the bourgeoisie don't usually have any; in that sense, they are the same as all the other classes, though that might be difficult to believe. Despite the human avalanche that had engulfed me, I decided to stay with it, more from lethargic curiosity than from any hope I might acquire the slightest scrap of knowledge. For a few months I remained part of that savage, unruly, unpleasant herd.

We entered the general chemistry lecture theater at a quarter to nine in the morning. The teacher, Sr. Vila i Vendrell, was middle-aged, medium height, the color of sugar candy, smiley, dapper in blue, with white piping on his waistcoat that matched his jacket lapels. He received his students standing at the podium, behind a large professorial table. He wasn't a sedentary teacher. Throughout the year he stood and explained unintelligible chemistry from a textbook written by a Professor Lozano from Madrid.

An array of test tubes, flasks, and stills stood on the table in front of him. He wasn't a man given to explaining chemical reactions simply with words. Not at all. He was an experimenter. He not only used the blackboard, where he drew figures holding the chalk between his fingertips so as not to soil his jacket, but also conducted concrete, practical experiments. He used to say that science has ceased to be a matter of words; it was a matter of acts. When Dr. Vila i Vendrell took a test tube between two fingers, the deepest silence fell upon the huge audience in the gray, icy lecture theater, thick with Barcelona's morning fog. We students could hardly hide our enthusiasm. Our morbid curiosity was expressed in much licking of lips and cheeky, ironic glances.

He poured some powder into the tube he was holding. The liquid was red and the powder was yellow. Then, no doubt to give the impression that it was a complex experiment, he took another tube containing a cloudy liquid and emptied into it a tile-colored powder. Dr. Vila i Vendrell carried out these operations with the utmost sangfroid, with elegant actions that were perhaps meant to suggest the august serenity of science. A moment came when two fingers of his right hand held both tubes—the one with red liquid and the one with yellow powder—while his other hand held the other two: the tube of cloudy liquid and the tube of tile-colored powder. You could have heard a pin drop in the lecture theater. A religious silence; in the meantime, he proceeded to mix. He was in no hurry. We, the students, were—up to a point. In our heart of hearts, we suspected that it would end badly. The fact is everything usually ended well. All of a sudden, the red tube the professor held aloft as if it were the product of some fabulous miracle turned a fascinating, astonishing bright green. A moment later, the cloudy liquid turned purple—a permanganate hue that wasn't as stunning as the previous change because it was a familiar color. Our eyes focused on the green: Those two inches of green in the tube became the geometric point on which every gaze, every direct and indirect vector converged in that immense, gray, impressive, dumbfounded lecture theater.

When this green appeared, a phenomenon occurred that might have impressed anyone who'd just walked in from the street, though it was one that had been happening for the last twenty years, a ritual reaction the student population passed on down the years. The students stood up and started to clap frenziedly to express their deep devotion. The first time I heard the applause, not realizing it was a ritual, I thought it expressed a deliberate lack of respect. However, when I saw that a grinning Dr. Vila i Vendrell welcomed the applause I started to clap in indecent haste—just in case, I reflected, my lack of enthusiasm ended up damaging me in some way.

Later, when I coldly analyzed what happened, I saw that those ovations weren't simply a sarcastic indulgence. Not at all. They were an obligation. From year to year, the advice was passed down that you must applaud Dr. Vila i Vendrell's scientific experiments. These ovations guaranteed him a fantastic standing in the hierarchy and contributed to a good husbanding of the course—I mean a reduction in the number of low marks and an increase in the number of passes. So we all applauded. But there is another factor: When two or three hundred people, especially if they are young and possess a relish for tremendous stupidity, which is the mark of youth, are concentrated in an empty academic space, a deadly phenomenon occurs, no matter how careful one is: Theater is staged. When Dr. Vila i Vendrell began to manipulate his tubes, theater—in the meaning given to it in this country—spontaneously erupted. The professor of general chemistry goodheartedly let the applause continue, though I have to assume that his attitude hid a degree of irony, an irony that was so well concealed it escaped everyone. When the clapping sounded too loud or lasted too long—something that was no effort for us—he stretched out his arm, as if trying to calm a frisky horse. He then uttered this sublime statement: "Gentlemen, gentlemen," he said, looking very slightly distressed, "hold your applause for when we succeed in synthesizing citric acid."

These regrettable scenes used to take place twice in every class: halfway through and at the end. The final ovation would scale frenzied heights. Standing opposite the clapping, Dr. Vila—now completely released from the glass tubes and miracles of chemistry—seemed to shrink in size. Then we undergraduates would leave, making a huge racket. The law courtyard—because the chemistry lecture theater looked over the law courtyard—would now become a scene of turmoil. The greater the ignorance, the louder the din created. Though, naturally, one could never have said such a thing.

It was ten o'clock and time for our mineralogy and botany class. The professor was Dr. Vila i Nadal, known as "Grandpa"—*Avi* in Catalan—within and outside the university. This gentleman held forth in a lecture theater on the first floor of the Law Faculty building. You had to climb very narrow stairs to get there. The mere thought that it was time for Professor Vila i Nadal's class sent students literally into a state of delirium tremens: The barbarian horde pushed violently upstairs, colliding head-on and screaming like zombies. It was a caricature—and a very unpleasant one at that—of an assault on a fortress. The most frequent cry was *"Avi! Avi! Avi!"* Others yelled down the gloomy stairway, "Shut up!" The response came from below: "Animals!" There was always a cowering student from the provinces whose hat would fly through the air, at times the result of a well-aimed swipe, origin unknown, and for reasons I couldn't fathom. It wasn't unusual for those clambering upstairs to throw the occasional punch. Meanwhile some would sing "Marina" or "I Love My Lovely Crooks," which a French songstress performed in a cabaret on the Rambla.

The mineralogy and botany lecture theater was dark and dingy in winter. It was an amphitheater embedded in a high-ceilinged cube, painted the color of liquid shit, with a neo-Gothic window that let in a dull light that filtered through the branches of the trees in the building's central garden. The podium, at the foot of the benches, was tiny in relation to the height of the amphitheater. Students poured in, creating an infernal din, and as the students adapted to the dim light, their peculiar—completely gratuitous—state of excitement seemed to intensify.

Professor Vila i Nadal stood there waiting for us, ready to fire, that is, on war footing. Stiff as a dummy behind a long table full of minerals and desiccated plants, arms folded, glaring violently, he was the poor caricature of a duelist two minutes before shooting commences. Nothing leads me to believe it was his natural attitude; experience had forced him to adopt such an extreme stance. He was small, lean, and swarthy, nervous, pigeon-chested, and twitchy-faced; he sported a salt-and-pepper mustache and beard, and generally wore a morning coat. Like many small, lean, and swarthy men, he acted like a reticent, Mephistophelian being. He was in fact well- meaning, good as gold, and unhappy to a degree that exceeded all imaginable bounds. His morning coat should not suggest he considered clothes were at all important. His morning coat was black, shiny, and shabby; his pinstriped trousers sagged and were baggy-kneed; his worn-out studded shoes were oversize, covered in dust, battered, and loose. All that might have made him look like an academic from a bygone era—that is, from the turn of the century—if under his morning coat he hadn't worn a white waistcoat that had yellowed ridiculously, an eye-catching, endearing anachronism enhanced by a frayed green tie streaked an aging lizard shade of brown and mounted on wire dangling from a celluloid collar visibly crinkled by sweat. It was all topped by a broad-brimmed hat rendered a diluted, watery black by dust and the passage of time—an unbearably, irrevocably sad hat.

We would find him, then, standing stiffly behind the table, arms folded, ready to challenge the entire world: snarling sardonically, glowering thunderously, and frowning defiantly. However, because of his small stature, the attitude his body struck inspired hilarity rather than terror. Bravado hardly becomes small men. White sheets of paper—the course register—lay on the table in front of him like a kind of small apron for his waistcoat. To his right was a little basket of rocks; to his left, a small heap of crystallized minerals. His weary hat sat becalmed behind this pile of rocks. The rocks in the basket and the crystals formed part of what is described as "teaching material" in educational parlance. I do assure you that even those rocks, when transformed into "teaching material" took on a strange, eccentric appearance. They were like rocks that had been "specially prepared."

The boys who aspired to high grades sat in the first row in front of Dr. Vila—quiet, pensive, polite lads, cold fish who never missed a class and nodded or shook their heads according to whatever the professor happened to be saying. In student slang of the time they were dubbed the ass-lickers. This species of student was present in every course but was most visible in Dr. Vila's; their limp tameness stood out sharply and unforgettably in the general tumult. The fact they were so few and located in such a small area made them stand out even more strikingly. Their little band included the smartly dressed boy from a well-off home, who turns out to be studious and disciplined and the poor, willing lad, who pays for his studies by working as a barber or clerical assistant and is hungry, ambitious, and pushy.

The avalanche of impetuous students created a violent racket as they entered the lecture theater, but in the end, naturally, it all more or less subsided. When that happened, Dr. Vila immediately unfolded his arms, picked up the sheaf of paper from his table, and began to call roll. I never could understand what the point of that was. It was absolutely unnecessary to control the attendance of students, to record who went to class and who didn't. It was plain that those who didn't go, didn't because they found it uninteresting. One couldn't have asked for a more respectable, spontaneous reaction. But that is how things were done and one could change nothing. I have suffered endless roll calls at university. It was a serious business in Dr. Vila's case because if it was a minimal waste of time with thirty or forty students, imagine the implications of calling out loud the names of three hundred brutes who would leap at every opportunity to instigate mayhem. The first thirty minutes of class—which officially lasted an hour—were spent calling roll.

Chaos was usually sparked by this operation. It was a drawn-out affair, in the course of which the professor frequently felt the need to scratch himself. Generally it was an itch behind his ear or on his shoulder. Now, Dr. Vila scratched most curiously: with the nail of his small finger, as if he were a caged monkey, in a nervous movement that climaxed in frenzied scratching. The elongated yellow nail meant his action was even more ridiculous. Most students collapsed in mirth before what was, objectively speaking, a comic spectacle and often even those who aspired to top grades stuffed handkerchiefs into their mouths to stifle their guffaws. The uproar began with a loud round of laughter, accompanied by shouts of "*Avi! Avi! Avi!*"

"Shut up!" the professor clamored nervously, in a hoarse, cracked voice, his eyes bulging out of their sockets, his whole body tensed.

But the moment he said "Shut up," hats rained down on his table from every corner of the lecture theater. Whenever I think of that flurry of hats flying through the room's gray, staid air, I quiver and burn with indignation. It was astonishing to see how those youths who had devoted so many years to their own education—spending thirty-five to forty thousand pesetas in the process—launched themselves into such a primitive, raucous melee.

"*Orden! Orden!*" the professor would shout in Spanish, jumping up and down, his whole body shaking, pitching himself from one end of his table to the other like a shuttlecock, his face contorted in horror, sweating, baring his teeth, spitting everywhere, hair tangled, eyes bulging, morning coat at sixes and sevens, tie dangling loose, and trousers in immediate danger of dropping.

"*Silencio! Orden! Orden!*" Dr. Vila kept repeating in a crescendo of nervous rage and indignation.

But the din increased, and his shouting and frantic gestures only fanned the flame. By the time he shouted "*Orden! Orden!*," the riot was peaking. A bread roll suddenly bounced along the professor's table; the soft thwap of the roll on the wood was usually followed by more metallic thwacks, a rock, a lump of lead, or a useless, rusty key. It was pure lunacy. On their feet, the students now abandoned the veneer of the most basic conventions and, like uncouth louts, screamed, shouted, sang, and hooted wildly. The more moderate sector laughed noisily and uncontrollably. All manner of voices, from every side of the amphitheater, bellowed "*Avi! Avi! Avi!*"

Suddenly an overcoat flew through the air. The students tossed it around like a ball. It was like watching a large, sinister bird as the garment soared through the gloom of the lecture theater. After a number of landings, the overcoat inevitably came to a halt on the professor's table; it sometimes fell next to the crystallized minerals near the basket of rocks. The professor's vocal chords eventually failed him. He continued to open his mouth and gesticulate with every limb more frantically than ever, but never succeeded in articulating or shaping a single clear response. He emitted muffled growls that alternated with the hoarse splutters of an impotent, cornered man.

Six or seven minutes of rioting subsided naturally into peace and calm. There was no specific cause: It came of its own accord, because it simply had to; perhaps it was exhaustion or perhaps that sad figure finally prompted overwhelming pity. The students sat down again, the noisy uproar gave way to relative quiet, and Dr. Vila's voice resurfaced, though it was still quite unclear. But then something strange happened. There was always a student—I never managed to find out who it was—who didn't agree with the cessation of these shenanigans (a student undoubtedly in favor of permanent, systematic rioting), who released a bird into the air the moment the professor's voice piped up again. The appearance of that poor creature in that hall of learning (a goldfinch purchased on the Rambla an hour earlier) triggered a return to the previous chaos with renewed vigor.

"*Silencio! Orden! Callarse!*" shouted Dr. Vila drawing on the last remnants of his voice, though by now he looked a wreck, drained and white as a sheet. His hands, arms, and legs were shaking. He was a man who could do no more.

It was as if he had said nothing. The eyes of the student mass focused on the bird's movements and roared a commentary at each twist and turn. First the goldfinch flew down the center of the lecture theater, flitted over to the walls, hit its head there, and then sought out the light from the neo-Gothic window that opened over the garden. It flapped up and down the pane of glass desperately trying to get a hold with its claws. Now and then it managed to cling to a part of the window, apparently hugging it, its wings spread wide. At such moments, a string of sharp, metallic sounds rang out on the glass. A student had aimed pellets at the bird from one of those catapults children use to break the bulbs of streetlights. The ricocheting pellets forced the bird to resume its flight and the riot restarted, wearily, intolerably.

"*Avi! Avi! Avi!*" they hollered without interruption. The cry resonated with a funereal, inhuman tone. The broken-winged bird finally fell to the floor and disappeared under the benches. Then the students began to burrow under their seats unleashing all manner of grunts, hoots, and farts. The level of din and chaos generated a shocking, depressing, barbaric atmosphere. Dr. Vila had long since stopped reacting and gesticulating. Standing erect behind his table, grinning sardonically, he looked like a man on the gallows.

Some days he spent three-quarters of the hour-long class calling roll in between the fracases. When the wretched professor was rendered hors de combat, the students calmed down to a degree, a calm no doubt brought on by the efforts they had expended in their heroic deeds. Dr. Vila took advantage of the precarious lull to pick up the list and call out a name. If the student was present—sometimes he was, though it was as if he wasn't—he would walk down to the table and stand in front of the basket of rocks. The professor picked a rock at random, and if, for example, it were a lump of lead, he would look at the student, hand him the mineral, and say with a wheeze, "Well then, Sr. So-and-so . . . lead . . . what do you know about lead? Tell me what properties lead has . . . come on, list them . . ."

It was all quite absurd and impossible to take him seriously. The scene brought tears to one's eyes.

The student might stand there, as if stupefied, staring at the rock in his hand. A long time passed and he would be unforthcoming. Now and then the professor invited him to break his silence.

"Well then . . . what are the properties of lead? Come on, list . . ."

Another kind of student wouldn't even look at the mineral and would recite, as if he were a gramophone—that being the era of the gramophone—what the course textbook said. I preferred the student who was speechless, apparently shocked to be interrogated about lead in the wake of the previous uproar, to the poor wretch who parroted a chapter from the unintelligible manual, which was pure hogwash. One imagined the former might in fact know something about lead when it was necessary, whereas the latter would take years to rid himself of the rubbish he had crammed into his head—that is, if he ever did succeed in doing so.

At that point, the mass exodus began. Indeed, the leakage of students started as soon as the uproar subsided. I suspect some left because they thought the teaching on offer was as derisory and irritating as the din that had erupted a few moments earlier. The students streamed out in groups of three or four. When the porter came and uttered the hallowed phrase from the doorway, "Time's up, Professor," the room was already empty except for those seeking top grades who stood out like sore thumbs.

Professor Vila i Nadal was, nonetheless, a man who had modernized his discipline and shown himself to be in favor of mineralogy and botany directly from nature. He was a Linnaeus who had appeared on the scene a number of years late, and undoubtedly a pioneer in terms of the methods currently favored in the university.

"Tomorrow we shall go," he exclaimed one day, out of the blue.

"*Avi! Avi! Avi!*" the students chanted mournfully.

"*Orden! Silencio!* Tomorrow we will go and collect minerals. A practical class! You have been warned! A practical class! Everybody must come! At three o'clock."

"In the nunnery," heckled one student.

"At three in the Law Faculty patio," admonished Dr. Vila i Nadal with the patience of a saint.

The notice was greeted with frenzied enthusiasm because they all knew, from what they'd been told by previous years, that it was going to be a hoot.

At three the following afternoon, the icy, barren law courtyard was a dark throng of people, a tuneless buzz and hum. The crowd was so huge I always thought—from the countless strange faces—that alien elements had joined up for Dr. Vila's experiments in practical mineralogy, students from other faculties, friends, and guests of regular attendees who didn't want to miss the riotous binge that was in store. The yard filled up long before the appointed hour of departure. People had galloped through lunch and rushed to the spectacle and now indulged in all kinds of antics while waiting for the signal to depart. One group of students was leapfrogging grotesquely. Beyond them, in one corner, another group had started a card school; farther on students were playing catch around the columns; others were embroiled in violent arguments. Everyone was eagerly awaiting the professor and the rumpus that had become an established tradition.

Dr. Vila i Nadal finally arrived in his morning coat and whitish waistcoat, with a sheaf of papers under his arm—the infamous attendance list—as edgy and nervous as always, smoking a poorly made cigarette, the classic smoke of the man who never has the peace and quiet to roll his own properly. If that fine gentleman in the hallowed space of the lecture theater was treated with the disrespect I have described, just imagine the figure he cut in the open air: broad-brimmed black hat on the tilt, dusty old shoes, frayed tie, yellow nicotine-stained fingers, slightly singed mustache, and the nervous twitch that always seemed to afflict him. He was greeted with loud applause, a raucous racket, and the usual howls of *"Avi! Avi! Avi!"*

Dr. Vila stood in front of the motley crew and, surrounded by those aspiring to high honors, began the forced march on nature. The crowd had to reach one or the other of the rocky outcrops of Montjuïc via the neighborhoods of plaça de Toros and plaça d'Espanya. Experience had taught him it was better to avoid the Gran Via, which was too central and busy a street to try to negotiate with that student carnival. So when we reached the corner of Aribau, we headed towards Diputació and turned down that street.

The appearance of this crowd of generally well-dressed youths created a buzz of excitement. Passersby stopped to watch; coachmen slowed their horses; porters and their families stood on their doorsteps; families peered over balconies, their attitudes quite different from when a funeral cortege passed by. The appearance on the pavement of a young woman or group of young ladies triggered a melee. Students surrounded them, attempted the usual indecent moves, and a swarthy scoundrel—generally from Lleida, with gleaming teeth, olive skin, and wavy hair—always went too far. Boundaries were easily crossed, a passerby bent on rescue protested, arguments ensued, punches were thrown, and police appeared. Somebody ran to fetch the professor who always walked far ahead, and Dr. Vila arrived after a while, huffing and puffing. From the start, he refused to become embroiled and began ipso facto to defend that individual against the police, saying that he fell within the jurisdiction of the university. This led to a dramatic confrontation. The professor stiffened, adopted a lofty, officious tone, declaiming, "Policemen, sirs, we have embarked on a journey to carry out experiments in mineralogy as determined by law. We are in the midst of our scientific endeavors."

The police looked at each other in astonishment, completely at a loss. They looked him up and down, bewildered, and were even more astonished.

"Long live Grandpa!" shouted one oaf.

"Long live the jurisdiction of the university!" bellowed another.

"*Orden! Silencio! Callarse!*" snarled Dr. Vila, brandishing his papers, working up a sweat.

The throng had split up and spread out as people set their own pace along the street; a group in the rear suddenly burst into the lead. This group had found a hurdy-gurdy—one of the countless hurdy-gurdies that brought entertainment to the streets of Barcelona at the time—and the instrument had been hired with the requisite player to accompany the outing with its musical offerings. When the young gentlemen discovered that Dr. Vila was arguing with the police, they decided it was vital to reinforce their professor's dialectic with music from the hurdy-gurdy they were dragging along. They placed the artifact behind him and while the miserable academic was gabbling away, trying to convince the representatives of the law that this was a scientific exploration and that its intrinsic interest vastly transcended any empirical, petty, or pedagogically routine consideration, the hurdy-gurdy struck up with the paso doble of "The Rooster" or "Come, Come, Come," which Chelito was performing at the Eden Music Hall on carrer Nou and which competed with the "I Love My Lovely Crooks" I mentioned before, the song in vogue in Barcelona that had swept the boards from the Buena Sombra cabaret to every café terrace and street corner.

"What on earth is that? What musical farrago is that?" shouted the professor, beside himself, yellow with rage, stamping his oversize shoes on the ground, hopping nervously up and down. "*Orden! Callarse! Silencio!*"

He had yet to utter "*Silencio!*" when the students handed another peseta to the hurdy-gurdy player. This character was not only ready to play "Come, Come, Come" as often as necessary but also to phrase the tune in the jolliest way possible. Balconies were packed. A sizable throng formed around his performance. Students practiced in the art of dance cavorted with the first member of the opposite sex they bumped into and, if they found none, danced effeminately with other males. The chaos was growing out of control. Increasingly unable to believe their eyes, the police put their hands to their heads and disappeared into the first bar they found.

At this, Dr. Vila chuckled contentedly—the chuckle of a man who has just won a battle. His feat was greeted with gleeful howls of "Long live Grandpa! *Visca l'Avi!*," a cry that was taken up by the people hanging over their balconies and the sycophants standing around him. He immediately began to scratch behind one ear with his little finger. Then he lit up a cigarette and broke into a walk with the fellow still playing his hurdy-gurdy trailing behind.

Progress along carrer de la Diputació generated two or three conflicts like the one just described and the band reached the area around plaça de Toros quite late. On the other hand, movement through plaça d'Espanya wasn't without its difficulties, particularly because of the trams—students gathered in such a riotous state were fond of derailing trams—and consequently the first contingents reached the rocky heights of the skirts of Montjuïc when dusk was beginning to fall. The hurdy-gurdy or -gurdies rented on carrer d'Aribau had accompanied the walkers the whole way with few interruptions. When we reached the wildness, these instruments disappeared. The terrain wasn't accessible to any kind of carriage.

As soon as Dr. Vila identified the presence of a few herbs or a rock on the ground, he halted, laughed, and announced, "Gentlemen, we have reached our terrain! Hands at the ready! The time has come to start our practical investigations!"

"It's dark. You can't see a thing!" shouted one student.

"*Avi! Avi! Avi! Visca l'Avi!*" bellowed yet another spoiled brat, gloomily.

And so the evening rapidly ended as twilight faded. Surrounded by those with head-of-the-class aspirations, the professor plucked the occasional herb or picked up a rock. He stuffed every item into one of his pockets. Two or three students had brought sheets of paper suitable for collecting plants.

In the meantime, one fact was self-evident: The number of students who had reached the terrain was much smaller than the number that had marched off from the Law Faculty courtyard two or three hours earlier. Tired of their larks and practical jokes, most had abandoned the hands-on class in plaça d'Espanya and jumped into a tram or taken refuge in a café or one cinema or another. When the first star of twilight appeared on the green, enameled sky, Dr. Vila was left with a few hangers-on. Almost all his class had vanished. The return of the select few in the pitch dark was a somber affair. Dr. Vila groped his way mechanically, tentatively through the dark wilderness.

Five or six of these practical classes were held during the year. The idea was to collect minerals in the autumn and herbs in the spring. I only attended the first two classes, but I expect they were all equally mad.

As a good, local product, I admit to being a mediocre, undisciplined student, but I always thought that what happened in that chaotic introduction to the sciences was intolerable, if not criminal. I don't mean to suggest Dr. Vila i Nadal was a good teacher. He was entirely responsible for many of things that happened around him. Nonetheless, I finally felt sorry for him—a feeling equal to the contempt I felt for my fellow students, those sons of the ruling class who were destined to be the ruling class of tomorrow. Their capricious pranks and permanent revolt against that weak, good-natured man, a repository of knowledge like others, filled me with indignation. These students seemed driven by a frenzied need to create disorder and anarchy in his presence, in stark contrast to the docile flock of sheep they became in the lectures of Dr. Alcobé, the professor of physics, a cold, lean fellow who was at once unpleasant and forbidding. The moment came when the chaos became too much. I couldn't stand any more.

One day, after the uproar in our mineralogy and botany class, a student got up from his seat, put on his hat in the middle of the lecture theater, and started to walk out. Dr. Vila challenged him: "Where are you going?"

The student tilted his hat, tightened the knot of his tie—the vogue was to wear them as small as an almond nut—grinned, and drawled like a cheeky lout, emphasizing each syllable, "I am go-in' for a be-er."

The student body greeted his reply with an ovation. Once more the teacher was under the gun. Dr. Vila blanched, broke into a cold sweat, and his whole body started shaking. He struggled to stop his tears from flowing. I didn't even want to find out what that rude idiot's name was. It was the last straw. I dropped out of introduction to the sciences and never returned to that class of shambles permanently instigated by the majority. I am sure other students reached the same decision no matter the calling they may have felt for the subject. That course was a sickness, the plague, worse than a flogging.

I said I'd like to have studied chemistry. Quite rightly too, my spirit of curiosity drove me to study chemistry alongside medicine. I've always been passionate about medicine, as many of my friends know and in particular my friend S. Perhaps the root of my curiosity in terms of chemistry and medicine—and of practical science in general—derives from the respect I have always felt for experimental materialism.

Consequently, I decided to see what studying medicine might be like. I went to the Clinical Hospital with various friends enrolled in this faculty. I expect that with more or less effort I would have survived the dissection room. I find it difficult to understand how anatomy can be studied by rote, I mean by learning texts by heart, as some of my student acquaintances do. I am able to retain quite a lot of things I have seen, but my ability to remember words is almost nonexistent. I attended various lessons given by Professor Batllés i Bertrand de Lis, who was an extremely courteous, stout, ruddy-cheeked gentleman of average height. Good heavens! The anatomy lessons given by Professor Batllés were seen by most students from a single perspective: either pass or fail.

They played the classic rite of passage on me as a novice student in the dissection room. A friend gave me a welcoming handshake. He withdrew his hand and I was left with another hand in mine that was icy cold and ashen colored—a dead man's hand with rather dark fingernails. It was a short hand—that is, it had been severed from the arm at the level of the pulse. I felt very tense for a moment but didn't start screaming as many people did who went on to become doctors, and distinguished ones at that.

I joined the Law Faculty by process of elimination—after my total failure in the introduction to the sciences, not because of the subject matter as such but because of the quantity of human bodies in play. I came there without any specific interest in law or laws—I don't mean I was entirely indifferent, because I have never felt indifferent in relation to life. As there were considerably fewer students, a sense of orderliness was much more present. Conversely, I found the demands so light that my university tasks (shall we say) were quite compatible with other more peremptory appeals to mental activity.

But that is quite another story. I needed to leave behind the sinister, wearisome disorder that reigned in the introduction to the sciences, a disorder that nothing could justify in a civilized milieu, not even that taste for the picturesque some people have. In that sense, the Law Faculty seemed like an oasis, much more pleasant and less stressful, picturesque too, but at quite a different level.

For reasons that would take too long to explain and that are quite irrelevant, as one who experienced the end of the classic heyday of student life, I can claim I lived in a relatively quiet and orderly manner. I can't say I visited the most sordid dives and I did manage to avoid the most wretched lodging houses, but that doesn't mean I didn't frequent cafés with billiards and tables for playing seven and a half, the music halls on the Paral·lel, and cafés with waitress service, because like a good number of my colleagues, my studies at the Law Faculty were more affected and ravaged by sensual tensions than by the civil code or judicial procedures.

When I came to Barcelona in 1913 to start my university course, the nineteenth-century cafés, with mirrors on the walls, red velvet sofas, frosted-glass lampshades, tobacco-colored ceilings, beady-eyed waiters, and traditional *conversazione*—all rather dingy and perfunctory, with the obvious exceptions—were already in decline. The student cafés in my day were Cal Pau and Cafè Gravina.

The former was on the Gran Via, opposite the entrance to the school of pharmacy. It occupied the ground floor of a modern house and was in the style of ground floors in modern houses in Barcelona's latest development: a huge hangar with cast-iron columns that supported the metal beams. A large glass door let in a stream of unpleasant, glaring light—except when the plane trees on the Gran Via were in leaf. This powerful glare reached almost halfway into the café. As you walked toward the back of the establishment, it softened and the space darkened. It got very shadowy right at the back because it always depended on artificial light. The brighter area—by the entrance—was for billiard tables and other innocent pastimes. The rear of theé was home to gambling tables that were positioned under a powerful white light that created a glow where it hit the green beige the color of seaweed in murky waters.

Cafè Gravina, situated in the street of the same name—a street that goes from Pelai to Tallers—was a sordid, shabby, gloomy, lively café that seemed to suffer from the dismal, black-and-blue shadow that the Military Hospital on Tallers cast on the surrounding buildings. The hospital didn't simply have a visual impact; it also had an olfactory presence that spread into the neighborhood air. Depending on which way the wind was blowing, whenever the door to Cafè Gravina opened it got a blast from the hospital. In the summer, that brought a stench of old, sweaty woolen mattresses—a henhouse, pigeon-shit smell. When these odors wafted in, the faces of the men at the gambling tables turned pale and sickly—as if they were convalescents who'd escaped from the hospital next door.

In both cafés they played snooker and billiards, and professional croupiers cut the cards for seven and a half—croupiers who years ago, so they said, had been students who'd gone downhill. You saw the odd silver five-peseta coin on these tables at the beginning of the month; from the fifth to the fifteenth, the odd peseta; from the fifteenth onward the smallest of small change.

On carrer d'Aribau you also found various student cafés that differed from those we have mentioned because of the presence of distinguished young peroxide blonds dubbed "tango-ers." These young ladies were full of pretensions but I don't think they practiced vice in a deliberately malicious way. Although I suspect that they were in the prime of youth, they simply aspired to some sort of retirement enliv-ened by the rearing of domestic animals—I mean that they aspired to a rabbit hutch or modestly populated hen coop. Although Cafè Gravina and Cal Pau were dives of ill repute, I never caught a glimpse of members of the other sex. There was a spontaneous division of la-bor. I don't mean that those vestal maidens—as they were dubbed by the decadent poets of the time in their more elaborate verses—weren't positively disposed or hadn't felt drawn at the beginning of their ca-reers to a somberly pallid student from Lleida with wavy black hair and an absolutely enviable granite marble head. In my time and in these matters, students from Lleida swept the board in a very real, palpable way. But I was quite uninformed on these questions. I never felt attracted by the establishments on carrer d'Aribau—probably be-cause of lack of money, but also because the street is on an upward incline and steep inclines have always made me hesitate.

In the gambling dens in Cafè Gravina and Cal Pau at the time I'm writing about, genuine students coexisted with a gang of croupiers, hangers-on, and boys who lived by their wits and the most devious wheeling and dealing. If those men had devoted some of their ingenu-ity to normal activities, they might have made a good living. Cafè Gravina was mainly frequented by poor—or at least apparently hum-ble—students from the countryside who looked out of place but were surprisingly passionate about their gambling. Cal Pau catered to better-off students from Barcelona who had greater leeway because they knew their daddies would cover their losses. The appalling spec-tacles let loose during the introduction to the sciences course were planned in this dive.

I spent many hours in these dismal establishments. In any case, I was always a small-time player, never a show-off—a quiet, gray, self-effacing player. When the moment came to lay a bet—you sometimes had to slip your hand through a crack in the wall of idlers standing around the table—I struggled to overcome a very strong, inexplicable feeling of timidity. I never managed to act in a valiant, determined fashion when I confronted a gaming table. It was beyond me. Nor do I remember ever voicing the slightest protest when some scoundrel claimed my bet and my winnings and pocketed the lot. When I realized I'd been cheated, I'd look perplexed and go completely blank; my inner turmoil was considerable. My cowardice was absurd but constitutional.

Sr. Pau, the bar owner, was a man for the morning: His was a student café, so his opening hours matched the academic timetable of our premier teaching center. It was a café that worked in reverse to all the others: There wasn't a soul in the place at night but at nine in the morning it was packed. One could spend hours arguing about the differences between morning and nighttime passions. Sr. Pau, as I was saying, would walk stiffly and solemnly from one table to the next. He was a respectable-looking, gray-eyed man of mature years, stoutly built, tall, burly, and pallid, with a spot of grease on his sleek, ashen white hair, and a round, pompous mustache, lightly singed by the Egyptian cigarettes he smoked. He was said to be a refined gentleman, a complete match for his clientele. He wore top-quality ironed shirts and collars, celluloid cuffs, and ties. There was one detail, however, in which his good taste deserted him: He wore too much brassware—too many rings on his fingers, too many shiny buttons, too many tie-pins—and the large gold chain adorning his estimable, splendid paunch was far too resplendent. Even so, despite such infantile lapses, he acted like a man who had lived life to the full—creating the impression that you had lived life to the full was a kind of general bourgeois ideal—and he had that world-weary, lukewarm manner of contemplating life, which stood him in good stead socially. It was a look that placed him a cut above the man in the street—that is, from ordinary people who, as a French novelist said, did nothing but work. His slightly gruff, solemn drawl added the finishing touch to his respectable demeanor—even if it could have been the voice of a practiced, scheming scoundrel. Some said Sr. Pau looked like a professor, and those who had dealings with him and were familiar with the political influence he enjoyed said he could have been one if he'd wanted, because he was a person with academic qualifications (perhaps) but hadn't bothered to flaunt them.

The truth is that in the vicinity of the university there wasn't a man who looked more like a professor—without actually being one—than Sr. Pau.

Leaving the introduction to the sciences course for the introduction to the arts was to move from chaos to fairyland. To enter the Law Faculty properly speaking, one had to attend an introductory course that introduced one to nothing, but the much smaller number of students meant it felt like an oasis. A crowd of two hundred and eighty students packed between four walls for the purpose of making them study is an untested educational practice. A group one-fourth the size isn't perfect for teaching purposes but is much less monstrous. The quantitative difference created a much pleasanter situation. In this sense, it was like entering another world. Apart from that, everything else was the same.

In other words, the university was an exact reflection of society in the country and not a selective body. The professorial terrain matched the general terrain in the country—except that the professorial terrain was much worse than the country's because it was pedantic and retrograde and could plead no extenuating circumstances. It was professorial mediocrity to match the mediocrity in the country. And finally a small minority of conscientious teachers with a sense of responsibility for their profession did exist, corresponding to the small minority, the derisory minority that seems serious about its mission to use its knowledge to benefit the country.

One could identify various phenomena in the introduction to the arts, the most outstanding being Don Josep Daurella i Rull, who taught fundamentals of logic.

Sr. Daurella was a splendid, excellent teacher; those of us who spent a year before his podium knew the meaning of truth. When, at half past one, the moment of truth under his auspices was at hand— "Time to stop, Professor"—we felt impregnated with the breath of truth and took it with us, echoing in our ears. Little did the men and women of Barcelona whom we met down Pelai or up Balmes realize that these obscure students had been exposed to the important things in life. Nobody could have imagined the transcendence of what had happened. If they could have, what might have transpired? It is quite beyond the power of imagination.

Sr. Daurella taught fundamentals of logic. When he crossed the faculty courtyard, often wearing a gown and miter, it was quite obvious he was on his way to perform something fundamental. When he sat down behind his table on the podium, it was crystal clear that he was about to perform duties that were at once remunerated and fundamental. When he began, one felt that ineffable emotion welling up in the lecture theater that one experiences when witnessing something fundamental. In the entire university syllabus you couldn't find any discipline or any other subject bearing such a dramatic epithet. In the exact sciences, where one supposes they exercised a degree of precision, there was nothing similar. Geometry, algebra, and integral calculus were not described as fundamental. Only logic, the logic of syllogisms, a kind of diversion invented by schoolmen and improved by Jesuits, was considered to be fundamental. It was simply that logic, as it was taught in the introductory courses to law, the arts, and humanities, and especially the way Sr. Daurella explained it, was considered to be the central, objective, genuine, and pure truth. If this hadn't been the case, that adjective would have been redundant.

It wasn't a question of being pretentious. I was there and can honestly declare scarcely a pretension was in sight. No. It was fundamental in such a real, heartfelt way, a truth so obvious, routine, and taken for granted, that Sr. Daurella would have smiled his best sardonic smile if anyone had voiced a single doubt. In any case, he possessed everything that one could need to profess truth. Firstly, his manner was tailor-made for gravitas. He was a most striking figure on his raised platform. He was medium height, chubby, with a dark olive, slightly Gypsy complexion. Rippling in small furrows and soft folds of flab, his face displayed a deeply indigenous seam that was half clerical and half mercantile. He dressed in black, the eminently respectable black of an undertaker. His neck was thickset and broad and set on vast shoulders. A heavy silk shirtfront, where a dark pearl gleamed, occupied the triangle not covered by his waistcoat. His cheekbones were broad, his eyes small and bright, his black hair flattened over his skull, and his mouth half curled in a snarl. His lively features contrasted sharply with their impassive, motionless Buddha frame. When it was cold in winter, he sported a red silk foulard that gave him a vaguely Episcopal air.

All these exterior qualities are wonderfully useful for a man on a podium. They contribute to an impression of natural strength. They lend a decisive air to any words uttered. Dr. Daurella was renowned for possessing these qualities. Nonetheless, we should be fair: He was an imposing enough figure not to require such an aura to assert himself. It sufficed for him to eat peppermints on his platform. Sr. Daurella loved devouring peppermints. He ate them green and he ate them pink. Eating sweets is a completely anodyne, non-transcendental activity. Eating sweets on a raised podium, while teaching fundamental truths, is to engage literally in a grandiose activity—who could ever doubt this?

However, I was a mere pupil and couldn't see some things clearly. What I now think of as normal academic practice—sweet-eating while executing one's duties is an activity accepted by academics and professors—at the time I felt it to be an expression of friendly bonhomie, delightful bonhomie. Seated opposite him in the small Chair of Logic amphitheater, suspended in the grayish silence floating in the air, I'd stare at him now and then. His cheeks moved as he sucked his sweet. He was licking the last of his mint. Peppermints burnt my palate, and I thought admiringly, "Sr. Daurella must have such a strong palate!"

When he had extracted all the sweetness, he took the remnants of the mint in his closed fist, threw them away like an olive stone, and started to suck the next one. I felt he was quite appealing, no doubt because that distinguished hack had to give me a pass mark. Today I find that extraordinary. This was the right adjective, because one must never forget that while he was enacting these homely niceties, we were in the presence of the truth, and all present endowed with a certain intellect were swayed by that truth's sovereign, gravitational pull. Syllogisms poured forth. One pupil piped up confidently: "Trees breathe through their leaves."

Sr. Daurella replied gruffly, in his baritone bass pitch: "The pear tree is a tree."

And the pupil completed the round enthusiastically: "Therefore the pear tree breathes through its leaves."

We were all so pleased as punch we would readily have gone on for another hour or so. It literally was a land of make-believe.

Professionally, Dr. Daurella sold cod wholesale. He was a convinced Thomist to boot. It would be rather an exaggeration to state that Dr. Daurella explained Thomism. No, we shouldn't go that far. He explained the barest bones, bones that had been picked clean—a mummified Thomism. But no matter, we were happy, ecstatically so, and you can't imagine how delighted we were to be transported to the era before Galileo, Newton, and Descartes. What a sense of well-being! What a land of milk and honey! Yes, I can say that I was happy, that my happiness lasted for a single academic year—one wretched academic year—and ever since my life has swung in an irremediable void. If anything could possibly cast a shadow over my happiness, it was the thought that that striking jackass, at the end of the year, might fail me with his fantastic bullshit in a totally *fundamental* fashion.

This unforgettable introductory course was blessed with another handsome professor by the name of Don Juan de Arana y de la Hidalga (a fine moniker!), who taught natural law and was vice-rector (Daurella was the senator), a member of the board of the Bank of Spain, etcetera ... that is to say, a past master at the game.

Around 1914, old Arana—"the frog," as we his spiritual offspring dubbed him—had everything sorted. He was a small, tubby figure who looked like an Easter egg. He was neat and tidy and very elegantly appointed; he looked like a baby rabbit whose fur had just been combed. He was extraordinarily energetic for a man between sixty and seventy years old. In the morning he dressed like a financier in the Maura mold: He wore light-colored overcoats, gray-buttoned patent leather shoes, sported an admirably smart mustache and small beard, a blue-ribboned white coffee fedora, and white gloves. Sometimes old age made his beard tremble slightly and that made him more fetching than ever. He was such a fine, elegant specimen of an old man you'd have said he lived on spoonfuls of undiluted milk from the bottle and the best buttered toast and that after he'd eaten he wiped his chops on a blue embroidered lace handkerchief.

He was a professor in natural law, the name given to philosophy of law in this country—that is, scholastic philosophy of law. Frankly, I don't know if such a thing as natural law exists. I never managed to find any enlightenment in Sr. Arana's lectures and, as I've never had any time since to reflect on these matters, I can't say whether law possesses immutable, eternal principles that are valid in any latitude, that are objectively natural, as natural, say, as the makeup and shape of a cat, a bowler hat, or a melon, or if natural law is a man-made law a number of respectable gentlemen declare to be "natural" because they live in comfortable homes, have inherited or married well, and sent their offspring to the best high schools. All I *can* say is that natural law, given its actual vagueness, had rather an expensive enrollment fee and that to "pass" one had to buy and learn by heart chapters from a textbook on the subject written by a fellow called Rodríguez de Cepeda, who apparently hailed from Valencia.

This textbook was a typical manual, a model for this kind of monstrous publication. In the prologues, its author solemnly established, in lengthy paragraphs, the importance of his subject, no doubt to convince us he deserved the salary he was being paid. That was followed by explanations of theories of law. These were legion. Everyone who had addressed the matter had expounded his ideas in a completely personal way, disagreeing with everyone else, no doubt, by dint of the immortal principle that every head needs a different hat. Rousseau's theory, Kant's theory. Theories by Hegel, Hobbes, and Spinoza, not forgetting theories from the Orient, by Greeks and Romans, and from the Middle Ages, the baroque period, the Enlightenment, and nowadays. Two names surfaced from this never-ending procession of theories that inspired immediate deference and interest: Grotius and Pufendorf. Men who devote their lives to theorizing and who are fortunate enough to have names like theirs are assured of immortality in the groves of academe.

I found the list of opinions very off-putting because it demonstrated that natural law was completely relative, a matter of speculation, given the diversity of opinions expressed by writers who have wandered down the misty avenues of the subject with their truths tucked under their arms. Faced by such arrant nonsense, one solved the problem by putting good theories in one corner, half-reasonable ones in another, and irremediably awful theories in very distant crannies. One had to know the first inside out, a great deal of tolerance existed in relation to the second, and the third required refutation. In terms of our work refuting impious theories, Cepeda attacked like a spoiled horse with an "I want this but not that." In this respect, Arana was more Cepeda-ish than the textbook's author. He wanted his pupils to be able to refute a bad theory rather than to understand and grasp it. This was quite monstrous. How can you refute something you don't understand or grasp? It made no difference. Every year the same episode was rehearsed, an episode I experienced and witnessed repeatedly, and if one ever describes it to anyone not deformed by our official seats of learning, they burst their sides in laughter because it reveals such stupidity—it is the legendary anecdote about Professor Arana.

"Sr. So-and-so," said the professor in his mellifluous Spanish. "Today we are doing Kant's theory (or Rousseau's). Tell me about Kant's theory. What do you know about Kant's theory?"

The student stood up, opened the syllabus, shifted his body slightly so his ear was better positioned to hear his prompter on the next-door bench, wet his lips, scratched the nape of his neck, and came out with drivel. The prompter, that day, for whatever reason, was a dreadful prompter. He was a failure as a prompter. A tense silence reigned in the lecture theater. In the meantime, Sr. Arana glanced at his student register through the gold-rimmed spectacles on the end of his nose. Finally, the wet fish of a student—to describe him accurately—confessed.

"I didn't find time to study," he said, looking distressed, oppressed, and completely at a loss.

"So, Sr. So-and-so," the professor replied, not at all sourly, smoothing his mustache, as if he were commenting on the weather, "you don't know Kant's theory. But I expect you know how to refute it. Now, be so good as to refute Kant's theory."

As the prompters were a waste of time, sometimes a holy spirit arose from the most unlikely corner of the lecture theater to help the person questioned to survive. The student heard various noises behind him (what was known as "rhubarb-rhubarb") and began to stammer. Sr. Arana immediately struck the pose of a man who is completely entranced. He wiped his chin as if he were stroking a goat's nipple. The rhubarb-rhubarb made sense and the student bore up. The professor listened with growing admiration. The amazing scene always ended with a professorial comment.

"You didn't know the theory but you did manage to refute it. That is quite an achievement."

I don't think high culture has ever scaled such heights as those exemplified by these absolutely authentic scenes.

After Christmas, when the refutation of evil theories concluded, one sector of the bolder elements in the class decided it was much more interesting to go and play billiards or seven and a half in Cal Pau. Another swathe of the register was convinced that Kant and Hobbes, Spinoza and Rousseau, the Greeks and Romans, the moderns and a good crop of contemporary thinkers were bad people, poor parents, barflies, enemies of the family, private property, and the state.

It was only then that we started on natural law "properly speaking" and it seemed we could breathe at last. It was a theological-scholastic hodgepodge of reasoning based on hidden, dispersed syllogisms that were set at Sr. Cepeda's intellectual level and presented in such a way as to please Sr. Arana. It was law that looked good, that was entirely photogenic and totally natural. However, something peculiar happened in my year: The textbook was calculated on the basis of a theoretically normal academic year, namely, a year without student strikes or extra holidays. Well, as many strikes were called as the state of the nation required and every holiday was respected completely, and when we reached 20 May, the last day of the academic year, we were only familiar, and even then only vaguely, as you might imagine in such an intuitive country, with half of what passes for natural law. If they had forced us to sit examinations on the other half, we'd have concluded that the slice of natural law we lacked was a complete fake.

And then the examinations were upon us.

Sr. Arana had absolutely sui generis criteria when it came to examinations—criteria I believe should be described as otherworldly. He ineluctably failed the last two students on his register. His decision was unshakable on this point. What was behind such strange criteria? How could the professor justify such an arbitrary, shocking attitude? I don't know. He must have had his reasons, but as I never heard him address the matter, I must declare total ignorance. The fact is that the last two on the register, even if they'd been reincarnations of Plato or Aristotle or the offspring of Pufendorf, would have failed.

However, in my view there was something worse than this arbitrariness: the fact that nobody took any notice and everyone thought it was perfectly natural.

For the other students, I mean those who preceded the last two on the register, the examinations were unimportant: A pass was guaranteed, even though we were absolute, fully certified idiots.

As the last two on the list knew what was going to happen from the first weeks of the course, they yielded to the designs of Providence. They didn't even turn up for the examinations. When a fellow student bothered to convey the news of the inevitable catastrophe, he would find them in Cafè Gravina or Cal Pau playing cards or potting billiard balls. They would shrug their shoulders when they heard the news and carry on potting.

Such is the news I bring from the introductory course to law at the University of Barcelona in the second decade of this century. It is not unlike the introduction to the sciences that was overwhelmed by numbers and ravaged by the hordes. It was an introductory course overwhelmed by the consequences of what I have just related.

23 March, Sunday. Xavier Güell invites me to lunch at his family's home. An apartment on Passeig de Gràcia: silent, at once daunting and muted. A succulent lunch. His family struck me as having lots of skeletons in the cupboard. His father is the typical gentleman from Tarragona: chubby, fair, bespectacled, and bald. He seems a very hard man with little imagination. One son has disappeared to Latin America in search of adventure. The daughter is a young lady brimming with vitality, a magnificent Diana. The mother is tall, fair, and ethereal, and looks vaguely irritable. The overall atmosphere is one of reserve and coldness. They all seem to be on the lookout to save their own bacon. A bourgeois family.

Yesterday I enrolled in the Institute of Education.

I was three times on the point of entering the Continental before dinner, to join López-Picó and sit in on his circle. Now that Folguera has died, I'm particularly interested in Carles Riba, who belongs to this group. What I have read of his work shows he's very passionate. However, my timidity got in the way.

In the afternoon at the library, Climent introduced me to Martínez Ferrando. Ferrando is a surprising Valencian: He speaks quietly, gently, and pleasantly; is never noisy, never gesticulates; and is modest in the most natural way possible. He speaks as if he were holding a handkerchief over his lips. I think his temperament is the opposite of mine, but I feel that we will be friends. He is a public librarian.

24 March. A general strike. Barcelona is transformed.

The situation seems to have come about (so they say) because the employers didn't abide by the agreement that led to the ending of the strike at La Canadenca.

I stay at home in the morning; in the afternoon I go for a stroll. Everyone is speaking more quietly then usual; the Rambla is so silent the sparrows sound as if they are screeching. It is pitch black at dusk. Candles are lit in the Athenaeum. Everyone is waiting tensely, even in the Athenaeum. As you walk down the street, you hear people in shop doorways discussing whether to put some light or other in their window. Many shopkeepers stand idly by. I walk down as far as Drassanes. The Rambla and the streets crossing it—in total darkness—are swarming with people. Escudellers is literally like a wolf's gullet and so dark people thud into each other. It's as if the city is a huge, dark, entangled skein of wool. Nonetheless, you can still hear the blind man's violin playing a tune somewhere or a beggar's voice along the wall. The market for love is flourishing in plaça del Teatre. The lack of light acts as an aphrodisiac. I walk back to my lodging house groping in the dark. From Canaletes onward, the human throng thins out. I am surprised the apartment isn't lit up at all. A silent night; Barcelona seems to be meditating. But maybe it is just asleep.

25 March. No change in the city. Judging by the movements, the military occupation has been extended. Order on the surface. Cannons and the Red Cross occupy a large part of plaça de Catalunya. I can see groups of armed vigilantes from the balcony in my lodgings: the Sometent. Soldiers in the streets. The soldiers stop passersby, who put their hands in the air while they are being searched. Late in the evening, very few people on the street. Scant light, but perhaps slightly more than yesterday. At night my landlady asks: What are we going to eat tomorrow? The general has given the order for shops to open tomorrow.

Today, the landlady's eldest daughter tried to commit suicide by leaping out of the window overlooking the indoor patio. I happened to be walking down the passage when I heard someone opening this window. I turned around and saw half of Conxita's body hanging over the rail... I ran and was in time to catch her by the legs and pull her back inside. She's not had much practice at jumping out of windows. That's not the way to do it. The girl is very pale—half fainting—leaning on the wall. However, perhaps I enjoyed it. Apparently it had to do with matters of the heart and the fact that her fiancé—whom I have heard is a policeman—isn't convinced by her. There is no reaction to the incident in the lodging house.

A splendid night. From the balcony that opens onto the street I look out at the sky with all its stars. There are no streetlights tonight so you can see the stars. Patrols are circulating slowly down streets. Occasional contingents of mounted Civil Guards. The sound of horseshoes on cobbles. A car speeds by now and then, making a raucous din—though not very often. I can hear snatches of hoarse rumbling from a phonograph blasting away in the corner of the gallery.

27 March. Things are still paralyzed, but the strike is weakening. I notice that barbershops have opened. I go into the one on Mallorca, by rambla de Catalunya. It is filled with silent people. Everyone is saying nothing and waiting. When somebody walks in, everyone turns around to see who it is. The display of force is impressive. The victors are being cheered in the streets. The men of the Sometent are in demand everywhere.

Institute of Education.

After his lecture on Catalan grammar, Pompeu Fabra introduces me to Joan Crexells: a very tall, thin young man, his spectacles in the air attached to a cord. I notice how he bursts out laughing at the slightest opportunity.

A history lecture given by Ferran Valls i Taberner. Extremely interesting. After five years at the university I had almost lost sight of the idea that there could possibly be such a thing as a pleasant, worthwhile class. Professor Valls, tall, pale, and strongly built, has a rather labored tone when he talks, which makes everything he says more interesting. I can't bear garrulous, fluent men.

Mid-spring. Delightfully starry, wonderfully soft nights. One feels the effect of a disturbing sensuality, which increases as everything moves beyond reach. A damp breeze that brushes your skin like a caress.

29 March, Saturday. Night. The strike continues—though it is petering out. I have worked very hard over the last few days.

Institute of Education.

First lecture by Xènius in the philosophy seminary. I really envy this man. I think he will become a powerful obsession of mine. He is a magnificent, exuberant orator who husbands his skills in the most fascinating manner. His lecture transports me to a world that I imagine is education outside this country.

A large audience. Estelrich resembles a rooster on a haystack. He is everywhere, with his artificial mess of curly hair; he wears light wine-colored socks with low-slung leather shoes I find quite perplexing. Millàs-Raurell, a face like a mask, pallid skin that looks as if it is covered in flour, almond eyes, and black garb. Josep M. Capdevila moves silently among the throng, sideways. Fair-haired, tubby Enric Jardí, with a thinker's features—or a romantic musician's—and a mania for counting arguments on his fingers. Tall, slender, elegant Joan Crexells, such a good lad and always laughing.

Three young ladies have signed up for the course. They wear dark clothes and seem delightful. One of them has a Greek nose—as they say—Climent has dedicated an amorous epigram to her.

The importance of Srta. Muntaner—Xènius's nymph Egeria. She is tall, dark, dresses very simply, is energetic and puts on a false show—I suspect—of svelte sophistication. The general public is not so attractive: There are young ladies in red, a cloistered nun, a lady dressed literally like a cockatoo. How sad fame must be!

It must have to do with being surrounded all the time by strange, rather uncouth ladies whose mouths, when they open, assume the shape of a hen's ass. The great knowledge Xènius has doesn't seem to do him much good!

Those who've enrolled and are already qualified teachers are somewhat pedantic. Don Eladi Homs is his own man.

Climent is being ironic.

30 March, Sunday. The Athenaeum, in the morning. A long conversation with Climent that prevents me from doing anything. Like all good conversationalists, Climent seems about to say something very important with every utterance, but never manages to. As we finish, he informs me, completely matter-of-fact, that he has become betrothed today.

Horrific lunch in my lodging house. Fortunately, the portions were minute.

In the afternoon, I try to write. I become discouraged and suffer nervous fatigue whenever I tackle the devilishly difficult act of writing. When I try to commit to paper something for publication, what I come up with seems, instinctively, pedantic, obscure, and pretentious. Moreover, Catalan is very difficult. It is virgin territory, land that has barely been tilled. Commonplace phrases that are an essential element in the literature of great languages cannot be used in Catalan because they are rural or too vulgar. It is diabolically difficult to achieve language that flows.

31 March. The general strike, which had died down, was declared officially over today. Countless arrests have been made. Màrius Aguilar comments sarcastically in the library that men in the Sometent are lining up right now outside military headquarters to remove from prison the people they jailed over the last few hours. Jaume Brossa died the moment the police broke into his house to arrest him. Brossa never did succeed in getting himself removed from the police files.

1 April, Tuesday. It is raining. Magnificent weather for the day after a general strike. Barcelona seems subdued. Completely flat. It clears up a little in the afternoon. The ground smells of spring.

I spend a moment in the Athenaeum. Books, pen, paper, tables, and desks are too much for me and I take to the street. At random: Passeig de Colom, the park, the area behind the park, the Somorrostro beach, and farther on. A strong, very aggressive southwesterly wind, a green, sick-making sea. Two loving couples—four silhouettes—alone and lost on the interminable, horrible beach. Seagulls. Depressingly damp.

On my way back, I see a magnificent adolescent girl skipping with some kids by the walls around the gasometers. Tall, lovely, full, soft legs, large eyelashes over big black eyes, shapely, sheer nylons. She jumps cheekily, without a care in the world. Thirteen years old? Fourteen? Firm, prominent buttocks, a loose dress, firm breasts flopping under her clothes, hair gathered behind her head. Her body is so full of grace against that awful landscape. When she jumps, she bares a round, wonderfully smooth knee. I think: Either you have to eat more or women won't ... feel hunger. Temptation fades.

At the end of the day, I walk back into Barcelona via El Born. Kids are rushing madly around Santa Maria. Everybody is skipping—I think even married women have joined in—an atmosphere saturated with a smell of oranges. When I walk past the church, I think of the Corpus Christi procession I saw there two years ago sparked by the Ramon Casas painting in the museum. Afterward I stroll up the Rambla to carrer d'Aragó, following some young ladies. Without any success. I'm hopeless when it comes to pursuing young ladies. I feel hungry again. The feminine forms vanish. By the time I get home I am exhausted.

2 April. Lack of light was perhaps what made the population of Barcelona suffer most during the strike. It was incredible. To spend one's nights in the dark, or with insufficient light, is naturally unpleasant. But material discomfort was not nearly as disturbing as the realization that something unthinkable had happened. And to realize that not so long ago electricity didn't exist and that I was born in the era of oil lamps.

Gritting his teeth, with his hissing voice and Catalan from Valls, Eugeni d'Ors was telling the gathering in the Athenaeum: "There are two kinds of man: those who are good at philosophy and those who are good for nothing."

"Yes, that's right," said Pujols, "but you always like to exaggerate."

For more than half an hour I gaze at *The Three Graces* by Raphael. The arm of the figure in the middle holding the apple has an infinite, disturbing grace that can't be translated into words. The vivid finish on Raphael's drawing.

Some of my friends think that the most attractive women are the virtuous ones who do all they can to hide the fact. I think quite the opposite.

Ugly women are generally very, very nice. But there are so few women prepared to recognize that fact.

4 April. University. Athenaeum, military training under the spotlights around the customs area. Nothing ever changes.

Spring is upon us, vast and mysterious, with the obsessions it insistently brings—but it's as if it didn't exist. As if it didn't exist—but still too powerful to keep me from taking anything seriously.

Xavier Güell. My friend Güell never loses the air of an enlightened rentier, of a dilettante rentier, of a rentier who subscribes to *Vogue.* Its pictures have the decadent quality of bread spread with sugar and olive oil.

I bump into Salvi Balmanya, from La Bisbal, on carrer d'Aribau. Two aperitifs with olives. A whiff of my country: health, peace and quiet, rudeness, everything is fine there now. What a din we people from the Ampurdan make! What a gratuitously noisy way of speaking! Balmanya is visibly upset when I mention Joan B. Coromina to him, because he speaks and gestures just the way Coromina does.

5 April. Institute of Education. A lecture on art history, in the museum in the park, by Joaquim Folch i Torres. Pitted by smallpox, with profound black eyes, he is lively, ironic, and robust. Those who think teaching or lecturing has to follow a conventional, set formula are surprised when they hear Folch. I think his spontaneous method of delivery is provocative. It is impossible to imagine a teacher if one doesn't start from his ability to evoke new horizons. Joaquim Folch's powers of suggestion are enormous. Above all, he has made me see the short-comings of the university.

I don't miss a single lecture at the institute. Perhaps there are too many—shall we say—career intellectuals, with no sense of spontane-ity at all and too strong a bent for mutual destruction. There is almost a general feeling of opposition to d'Ors. Xènius's manner is fated to create a host of miniature Xèniuses.

I have met many people at the institute and the Athenaeum.

Ventura Gassol. He has the peasant cunning of someone who has passed through the seminary. He is never natural—despite his efforts to simulate naturalness. When he was talking to me about the last strike, he said, "I am surprised how much I can be provoked by things that don't interest me at all, the problem of the workers, for example. Is it true we are sad because we cry?"

With his deliberate mess of curly hair, Estelrich could be taken for Italian or Portuguese. He is Xènius's number one enemy at the mo-ment. He has fatal love affairs. He is a cosmic individual. He lives in a bubbly magma and his mentally primitive spirit spills out in every di-rection. He is more greedy than ambitious, more sensual than domi-neering. If he were given the opportunity to choose between a woman and a lecture on women, he would grab both—a sure way to end up with nothing.

Joan Crexells. I was slightly disheartened when I discovered Joan Crexells had been a rhapsode at the Popular Encyclopedic Athe-naeum. Rhapsodes annoy me as much as iconoclasts. I belong to a world that is more reasoned and plausible. I was afraid momentarily that these adventures—for heaven's sake, one never can tell!—would lead him to lose his sense of the absurd. I must confess that none of my fears were confirmed. Crexells is an open, affable man, with a positive, wide-ranging sense of curiosity, who works with great enthusiasm and relishes activity. Even though he has had a smooth passage so far, he has an innate wit that means he will easily overcome obstacles.

Enric Jardí. What I most admire about this man is his vast culture and his ability to think calmly while appearing to scale heights of mediocrity. He is the only person I have ever known who approaches metaphysics with an adorably childish enthusiasm.

The resident pedagogues are Don Eladi Homs and Sr. Palau i Vera. Sr. Homs is a stiff giant of a fellow with a morose, funereal, overbearing, persnickety, rather halting manner. Physically he looks like a bored but conscientious engineer. Sr. Palau i Vera listens to Xènius's lecture while twirling his mustache—he is a thin man—and squinting at his manuals.

Millàs-Raurell. I like this small young man's admirable sense of ambition. He is so lively, self-confident, active, and tireless, and he has that cheeky edge, which people here usually possess.

Josep M. Capdevila, from Olot, is reputed to be very intelligent. He is a fervent supporter of Xènius. With Srta. Muntaner he comprises the nucleus of Xènius's fans. He must be intelligent; he thinks clearly and coolly. He is a bold man who acts with a somewhat soporific sense of discretion—a discretion bordering on the sanctimonious.

Climent is writing epigrams inspired by this course. He tells me I should write my novel. I'm not at all ready for that. Anyway, I think it's a heady brew.

6 April, Sunday. I read John Dewey's textbook on pedagogy, with Climent. I tell my friend, "All this is very elementary."

"It's very elementary but well worth knowing," Climent retorts.

I waste an hour and a half trying to put together four lines of verse. A total failure. Nonetheless, the exercise makes you understand how easy it must be for individuals endowed with an instinct for doggerel to write them at the drop of a hat.

Drill at the Military Academy in Drassanes, learning how to march in step, bolt and chamber, belt and cartridges in Castilian makes me feel as if I am starving. Afterwards, when I get to my lodgings, I find there is nothing to eat for dinner. I suspect that I might have become an excellent soldier if I'd been able to eat at the Suís when it was time for drill.

Couples, on the Rambla.

To watch a mature man with a young girl gives one food for thought; a mature woman and a very young man is a bad business; two young people of different sexes is a miserable sight. I know only too well what a thankless task it is to attempt writing about a first love if you are a writer who has not been completely corrupted by the lexicon of third-hand romanticism and the clichés of risqué novelettes.

7 April. The Pompeia Sporting Society. Reminiscences of student life. Today, in a pharmacy on the Rambla, I saw the apothecary's final-year diploma hanging in its baroque frame. The professors were at the top in their gowns and miters, displaying the customary bearded respectability of people of the time. At the bottom a series of young men with blurred features set in oval frames. My friend's considerable nose, supporting his spectacles, filled one of the ovals in that solemn composition.

I thought how I am nearing the end of my university course, and in next to no time will be posing in front of a photographer who will record my face while waving a rubber switch. And this photo will fill an oval in my year's diploma, and will have to hang on one stretch or another of my wall. I would feel most pressed if I were forced to say which particular stretch should take that piece of junk. I couldn't, frankly.

All this led me to ruminate a while on my life as a student. People usually say students lead a happy, cheerful, carefree life. I have been leading a student's life for many a year. But as yet I haven't found it to be happy, cheerful, or carefree. Perhaps it was, but it quite passed me by.

As a student I belonged to the Pompeia Sporting Society, not as a sportsman but as an assistant secretary. The need to work, to earn some money has hounded me cruelly from my most tender, adolescent years.

"Two hours a day for sixty pesetas a month. Is that all right?"

"Thank you very much," I replied gloomily, leaning on one of the columns in the Law Faculty courtyard.

"You have to write up the minutes of society meetings, draw up receipts, and see to correspondence."

"That will be fine."

I was talking to Bonaventura M.P., a very lively, active and entrepreneurial fellow student. Of all those in my year, he was the one with the most extensive social life. He was very affable. He was one of the faculty students who ate large numbers of sandwiches in Canaletes every day. He was from a famous family—known for its role in politics. He would spend an hour from one to two o'clock greeting a host of adorable senyoras and senyoretas on Passeig de Gràcia. Additionally, he was secretary of the Pompeia Club and one of its most active members. Everything indicated that his future would soon be settled. All in all, it is better if the people who are going to do us a favor are well positioned, particularly with an eye to the future favors they will have to grant us.

P. gave me the address of the office situated on a street across carrer de Salmerón, next to the Pompeia Theater.

Thus, at five one October afternoon, I walked up Passeig de Gràcia, my head buzzing. It would be an exaggeration to say I was happy, but I was very curious, very curious indeed. I had been given so much information over the last few days about my job!

Some had said, "Friars from the monastery of the same name are behind this Pompeia Society. If you behave yourself, you will be set up for life. They are rich and powerful, and can make and unmake people in this country. Work hard and you won't regret it!"

Others said, "The Pompeian Sporting Society was created to wean good families away from the Jesuits and place them under the sphere of influence of the friars on the Diagonal. For the moment, it seems to be working very well; young men and women are pleased with it and lots of good marriages are being arranged."

My curiosity was aroused immediately. I thought I'd been given the post of assistant secretary, and in fact what P. had done was to enormously complicate the way I saw the world. I refer to a period in the early years of my university degree, when my thinking was at its most ingenuous. Well, I have always been a slow, innocent young man. Often, when others see tangled motives behind events, I see only a single mechanical explanation. I often wondered, "How can people be so difficult to understand?" My own shortcomings, my own lack of understanding, were most evident: I was at that age when you can't imagine the other strange, entangled realities that lurk behind what you read in the newspapers.

"We'll see how it goes," I told myself as I turned into the street where the office was located, a street full of noisy children and carts, strewn with wastepaper and orange peel. Before I crossed the threshold, I looked back from the end of that sordid street: The blue-black, slightly golden light of dusk and the tumult on the street seemed quite wonderful.

A voice brought me to a halt inside the dark passageway: "What do *you* want?"

I explained what I'd come about. As we spoke, we walked down the passageway until we stood under an electric bulb that flickered painfully. The man addressing me was small, fair, and pink-cheeked, with deep-set blue eyes. His hair was tidily combed and plastered down. He wore a blue suit, a white silk scarf around his stiff neck, and rope sandals on his feet. He belonged to that unmistakably tubercular species you find on the backstreets of Barcelona.

"Follow me!" he clamored. "You need to speak to Sr. Codina."

I couldn't say which way we went. The house seemed a vast warren; at one moment I thought we were walking behind the stage of a gloomy, empty theater. In any case, the lighting was very poor. There was a thick layer of dust on the lightbulbs, some cloaked by a curtain of cobwebs. After crossing various passageways we reached a square door, which was lit up.

"You first," said the man in blue.

I looked inside. The room was thick with blue smoke. At the precise moment I entered, I saw a man at the back, behind a table, in the midst of a coughing fit; his eyes were bloodshot and he was holding an herb-scented handkerchief to his mouth. I glanced around. It was a square, low-ceilinged room that didn't seem to have windows. The walls were covered in glossy posters advertising sporting events, with bronzed athletes throwing the discus, young ladies in red or green sweaters playing tennis with an air of great refinement, and automobiles speeding around bends generally against the backdrop of a synthetically blue sea. There was another table, apart from the one where the man I assumed to be Sr. Codina was sitting, and seven or eight chairs lined up against the walls.

I waited shyly for the aforementioned gentleman to end his coughing fit before I introduced myself.

"Come in, come in ... Sr. P. mentioned you. Very pleased to make your acquaintance."

Sr. Codina stood up with difficulty. He held out his hand. He was in his mid-forties, tall, thin, and doe-eyed, with big, transparent ears and lank, jet-black hair splashed with brilliantine, a great mop of which hung down over his narrow, hard, wrinkled forehead. He spoke in a tenor's voice with a vaguely sarcastic tone. I saw right away that he liked to leave his cigarette to burn suspended on his lower lip while he twirled his singed mustache with huge white gorilla hands covered in red blotches. He wore a celluloid collar and cuffs and a tie molded around a strip of wire. A yellow pencil stuck ridiculously out of his waistcoat pocket.

"If you wish," I said, after exchanging the usual pleasantries, "we can get down to work."

"Why be in such a hurry? Take one and have a smoke," he said, holding out a forty-five cent packet.

And immediately after: "Did you read his little speech? A good one, I can tell you. We don't deserve him."

I couldn't guess which speechifier he was talking about, but I had the presence of mind to proffer the broadest, most supportive smile I could muster from my repertoire.

"I can see we are going to get along!" he said warmly, his gleeful smile revealing yellow, nicotine-ravaged teeth. "That will make life so much easier."

After a long conversation, in the course of which I agreed systematically with Sr. Codina's point of view, there was no option but to start work. I did so willingly, because that was what it was all about. Sr. Codina seemed rather weary and bad-tempered. Nothing could be more boring than having to teach someone what you do every minute of the day.

The minute book wasn't up-to-date, but notes within its pages could be properly expanded to give the impression of magnificent, well-phrased minutes for signing, though they were in fact entirely trivial, the most important sentence being "May God preserve you for many years." Afterwards, Sr. Codina, in more paternal fashion, showed me how to make out receipts. It was the office's basic operation. He handed me a giant book. Every page corresponded to a member, whose name figured at the top. Twelve green slips of paper were appended, one for every month in the year.

I sat at the empty table of the secretary-to-be. Sr. Codina handed me pen and ink.

"In this book," he told me, "you will find the great and the good of Barcelona. We have to prepare the receipts for October. Write clearly and away you go!" he added, giving me orders me like a good secretary's assistant.

He then collected his smoker's kit—the packet, the Job cigarette papers, and the box of matches—bid farewell with a "See you soon," and disappeared. I started work after reviewing my range as a calligrapher. I decided to write the member's name in the most Gothic hand I knew, the address in crystal-clear italics, and the monthly quota in the most flowing, round figures my hands could manage. Later on, these initiatives were deemed to be satisfactory and received generous praise.

Between one receipt and the next, I glanced through the book. I found the most impressive names, the great and the good in the city of Barcelona, people who devote themselves to society life and appear in free newspaper copy—because those who pay are less important than the people who have an almost implicit right to coverage; those who practice expensive sports, as well as the ones renowned for their wealth, virtues, and savoir faire when it comes to dining out, who think they are top notch. There were even others I didn't recognize at all, who'd passed me by, as they say, and I felt they seemed equally respectable. The light from some lent a glow to the slight shadow over others and the whole array was thus perfectly illuminated. I was deeply moved. I was bedazzled.

When I left the office, I asked a passerby for the time of day—because I have never owned a watch—and it turned out I had stayed on an hour longer than necessary. It was nine o'clock. Gran de Gràcia, illuminated by a magnificent white light, was full of people strolling and making a lot of noise. The yellow trams gleamed. It was a warm night.

On subsequent days I arrived at the office punctually. Initially, the young man in the blue jacket accompanied me through the labyrinth of corridors. He switched on the office lights. Later I made my own way. I didn't see Sr. Codina for many an afternoon. So I was completely alone between those four walls decorated with sporting posters, handling the receipt book that had made such a profound impression. A receipt book is an extremely ordinary object. I recognize that now. But at the time I didn't see it that way at all.

Anyone who hadn't known me at the age of seventeen or eighteen could never understand the intensely magical impact this book had on me. I was primitive, elemental clay readily molded by the mechanical assimilation of the most mundane clichés. Evidently the only things that made their mark on me were the prejudices of the man in the street: the fetishes of wealth and glamour, admiration for glitter and show, and worship of accepted virtues. At that mythical, naïve age, the conventional is what's most hallowed. I completely lacked then what I had to strive hard to carve out later: namely, a reasonably critical mind. And there were other reasons that predisposed me to adopt such a stance: Family life, which was so cold, puritanical, and severe in my childhood years, led me to be so emotional and sentimental that I never quite knew what to cling to. At the time, these excesses led me to embrace a range of intensely vibrant yet hackneyed clichés. I was literally dazzled, grotesquely dazzled.

Can you believe it? I almost blush to acknowledge it: A receipt book containing the great and the good of Barcelona awoke my need to feel secure, a permanent instinct of mine. I found shelter in its pages, like a chick snug under the warm feathers of the mother hen. A lovely feeling. It was like finding a warm den, and each day I was forced to endure until I could head there was like being exposed to a horrible storm the elements had unleashed. The feeling you get when you reach the fireside after a day spent trudging through snow.

I now find it difficult to believe that the profusion of illustrious names the book contained actually existed. But things were different then. My anthropomorphic wonder led me to imagine the physical characteristics of the people who were members of the Pompeia Sporting Society artistically surrounded by charming, fascinating ladies, refined young ladies with a cherry on each cheek, young, winged creatures in the form of cherubim. I'd been marooned in a molten flow secreted by red-hot spasms of bourgeois mystification. I'm not afraid to say so because it was a fact: I felt proud, intensely proud to serve. I was spontaneously filled with a fresh moral evaluation of my own status.

"What a good chap you are!" I told myself, expressing what I vaguely felt, as I plunged myself into a sea of self-satisfaction.

Those days were the heyday of an era of childish thinking, tardily re-created by adolescence. A double dose of childishness. I forgot everything else and anxiously longed for it to be time to go to the office. The names in the book were completely unknown to me; nonetheless, I imagined the silvery beards of some of those pillars of society and the respectability they must represent; I conjured up the jewels some of the ladies must possess, vivacious younger ladies, the huge fortunes linked to some names. The green receipts evoked a dazzling, stupendous world. I entered the Pompeia church and effortlessly imagined the friars of the establishment with their martyrs' palms. It all seemed perfect. My pride in serving gave my soul the shape of a dove. I also went to take a look at the sports field. I'd never have dared to go in. I peered in from the entrance. It seemed a most pleasant place. Wooden chalets painted the color of ox blood, white window frames, very elegant and mathematical tennis courts, wrought-iron chairs, cane armchairs, numerous distinguished attendees afforded me the vision of a true paradise. I thought I saw my friend P. in white trousers and a buttercup-yellow jersey talking to a tall, willowy blond. That scene warmed my heart and I waved my handkerchief, a friendly gesture signaling my presence. He didn't see me. What reason did he have to see me? I was so bewildered that an automobile entering fast almost flattened me. I stepped back in a comical manner.

"Idiot," I heard someone shout from inside the car.

I was so embarrassed, I blushed a deep red. However, all things considered, that wasn't the right place for me. My place was in the club office. I thought the epithet that gentleman bawled at me was completely deserved. Why not be frank and admit it? I thought the driver of the car was in the right.

Sr. Codina came to the office more frequently at the end of the month. He scrutinized my work. He didn't make any explicit comments but I think he liked what he saw. We became friends.

To avoid exaggerating my importance, I won't talk about the receipts. Filling them out was infinitely pleasurable, and I would gently run my tongue along my lips to the movements of my pen, with just the right turn of the nib, to ensure my calligraphy remained graceful. Modesty apart, the receipts were presentable and weren't visibly flawed. I mentioned that Sr. Codina was rather behind with the minute book; I had the agreeable task of bringing it up-to-date. I spent divine moments doing all I possibly could to be a decent secretary. In the end I managed to give the correspondence an exquisitely agreeable, fawningly polite form and content. I suffered when I thought that Sr. Codina might be rather careless and not duly post them.

At any rate, his company was amusing. His forte was highlighting contrasts. If he spoke, for example, about Sr. Cambó's "little" speech, you can be sure it was a supremely significant oration. He usually made comparisons by playfully deploying the diffident diminutive. While solemnly twirling his mustache, he once said, "The Reverend Father Rupert is a very enlightened chappie."

I stared at him without blinking. Not a single muscle in his face flinched. He'd spoken with utmost seriousness. It was simply the strange way he had of talking.

Another day I greeted him politely and asked, "Is your wife well?"

"My wife is in fine fettle, thanks be to God!"

I thought that an odd reply. I eventually had an opportunity to see Sra. Codina: She was thin as a rake and seemed extremely feeble.

Sr. Codina, sour Sr. Codina, I harbor such a tangle of memories of you! What lurked behind your strikingly serious appearance, behind your melancholy smile? Were you a comedian, or perhaps a defrocked monk lost in a world of contingencies, or simply a valuable, distinguished member of the establishment upon whom one had of necessity to rely?

As I was feeling so affectionate toward the organization I describe, it came as a surprise one day when I heard from the passageway a voice rasping in the office. I tiptoed to the door and soon summed up the situation. It was a club member—the son of an extremely wealthy manufacturer—who'd been playing tennis. He'd changed in a dressing room and gone to the courts in his whites. He'd apparently left everything he was wearing in a wardrobe that he'd locked. When he came back from the courts he'd had an unpleasant surprise. Language is too poor to express it politely, but it was straightforward enough: Someone had—how shall we say?—stolen his wallet. The obvious inquiries were made immediately. The staff on duty were cleared of any blame. After making the protest that was within his rights, the honorable club member had come to register a complaint at the office.

"We will duly notify the people who can help," said Sr. Codina, more dead than alive, his ears drooping, a sorrowful, despondent look in his eyes.

"You do understand this must be dealt with and without delay. Would you please show me the list of members?" asked the visitor, red with rage.

"It is a delicate matter and we will do everything in our power. In any case, you shouldn't forget there can be alien elements, unpleasant intruders, and devious characters in even the best-run club in the world."

I was quite overwhelmed; if Sr. Codina hadn't adopted that overly emphatic, sad but sour tone that day—which I immediately thought was an overreaction—I would have immediately forgotten all about it. Much to my dismay, there was a repetition of the incident a few days later. A daughter of the aristocracy entered in an unpleasant huff to inform Sr. Codina what had come to pass that morning.

"It is the second time it has happened," she explained. "*My* purse was stolen at the Polo Club not long ago. Today my bracelet disappeared during a game of tennis. It wasn't valuable but had special sentimental, family value. I find all this quite unpleasant and unacceptable."

"Senyoreta," piped Sr. Codina, his voice shaking, absolutely beside himself, "we will do everything humanly possible—"

"It makes one feel quite desperate!" the young lady interjected.

"Intruders, alien elements, undesirables are all around us."

These words affected me when I first heard him utter them, but now they sounded very strange. Wasn't Sr. Codina exaggerating? Alien elements, undesirables, dubious intruders, this was all new to me! What did it mean? I began to turn this disturbing news over in my mind and drifted into a state of inexplicable sorrow. The look of total despair on Sr. Codina's face that evening plunged me into even deeper gloom and confusion. Before departing, I went over to the table of the first secretary, in that muted, lugubrious ambience, and asked, "What *is* all this about, Sr. Codina?"

I asked the question, barely concealing my state of anxiety.

Sr. Codina looked at me with downcast eyes and his head lowered in sorrow.

"Aye, my poor lad!" he said blankly, with a limp wave of the hand.

I waited for him to say something else. But he didn't say another word.

That night I was shocked into experiencing the reverse process of what I've attempted to describe. My instinct for self-preservation tried to halt this reverse: I did all I could to maintain my previous attitude. It was to no avail: I was being swept along by a torrent of disillusionment. Some people are born with a reasonably accurate view of life. It was not my fate to be so fortunate. I have had to learn everything in the most impressionable years of my life, when an excess of sentimentality and emotion prompted childish, ingenuous euphoria. I had to throttle my youth and develop a thick skin—that is to say, gain experience. My every contact with real life was extremely painful. I should have been be born with a hard wooden head and sharp, pointed teeth. But some things are not of one's choosing. My last afternoon in that office is etched on my memory, and when I think back to it, it is no laughing matter.

Sr. Codina had sent word that a cold was keeping him in bed. I was by myself in the office when a gentleman whose accent seemed to betray that he was a foreigner walked into the office. His situation was similar to the young aristocratic lady's. In one of the most desirable clubs in the city, he too had been the object of the reiterated attentions of the infamous undesirables. He was in a great state of shock. I tried to pacify him by repeating Sr. Codina's wretched formula. To absolutely no effect. I decided to shut up and ride the storm. I felt helplessly exposed to that gentleman's justified rage. My silence solved nothing. His monologue became increasingly strident. He ended up threatening me.

"As a last resort," he said, "I am prepared to take you to court."

I laughed and replied, "You are going too far! Please be reasonable! In any case, you won't report me."

"And why not, pray tell?"

I stood up, put on my overcoat, and took my hat. I put my hand on the switch and added, "Be so good as to leave ... I will accompany you."

I switched off the light in the office.

"My dear sir, have a good night!" I said, waving my hat at him when we were in the doorway to the street.

I never went back to that office, but that doesn't mean I never will. I am now much better equipped to be a clerical assistant than I was when I was seventeen or eighteen. There are few things that surprise me now: I am not even surprised to be writing afresh these pages that seem so burdened by naïveté as to be an unpleasant fiction. However, I have already noted—by way of an excuse—that these observations should be located in the most infantile phase of my thinking.

And such are my memories of student life: the life that people say is happy, carefree, and comfortable.

8 April. I spend a good part of the night in a small room at the Athenaeum with Joan Estelrich—an Estelrich driven by a desire to confide.

He is physically leonine—and has been leonine practically from birth, which is extraordinary because the leonine species of human usually emerges in maturity. An astonishing species! Moreover, he is histrionic. He dramatizes everything and has a natural tendency to overplay everything. He is enormously vigorous, on all fronts. He makes an extremely good living playing the role of an intellectual. He has traveled a long road. He has written a lot, lectured, dueled with a military officer, and been warned off by a bishop. They seem like the makings of a good life. He has also had a religious crisis, as if it were a trifle. He is now a can't-make-my-mind-up—an agnostic, as he calls it. He is furiously anti-Ors. He says Ors can't tolerate individuality—and that's tantamount to justifying summary judgments and executions. Externally he reminds one of those intriguers and poets in small Italian courts in the baroque period. But it is strange he doesn't like intrigue. Unless you get in his way, he comes out with systematic praise, permanent eulogy. His sugary Majorcan spirit palls somewhat. He strives to keep himself in a constantly wild, enthusiastic state of erection.

As I'm going to bed I tell myself that personally I wouldn't have liked an Italian moment in my youth to be at all visible. Nevertheless, I recognize that others have a perfect right to want such a thing. Caution has always been my byword. But such are the youth of today.

9 April. The circle at the Athenaeum.

I don't think two men could be more radically different than Ors and Pujols—just as I think there can't be two who profess the same deep, inner, secret reciprocal empathy these men do. It is one of the most complex phenomena I have ever witnessed.

They are, as I said, radically different. Ors is the great actor permanently playing a variety of roles. Pujols is natural, direct, and establishes an immediate, fresh rapport. On the surface they hate and scorn each other. Some of the arguments between Ors and Pujols have led to the bloodiest fallouts, the most horrendously rude clashes seen in Barcelona for years. Moments that left even those used to such incidents speechless. The desire for blood in these reciprocal attacks isn't simply expressed in head-on clashes but in any situation related to any matter.

Nonetheless, there is another aspect to their relationship. Ors finds Pujols immensely witty, and Pujols believes Ors is a remarkable individual. Nothing explicit supports this assertion of mine. You have to search out the evidence. You must find it in the course of everyday trivial dialogues, in glances of real affection, in the delicious little smiles of pleasure Ors stifles when he listens to Pujols speak and Pujols's nervous, rather convulsed laughter when he hears Xènius embark on some elaborate conversational gambit.

Perhaps, for Ors, Pujols embodies the fantastic concentration of the country's deepest, most primitive ancestral roots, its most authentic nature. On the other hand, I can't pinpoint what Ors signifies for Pujols. I exclude the possibility he might envy him. No. It is something I can't fathom. Pujols is less effective than Ors but much more complex.

10 April. Fresh and ruddy, stalwartly resisting his arthritis, my father has arrived in Barcelona and invited us to dine in his hotel, the Internacional on the Rambla. The noise from the Rambla enters the hotel via its countless balconies. A meager dinner. Afterward, we drink coffee in Petit Pelayo. Excellent beverage. It is a pity, nevertheless, that the coffee isn't strong enough to transmute third-rate dinners into first-rate ones in our imagination. The opposite tends to happen, and after a very ordinary dinner, the coffee, however good, suffers a loss in quality.

The eruption of spring is too violent. Streets are already starting to stink of smelly armpits. We stroll for an hour along the lower part of Passeig de Gràcia. The trees have begun to blossom magnificently. Pink-green velvet in the glow from the streetlights. A sliver of moon, hazy distant stars, and a gentle delightful breeze. The quality of the air in springtime is one of the most likable things about this country.

11 April. I accompany my father to Sant Gervasi. He's going to visit a friend who is in a clinic. I walk the streets while he is visiting. I remember wandering up and down the streets of Sant Gervasi in my first years at the university with no particular object in mind—especially on Sunday afternoons, divinely sad Sundays in spring.

I thought it most strange. It is a village of small mansions and houses with small doors and windows, gardens with little trees and paths with little fountains with toy fish and vistas of stones, grass, and terraced roofs, all in miniature. These small gardens usually house small chicken runs with chicks and a little rabbit that occasionally sticks his little snout out. There are monasteries with little monks, clinics with the sick little people, little factories with little workers, and small trams on small tracks. My use of "little" and "small" comes spontaneously, not because the monks, fountains, and sick people of Sant Gervasi are on the shorter side compared to those elsewhere but because, accustomed to the grandiose scale of things in Barcelona, my eyes lead me to see Sant Gervasi as a village in miniature. The proximity of the contrast increases that illusion. Obviously people in Sant Gervasi have the same measurements as others and eat from plates and wear shoes that are the same size as those used and worn by others. But that doesn't mean Sant Gervasi doesn't appear miniature.

Twilights on those spring afternoons were beginning to lengthen and the sunset was a creamy yellow the color of a cream roll. A loving couple passed by the ocher wall on a quiet, almost deserted street and looked languidly into each other's eyes, not saying a word. Now and then clumps of branches draped a delicate tracery of leaves over garden walls. Two monks were whispering opposite a garden gate, holding a religious print, ready to smile when the gate opened. Farther on you bumped into a countryman dawdling along with his nose in the air. He was sick. He was the sickest man in his village. They had allowed him out of the clinic for a few hours to distract him and put him in the right frame of mind. They would soon be cutting him open down the middle. In the meantime he gapes and grimaces, strolls along the streets, his smock over his shoulders, flourishing his switch. Between two bars of a grille, at the bottom of a tiny garden, I can see a rustic fount trickling over moss and shells, and a concrete bench imitating a tree trunk. A cottage the color of scrambled eggs sprinkled with cinnamon lurked beneath the foliage. Beyond that there was the precise brushstroke of a garden terrace and, against a background of bitter green broccoli, I watched a black-bearded gentleman in shirtsleeves, with an ironed collar, round fists, and a medallion on a chain, swinging a fork. Next door a pink house came into view, a summerhouse with green shutters and a small patch of sand in the entrance, with swings and a table, and on it, a newspaper. Meanwhile we walked past three tiny factories, those absurd little Sant Gervasi factories! The first was a sweets factory, the second an elastic factory, and the third manufactured petits fours. A little finger-biscuit factory! They were three different, perfectly tolerable smells, but with a very distinct aroma when they blended. However, I couldn't stop. On the corner, a couple of mounted security guards and a housemaid were doing their best to enact an allegorical version of *The Rape of the Sabine Women*. A cat meowed on the bank of a stream and a dog barked on a terrace. A friar walked by, eyes down, followed by a young man who looked like a poet. An uncommonly small convent bell chimed, sounding cracked and monotonous.

And twilight came and went in Sant Gervasi de Cassoles. Then the moon rose above a roof among a tangle of electricity wires, and the smell of camphor wafted from a crevice in a window; first, the smell of beef with peas, then baked cod . . .

12 April, Saturday. I travel to Palafrugell with my brother for the Easter holidays. On the afternoon mail train from estació de França, from three to nine: a six-hour journey. I am quite tired by the time we arrive. The house on carrer del Sol strikes me as very cold. An excellent dinner. I feel revived. I go to Cafè Pallot and drink coffee with father and his friends. It is a bad day for table talk: no local content. After lunch, those present simply repeat from beginning to end what they have read in the daily newspapers.

13 April. Palm Sunday. I go to church. The smell of laurel branches—*llor* in the Ampurdan—and of strawberry and cherrywood. The church is full of them. The noise of branches being dragged along flagstones in church. The scent is potent, rural, and appealing. It impregnates the gilded legs of the small angels on the altar, the congregation's clothes, the dark nooks and crannies, the air, the wood and wrought-iron grilles. One's sense of smell is so saturated it seems everyone must be giving off an aroma of laurel. This is perhaps the only day in the year when another smell crowds out the sweet odor of incense, the bitter tang of pious women, and the taste of wax. This aroma of laurel returns to our nostrils whenever stew is cooked at home.

As I leave, I greet Almeda the pharmacist on carrer de Cavallers. As always, he speaks in the diminutive.

"I am going to drink a little milkie," he tells me, as he wipes the lenses of his spectacles with a white handkerchief.

I have an aperitif with my friends. Two or three healthy shots of orange liqueur that we down without noticing as we chatter on as people do here. Family lunch, the tastiest black rice imaginable, with squid and shellfish; chops cooked with turnips from Capmany. Tender lamb chops in Palafrugell are delicious beyond words. Huge quantities of coffee and cognac. Sunday afternoon—with the usual gravitational pull of the emotions. The small deserted town oppresses me. I feel as if I were inside an empty nutshell being rocked by a dying breeze. A lovely day to run your lips over pink female skin, but quite horrible for walking down streets with your hands in your pockets. Through windows you can still see people holding their legs over the embers in a brazier. The cinema. The heavy smell people give off. Young ladies' wretchedly cheap perfumes. I think of poor Roldós stooped over that piano in the dim light. I leave the showing. Absolutely nobody on the streets. A cold, unpleasant twilight. I meander by the town wall. It seems that I am fated to be a wanderer. I go back for more aperitifs. Absinthes. Dinner. Coffee and cognac. Feel stuffed and feverish. Galloping heartbeat. Impossible to lie flat in bed for very long. My heart aches. My head reels and aches. I sit down on one chair and then another, gripping a handkerchief. The icy draft blowing through my bedroom makes me shiver. Quite impossible to throw off the scent of laurel from the morning. A repulsive, obsessive feeling that you're living inside a stew. It must be very late ...

14 April, Monday. I get up feeling ill, numb, absent, depressed. My father doesn't say a word at the breakfast table but gives me an almost theatrical look of contempt. "You must be tired of Barcelona," says my mother, as if she were talking about the weather.

Holy Week weather. As always, it is a gray, still day, with no wind or sun. The low ashen sky glowers with a gooseberry-tinted lining. My mouth is so dry I find water a comfort and joy. The tendency of alcohol to trigger thirst, to produce increasing thirst is the most vicious circle in human life. I stay at home. Interminable dusk and night. The books I have at hand don't arouse my interest. I would prefer to read others I don't have at hand. I stare at the ceiling for hours with the light on, breathing in the air in my freezing bedroom.

15 April. Carrau's story.

These Lenten days are diamond bright. The year approaches adolescence without turbulence or tumefaction. Every day is brighter and more open. Beneath white afternoon clouds, the landscape stretches and sprawls under the sun as if recovering from a long bout of delirium. It is an intense landscape, without clutter or clatter: the pure sod of life. It is a primitive landscape jagged in its outlines.

In the immediate foreground, the land presents a simple palette of colors. The moist, pale purple Lenten wind darkens the green of the small, restless allotments and fluffs the mother-of-pearl field of rye, adds a touch of smoke to the lees of fallow land and warmth to a luridly yellow turnip field. Asparagus grows on the wayside and watercress blooms on irrigation channels. The far country is drawn sharp and delicate; the mountains on the horizon, foreshortened and pale, seem mountains of melancholy. At such times the infinite oppresses.

Twilight and a violet vapor shroud all. Now everything seems vaguely spongy; at times the senses liven up, then depression descends and spirits dip. Now it's a delight to light a fire of dry grass in some corner and let your thought drift away on the bluish smoke. The land is full of acid smells that cleanse the head.

This is the best time to stroll in the sunlight. You walk for an hour or so, breathe in the fresh, tart air; then nothing could be more relaxing than to climb a small peak, lie down, and contemplate the yellowish brushstroke of the road wending between the fields. A cart passes, the tiny figure of a wayfarer stands out; the huge automobile that drives by seems to roll along like a bumptious monster.

Gazing at that road reminds me of an incident in the life of Carrau, who has since died. Carrau was a cardsharp who specialized in playing *burro* and *canari*, that is, five-card *burro*, also known as Majorcan *burro*. In winter or summer, Carrau would have walked for an hour to play these games, even though, like all good gamblers, he had very delicate feet and was forced wear black canvas boots with a hole to allow a stubborn, unruly big toe to breathe.

Carrau had a small inheritance, lived frugally, and was eating into his capital. His great desire was to have a buggy and one of those almond-rumped mares that fly along the road, to be able to follow markets and fairs and play at *canari* with the most flourishing folk hereabouts. Carrau gambled in the expectation he would get his buggy, and when the game began, as he sat down and took out his money, he would say, with a knowing wink, "You do understand, don't you? I am going after what is mine."

As Carrau was a bachelor and his friends weren't the prying sort, this reference was never clarified and no one knew what he meant. But he cherished it in silence. He thought only of his little mare, dreamed of the buggy, christened the animal, made it stop and go with his ritual cries. He mixed up his card dealing with the conversation he'd have with the Gypsy from Figueres and his friends' reactions.

"You go and stand in front of the Gypsy," he'd say. " 'I want a beast like this.' The Gypsy says, 'Do you want the little mare for yourself?' And you reply, 'No, it's for a gentleman who'll see to everything.' And the Gypsy shows you the best in the province, and, when you say in the province, you mean in the country."

Or else: "Imagine your hand is the nine of golds, two small trumps, and two dead cards. It isn't a strong hand, but you can keep your cards to your chest, bluff it out, before calling it a day."

He also liked to imagine the impact it would make on his friends if they were to see him arrive by such airy means. He conjured up the expressions on their faces and now and then came out with a "I'll give you a shock you won't get over in a hurry."

Carrau went to Figueres on a market day, walked into a café, sat at a six-peseta all-bets *canari* table and won four thousand pesetas in less than an hour. It was like gimme, gimme, gimme. When he walked out, his head was in a spin. He went for a boiled egg, coffee, and a shot of anisette; he spread the word and in no time was off to buy a yellow, blue-striped secondhand buggy. He went to see the Gypsy.

"You want a mare, my son? This little darling is the one for you," he said, pointing to a dainty dapple-gray that was plump, gleaming, and frisky. "You don't deserve her," said the Gypsy. "She's as in the pink as any priest and lives on the stars."

While Carrau walked around her and inspected her teeth, the Gypsy continued his running commentary: "You want a lovelier one? Look at her, my son. You won't find one better. Isn't she a beauty?" whined the Gypsy, his crooked mouth coming out with the sweetest words.

Carrau bought her and put a golden bell around her neck and a flower behind her ear. He harnessed her and rode his "purchase" around. He was pleased with her performance. The animal responded, pricked up her ears, her veins quivering.

"The best in the province," declared Carrau, taking the reins.

It was ten o'clock. The day sparkled like a diamond. They left the white, sunny outskirts of Figueres behind them.

At first the mare trotted daintily. Her bell tinkled cheerfully. Carrau, bareheaded, gripping his whip, fantasized, called out to people working in the fields, held a picturesque dialogue with his animal. The buggy swept along, sails and curtains billowing, between bright sunny fields, as if it were out of control. They left behind one village after another. Women washing clothes in streams and spreading their sheets over bushes gaped at the quicksilver buggy. Then the tinkling disappeared as the buggy swerved around the corner.

The ford over the Fluvià was very shallow and Carrau decided to cross it in his buggy. The blissful mare clip-clopped sweetly through the clear water. Once they were on the other bank Carrau, trying to upset the animal, clipped it sharply and the mare galloped flat-out for a mile or two. Then, when Carrau's buttocks were sore, the animal resumed at a lively trot.

With that Carrau reached Verges and came to a halt. He went into the roadside tavern and ordered food. He was hungry. They cooked chicken with rice and half a homegrown rabbit in herbs and white wine.

"Make sure the rabbit's tasty, lady!" shouted Carrau, smacking his lips. He stretched out on the red upholstered sofa in the tavern. Lolling, smoking a cigar, a thin wisp of smoke curling from his nose, he thought *this* was the life. Carrau had a gambler's pallor and a hard, round paunch from sitting at so many *canari* tables and never exercising. Though bald, he had a great shock of hair combed over his head so it looped grotesquely from his left ear to his right.

"A buggy," said Carrau, "is worth half a lifetime. I'll live at least twenty years longer."

He was in that state of bliss when suddenly he heard shouting outside. He looked up and heard the waiter say, with a mysterious, sibylline air, craning his neck to look through the glass panes in the door, "The card school is here."

Five or six cocky village youngsters strutted in, creating a din, and asked for cards. They sat down and started to play a lower form of *canari, de tres al quarto*. Carrau left the sofa, walked over to their table, poked his nose out the door, and seeing that the sun was still high in the sky, decided to sit for a while and have some fun.

They played first, as usual, for a laugh; then they began to take it more seriously. The result was that after an hour and a half, Carrau gambled away his buggy and mare and had just enough money left to pay for his rice and spiced-up rabbit.

Disheveled and deathly pale, Carrau walked out onto the road and resumed his journey on foot. It was late afternoon. People were returning to the village with bundles of grass on their backs. You could hear the bells of flocks of sheep. Young kids were throwing stones at one another in front of the tavern and making a hellish racket. As soon as Carrau left the last house in the village and was alone, he began to swear like a trooper. Each oath was like a clap of thunder.

When he had blasted the whole heavenly host, he started walking. He took fourteen or fifteen steps in silence, stopped for a moment, saw the lights from the village, and started walking again.

At twilight, a rather damp, pale purple Lenten breeze began to blow, and the stars twinkled in heaven's fields.

Holy Week. I meander through the countryside. It is an overcast, sad, murky day—just right for people who have things to do. A damp wind from the south. Solitude amid the fields. The country is beginning to turn green. The wind flattens the short ears of corn—as if a wandering shade were passing over them; a bass organ growls through the pines. In the distance, the sea is so murky I instinctively turn away. Only concrete, tangible things are pleasant; murk is evil. I remember little A.—fourteen years old—when she was sucking a soft, golden grape last autumn, with her eyes closed. I walk along paths through pine groves, a dry, bitter smell of pine resin. Late at night, the noise of the wind in the treetops is a basso profundo, striking in its solitude.

In the café, Enric Frigola is analyzing set phrases. He says, "For example, the sentence 'Paquita was the tinder to sin' is a complete anachronism. There is no tinder anymore; the tinder matches, which used to make that dreadful sulfurous smell, are no more. If we want to be à la page, we should be saying, 'Paquita was the lighter to sin.' Then comes the sequel: Why this keenness to compare sin and passion with fire, what sense does that have? Is it trying to suggest that all sin implies a degree of vitality and the state of grace is repose, indifference, and limp, blank stares? What does all this mean? Does it mean a different level of biological intensity is all there is between one state and another, and that one should stick to vegetables, soft food, and water? It would be as well to scrutinize the meaning of these words with some proper criteria."

That night, the Reig restaurant. J. B. Coromina tells me, between one roasted almond and the next, that despite everything there are two beautiful lines in "Marina." These are: "My hopes saw her float—on the wings of desire." Maybe, but so what? As the night seems off to a bad start, I leave.

16 April. Holy Wednesday. I go to our farmhouse. It is a slightly brighter afternoon. I hear water trickling along irrigation channels. Cress and water herbs, which add a delicious flavor to a salad, must be growing in the pools. The asparagus along the wayside is now over. One the other hand, peas and beans are about to start appearing in the market. Carrots are sweet. Spinach is really tender. Beets hardly seem so. Lettuce melts in the mouth. Now is the time to eat herbs. In the spring, botany is a heavenly, angelic thing.

Swallows swoop over the farmhouse. They sometimes swoop down and skim the dark mirror of water in the tank with their beaks. Cats are on alert in case a young swallow tires of flying and falls. Nothing ever stays still in nature.

I enter the kitchen. Nobody is there. They are out feeding the animals. The fire is lit in the hearth. I sit for a while on the comfortable, shiny wooden bench in front of the sparking pinewood fire. Darkness descends behind the barred window. The house is huge and ramshackle, but now that there isn't a living soul about, it seems enchanted—and that's depressing.

The two great vistas in this country are the ones from Pedró in Pals and from Molí de Vent in Begur. However, there is another less known, which is the one you see before reaching the Morena saddle, a hundred and fifty meters above our farmhouse, with the olive grove in the foreground, over the road from Girona to Palamós. It is absolutely perfect—even if it is not quite right to describe a vista as "perfect."

A stormy evening, an unpleasant breeze. The town streets are deserted. Sr. Roig is the only one walking up and down carrer de Cavallers—bareheaded with his cane on his arm. Whatever does Sr. Roig think during those endless hours of solitary strolling? Does he compose music in his head? Is he planning a sale of cork? Is he imagining a plate of tasty food? We know Sr. Roig is a composer. We know he is a hard-nosed, successful trader. That his palate is the most discerning in Palafrugell, an excellent gourmet. But what do we really know about Sr. Roig? What do we know about people we never see?

17 April. Holy Thursday. I bump into Hermós in his gentleman's attire. He is still in Calella with the Barris family but wants to leave. He says it has been a very, very long winter. He says life in Palafrugell is desperately boring. He would like to live alone, by the seaside. He'd settle for a small rowing boat, four lines, a fishing net, and a cuttlefish pot. "I'd go for a row," he tells me. Then he adds: "Now I have to play *tresillo*, eat chicken, and put shoes on to visit the Monumental. I can't take any more."

I was curious to find out the state of play with what we call "Jew killing" around here. On a day like today, when I was a child, the children in the village would go to church after lunch to kill Jews. We went with all kinds of tools for making a racket. Some beat the ground with clubs; others banged on an oil drum with an iron bar; small shops sold hammers to hit anything in sight; you could also buy a rattle with a wooden handle you turned to create a horrible, dreadful sound. There used to be a huge uproar in church. The pandemonium represented a hypothetical killing of Jews.

What was the origin of this event: revenge for the death of Our

Lord, a theoretical revenge but one that gave out a very clear message? Does it hark back to a pogrom avoided by a diversion—and enacted only symbolically?

This evening I noticed that many fewer children had come to kill Jews than in my day. In that era every child from a good home in the village was there. Today only the hungriest came: They'd probably been promised bread and chocolate to come and kill Jews. This was one way to prolong the tradition for another year.

I feel very glad to see this grotesque, ugly tumult in rapid decline.

There is such dense smoke in the café that two or three friends and I walk up carrer de Pi Margall, as far as the holm oaks of En Frigolet. The holm-oak wood is marvelous. This noble tree casts a rustling, spongy, bright, serrated shadow. We spend two wonderful hours there.

How strange: The first thing an inhabitant of Palafrugell does when he feels sick, when he notices a spot has erupted on a part of his body, is to wrap a white silk scarf around his neck. When some people reach a certain age, they put the scarf on and never take it off. Perhaps the idea is to suggest that they are in danger?

19 April. Holy Saturday. These few days have been completely barren. I tried to write...I shuffled my sheets of paper and thought about Josep Ferrer...I tried to read something difficult. Nothing happened. Nothing gelled. Sterility is depressing because it makes you wonder if you aren't a complete idiot.

Conversations at the Fraternal Center with friends.

Enric Frigola states that, according to the English, one of the central aims of intelligence is ensure men have style and are amusing.

"What does it mean to be 'amusing'?" asks Coromina.

"It means," replies Frigola, "that a man has a sense of humor."

"Is it true that a man of irony can be thought amusing?" I ask.

"It depends on boundaries," says Frigola. "Irony cannot go beyond certain boundaries."

"Which boundaries?"

"Dickens, for example."

"Are we to understand that Napoleon had a sense of the ridiculous?" asked Frigola. "Or that Dato and Romanones have such a thing today? In certain situations nobody pays attention or lends the slightest importance to a sense of the ridiculous. Where is it when one is in bed with a woman? The systematic, permanent defense of the idea that a sense of the ridiculous is sacred and untouchable is a symptom of mediocrity, is mediocrity itself—and the total negation of a sense of humor."

Everyone was rather dumbstruck by this sudden outburst from Frigola, who is usually unable to generate the least fervor. When he sees our astonished looks, he retreats into himself and makes a rather timid confession: "I say all this because my sense of the ridiculous ruined my life!"

21 April. Easter Monday. Today, like every year, sardanas are danced in the sanctuary of Sant Sebastià and the insect procession takes place. From the boundary cross, fields are blessed and insects—parasites and plant insects—are quite deadened, if not actually killed. It is a fine thing. For centuries and centuries, this was the only insecticide. The strong-minded—such people abound in the Ampurdan—say: This is grotesque. No, it isn't grotesque. It is admirably well-intentioned. A pity it is hardly effective.

I enter the chapel for a moment; tiny Sant Sebastià, wearing a blue dress coat and red trousers, sword at his waist, his hair blowing in the wind under his three-cornered hat, is very elegant and svelte.

A rather off-color pastry gives me a needling stomachache that puts me in a permanent bad temper.

In the café, Lluís Medir, who is reading the newspaper, throws it impatiently on the table and says, "This world is a stewpot."

"Of course it is!" says Frigola with a frosty little laugh. "What did you think? If you didn't have such high expectations, you could have finished reading the beastly things in your newspaper and not batted an eyelid."

22 April. Back to Barcelona. We catch the express in Flaçà. My brother looks out the window at the countryside. I read a French novel at the back of the third-class carriage. Night is falling. When it is pitch dark, a small light in the ceiling is switched on. The light flickers and I have to stop reading. I roll a cigarette, ask what the time is. I think: This to-and-fro from Barcelona to qualify for a degree I will never turn into a profession, I will never use, has perhaps become a farce that has gone too far. When I think coldly about how my parents still believe in me, I am bewildered by the power faith continues to wield in this world.

My lodgings. The usual horrible atmosphere. In the evening I go to the library. Old Costa, coattails waving, serves me coffee. Nothing has changed. The library is equally funereal. The green lampshades create a dense murkiness the color of stagnant water. The green turns the sparse readers deathly pale.

23 April. Institute of Education.

Most of the students attend in good faith. Besides, I personally have learned a huge amount. But those we might call the leading "figures" this year don't set a very good example. The infighting is constant and relentless and becomes childish—to the point of seeming gratuitous. Almost all these characters work against Ors, behind the scenes. The man must find it strange to be surrounded by so much fake friendliness and so much real, palpable hatred.

The smaller things are, the more likely they are to turn into nests of intrigue. For people to like one another, it is vital they live far apart and don't cohabit.

After his art history lecture, Don Joaquim Folch tells me to research artistic influences in the era of Saint Francis. In the café I tell Gassol how pleased I am to do this for Folch. The moment he hears the name of Folch, Gassol reacts surprisingly violently.

"Did you say 'Folch'?" he grunts. "Don't mention that fellow to me! He is a scoundrel!"

"If you say so, but could you be kind enough to tell me why?"

By way of response, he gets up and walks out of the café in a huff.

These scenes—I imagine—are only possible because we live too cheek by jowl in this country.

We plan two excursions with Climent and Martínez Ferrando: one to Majorca and the other to the Ampurdan. Ferrando knows Girona. He worked there as a librarian. There is always a local archivist in Anatole France's novels. My friend held this position in Girona. What a wonderful job! We share fine memories of Girona. It rekindles my lasting obsession with the city.

When we finish our conversation, in an almost inaudible voice that his tendency to keep a handkerchief over his mouth makes even fainter, Ferrando says that when Sra. C. goes down to the station to meet her husband, she welcomes him with a loud kiss; when that encounter takes place at their apartment and nobody is around, the good lady simply says "Hello!"—and doesn't even shake his hand.

24 April. As usual at this time of the year, we begin to worry and obsess about examinations. There are only twenty days to go.

What choice do we have? We must *cram*. (This is one of the most horrible words in student parlance.) I rise early in the morning and soak up coffee. I am terrified by Don Magí Fàbregas's subject—judicial procedures. I am quite out of my depth. Sometimes I wake up at night and toss and turn thinking they will ask a very precise question about something I know nothing about. Dreaming you are in an examination must be one of the saddest, most pointless things one can do in life.

I tell Climent that from now on it will be difficult to attend the Institute of Education as frequently as before and that I may possibly have to ration my visits to the Athenaeum.

"No matter," he replies. "Finish your degree. You really won't be missing anything."

Out of curiosity I go into Cafè Gravina to see if the imminent examinations have changed its human profile. However, I can't see anything that is any different. It is as animated and busy as always.

"Two reals bet," I hear the croupier say.

And immediately: "A peseta against a real, agreed!"

When we speak about good or evil (in the abstract), we are referring (I suppose) to (tangible) pleasure or pain.

If the earth is for the strong, heaven must be for the meek.

The requisite stance implicit in the Orsian conception of the classics and romantics is useful in the evaluation of art and individuals from the past; it is useless when it comes to the living. "We aspire to classicism!" says Xènius. That is all well and good. But wanting to be classical doesn't necessarily mean you are. Perhaps being classical, like being romantic, has to do with temperament and intuition. At certain times, being classical has meant preferring not to be that. I think Molière is much more classical than Racine. However, refusing to be classical, refusing to accept the predominant canon of what is classical at a given time, doesn't necessarily mean one is romantic. Molière is a tremendous realist.

26 April. The more complex and difficult a situation is, the more energetically some people react and the more tenaciously determined they become; others become increasingly doubtful and hesitant and give up without a fight. Success or failure notwithstanding, some people tend to stride ahead instinctively, while others tend to flee, to beat a retreat.

"Your shyness is sometimes so visible," Alexandre Plana was telling me today, "that you give the impression you believe that using one's legs for the purpose of walking is some kind of exceptional privilege."

He is very perceptive.

One should add that, like all shy people, I have my audacious moments. They usually come when I am holding my pen.

My lodgings.

The food is horrible. The best dish here is the local, mild climate. It doesn't seem possible that in such a nutritious, substantial climate one can eat so poorly yet lead a life that, though wearisome, remains reasonably normal. The meat is particularly dreadful. These leathery beefsteaks, sliced as thin as a cat's ear, served as flattened and hollowed out as a skein of esparto. The haricots are so tough and stringy they seem less a product of nature than something manufactured for the establishment. It is dismal to decide so early in life that if one doesn't eat well, one may not be intelligent.

I must say that I have been eating badly for more than ten years: From the time I entered that boarding school in Girona at the age of eleven to the present day I have eaten decently only in the interludes spent at home. I am not resentful of society. Nonetheless, I understand the conditions for feeling as I do are easily generated.

At last something has happened in our year. Fellow student A. has impregnated a young lady he was courting from a good family. As one can imagine, it has led to a big scandal.

The excitement has spilled out into the faculty courtyard and people talk about nothing else, even if it doesn't seem that way because it's being kept so hushed. Reactions are diverse and shades of opinion vary widely.

Those aspiring to starred first-class grades have located themselves on the side of conventional morality and believe it is an appalling development.

The mere outstandings wrinkle their noses and say it is rather bad form.

The goods are more reserved and discreet and have sealed lips.

Those of us who are borderline passes—if not outright failures—are very happy a colleague has done something to enhance us so. We only hope everything turns out fine, follows its proper course, etcetera.

To see a woman melt into one's arms must be a magnificent spectacle—if, whenever it happens, it weren't so expensive...

27 April. The airiness of spring puts an intolerable pressure on the body. It represents a genuine, physical gravitational pull; light mornings, almond-scented air, swelling branches, fluffy leaves—the blossoming of spring is so disturbing. If the senses were on edge like this for the whole year, life would be quite intolerable.

I now leave the house before eight o'clock. The breeze at this hour is delightfully gentle. The sunspots are bright and strong. The light seems to spread a layer of golden oil over everything. The town hall is washing the streets down; the ground and the pavement seem to be alive and kicking. The girls going to work still have the warmth of bed on faces that shiver in the sharp, morning cold. Today, Sunday, I have spent a couple of hours revising my notes on a bench in plaça de la Universitat.

I had pledged not to read the newspapers until after the examinations. I read the *Glosari*. I am not at all embarrassed to say that I was longing to do it—I was missing the *Glosari*, in spite of everything.

I also read an article by Azorín on Gracián. Azorín reproduces the following paragraph by the Aragonese Jesuit:

> Fresh vegetables temper the heat in July, and heated they give comfort against the rigors of December. One plant follows another thus, can be easily picked and stored, providing pleasant,

abundant sustenance throughout the year. Ah, the generous bounty of our Creator! And who can deny such attentive providence, even in the secret depths of his foolish heart?

It is all so well and good. Here we have—I think—a demonstration of the working of Providence not based on a succession of syllogisms but generated by the example of fresh beans and dry beans—the "dry 'uns," as they say in Barcelona. However, I can see nothing providential about the green beans we are currently eating in our lodging house.

Azorín. He is a great writer; I have read a great deal of his work. He is subtle, sensitive, and incredibly elegant. The way he writes is simple, clear, and diaphanous. He never falls back on traditional, flowery sentences—on the curlicues of Castilian. In this sense, the rhetorical residue in Azorín is always negligible. One could make a comparison between the style of Azorín and the style of Pérez de Ayala. Ayala is a writer in the wake of the generation of 1898 who has reverted in the most direct, explicit manner to traditional Castilian sentences. Ayala always survives, however, because the sharpest of minds is at work underneath the often heavy rhetorical frame. Stylistically, Azorín and Pérez de Ayala are polar opposites. Ayala writes Castilian as well as Castelar—if we can agree that Castelar is one of the last representatives of the golden age of Castilian rhetoric, a phenomenal writer in terms of form but devoid of the slightest human interest. Azorín has invented a language that is Castilian only in word, he has shown himself to be completely impermeable to elaborate stucco rhetoric, to traditional Castilian sentence structures. He has simply created a strikingly original language.

If Azorín isn't a rhetorical writer, he is, on the other hand, a static one. The characters and landscapes he has created are static. They are self-absorbed characters and frozen landscapes.

Whenever I walk down the street and look at people, I understand ever more clearly how important the issue of proportion is. A broad forehead, slightly broader than normal, is the forehead of an idiot; a narrow forehead, slightly narrower than suits its owner's face, provokes the same anxieties as a gorilla's forehead.

People's faces tell you if they have been or are being humiliated.

28 April, Monday. The scant food, the excessive consumption of coffee, cramming, being closeted in my bedroom, the extreme chaos in my lodgings—I can tell you that being forced to study next to an unmade bed is the most depressing way to do one's duty—make me feel like someone who has been given the evil eye. My permanent state of exam anxiety is turning me into a complete moron. In a few days, I will start blinking, as if the air was one mass of bright twinkles.

Early in the morning I walk up Pelai to the judicial procedures lecture theater. My memory is stuffed full of a thing called "recourse to appeal." In the meantime, I feel morose and invaded by the quasi-indecency of spring.

With that I bump into Joan Estelrich before I reach plaça de la Universitat. He is carrying a briefcase full of papers and is fresh-faced, bright-eyed, bubbling with life, amazingly lively. Estelrich also lives on carrer de Pelai in a proper boardinghouse, with Martí Esteve for company. The place has a huge bay window, with white tulle curtains behind an impressive set of windows.

"You don't look at all well," says Estelrich. "Your face looks terrible!"

"Life is pleasant; studying is the pits."

In light of which Estelrich launches into a crazily enthusiastic hymn to Barcelona in springtime. These outbursts usually bode ill, particularly if they are protracted. Fortunately, the tram my friend intends to jump on is approaching. It is inevitable: He resumes his hymn.

"My friend, women will be the end of me ... that's a fact!" he says as he raises his arm to stop the tram.

Then he waves cheerfully from the platform.

Head down, I return to "recourse to appeal."

When I pass through the entrance to the university I feel genuinely surprised: I mean surprised to be walking through. It is strange how, with this weather, the mechanism for human freedom still galvanizes.

In the afternoon I go to the Athenaeum library for a moment to dry out.

Climent points out a book entitled *Quelques intentions du cubisme*. Author: Maurice Raynal. Monsieur Raynal asks at some point, on one page: "*Est-ce que le Créateur, lui-même ne serait pas le premier cubiste?*"

What do you expect me to say, Monsieur Raynal? If he is, he keeps pretty quiet about it.

As a result of the influence of the book by Joseph Joubert that Climent read at the suggestion of Josep M. Capdevila, who became infatuated with him (with Joubert) on orders from Don Eugeni d'Ors, my friend is fond of stating that the essence of being well-bred (*la politesse*) is systematically hiding one's preeminent qualities.

"But that," I tell him, "is only applicable to people who possess such things. For the majority of mankind, being well-bred is about consistently hiding one's most glaring defects."

Sometimes when you walk down an old street in Barcelona, you are pleasantly and ineffably surprised to hear a carpenter planing. Today, when I walked past a mezzanine with its windows wide open, I heard a paperhanger, a cigarette dangling from his lower lip, singing "The sparrow when he's roosting, likes to chirp . . ." in a playful, muted voice.

29 April. Clearly now is probably when I should be ditching these regrettable, infantile notebooks and dedicating myself full time to studying, to cramming. But it is a real effort to give them up. The first point of interest these papers have for me is that they will probably never be published. In any case, if they are one day, it will be so many years from now that what I write here will be beyond any suggestion of vanity. I find these pages tedious and annoying, but I'm making a huge effort to keep them up-to-date, perhaps for the sole reason that when I'm face-to-face with my notebook I rediscover myself and can assume that the day's dramas are over. These scribblings are written too naturally and loosely, given that as soon as I start to write for publication I tend, prompted by shyness, to write pretentiously, obscurely, and pedantically, while the lines I write here every day are as necessary to my life as the act of breathing.

To add to my self-portrait: Perhaps I am simply a chatterbox. I will never tire of talking, to such an extent that if I've ever felt fatigue, it was precisely during a debate. I feel the need to approach people and ask them questions. Any—the most trivial—pretext will do. The most banal. However I don't like to keep conversation at the level of gossip, of meaningless banter. A kind of spontaneous urge leads me to shift from small everyday things to general ideas. I am a man who likes to relate things to general ideas. This urge is like an illness—a child's illness, to be precise. I have noticed that other individuals suffer from a similar illness and strive to contain themselves. They believe it is dangerous and childish to generalize. They prefer to hold themselves in a state of systematic contradiction. I can't do that. I tend, frivolously, to generalize. As my conversation partners are surprised by this urge of mine and in the end simply shrug their shoulders, almost all my dialogues turn into long, wearisome monologues. In the end, people walk off, their heads (I imagine) spinning.

This extreme sociability of mine is perfectly compatible with long periods of solitude. I often experience these alternating states, though they never coalesce into anything continuous. In a solitary mood, I generally feel like walking. When talking to people, I prefer to be seated and when alone, I tend to stroll. I am very fond of meandering, particularly at night, especially around Barcelona. My desire to meander never comes as a fully premeditated act; a mysterious force is always driving me to roam the streets—linked, I suspect, to certain meteorological conditions.

During the first three or four years of my degree I fled the apartment on carrer de Mallorca an infinite number of times and simply left the door ajar. When I saw that my brother—I shared a bedroom with him—was sleeping like a log, I got up, dressed, tiptoed silently in the dark to the front door that I opened almost as carefully as a professional. I went out to the landing and left the door ajar. I went down a few steps and put my shoes on. The success of the operation depended on the absurd hypothesis that nobody in the apartment would dream of waking up. I never thought that someone going up or down the stairs might see the door ajar. Strangely, the first hypothesis was confirmed. Nobody ever did wake up, and if anyone did, they didn't notice that the door was open or that I had gone out.

When I was in the street—having a key to the front door was never a problem—the cool air revived me.

I would walk down rambla de Catalunya, but I'd always ask myself the same question after crossing a street or two: "Fine, but what now? What are you going to do? Where are you going to go?"

I would go out with next to no money in my pocket—as broke as usual. The small change I carried on me wouldn't even extend to a miserable glass of cognac. I never dared filch a peseta from my mother's purse. This led me to think about moral issues. For a man with a Catholic upbringing, I came to such considerations late in life. Anyway, I was lucky. Some people never do reach that point.

Nonetheless, despite everything—despite the fact I had no answer to my own questions and lack of money shut down every option—a strange impulse always drove me down the street.

All I ever did was stroll along the Rambla. It was full of life, light, and movement. But I rarely lingered. There were too many people. At such a time, the women were busy. Their provocative poses intrigued me and left a bitter taste on my lips. So many platitudes and clichés collapsed on the Rambla! Sometimes when I reached carrer Nou, I would plunge down the backstreets in the lower part of the fifth district. But I couldn't stand it for very long. The streets gave off such a repulsive stench of piss I was soon forced to put my handkerchief over my nose and mouth. I was choking. The likelihood that I might place the soles of my shoes on some dubious liquid sent the most unpleasant shiver down my spine. No. It wasn't the neighborhood for me. I came out by Drassanes and headed toward the quayside—occasionally to the coal wharf or the Barceloneta; it made no difference. After a short walk by the water's edge, the calm there soothed me. It was a silence that seemed empty—a silence that seemed to reflect movement in times of repose, the repose not of dead things but of life that has halted. I walked around the areas of water that were vaguely lit by arcs of light and closed off by the quay. The lights of boats were reflected on heavy, greasy, colloidal waters. The dense water plashed, moorings wheezed and whined, the hard shoes of a solitary mariner resounded rhythmically, and the elements in the spotlights sputtered in the stillness. I met the occasional long-suffering fisherman sitting on the jetty, a basket by his side. The stacks of merchandise—boxes and sacks— were guarded by night watchmen who lit small fires in front of their stiff canvas sentry boxes. Among the merchandise, you could always spot a fleeting figure on the edge of the gray, hazy shadows on the dockyard walls. These were long strolls; my head and body felt so light I found everything fascinating. The ships were a great pleasure. I was astounded by every little feature. All my old passion for the sea poured into this visual feast. English coal ships, Scandinavian cod-fishers, slender-lined Italian schooners transporting blocks of marble, Germans from the Baltic with piles of aromatic timber on their decks launched my imagination on a fabulous journey. As they were moored one after the other, they aroused my curiosity in turn. Now and then I stopped and lit a cigarette. It was on one such break that I felt a twinge of pain in my feet. If I waited before resuming my walk, the pain increased. My feet hurt, they were on fire. This onslaught was usually accompanied by general body fatigue and tremendous hunger. Exhausted and depressed, I slowly began to retrace my steps. The slower I walked the more the pavement hurt. But I couldn't walk faster because my body wouldn't let me. Then I began to have strange hallucinations. The weaker I felt physically, the more vivid the erotic images flooding my mind. Women filled my field of vision, female faces that seemed to beg me to approach them. And I did so, naturally. They were pure fantasy. Those female forms were usually patches of light, blurred shadows, a passerby lingering in the distance. On the Rambla I usually drank a glass of milk. Then I felt a void in my stomach—as if it were carrying a heavy weight. Early-morning trams were few and far between and I was too impatient to wait. I continued on foot.

The members of the public the tram transported seemed the height of self-satisfied stupidity. Although my imagination was still awash with the erotic, the eroticism of others repelled me. When I reached the warm, gentle half chiaroscuro of rambla de Catalunya, my hallucinations began again. Sometimes I thought the trunk of a tree, the glow from a shopwindow, a distant passerby were female forms. I hurried on. Then ... I was back home and exhausted. I climbed the stairs, holding my shoes. I closed the door very carefully—shut my eyes, shrugged my shoulders. I undressed in the dark. And then began a sleepless night brought on by overtiredness.

30 April, Wednesday. I observe the impact of approaching examinations on the students in my lodging house. Nerves are tenser. The most trivial incident and they go wild; their nerves are frayed to the point of frenzy. Today, during lunch, there were almost full-scale fisticuffs. We had to pull them apart. They were arguing whether the coffee served at the Tupinamba was better or worse that what was on offer at the café next door—the name of which now escapes me.

When I reach the first floor of the Athenaeum, on my way to the club, I often see Don Miquel S. Oliver at the back of the office. He is fat, imposing, and apoplectic, with huge, bulging black eyes that literally ooze with melancholy. I have occasionally passed him in a corridor; he walks slowly, slightly out of breath, holding his black hat, his brow flecked with small gleaming beads of sweat. I don't know him personally, but I feel he is tolerant, sensitive, and most polite.

Every year, spring comes and López-Picó publishes his small book of poetry. Picó has taken to heart Xènius's rallying cries about the hallowed nature of continuity, perseverance, and regularity, etcetera. They are sublime rallying cries but perhaps they are followed too eagerly. There are a lot of bones in Picó's inevitable annual stew. Too many, perhaps. You sometimes find a small bone in Carner's poetry— a small bone from a chicken wing. On the other hand, the surfeit of flesh in Sagarra's is rather cloying. The regularity of Picó's poetic production demonstrates at the very least that we are dealing with a paterfamilias who feels a true vocation.

1st May. Punctually, at twelve on the dot, Don Cosme Parpal i Marqués, a professor in some branch or other of the Arts Faculty, walks across the Law Faculty courtyard. He is wearing civilian clothes. A morning coat. He looks like a pigeon: thin legs, tight trousers, prominent high stomach, small head, receding forehead, hair to the nape of his neck, body leaning so sharply backward that when he uses his walking stick, it never touches the ground. His coattails flap in irresistibly comic fashion.

The remoteness of women.

I am quite sure I'd have found it both positive and practical, so as not to waste time, to have access—at least conversationally—to a lady inclined to be warm and generous. Pleasant enough to wear clean clothes, say. I fully understand why Rousseau was so grateful to Madame de Warens.

I would have particularly liked for them to ask me questions or at least to let me ask them some. But it was impossible. My total lack of social savoir faire blocked this avenue, meaning it was never an option. In this sense, I have only ever dealt with women of no distinction at all. This leads me to give too much importance to sexual problems. Feelings of unease and wasted time.

Moreover, it would have been very useful from the point of view of health. I could have cast off that inner vanity men have, and that would have been a great accomplishment. For a man is never happier than when sashaying before a woman. The more ridiculous the performance, the more maternally female the instinct aroused, the more words of consolation uttered: "Poor fellow!" These are the words that mean the most to the other sex.

Then everybody would undoubtedly have emerged a winner.

I can easily imagine a man and a woman sitting down to lunch together, pleased and delighted with their mutual company. However, I cannot imagine there is any rule or art when it comes to happiness. Being happy is a subjective matter that is considerably strengthened if your friends agree to decree, if only by majority vote, that you are really happy. In my case, I've been waiting for such support for years—but it never comes. The reason for the delay can be found in the previous entry. At least that is what I suspect.

4 May, Sunday. Three interminable days when I couldn't write a word. The fact is you stuff your memory with countless items about which you haven't a clue. It is absurd. Not absurd but farcical.

Your memory has a wonderful capacity for keeping the things you intend to remember visible on the screen of your mind. When I studied repurchase law, I had a toothache. I wrote "toothache day" in red pencil by the questions referring to repurchase on the textbook. If that subject comes up, then the tangential reference to toothache will help me write about repurchase with greater facility. These parallel aids are my memory's crutches. The more crutches there are, the livelier the memory and the more likely you are to remember. If you want to light the fires of my memory, a spark is indispensable—whatever it is and wherever it comes from. If you could harness things you'd like to remember to recurrent obsessions—generally referring to moments when your pride has been wounded—you would possess a magnificent memory.

Nonetheless it all sounds vaguely sinister.

The line by Victor Hugo, a miracle of imitative harmony, "*Waterloo, Waterloo! Waterloo! Morne plaine…*" often comes to me in the long hours when I am revising my different subjects, "Cram! Cram! Cram! *Morne plaine…*"

Personally, I couldn't care less if they passed or failed me. However, though my friends think I am a man without feeling, I must confess I'd feel the deepest remorse if they *did* fail me because of the sacrifices made by my family (economic sacrifices, that is).

I met Alexandre Plana on carrer de Pelai. Plana, who is famed to have almost no female friends, is affectionate toward his friends. When he sees my anxious expression, he gives me a bovine glance with that smallpox-pitted face of his and says, "It will be all right . . . it will be all right . . ."

And puts his hand gently on my shoulder.

His glance seemed so pitiful for a moment I think he'd have glanced at me exactly like that if he'd seen me laid low in bed with pneumonia.

Thought always leaves one dissatisfied; action is more satisfying, although often not entirely so. Space is sad and indifferent; time is sad or happy. Reason focuses on space; sensibility on time.

6 May. I stroll down the Rambla at night to escape for a while from the nervous exhaustion brought on by judicial procedures and mercantile law.

One of the things I find most striking about Barcelona is what we could call its dualism, the way a street like the Rambla, that is so carnal, earthly, and sensual, so directly and straightforwardly human, is overlooked by temples (the cathedral, Pi, and Santa Maria) that are so lofty, so spiritual, so sensitive, so suggestive of warmth—an almost divine quality.

In my room at the lodging house I don't know what distresses me more: the unbound, dog-eared textbooks or the trail they seem to leave behind; the ashtray full of disgusting butts; the empty cup of coffee with a circle on the saucer where a fly is always buzzing; the dank smell of cigarette smoke floating in the air, etcetera.

Of course, I'd much prefer to ditch everything and go for a stroll. It would be very pleasant, but I'm not sure I could. I say so using an expression that has become fashionable in Barcelona and that I detest: I don't know if I have the cheek. Evidently the thought of my family's situation influences my dearth of cheek. All the same: I feel yet again that behaving properly induces genuine pleasure—a literally physical sense of satisfaction. This undoubtedly means it deserves less praise.

But this really isn't the problem. It is quite something else. At a very early age, I discovered that money is hugely important in life. It is simply vital to possess a minimum amount. Likewise, I grow more convinced by the day that I am absolutely unequipped to earn money. This tension is a permanent obsession of mine—a permanent, onerous obsession that I am sure will leave its mark on (derail?) my life. I feel I will always live in fear.

11 May, Sunday. More days when I haven't written a word. I barely recognize my notebook when I put it on my table.

My university plans aren't crucial, obviously, but here they are: I intend to sit all the fifth-year examinations and one or two sixth-year ones now and leave the others for this year until September. That way— if it all turns out fine—I will have completed my degree in a little over five years. Now that I'm about to sit my examinations, I'm only interested in one thing: getting them over and done with, and quickly.

I have drunk an excessive, crazy amount of coffee over the last few days (I am mad about coffee) and my stomach aches. I feel constantly empty inside as if somebody had sandpapered my tissues. I can't clear my pituitary gland of the ever-present smell of tobacco—concretely, the stench of butts in the ashtray. It impregnates everything in the room: especially the pillow on my bed, the sheets and general atmosphere. I can't open the balcony door wide because the noise from carrer de Pelai—the trains whistling to Sarrià, the clanging trams, the hooting automobiles—is excruciating. Coffee, tobacco, and ... judicial procedures! Something to look forward to. The pervasive odor often sends my head into a good long spin. I prefer short, swift stabs to dull, indefinite pain.

Judicial procedures is probably the touchstone subject of the law degree—I mean, for a student of law. The young man who takes to it spontaneously, almost effortlessly, is more or less on his way to becoming a lawyer and will be sensitive to court issues. I don't believe this is actually true, but it's the idea that floats in the air at the university. Justice is the essence of law—relative justice at least; procedures, methods of debate, are secondary. However, in this atmosphere, fiction always carries more weight than reality and guile more than substance. This is at the core of the system, as I have said repeatedly.

Now if this really is the touchstone, I will be a very minor lawyer. The mere name of the subject makes my temperature soar. As I learn by heart the icy articles on civil judicial law, I think I can smell the odor given off by judges' and magistrates' offices—the smell of wax-sealed papers piling up on their shelves and desks.

13 May. The slippery slope.

A long (amusing) conversation with S., a fellow student who's from the mountains and has a reputation for being a sly scoundrel. As we walk around the cloisters, he tells me, "You take these examinations too seriously."

"Oh, do I? Do you think so? How do you take them?"

"Very differently," he says, scratching the back of his neck. "Like most things in life, taking exams simply requires a little cunning."

"Tell me more, please," I ask, quite blasé.

"The first thing I can tell you is that you made one big mistake: Your number's too high on the lists and you will be one of the first to be examined. That was a wrong step to take. I always enroll late, as late as can be, and am one of the last on the lists."

"So what?"

"You'll soon see. Those of us near the bottom of the lists can always make the most of the fact that the professors get tired—I mean, tired by the effort they put into the exams—and they just want to get them over and done with. When such a situation arises (unthinkable in the first hours of the examination) and the number Lady Luck throws up relates to some unknown topic, you can always decide to recite another set answer, imagining that you actually did get the number you wanted. I've often done this very successfully and the teachers couldn't care less because they are so tired."

"But is there a technique for spotting when an exam jury is tired?"

"No, none at all. But it's like clothing: I can tell good cloth from cheap stuff simply with a touch of my fingers. What I'm saying is that there is a technique to passing exams. It is all about coming to them fresh and not dead tired—I mean, being in a stronger, more alert state than the gentlemen sitting half asleep on the platform."

"So you mean you must be devious!"

"Right. You have to come to the exams feeling fresh and cool and ready to take advantage of whatever turns up, to be in complete control of yourself. And when your opportunity comes, go straight in for the kill."

"Naturally, you have to play your hand smartly."

"No, not really... only the minimum guile is necessary."

Explained by this sarcastic knave from the sticks, it all makes me laugh. In fact, I take it much more seriously than it might appear.

"That's why I was saying," he says by way of goodbye, "you aren't on the right track. You look tired."

"So I see, so I see..."

Examinations.

Josep Calonge, from Palafrugell, a friend at the university (studying in the year immediately before mine), tells me how Don Joan Permanyer had this conversation with Don Josep M. Trias de Bes on an examination day (they were part of the same jury) before settling down to work:

"Trias my friend, we will have to pass everyone today."

"Oh..."

"Yes. We will have to pass everyone. Just imagine, the notary in Manresa recommended one young man in particular and... I can't find his letter anywhere. I must have mislaid it, I'm really sorry. Now, as I don't remember this highly recommended student and can't afford to upset anyone, we have no choice but to pass everybody and avoid putting our foot into it."

"That's fine, Don Joan," Josep M. Trias replied, chuckling to himself, elated, bursting to relate the anecdote to the whole of Barcelona once the jury session was over.

16 May. I have slept very badly over the last few days. I find my bedroom makes me feel sicker by the day. Time passes desperately slowly—but as the first day of examinations approaches I feel anxious, unpleasantly so. All the same, however, now it's about finishing them once and for all.

20 May, Tuesday. Exams begin today. Everybody puts on a brave face; except for those who have it all tied up and never played truant, the real process is an inner one. Everybody is extremely cheerful, but their mood hangs by a thread. Some people have such yellowing cheeks they look as if they have pledged a candle to the Virgin Mary.

24 May, Saturday. I finished my exams this afternoon, late. I passed, just in time, but I passed. I was obviously lucky. I ignored the rural knave's suggestions. I am really very exhausted. I shivered with cold on my way from the university to my lodgings—I assume because I was thinking I've passed the subjects that are said to be lighter. I eat a sandwich. I drink a glass of cold beer in Canaletes. I feel sleepy. I am going to bed.

25 May, Sunday. I don't know how many hours I slept: fifteen perhaps. While I am getting dressed, I look through the half-open balcony door: A wonderful, golden afternoon has just begun; the gentlest breeze is blowing; white clouds in the sky. I feel face-to-face, once again, with the delightful, morose Barcelona spring. I think how tonight will be so pleasant and enjoyable. I am in no mood to eat in my lodging house. Anything that reminds me of the previous few days puts me in a bad mood. I even seem to be off coffee. Less so, tobacco. I smoke the twenty-five cigarettes I roll a day. Before the examinations, it was thirty-five. My purse allows me to eat two ham sandwiches in the American Bar and drink a large glass of beer. The draft beer is excellent. I walk up the Rambla. Spring. Delicious air! Women have a striking presence in this air. It tastes of the flesh of fruit. On the corner of carrer de la Canuda, the opening to the drain melds with the scent from a bouquet of roses a bellboy at the Continental Hotel is carrying. The roses smell vaguely of death.

In the midafternoon I start a conversation in the Athenaeum library with the elegant, gentle, wondrous Mossèn Llorenç Riber. I have the impression the whole time that I am chewing a strawberry toffee.

I try to write a short story about the ins and outs of examinations. I realize that everything seems very confused—that I don't really remember anything. It all seems distant now. On the other hand, I'm beginning to be obsessed by the subjects I have left for September. Naturally, I am going to have a bad summer. For how long, I wonder, will this horrible institution on plaça de la Universitat persecute me? The mere thought of that cold, symmetrical building the color of brown stew gives me goose bumps.

After dinner I stroll leisurely along the Rambla, hands in my pockets, a cigarette between my lips, nose in the air. A large number of imposing, statuesque ladies from the south of France—overplaying in my taste their matriarchal tendencies. It seems as if everybody can speak French. It is all subterfuge, thank God! If it weren't, I might as well just beat it. The Rambla is impressive with its lights, hustle and bustle, and money. You're offered cocaine in almost every establishment. A lot of foreigners. Gentlemen I think must be Scandinavian seem very amused by the mess a sparrow has dropped on someone's hat. I struggle to stop myself from bursting out in laughter.

For a while I follow a small, plump, shiny, bald, hatless gentleman with a big nose and substantial rolls of flab, dressed in black (a jacket with piping like the one worn by the poet Joaquim Montaner); he is walking down the Rambla with an imposing courtesan on each arm. If this gentleman doesn't have great expectations, he is hiding them very successfully. If expectations are the sign of a great mind, I think this man's mind must be immense.

I meander for ages along the Rambla and side streets—to the west and to the east. A moment comes when I cannot tell shadows from real, palpable forms. I wander, gape into doorways, in the streetlight, through cracks. There is no way to conduct myself to bed. I finally surrender with the first light of dawn. Drowsily I start packing my case.

27 May. Palafrugell. I go to the café in the late afternoon. People are washing the streets down. A delightful smell of earth or white acacia blossom on carrer del Sol. I meet my friends on the club terrace. Linares wears a hearing aid on one ear—his mushroom—but looks distant and prickly, the attitude of someone who is completely deaf and wants to give the impression that he is deaf even with a hearing aid. A small motorbike is parked by the curb's edge. It is a small English model Tomàs Gallart has bought himself. He sits astride it and is so tall he seems to carry the machine between his legs rather than ride it. Joan B. Coromina, with his beady partridge's eye—over the years, this eye will turn into a cockatoo's—looks small and on edge like a bastard son of a Roman Caesar. Bofill (Gori) is ruddy, happy, and beaming. I suspect he has already eaten dinner.

"Hellooo!" he booms in a sonorous, all-embracing, patriarchal fashion.

Apparently the earth revolves solely to allow Gori to go hunting, shoot four times, hear the bells chime, and observe the birds flying over the open fields. Apparently strong wine from Jaca and fifty-cent packets of cigarettes and cheap broad-leaf cigars are also manufactured for the sake of his human well-being. I feel embarrassed by his "Hellooo!" that fills the street for a moment.

A proliferation of aperitifs.

It has become fashionable to embellish front doors with a brass plaque displaying a Sacred Heart above an inscription reading something to the effect of: "This is a Christian household; blasphemy is banned." It transpires, however, that in some of these households the husband and wife who have put up a brass plaque are on bad terms, so some husbands have stuck a strip of paper over the motto stating "blasphemy is optional."

It is an absurd statement, especially because going back on one's word in this country is horrendous. If one considers things objectively and takes into account their age-old standing, all such inscriptions are unfortunate because they show how one attitude is as deeply rooted as the other.

In bed, his head rested on two pillows and his prostrate position had an ex cathedra touch.

Having a quiet voice is no defect in and of itself, quite the contrary. What is sad is having a voice that is unpleasantly and unexpectedly quiet. In this case, better to be heard shouting, even if it is wearisome.

28 May. Coromina, who is rather jealous of the motorbike Gallart bought, invites me to ride to Girona on his device. I have no positive experience of these machines being at all comfortable. We ride along at top speed. When the noise stops in front of Cafè Vila, on plaça del Vi, I feel as if my whole body has been pummeled. These things are not for me. Some people seem rejuvenated by contact with one of these machines. They give me gray hair.

When we go under the arches, in front of Can C., we see D.S. He is a small, vaguely iridescent old man who wears a morning coat. His face is a flabby, pale sheep's face.

"There you have," Coromina tells me, "the noblest man in the city. The ideal of this little old man who isn't completely bankrupt yet is to keep embroidering his cushion and stroking children's legs. When he pursues his pleasure, his eyes cloud over and his lips slaver like a snail. He is knowledgeable and not without talent, but like a good aristocrat he lives in a world prior to the French Revolution. He has a priest in his household who wheels and deals. When D.S. dies, almost all his fortune will go to the bishopric. Families end on such a note if they are lucky."

He has the good taste to spare me the prognosis for families who have no such luck. Restraint is always pleasing.

For nearly our entire stay in Girona, Coromina talks to me very enthusiastically about Dr. Dídac Ruiz. He met him in Girona, when Ruiz was the director of the lunatic asylum in Salt. He was half crazy and bad-tempered—Coromina tells me—but knew a lot and was precise and confident in his knowledge.

That evening, in our café conversation, I played a naughty little trick on Coromina. I show him Ruiz's preliminary notes to Nietzsche's *The Antichrist*—the only work by this author translated into Spanish directly from the German, if I'm not mistaken. In these notes, Ruiz mentions Callicles's famous speech on the superior rights of the strongest—the speech that inspires the whole of Nietzsche's anti-Christian doctrine—and Ruiz says that Callicles's speech is to be found in the *Phaedo*. Now that isn't quite accurate. Callicles's speech is in the *Gorgias*, if I'm not mistaken.

Coromina smiles at me for a moment with the necessary minimum of contempt. I think that's the least you can expect in this country when self-respect is involved. However, this is all very trivial.

In the translation (which I am reading in bed) from Latin into Spanish by Fabié, of the travels of Lleó de Rosmital de Blafma, the Bohemian noble, through Spain and Portugal in 1466, one reads (on page 150) the following—which I will transcribe in the language of the translation: "I don't know what else he says of this province (Catalonia) except that its inhabitants are the most treacherous and wicked of men and there are none like them in any land. We traveled through three provinces of infidels, barbarians, Saracens, and Granacerens, and we were much safer with them than with the Catalans."

29 May. When spring comes, it is the same every year: Our conversations contain little storms in a series of little teacups. Today we were witness to a few picturesque skirmishes that endow small-town life with a certain charm.

Joan B. Coromina felt duty-bound to speak about pious old dears in a barbed manner—and in the name of religion. At the very moment when he was about to add a little spice, when he was curling his lips into a grin, Gori stopped him in his tracks.

"It makes no sense to speak in this way," Gori interjected, indignantly. "It makes no sense to joke about pious old dears in the name of religion, when there are so many arguments in their favor from other points of view. I have noted that these timorous, deathly pale little spinsters, who are quite tedious and irritable, show a special touch when it comes to making peach and apricot jam, delicious sweets, and the richest creams. If you don't want to taste any more jam, then keep mocking these pious old dears as much as you like. Now, if we want their jam, and I am a great fan, I don't see why there shouldn't be pious old dears."

"You are a fine old fool!" exclaims Coromina, scorn all over his face.

"And you are a great windbag," answers Gori, pouring beer from his bottle into his glass.

They sit there eyeing each other like cat and dog. Their stares harden intermittently; the scene is unbelievably comic.

Later on Coromina—who seems to be talkative today—speaks to me as if he's furious: "One day we must talk about the university. The university is our bourgeoisie, our horrible bourgeoisie's most obvious creation. If you want to understand what I mean, try this exercise, I beg you: You can always reach an understanding with an illiterate; it's more difficult with a man who reads the newspaper and is aware of the rule of three; you will never establish a serious dialogue with a man who has a university degree. I don't want to start discussing bourgeois taste because we will be here all night, but you ought to at least realize that the bourgeoisie has corrupted the taste of priests and laborers, who were the people with the most refined taste in this country. It is a class without imagination or taste . . . or the least desire to let go of its cash. It is the most wretched, pathetic class in the country. Through their fathers, their university, and their women, they create the ruling class, a class that has only one principle: to conspire and command; and one aim: to leave things as they have always been."

When we reached this point, Coromina looks at Gori, sees that he is smiling, and goes quiet. After a short pause, Gori glances around the table and asks, "Is anyone, who isn't a complete Neanderthal, up for a game of cards?"

Once again, the hilarious, thunderous glares.

People in this country practice a strait-is-the-gate form of Epicureanism, and do so as if they were ashamed, as if they ought to be apologizing. The confectioner defends a full-blooded strand of Epicureanism, but his poverty doesn't allow him to practice it even in its most minimalist forms. Perhaps this indicates how poorly the things of this world are distributed.

"The Ampurdan," Salvi Soler likes to say, "is a very strange place. There are people here who prefer to risk selling something for the promise of a thousand pesetas than selling for five hundred with cash handed to them on the spot."

August Carbonell has a magnificent, splendid Adam's apple. When he swallows, his Adam's apple makes such varied, amusing, and surprising movements that the beauty of a goose's neck pales in comparison.

"Sr. Carbonell," says Frigola, "can be positively grateful to the designs of Providence. Providence sometimes allows a man to be deformed so he can earn his livelihood. Not that one can say that Sr. Carbonell is in any way deformed; he is in the best of health and enjoys an Adam's apple that is literally worth an empire. He can take it anywhere and be sure to find a solution to all his problems. In Latin America, he would be invited to a different house every day because nobody would want to miss the opportunity to see something so amusing."

To put an ice cube in one's mouth—or to see someone else do it—gives me the physical sensation of crass stupidity.

30 May. My father summons me into his office. This was always going to happen. My father's office is a well-ordered, icy room, the room I know the least in the house. There is a copy of Montaner i Simon's *Enciclopedia Universal Ilustrada* on one shelf.

He watches me walk in with a great display of affection—behind a slightly sour smile. I look away. I have always been rather uncomfortable to look my parents in the eye (a form of embarrassment).

The conversation is direct: "So what are you intending to do?" he asks impassively, as if he is inquiring about the weather.

"I'm not sure. Take my final degree examinations in September."

"But if you're going to do that, you need to study. Where do you intend to do that? In Palafrugell? Can you study in Palafrugell? I don't think you ever have."

"Fair enough."

"Distractions are endless here."

"I agree, I thought Barcelona would be the best place to study, if I want to ensure a pass."

"Probably. It is very hot then in Barcelona, but it is possible."

"Of course, it is very hot everywhere."

There is a long pause.

Then the conversation resumes on a more insistent note.

"Fine. Let us imagine you qualify as a lawyer. When you reach this point, what plans do you have? Do you feel a vocation for the profession you have been studying to enter?"

"Not at all. Absolutely not. I am not interested in civil service exams or joining a law firm. Besides, that all takes a long time, it is a very slow process . . . and I imagine there's no money left."

When my father hears that last sentence, he widens his eyes. Then he takes a deep breath as if a great weight has been lifted from his mind.

"What you just said is unfortunately only too true. We have made a great effort. We have given you a profession. Things have not turned out so well for me as they might have."

I immediately preempt a possible bout of self-pity.

"We can talk about that some other time," I say. "Perhaps now isn't the time."

"No, of course it isn't."

"Now is the time to make a start, to reach a decision, and the sooner the better."

"No need to do anything in a mad rush either."

"I will go to Barcelona at the beginning of the month. I will take the remaining examinations in September. As soon as I get to Barcelona, I will look for something to help pay for my lodgings and everything else. Is that what was on your mind?"

My father is struck dumb. He had been planning this exchange for months and months. He hadn't dared to suggest it. He found it very upsetting. I had been expecting this conversation for more than a year. From my point of view, the delay was a windfall, though it was probably a burden for my family. Fortunately, the equivocating is at an end.

When my father started the conversation, he feared two things: First, he thought I would be annoyed if he suggested a conclusion to my degree that differed from what other households would usually suggest; second, he was afraid of being direct, of showing all his cards. Naturally this reveals his sense of tact and is to be warmly applauded. But getting upset over a matter of tact is complete nonsense.

When he saw that I didn't take it personally, that, in fact, I preferred a little plain speaking, his immediate reaction was one of vague disappointment. He had been stocking up on arguments to convince me and had struggled to flesh them out. It is always rather vexing when the efforts one has made prove useless because they are unnecessary.

Later, when he recovered from his initial reaction, I am sure he felt happy. In any case, he got up from his armchair looking pleased and almost smiled.

31 May. I have been turning over yesterday's conversation with my father for hours and hours. Temperamentally, I tend to see the difficult rather than the agreeable side of things. Even so I don't feel I am facing a dead end. My lack of awareness—probably—makes me feel confident. It isn't a very pleasant situation, but I expect I will find one way out or another.

I think this should be my strategy: First, leave for Barcelona at some point; second, not go back to the place on Pelai; third, establish myself in a more wholesome lodging house; fourth, realize that the solution to my problems will be found in the Athenaeum, in the circle around Dr. Borralleras, not in the library; fifth, accept any solution aligned with my passion for literature and reject all others outright.

After writing this, I feel an immense peace of mind. Why is it that when I am worried by something and write about it, my worries disappear, at least momentarily? How infantile!

I had a nightmare last night: I dreamed that I was taking an examination. As an adolescent, I would dream of something scary: that I was trapped in a labyrinth of stone. But the examination nightmare is more upsetting, precisely because it is much more realistic.

It isn't the external details in the dream that create my unease. It is the fact that I face gentlemen who formulate a question that nobody could answer. The situation is quite absurd, but so absurd I cannot throw off the anxiety I felt.

I sometimes wonder: Was the fact I didn't fit in at university a shortcoming or a positive quality on my part?

1 June, Sunday. Before bidding farewell to Palafrugell—because I assume I won't be returning for quite some time—I should like to go and plunge myself into town life, take a refreshing dip in the everyday.

Gori commented today in the café: "When our friend the musician Paradis states that he is going for a stroll out of town to find inspiration and catch the melodies floating in space, he isn't telling the truth. Our friend Paradis goes out of town because he is hungry; he goes to pick peaches, apples, and figs that belong to other people. And it is his stomach's voice that never lies. The day our friend decides to write the 'stomach song' we will be regaled with a piece of music that is absolutely sincere, magnificent, and original."

Obviously these remarks are unacceptable. But today I like these savage barbs. All the same, how can one square Gori's anti-conventional, rebellious attitude with his ambition to be someone important? Gori wants to be prominent. He would like to be a judge—a kind of judge for the duration. Does he feel the need to redeem a large quota of the human stock? Is he really imbued with the talents that can serve to manage and settle the differences others have? In fact, his tendency to manage is quite notorious. "This must be sorted out!" he keeps repeating. "We must ensure we sort this out! Things won't be right until we do."

Perhaps this man's personal stability depends on unraveling whatever he finds and then making all kinds of efforts to put things back together. Such characters aren't uncommon on this peninsula.

Enric Frigola declares that years ago the two individuals in town who chased the most after women were Don Manuel Fina and Sr. Melitó Dausà, a bottle-cork manufacturer. They were friends. One day they had the following conversation:

"I have just the woman for you, Melitó."

"You don't say! What kind?"

"A superb specimen, naturally! But I should warn you, she will cost you."

"What do you mean 'cost you'? I've still got a fine head of hair."

"I just mean that she won't come cheap."

"And I've got all my teeth."

"I know, I know!"

"Besides, I don't have any nasty vices and couldn't be more straightforward."

"That's enough of that! If you carry on like this, it will cost you an arm and a leg."

In the café I hear one man tell another, "It isn't true that musicians have a better ear than other people; musicians simply hear things, you know, that have passed through the prism of the solfège."

The person listening responds after a long pause: "Quite honestly, I don't really understand you, but it could very well be."

We are back to summer. There was a northeast wind this morning and in the afternoon the southwesterly. Such swings are quite normal.

The southwesterly is a turbulent, gusty, damp, murky, loud, and disorderly African wind. The northeasterly is a more academic wind. It has come via Greece and Italy, and before reaching this far has brushed against divine forms, which seem so distant to me. It comes off the sea, a calm and judicious wind.

I could never bid farewell to these winds. I carry them in my blood—with the north wind.

3 June. Barcelona.

I reached Barcelona with two hundred pesetas my father gave me. Tarrida—the villainous student from the heights of Montserrat— took me to a posh-looking lodging house, aspiring to pension status, up rambla de Catalunya, near the Gran Via. It has a clean, light stair- case made from rather pale but good imitation marble. It is many flights up, a real climb, but nothing to be done about that. It is a small bedroom—a lovely room, according to the landlady. Let's agree on that, it is lovely. The landlady, a widow, has two daughters. The eldest one is an office worker. The other is always in the company of a South American student from the conservatory who wants to be a violinist. Although I've been here hardly any time at all, this violin has given my ears a fine drubbing.

My two hundred pesetas will last me to the end of the month, if I am very careful. After that, who knows?

I go to the Athenaeum circle at night. The temperature on the Rambla is divine. People walk lethargically up and down rambla de Canaletes.

The scents the ladies wear are perhaps a bit cloying. The aroma from the Havana cigars is quite wonderful. Lots of people sit on the benches along both sides. Some are sleeping peacefully.

Hardly anyone at the circle. Borralleras and his friend Albinyana are at a concert. The conversation is flat and placid as the night. The worst thing about this kind of night is it sends you to sleep.

Borralleras is such a fantastically social animal that his gregariousness is quite refined. He has a friend for every mood. He goes to concerts with Albinyana and to exhibitions with Joaquim Sunyer and Pere Ynglada when these gentlemen (who live in Paris) are here; Josep Maria de Sagarra is his mentor in theatrical matters; Màrius Aguilar is his journalist man for all seasons; López-Llausàs is his expert in the world of books and bookshops. He is an idler who is a very busy bee. He literally can never stop, he is so busy.

I have resolved to explain my personal position to Borralleras and let him give me the solution he thinks fit.

He finally turns up—by himself—before two in the morning. Sensitive souls usually come out of concerts looking as if they have been beaten—as if they'd been knocked around with a vengeance. Borralleras walks in looking dreadfully depressed, his face a ghostly white, big bags under his wan purple eyes. He greets us wearily and sits in his usual place. His glance around the room communicates melancholy, tragic resignation. Then he lights a cigarette, slowly, mechanically, seemingly drained and apathetic. He reluctantly takes out his cigarette case, a black-and-white paper packet, and a box of matches. His first drag that he eagerly inhales (an eagerness usually accompanied by a grimace) appears to revive him slightly. Borralleras is a committed smoker: He smokes because he needs to. Then he smokes and listens in silence to the conversation without moving a muscle on his face, peering at those involved—a present or absent gaze, I can never decide.

Borralleras is thirty-seven, but you might easily think he was much older. He is tall, full-faced—very fat-faced when he was young—smooth-cheeked, with his hair combed back. His features are nothing out of the ordinary, but the whole of his face is like a pale mask from which his tired, deadpan, passionless eyes stand out inside the purplish circles of his spectacle frames. He wears a hat that is almost broad-brimmed, a high starched collar, and almost always dresses in blue; his excellent, sturdy shoes are light in tone. His hat and collar are reminiscent of modernism. I have heard him say he would like to replace them with more comfortable, fashionable items.

While the conversation continues, ignoring Quim's recalcitrant silence, I wonder if it's a suitable time to ask him for help. When he gets up at just before three to go to the Gambrinus, I have my doubts and don't know what to do. I finally get up and we go downstairs together. Then I walk down the Rambla with him. He drags his feet, as if they were hurting.

"Are you unwell?" I ask.

"No, I am well enough today. I haven't got a migraine, rheumatism, or gout. Those things that help me to get through life. It was a long, boring concert. A concert for snobs. Albinyana couldn't stand it and left before the end. I am in fact worried about the circle at the Athenaeum."

"What's wrong?"

"On the surface, nothing, but I am sure something *will* go wrong one of these days. It is changing. Now, it is barely a circle—it isn't what it used to be: a meeting of friends brought together precisely by the differences they had in almost every regard except in their friendship. Anarcho-syndicalism and the workers' movement have led to a change in the atmosphere and emphasized sharp differences. Today the circle is a mixed bunch, a tutti-frutti that cannot possibly gel."

"Now I understand you."

"From its early days, at the Athenaeum on plaça del Teatre, the circle always included intellectuals, artists, and members of the bourgeoisie, including lawyers, doctors, etcetera from this class. The circle contained people with a conservative bent or temperament and those with quasi-liberal or, if you will, quasi-anarchist leanings. People with different outlooks on life who could disagree on many things but be united by mutual tolerance and respect. That is now beginning to disintegrate. Not everybody around the table is equally conservative. Twenty years ago, Brossa, Ferrer i Guàrdia's son-in-law, and Don Teodor Baró of *El Brusi* were much closer than Màrius Aguilar and Jardí can be today. There are elements who are out-and-out supporters of anarcho-syndicalism: Aguilar, Montaner, and Pinilla, that fool of a lawyer. I suspect that Ors has tendencies in that direction too, albeit with his stiff prima donna manner. Estelrich, who never stops, has massacred Ors before the big shots in the Lliga. The heavy artillery reckons that Ors is a soft intellectual with bad habits who is poorly organized. But what do they expect? The time will come when Ors stops coming to the circle. When he feels he is being choked, he will turn anarcho-syndicalist. In the long run, he will leave for Madrid. The Majorcan is a practiced sycophant. In the meantime, the opposition party in the circle—the conservatives—is hardening. Up to now, Enric Jardí was the only systematic hard-liner. Reading *L'Action Française* has gone to his head. Solé de Sojo, Rafael Dalí, the textile manufacturers, are starting to react like cavemen. Some people are starting to feel ill at ease. This is a new development. It isn't a circle anymore but a set of antagonistic groups who will start fighting any day now."

"All the same, there are still plenty of members who represent tradition, that is, who are in favor of tolerance." And I mention Pujols, Camps Margarit, Palà, Sagarra, Rahola, Antoni Homar, López-Llausàs, Lau Duran, Drs. Manou and Ventosa, Professor Tayà, Canyelles, Sandiumenge, Lluís Llimona.

"All these you have just mentioned, except for Pujols, who is a man who dances to whatever tune is being played, are becoming more and more conservative. The same is true of Plana, Valeri, and almost everyone else."

"Don't you hold Pujols in high regard?"

"My dear Pla, I think there is something you still don't grasp: I can criticize Pujols fiercely and be enormously fond of him. That is the circle's tradition."

"Of course." I bow my head slightly and learn my lesson without blinking an eyelid.

At that point we were standing in front of the Teatre Principal. When he realized that, Quim turned around, looking quite bewildered. It wasn't his kind of district, evidently.

"And what are you intending to do now?" I ask as we start walking back up the Rambla.

"I want to go to the Gambrinus for a while. I expect I will find the de-cloistered nun and other friends there."

"No, I didn't mean that. I meant what are you intending to do in relation to the situation in the circle?"

"I am thinking of going to Paris. I promised Pere Ynglada and Sunyer years ago that I would and I can't put it off any longer. And what about you? Wouldn't you like to go to Paris?"

When I hear him ask that, I decide the moment has come to air my own concerns. I make an effort to be as natural as possible —though maintaining a suitable tone for asking favors. I start with a short statement as to my family's economic situation. When Quim assumes the burden of what I am after, he becomes absolutely attentive—a quasi-religious kind of concentration. He listens to me like a confessor. That confirms everything I have been told about this man.

He is a complete idler. He seems totally apathetic. But strangely, he is nothing of the sort. Quim works extremely hard, is very diligent, highly productive, one of the men of his generation who does the most. I don't think he has ever worried about himself except when he gives a detailed account in conversation of his attacks of migraine or gout, because Quim is one of his own conversational gambits. Nor do I think he has ever worried about things that worry most people. But as soon as there is a favor he can do, or help to provide, or support to offer, as soon as someone else has a problem he can solve, he is prepared to work night and day to overcome every obstacle. The words don't exist to describe his goodness and generosity. He is a man of demanding taste, subtle and highly intelligent, but the radius of his goodness reaches out beyond his own tastes and preferences. However, it only needs a greater interest to be at stake, involving a friend or acquaintance, independent of claims of clan, party, or coterie he will put all his energy into it. When things reach such a point, this man who is reputed to lead the most chaotic life in all of Barcelona behaves in the most orderly way imaginable. He uses a notebook to jot down the strategy he will pursue in each individual case, the visits he must pay, and the arguments he must deploy. These jottings become a kind of precise emotional accounting—the precision of which contrasts with the absolute lack of precision that characterizes his handling of his own affairs.

I continued with my explanation of my little problem and he listened in a spirit of attention, which didn't slacken for a second. He finally made his great dramatic move. He stopped in the middle of the Rambla and out came the renowned notebook. He jotted down a few notes with a small pencil I thought must be made of silver—after gazing hard at me in a questioning fashion I found disconcerting for a moment.

"We must first clarify matters!" he finally exclaimed. "I have seen that you have published four little pieces of 'nonsense' in small magazines. You recently published something in Picó's *La Revista*. You will be a writer. Junoy and Plana have told you as much repeatedly. But I haven't liked anything I have read by you so far. You write in a style that is dark, sinewy, and dry like the meat eaten by families in Barcelona. You are probably a man who has things to say but doesn't have control of how to say them. The most urgent task in your case must be to lighten your style, make it less intricate, and apply a proper order to things. Now there is perhaps one good way to lighten your style: It would be to work for some time as a journalist. You would have to learn to write short reports, do you understand?"

"Yes, absolutely."

"Journalism is not a good trade to be in, and I'd advise you to abandon it once you have sucked it dry. On the other hand, journalism is useful because it forces you to face things head-on and describe them clearly and simply. You would have to accept whatever terms you are offered, and it won't be very much. Perhaps it won't even pay for your lodgings. But you don't have any choice. If you have any objections, I would be pleased to hear them."

"No, I have no objections to raise."

"I say that because this country is full of people who ask for things and the second they have them, they start to scowl as if they'd been tricked like a pack of country bumpkins. I hope you won't be one of these. That would make me the cuckold who's forced to pay for the drinks. Very well, then, I will make inquiries and let you know... anyway, see you soon. Good night!"

And without allowing me to utter one word of thanks—we'd reached the entrance to the Gambrinus—he walked into the café. I watched his back disappear around a corner toward the back of the establishment.

I dwell on my situation as I return to my lodging house and feel my optimism surging.

5 June. As I thought about yesterday's conversation, the great surprise, apart from Borralleras's kindness—was my sudden awareness of Josep Maria Junoy's apparent interest in me. I have talked to him from time to time at the library, and seen him in the club, where we've drunk the odd beer together on the terrace. We are friends, and will surely be even closer, but I don't think you could imagine two men who are more different. He is a man who has done everything. He lived in Paris for a long time and has traveled widely. He is a pioneer in various expressions of modern European art. Maurras's praise of his calligram to Guynemer truly hallowed his name. Maurras's article was for Junoy what Rémy de Gourmont's praise for his drawing in *Iberia* magazine represented for Pere Ynglada. Junoy is a cosmopolitan dandy, sophisticated in matters of art, with a sensibility few would dare dispute. Contrast is the only explanation for the interest Junoy is now taking in a man as deeply rustic, elemental, and simple as I am.

He is a fop. His skin is always so iodine—perhaps he is a skilled makeup artist—with beady eyes, a sprig of mint in his mouth, and cinders under his felt hat (*alla cacciatora*) with a small feather in winter, his straw boater (with red-and-blue ribbon) in summer. Josep Maria Junoy appears to have a sense of well-being, possessing a heady, most delightful air. His magnificent, English-officer trench coats, comfortable, belted overcoats, and thick, oxblood foulards are worn not so much with bourgeois restraint as with the desire to impress as a man of wit and standing. Moreover, Junoy moves in a responsive, well-disposed Barcelona milieu and enjoys a very good press—especially the left-wing variety, because of his brother Don Emili. Don Emili, whom Josep Maria adores, is a militant republican yet he has a very positive friendship with the king, a striking contradiction that can make life complicated for him. Apart from those interested in the game—like Cambó—the one man who can plumb the depths of Senator Junoy is a man who is equally complex, namely his brother Emili. This is my way of saying there can only be a relationship of very striking contrast between him and me.

He is fond of literary virgins and genuinely excited by unpublished figures, and this may be the secret reason for his interest in me. Apart from that, he is smart and scintillating. You sometimes feel he must spend a couple of days at home honing his repartee, his subtle shafts of wit, and when he has gathered a sheaf together he rushes out to try them on those he thinks most likely to appreciate them. I have some experience of this because I've occasionally figured among the ranks of the chosen. He is very clever at firing his rockets, as if they surged spontaneously in the course of conversation, but I've always felt his pyrotechnic talents are too perfect, his rockets too well-endowed with light and shade not to be prepared well in advance. I don't say this with any ironic or scornful intent. On the contrary, I'll always be grateful to Josep Maria Junoy for his keenness in allowing his friends the pleasure of sharing his subtle barbs. Junoy is a fascinating individual in a land of highly tedious, inward-looking, closed people. His working style is also highly appropriate. Persons of wit only come into view every so often.

He is currently obsessed by religion and, after spending years out in the cold, is ready to accept the warm shelter of faith. It has been a lengthy process, with many dark hours of anguish, accompanied by much reading. One day when Alexandre Plana was quoting Pascal and Fénelon at him and voicing doubts as to whether he had taken the best path to arrive at faith, Junoy responded, "Don't you worry... the more I read, the less I understand."

The day Junoy told me he was preparing himself to embrace orthodoxy, we went for a long walk. He was wielding a very thin, gnarled walking stick, a fragile cane that curved like a snake, and he was carrying a parcel of books under his arm—which looked like a folded wing. We visited the bookshops on the Rambla, drank a beer on the terrace of the Lyon d'Or, went into the Schilling establishment, walked up the Rambla. Junoy skipped along and this gave him a light, elusive air. A table on the terrace of Petit Pelayo—next to which a large, sallow gentleman who was eating half a dozen oysters—was the place my friend chose to bring me up-to-date on his exact location on the path toward faith. He told me, looking quite anxious, "It has been a long, difficult path and I can't say I have reached the end. The dogmas were not so onerous to assimilate. It's like swallowing a large spoonful of castor oil, but once you've swallowed them no more thought is required. There are other things, however, which I found very, very difficult. One might say they are issues of minimal importance. Right now, I've encountered a rather large obstacle, an obstacle I find paralyzing. Can you imagine what it is? The hats priests wear, I find the shape to be in such execrable taste. Can one belong to a religion that tolerates such ghastly headwear?"

I relayed this anecdote to a few friends and they spread it around Barcelona giving it a literal meaning—that is precisely the meaning it doesn't have. Using the example of clerical hats, with his customary wit, Josep Maria Junoy wanted to suggest that the biggest obstacle on the road to faith was his own selfishness, his lack of charity, the way he hardened his heart before a trifling problem, all related to his sense of the ridiculous.

The way Junoy writes isn't exactly my favorite kind of wine. When he writes, he permanently worries about elegance, in a subtle, harmonious, dry manner. "I would like to write," he has often told me, "in a style as dry as whiskey." I prefer simplicity to elegance; something lifelike in contrast to the orthopedic rattle of his harmonies; tense muscularity as opposed to his anemic staccato sentences.

"In the end," he often tells me, "you find a way to mix the sauce for mayonnaise. Mine always comes out watery."

He is a man who constantly surprises, and he gave me a real shock the day I realized he so disliked Eugeni d'Ors.

"You will understand," said Junoy, very excitedly, nervously toying with his sprig of mint. "There are things one simply cannot stomach. I went to visit him one day in Paris. It was when people wore button shoes—I did as well—a disastrous fashion. He opened the door and I was astounded to see how he received me with his shoes undone, their tongues hanging out, and his trousers tucked inside his shoes. Button shoes with their tongues hanging out are not a pleasant sight . . . and I could probably have tolerated that. But do you know what he started talking about? Mallarmé!"

I could hear the indignation rising in Junoy's voice. His eyes were glinting and the iodine in his skin assumed a brighter, sharper yellowish-clay color.

"No, no . . . there are certain things one should never stomach! I imagine you agree! Dandyism, button shoes, their tongues hanging out, Mallarmé! It is more than anyone can take! You tell me where it all might end? He is intolerable, however great a philosopher he may be!"

7 June. A long conversation with Quim, along the Rambla, in the early hours. He tells me he isn't going to the Gambrinus as he has to get up very early in the morning to make a number of visits. I say I will accompany him home. He lives in a small apartment on carrer del Bisbe, the balconies of which open onto plaça de Sant Jaume. As we walk up carrer de Ferran he tells me he can't give me any news yet.

"I've made some inquiries, I've tested the waters," he says. "I will let you know as soon as I have anything concrete to tell you."

Quim, who has a small income, is a bachelor and lives alone on carrer del Bisbe. He has an old servant: Maria. There are two things about which Quim can talk for hours and hours, inexhaustibly: his physical ailments (migraine, rheumatism, gout) and old Maria. I imagine Maria has similar experiences to her "senyor." To judge by his long descriptions, these two solitary beings spend their lives in mutual contemplation, trying to grasp the way their actions mesh, with an interest that constantly renews itself. When we reach carrer del Bisbe, Quim glances at the entrance, looks at the town hall clock, and says, "I'll accompany you as far as carrer d'Avinyó. It's still early. I can never decide when to go to bed at this time of night."

We begin to retrace our steps. This man, who lives surrounded by people, in a tonic of constant table talk, sometimes gives me the impression that he prefers quiet conversations. In our table talk, which is generally brilliant, if schematic and continuously interrupted, there seems to be no place for his more complex, diffuse, highly subtle insights. When Borralleras embarks on one of his confidences or descriptions, he becomes a very analytical kind of voluptuary. His sharp powers of observation allow him to capture an infinite range of minute but lively details and connect them up in infinite, occasionally musical ways with a series of tangential remarks of the utmost interest. His descriptions aren't those of a miniaturist.

A miniaturist takes a great device and reduces it to fit through the small eye of a tiny needle. Borralleras works in the opposite direction: He can transform something small into a great device by lingering on the details. He isn't a narrator who opts for broad brushstrokes in a superficial, amateurish fashion. Nor is he a naturalist or a verist. He is in fact symphonic in style, with a mind that combines an infinite range of facts, emotions, allusions, and feelings with the most diverse points of reference. With all that, we'd reached carrer d'Avinyó and, to my great surprise, Quim said, "Now you accompany me back to carrer del Bisbe. I imagine half an hour makes no difference to you . . . then we can say our goodbyes, because I must be up early tomorrow, as I told you."

Borralleras talked about Maria. He described the way she had acted last summer in Prats de Lluçanès (a small town where he spends the summer), her troubled relations with farming folk. He then began to talk about farming folk—another of his favorite topics, especially in the autumn, when he returns from Prats de Lluçanès. His ironic affection for countryfolk leads him to imitate their gestures, tone of voice, and dialect. He is a stream of inexhaustible comment, a kind of (musical) flow of conversation that knows no bounds. Excellent descriptions that Quim elevates by shading in the details to give them a mysterious aura, a hint of pathos. Prose gains greatly from such shading. Sterne, Voltaire, and Renard are linear writers, who use no shade and are perfect in what they draw. Ruyra is gifted in the use of shading. The master among masters in this respect is Dostoyevsky. The most trivial, banal, and commonplace sentence in Dostoyevsky has a hint of mystery. The spirit of Quim, I was thinking . . .

However, we'd now reached carrer del Bisbe for a second time and, after looking at the town hall clock and surveying the street, Quim said, "I see it's still early. The night watchman hasn't come. I'll accompany you back to carrer d'Avinyó and we can say our farewells. This untimely subscription to purchase Sunyer's painting is what's behind these visits."

The spirit of Quim—I was thinking—derives from the spirit of the music that has surrounded his life with resonances, impulses that suggest the vaguest, most diverse things and arouse his curiosity. Perhaps this first impression should be rounded off with what the poet and lawyer Solé de Sojo usually says in small gatherings. "You cannot understand Quim," Solé would say, "if you haven't read Proust. Quim is one hundred percent Proustian." (I have yet to read Proust.) Solé is the first person in Barcelona I have heard speak at length about him. Quim was possibly one of the first readers of Proust in Barcelona. Was it Pere Ynglada who encouraged him? I suspect not. Today Ynglada is in the full flush of his passion for the Far East and his favorite literary repast is Chinese poetry. Nor do I think Joaquim Sunyer or Josep Maria Junoy pointed him in the direction of Proust—despite the fact that Quim receives his news about Paris from this trio. Junoy can be ruled out—he is the anti-Proust. Good painter that he is, Sunyer reads very little. The book that painters prefer tends to be *Daphnis et Chloé*. Quim's enthusiasm for Proust is a typical case of elective affinities.

We talked about elective affinities and there we were back on carrer d'Avinyó, and so it was time to return to carrer del Bisbe yet again. Which is what we did.

It was now very late. We began to see the occasional person who'd just got up and was heading to work—the people who constitute the guilty conscience of birds of the night, to the point that they feel ashamed when they spot one. I understood from the gusto with which Quim spoke about Proust that he much adored this author about whom very few had spoken to this day, with the exception of Léon Daudet in *L'Action Française*. Quim never knew when it was time to sleep and, when the conversation centered on one of his favorite topics, his use of *never* could always be taken literally. Never. When we reached plaça de Sant Jaume I dared remind him of what he had repeatedly told me: namely, that he absolutely must be up early. Visibly displeased, he listened to my comment and I'd even say scowled, suggesting—perhaps—that he felt it was ridiculous for me to remind him of a duty he himself had to see to. Once we'd said our goodbyes and wished each other good night, I watched him walk toward a small bar on the square and start a conversation with a night watchman—whom I supposed worked on his street. I suspect that by deciding to do that, he wanted to teach me a lesson that I think I deserved, to the extent that, from then on, I determined never to prompt any birds of the night, however often they may have previously said that they really did need to get up *early* the next morning.

9 June, Monday. By ten o'clock I am in and around Canaletes. It is a glorious day, a wonder: The air is like a pillow filled with canary fluff; white clouds are furnishing the monotonous blue of the sky; the bustle of traffic prevents me from hearing the birds sing, but I am sure the birds *are* singing everywhere. The famous kiosk's orange-juice fountain is spurting and spluttering between the globe of the Teixidor Cyder bar and the globe for Bragulat sparkling wine. The spears of the palm trees on plaça de Catalunya flash and dazzle in the sunlight. If I look around, I can see that, apart from those going to work, almost everyone is holding a croissant and striding along like a conquistador. I dislike only one thing in this prosperous, endearing cityscape: the yellow of the trams. Yellow is the color of lunatics.

The first sign of differences between the Allies in relation to defeated Germany. When one loses a war—or anything else—to a coalition, the vanquished make easy advances on favorable terrain, on the terrain of conflicts between coalition partners. It is an ancient game and, if one knows how to play it, can be very fruitful. Reading the newspapers over the last few days takes me back to that marvelous time I had three or four years ago reading Thucydides.

It is very unpleasant to be waiting for a person who should have come and didn't; but waiting to say goodbye to a person we find irritating—who is never in a rush—may be even worse.

Despite my passion for literature I have never been able to warm to novels. I take no issue with the way novels begin and set the scene; when tensions and the fiction of the denouement begins, I can read no more—the book inevitably falls from my hands. Novels are children's literature for adults. When we were small and Grandmother Marieta told us stories by the fireside, if she ever paused, we'd ask, bright-eyed, "And what now? What now? What happened next? How did it all end?"

People who read novels look for the same effects. But novels aspire to do much more than spin yarns; they want to reflect life. A novel is a mirror, etcetera. Now, it is true that novels reflect life when they describe a situation and specific characters, but when they create and resolve a conflict they reflect nothing, they are merely being fictitious. In real life nothing ever ends, except as a result of death or oblivion. However, novels don't usually end on that note. Novels seek to demonstrate one thing or another—generally the greatness of whatever moral code is in vogue. I think that the seven or eight great novels that represent masterpieces of this genre would gain in stature if they had no endings.

12 June. The circle at the Athenaeum.

Social microcosms like this can be a substantial help, if one fits in. If this is the case, they can extend one's range of contacts in unsuspected ways. When it doesn't work, it can have tragic results. I tend to think I've landed on my feet. Francesc Camps Margarit was one member who looked favorably on me from the start. Two or three days after we met, he told Alexandre Plana, "This is a country lad who will go far. He is the sort from his generation who plays hard. He sometimes seems quite unaware."

A few days later I was telling friends on a café terrace—Junoy, I think—how distressed and horrified I felt at the idea of going to my lodgings and eating those dreadful haricots. It was before dinner. Camps Margarit was listening to me at the next table. The moment I got up to wend my ill-fated way to my lodgings, he came over and slipped me a silver five-peseta coin (thus signaling it wasn't the first time he'd done such a thing) and said, "Go and eat in a restaurant. The description you gave of those haricots was worth more than five pesetas. Then come to the Athenaeum."

This is something one doesn't forget. Later, at the circle, he invited me to coffee, French cognac, and a Havana cigar. After that I thought I had the right to think of him as a friend. I'd like to write a portrait of this man. But perhaps I don't know him well enough to.

He is a man of average height and very changeable in appearance (there are days when he seems plump and others when he's a bag of bones) with pronounced features: red cheeks; black, bristly eyelashes; canonical cheeks; the brightest, liveliest eyes; a bushy, freshly trimmed beard; a fine head of gray hair; a thick trunk of a neck above a sternum that juts out willfully. He dresses casually, and with great verve and a sense of mischief wears those gleaming ties so in vogue in Barcelona. His mischievous presence is perfectly compatible with lapses into the most obvious shyness. This vacillation suggests a degree of indecision. When he laughs he goes "Hee, hee, hee!" and places a handkerchief over his mouth so as not to overdo it.

I have never met Albert Llanas, but I have seen photos of this gentleman. I have the impression that Camps bears a physical resemblance to Llanas, particularly to Llanas as a young man. The only difference is that Llanas's hair was more abundant and copious than Camps's—two different styles. If the hairstyle of Llanas's era had survived, Camps would have made it his, because the physical constitution of the two men is similar and, consequently, he'd have responded automatically in kind.

When Camps sits down, he loses a lot. One should see him walking along the Rambla, up Passeig de Gràcia or entering a textile shop, squeezed into a jacket with its middle button done up, a newspaper sticking out of his pocket, his nose in the air, and a cigarette in his mouth—a cigarette pointing at the sky, like the boom of a brig. He sways provocatively from side to side, weathers the ladies' stares, and simulates the air of a prosperous baritone—an ineffable, simultane-ous mix of friars' cat, condottiere, and simpleton. People stare at him, slightly taken aback. The poor ask him for alms more than they do ordinary people; newspaper and lottery-ticket sellers approach him more than anyone else. I imagine he adores this. There are a lot of show-offs in Barcelona, particularly among the upper classes. Men in Barcelona tend to show off spontaneously. Don Trinitat Monegal is one such delightful swaggerer. And despite his middling status, Camps has made up a lot of ground in this respect.

Most of the pungent phrases, caustic barbs, and entertaining sal-lies uttered in Barcelona over the last fifteen years have come from Rusiñol, Pujols, and Camps. The mechanics of Rusiñol's humor have yet to be analyzed. I deliberately use the word "mechanics" because his humor *is* rather mechanical for my taste. Pujols is unique in the witty way he handles contrast. His use of the language's most colloquially vulgar turns of phrase in certain situations has created moments of genuine comedy. His exchange with Sr. Taxonera on the subject of the eclipse, as they were leaving the Continental, was the talk of the town. Taxonera: "The eclipse will take place at four o'clock." Pujols: "No, they're always around half past four."

Overshadowed by these two giants, Camps has defended his turf remarkably well. One day a woeful Dr. Dalí said, "Bad news, Camps! Sr. Llavoll has been injured. Half his body is paralyzed, as if it were dead."

"So, God has half forgiven him!" came Camp's lugubrious re-sponse.

It goes without saying that Camps has been a key element in all the humorous magazines published in Barcelona in recent years, in par-ticular the unforgettable *Papitu* in its first period—which won't be easily surpassed. His trade as a textile packager means he makes in-numerable contacts and visits many offices. This provides him with an almost infinite amount of human material. He knows everybody, and since telling Camps an anecdote ensures it will receive maximum ex-posure, people are quick to tell him the juiciest gossip from Barcelona and surrounding towns, and the textile industrial area in general.

And it is odd that this arsenal of anecdotes and supply of bons mots, incidents, and reminiscences don't turn him into an excellent conversationalist. He is very good when he begins his descriptions, in control, giving color to things, and life and movement to a character, but he is suddenly derailed by an attack of shyness. He seems to say to himself, "It's all too long, or uninteresting, or too tedious," and he loses his way and his conclusion is lackluster. I have heard him come out with his best witticisms at moments when he is confused, when the conversation has become heated and everyone is speaking quite spontaneously. In the midst of such banter, Camps's shyness seems to retreat, as if he felt confusion offered a kind of impunity. Camps's character is most peculiar in the sense that he seems permanently mischievous and brazen but is one of the least insolent performers one can meet in the crowd in Barcelona.

He is a warmhearted fellow. His warmheartedness is generous and open—from good manners to acts of charity. He possesses a quality that is quite unusual in the country: He likes to cushion other people's lives. He will move heaven and earth for others. He is particularly adept in conversation at highlighting things that may interest the person he is talking to, and passing on praise and compliments he has heard about the individual concerned. Obviously he sometimes forces his hand, is inventive and says one thing rather than another. He can land himself in absurd, extremely comical situations. Sometimes he's been compelled to tell so many lies to keep people happy that he's risked a beating. Snide critical cynicism is unpleasant. The cynicism involved in wildly exaggerated praise can turn to venomous lucidity or dazzling glare. Pujols and Camps have cultivated this tone to oil the conceits of others, not to cause mischief.

Camps is inexhaustible when it comes to being charitable. He's never been known to say no. He has always been generous, elegantly solicitous. Before he went to live in Madrid, Xammar said Camps was the only person in Barcelona prepared to give a secure, long-term loan to a journalist. If anyone ever doubted this claim, he'd say he was a fool, a man with no critical sense.

"It isn't simply enough to give out a loan," Xammar would say. "It is vital to keep on good terms if one can't repay the loan. In this country, Camps is alone in this category."

For months Camps had been giving five pesetas a week to my journalist friend V. This journalist waited for him at an agreed time in the
entrance to the Athenaeum, and Camps slipped him the money as he
went in without saying a word. One day V. didn't make their rendezvous. Camps searched the Rambla for him.

"I'm sorry...there was a mix up today," Camps said when he saw
him, looking fearful rather than pleased as he handed him the silver
coin.

You often hear people say, "Camps would sell his father for a good
joke."

And it is clearly true. The flair Camps displays when it comes to
wit, sauce, and frenzied wordplay means that now and then he, like
Pujols, acts like a monster that has slipped its chain. If people ever
noticed, they would beat them to pulp. They don't, I suppose, simply
as a measure of self-defense. On the other hand, I don't believe one
can make an omelet without breaking an egg or two. I don't believe
anyone has discovered other means to achieve that end.

It would be fascinating to review Camps Margarit's ideas on literature. He wants literature to be successful, and by that he means success in the wide, wide world. In this sense, if anything is to be any
good, it must be in the style of Rostand and Cyrano high and low. It is
not difficult to observe how everyone of his generation, even Camps
Margarit himself, loves to "Cyranize" a little or, if you prefer, to be
quite clear, to "Rostandize." It is likely that Camps's friendship and
admiration for Màrius Aguilar and his literature derive from this vein
of Rostandery. One can see Rostand's impact increasing by the day. It
is remarkable how he is penetrating the society of Barcelona, how
Camps and his generation have embraced the work of the author of
Chantecler. The literary writing of Màrius Aguilar, even his most everyday columns, has panache—feathers that flutter in the wind.
Camps thinks that Aguilar is the best possible kind of writer. I have
heard him say, "He is interesting even when he has nothing to say." I
marvel at the influence Rostand still has, which allows such boutades
to abound.

Apart from this, Camps likes literature that allows its authors to
go into a shirt shop and receive an automatic discount from the shirt-

maker—or, if you prefer, when its authors walk down the street and people think or say, "Golly, Sr. X, that was a wonderful article you just wrote!" In other words, literature for Camps must imply immediate, direct, palpable, outright glory. His ideal is equine folkloric literature or prose that would please Sant Medir gatherings. In fact, one of the happiest days in his life was a Sant Medir day, I can't remember the year, when he rode in the carriage of the *Papitu* editorial board and heard people on Gran de Gràcia say, "Look, that's the carriage for the people who write for *Papitu*!"

Indeed, if being a writer doesn't bring one immediate entry into this or that carnival procession, what *is* the point of being a writer?

All the same, his literary ideas and the great admiration he feels for Màrius Aguilar don't challenge his social ideas. Camps has a chemically pure bourgeois mentality, whereas Aguilar leans toward anarcho-syndicalism. They often argue. They can never agree. When they argue, Camps displays his off-the-cuff wit.

"I see you are calling for more justice in your article today," remarks Camps.

"Exactly so. I call for more justice!"

"And what is justice?"

"Justice is fairness, a fairness that isn't upheld by the Employers' Association."

"I see now! You ask that the blind have the right to a dog, and the one-eyed the right to half a dog. Is that your idea of fairness?"

Aguilar leaves it at that—out of friendship more than anything else—with Cyranoish presumption. Camps takes command of the territory with the mischievous air of a Chantecler.

13 June. The lodging house.

The lodging house where I live now on rambla de Catalunya is very different from the one on carrer de Pelai. Spiritually, it is possibly more disorganized. From the outside it seems much tidier and well run. The old place was for slack, poverty-stricken students. The new one is populated by office workers and clerks—and we know these people share the tastes of their respective masters and express themselves in like manner. That was a home for the down-at-heel; this is a home for people who may not be wealthy but aspire to be one day. Knowing the right road is crucial if you're planning to go somewhere.

In its fantastic disarray, the lodging house on Pelai was raw, obvious, and amusing. Everybody acted as they were, spontaneously. Here you have to be extremely careful about what you say in order not to put your foot in it and be exposed to general ridicule. I now have the feeling I'm living among important people—who are simply being acted out by their employees. When someone around the table says, "It was very hot today," the others look at you as if to say, "I'll let you know about that tomorrow after I've spoken to my boss."

This place is a stifling hothouse of clichés and commonplaces. The philosophy of the house is dictated by the grace of *El Ciero*, that is, *El Noticiero Universal*, our Universal Daily Post.

The differences between a poor man in a house for the poor and a rich man or simply men with aspirations to riches are unending, infinite. There are as many as there are between black men and white—not forgetting the different smells that whites and blacks give off, or so they say.

My move from Pelai to rambla de Catalunya has changed my daily vision of humanity. I often saw Joan Estelrich and now I never see him. The stew-colored university building is no longer part of my field of vision. My new situation, focused as it is on the circle and my forays into journalism, has removed from view Joan Climent, my colleagues at the Institute of Education, and even at the Military Academy in Drassanes. My cityscape has suffered a huge metamorphosis. For better or for worse . . .

Scene at the club.

It is half past five. The weather is muggy. The doors over the Athenaeum garden are open and admit the dull rumble of the city. Not many people have come. The conversation proceeds very quietly. Don Pere Rahola is asleep in an armchair. He has been enjoying blissful sleep for the last half hour, his head resting on his chair back, mouth drooping open, under a large mustache with Cyranoish twirls.

He is breathing deeply and when his lungs refill he snores long and loud. Whenever he makes that noise, those in the room regard the sleeper with respect and surprise; then they look at each other, at a complete loss for words. Every afternoon, over many years, the same startling performance. Don Pere wears nothing on his head. (I have sometimes imagined what the effect would be if he were to wear a hat.) His baldpate gleams a light pink. His body emanates a Piver scent, rue de la Paix. The hair around his pate curves upward—a kind of miniature coat hanger. Don Pere's mustache and beard are neatly trimmed. His beard is neither big nor small; it isn't flowing or African like Jaume Brossa's used to be, nor Mephistophelian and sharp-pointed like a goat's nipple: It is a sturdy, handsome beard in keeping with the social standing of the individual who has spawned it, under which Don Pere sports a rich, luxurious shirtfront. A pale pearl on his shirt. He is dressed in gray. A small diamond glitters warmly on a ring worn on the small finger of his left hand which is resting on a chair arm.

15 June, Sunday. Sr. Dalmau, from the renowned Dalmau Galleries, on carrer de la Portaferrissa, attends the Athenaeum conversations on Sunday afternoons.

There is an entrance on Portaferrissa that leads into a very long passageway. If you walk along the latter, you come to a rather damp inner courtyard, with broken flowerpots and spindly plants that give off a dank, mossy smell throughout the winter, at the center of which is a kind of cage with a glass-paneled roof. This cage could well be a photographic studio. In fact it is a cage that belongs to the Dalmau Galleries—namely, the shrine to avant-garde art. I started going there when they held the Van Dongen exhibition, namely, when this artist, in the middle of the war, gave his first exhibition on the Continent of paintings he had painted in North Africa, especially in Algiers. I later followed the exhibitions of members of the group that first called itself the Courbet Group and then transformed into the Evolutionists with Sisquella, Serra, Miró, Viladomat, etcetera leading the way. The master of this group, at school, was Labarta, Lluís Labarta, the son of old Labarta (one of the long-established affiliates of the Athenaeum library), and in terms of polemics and style, Joan Sacs.

The most turbulent, anarchic youngsters on the Barcelona art scene head for the Dalmau Galleries, along with the strangest birds of passage. Some amazing characters passed through the gallery, particularly during the war. Even so, the strangest man in the place is Sr. Dalmau. He is a small, pallid man with a languishing black beard, who always wears oversize dark, shiny clothes. They are too long and too wide: His trouser bottoms concertina on his dusty shoes; his loose baggy jacket is more like an overcoat; the objects he carries in his pockets are always weighing it down; his waistcoat is like a waistcoat for three Dalmaus. In the winter, he wears an overcoat he can barely hump along in and a broad-brimmed black hat. I think it's obvious that Sr. Dalmau is a notoriously reluctant dresser. However, this indifference to clothes pales beside what we might call Sr. Dalmau's indifference to his physique. His voice is so feeble and faint—his mouth movements so minimal—you have to be accustomed to it to catch anything he says. He walks so wearily, so droopily you sometimes feel like holding his arm to keep him from falling down. It's as if he has been starving for the last three or four months. His general appearance is of someone who has journeyed beyond the frontiers of neglect, waste, and apathy. He is an anemic man par excellence, a being in the process of becoming a cadaver.

The only thing that seems to give him energy is smoking the cigarettes he rolls himself. On Sunday afternoons he enters the room where the circle is assembled, orders a coffee—which he drinks with the tiniest sips—and places his cigarette case on the marble table. He smokes very slowly and is a champion at keeping a dead butt hanging off his lower lip for as long as possible. He doesn't usually join in the conversations. He sits, listens, smokes, and is silent. If he is asked a question directly, he responds with the smallest number of words possible—though it often seems he says nothing because he articulates his words so haltingly.

"By the way, Dalmau," Quim Borralleras said to him today, "you have a very strong show at the gallery this week."

(It is an exhibition of cubist painting with Juan Gris and some Polish artists in the same line. It is the last of the season.)

Dalmau said something that was only heard by Solé de Sojo, who was sitting next to him.

"What did he say?" someone asked.

"He said," replied Solé de Sojo, "that everything is always strong and vigorous at the Dalmau Galleries, starting with the boss."

"Now pull the other!" whispered Camps.

"Hee, hee, hee," tittered an amused Dr. Dalí.

18 June. As I had to start sooner or later, I have begun to study the remaining subjects I still have to sit. There are two: private international law, the chair held by Don Josep M. Trias de Bes; and forensic practice, by Don Magí Fàbrega. I like international law; it is a reflection of life itself, of the inextricable chaos that strikes human life at times. I can't think of a single novel as incredibly rich. Forensic practice is a deadweight, the mere thought of which gives me a temperature.

20 June. In quantitative terms, this notebook is assuming extraordinary proportions. When these papers are published in thirty or forty years—if they ever are—how will readers react, that is, if they find readers with time on their hands? I only ask one thing of this hypothetical reader: I ask him to read it slowly and calmly. Books that have been written without great motivation, on a whim, books that don't respond to any inner need, gratuitous books, can be read, as Pujols likes to say, in fits and starts. But the fact is that this notebook, which I started quite lightheartedly, has now become a burning inner necessity.

In the first place, this notebook imparts an element of discipline to my life—one of the few elements of positive discipline in my life. Climent asked me one day in the library, "If you had money, would you still feel the need to write?"

I answered immediately, without hesitation: "Of course, I would. I might write even more."

No doubt about it: It is dismal to be poor. The things of this life are very pleasant. Everything invites you to partake, and ladies are—sometimes—magnificent. When one is poor, one can only look at these things from afar because we poor have no purchasing power. I suppose that in old age this lack of purchasing power makes no difference. In one's youth, however, poverty is tragic because a lack of money intensifies one's lust for life. The less money one has, the more life stimulates desire. Unfulfilled desire makes one believe that human life is full of mysteries, of treasures that beckon with a magical, hedonistic allure. Thus one ought to have money in one's youth, mainly to establish, by virtue of enjoying them to saturation, that human life contains no mysteries and that the allures of hedonism are stuff and nonsense—nearly. That's why I, personally, would like to have money: to be able to walk past a restaurant, a lady, or a shopwindow and remain aloof. That way I would avoid the huge tracts of time wasted and the pain inflicted when life becomes a constant thirsting after temptation. In a word, I could write more.

Consequently, given my youth has been imperiled by poverty, I am grateful for any activity that imposes discipline. This notebook is one such activity because its childish joys fill my time. I am unable to set aside its pages and on the days when I don't write—because I feel uninspired—I feel most upset.

The overall tone of my notebook is critical and, given the prevailing mentality, possibly even subversive. I don't regret it. To improve anything whatsoever, one must first analyze and describe. No self-interest binds me to the establishment in this country—either from the position they occupy in the present or from the one they will fill tomorrow, as mere memories. This notebook responds to my need to take a stand in relation to my times. If Taine's theory were true in all its extremes, I should be a mere product of my time. Environmental determinism works with writers who surrender to the current. I sail against the corruption brought by that current. I am not a product of my time; I am a product against my time.

These pages help me to learn to write. Not to learn to write well but simply to learn to write. They imply a huge, continuous effort, which goes unrewarded but is innocent.

23 June. Xènius has now come out in summer fashion and occasionally drops in on the circle. He creates a stir: He wears a light, cream-colored jacket; gray trousers with a leather belt and waist strap and a collar and tie; he has changed his bowler for a boater, which he wears tipped ever so slightly over his ear. His summer outfit makes him look fatter; his double chin, neck, and rear take on a notable solidity. Rather than being sinuous, his body now begins to seem modulated—modulated by the bass notes of a cello.

Xènius has seated himself in a wicker armchair and adopted a mysterious, sibylline air. He has come resolutely determined not to say a single word. Pujols asks him questions in the sweetest, most cheerful manner he knows. He extracts no response. Borralleras looks at him askance. Jardí follows suit. I do as well. Borralleras winks at me: He is suggesting, I imagine, that the situation has reached its climax and the pantarchy's anarcho-syndicalist crisis has entered a possibly decisive phase.

This individual has shocked his contemporaries far too often.

One of the greatest mistakes I ever made was to become personally acquainted with Xènius. The ideal for our generation when it was beginning to make its presence felt would have been to be acquainted with a Xènius already transformed into a classic, surrounded by all the attributes of fame, his life turned into a legend—a Xènius, namely, who had died dozens of years before we appeared on this earth. In fact, everything is interchangeable: If one must live, it makes no difference whether one lives yesterday, today, or tomorrow. That solution would have spared us the torture of being his contemporary, and perhaps spared him even more. This man will have been fated never to establish contact with his contemporaries; on the other hand, I think he will be worshipped by future generations. I would have preferred to belong to that future.

If only I could have avoided meeting him, if only I could have stayed far away from him—say, the distance from Barcelona to Palafrugell—he'd have lodged in my memory with a fascinating aura. He'd have represented *the* great writer, the distinguished orator in French, before Henri Poincaré: the prompter of intellectual concerns; the man with an immense culture; the person who restored education and good taste in the country. Xènius has unique qualities that provoke adoration in all those who don't know him. I know him and still like so many of the things he stands for! I am hugely indebted to him! Nevertheless, it is true that he doesn't have the characteristics that make him a contemporary—you can only stomach him from a distance, appreciative of the potential that remoteness creates. There is a lack of consistency between his life, his appearance in society, and the aims of his teaching. Young people rarely accept such a lack of consistency.

He is very affected. He doesn't act in a simple, straightforward way. He continually strains to be seen as exceptional, different from others, not so much in the things that distinguish him naturally but in the most trifling aspects of life. He is an individual who has spent his lifetime preaching classical values, normality, continuity, the superiority of the categorical over the anecdotal—yet he is in fact an entirely anecdotal, eccentric, whimsical, extravagant, and romantic figure. He constantly seeks to highlight himself. He speaks in italics. He writes—a man who writes so well!—in a stiff, symbolic, priestly mode. He wouldn't know how to ask naturally for a couple of eggs. He is a man increasingly dominated by his mask—a mask that appears to be porous but is fiendishly hermetic.

The features of this mask are its intense charm, its concentrated sugary sweetness; a syrupy, morbid, bland quality that can verge on the pornographic. All this splendid candy probably conceals an inner temperament that is completely unstable and insecure, along with highly charged violence, bitterness, and contempt. Candy calls out for adulation; if adulation isn't forthcoming, then violence inevitably ensues. That is why Xènius's stream of sweetness transports me to a virgin jungle. Particular movements of his mind—and his body—are slowly, silently, tropically lubricious. That doesn't mean it isn't gratifying, that the presence of Xènius doesn't provoke pleasure, bordering on ecstasy, in certain sensibilities. I personally find his lowered eyes and sleepwalking rituals less appealing, precisely because he promised us something quite different. What ever became of the clean, pure lines of his much vaunted classicism of the golden mean? Or of Don Eugeni's eighteenth century? He is such an unbearable playactor! When the man has spent his entire life exploiting the romantic-classical antithesis and stigmatizing romanticism as the sewer of all human error and abjection, it strikes one as rather pathetic that the supreme legislator in such matters should take romantic virtuosity to such an extreme that the skeletal *racconti* of Puccini's and Debussy's massaging of the senses, etcetera, pale in significance. That wasn't the deal.

Xènius writes sibylline, undulating prose, with a tendency toward a civic, quasi-intellectual liturgy. But didn't we agree to combat everything that comes from the East? Didn't we agree to wage systematic war on the podium? Through Xènius, we learned about Nietzsche and the sense of individual, incorruptible independence that some ancient philosophers gave to their lives. We think of this pride as the Magna Carta of the lay, civic spirit. So if words mean anything at all, what kind of purifying, lay classicism is behind his tendency to inflate, embellish, puff up, mystify, and pontificate? His is a case that goes beyond my poor powers of comprehension. His is the case of a man who has suffered huge disappointment in life.

Don Eugeni's latest theory is that he owes his country nothing, that the fact of his birth in a specific landscape is a completely fortuitous phenomenon—that, at the end of the day, it is the country that is indebted to him. (Josep M. Junoy is of the same opinion, but his case is less dangerous than Xènius's.) He simply exacerbates everything we have noted; his is the most vulgar form of individualism, romantic exceptionalism taken to its worst extremes, to the frontiers of the worst excess.

When I was twenty, at an age when remoteness led me to confuse intelligentsia and intelligence, I might still have managed to separate a distinguished work from its author. Now I am twenty-two and I find it completely impossible.

25 June. I have never been one to roam the suburbs of Sants and Hostafrancs. Though I have lived in Barcelona for five years, I have never been up to Tibidabo. I am not familiar with Pedralbes, Sarrià, or Horta. I have made brief forays to Sant Gervasi and I have reached the first bulwarks of Vallcarca in the district of Gràcia. On the other hand, I am familiar with the mountain of Montjuïc, particularly around the castle and the slope facing the sea, and the suburbs to the east: Sant Andreu, El Clot, and El Poblenou.

I have read a limited amount of literature from the suburbs. It is rather monotonous: variations on a tragic theme. Dickens has many suburban pages. My view is that Barcelona's outskirts aren't at all tragic. They are dismal, not tragic. I find some streets in the fifth district much more irredeemable than the city periphery. The gray mediocrity of these outskirts is what strikes one.

I spent a large part of this afternoon and evening meandering along the streets of El Clot and El Poblenou. Meandering aimlessly, randomly. Now that it is summer, poverty, in short sleeves, seems warmer and more reasonable.

The Barcelona suburbs are composed of low-built housing. They provide a horizontal perspective. But suddenly a tall, isolated new house looms above the expanse of low construction, in an impressive display of naked verticality. It is a premature building, a trailblazer, and an excrescence that didn't follow the normal process of growth. One would think the horizontal expansion of a suburb should be accompanied by vertical growth: from single-story, to two, then four floors, etcetera. But it's nothing of the sort. The development spreads out in individual units and can lurch suddenly from one to seven floors. In my view these houses with their naked, skinny, skimpy walls are the grimmest feature of the suburbs, and this is perhaps because they are outlandish and anticipate how unappealing they will be when finally connected to the city.

From the outside, these houses always seem new. The tiles on their side walls are blood-colored. They have been constructed according to current taste. But when you examine the detail at close range, you see how these houses tend to be the most forlorn and dilapidated in the area. They seem to have aged prematurely. They have grimy, filthy, or broken windows, with pages of newsprint held in place by glue. The washing hanging over balconies, dirty stairs, dripping walls, poverty crawling up to each floor—a sorry sight. These houses seemed marked by the stigma of subversion in the dark twilights of winter. In summer, human life spills from doors and balconies. When it is windy and sunny, the clothing that flutters on the terraces is the single cheerful element.

Barcelona is surrounded by the soft outlines of small mountains and hills with a thin scattering of trees. The contours of the hills are sporadically adorned by the silhouettes of spindly, rickety pine trees that, against the light, occasionally look like delirious shapes—like a herd of phantom horses flying over barren earth. These miserable trees on the outskirts of Barcelona are hardly one of the most pleasant sights the city has to offer. In my imagination the silhouettes of these gloomy, frantic pine trees always accompany the tall, sad, isolated houses on the city outskirts.

28 June. I meander for hours down the streets in the slums of Barcelona's fifth district. A hot night. Like so many, I leave home intending to give myself up to pleasure. However, after walking the streets for a while, I see only poverty, filth, and suffering. The stench is stifling. For every pleasant person you see, you must withstand the presence of a thousand monsters—yours truly included, obviously. The liquids on offer in the taverns, the food they serve up, are disgusting. The brothels are unbelievably sordid. People are bitter, tense, and ready to lash out. It is depressing to see the extent to which they have managed to transform this world into the quintessence of all that is unpleasant. It is impossible to imagine experiencing any pleasure at all if you don't have loads of money and a lively imagination to help you over the hurdles that always seem to present themselves. In this country, everything conspires on behalf of the sordid. Woe to the person who tries to act in the Grecian manner!

After an hour of roaming the streets, all my hopes of pleasure have disappeared into an emotional morass dominated by self-pitying melancholy. If it weren't for short bouts of intoxication and a blind obsession with your instincts, the idea that you could make the slightest contact with this world is inconceivable. You left home with a few pagan expectations and within a couple of hours have become a Christian who champions asceticism. It would be of interest to chart the parallel transformation in the human body. You left home feeling quite cocky and slightly arrogant, but the inner process now deflates your body, depresses and bends it low, empties it out, and you finally see yourself as a punctured flat tire. You end up dragging your feet along the sidewalks, head sunk between your shoulders, eyeing things with anguish and dread, registering only the thick veil of sadness that drapes them.

Perhaps I am simply too sensitive when it comes to these morbid attractions—which seem somewhat infantile once I am back in plaça de Catalunya. But I can do nothing to alter it. I sometimes think that if I dressed more smartly and less shabbily, it would give me a sharper, colder outlook on life. I should order a good suit, made to measure by a good tailor. All the suits I have ever worn have been like charitable gifts, clothes passed on to me, even though my family has paid religiously for each garment. If I ever *had* worn a suit that had been passed on, it would have hung on me just like one that had been paid for, which is rather a sad thought. I shouldn't wear trousers dotted with cigarette burns. I should wear suspenders. I have only once worn suspenders—on the day I received my first Communion. Why? Everyone who knows me must have noticed my trousers are always too loose. It is a horrible faux pas. I should own a watch. That would spare me from anguishing over the time and arriving absurdly early. I should own an umbrella, a mackintosh, half a dozen shirts, three or four ties. I should shave daily. One day Sr. Totusaus, the Athenaeum barber, asked me, "Where do you have your hair cut, Sr. Pla?" How embarrassing, for God's sake! Luckily Sr. Totusaus spoke softly and nobody overheard. When I think of the delightful charm, the soft black sheen of Mossèn Riber when he leaves the barber's! I should have my shoes cleaned—at least on alternate days! And what about my hats! They are cheap hats on the whole, unfashionable hats, I imagine, and they seem old after I've worn them two or three days.

I should see to my nails, have them trimmed and polished from time to time, and use a little scent. Everybody else does—a light touch. This "light touch" unleashes uncontrollable mirth. But could anyone imagine me prostrate in a barber's chair? When Sr. Totusaus invites me in, I tell him I don't have time. That's simply an excuse. The very idea disgusts me. I should make the supreme sacrifice. But the fact is that my greatest defect—in terms of the attitudes in our country—is that I am no exhibitionist. I have the lowest opinion of myself. I don't like myself at all. I think I could commit the most abject blunder, the most wretched error at any moment. I have great doubts as to my inner moral drives. My defenses—especially those that derive from vanity and self-esteem—are almost nonexistent. I may be a shallow fellow, but I am no braggart. And mighty shallow at that. A day doesn't go by when I don't produce the requisite lies, don't voice the requisite gratuitous platitudes—checks that will bounce—don't talk frivolously or surpass myself in whimsy. There are people who can justify their own lies. They think everything they do is absolutely necessary. Lucky them! I lie and am very conscious of the fact. It is obvious from my face. I can't pretend; I haven't the necessary self-confidence. And it is precisely because I have no self-confidence that others have no confidence in me. I never succeed in inspiring confidence and that is the truth. When friends of mine have applied their intellect and scrutinized me, they have made a cruel diagnosis. Màrius Aguilar once wrote that I am a sort of Mediterranean Russian. And that is very sad coming from a Latin, Cyranoish spirit like him! Josep Maria de Sagarra says—and has said this to my face—that I am a fake. I don't know how Dr. Borralleras regards me. He looks at me, looks at me again and again, and I suspect can make neither head nor tail of what he sees. Well, I don't want to think that I am right or above everyone else. I am not equipped to be a hero. But I am sure of one thing: It is absolutely vital I do something about my appearance—at least wear a new suit.

1 July. I have started at *Las Noticias* on a recommendation from Dr.

Borralleras to Sr. Miró i Folguera. Journalism. A strange departure. It was the only possible solution after that last conversation with my father.

5 July. For the past few days, when the sun began setting, the circle has met in the garden under the palm trees. Apparently it happens every year.

The shift to the open air—open air surrounded by high walls—has its drawbacks, given the mentality that predominates in our conversations. Discretion is vital in the garden: One cannot talk as forcefully, since someone could always be eavesdropping—undesirable interference from the outside. So at this time of year the club loses its vigor; a hint of tedium is apparent. Besides, in the summer people seem different. When they aren't fully dressed, they lose something.

Francesc Labarta likes to argue and debate more than anyone else I know. He is amazingly vigorous. He is an early-afternoon participant. As soon as he arrives, he gulps down his coffee, as if he were in a hurry, and after the last drop of coffee orders a large alcoholic concoction such as students drink, which he sips to curb his aggressiveness. Once he has taken his "chaser" to use his words—Labarta employs, thankfully, the language of Barcelona artisans—he starts debating. When he debates, he twists his mouth, his voice cracks, and his face is more like a two- or three-year-old photo of a male face than a real one—a photograph of a face that is there but has already started to fade. His favorite topic is art, on which he can hold forth almost indefinitely. You can understand why the young artists in the Evolutionist group find him so fascinating—though I have to admit I often find him difficult to fathom, no doubt because of my ignorance rather than his lack of method. Borralleras, Carles the painter, and Pujols give him a wall to bounce off, by more or less arguing against him. Then he is in his element. However, if he finds the conversation lackluster and uninspired, he doesn't abandon his usual vigor, he simply opts for a somewhat monotonous monologue that flows endlessly all the same. With the change in the panorama that summer brings, Labarta says less. This saddens him and bewilders the circle; they can't decide whether a weight has been lifted from his shoulders or he is missing an organ that has been extracted with a scalpel.

The end of the opera season catapults Borralleras and Albinyana into the limbo of boredom. Albinyana is one of the thinnest men in the circle, one of the most pale and skeletal, impoverished and ascetic. If people's bellies are generally visible because they protrude, in a more or less distinct curve, Albinyana's belly curves inwards, making his body look bent, as if he were almost doubled over.

There are magnificent representatives of every tendency in these conversations. There are stout, succulent specimens like Dr. Dalí, Eugeni d'Ors, Josep Maria de Sagarra, and mere shards like Josep Maria Albinyana, Carles Soldevila, and Lau Duran Reynals. In the last issue of the *NRF*, André Gide, no doubt in a bad-tempered moment, wrote: "It seems that stout men tend to putrefy and skinny men to ossify. It is quite unavoidable."

Albinyana has a large nose, elongated arms and hands, and a broad expanse of earlobe. He is very rich and cultured. He is a man—like many others in this country—who couldn't enter the family firm, and he has become a wholehearted, systematic adept of these conversations. He owns lots of books (the whole of modern French literature); he has a mania for music; he has started to collect paintings—Sunyer has painted his portrait; Josep Carner has dedicated sonnets to him. If the country wanted to function properly, it would require three or four hundred Albinyanas.

He belongs to the most reactionary group in the circle, that is, he is very close to Enric Jardí. His bedside daily read is *L'Action Française*. He reacts violently to the tragic situation the country finds itself in— overrun by bands of gunmen. I heard him say, "Fortunately, our discovery of Maurras allows us conservatives to walk the streets holding our heads high."

However, if it weren't for these current acts of frenzy and their repercussions, I don't think Albinyana would be interested at all in politics. His natural state in these conversations is one of deepest unresponsiveness. He leans back comfortably in an armchair with a huge Hoyo de Monterrey between his lips, nose slightly on the slant, always shivering a little, and stares into the distance, sometimes humming a few phrases from Debussy—*Pelléas et Mélisande* is his favorite piece of music—while listening vaguely to what people are saying around him. Even so, the slightest reference to music—if only the statement of a mere cliché—has the virtue of swiftly bringing him back to life. All his feelings bubble to the surface. If the conversation enthuses him, he becomes uncontrollably nervous. As is often the case with music buffs, he tends to become quite aggressive. He cannot conceive that someone might like a piece he hates. He soon assumes a scornful, unpleasant tone in debate. His body reacts with all manner of ticks—nerves that erupt on their own account, unleashed from the pressure of repeated constraint. He soon loses control of what he is saying. His imagination gallops at a swifter pace than the stream of words he is uttering. And that leads to incoherence, disconnected words he spits out as if on the rebound, and his body begins to shake violently: hands, arms, head, eyes, shoulders, legs, and everything else. It seems as if he is struggling against an invisible force. It is an amazing spectacle because it always comes as a surprise. Although nobody can ever know what anyone's inner life might be like, one *can* interpret Albinyana from what he seems to be like on the outside: a suspicious, pusillanimous, shy man, full of intellectual prejudices, possibly deeply embittered, and possibly emotionally resentful; a man overwhelmed by the tedium of life who has found in music an escape from the sorrows of this world. Consequently, issues of reality are negligible as far as he is concerned, while anything related to the spirit of music is vitally important.

Camps sums it up like this: "You can insult him as much as you like and he will smile most pleasantly; you can argue against Debussy with him and you give thanks to God if he doesn't wipe the floor with you."

Borralleras also lives within that spirit of music—now enriched by his reading of Marcel Proust, which is essentially a musical reading because of the effort involved in transforming the past (memory) into reality, into the present. Life also seems to weigh heavily upon Borralleras. But his sensibility doesn't seem so susceptible. On the outside at least he seems to be more measured. However, I wouldn't want to be conclusive about it or to risk a prognosis ...

Now that Barcelona is without music, these two wander like souls in limbo. They made one last attempt: They went to listen to some opera or other in a theater in Gràcia (I can't remember which) that organizes a short season every year at this time. But I notice how much they smile and latch on to picturesque anecdotes when they come back. When they don't return from a concert as if they'd been given a battering, it means the music wasn't up to scratch. Borralleras talks of leaving the city, of going to Prats de Lluçanés.

"I have no choice," he says. "I must be off on my summer holidays. There is nothing happening here."

11 July. Library.

Josep Maria Junoy encourages me to read Charles-Louis Philippe, *Le Père Perdrix* in particular. Although this writer died some years ago, he talks about him as if he were still alive. That gives me some idea of how interesting he finds him.

Ever since Junoy entered a crisis over his Catholicism he can't bear the sight of anything that smells of French, from near or far—not even in a painting. He has peremptorily presented me with the Mercure de France edition of Rimbaud's poetry with Paul Claudel's famous prologue.

"Here you are," he said. "I find this book loathsome. It is quite amazing how people in this country are driven to simplify at times. It is an unbridled elemental, hysterical tendency to react fanatically."

All the same, leopards never change their spots ... Josep Maria Junoy has been a simplifier in his time, though I suspect we are only at the beginning and that it will get worse. He is entering a crisis over France and reacts in the way he likes to speak of many things here—hotels, for example: how they are generally bad; one can only rarely find a good one. He detests France and anything French—but now recommends I read Charles-Louis Philippe.

"What kind of author is he?" I ask.

"He is your kind of author: country life, landscape, and people."

"Is he a naturalist? I confess I sometimes find homegrown naturalists rather tiresome."

"He is light, airy, incisive, synthetic, realist. You will recall that sentence of his: 'Illnesses are voyages for the poor.'"

"That's really quite good."

He then encourages me to read something else: *César Capéran: ou la Tradition* by Louis Codet. He asks me for a short note about this book, for a magazine he is bringing out or wants to. Then he departs, a sprig of mint in his mouth, his boater tilted slightly over his ear, and a sheaf of papers under his arm.

Ricard Permanyer is a lad who spends long hours in the library; he is sometimes there early in the morning or very late at night. He is tall, thin, pale, fair, and wears a dark, shiny-elbowed jacket. His books often don't fit on his desk and he has to use an extra chair. I rarely see him speak to anyone and he is one of the few literary acquaintances of mine who is not gregarious. Nor does he seem in a great hurry to publish. I would like Permanyer much more if he hadn't told me one day, with his characteristic energy, "I'd like to impregnate my poetry with all that is puerile, innocent, and childish."

While he was saying this, I was thinking, "I'd like to impregnate my prose with all that is sly and malicious."

Alfons Maseres looks tired and weary, his back slightly bent, his arms seeming to dangle loose; when he carries his walking stick under his armpit, he doesn't hold it tight and it tends to slip down; when he stops to talk to someone, he rests his stick on the ground, leans on the handle with both hands, and his legs seem to give way. His voice is faint, his smile sad and bewildered. All this may be the result of the intellectual work Maseres does, which is paid like piecework.

In *City of God*, Saint Augustine establishes a hierarchy in human labor. He places intellectual labor at the top; then agriculture, because of the way it relates to God's work; then the labor of artisans; trade comes last, for reasons that are obvious enough. Could Saint

Augustine ever have imagined intellectual labor might be paid for as piecework?

Most likely I'll be paid for my intellectual labors as if they were piecework too. I see that most clearly—intuitively. The sight of Alfons Maseres is most depressing.

13 July. Roulette.

Obviously I'm not a member of the Arts Circle, but a large number of friends from the Athenaeum go there to play roulette. I sometimes spend a while with one or another of these friends in the gambling room.

When you are practically broke, you start to think that the idea of winning the jackpot at roulette is a good one. I could soon become addicted. The only drawback is that when I enter the gambling room I am practically in the same state as my friends when they leave the place: skint as a brick.

On the rare occasions when I've tried my hand, I soon understood I had little aptitude for a life of vice. I had no presence, no flair, no spark. I can't even take it seriously. Borralleras gambles as if he were indifferent, in a phantom faraway place. Sagarra watches the ball move with an extra double chin. Canals the painter nibbles his mustache nervously. Labarta, Casanovas, Nogués, Carles, Padilla, and the Soto brothers are also roulette adepts and take it seriously—Carles less so than the others. They are individuals who stand out in a gambling room.

Now, probably because of my lack of awareness, I think I have a certain advantage over my friends. I think that playing and losing are two things that are closely related. In contrast they believe that playing and losing is a nasty trick deliberately played on them by Providence. If they leave the room on a winning streak, you can read it on their faces and they swagger unpleasantly. If they leave after losing, they look as if they've been given a beating—like dogs searching for a quiet, remote spot away from the world. In my view they allow themselves to be overly influenced by the unwarranted powers they grant themselves. Naturally I would like to win, but I find that losing —and I always lose—is so much a part of the nature of things it isn't worth worrying over for a moment. I leave the room having almost forgotten what just happened inside—and feel incredibly hungry.

I sometimes suspect that gambling would have no appeal for people who aren't egotists or extremely conceited.

Don Francesc Pujols, who attends the Arts Circle and the gambling room, is not fond of roulette. Today he remarked, "I could play because I have something to lose. My fifty pesetas a day arrive, come rain or snow. But losing to a bunch of croupiers would be far too asinine."

The ambience at the Arts Circle, a group of artists aspiring to be merchants and merchants trying to be artists, is—while we're at it—a complete jumble.

We continued to read Rohde's *Psyche* over the last few days; fortunately, Pujols's conjunctivitis had improved. Despite the hours we spent reading, I can't say that Pujols let his mask drop for a single moment. Sometimes when he attempts to show himself in a different light, his capacity for self-denigration verges on the fatuous. I find him tiresome.

"Can I ask you something, Sr. Pujols?" I asked him today.

"Do, please feel free."

"Could you tell me why you are so keen to appear other than you really are?"

"I don't really follow you, quite frankly."

"Could you please tell me why you're so keen for me to think you are a fool?"

"Not true, my dear Pla! I treasure nothing like a friend. I appear before you as innocently as if I had been born yesterday."

"And if I refused to take you at face value, what would be the up-shot then?"

"Don't take it so to heart, I beg you!"

"At times I find you frankly tiresome."

"Well, I find you simply delightful."

He uttered that last sentence as if he were performing in a comedy. One has to smile. One is left disarmed—and totally in the dark, as at the start of a conversation. Pujols slithers like an eel, constantly looking for that witty remark, ready to perform any role in the book to avoid saying what he really thinks.

"And what do we make of this book we are reading? What is your opinion?" I ask him after a pause.

"It's a plate of boiled rice. And just imagine, we are reading it in French! If we'd been reading it in our mother tongue, we'd have lost our way a long time ago. Nonetheless, this professor seems a very good person and writes very well; he writes in a gossip-column style, as you do in *Las Noticias*."

15 July. An extremely pale, upset Quim staggered into the club today. He came in gripping his hat tight, looking dizzy, sweat streaming down his forehead. The old coffee merchant, Costa, came after him, depressed, as if he were in mourning. For a moment our friend seemed to sway as if about to faint. Costa held his arms out to shore him up. Quim finally made it to his usual seat where he flopped down in a state of exhaustion.

Quim's appearance shocked the circle and the news spread quickly around the building. People wanted to know what had happened. We made all manner of lengthy conjectures without reaching any conclusions. It was impossible to ask him anything while his head lolled on the back of his chair, more dead than alive, semiconscious. So we whispered at length and made the least noise possible, as if we were in a sick man's bedroom.

In any case, once Dr. Dalí had loosened Quim's trouser belt slightly, removed his tie, and given him a few sips of cognac, Quim seemed to revive. But it was a good hour before he was in a position to speak. Quim has extremely talkative days and others when he is at a loss for words. I suspect today belonged to the latter category. If he said anything it was because everybody around him was very curious. Obviously his story was rather incoherent because of the state he was in.

In a quite arbitrary, spontaneous fashion, Quim had found himself caught up in the middle of a most alarming occurrence—although there have been dozens in Barcelona since Sr. Barret the manufacturer was murdered at the height of the First World War. This city is unreal. There are so many incidents that people read the news of attacks on individuals as if they were glancing at theater gossip; it is enough to drive you crazy.

Quim related the episode as follows: "I left home, as I do every day, ready to come to the Athenaeum. Today I decided to take carrer del Duc de la Victòria to reach Canuda. It isn't my usual route but I decided to take it today. After lunch Duc de la Victòria isn't usually very busy. I walked along the pavement, the pavement on the left, from carrer de la Portaferrissa, in the shade. A small, chubby gentleman was walking slowly along, seven or eight paces in front of me. From the back, this gentleman looked like a shopkeeper. Suddenly I thought I heard a strange noise, very close. I saw an object rebound off the wall in front of me, barely half a meter from that gentleman's back, taking out a chunk of limestone. It was a bullet hitting hard. The shot had come from behind me, because everything looked normal in my field of vision (the section of the street that comes out on Canuda). The second I turned my head to see what was happening, I saw the citizen in front (who had just registered how close the bullet had come) break into a run with his hands over his head. The interlude between the impact of the bullet and his breaking into a run was so short, and the fact he hadn't looked around was so surprising, that I concluded the man was one 'in danger,' a man who had received death threats. Well, naturally, he didn't run very far, because he ducked into a doorway, as quick as a hunted animal. The moment he stepped inside a shower of bullets rained down on the entrance. The man's disappearing back and the crackle of bullets created a scene of dramatic, rapid action."

"So you found yourself," said Jardí, "between the gunmen and the man they were attacking."

"Right in the middle. The gunmen were behind me and I thought they were firing from the other curb. I couldn't see them. When the fugitive dove into the entrance I thought he must have escaped and I looked around. I saw a car with its engine running and two young-looking men climbing into it. The car calmly reversed and drove off up Portaferrisa. Meanwhile, the people coming from carrer de la Canuda huddled together. You can imagine what an unpleasant scare it was."

"Well, you know," said Jardí, beside himself, "this is intolerable! Soon you won't be able to step out of your house. We should all be ashamed of ourselves!"

"Yes, sir…I totally agree. But the fact is people exist who are prepared to defend these monstrous acts…and defend them in the press!" shouted Solé de Sojo, turning purple with rage, his whole body shaking as if he were about to have a fit.

Solé had only just uttered the words we have transcribed when we saw him stand up, nervously do up his jacket button, grab the neck of the bottle on the nearest table, and head toward Màrius Aguilar, who was sitting three or four armchairs away. Aguilar, who had watched him move, also stood up and grabbed a bottle of water. When they were face-to-face they raised their respective bottles simultaneously to hit each other on the head, but too many people intervened for either to actually strike. Solé's bottle was empty; Aguilar's was half full. When he went to strike Solé, his bottle poured its contents over the skull of the first person to come to separate them: the head of Antoni Homar.

Given the bodies separating them, the adversaries were forced to calm down. They went back to their normal seats. Despite the grotesque end to the scene, the circle was reduced to silence, dumbstruck. In the midst of this strange silence, Quim stood up, took his hat, and left. Aguilar also left shortly afterward.

I heard it said later that Solé had acted in the manner he did because he had glimpsed a smile on Aguilar's face while he was speaking.

My God, what a situation exists in this country, in Barcelona! It isn't a revolutionary situation; no revolution is being called for. I don't think anyone believes the foundations of present-day society are threatened. The bourgeoisie isn't afraid of revolution and the gunmen have never thought they were carrying through any kind of revolution. It is just that anarchists have taken possession of the streets and are brandishing pistols. Their presence is so visible, so defiant, that many people find this situation entirely natural. We cannot seem to escape this impasse: tyranny or anarchy. It is a situation that is not easily understood even by people like us who are eyewitnesses to the events as they unfold.

16 July. I joined the editorial staff of *La Publicidad* (the evening edition) after the sacking announced yesterday by Sr. Miró, on behalf of Sr. Barco, the director of *Las Noticias*. Professional journalism. There was no alternative—it was inevitable. How sad. Being a journalist in this country amounts to very little indeed—if only it amounted to that! But there's not much we can do about it . . . that's how it is . . .

19 July. Vicenç Solé de Sojo.

The poet Vicenç Solé de Sojo, a relative of Anguera de Sojo, the famous expert in canon law, and of a sanctimonious old woman on her path to sanctification, works as a clerk in the office of Sr. Anastasio, who specializes in maritime law. He is a very important member of the circle. He is one of the first to arrive after lunch. He is immensely loyal to Borralleras. He really admires Camps. He is not one of the most emotional participants. He is a rather tolerant, liberal man. He is famous for his politeness. His run-in the other day with Aguilar is more a symptom of the general situation in the country than of his character.

From the outside he looks swanky, but his swankiness is only apparent and is involuntary. There's not a more discreet, pleasant person in the whole of Barcelona. His head and face are a tiny oval shape; his chest and stomach (two things that don't fit together) a large oval shape. Seen as a whole, he looks like a pumpkin on legs and, as he walks rather stiffly, like all shortsighted people, he does a good impression of a radish. He dresses in superb English style and his hair is always impeccably combed and greased. His eye-catching clothes would be even more so if he weren't so plump. When he was poorer than he is now, I saw him wear wonderful white-coffee-colored, embroidered waistcoats in the spring and waistcoats made of dark, sumptuous red polka-dotted cloth in the autumn—as well as black silk sashes and a gold coin on a chain. In the winter he wears genuine Bond Street, oxblood foulards over the blue velvet collar of his blue overcoat. And the most wonderful bowlers! People say that Xammar (a renowned connoisseur) covets them. He smokes a (Dunhill) pipe and the smoke it produces is delectable. Excellent English tobacco. Pompeu Fabra and Solé de Sojo are the only people I know who have definitively liberated themselves from dependence on the wretched, primitive tobacco that is produced nationally. Pipe in mouth, his lip moistens and he starts slurring his *s*'s into *sh*'s.

Pujols once summed him up in a quip that has stuck: "Poor Solé is a gentleman, but his face lets him down."

When you scrutinize him, Solé seems an assortment of odd elements. His head and face form a piece that doesn't seem to suit his body. It is quite extraordinary; it's as if his head—or his body—didn't belong to him and belonged to somebody else, as if they were disconnected. One gets used to it in the end, but for a time you harbor the feeling that Solé will most likely come to the circle wearing another head, a head he perhaps hides away in his wardrobe.

His face is solemnly oval: lots of flab and big cheeks. It is a face characterized by a lack of proportion in its component parts. The top part and flabby bottom are out of proportion. His nose, eyes, and forehead occupy a much smaller space than the bottom part of the oval: as if the top suffered from having to tolerate his huge rolls of flab. His neck is short and rather compressed.

9 August. Girona. Military service. I did my military service in Girona, in the Fifty-fifth Asian Infantry Regiment garrisoned in that city. I was part of the call-up quota but exempt from the draw—the horrific realities of the current situation of inequality. Twenty days of military service. All the same they say the situation has improved. In my father's day, you could pay your way out and only the poorest of the poor actually served.

The first days in the barracks were drawn out and insufferable.

We had to be in the company quarters at six in the morning. Rubbing his eyes, his trouser belt hanging down, shirt and army jacket open, exposing a hairy chest, a drowsy corporal read the roll call, screaming like a madman. Nobody of rank would appear until eleven, but you couldn't sneak off.

The so-called company quarters was situated in an extremely long passageway, with a four- or five-meter-wide creaking beam ceiling that was dimly lit night and day by three dirty bulbs that occasionally flickered and sprouted spikes like illuminated sea urchins. It was a gloomy atmosphere, rather dramatic, though shabby. The St. Dominic's barracks is in the upper reaches of Girona and occupies a bend in the northeastern wall. It is a former Dominican convent—Domini Canes (Dogs of God)—which was sold off and is now slowly falling apart and being patched up. The church is thirteenth-century, built by the preaching fathers, and is Girona's oldest Gothic temple. Today its walls are covered in filthy grime, thick layers of dust, and the place serves as a dormitory for soldiers.

Originally the monastery had a Romanesque cloister that was destroyed at the time of the war against Napoleon. In the coldest, most sober Gothic style, the present building strikes a good balance, with arches decorated with trefoils, supported by columns with carved capitals that rest on a stone base that runs around its four sides and is the central part of the barracks. There is a well in the middle, ruins to the right, prison cells to the left, and the center acts as a refectory. On Sundays regimental mass is held here.

At a later date, a second floor was built over this cloister with semicircular arches, on slightly swollen columns, and it is a real pigsty. The regimental band and offices are lodged on this floor. When they rehearse, the whine of wind instruments, the strident, metal din of bugles and visceral gurgles of oboes reach as far as the courtyard. The current music master was Maestro Juncà, who had written a lot of sardanas, a small dun-colored man who wore blue spectacles and seemed exhausted. In the interludes between the tunes, a typewriter clattered like a partridge pecking the bars of its cage.

The company I belonged to occupied the second floor of the west wing of the barracks. The beds were lined up alongside the wall. Short black poles extended from the wall above each bed for the soldier beneath to hang his plate, trousers, and cartridge belts. These poles were also what supported each individual wardrobe. The latter were wooden cupboards draped with a flag covered in lances, chains, lions, and castles. Two shocks of rifles stood at each end of the passageway.

We spent our free time lying on our beds, smoking, chatting quietly, or reading five- or ten-cent novels—the only literature that wasn't frowned upon. There were lots of bedbugs, but as nobody did anything about them, we could study their movements at our leisure, because the insects enjoyed complete freedom. I have never found the observation of bedbugs to be at all exciting, so I would sometimes go and stand by the barred windows that opened every fifteen yards opposite the line of beds.

From these windows you could see the dome of the cathedral belfry, the hallucinating decapitated angel, a few housetops, a collection of roofs, terraces, balconies, chimneys, and yellowish to purple walls. To the north you could see a stretch of marrow-colored city wall. This stretch of wall was a kind of path running between stones, grass growing out of the walls, and bracken. Every afternoon, between two and three o'clock, a fat, pink priest walked that way, smoking a pipe. A flaccid, fat black-and-white dog always followed the priest, wagging its tail affectedly.

That collection of stones had a life of its own. In the morning two or three women appeared on their balconies and shook the dust off their blankets. At nine, a tall, thin, fair girl in mourning clothes came out onto a terrace strewn with pots and languishing flowers and watered her tiny garden with a can. From time to time, someone who stayed out of sight closed a window and the sun's rays hit the panes of glass to create a mother-of-pearl glow. One of these windows was usually open and you could see a painting of a crucifixion that the breeze sometimes seemed to move. Later, the brightest shape on the black background of the painting seemed like a globule of light suspended in the room's sad, shadowy air.

There were damp, dirty, abandoned terraces. You could see the rubble from a pigeon fancier's loft on one. Another sported a vine, some carnations in brass pots, and a discreet air of respectable poverty. Others were full of old junk. Cats and dogs roamed these heights. I remember two puppies playing and fighting, frolicking and acting as if they were biting each other for hours on end. Cats reached the most unlikely places, as if they'd thought it all through.

All these scenes loomed large under the pale gray Girona sky. They were our entertainment in empty, idle time in the barracks.

The sergeant would arrive at eleven, book under arm. This fellow, Castellà by name, was Catalan and wanted us to think he was Aragonese. He was in his mid-thirties, small, fair, with a bumpy narrow forehead, dull sallow eyes, trembling thin lips, and a drooping handlebar mustache. He was very conscious of his appearance, wore high heels, and walked stiffly, leaning his head slightly backwards. He had a magnificent bass voice, splendid for giving orders that contrasted with the timorous tone he adopted with his superiors. When his officers reprimanded him, his face turned deathly pale, and, in contrast, when he could stand proud, he grew in size and acted as if he had spent a lifetime winning battles.

Castellà was our drill sergeant and faithfully repeated from memory all the set phrases in the manuals.

He was renowned for his bad temper and a number of anecdotes about his character were in circulation. Apparently one day he was caught doing something he shouldn't and arrived home fuming. The previous day his wife had bought a couple of chickens for fattening. Caged on the balcony, the chickens sometimes walked up and down the passageway in the apartment. They were skinny and lived for the moment when their mistress fed them; they sometimes pecked her skirts. Her name was Neus, though her husband called her Niña; she was small, thin, and spritely, with large dark eyes.

When the sergeant walked in, he glanced at his wife in a rage. He quickly threw off his military gear, unbuttoned his army jacket, took off his trousers, and walked to the wardrobe in his underpants to find some different trousers. At that very moment the chickens that were loose in the apartment ran into the bedroom. The sergeant looked at them askance and kicked them away.

"These chickens are getting on my nerves, Niña," he snarled.

The chickens reacted by making their usual din. They started to flutter. The sergeant became more and more furious.

"Would you be so good as to shut those chickens up?" he roared at his wife, who was cowering in a corner.

Neus tried to remove the chickens from the bedroom. She couldn't catch them. One leapt onto the table. The other flew onto a chair and hopped from chair to sideboard, its wing breaking the cruet dish on the sideboard in the process.

The sergeant despaired. His eyes glazed over. He suddenly grabbed his revolver and fired it at the chickens until they were dead.

When they heard the shots, the neighbors gathered in the lobby, made various conjectures, but weren't sufficiently moved to go upstairs. After a while, they saw Sra. Neus come out to go shopping. When they realized no blood had been spilt, the neighbors were much relieved. After lunch the sergeant strutted off to his café, heels and head high, as if he had just won a huge battle.

My military service in Girona was short, interminable, and slightly crazy.

10 August. Barcelona.

I return to Barcelona from Girona after finishing my military service. The journey was stifling. Everybody on the train was in shirtsleeves. If it hadn't been possible to open the windows in the third-class compartment—in mine they could be opened slightly, to much protest—the human stench would have been dreadful.

One day, during my military service, my friend Alexandre Plana turned up in Girona. He had come to see me. I felt so grateful. We idled around the center for hours—going from café to café. Plana is not fond of cafés. He felt uncomfortable and out of place. But I didn't think there was anywhere else we could go. It was very hot and occasionally the stench from the drains hit us. In a dingy, shabby café under the arches, he told me that he would be publishing a small article I'd sent to him about the Sant Daniel valley in *Diari de Girona*. The flies inhabiting the establishment buzzed drowsily in the murky light. The ever-generous Plana said, "The piece on the Sant Daniel valley is fine."

"You really mean that?" I asked.

"There's only one thing wrong with it, naturally: I find it rather overliterary. The adjectives are recherché, the phrasing very unnatural, the desire to be original too evident. But what can you do about that? It is a defect that comes with your age. The best style is the style used in letters to family, but without the surfeit of emotion they usually have."

"What must you to do to write like that?"

"Get rid of the small literary tics that seem perfectly foolish. You like Girona. Girona is a fantastic literary subject. Write about Girona, but straightforwardly, avoiding rhetorical flourishes. Look at things closely, scrutinize them, and then describe them in words."

"When I was just in Girona, things didn't seem as easy or as simple as when I was at school there."

"And will appear less and less so. Writing is difficult. If you aren't prepared to make the effort, you should forget it and take up some other trade."

On my way back from the station, where I had accompanied Plana, I decided to forget the article on the Sant Daniel valley and not even make an effort to reread it.

For the twenty days of my military service I lived in lodgings on Cort Reial, near plaça de l'Oli. There were various other soldiers from Palafrugell: Narcís Bisbe, my schoolmate; Sarà, the son of a stout guttural man who sang bass in the Cork-Lid choir and was very fond of drinking martinis; etcetera. The young ladies in the nearby houses were very expensive: They cost three pesetas. Lunch visibly deteriorated. In the lodging house we ate amazing amounts of haricots—which were tough and stringy. I didn't hit the target once in my shooting practice in Montjuïc—not even a consolation hit. I cut an absurd figure as a marksman. It is likely that my lack of skill was due to the fact that I was so worried about the kickback from the rifle butt. On the other hand, I think I was quite good at finding shelter in the undergrowth in the gullies in Les Pedres, when the battalion was on guerrilla exercises. The latter made us really hungry, but the thought of the string beans awaiting us at dinnertime made us very depressed.

14 August. I leave for Calella. It is the eve of Holy Mary's Day, my mother's saint's day. It is a very important family celebration—all the more so because it is summer. Celebrations seem more exuberant in summer than in winter.

As usual, I catch the early-afternoon mail train from estació de França. This station is chaotic and dirty. There is a long line in front of the counter. Very crowded and hot. Sometimes the damp sea breeze fills our nostrils, combining with the steam given off by the piss of the horses pulling the carriages, buggies, and stage coaches waiting outside the station. This liquid vapor, added to the stifling heat and coal fumes from the engines, creates a symphony of smells that's hardly appetizing.

The train finally moves off and because everybody, quite unusually, has agreed to open the windows, there is a very pleasant breeze. But the light is harsh and unpleasant, even though it is so humid. Out in the open air the heat of summer is bearable in this country because there is always a slight breeze. In contrast, the light is oppressive and trying. It is a monotonous journey. The train stops in every station. People get off and on. Bells tinkle. Every station has a different tinkle. Engines whistle. When you think about them, these whistles seem ridiculous, but they help the time pass. One must do something. It is very difficult to read. The rocking of the carriages means the letters on the page move too much and it is hard to decipher anything. The train journeys I have taken have made me realize how lots of people are happy traveling once they have a seat—even an uncomfortable one—and their faces and bodies exude what we might call railway bliss.

People like traveling by train, as they like eating in an inn—perhaps because it is such a rare event in their lives.

After Granollers the track begins to climb. The train slows down. The engine puffs and pants. A time comes when we progress at the speed of a turtle. My God, how it pants and puffs! Two blasts of white steam alternate from either side of the front of the engine and blow a cloud of dust over the dry grass along the side of the track. "Can you hear it panting?" asks a smiley man sitting next to me. This gentleman is blissful. Perhaps he reckons this panting entirely justifies the cost of his ticket. A moment comes, inside the tunnel, which is as dark as a wolf's gizzard, when the train reaches the top of the incline and starts going downhill. In a flash, we progress from slow and silent to a horrendous din of clanking metal, creaking wood, and human bodies bumping and jumping on their seats. The engine gives a long whistle. It is a happy, drawn-out whistle. There is a dramatic feeling of speed. It is as if the huge, gleaming hulk of the train has begun to hurtle down a precipice. The wind ruffles people's hair. The brakes squeal. "Can you hear those brakes?" asks the gentleman next to me, as smiley as ever. This gentleman follows every single movement the train makes; he misses nothing. He registers every palpitation. Perhaps he is a true Orsian. After a while the train seems to calm down and resume its normal, reasonable speed. Now a gentler breeze blows in through the windows. People sit still. At the stop in Llinars, heat permeates the silence. The acacia leaves in the station are completely still, a blotchy, tepid green. Passengers sweat in their seats. Fat women look hot, flushed, and weak, as if they've been choked and would topple at the slightest push. Those carrying less weight are less out of sorts, but the sweat lightly covers their skin so they don't seem so leathery. The evening proceeds.

The poplar groves start after Sant Celoni. La Tordera and all the streams flowing there create these poplar groves. In my view, it is the main scenic charm of the journey. The area of La Selva, as it nears the undulating line of the Montserrat and Les Guilleries mountains, creates groves much like the dark, symmetrical pine groves in my part of the country close to the sea. La Tordera and the lake in Sils, that always used to have reserves of water and now has them only when rain floods the countryside, are the elements actively feeding these poplars. Sometimes the groves run alongside the rails. I have seen them in all weather: in the winter when the trees have a purely linear nakedness, often near vast pools of dark water, as in a great lake where the trees stand stiff and straight as if they had died vertically; and naturally in good weather when the poplars display their beautiful mass of elegant foliage.

Do these groves constitute a wood? Yes and no. For a wood in the literal meaning of the word, they lack the necessary cosmic quality, namely disorder, geological and botanical chaos, and the fact that it is impossible to see—even in our modest forests—the wood beyond the end of one's nose. The German saying—that you can't see the wood for the trees—is perhaps the quintessence of a forest, not only when it is virgin forest but also when it has arisen as a result of natural occurrences in the terrain, not to any order or plan. In contrast, a grove is a wood in the form of a garden, in lines, following a set perspective, planted with standard trees and, consequently, a repetitive sequence, with an eye to the inevitable revenue. Nonetheless, conversely you cannot say it is a garden, even a very basic garden, because although a grove requires level space and has perfect, mathematically drawn lines, it has no whimsical decorative detail. I have a weakness for groves, not simply because they don't tend to exist in my part of the country but because it is a form that is midway between garden and wood, the form of natural garden most suited to our temperament, a graceful form that isn't affected and satisfies the most genuine good taste. The defense of gardens against woods, of culture against nature, waged by the *noucentistes* is all very well, but I am not in favor of extremes. I prefer an intermediate state that doesn't lean too much one way or the other, that lets me breathe naturally.

I would like to become familiar with French and Italian geometrical gardens and the freer English gardens. Perhaps it will happen one day. Heavens, who knows! I have been hearing about them for years as a result of the polemics over *noucentisme*. I don't like chaotic gardens with rocks, exotic plants, and "grotesque" elements (a word that comes from the Italian *grotta*) which is merely mechanical decorative whimsy. They seem like gardens for geniuses. I prefer cheap, relaxing, genuine gardens. A grove is the simplest, most basic garden, the archetypal idea of a garden stemming purely and simply from the owner's account book. Trees are planted at a distance from each other that maximizes growth—and income. I believe the most beautiful countryside is always the most useful, creating the most income, which is the essence of a grove. At the same time, groves are very elegant. What more can one say?

When the train reaches poplar-grove terrain—roughly the area between Sant Celoni and Riudellots—dusk starts to descend. In the winter, it would get dark in the afternoon. When the grove was near the side of the track and the train skirted it quickly, making a thunderous din, leaping from one stretch of rail to the next, the lines of trees spun round and round like a carousel. It was as if the train came to a halt and the trees circled it on an invisible axis, a movement so perfect it seemed powered by a hidden mechanism. On that long, monotonous journey, this movement—like the dazzlingly yellow omelets, apparently made from canary eggs, that were sold in bread rolls at the junction station—held two genuine surprises. In the winter, when it was dark, a full moon sometimes shone on the groves. The pools on the ground from the last rain were so extensive they seemed like one huge lake. The lines of skeletal trees kept perfect order above the dark, melancholy waters where the moon glittered. It was an unreal landscape, at once sleepy and slightly threatening, though with a strange kind of warmth—probably the subtle warmth of the landscape of La Selva. When it was fine, I could see the groves from the train in their humble, usually solitary splendor, their bright shadows fleeing across the land, over cool grass and small wildflowers. I'd have liked to spend an afternoon or two in one of these spots with a young lady fond of nature's charms. However, such a situation, which a priori seems simple and straightforward, has yet to materialize and it is unlikely it ever will. It is more probable that I shall be fated to travel in this train across these groves without ever stopping. I am sure they will remain an imaginative detail within my precarious phantasmagoria.

The poplar is typically grown in groves and in many varieties; it is tall, svelte, and elegant and seems specially created to give the groves their unique harm. The poplar has a leaf that rustles cheerfully and deliciously when a light breeze blows, so that in these parts a small, more or less spirited noise is always present to fascinate the senses. Moreover, the leaf of this tree—like the leaf of the olive tree—turns over when blown by a breeze, and when the full light of the sun hits the back of the leaf, which is very spongy and lighter, though never quite silvery, the foliage seem be covered in a foamy spray that isn't metallic and hard like an olive grove's but ineffably soft. In the train this afternoon I thought how delightful it would be to stretch out on the grass in these groves, to look up at the sky and while my time away contemplating the innocent, delightful way the vegetation moved.

Of all the natural spectacles created by vegetation these groves perhaps come closest to our way of being. It is a changeable spectacle— and its variety is difficult to describe at times, or at least seems to be. Perhaps light is the key element of its spirit. A particular light makes the groves cheerful, radiant, and pleasant. They can also seem sad, depressed, and crestfallen. Sometimes, toward dusk, they are so solitary they trigger indefinable fear.

When we reach Girona station, it is dark and already nighttime. For heaven's sake, seven o'clock and already dark! There is hustle and bustle in the station. A railway worker walks by, flashing a red light. Another wretch, dressed in blue, taps the wheels with a hammer to check that the metal is sound. "Can you hear that hammer?" asks the jolly gentleman sitting next to me. It is amazing how many bright sparks one meets in this country. The station bell tinkles once. After a while, it tinkles a second time. After another interlude, it tinkles for a third time. "Can you hear that bell?" asks the jolly gentleman sitting next to me. The time comes when this gentleman's repeated statements of the obvious allow me to see him in a strange, enigmatic light. It seems evident that he is not quite right in the head. But perhaps it isn't simply that he isn't quite right in the head. Perhaps he is just an Ampurdanese barrel of laughs going home for the holidays.

The train moves off and across the bridge over the Onyar. The large park of La Devesa is on our left, in complete darkness; the urban conglomeration of Girona, on our right. Sad, miserable lights dot the impersonal buildings. The terrible impression human constructions make in this country of being eternally unfinished. The precarious light from the small electric lightbulbs reminds me of erotic moments at school in my adolescence. It all seems long ago, a blur in my remote past. The train slows down; the track must be going up an incline. I shift so I am by a window that isn't shuttered. There are passengers who always keep their windows shuttered. The lights from the apartments on the bend in the Onyar shine through the bridge's metal stanchions. A faint light color gleams on the wan, oily waters: a bar of honey-toned, dark gold. An arc light crackles over the bridge now receding into the distance; the spasm of bright light vaguely seems to illuminate the Sant Feliu belfry. We cross the bridge and the Sant Pere de Galligants neighborhood appears in the window and seems suspended under the massive hazy outline of the cathedral. The lights from Sant Pere are, as in previous years, the most melancholy and yellow in the city—a rancid oily yellow. It is a light that seems inseparable from the old stones and the poor, shabby crust of these buildings. So many memories spring to mind! I see the wooden footbridge we used for crossing the river, the water in the adjacent ponds, dotted by the most wretched of the city's lights. I hear frogs croaking above the noisy din from the train, a wind whistling through the spindly reeds, notes from a distant hurdy-gurdy, and I see the moon's dull shimmer on stagnant waters. But the train moves on and leaves everything behind, in the impenetrable blur that is the past.

15 August. Calella de Palafrugell. Holy Mary's Day. By the time I arrived, mass had been over for some time, and people had disappeared into "the gentlemen's houses," as local fishermen like to say. It is hot and bright, with a northeasterly light and luminous air. The beach is almost empty; the summer people are dressed in their best and only the rougher elements are swimming. There are so many Marias in El Canadell that one can exchange pleasantries outside every small front garden. As I enter our house, I see Mossèn Narcís—skullcap, short cape, walking stick—coming to give my mother his best wishes. He is sitting rather stiffly in the shade from the acacia, a warm smile on his face. My mother, who is busy in the kitchen, receives these best wishes between the rice pan and the chicken pan, and interrupts her toiling to listen to Mossèn Narcís though she finds it rather a strain. The reverend, however, has his program mapped out and will arise from the rocking chair at a specific time on the dot. He is an imperturbable, punctual man.

In ironed collar and tie, and shirtsleeves, my father sits opposite the parish priest and gloomily tries to prove to him that the march taken by time is simply catastrophic. The priest nods in ready agreement.

"Do you know what time we'll have lunch today, Mossèn Narcís?" asks my father. "It will be well past two o'clock. It's quite intolerable. Well past two o'clock! If the old folk were to come back from the other world!"

"Too true, Tonet, too true! No sense or reason to it. If the old folk were to come back from the other world . . . no need to say another word!"

It is the same conversation Mossèn Narcís and my father have every year on Holy Mary's Day. I've heard it ever since I could reason. Their annual mechanical repetition of the same conversation is impressive. "Is it possible," I wonder, "that when two people meet they always repeat the same conversation?" I sometimes suspect that this robotic repetition is a feature of civilized society. In small towns, where people know each other better, it is obvious and can be heard day in and day out. A good observer, familiar with the individuals concerned, could anticipate their dialogues almost without fail.

We finally have lunch at just before two. Aunt Lluïsa has come to spend the day with the family, and the sight of bathing suits triggers her continual attacks of embarrassment. Traditional lunch. First is a large dish of big rock mussels scented with a strong tang of the sea. The rock mussel is the most delicately flavored in this country. Followed by local black rice, fish, and chicken in a succulent sauce. Then the usual portions of grilled lobster. The lobster shell singed by the flames fills the dining room with a delicious smell. As it is hot and everyone is eating with their windows and doors open, El Canadell is full of the most evocative clatter of plates, spoons, and forks, which I find inseparable from the aroma of lobster shells. Then a cream roll from Comas's pastry shop makes its appearance and the delicious, light sponge cake, with a dash of lemon and cinnamon, sent by Grandmother Marieta. And to round off the meal—another tradition on this day—ice cream made in a wooden bucket full of ice and a container with the necessary ingredients, a container that revolves when the small handle on a mechanical device is turned. This gives way to coffee, which is usually extremely good, aromatic and most pleasant, tasting of the softness of the water in local cisterns as people always say.

The wind has changed during lunch: The morning northwesterly has shifted to a southwesterly blowing very gently, slightly moist and cooler. When we go out on the terrace to contemplate the sea from the shade of the acacia, we feel the wind on our faces: a lovely caress. These saint's day lunches are always accompanied by the wind—the southwest wind, to be precise. Initially the splendid bright light dazzles us. Then immediate details appears more clearly, and we see the white, bluish blotch of Sr. Narcís Ferrer, alias Narcís the watchmaker, rod fishing as he always does on a holiday on Barret Rock. He is wearing his broad-brimmed brown straw hat and a proper gentleman's shirt: white, ironed, with a knotted metal-green tie, tied at the back. He is a tenacious, enthusiastic fisherman who never catches a thing. The people of Calella are very fond of Sr. Narcís, who is a watchmaker and jeweler, not simply because of a temperament that is suited to the needs of his public (he is a comedian whose touch is so light few people even notice it) but also because of the presence of his wife, Sra. Tuietes, a tall, fat, exuberant, somewhat squint-eyed woman, who wears a high bun and is given to loud, imperious declarations. Sighted in her bloomers, Sra. Tuietes must be awesome and off-putting.

A large part of the afternoon is spent in mutual congratulations and the usual saint's day exchanges.

I walk to Forcats Point along the coastal path. From Forcats—or from the sea—Calella is a wonderful sight.

The town lights at dusk, the streetlamps moistened by the wind, a tranquil silence. At ten o'clock, everyone is yawning, a sweet slumber you cannot fight off. In the Mediterranean, the southwesterly wind induces a drowsiness that is sticky, rather uncomfortable, but practical—if your body has adapted, naturally.

In this area, with this weather, it is never hot. One wind or another is always blowing. I mean that days of intense, concentrated heat are few and far between.

It is very likely that the feeling of heat—the false feeling of a heat that is genuine enough—is caused by the light, which can be difficult to absorb, when it isn't simply horrendous. At ten in the morning, when the northeasterly has settled in, the light is sometimes so strong, insidious, and dazzling it hurts the eyes. This visual onslaught means your body can be very hot even though you stay in the coolest shade. When the southwesterly blows in the afternoon, things improve remarkably: Horizons blur, the air is gentler, details haze over, everything is bathed in a vague pale pink, the light becomes pleasant, and distant space seems to drift. Glaring light induces a dull throbbing headache between the eyebrows. If you put on dark glasses, it feels as if you're losing your head. But nobody likes dark glasses. People think they are for blind men.

17 August. Calella–El Canadell.

Two hot days, the usual light winds and sultry, sweaty nights. There was an electrical storm this afternoon—what sailors and fishermen call *el grop*. I think there are two kinds of *grop*: the nearby, immediate sort that begins where you are, with a whirlwind or swirling gusts, coming from nowhere in particular, sometimes from several, often opposite directions, stormy winds, accompanied by apocalyptic thunderclaps and lightning against a gloomy, deathly sky, crackling and booming accompanied by a succession of violent downpours that usually end in a fishtail; and the distant *grop*, which is a great display but restricted to a spectacle of merely visual effects. Today's was one of the latter.

The wind dropped at six. The sea was totally calm; an oily silence descended. In the west the pallid sky yellowed and turned everything almost an egg-yolk color. Suddenly there was a distant, muted thunderclap which lasted for two minutes, a wave of sound that seemed it would never end, followed by a quick, nervous, frenzied flash of lightning that glowered green in the haze retreating in the western sky.

Then a shorter, weaker thunderclap. Another less intense flash followed by an even feebler one. Another diffuse thunderclap, a sound that fades and vanishes. The sky is no longer pale, the egg-yolk yellow having given way to the usual color of sky at that time of day. In the meantime a few large drops of rain have fallen and created bubbles in the dust on the road. A lighter, colder breeze springs up. Then nothing at all. It was a dry *grop*, as the fishermen say.

During this whole operation—which must have lasted slightly more than ten minutes and made the usual impact in the place where it erupted—the sea stayed completely still, in a state of total indifference. When the *grop* disappeared, a faint southwesterly began to blow—the twilighter, as Sr. Pere Jubert liked to say.

"Red sky at night, fisherman's delight," I hear a fisherman say in the tavern.

In any case, this is what it was like.

The night was slightly less sultry. It was cool in the early hours.

18 August. After lunch I catch sight of Hermós mending a trawl line in the shade of a boat. I go over to him. His baldpate is gleaming. When he sees me he looks happy and curious. His eyes are quite bloodshot. He is like a cheerful gorilla.

"I thought you were in Aigua Xal·lida," I say.

"I came for Holy Mother's Day. I'll go back this afternoon with the southwesterly. I have brought Marieta some fish. Today we'll eat red-grouper stew."

"Yum, yum."

"You need to do something to celebrate. I took so much quinine in Algiers I went stiff as a rake. I'm still taking the stuff. I sometimes think I have gone mad. The fever gives me the cold shivers even when the sun is scorching, but quinine turns your backbone inside out. You'll never see the old Hermós again. Fish stew is my only relief. Marieta has the right touch. She knows how to prepare them. She makes them like they used to in rich households, like Can Barris, years ago. I don't mean that poor households in Palafrugell don't eat well, but however good the cooking is in these homes, they always leave out one ingredient or another, and nothing is really perfect. Sr. Tintorer, who was a friend of Master Joan, would sometimes say of a sauce: 'This sauce is sublime.' Hey, do me a fucking favor and tell me what 'sublime' means?"

"I'm not sure...it's a word used by gentlemen who wear stiff collars on a working day. We can do without it, right?"

"That's just what I thought! But there are so many different ways of talking, for God's sake! Some people know nothing...and talk about everything. Did you realize there were so many people like that? There's a young French lady in Can Batlle who's asked me to teach her to swim. No kidding. Paying, naturally. Half a peseta a lesson. Who'd want to go net fishing in winter?"

"But you never learned to swim."

"That's right. Who do you think I am? No fisherman around here can, not even Pere Benet. Naturally, as we don't like water, we'd never go to sea if we thought we were going to fall in! If we thought that was at all likely, they'd never drag us out of the café, not for all the tea in China."

"So have you got anywhere with the French lady?"

"Not really. I told her I'd teach her to swim but would keep my long johns on, but as she speaks so oddly, I don't think she understood me at all. What do you expect? It's what Dr. Martí always says when he's in a bad mood: In this country, we are uneducated, have been taught nothing, and know nothing. At my age I still can't read or write. I am thicker than if I'd been born in Begur...we are as thick as if we had a slab of lead for a brain. And by the way, don't you want to come to Aigua Xal·lida? There's still a mattress for you in the cabin. What should we do with it? I just hope we don't get any leaks in the winter."

"No, I've work to do."

"So will we ever meet up again?"

"I wouldn't say never!"

"Time passes so quickly."

"I heard you were off right away."

"Yes, the day after tomorrow more than likely."

"You must be very busy."

"Don't make me laugh."

"What's your trade?"

"I'm a journalist."

"People say that is a fishhook brand of trade."

When Hermós wanted to speak highly of something, he would say it was the fishhook brand. He'd learned that from boxes of sardines from Nantes. The sardines that were reputedly the best had a fishhook on the lid—the hook for catching sea bream.

"Do you like your trade?"

"It's quite strange."

"So you won't be eating any more grilled sardines, like the ones from Escala, years ago."

"What can I do?"

"It's really nice in Aigua Xal·lida in September. It's mushroom-hunting season. Someone or other turns up, mainly from Begur. The sharpest characters come, the best from every household. Miner is a sly fellow who can never get it right. The carabineers are always after him. Luckily he always gives them the slip. He has ended up in a bad state. He never says anything. He never talks. You never know where he is. You find him in the strangest places at any time of day or night. Pelayo Taler is very different. Taler is a smooth operator, never shuts up and likes to gossip. He is useless when it comes to smuggling. On the other hand, nobody can rival his fishing with dynamite. Compared to him, the poor fellows in Tamariu are worthless."

"They're our ancient stock, the best."

"What do you mean 'ancient'? They are poor people who'd like to eat and drink well. They'd also like a woman now and then, but those who show a leg want a good bed and cash and the whole works, not to be left as poor as a church mouse when the wind starts to howl. They're not in it for the laughs. In their pink nightgowns they look as if they might be from fairy land, if you get me?"

"And have you never tried your hand at smuggling?"

"When I am in my cabin in Aigua Xal·lida, I do sometimes hear people. Just footsteps, they never say anything. I find them frightening, not exactly what you call cheering. My cabin door is always open, but when I hear the slightest sound I bolt and bar every hole I can find. I shove my table against the door. I am no good at this kind of thing. I don't know how to defend myself. If you want to be a good smuggler, you need to be able to read or have a secretary who knows how to spread the business around. What can I do? I'm on my own now. You're leaving for good. The Begur rabble is decent enough. They wouldn't have bothered us."

"That might have made the most sense."

"Perhaps! But that's all in the past now. You want to be a gentleman, wear a tie, hat, and braces, and speak posh. You want to be rich and strut around. It makes no odds. A rich man can afford a second supper. You don't want to live on smoke, on hot air."

"All the same, you must have something."

"Yes, a thousand pesetas in my post office account, in my post office saving box."

"It's a good one."

"I wouldn't know because I never see it."

"You're richer than I am. I don't have a cent."

"Wait until you're my age and we'll see."

A very light, pleasant breeze blows across the shade from the boat and makes me feel drowsy. Hermós goes on, after a pause: "Are you going to live in Barcelona?"

"I am for the moment."

"There are lots of nice women in Barcelona."

"Maybe. But you have to pay."

"I wasn't born yesterday! We always have to pay."

"I like talking. It makes me sleepy. Give me the top of the trawl net so I can use it as a pillow. It has a dirty saltwater smell I think is wonderful."

I fell asleep immediately. The breeze is so gentle! Hermós's apish face gives me an unfailing sense of security. Two hours later, I wake up and realize we could have excelled in the simple style of life. Dusk closes in. A yolk-yellow color hangs in the air. Hermós has disappeared. The only trace I can find of him is the vague aroma of a thin cigar.

19 August. El Canadell.

I bumped into Sra. Rosita. I hadn't seen her for some time: perhaps since the war years. She had been to mass and was strolling leisurely along, carrying her mantilla, rosary beads, and a prayer book with a mother-of-pearl cover. Pleased to see her. She forced a smile and didn't quite succeed. She wants me to realize—as she did years ago and perhaps has always done—that she is constantly worrying, that something is always vexing her. The way she flutters her eyes creates a wonderful lingering expression of tact and sadness—just perfect. The baroque excelled at this and she does a good imitation. In any case, she walks so stiffly, so straight-backed, that she is a striking presence. She used to speak very sententiously and still does, I expect. When she speaks, the words sound nasal and bad-tempered: her French education. I imagine she is still horrified by the frivolous air of the most innocent conversations. It can't have been easy to guess what she might have liked to hear at any given moment.

During the war, when she dropped in at home—and I did stay in sometimes—I saw how skilled she was at slicing ham and sausage. She sliced it very thin, miraculously thin. I don't know how she did it. She produced slices that were transparent and ethereal. She believed these things should be cut very thin. She was right. It makes them tastier.

But she did perhaps take her skills too far. In the afternoon, when it was time for a bite, her light, fleeting ham left us feeling very hungry.

"Sra. Rosita, it is a such fine day," I tell her.

"Yes. It is quite splendid. Let us give thanks to God for allowing us these wonders."

While she is making this last remark, I notice how she rolls the whites of her eyes and wags the finger on her right hand sententiously. She immediately adds: "It is quite a splendid day, however."

"Go on, Rosita . . . do go on."

"It is a wonderful day, but what if we go to hell, if we don't find salvation?"

"You will be fine, Sra. Rosita . . . you will be fine."

"That's easy for you to say: You'll be fine, you'll be fine . . . I'm the same as everyone else: a recalcitrant sinner. The Gospel says it all: 'Many are called and few are the chosen.'"

"Though the Gospel may say that, and even say it in Spanish, I can't believe it. Sra. Rosita, you are goodness itself and exemplary in every regard."

"By the holy saints! The devil makes you mistake like for unlike. 'Many a slip betwixt cup and lip.' One cannot speak lightly of these things."

"All the same, a few will be saved. It would be a pity if a person like you were left out in the cold."

"Yes, truly, it would be a pity. And that is why one must be vigilant, night and day, and always be on the alert. One can stumble at any moment."

Sra. Rosita uttered these last sentences with a tiny but visible smile, a self-satisfied smile I mentally interpreted as indicating that the literal meaning of her words wasn't a true reflection of what she really thought. I mean to say—though I might very well be mistaken—that Srta. Rosita cherishes a cast-iron conviction that she will be saved.

We talk about a gentleman in El Canadell, a mutual acquaintance, and to give her an idea of my opinion of him, I say I think he is a happy bum. When I say that, Sra. Rosita flinches, sticks a finger in the air, and looks indignant.

"Please, I beg you," she says mutedly. "In conversation with a well-educated person, in fact, in conversation with someone of any class, never use the word 'bum.' It is a vulgar, common word I find most upsetting and unpleasant."

In the belief that Sra. Rosita's indignation might spring from the sharp, overemphatic sound the word has, I try to calm her nerves and say, "But would it be more acceptable if I were to say he was a happy bunny?"

"By the holy saints, don't make it worse! The way we speak is already bad enough without damaging it any more, dirtying it with intolerable swear words."

When I leave Sra. Rosita, who resumes her stiff, straight-backed walk, I have the pleasant feeling that I have been freed of a great weight—a hundred-year-old weight.

On the table in the small terrace I see a book that must belong to one of my sisters. I pick it up. They are poems by Lamartine. I find this line: "*Un seul être vous manque et tout est dépeuplé...*" This line describes the state of mind of young people most exactly, the tendency one has at this age to sink into indescribable sadness, which is almost automatically irreversible.

A moment comes, nonetheless, that is quite common, when things lead one to depend on an *être* or you are at someone else's disposition, and then the only solution is to marry for the four hundred and fifty years that one thinks life will last, when you are my age.

19 August. El Canadell.

From time to time I see calls in the paper to participate in some poetry festival or a description (usually the same, with identical adjectives) of one of these festivals. Josep Carner's name often appears in reports of these poetic debacles, and he must have won countless prizes in cash or art objects. The people on the juries are almost always the same, which perhaps suggests we have a set of renowned, lyrical, vagabond judges we can call upon. On the other hand, many small towns must have a group of people ready to join this kind of competition whenever the opportunity arises. The country must possess an ill-defined, though real enough, reserve of cash for such revelries.

I don't know why these festivals leave me absolutely cold—or even uneasy—when I read about them in the newspapers. Perhaps it is because I am so shy. When I am with more than four people, I dry up and can never hit the right note—as most people can. In any case, even if that isn't why I feel so indifferent, it's not as if I don't think it worthwhile devoting a moment to them.

These poetry festivals may have been useful in the history of the literary movement. But it is also true they have helped to create a typical kind of literary triteness in their references to the fatherland, faith, and love. And especially because of the way they relate to a diffuse form of sociability, conversational exchanges, and the use of certain expressions, this literary triteness—which clearly relates to the voices and practices of actors in the Catalan theater—is horrendous, has existed for years, and is inseparable from the petty bourgeoisie of Barcelona whose fondness for artistic exhibitionism makes one's hair stand on end. If you imagine a Palafrugell mentality—one that exists in the country's small towns—its most marked feature is a certain loathing of triteness, an antitriteness that can be very strong, a hostility to the conventional that at times leads to coarseness, which I personally much prefer.

While all we have is brittle, weedy, Sunday-afternoon literature, a literature created in the odd spare moment—the free time allowed by other tasks—we are permanently threatened by these romantic outpourings. The less of a calling the mind possesses, the more emphatic and hyperbolic will be its products. One of the best things Sr. Ors has done (Sr. Prat, in other words) is to create a modest, if genuine, level of professionalism.

The first muscatel grapes have appeared on the table. It's been very hot this year and that must explain why their appearance is premature. "They are from abroad," I hear the family maid say. They might be from vineyards on the frontier. They are excellent.

As far as my taste goes, muscatel grapes are the best fruit I know and nothing can possibly rival them. They shouldn't be too ripe or too sweet. The skin of the grape must break on the tooth. They should be full and firm. Grapes, more than any other fruit in the country, define fruitiness.

20 August. El Canadell.

Sebastià Puig, alias Hermós, is still wandering around Calella with his fishing tackle and he tells me, before his favorite aperitif of vermouth and olives in Cafè de les Voltes, what happened to the *Franca Fassio* a few months ago.

"When the war finished," he tells me, "the steamship service between Genoa and Barcelona was resumed and the *Franca Fassio* was allotted its weekly trip. I was very familiar with the ship because I had seen it sail by so often from my cabin in Aigua Xal·lida. I had also seen it moored in the port of Barcelona, when I went there with Enric Vergés and we stayed in Hotel Lloret on the Rambla. It was a rather small ship that shuffled along like an old man, painted white and very well, but the moment you got closer a smell of rancid vomit made you turn away. Lots of people must have been seasick because it was always very full. One day last winter, it must have been in mid-March, I set out from Aigua Xal·lida to catch some fish for supper, and I cast the argentine net in some inlets on the Aiguablava coast. There are excellent argentines in March—they call them *joells* in Cadaqués; they are slightly bitter and when the sea bream hunt them, they swim into coves and inlets like blue fish, almost always in shoals. It was very early but even so it was very misty. The sea was silent: totally calm. However, there was a thick white fog that was wet and slimy. As no wind was blowing, it seemed to be fixed there. I don't like fog, especially at sea, because I'm always afraid that, like an idiot, I will get lost. I was intending to try my net out in Es Tramadiu, which is the best place for argentines. I bundled myself up well, because it was pissing it down, and rowing from the hip, near the coast, almost touching the rocks, I moved on. When I reached the Bishop's Cave coastline, which is hilly with that yellowish patch people say looks like a bishop's face, I thought I saw the strangest shape looming above me, melding into the fog, huge, whitish, and alarming. When I spotted the apparition I was but a thick rope's length away: I rowed closer and closer, slowly, astonished and intrigued. If I'd any sense, the sight of that strange object would have turned me right around and made me head home. But the fact is that bulk I could see in the fog lured me on and sent my head into a spin. I drew gradually nearer. People like me who live alone, like an owl, are birds charmed by a snake: We don't know what is about to hit us. The sea was still. The fog was thick. The silence was absolute. The silence of the coast in winter, when there isn't a soul about: the solitude of such spaces. Nonetheless, I did think I heard the dull hum of an engine. It was an extraordinary effect, something I'd never heard before, reaching me through the fog, like a noise created by the fog itself, a noise that seemed to come from my body rather than from the spectacle looming before me. Now I was close enough to see detail: a funnel, topsides, portholes, a mast, and rigging. All painted white. It was a steamship that had hit the rocky slope of Bishop's Cave and run aground there. Its prow had hit the coast head on, no joking. Of course, the fog had dragged it off course. At least that's what I imagined had happened: It was so strange. I was so close the noise from the ship's engine deafened me as it tried to reverse off the rocks where it had gotten stuck. The engine made the vessel vibrate but couldn't move it. It was as if they were shaking the topsides and opening up its insides. You couldn't see anyone on board. It can't have been carrying many passengers. The crew was at their stations and had their work cut out. I peered as far as the fog would let me and thought that shape indicated it must be the *Franca Fassio*. I was right by the prow, with my boat next to the topsides. All of a sudden I saw a man with an open shirtfront on the ship's bridge: a pale white face, like a ghost, under an officer's hat. I went nearer, waved my arm, he saw me, leaned over the side of the bridge, and I shouted using my hands as a megaphone, 'Can I help?'

"Please don't laugh, don't laugh or I'll stop telling my story.

"The moment he heard my voice, the officer—perhaps he was the captain—raised his arms, and his face creased as if he were in a rage. Fog trickled down his face. I don't think he understood what I'd said. The fact is he seemed out of his mind; his whole body convulsed as if he'd gone mad. It must be quite unusual to hit those rocks head on. And he'd been lucky his ship had been chugging slowly along or it would have been holed. I looked at him, more dead than alive, and all at once he started shouting. I didn't understand what he was saying because I never could understand the Italians in Algiers.

"'*Mascalzone!*' he shouted. '*Figlio d'un cane. Va a farti ammazzà …*' The same things I'd heard in the cork forests in those mountains belonging to La Calle, in Algeria. The man was obviously insulting me, but I didn't have a clue what he was saying. I didn't understand a word. I didn't think I warranted that outburst. Don't you think he was going too far? I'd said what you must say in a situation when you are facing disaster. The man had gone crazy. The ship had run aground, and if it wasn't deliberate, it meant a bad stormy season was upon us. The engine was straining and panting but not budging it off the rocks. Perhaps my presence in those waters had sent him into a frenzy, the fact I'd seen what had happened. That was the last thought I had. Once I grasped the situation, I didn't hang around. I grabbed the oars, rowed hard, returned to Aigua Xal·lida, and shut myself in my cabin. I've never liked getting mixed up in quarrels or difficult situations. What would you have done? When you're not wanted, best beat it . . . that was what old Roig said, the man who made counterfeit money, when they let him out of Bisbal castle."

Hermós pauses, nibbles an olive, takes a sip of vermouth, and with a slightly sweeter face says, "When will you stop laughing, you idiot? You thought what I said to the officer was funny . . . but what else could I have said? What would you have said? Obviously you speak more poshly. You sometimes forget who I am. I am the offspring of Can Cuca in Vila-seca. When I was a kid I often went hungry, I never went to school, I don't know how to read or write, I've had to learn a lot of different trades; if Donya Rosa Barria and Marieta Batlle hadn't taken me in, I'd have spent a long time out in the cold. Your lot had everything put on a plate for you while I've had to sit and wait. In my time, there were lots of people like me; you keep a low profile and stay out of sight. You're different and you know what you must do at each step. Your lot has got everything signposted."

"Hey, come on, Hermós . . . I'd never have dreamed you were so good at plucking the violin strings."

"The only thing I will say is that when a friend of mine dies, I go to his home and pay my respects and say, 'Can I be of help?' It doesn't take much to please! People have often said, 'Hermós is a good man. His heart is in the right place and he is generous.'"

"So do think you are a good man?"

"What do you expect me to say? That's what people tell me. And quite a few, too."

"And what happened to your fishing in Es Tramadiu? There must still be argentines swimming around."

"Yes, of course. I'd have had a bad day if I'd not found a slice of dry cod in my cabin. I made rice with strips of cod and wild rice. That's how it always ends up when a boat runs aground."

As I walk through Calella on my way to lunch, I smell the home-made sauces. Wafting on the light southwesterly that has just blown up, the aromas are quite delicious.

22 August. Although I am parochially minded and really don't like generic adjectives, symbols, and abstractions, and do like small-town life, and although most of my friends here are very interesting and I have never been bored (I don't know if the reverse is true), and some have taught and helped me to understand many things, and I won't find anywhere else like it—probably because of a mysterious and obscure affinity my roots created with this piece of land—I am basically pleased to be setting out on a path that will lead me far from Palafrugell and this area. It isn't that I think that small-town life fatally stifles and destroys the personality—big or small—that one has or might have. In small towns it is possible to educate oneself and be productive (sometimes very productive) no matter what scholars of metropolitan societies may say. I know it is difficult because the environment is too restricted, familiar, and precarious—and that it requires more individual effort. Proximity, moreover, gives way to tedium and tedium finally shatters the will. However, that doesn't mean one cannot survive. Although life in a small town is difficult, I think there is something that is even more difficult: making the effort to leave. And that's precisely why I have chosen this path—not with an eye to the results that might accrue, which will almost certainly be third-rate, nonexistent, or perhaps counterproductive—unless something unanticipated happens. I chose it precisely for the difficulty of the path that I must overcome.

23 August. I leave for Barcelona. I catch the small train in Palafrugell—the three o'clock train. After the climb to Terranegra the train hurtles down to Flaçà in a violent racket of wood, glass, and iron. Sometimes the engine whistles triumphantly, which upsets people even more. Passengers are thrown from side to side, often on top of each other, depending on the angle of the track and the movement of the train. A tall, thin, gaunt, sweaty countryman in his Sunday best is sitting opposite me. When he is thrown onto the lady next to him—a sturdy, static lady, with three double chins and a permanent bouffant that remains intact—I hear him say, "The things one has to suffer, senyora!"

"What can one do? One has one's hair done only to find oneself in this dump," says the lady sourly with a frown.

While I am in the line at the Plaça station to buy a ticket for the express, I decide to spend the night in Girona and resume my journey on the six o'clock express. I think it may be a long time before I am back in Girona again. I have always found it hard to resist these waves of primitive sentimentality. I don't know if I ever will. It is my call of the wild.

When we reach the station, I leave my case in the checkroom and walk along carrer del Progrés to Pont de Pedra. When I reach this bridge, I light a cigarette and feel I'm acting like a real fool. It's always like this. A string of memories, images, and confused reminiscences come to mind and I falter and drift. I don't know where to start...I walk slowly up the Rambla. The cafés under the arches are almost empty—a kind of provincial and lifeless summer silence. The waiter in Cafè Norat says a lot of people are still on holiday. These cafés have their moment of glory on market Saturdays, when spoons, cups, and glasses clatter and tinkle and there is lively chatter over trade. Now they seem like different cafés. Even though it is seven in the evening, it is very hot and the sunlight is bright. A summer sea breeze is blowing up the Onyar and in the shade under the arches remains delightfully gentle, but then the breeze seems to vanish. A still, intense sultriness remains. I wonder why I have come to Girona on a day so unlike what I was after. Naturally I would prefer it to rain. I'd like there to be gray sky, gray air, gray stones, grayish people, the sound of rain splashing on the cobbles or on people's umbrellas. The grays of Girona fascinate me. What I am saying is ridiculous, of course. This is just the right weather for August 23. I've simply chosen the wrong moment to come. Some people choose the wrong master, others, the wrong moment. I decide to sit in a café and wait for dusk to fall—the moment when the violent colors break through. It isn't much, but there isn't much else I can do.

While I kill time at a solitary table in the café, I suddenly think of the face of a gentleman I once met in this very establishment—perhaps at the very same table where I'm now sitting. I mean Sr. Bernat Pinyol, the father of a schoolmate who was rather slow and at a loss for words, though he could be lively, and whom I was able to help in exam periods—something for which his family was quite grateful. Sr. Pinyol was an extraordinary man because he was so normal, straightforward, and unambiguous. I have never liked eccentric, strange, bohemian, overly clever, or mysterious individuals. There are enough mysteries in the usual course of life. Such individuals exhaust me.

There was nothing special about Sr. Pinyol. He was like we all are: slightly unclear, slightly odd, vaguely unaware, reasonably sensible, quite careful, forgetful, confused, and predictable. He could be a tad theatrical and histrionic, but at the moment of truth he was humble and very clearly a good person—a man of sound good sense. He carried a stick and when he was talking and warming to what he wanted to say he would puff out his chest, particularly when he was showing off in debate, when he was being sententious and annoying and wanted to demonstrate hallowed truth, like, for example: "Knowledge doesn't occupy space" (an obvious untruth); "Better a bird in hand than a hundred in the bush" (an undeniable commonplace); "A decline always follows an incline" (not necessarily); etcetera. And many other things in the same style. When he made these declarations, he swelled his chest and flourished his stick in the air, as if staking his claim to a remote, exotic land. One day Sr. Pinyol told me, "When it's time to sleep, I sleep; time to eat, I eat; time to work, I work; time to stroll, I stroll; time to get it in—I get it in—though struggling, at my age, obviously. When I do one thing, I don't think about another. I have reached the age I have, with all my teeth, by never letting the obsession of the moment interfere with the task at hand."

"Well, Sr. Pinyol, you are quite remarkable, the perfectly organized man," I responded, by way of continuing the conversation.

"Yes, sir. And there is more. I am under the impression that my mind is a set of small boxes: one box for behavior, one for work, one for hobbies, and one for vices—small ones, of course. If the things that crop up—and so many crop up I never know how the chaos will sort itself out—fit in my little boxes, I consider them to be *un-ar-gu-able*. Do you follow me? If they aren't suitable, if they don't fit easily and don't match, my consciousness rejects them without qualms, lock, stock, and barrel. That's the way I am, and the way things are."

"Lots of people in this country are like you. Sr. Pine Nut, you seem to be a seed in name and a seed in deed."

Sr. Pinyol was particularly well equipped to grasp things simply and schematically and gave the impression he was acting spontaneously, prompted by what came from within. His conversation was as thin as onionskin—but onionskin that soon stopped you from breathing and became asphyxiating. On the one hand, I liked the fact he was so stunningly normal and so characteristic of the country; on the other, I found him totally repugnant and indigestible.

Sr. Pinyol often used the phrase "It's not worth it" when estimating the value of some thing. It's worth it, it's not worth it . . . One day he said to me, "Religion? Best leave it as it is. It's not worth bothering about, you know? I mean, it's something purely expeditious, generally speaking, do you see? It's like taxes, the Civil Guard, the active and passive classes. Personally, I think everyone should be able to think what he wants to think, if he actually has the time to think about it. Generally speaking, it's not worth the worry. Just forget it."

I thought about Sr. Pinyol for a long time. Now, when writing these lines, I suspect that if I'd concentrated on remembering something else, it might have served more purpose. However, it is often the case that your memory hinges on particular images and it is very hard to rescue it from them. Time went by, daylight disappeared, and the urban scene now extended under grayish starlight. I left the café and started to walk at random through the city. I was still obsessed by Sr. Pinyol, particularly by the general issue the man posed: the recognition that the most normal of men can give rise to a feeling of abnormality. That monster of order and pragmatic wisdom helped me understand that life is a long haul down a rocky path.

On that note I reached a completely deserted carrer de Ciutadans and observed how the windows of Sr. Pujades's civilian and ecclesiastical hat shop were shuttered. I would have liked to take another look at the striking headgear we wear, at shopwindows that are some of the most vivid memories from my schoolboy years, particularly after the great stir hats have created in the church over recent years. There had been a singular lowering of standards and a small, flat, round, rather plain hat seemed to have won out—with a touch of fur that was soft and decorative.

I next saw a very narrow, stone side street that crossed carrer de Ciutadans: carrer de la Llebre. I once lived in a room on the top floor of a large old house on this street—a small, dark, interior room, full of family photos and portraits I found quite scary. At first glance everything seemed very tidy and well organized; later, a closer look revealed a place that was much less straightforward. Besides, it was summer and very hot: an unventilated heat.

It was a boardinghouse ruled by two pious ladies in their early fifties, sisters and spinsters who never stopped talking and knew many well-to-do people. They were typical products of a city of Levites, which is what they say Girona is: pale, abundant flab, scant hair, fussy, full of little questions, gossip, indiscretions that were quite discreet, mantillas, and missals. In a word, the usual around here. Those good ladies spent most of their time in the nearby parish church of El Carme. They went to this church in the morning, afternoon, and early evening. They went taking turns. When one didn't go, the other did.

"Srta. Quimeta?" asked someone or other knocking at the door.

"Srta. Quimeta has gone to El Carme."

Then Srta. Pura would go. Srta. Pura had also gone to church. They were always in church. What did they do there? They spent huge amounts of time there; morning, afternoon, and early evening. El Carme was the local parish church; it was very near, on the side street that ran parallel to Lebre, which was home to the headquarters of the civil government—an old convent. It was a dismal church, cluttered with baroque objects: a dark morass of dusty, gilded wood that sometimes injected a rusty hue into the air. They attended different kinds of mass (the favorites were funeral masses) and all the Trisagia, forty-hour devotions, novenas, sermons, marriages, and baptisms—the whole gamut. On days of copious ritual, beds were left unmade but, as I never met the other people who slept there, I have no idea whether there were any repercussions. You do feel your spirits slump if you go to bed only to find it still unmade. It made no difference as far as I was concerned because I'd learned how to make my bed at school. It was one of the most worthwhile, positive things I learned there.

It was a hot night and the air was still and warm. People sat in their doorways looking drowsy and enjoying the fresh air. People in vaguely light-colored garments leaned over their balconies. There were patches of color I associated with a particular smell. Some people sat on rocking chairs on their balconies. Electric lightbulbs flickered in a distinctly anemic yellow glow. The occasional shopwindow shed a little light, a vaguely straw-colored patch on the sidewalk. On plaça de l'Oli, almost on Cort Reial, was the lodging house where I lived when I was doing my military service—with other soldiers from Palafrugell. It was there that one of those lads—who had gone back home without leave—told me that Hermós had shot his cat in a rage, the cat that he'd named Pernales after the bandit, because it had eaten a sea bream he'd caught, perhaps the only one he had ever caught in his life. Hermós was furious because he had decided to give the fish—which weighed more than two pounds—to Donya Rosa Barris to make a good impression on her. It was in fact rather strange that Hermós, who was so sensible despite his wild appearance, should cohabit in Aigua Xal·lida with that insatiable, skinny, cheeky, bubbly black cat. So I concluded that its death must have been necessary. Hermós must have been fed up! His expectations are all earthbound. He is a man who predates Plato, the inventor of idealism, of ideal expectations. The damage those ideas have wrought! The sterile grief it has brought! His expectations are earthbound and it's right and good he should have killed Pernales who ate the fish he was going to give Sra. Barris as a present.

I glance at the façade. The balconies of the boardinghouse are still lit up. That house was so untidy, so messy, so fantastically chaotic! It was, nevertheless, a spontaneous form of chaos, created by the nature of the people living there, in which nobody was authorized to interfere or set rules for the incumbents. Everything was optional: meals, going in and out, and curfew at night. Whoever wanted to sing, sang; whoever wanted to harangue, harangued; whoever wanted to weep, wept; whoever wanted to shout, shouted. There was a lad from Olot, another soldier, who slept in the bedroom next to mine and used to kick the partition wall with his shoe heel.

"I am hungry," he would say in a stentorian voice at seven in the morning. "Where *moight* we get a bite to eat? I could eat a sheep."

The lad on the other side slept like a log and never gave any signs of life. But the lad from Olot—a stocky little fellow with watery eyes— kept hitting the partition wall with his shoe heel until he got tired. I never saw anyone protest at that deeply annoying habit. Those who were sleepy weren't bothered by the noise; those who weren't—a mi- nority—weren't bothered by yet one more act of idiocy. The lodgers were mostly young and light-headed: village lads, who were dazzled by life in Girona, which they found fascinating. Everything was fine be- cause staying in Girona had to be an improvement over being at home. I must say that, like one or two others, I found the chaos quite de- pressing. And chaos has depressed me ever since. The revulsion I have always felt in the presence of disorder and untidiness—a repugnance that has never deserted me, thank God—began in that household.

I turned into Ballesteries. All of a sudden a man walking in front of me stopped at a door, put a key in the lock, and I heard metal grat- ing. I like to hear keyholes grate in Girona—as I like to hear a black- smith hammer on his anvil in country villages—because I think it is an inseparable part of the old city. It was the purest, longest, screechi- est grating: That lock hadn't been greased for many years. The noise brought me to an immediate halt. There must have been just over a yard between the back of the man opening the door and me. In a flash he turned around, looking intense, if not suspicious. In fact, the streetlight cut his face down the middle, turning one side darker than the other.

"What can I do for you, sir?" he asked, after he'd given me a good long stare.

His voice was loud, deep, and well modulated. I smiled and held out my hand.

"But aren't you Joan Ferret from school?"

My outburst had sparked no recognition from him. He took a step back to get a better view of me.

"Yes, that's right," he said finally, "and you are that boarder, now I can see you. And how are you?"

"I have to say I am fine."

"Just wait a moment!" he said, turning around and locking the door again.

Joan Ferret was a schoolmate, except he studied commerce and was a day student and I was a boarder studying for my school certificate. He must have been two years older than me. We became very close friends. He posted my letters so as to avoid school censorship and bought me my first fifty-cent packet of cigarettes. At the time he was of average height, chubby, fair, and ruddy-cheeked; he always kept his hands in his pockets and loved whistling. Now he seemed taller, not so plump, though still well built and sturdy. He may have been paler in complexion. A small finely turned mustache seemed to give his face style. At school he was reputed to find studying hard; however, even though he looked foolish, he was neat, well organized, and calm, and his books always seemed just out of their wrapping paper. I imagined he wasn't very interested in what he was studying, which was natural enough because commerce, at the end of the day, is more fun to practice than to study. He was the only son of a small-business man and his father owned an important, prestigious wax chandler's shop that was extremely well regarded in the pious, ecclesiastical world of the bishopric. They made pale white tapers for funerals; large candles with a minimal drip for processions; altar candles that were yellowish and matched the baroque ornamentation; and spiral candles. They made the green spiral candles that were like peppermints and were inseparable from the Easter Lamb. One of Ferret's sisters had the most perfect legs in the entire petty bourgeoisie of Girona and most pupils at school were crazy about them.

"Aren't you at work?" I asked, as we started walking.

"Oh, no! We've just finished a game at the Moral Center. In this heat, you don't feel like going home. Besides, the family sleeps best early on. My wife and kids sleep like logs."

"What? Are you married?"

"Yes, I am married. I have a boy and a girl."

"Congratulations! That's impressive!"

"Yes, I know! It is a very important step. I married three years ago. My father believes we businessmen should marry young. I expect he's right . . . and so I did."

"And is Lola married as well?"

"No. Lola, who was so much in demand years ago, isn't married, whereas I was the one reckoned to be shy and simple, and I've gotten there. Lola has gotten much thinner; in contrast, my wife has gotten plumper."

"That happens."

We were by the tobacconists at the crossroads. A small fat man was lighting up a large-leaf cigar by the entrance. Both of his eyes seemed to be squinting because he was focusing on the flame.

"Do you smoke that kind of cigar, Joan? I'd like to offer you one."

"Don't worry . . . no need to bother."

After he'd lit his cigar, which I thought gave off a strange, repellent smell but was no doubt simply the standard aroma from those large-leafed cigars, I asked him, "Your business must be doing well. Do you like your work?"

"Yes, we can't complain. We sell candles to the whole of the bishopric and all the towns that don't have electricity. On the other hand, we don't have high hopes; the consumption of candles is on the decline."

"All the same, I won't worry on your behalf. You'll have enough for what you need. And I must say I am so pleased to have bumped into you—and in such a haphazard way. We've not seen each other in so many years. Not that I come to Girona very often, though I did do my military service here. Funny we never crossed paths!"

"It's not really so strange. I lead a very quiet life. I never go anywhere. From home to the café and back."

"To the Moral Center?"

"Yes, that's right."

"And is your center really moral?"

"It's like all self-styled respectable cafés managed by priests: It's good for a game of cards. I might prefer to go to the casino or Cafè Norat, but what choice do I have? Though they're really about the same. My father went there and is a founding member. Business means I must follow suit."

We crossed the Saint Augustine bridge and reached the dark, deserted square of the same name. This square contains a statue of a general in a rash, heroic stance. We crossed the square; the ill-lit arcades have a mysterious, suspicious, solitary air.

"Can you believe how hot it is?" my friend asked with a wave of his hand, as if his clothes were too heavy for him.

"Yes, it's hotter now than when it got dark."

"It's like the sultry heat that comes with thunder and lightning."

"Who knows? I don't. What I really meant to say, my dear Joan, is that I never expected to meet you and in particular to find you so well set up. I've only the faintest idea about what happened to the rest of our schoolmates. You must know more. Though years have passed, lots haven't found jobs. Fortunately most could fall back on their families for help. Even so, some have not fared well at all."

"Better not to exaggerate in my case."

"Who's exaggerating? It's obvious enough. You've a good business, a wife and children, you must be in clover—"

"What do you mean 'in clover'?"

"I mean you must be doing well, you must be happy, as happy as one can be in this neck of the woods, the same as anywhere else, I imagine. On the other hand, you pay your taxes, go to the Moral Center, and are well respected—"

"You were always ironic and sarcastic at school. I see you haven't changed."

"No, really . . . and I say it with my hand on my heart. And I confess I would have liked to come to Girona—then perhaps not come back for many years—and meet a man, indeed an old schoolmate, who has done rather well, is happy, and looks well. I thought you were that man, but I see I got it wrong."

"Yes, it would take a long time to explain . . . you got it all wrong."

"Don't think that makes me happy."

"Although you've been overoptimistic in the conclusions you drew about my life, the whole thing is so petty it's hardly worth talking about."

"So you'd like to extend yourself, be involved in something larger. You're somewhat of a dreamer?"

"I don't know what I'd like ... I'd find it difficult to pinpoint."

"Altogether I can see you aren't happy. Not even living off something so precarious and uncertain as wax strikes you as being of interest?"

"Lots of people earn a living from light."

"Yes, from another kind with a much brighter light. And when you suggest that the life you lead is wretched and wearisome, are you serious or simply grumbling as people like to do?"

"Perhaps we should leave that for another time."

"As you like. In this country, we like to leave things for another day. There used to be a cinema in this square. I feel I can almost hear the noise they made with that bell, that bell they were always ringing to remind people that it existed."

"Today isn't a cinema day. They show films on Saturdays, Sundays, and Wednesday evenings."

"On Wednesdays! That's an excellent day to go to the cinema, don't you think?"

"People like going on a Wednesday. It makes the week seem shorter."

"They think the week seems shorter? But a week is so short as it is, it flies by, only seven wretched days."

"My wife thinks a week is interminable, far too long."

"Is she in good health?"

"For the moment."

We walk through plaça de Sant Agustí, under the mainline train bridge, and into the Devesa. The Güell was a dribble of water. On the right, past the gardens, under the trees, we see embers dying on the ground: the remains of a fire from a Gypsy encampment. The humidity must be high because when we turned into the broad avenue we were hit by the stench of roots, leaves, and earth. The height of the trees creates tranquillity. Some gas lamps—splashes of dingy light— lent a hazy brightness to tables set around a refreshment kiosk. A figure moving around that area walked in and out of sight; he looked like a scribble on a sheet of gray paper held against the light. In the dim glow the lofty plane trees seemed to frame that mysterious, forlorn, intriguingly shabby scene. We sat on a bench on the avenue. The silence was dense, almost palpable. Not a leaf rustled, not a single sound. Everything encouraged you to speak in hushed tones. The Devesa seemed to be a real jungle; Ferret smoked his cigar.

"And while we are talking," my friend said suddenly, "why did you come to Girona? I expect you've work here tomorrow."

"Not at all. I came to spend the night wandering around."

"But you must be staying somewhere or other."

"My case is in the checkroom at the station. I intend to catch the Barcelona train just before six. The train we used to see from school when we were washing our faces."

"All the same, you can't just be wandering at a loose ends ... or are you training to be a tramp?"

"Of course not, I like tramping around, that's all."

"What's in it for you?"

"Nothing."

"I expect your meandering helps you write. You have to find something to write about."

"I'm not sure. Who knows? Do you like reading?"

"Not really, but that doesn't mean I don't read the odd novel. Though I find novels boring, believe me."

"Which ones do you like?"

"I like novels that are like films: lots of speed ... and lots of emotion, galloping emotion."

"I've got you. You want action."

"That's right. That's entertainment: I have enough work with our candles."

At that very moment, the cathedral clock chimed.

"What's the time?" I asked.

"The cathedral's chiming midnight."

They were deep chimes that seemed to come from the center of the earth rather than from the air in the sky. They came from the center of the earth but never lost their metallic timbre, between bass and husky—a solid, slightly cracked *drring* that seemed to make the earth shake. After the cathedral clock chimes—which Ferret and I listened to in silence, clearly bewitched—a lot of other bells, big and small, started ringing, with clear or blurred *drrings*, solemnly or like cowbells. For a few seconds, the air seemed replete, saturated with a delightful ringing that had no rhyme or reason.

"These bells don't strike together, they aren't exactly in harmony," remarked Ferret, as if apologizing to an outsider.

"That's of no matter. The bells that ring later are the ones I prefer. Do you really think they all ought to ring at the same time? It would be a terrible noise. It's good that they are strung out."

"We locals pay no attention. It's as if we heard nothing."

"Obviously, on your bedside tables you all have four-peseta alarm clocks that make a horrible racket."

"Something like that."

We left our bench in the Devesa and the moment we stood up, I felt as if I was starving. I gave a loud, hungry gasp—the kind that inevitably accompanies an empty stomach and general weakening of one's body, a kind of partial collapse, like a wing dropping off. When I started walking, I thought I might faint. I clutched my friend's arm. When we reached the first streetlight, he looked me in the face. I must have turned very pale. He asked, "Don't you feel well?"

"It's quite silly. I'm just hungry. I didn't eat anything for lunch. I should have eaten dinner, obviously, but it passed me by. The thought didn't even enter my head."

"Are you usually so careless?"

"No, only occasionally. My timetable is quite flexible. But don't worry, it's nothing serious. If it weren't so hot and if there was some fresh air, I'd have come around by now. It is so sultry and oppressive."

"What do you want to do now?"

"We should find an open hotel or restaurant."

"That won't be easy. It's late. That kind of establishment is shut by now."

"Don't worry. We'll say our goodbyes at Quatre Cantons. I'll find someplace. I know the neighborhood. And if I don't find, the waiter in Cafè Norat will give me a bite to eat. I suppose Cafè Norat will still be open?"

"Yes, because people gamble upstairs."

We retraced our steps and came to Quatre Cantons past the Saint Augustine bridge and said our goodbyes as agreed. The walk *had* gradually brought me around and I now felt more at ease and self-possessed. Conversely, it was getting late for my friend Ferret. He had been very pleasant company and I was very grateful.

As we shook hands, he said, "I hope you don't make a habit of forgetting to eat dinner."

"Yes, I know, it was poor judgment," I replied. "Don't think anything of it. It won't happen again."

I reached Cafè Norat, on the Rambla, which was open, deserted, with its lights switched on. The waiter, whom I'd known for years, was snoozing with a white napkin on his shoulder, near a barrel of beer by the counter. I was sorry to have to wake him. He was sweating in his sleep. I told him about my plight. He listened, half asleep.

"I can't offer you anything hot. We don't have a restaurant."

"Too bad, that's a pity. I could eat a horse."

"I've got ham, a few slices of cold sausage, a hunk of Dutch cheese, biscuits . . . and bread."

"That's very kind of you."

"Oh, and cold beer and coffee. It's not dinner, more of a snack."

"Thank you."

Very shortly the things the waiter had mentioned—and then scraped together—were placed in front of me. What I really needed, of course, was a bowl of soup and a fine cut of meat. But I was grateful all the same.

It was tasty sausage or at least seemed to be. Everything seemed top quality. I asked for some more sausage and received my seconds. The biscuits were on the stale side and slightly soft. The beer was cold. Clinging to my plan to catch the train before six, I drank two cups of coffee—so I wouldn't fall asleep. When you are sleepy, however, coffee isn't much help, none at all, practically.

While I was eating the string of items the waiter had called a snack, I made a decision: I decided not to leave that pleasant place until they shut. It was relatively easy to deal with my hunger, but I felt tired and the heat had depressed me. My last few days in Calella had been chaotic and futile and the hustle of the journey aggravated by my long fast had brought on a sort of torpor. I felt comfortable in Cafè Norat, which was more or less open, brightly lit, and deserted. It seemed cool in the early hours there—not very cool but sufficient enough to spare me the warm, damp sensation around my shirt collar and the weight I'd felt on my feet now that I was wearing shoes after so many days barefooted.

On the other hand, while I ate the figure of my schoolmate Ferret was ever present in my imagination in a very vivid fashion. That lad, whom I'd found so changed now, was part and parcel of my adolescent years and associated with those years by their most characteristic feature: the erotic. School, adolescence, eroticism...an inextricable bundle of threads that were difficult to untangle. I have never tried, but I think it would be impossible to separate one from the other. Nevertheless, the fact remains that memories, if they are sharp and distinct, however unconscious and confused they may be, tend to appear in a synthetic, comprehensive form. Syntheses of this kind can be overfacile and shockingly incomplete, but they are useful and positive. So I synthesized those long, interminable years and concluded one could sum everything up by saying that at that time, as a result of any minimal erotic titillation (which I now consider absolutely trivial) and the gratuitous arrogance of adolescence, the pressure from your member was so invasive you sometimes felt, particularly when walking down the street, as if you were displaying it under your arm— like a baguette. Some seemed able to carry it off in their lively, contented stride; others looked more downcast.

My schoolmate Ferret was one of those who walked to the Sanctuary of Angels every Thursday with the horde from school. Every Thursday we marched to the Angels—sometimes on Sunday too— and on our way back, some of us, with Ferret leading the way, did something I now feel was gross and crazy. The return walk was always wild, uncontrolled, with a couple of friars bringing up the rear. It was difficult to linger but easy to race on in front. The gang of adolescents I'm referring to, welded together by one erotic obsession after another, occupied the front line in the group placidly strolling along until at a sudden bend in the woods we would break into a frenzied run. My God, how we ran! We knew the path well, even a number of shortcuts.

We simply had to run fast enough to give ourselves twenty-five minutes in one of Girona's brothels before the compact host of schoolboys—thoroughly disciplined by this stage—appeared on a street leading into the city. When we reached the small door to the stairs that led to the "establishment," we were sweaty, red-faced boys panting like cornered dolphins. We had run, jumped, and slithered for a good hour along a hellish track as if possessed. Our initial erotic impulse was incredibly strong; this drive erased any notion of discipline, even though we knew we were committing a grave error that could cost us dearly. When we came to that narrow, ill-lit staircase, after exchanging the delightful smells of the wood for fetid emanations in the most wretched, stinking part of Girona (an exchange that often made my senses want to turn tail and run for it), we must have looked like a bunch of desperadoes, our outer appearance (clothes and shoes) giving the impression that we'd been pulled through a hedge backward and were about to commit a dastardly deed. The truth is, however, that exhaustion from our long cross-country run had diluted our original urges, lowered our temperatures, and I for one sometimes felt that my body had even shrunk. In single file, we passed silently through the door, and although the individual opening the door to us—a fat woman, with two or three double chins, elephantiasis ankles, and a high, greasy hairdo—uttered a few obscenities, no doubt wanting to arouse us, we walked into the main lounge (with shuttered windows over the street), more dead than alive, struck dumb, peering out of the corners of our eyes, as if someone had just clipped our wings. At that time of day, the lounge was usually deserted (except for the odd shabby, foolish farming fellow smoking a thin cigar, hat over the nape of his neck, next to a glass of cognac, the type of man who people say keeps his thoughts to himself, if he has any), and we sat down at a corner table that was probably best suited to our timidity— the farthest from the devilish spirit our imaginations had anticipated. We flopped down on the seats and chairs around the table like heavy, shapeless sacks. We must have been fifteen years old. After sitting there for a while we felt our bodies recovering, but we realized that our arrival hadn't made the slightest impact and that somebody had merely come to ask us what we wanted to drink—the mandatory purchase. Obviously it was too early for any other kind of business. At any rate, someone must have been up to something in that maze of bedrooms, dressing rooms, alcoves, and passageways that comprised the establishment—a very old house refurbished into an even greater warren. The inane manner of our arrival was of a piece with our poverty-stricken, shabby appearance; they obviously must have taken us for customers of no monetary interest whatsoever. In this kind of place, such judgments are crucial and the news spreads quickly through the maze. Thus it was quite obvious that our presence around the table simply amounted to a sad, silent circle of bleary boys. And as our imaginations had raced with hazy, if spicy scenes, we felt bitterly disappointed. I say bitterly because it is the clichéd adjective; in fact it was much worse than bitter disappointment: It was mental disappointment. Meanwhile, a schoolmate, full of rural spunk and energy, whose family had a small farmer in the area of Santa Pau, must have found the lackluster atmosphere unbearable and, being a great admirer of mechanical music—pianolas were now the height of fashion and one occupied part of a wall in that room—got up intending to find someone to start that piano, naturally for a small fee. When he made that move, another schoolmate, Malgrat's son, made a gesture that, even in our state of youthful blitheness, stunned us, really stunned us, I mean, from a rational point of view: He put the fingers of his right hand into his waistcoat pocket, took out the watch he was carrying, and stared at it for a good while, no doubt calculating how long we'd been there and how long we had left before we'd have to rejoin the line returning from the Angels. He was the one of us who had never, at any moment, lost sight of time in its most dramatic aspect, given the situation in which we found ourselves. He was a thin, gaunt lad, all black curls on a slightly goatish head, and spoke in a shrill falsetto. His thin, piping voice informed us that we had been in that establishment for barely ten minutes, in other words we had fifteen left. He spoke in a reprimanding tone, underlining the fact that he personally was not prepared to arrive late. Given our semiconscious state, our friend's timekeeping helped clear our dazed senses—which were, however, increasingly settling down. A long time elapsed, during which we listened in total silence to the unidentifiable sounds

coming from the house and looked eagerly at the different doors leading into the lounge, which seemed more and more of a dump. Nobody
came near our table ... nobody registered our presence. By the looks I
caught on the faces of some of my schoolmates, I suspected one or two
had caught a fleeting glimpse of a young lady of the house in the dim
light of a passageway. Or perhaps had imagined they did. I can say
that, for my part, I saw no sign of a single one, whether nearby or in a
remote corner of that maze where we found ourselves. The schoolmate from the area of Santa Pau came back at that very moment and
told us—with that deadpan expression of his—that it was impossible
to start the pianola because it was too early, and also that Perlita, the
girl who possessed quite a reputation in the city's General and Technical High School, had left this place for a similar establishment in a
small town that was holding its fiestas that very week, which she
hoped to find highly profitable—at least to generate an income to
cover the many obligations the said young lady had to meet, some of
her relatives being in a precarious state of health. This last piece of
news helped cool our ardor even further. We would have been delighted to see, let alone meet, that girl who was so renowned, a kind of
summa of local erotic potential. I am sure each us was carrying enough
money to approach her. In our adolescent arrogance, it never occurred
to us to think that if one of us did manage to sleep with her, the rest of
us would have been left with our tails between our legs. Our time was
so limited it would have been filled by the money one or two at most
had, and everybody else's would have been surplus. In any case, I don't
think we were at all moved by the family concerns of the fascinating,
ever invisible Perlita; we simply wanted to see her with our own eyes.
Adolescence is the saddest, most deprived time in life because it is
when one has the most intense expectations but no means of fulfilling
them, consequently one is subject to serial disasters—large and small.
The fact that the schoolmate from Santa Pau had only meager powers
of expression meant his description of her movements seemed endless,
and more of our time disappeared. Twenty-five minutes in that kind
of situation are laughable: hardly enough for my pituitary to savor the
blend of aromas from the poor, bitter vegetables being cooked and the
warm, sweaty sheets floating in the brothel air. As a result my school-

mate, who was Malgrat's son, put his hand in his waistcoat pocket, stared at his watch, and declared we had barely five minutes left. Another companion I can't pin down for the moment, though after all these years that have passed I still remember his cold, quizzical smile in the face of misfortune, which confirmed what we'd just been told. Chairs clattered and we quickly jumped to our feet, no doubt to show that the huge disappointment we'd experienced had in no way diminished our will. We started to leave, but we didn't even say boo. The lady with the double chins and elephantiasis ankles opened the door for us, glaring severely as if we'd done something dreadful. We must have looked pathetic and our chilled spirits can only have underlined our wretched appearance. We went downstairs not saying a word or making the slightest sound. The street was dark and deserted and we felt even more downcast. We followed our companions who knew the neighborhood, walked down alleys I couldn't now describe, because we didn't notice them, obsessed as we were with the more difficult maneuver of re-joining the line that was returning from the sanctuary. I can only remember the stone mass of the Sobreportes city gate suddenly looming out of the darkness. We lurked in the shadows of the church façade opposite the city gate and waited for the procession to appear, which arrived rather late, stoking our insecurity because we all imagined to a greater or lesser degree that the friars had caught wind of our prank. Finally the line appeared, in double file, dragging its feet, not saying a word. They looked exhausted. Aided and abetted by the darkness we gradually rejoined their ranks, taking great care, naturally, and so we reached school as we did every Thursday: on our last legs. I remember how we slept like logs that night and how in the morning they had to shake us to wake us up. Our disappointment was so great that our erotic obsessions vanished for a couple of days. Then returned. The next Thursday came around as frenzied and blind as ever. It was a never-ending story.

I had already resolved to stay at the café until it closed, so I ate my snack very slowly and lingered over my drink. After serving me, the waiter resumed his snooze next to the barrel of beer—now without the napkin over his shoulder. The place cooled down. The air was more breathable despite the concentrated smell of cigarette smoke stubbornly impregnating the place. I concluded that the waiter's nap was doing me a favor and left him in peace. The clock registered a quarter to two although clocks in this kind of establishment tend to be fast. I enjoyed a long stretch of total peace and quiet, which I spent daydreaming, as you do when you are idly waiting. In any case, I felt much better, in a brighter, livelier frame of mind. As time passed, I felt perkier. Obviously, sleep might get the better of me at any moment. It was unlikely that at that time of night I would find another friend to talk to, as I'd bumped into Sr. Ferrer earlier on. Though at that moment I didn't feel at all sleepy.

When the waiter moved suddenly in a strange, surprising, spontaneous way, raising his shoulders, opening his eyes, and standing up, I glanced at the clock: The hands had only just passed the two o'clock mark. He'd woken up with a start. I had never seen anything like it. Why? I don't think anything in particular had happened in the café. Perhaps the waiter is more perceptive in his sleep than I am awake...I mused. Such strange things do happen! He quickly put a napkin over his shoulder and grabbed a tray. When I was about to ask him why he reacted like that, he came over and said, "They've finished."

"Who has?"

"They've just finished gambling. They play upstairs. They'll be down any minute."

"The gamblers?"

"That's right, the gamblers."

"They'll walk through the café?"

"One or two always do."

"Are they gamblers who like to have a second supper and go to bed late?"

"I couldn't say. Some drop by for a coffee and then go."

A bunch of complete strangers (as far as I was concerned) walked past the café; they seemed highly respectable in appearance. I thought I recognized one: a teacher from my secondary school, a mathematics teacher to be precise—a wheezing, herpetic, chain-smoking Andalusian gentleman who wore a cloak in winter. These gentlemen wore light summer clothes and represented a wide range of human types, though they were all mature men—not a single young blood to be seen—as they passed and went their separate ways. Only two came into the café and ordered white coffees. They downed them quickly and left. Once they were through the door, I asked the waiter, "Are these gentlemen from Girona?"

"No, sir. They are from Figueres."

"Are they professionals?"

"As professional as you can be in this walk of life. They act as bankers in all manner of games, you know."

"Are they wealthy?"

"These people don't miss a trick. If they can't be bankers, they don't play. They are sharp customers."

With that, the waiter starting stacking chairs upside down on tables. The café suddenly looked quite different. There is nothing more unlike a café than a café with its chairs upside down on its tables. Most off-putting. He turned various switches and the establishment was almost in pitch dark; a bulb over the bar dimly lit the nearby table where I was sitting. Then he addressed me in a earnest tone: "I am very sorry, but it's time to close up shop."

"Not much I can do about that. I must say I was very comfortable here, but if I have no choice..."

"It's not that I'm in any rush to get to bed. It must be unbearably hot at home. There are houses like freezers in winter and in the summer you could boil eggs in them...but there we are...that's life. What are you going to do now?"

"I want to catch the express that leaves before six."

"So you've got almost three hours...not long enough for a hotel and too long to cool your heels."

"Isn't anything open in Girona?"

"I don't think so. Of course, there are always brothels."

"No, I hate them. Isn't there anywhere else?"

"No, sir. Everything is shut."

We said goodbye and I resumed my walk. Meandering at random. It's not an unpleasant way to spend one's time, though it's underappreciated. When I reached Quatre Cantons, I set off down Ballesteries. The street was deserted and totally silent. People were sleeping with their balconies and windows wide open—the heat inside must have been stifling—and occasionally I heard someone snoring at a perfect, even pace as I walked by. The rhythm swung like a pendulum, though the snorer occasionally had a chesty cough and the sound then became part nasal, part guttural, like the loud rumblings of a prehistoric troglodyte. Then normal rhythms were reestablished. Sometimes the balcony doors of houses over the old streets in Girona are huge, as you would expect, and reveal large, high-ceilinged rooms. Which means the shutters are big. When a shutter curves charmingly on a balcony, and someone is snoring in the immediate bedroom, the sound reaches you in a more human, distant form, something inseparable from the activity released by a summer's night. I also occasionally heard water running from a tap that splashed monotonously, all the louder because I couldn't track it down. As I roamed these streets, where the heat seemed to bring me closer to ordinary human activity, I occasionally heard someone talking in their sleep. Some people do this in a chaotic, disorderly manner that is incomprehensible; others do so in a flat, normal tone of voice, pronouncing every word distinctly. Initially it is like a monologue that will lead to dialogue. To hear a nighttime dialogue firsthand without offending the usual sensibilities might be rather amusing. But that's wishful thinking. The monologue becomes interminable and finally quite incomprehensible. You understand disconnected phrases but overall the words are disjointed and opaque. That night I heard nobody talking in their sleep.

When I reached the slope to Sant Feliu I was distracted and continued along Ballesteries, toward the Galligants bridge. When I reached the bridge—and found myself in the heart of the Sant Pere district—I realized my mistake. I retraced my steps. I wanted to go to the cathedral square via the street to Sant Feliu and Sobreportes and then, via La Força (the street where my old school is) to find my way back to Quatre Cantons and the Rambla, that is, the former plaça de les Cols. It is one of the most wonderful walks in old Girona. By that time the neighborhood was deserted and the vice, as they say, that was practiced there seemed out of sight, was very much "scraping a living"—to use Pujols's expression. I could hear a gramophone vaguely in the distance. A man was standing in the entrance to carrer de les Mosques. He was around thirty-five, small, fair-haired, with a bulging narrow forehead, a furrowed face, dull eyes, a drooping mustache, and sore, tremulous lips. He broke into a steady walk. He was wearing highish heels and strutted a bit. As I was by the Galligants bridge, I wondered whether it wouldn't be better to go through the Sant Pere gate before retracing my steps, so I could listen to the frogs who sang in the marshes left from the last time the Onyar flooded its banks. There were so many they made the air vibrate. The memory of the frogs' croaking, which had floated in the air when we walked back to school from the Devesa, has stayed in my imagination despite the years that have passed, inseparable in my mind from the wan, multi-colored reflections of the illuminated windows in the houses over-looking the river's murky waters and the fires lit by the itinerant Gypsies in their caravans on the open land. Evidently it might have proved a futile excursion, because the songs of frogs belonged to late spring, the end of the school year, the middle of May, to be precise, and I don't remember if the frogs croaked in late August, which was where we were now, particularly in summers like this when there was a hot drought. When I walked past the street I mentioned, I saw the local night watchman asleep, sitting on a chair against a doorway, be-tween his truncheon and the streetlamp, and the very moment I glanced at his placid, sweating features (he must have been almost sixty and had healthy, ruddy cheeks), I was distracted by the sound of a window opening violently. I looked around to see where the noise was coming from, saw a patch of light in the first-floor window of the house opposite, and all of a sudden, a shrieking woman stuck out her head. It was only for a brief moment, like a flash of lightning, because the window slammed shut loudly. I don't think the night watchman noticed a thing, because he was still sleeping among the tools of his trade. Nor could I say what the woman looked like, whether she was fair or dark, let alone whether she had shrieked from pain or because she was under the influence of an excess of alcohol, say, or some other madness. I then remembered how when I was at school a party had been held in that apartment, the sort thrown by *matur-rangues* (strumpets)—a word heard less and less nowadays, especially in Barcelona—a party with barrel-organ music, that was later replaced by a pianola with the rolls of perforated paper used by those musical instruments that had suddenly come to mind. That strange scene was short-lived, and when the window closed and the woman's shriek faded, the street relapsed into its previous silence. I then reached the slope to Sant Feliu; on the other side of the street was the kiosk by the bend you had to go around to get to the footbridge over the Onyar. It is an attractive kiosk. Two or three doors away there was, or is, a pokey, old-fashioned shop that gave the impression you could find anything there even though it was so dingy—the typical pre–gas age nineteenth-century grocery store. When I was a schoolboy, we used to buy licorice and candy bars there, each of us with a sweet tooth we'd brought with us from our small towns, which Girona students didn't seem to share. The shopkeeper himself used to serve us, a physically odd man, who has lodged in my memory as the quintessential old-fashioned shop-keeper: He was tiny and wore a skullcap pulled down over his fore-head that in its day had been embroidered, and a short, ash-colored gown that nobody would ever have claimed was alpaca. His nose was round like a little ball and his eyes were like a ferret's; he was clean-shaven with a flabby double chin and a potbelly that stuck out over the top of his trousers, with kneepads, which sagged down to shabby slippers that exposed his bare heels. He was renowned for being a man with an eye for the ladies—what Jules Renard calls a *juponard*. In any case, he always gave the impression he was hiding something up his sleeve, and he preened himself and bristled fiercely as if his small but substantial flashes of business insight might have poisoned the atmo-sphere. When it rains, it pours. When your eyes got used to the dismal gloom inside, the first thing they saw was a piece of paper with this warning: "No credit here today." The first time I saw this legend was in the only grocery store on the cathedral square.

As I walked toward the Sobreportes gate, the streetlamps seemed few and far between. An occasional anemic bulb flickered. The ex-posed stonework deepened the darkness. It was hot, but the air was perhaps less oppressive in the early morning. There was total silence. To my great surprise I heard a rooster cry. It was almost the right time for roosters to cry, but that throaty shriek struck a strange, not to say grotesque, note in that architectural ensemble. Where was the rooster? Perhaps there was a chicken coop in a convent or perhaps it was a present to a cathedral canon or bigwig who was awaiting the day when it would become a roast on his table. The stone mass of the cathedral loomed in the dark haze. Its clock struck a quarter to four. It was still very early. Although I was walking slowly and stopping with every step, time hardly seemed to pass—it was desperately slow! Why "desperately"? Your body responds in a purely personal manner. It takes a huge effort to stop that. We only find truth in what suits and pleases us. I would have liked to see the cathedral in daylight. However, it seemed rock-solid. What a stupid thing to write! Can one imagine a cathedral that isn't rock-solid?

The very narrow carrer de la Força was pitch-dark: Bible black. Just after I walked past the institute—I mean the General and Technical High School—I felt my whole body weaken, as if my head was slightly off-balance. I approached a doorframe and rested against it. After a while, I felt the hot flush that had swept through me give way to a more pleasant coldness on my skin. Keeping close to the houses, I reached the post office and sat down on one of the steps close to the street. I felt myself recovering quickly. I heard a cart roll by Quatre Cantons. I saw two or three people walk by—a woman with a basket—but didn't know whether they were going to bed or had just gotten up. It was a vague, imprecise time of night. By Quatre Cantons I had hopes I might find a taxi or a trap to take me to the station, but I realized that was quite ridiculous. Naturally everything was closed and not a soul roamed those streets. The Rambla came to the rescue with a bench where I could sit. And that was how I got as far as Pont de Pedres without major mishaps, by resting for a while on every other bench. By the bridge parapet, I thought that in the east—that is, from the area of Les Pedres—dawn was beginning to show its first light. I'd thought I was close to the station, but at the moment it seemed far too distant. I was afraid of losing consciousness—of fainting. Indeed that wouldn't have been at all unusual. Nonetheless, I put my best foot forward, went up carrer del Progrés to plaça del Marquès de Camps. I sat on a bench in this square for a long time. The cool breeze in a much less built-up area did me a world of good. Now I had to walk and make it to the station restaurant. When I reached the small front garden I saw it was still shut. Dawn had brought considerable light; the odd cart trundled by and the occasional passersby: A man skipped and hopped by, hands in his pockets. I saw that stout fellow who sold lottery tickets and carried a huge knotted stick with a mushroom hunter's metal rod. He sometimes seemed to sell his tickets by flourishing his stick. They finally opened the station. The clock read just past five. As a recognized customer I managed, with a struggle, to get them to cook me an omelet, which was a long time in the making. In the meantime, I collected my suitcase from checkroom and asked a young lad who was a friend who bought tickets for other people to purchase mine. I was in no state to join a line; indeed that kind of task has always irritated me. The omelet was a magnificent yellow: It looked like a canary. I ate it with a salad of endives, peppers, and tomato. Pear tomatoes: They are the best and now, at the end of August, is when they start to appear in the market. It was a good plateful—with salt and olive oil. Then, a few roasted almonds and a thick kind of liquid like chestnut water. That small breakfast brought a degree of euphoria and I had no further need to call on my imagination. I waited for the train on a bench under the station clock. It was getting lighter and lighter. Railway workers put the lamps out. People started to come and go; the day was beginning to stir.

Finally the train arrived. I got into a third-class carriage: I have never traveled in any other. There are very few passengers. I settle down in the carriage with the everyday customers, some whom I know, so the conversation helps keep me from feeling so sleepy. However, I soon find almost everybody is asleep, heads back and mouths open. Some snore surprisingly naturally. The bell rings, the engine whistles, the train moves off. I feel sleep overtaking me in Fornells de la Selva. I have two or three long naps, one from Breda to Llinars. I am so sleepy that in spite of the bright light, the noise from the train, and an uncomfortable seat, I could have slept on a bed of rocks. The fact is that if I hadn't nodded off and napped, the journey would have been tedious in the extreme.

24 August. Barcelona.

We reach the station in Barcelona well before nine. A taxi takes me to my lodgings on the Rambla. Before going up, I drink a coffee in the café next door. Then straight to bed. I struggle to get to sleep, but in this state once I do manage, I sleep for hours on end.

The best part of the summer day in Barcelona is the morning, before the sun hits the city. The city is attractive, the trees are pretty, the air is pleasant, and everything feels cool. Later, when the sun beats down, the heat is clammy and oppressive.

I wake up in the evening just before eight. I eat fried hake and steak and potatoes in my lodgings, which are almost empty. It seems as if it were yesterday. I go back to bed. I start writing down my memories of my stay in Girona. It should be written without filigrees, stripped of any heroic tone. It's a short blast. I finish straightaway. I doze off again. I was really tired.

26 August. I meet Álvarez, one of the news reporters, in the editorial offices of *La Publicidad*. He is a friend. He has a long, deep scar down to his lips that forces him to speak in an awful, soft, gummy slur. The scar disfigures his face and gives his whole body a dramatic crippled look. It must rankle with him because he is constantly striving to show he is normal. His speech difficulties encourage him to chatter endlessly; he is never silent and is bilingual to boot: He constantly switches between Spanish and Catalan. He is also hyperactive, tireless, nervy, always rather hot and bothered and disorganized, ready to go anywhere at any time of day or night, hounded by paperwork, errands, telephone calls, and visits. He has another peculiar trait. Our editorial boards are full of people who write neat little gossip columns, roll out the standard four sentences and yet show no interest or fascination for real news. They can write the news in formulas they know by heart but find it impossible to search for news and track it down. Álvarez works in exactly the opposite way: He has a special nose for trailing, locating, and pinning down a newsworthy piece but, conversely, as he is the first to admit, he can't write it up. He finds it impossible to write the simplest, most schematic article—if we accept the hypothesis that this kind of thing actually exists. I have seen the results of his way of working: His drafts contain random words, odd staccato sentences, squiggles he alone understands. His work is excellent, and Álvarez is today one of the reporters who knows Barcelona best, but he assembles the information he finds into a magma of words, a shapeless monologue, nonsense. There was only one solution: persuade Álvarez to report everything to Manuel Fontdevila, the lead journalist, who could polish it up—that is, recount it in an intelligible fashion. Fontdevila is experienced; he strikes the right tone and Álvarez has become one of the newspaper's most distinguished reporters, even though he cannot write.

In his hands, a most common fault becomes a disaster: He hates generalizing, putting things in context, ideas. His eye focuses solely on the detail, on the anecdotal, on events as they appear at first sight. Other more crucial, more decisive events lurk behind them, but he is completely blind to them. His way of understanding things may be prompted by a variety of causes: a mania for objectivity that has turned into a persecution mania. We shouldn't exclude the possibility—defended by Josep Maria Junoy, a close friend of his—that Álvarez is a purely elemental being like so many in this trade, as I have noticed during my short but concentrated stretch of experience, which has been confirmed by people who have been involved in these circles for years and years, like Sr. Miró i Folguera.

On the other hand, Álvarez behaves exquisitely; he dresses well, is pleasant, affable, extremely generous, and friendly. One can't ask more of a work colleague.

1 September. López-Llausàs, a member of our Athenaeum circle, told me that his father, the famous, controversial publisher of *La Campana* and *L'Esquella*, has for some time been planning to publish a facsimile edition of *Un Tros de Paper*, a nineteenth-century magazine published by his grandfather Innocenci López, the founder of the generation of publishers who bear this surname. I must confess I don't know this publication at all, that I have never seen it—something that doesn't say much for my curiosity, particularly after the praise showered on it by López: cartoons by Padró, articles by Robert Robert, Albert Planes, etcetera. Coinciding with my conversation with López and wholly separate from this project, I remember Alexandre Plana, or perhaps his friend Lluís Valeri, telling me that Carles Riba is a great admirer of *Un Tros de Paper* and intends to select what he considers the best pieces from the weekly for an anthology.

As I have no time to go to the Athenaeum library, or the least contact with López senior so that I might gain access to the family archive (father and son aren't on the best of terms), I have tried to investigate all this by using the means that I have freely at hand. *Un Tros de Paper* was published in Barcelona in the years 1865–66 and that means a complete run is rare, though not impossible for an ignorant dilettante like myself to find. I'm particularly interested in the articles written by Robert Robert, which Riba has praised highly, according to the testimonials I've mentioned.

I have been reading the small volume entitled *Barcelonines* published by L'Avenç in its Biblioteca Popular—number 73—which includes a few pieces by Robert Robert. His prose still makes a real impact and some pieces like "The Backroom" are the best writing in Catalan from the time of the so-called Renaixença—a very difficult period, hence its great value. The L'Avenç volume carries a prologue in which Robert is introduced as being a highly original writer. The last paragraph of this anonymous introduction says the following: "One very much regrets that Robert hasn't written more in Catalan, because hitherto no writer in our language can rival him as a satirist." Perhaps this is a rather exaggerated claim. We have Jaume Roig and the satirical poets. It is a claim made before the work in progress now being written by Bofill i Matas and Josep Carner. Moreover, everyone in this country starts to exaggerate the moment they pick up a pen.

One often hears the view voiced that the best book of Catalan prose from the last century is *The Diary of a Pilgrimage to the Holy Land* by Jacint Verdaguer. Yes, it is true his description of the journey has great normative value, that it is written the way people speak, yet with a certain style. It is immensely important. Verdaguer has a gift with language and writes—in prose especially—in a manner that seems hard to believe, given the period when he was writing. It is the language of his fellow countryfolk from the Plana de Vic recorded by a genuine writer. All the same I think Robert's writing can stand up to comparison with the *Pilgrimage*. Of course, it is very different. Verdaguer's language is always inflated by his religious sensibility, by a degree of religious, mystical rhetoric (mysticism he has plagiarized), and the way he inflects the language is interesting but often unengaging. All the same, Robert Robert is no insignificant writer of prose. He was a man who noticed things, who had a great sense of observation. In any case, one cannot ignore or minimize the period: 1865–66. The influence of Castilian in these years is all pervasive. Pitarra was attacked by the most important dailies of Barcelona for being the height of vulgarity. Society—which was very Castilian-oriented— thought differently. No, Robert Robert is a significant writer who wrote rather messy prose, to be sure, but was very important and preceded Verdaguer's *Pilgrimage*. They are undoubtedly different but Robert's commonplace descriptions are much more interesting from the perspective of today's taste than Verdaguer's rhetorical clichés. The idea that a writer is good because he is Catholic makes no sense at all.

In the meantime, I meet Sr. Bo i Singla in the daily's editorial offices. He is a renowned republican, small, bald, with a forlorn orphan's face and a dogmatic, fanatical, reductive expression. The moment he sees me, he says, "I've heard you are interested in the figure of Robert Robert."

News can spread with startling rapidity in Barcelona.

"Yes, that's true," I replied. "But, you know, I don't have time to apply myself."

A short pause followed, during which I presumed Sr. Bo i Singla would say how pleased he was that I was so interested in a contemporary of his—and a fellow believer as well.

"You mean you'd like to?" asked the renowned republican.

"I'm not sure," I replied. "I have only a very vague notion of Robert Robert; you must have known him."

"Yes, very slightly. I was quite young, but I am a man from the days of the September Revolution. I am quite old, too."

"And what is your opinion of Robert Robert? He played an important role in the September Revolution."

"That's for sure, but he was such a coarse man and such a coarse writer... I can't understand how a man like you can get so worked up over such a petty-minded outlook and literature."

"Do you really believe he was petty-minded?"

"Petty-minded, trifling, mediocre."

"All right. Yours is a view that commands respect."

"I liked Castelar. I was mad about Castelar. His speeches, his writing, were like the sea, do you understand?"

"No, I don't understand you at all. You say you think he is like the sea? I think he is impenetrable."

"And, as Castelar was like that, how on earth could I ever be interested in the small-minded, sarcastic, bilious literature of Robert Robert?"

"Bilious, but he has been dead for years and years. I gather he died before the Restoration. Don't you think it is time to see things with some objectivity?"

Sr. Bo i Singla defended his literary ideas: I mean the high-flown, baroque, pseudo-aristocratic literature he so adored. He came out with this curious statement at one point: "A man like Robert, who was so visibly tubercular and crude, so unsubtle, and indecent in his style ..."

His criticisms were so visceral, it would have been difficult to imagine that Robert even existed in literary terms.

Robert Robert was a bilingual writer. Like so many Catalan writers in the last century, he lived in Madrid for a great part of his life. I am not familiar with his work in Spanish. I have read his Catalan writing in the small volume published by L'Avenç. In my humble opinion, he was a significant writer. It is excellent news that Carles Riba is interested in *Un Tros de Paper*.

3 September. The Athenaeum circle is gradually reestablishing itself. After the summer defections. Those returning have healthy complexions or are quite tan. Those who didn't leave retain their Barcelona pallor. So the skin color of those attending now varies. Only Dr. Borralleras has returned from Prats de Lluçanès, where he goes every year, with the same pallid skin he had when he departed.

Josep Maria de Sagarra came back from the Montseny today. Sagarra is currently the rising star of Catalan literature—specifically in the field of poetry. He received an enthusiastic welcome. As there was an empty chair beside me, he sat next to me. He ordered coffee and cognac and lit up a large, magnificent Havana.

"This lad has everything!" I hear Camps Margarit whisper.

The *noucentiste* poets will make Maragall unfashionable but it will not last long. The *noucentiste* poets are most in vogue now, particularly Bofill i Mates and Josep Carner. However, people have begun to say that these two poets are versifiers and, consequently, a cooling-off period is inevitable. This won't last very long either, unless the notion of what is valuable has been lost in this country. Sagarra is on the rise and isn't exactly a *noucentiste* poet, nor does he add to the enormous contributions the *noucentistes* made, especially in the linguistic realm. How far will he go? He writes extremely fluently and is gifted with language. He is very young. One cannot say how far he will go. We shall see. The business of literary conjecture is extremely difficult and strange surprises abound.

Quim Borralleras was the only person to welcome Sagarra normally, without exaggerated words of greeting or gesticulations. They are great friends and the doctor holds him in the highest regard, but remains unsure—I mean unsure about the way he writes poetry—and is simply observing how he develops. He has discreetly told people he can trust, "Sagarra has the most diverse talents and you never know what to expect from him. He acts sometimes like an atheist (I don't know if he is one really), and then seems like an excommunicated nun. At other times he acts as a Catholic (again, I couldn't say if he is one or not), and then like the priest from Bethlehem church. He can be superbly open and friendly, fantastically polite, and extremely good company! Then all of a sudden he adopts the stance of a man betrayed, looks at you askance, screws up his eyes as if you had insulted him. Whenever I have found myself in this situation, I have tried to remember whether at some point I *was* ever impolite toward him, consciously or unconsciously, if I offended him, so I could clear up the misunderstanding immediately. I have always acted like this. The truth is I could never recall anything of the sort, and thus could never discover anything between us that needed resolving. Sagarra is obsessed, hugely obsessed, by slights, which must be why he sometimes imagines them. He invents slights, believing they happened without any evidence. In this respect, he is quite superficial and his judgments aren't consistent. His greatest psychological fault is that he is highly suspicious. That is his defense. He is too immature and his character is prickly and difficult."

Dr. Borralleras's observations are quite true and I've often noticed these things myself.

As the afternoon progresses, the gathering thins out and the general conversation splinters into different smaller conversations. I ask Sagarra if what editors are saying is true, namely that he has been appointed as the Berlin correspondent for *El Sol* in Madrid and *La Publicidad* in Barcelona. He confirms the news in an irritated tone, as if he is about to doze off.

"Yes," he says. "I shall soon be departing. They are now bringing me the clothes I have had made."

"Clothes, did you say? But you always give the impression you have many already."

"That's right, but you understand, in such situations, it is better not to be caught with everything hanging out."

Sagarra's habit of speaking indecently, using the most vulgar turns of phrase, has always seemed grotesque to me though many people find it amusing.

"I have had dozens of shirts made and I have purchased socks and ties, several suits, a dress shirt and jacket, and a tailcoat."

"What about a frock coat?"

"No, they are out of fashion. Nobody wears them anymore."

I asked that last question timidly, anticipating the poet's hostile response, that is, imagining he'd consider it an insult to his sense of fashion and social propriety. I was surprised he didn't blink an eyelid—very pleasantly surprised.

"And have you had overcoats made to measure? I understand winters in Berlin can be very cold."

"Naturally, several and some with a fur-lined collar!"

"Very good. Fantastic. You will be the best-dressed journalist in Berlin. That's a good way to start. On the other hand—how can I put it?—all this clothing you will take with you would perhaps be more appropriate in a country that had won the war rather than a country that had just lost. I imagine Berlin is very impoverished and shabby. The clothes you have had tailored call for Paris, London, or the United States."

"Not at all! I want to write another kind of journalism. I don't want to be seen as starving, as yet another beggar in the trade. I intend to go to the very top, do you see?"

"To the very top of what?"

"To the very top of the top."

"Ah, I see now…"

At that point Pujols sidles over—he was sitting a few tables away talking to Josep M. Albinyana—and we break off our conversation. Pujols, who already knew about the poet's appointment in Berlin, congratulates him and predicts that he will be a great success with the ladies in Berlin and with Germans in general.

"You will," he says, "be the true representative of the Latin race in those northern mists, our most warmhearted and, we hope, most effective representative, and women will melt in your hands, in your divine hands, as dear Ors would say. And, certainly, you must hang a sign on the balcony of your house, advertising your presence."

Sagarra's outburst of laughter at Pujols's quip is loud and hollow, but occasionally he seems to laugh as if he meant it.

5 September. Politics in this country are in a perilous state. Social unrest is rife both externally (terrorist attacks) and internally. There is great confusion and incomprehensible debate and the perspectives advanced are derisory. It seems as if everybody couldn't care less about the country. Hardly anything positive has been done since Sr. Prat died in 1917. Sr. Cambó, who has led so many initiatives in his lifetime, now seems hesitant and worried, or so the political journalists say. That's hardly surprising. It sometimes seems as if the country has lost what faith and energy it had and by which it achieved so much years ago. Conditions for a dictatorship are being created. It's hardly worth talking about the state: It only seems to work when there are no problems.

It is raining. When it rains early in the afternoon, the national smell appears in the countryside, namely the smell of mushrooms. You can smell it in Barcelona too, but not as strongly; it is less distinct and less pungent, though still present. Literary people sometimes describe the scent of the earth: It's the smell of mushrooms.

I have never sported a mustache, or button shoes, long johns, a cane, a wing collar, rings, tiepins, watch chains, perfumes, a cravat, or long hair . . . so many, many things that were typical of the previous generation. For the moment, I have yet to use the spittoons that once were ubiquitous. The fact that I have bypassed this entire assortment of items may be for better or for worse. Perhaps for the better. At any rate, now you know!

7 September. In the early hours I spot Dr. Borralleras sitting at a table on the Lyon d'Or terrace accompanied by a member of the female sex and our mutual friend, Lluís Foyé the aviator. It is a splendid night and wonderful to be on the Rambla. Quim, who sees me hovering there, beckons to me to go over and join them, which I do. I know everyone present. The member of the female sex at the table is an acquaintance of Dr. Borralleras, whom he had introduced me to on a previous occasion. She is a kept woman, mature in years, slightly squint-eyed, thin though rather sickly looking, smartly dressed, extremely amusing and lively—though rather past her prime—that

Quim introduces her to me as a someone very well read and cultured. At the moment Quim seems greatly influenced by Marcel Proust's work. It fascinates him. He speaks about it night and day. He does what he can to encourage people to read Proust. I imagine he would be happy if this young lady were to.

My inopportune arrival hardly interrupted the flow of their conversation. They were talking about human vanity. The young lady was actually speaking. She spoke vivaciously.

"From what people say," she was saying, "women apparently have a monopoly where vanity is concerned. Elements in their visible life—fashion, for example, their facial expressions, the way they argue—seem to confirm this. Currently, the dresses and hats people wear furnish further, very positive evidence. The case for what is visible isn't simple and straightforward, as a matter of fact: Everything becomes blown out of proportion. Even so, I don't agree for one minute that women exercise this monopoly, generally speaking. Men are infinitely vainer than women. I have no small experience in the matter. A moment comes when men reveal their vanity in exaggerated style: in bed. They are quite unbearable, tedious, and objectionable. They go to every extreme, sometimes the most violent extremes. Their affectation is childish. The worse their intentions, the more childish they become. One has to be very patient indeed to put up with them."

Foyé listens with a skeptical smile, with a smile that is in fact vain. He appears to be a man completely impermeable to any vanity that isn't his own. Quim's expression is entirely serious; he doesn't move a single muscle of his face, which is set like a mask. I am sure he is interested in what his friend is saying but is probably astonished by her considerable range of expression. Perhaps he grasps that it may be possible to induce her to read Marcel Proust—not an easy read by any means—his main obsession at the moment.

"It is male pomposity, male lack of naturalness, the vanity of men that causes so-called feminine perfidy, which is prompted by intolerable boredom and desperation; it is one of the subjects literature has explored in great detail, in all eras. Perfidy, feminine guile exists: It is women's way of wreaking a natural revenge on the intolerable pomp and circumstance of the opposite sex. Men think they possess every virtue, every talent, every kind of intelligence, even the potency behind life itself, which soon shows itself to be rather mediocre and meager. They rarely tell the truth. They aren't generally what they seem. They are intolerable. It is this disappointment that creates feminine perfidy. It is the normal form revenge takes. In a country like ours the social system seems to put every possible obstacle in the way of feminine movements and to assure the impunity and absolute invulnerability of men's pompous excesses. The lack of coherence and fickle moods novelists assign to women are simply their way of exacting revenge. It is highly amusing to see men accuse women of displaying these defects when men are in fact the authors of the most typical feminine reactions. If men weren't so vain, women wouldn't be so dangerous."

The skepticism of Foyé's smile hardens. He is perhaps riled because he can't see exactly where the woman articulating these thoughts is heading.

"Young lady," asks Quim, "have you ever come across a straightforward, true, natural man in the course of your work?"

"Some, very few. Obviously there are men who are driven by such a sense of the ridiculous that they seem immune from vanity. However, that sense of the ridiculous sometimes pushes things to another extreme, and those unfortunate enough to have it in excess are hollow and mealymouthed. Almost all the rest are boring and thoroughly vain."

As the sky is beginning to brighten behind the monument to Columbus, Quim asks if the time hasn't come to leave the café terrace and start on the return home—that is, to his apartment on carrer del Bisbe at the point where this street branches off from plaça de Sant Jaume. One can see the square and the two large buildings on either side from one of the balconies in this house. In the early morning, plaça de Sant Jaume has a bureaucratic, icily provincial air.

8 September. Before the war, all the couples one came across in Barcelona appeared outwardly languid and faint, as if touched by moonlight, especially if they were comprised of the offspring of well-to-do families. They sometimes held hands with long, languid fingers. For the moment, the languid look seems to have disappeared and people now behave more directly and thoughtfully. People say this change is the result of the war. I prefer it. Neither languid, twilit beauty nor idealized beauty did very much for me. I feel excited by real physical beauty, although it can sometimes have its own kind of stylization. I struggle to believe that Stendhal could possibly have written this sentence: "The angelic soul in that beautiful body departed life in 1825" (*Souvenirs d'égotisme*). This is Stendhal idealizing Mathilde, who cuckolded him so often. It is a silly sentence that rings false and sounds grotesque.

The other day I mentioned the smell that invades the country when autumn begins, especially if it has rained or is very damp, the smell of the earth, namely, of mushrooms. This time of year has a single smell—or at least a diffuse smell, which prevents us from smelling anything else and sometimes seems deathly, depressing, and often dubious. The recent downpours—it will soon be the Mercè holiday and the autumn equinox—made me think of spring. Spring is full of the most varied, diverse smells, of subtle scents that don't meld—bitter and sweet, dry and hot, gentle or intense aromas that are complex and fascinating and revive the dimmest memories. I find the smells of fennel, acacia blossom, honeysuckle, and gorse more intense than scents from flowers people grow—the flowers found in gardens. No matter that they lack external presence or have poor display of color.

One of the few useful, sensible things I did during my years in the Law Faculty was to enroll in an Italian-language course taught at the Casa degli Italiani in Barcelona—I don't remember the precise year. The class—which was crowded—was so intensive I think I only got to know the other students by sight. People were there to work and we had no interest in wasting time. There were Italians who wanted to improve their language skills and locals who had decided to study Italian of their own free will, out of genuine interest—or by necessity, of course.

Until that point I had lived in a Francophile ambience. The circle at the Athenaeum, which had played such an important role in the course of the last war, was passionately, fanatically Francophile. France and nothing else! They could entertain the most ridiculous ideas: The only thing not up for discussion was France and their own Francophilia. In sporting matters—which for many members could be highly contentious—there were supporters of Barcelona and L'Español who peacefully coexisted. It would have been impossible to coexist with anyone who wasn't a Francophile. Italian-related things were looked down upon and disregarded. Italians were considered frivolous, gossipy, inconsequential, highly verbose, and dangerously cunning. Eugeni d'Ors had spoken with seriousness about Italy in the circle. He had spoken about Italy in order to use classical Italian design against Gaudí. Pujols's extravagant praise of Italian poetry and opera had been criticized because it was deemed excessive. The first people from the country to go to Italy, apart from those who made pilgrimages to Rome, were the *noucentistes*. *Noucentista* art had Italianizing pretensions: Galí, Aragay, Obiols, and Riba were planning if they hadn't already done so to take an Italian tour. López-Picó's *La Revista* had devoted space to Italian matters. Estelrich was an outright Italianizer—perhaps because of his love for Majorcan culture. However, they had all occupied slightly equivocal positions during the war. D'Ors, the most Frenchified person I have ever known, Frenchified to the marrow of his bones, has publicly defended Romain Rolland and his *au-dessus de la mêlée*. Riba had believed a German victory would favor the political interests of our country. (Prat de la Riba had thought similarly.) Nonetheless, this movement kept a low profile and remained a minority affair. The main block of intellectuals—from Santiago Rusiñol to Pere Ynglada, from Quim Sunyer to Enric Casanovas and Josep Maria Junoy—had remained unquestioningly pro-French.

I began to study Italian in order to read *History of Italian Literature* by Francesco De Sanctis, a vitally important book according to Josep Maria Capdevila and his inseparable companion Joan Climent. Josep Maria Capdevila seemed to have three obsessions at the time: Saint Francis of Sales, Francesco De Sanctis, and Joseph Joubert.

Climent followed suit. All three obsessions were the creation of Eugeni d'Ors, naturally. For many of the country's intellectuals d'Ors uncovered inexhaustible treasures that were in infallibly good taste.

The classes were held in a clean, bright, spacious room in the Casa degli Italiani—situated in a mews in the Eixample whose name I can never remember: the one where Dr. Arruga has his office. A large podium. A portrait of wondrous Dante. Clean materials for the students. When I think of those benches in the university lecture theaters, my God!

Cavaradosi, our grammar teacher, is small, stout, pallid, and sad, dressed in black, middle-aged, with a white piqué waistcoat, where a silver watch chain swings. He generally speaks standing up, pacing across his podium. He sometimes uses the blackboard. I don't know what accent he uses because I can't understand him at all. (At the end of the course I discovered he spoke with a very marked Neapolitan accent.) Professor Cavaradosi is the author of the grammar we use. I think the book is clear, intelligible, and practical. His explanations are straightforward and coherent.

I'm not suited to this kind of thing, which I find rather boring and quite unappealing. You can only learn things you like by applying some discipline. Thanks to my teacher and his grammar I may perhaps have made some headway—I don't know, probably not very much. A few days after starting the classes I order De Sanctis's *History* from the Athenaeum library. I can't decipher a thing. I read a paragraph and it was as if I'd read nothing. I try out a volume of Croce's *Aesthetics* in the same spirit and with the same result. Days later I open *Corriere della Sera* and understand the odd simple sentence. My first contact with this newspaper makes a big impact. It is the second daily I have read in my life that I found interesting—intriguing, that is. The first was *Le Temps*, from Paris.

My attendance at the Casa degli Italiani classes makes me decide to head for Italy as soon as I can. When will that be? Who knows? I don't covet wealth, but with every day that goes by I increasingly understand one can do absolutely nothing without money—without a small but adequate amount.

10 September, Wednesday. I have no time to write. The examinations in the subjects I still have to sit for my law degree are fast approaching. I have to read my textbooks and learn by heart (if I can) the contents so the examinations aren't a complete disaster. I do so reluctantly, with no interest. I understand nothing. My only hope is for my memory to retain as long as possible (no time at all, I suspect) what I am reading.

The newspaper is a lot of work as well. I have no choice: I have to do it. Between one thing and the other, I hardly have any time to sleep; I am consuming too much coffee and tobacco. The food is dreadful. The monotony and mediocrity of all this make me very bad-tempered. Luckily, I have some powers of resistance. I have had to swallow so many noxious things in my lifetime! And will swallow many more, so help me God!

25 September. I passed the remaining subjects for my law degree. Better not to think about it. What with my leaving certificate and degree I have had to sit many exams in recent years, but I have never been able to get used to this kind of pedagogical ritual. They have always scared me stiff, sometimes grotesquely. To this day I don't dream very much—pleasantly or otherwise—but whenever I do, the dream has been inspired by an obsessive, disagreeable panic over examinations: an obsessive insecurity. The outcome—whether good or bad—has brought a sense of relief. Preexamination insecurity and the examination itself created unease in the consciousness of my unconscious life.

To become a lawyer, I will now have to buy the title—that is, pay the state the necessary amount to obtain it. I don't know how much it costs. But where shall I ever get the money? I don't have a cent—and what I do have I need to use for my board and lodging. My father can't be very well set up. It is a waste of time asking him—and besides, it would generate ill will. Where will I get the necessary money? Will I ever be able to pay for my law degree? I think it must be easier to make it to the framed record of my year with my fellow students, under the oval portraits of our professors, than to buy the degree.

This situation has only one solution: a serviceable relationship with a rich lady. But one can only enter this kind of relationship by means of patience and effort, that is, over time. I have always felt women are a big waste of time. I tell myself I must be mistaken. I have always preferred to waste my time idling, listening, or reading. I've been what they call an unhappy man.

26 September. I escape to Palafrugell for a day to celebrate passing my final examinations. My family is clearly pleased, though without the usual excessive outpourings at such news.

When I have finished telling them all this and enjoy a moment to myself, I realize I've nothing else to do in Palafrugell. That comes as a surprise.

It is a magnificent, bright afternoon and, seen in perspective, typical of autumn in this country. I walk to Ros and the Sant Sebastià mountain. The local vistas. When the afternoon slips by and brings that vaguely egg-yolk light, things seem even clearer and more precise in outline. On my way back, I linger for a moment on the En Casaca bridge. Sunset. The embers of sunset create a golden, greenish, reddish haze that slowly wraps around everything before sinking into a dark blur. The formless mass of Palafrugell becomes incomparably soft and gentle—as if seen against a backdrop painted by one of the old masters, reminiscent of reproductions I've seen.

During dinner—delicious Caesar's mushrooms, the best in my view—Mother says, "Don't take notice of other people. Easy come, easy go. Everything's uncertain, so brittle."

I take the first train back to Barcelona in the morning: the five o'clock train. After spending a mostly sleepless night in bed, I'm more tired than ever.

28 September. A manservant pokes his head around the clubroom door and says, "Sr. Solé de Sojo…wanted on the telephone!"

"Sr. Solé de Sojo is in London," responds Camps quickly, looking at Pujols with a sudden grin.

"That lad's a shuttlecock. He's always on the move," Pujols adds, paternally.

And in effect, when Solé isn't in Barcelona, he is in London or about to go there. When he returns, he is always fatter, more oval, and sleeker. He is one of those people whom Europe tones up and extends. He needs that air. He brings back the latest fashions from London and Paris. His close friend in Paris is Pere Ynglada. He brings with him not only the latest news from the worlds of art, literature, theatre (ballet), and music (cabaret) but also the latest model of cigarette lighter, shaver, watch, tie, suspenders, belt, hat, socks, sticks, garter, pipe, tobacco, matches, records. In Solé's hands, these trifles assume fabulous, extraordinary proportions. He must have large quantities of such things at home that have gone out of fashion—things that lasted for a moment and then had had their day. The people he feels most affinity toward appear to be Josep Maria Junoy, Lluís Garriga, Pere Ynglada, and one or two others, very few, in fact. Nonetheless, he seems to have dazzled them with his tireless, lurid displays of the latest fads and gadgets. From a political point of view, this man on a constant quest for new sensations is an outright reactionary. People who know the circle's makeup say Solé attends not to develop himself philosophically, to catch up on city gossip, or to serve his legal vocation—which is apparently considerable—but to nurture his sensibility. Solé acts as the poet in our circle, and it is probably the only time in the day he does so. I'm vaguely acquainted with his poems. They have a railway touch: overnight sleepers, restaurant cars, the Orient Express, and high speeds.

The combined influence of Rusiñol and Pujols is most visible in the lively way Francesc Camps Margarit expresses himself. Despite these pressures, Camps has retained a very real, individual personality that is sometimes unique. This is noteworthy. Catalans are very prone to imitation, parody; it comes naturally, we might say—a keen fascination for achieving complete identification. After meeting Manolo

Hugué, Ramon de Capmany imitated him, especially his way of speaking, and did so astonishingly well.

D'Ors tell the circle he wants to come up with a commentary against Krause.

"Please don't!" I hear Pujols react. "Please don't! Don Tiberio Ávila only discovered Krausism two or three weeks ago, and if you do that, he'll be mortified: He will never recover."

29 September. In the circle, Francesc Pujols has his days. There are afternoons—and nights—when he seems absorbed in a morose, apathetic silence, emphasized by his body weight and size. He always sits there holding his stick. On days like this he simply twists its knob over the floor tiles—or pretends to, so as not to make any noise—and when he is absentmindedly thinking about the outside world, he sometimes looks vaguely up at the ceiling. On other days, he finds it easier to kick-start the engine, as he likes to say. His monologues then gain momentum and nothing will stop him; he employs gory adjectives with ease, words which in his usage are unusually appealing and slightly tragic.

I heard him talk about the repercussions of shifting the center of gravity in the Athenaeum, from the room above—the circle deemed to be conservative—to the circle downstairs. Pujols and Borralleras were the ones to execute this operation. They campaigned well, won the elections, and now are the masters of the house. The operation gave rise to great arguments, much unpleasantness, and serious altercations. One of the members of the upstairs circle who most distinguished himself for his frivolity and lack of substance was Dr. Josep M. Roca, known in Barcelona as Rock of the Union (meaning the Catalan nationalist Unió Party), an academic with considerable weight in the right social circles. Pujols felt raging contempt for him.

"When I heard the news," Pujols said, "that Sr. Rock of the Union was claiming we had carried out this operation in the Athenaeum in order to transform this establishment into our bread basket as well as a house of ill repute, I sought him out and told him, 'Look here, Roca, I'd much prefer to be deceived than to deceive. I'd like to make it crystal clear…' When I said that, Roca seemed astounded, as if taken by surprise. 'I find your surprised expression somewhat suspect, Sr. Roca,' I added. 'Perhaps you don't agree with what I've just said. My words are, in any case, only by way of a well mannered response…so, I think we should understand where we stand now. If you continue to speak the way you have been…' Roca tried to articulate a word or two. He seemed unable to overcome his state of shock. I left him open-mouthed, striving to move beyond his blighted state. I walked away. After this exchange, I gather he *has* stopped speaking the way he was previously. Exit, lips sealed!

"Josep M. Roca," Pujols would add, "was important in my time, a mixture of improvisation, ignorance, bilious vanity, envy, and intolerance—and at the same time he was completely lacking in seriousness. I sometimes wonder if this country will ever get anywhere while people like him abound. A lady from Vilafranca, a Sra. Carbó, once fell passionately in love with Roca. As he was thought to be a sage, and he himself believed he was one, her attentions puffed him up like a pumpkin. He bought a snow-white hat, flashy cane, and fantastic shirtfront, and he had a suit made from the finest canary-yellow cloth. He wore such shiny shoes with white, Eucharistic gaiters that his extremities looked like the lake in Lamartine's poem after a snow storm. In this outfit, Sr. Roca strutted around like a dandy and made quite a splash. In the Sra. Carbó era, he had his hair washed with egg whites by the Athenaeum barber and his beard brushed with a toothbrush.

"Sra. Carbó swooned so tenderly over Sr. Roca," added Pujols closing his eyes and fluttering his eyelashes, "and when she exclaimed 'Ay my Roca, ay my Roca!' so lovingly, so suggestively, it was highly amusing, not to say amazing, to hear such a hard, weighty word being uttered by this flushed and trembling woman.

"There was a little man who exercised a lot of influence over him: Dr. Font Turner, known as Font Nano, a sort of monster from a mystery book, who acted like his tail. The main biological reason for Font Nano's presence on this earth was his extremely anti-Cambó stance. Dr. Roca is of the same mind. In this century we have known a lot of

Catalan nationalism and talk of this kind. But only one thing was beneath their show of words: a stance for or against Cambó, sympathy for Cambó and for what he stood for, or hostility. Everything else was secondary. The upstairs circle was the center of the anti-Cambó position. Dr. Roca and Dr. Font Nano are the quintessence of this anti-Cambó-ism: They are opposed to Cambó in a permanent, visceral manner—just as passionately as they opposed the grammatical norms established by Pompeu Fabra. Why are they against the institute's norms? No one has ever worked that out. We have waited so long for them to justify their position that one can only conclude it is a product of their levity and ignorance.

"Another close friend of Dr. Roca is Sr. Pelegrí Casades i Gramatxes, a terrible, grumbling, bilious, snarling, tiny satrap with a poisonous tongue. Don Pelegrí is such a short man that he has to have a series of tomes stacked on his chair if he is to reach the table and conduct his research. These books include the most valued works of the human mind: the Holy Bible, the Patrology of the Holy Fathers, and the Commandments. It is quite possible that many more important books have passed under his backside than through his hands.

"Dr. Roca's first devotion is politics. He was elected president of the Unió Catalanista and was a total failure. The only thing people remember from his term as president is his nickname, Rock of the Union, which has stuck to him. When he was president of this body and in Berlin one day, he joined in a homage being paid in Roda de Ter to a fellow believer, by sending a telegram with these very words: 'Body Berlin. Stop. Soul Roda. Roca.'

"In the years when the upstairs circle controlled the Athenaeum, Roca was elected president. He swaggered enormously. The streets of Barcelona weren't wide enough to accommodate him. As a result of this post he undertook a limited amount of academic activity, which perhaps gave him more satisfaction than life ever had."

30 September. Lunch in Can Soler in the Barceloneta with Joaquim

Sunyer and Josep Maria Junoy. We were beginning to enjoy the sun and the Barceloneta was delightful. It was a magnificent day. Rice and fish with perhaps a touch too much saffron and grilled fillets of sea perch. Sunyer is extremely affable, a man with a humanity and depth of understanding that I find rare in the world in which these gentlemen move. He greatly admires and supports Joaquim Borralleras. Every day I meet people who say the same things about Quim. The impact Quim has had on all intellectual circles in Barcelona is quite stunning, despite his outward detachment and apparent indifference. He is a unique, singular figure.

After lunch, it is so sunny Josep Maria Junoy suggests going for a stroll along the breakwater. And we do. There is hardly anyone there: the usual sailors and fishermen, some mending fishing tackle and others looking at the sea—I mean the open sea. I mention this to Sunyer the painter and ask him to tell me why the sea fascinates some people—he is after all a contemplative landscape painter.

"It is exactly the same in Sitges," he says. "When sailors and fishermen don't know what to do next, they look at the sea for any amount of time. When I went to Banyuls to see Maillol the sculptor, I observed the same phenomenon."

"Sunyer, have you ever looked at the sea?"

"From a distance and vaguely."

"Have you ever noticed a woman look at it for any length of time?"

"I don't really remember . . . I don't think so."

"What do these people find in the open sea that they can spend so long staring at it?"

"Frankly, I don't know."

It is a fact. There are people who are fascinated by the open sea. In fishing villages along the coast, they spend hours and hours observing it, generally not making a single movement, particularly if there is a wall to rest their arms and elbows on, and if they have no work to do—and sometimes even if they do. I have often wondered: Why do they look out to sea? What do they find there that is so fascinating?

In Calella de Palafrugell, a small town on the coast that I know well, one of the fishermen who looked at the sea the most, in recent years, was Josep Tort, the barber's uncle, an elderly man who is plump, round-faced, and potbellied, a sententious bachelor who is rather sibylline in the way he talks. He isn't a solitary, individual fisherman, but one who first embarked on sardine boats and then on trawlers. On land, you could always find him at one or another renowned vantage point, staring at the waters of the open sea. He never went to the café, to mass, or to the tavern, and never left town: By night he went fishing and by day he looked at the sea. What could he see? One day I said to him—he was a friend of mine: "Tort, you are always looking at the sea."

"Yes, that's right."

"Do you find it amusing to watch steamers and sailing ships go by?"

"I like sailing ships but I couldn't care less if they pass by."

"But you must see something out at sea."

"No, I don't think I do."

"So why do you look at it for such lengths of time?"

"I don't know…I couldn't say…"

One summer I looked out at the sea as long as I could to try to understand this enigma. I found nothing. In fact, I reached the conclusion that the waters of the sea, of the open sea, were horrible. I couldn't find any kind of beauty—or anything fascinating at all. Clearly the sea can trigger all manner of different reactions: It can arouse the desire to depart, to flee, to escape, to see the world, to find a different habitat. But the fact is the people I've known who were most fond of looking at the sea were the most immobile and sedentary. The sea offers various scenarios. The sea *is* a varied spectacle. It changes, especially in the summer. It is different in winter. In winter, a persistent, continuous, tiresome outlook can settle in. The sea's diversity depends on the weather. The weather is the sea's prompt. The sea does whatever the weather dictates. The sea is a passive element in the games the atmosphere plays. The sea is a harsh, horrendous form assumed by nature.

One day I carried out a test. In the presence of Josep Tort, I paraphrased the famous phrase from Aeschylus, "The sea, ineffable smile," to see what impact it made. It was a day when the sea glinted in the sun and was full of eddies and foam stirred by a cool northeasterly.

"This sea," I said, with a deadpan expression, "seems like one continuous smile remaking itself."

"What was that?" the fisherman asked, looking rather shocked. "A smile that is remaking itself? Have you ever seen the sea smile?"

It would be curious to see what effect the old Greek's phrase has on seafaring people. It's more likely they'd consider it a purely artistic-literary turn of phrase, namely, a futile fiction.

On another occasion, I carried out the same test with the Eugeni d'Ors phrase "The sea, in its stark nakedness." Not many things have been written about the sea—ones which have stuck, I mean. Lord Byron uses a lot of adjectives to describe the sea in the French translation of *Childe Harold* I read not long ago. Xènius also wanted to say something—something that would last—and he came out with "in its stark nakedness." I repeated his phrase to a sailor, who had plied the route to the Americas, while I pointed a finger at the sea.

"Did you say 'in its stark nakedness'?" the sailor responded. "What do you mean? You do mean something or other, I suppose."

I didn't insist. It was simply an artistic-literary concept and was unintelligible to nonliterary beings.

At one point I decided that sailors and fishermen look at the sea because it inspires an obscure panic in them that is sometimes justified—because they feel the lure of fear.

"If you look at it for so long," I told Josep Tort one day, "it must be because it frightens you."

"It isn't that I really like it, frankly," replied Josep. "I'd have preferred a trade on land to a trade at sea."

"I understand."

"But it doesn't frighten me. If it did, I wouldn't look at it, I couldn't stand it."

"Has it ever done you any harm?"

"Frankly, no. Never!"

Water on its own, the open sea on its own, is horrendous, oppressive, and unpleasantly sterile. The view of the sea one has from the land around the Sant Sebastià hermitage is almost instantaneously unbearable, if one looks at it with any degree of sensibility. On the other hand, a mixture of land and sea is magnificent—a continuous, surprising source of beauty. Cadaqués is splendid because its bay makes it impossible to separate the sea from the land. The sea, as seen from the town of Calella, is relatively—minimally—attractive. Conversely, seen from the sea, from over the sea, the town of Calella is splendid, fascinating, and never tiresome. It is the mixture of land and sea that is attractive. That's why people like lakes and rivers so much—that mixture is their essence. From the top of carrer de Claris, you can see two inches of sea. This sight, with the city before you, is quite dramatic. Generally speaking, the sea you can see from the heights of the sloping plain that constitutes Barcelona is one of the most beautiful things about the city.

1 October. A dark day, many hints of rain in the early morning, but the water that does fall hardly wets the streets. The early afternoon is bright and sunny but already shows signs of autumnal melancholy. By early evening, the sky darkens again with the occasional slight rain.

Every editorial board has writers who write about Barcelona—the so-called *barcelonista* writers. This kind of writer exists in every city of a certain size. They are usually excellent writers. I don't think they do any harm. They write about things they find in archives. You can find so much in archives! I don't think what they do is difficult; there is an endless supply of all kinds of historical papers. Sometimes these writers are lyrical and full of hyperbole. Now that the leaves have begun to fall from the trees, one of these writers has just penned this sentence: "The plane trees on the Rambla, with a little goodwill and sparrow fluff, seem like almond trees in blossom."

These writers are often intolerable and unreadable.

I go to the cinema from time to time—rarely—and sit and watch a film. I try to go to cinemas where they show the latest films. Then I bump into someone or other and say—because you have to find some-thing to talk about—that I have seen such-and-such a film. My inter-locutor scowls and says bumptiously, "I've seen it." I occasionally tell a married couple, only to hear them chorus the reply: "We've already seen it."

At other times I am reading a book that has just come out or one that came out years ago—which everyone has forgotten—and, of course, I tell the people I think are interested in the world of books. They invariably grin and say, "Good heavens! We've read that."

If I buy a shaver sold as being the latest model, it turns out that everybody owns one. If I go to a restaurant that has just opened, which some gourmet has recommended, I discover that everyone has already been and found it so-so, and is hypercritical.

This is a city in which everyone knows everything, has read every-thing, owns everything, and has seen everything. I imagine this must be a very small city, but I can't vouch for that. As the reporter in charge of the section of a newspaper called Crime Reports, at seven o'clock one evening I saw a man's corpse on carrer de la Cadena—he had just been killed as a result of a terrorist attack. At seven thirty I told a friend; he had already heard about it. If you are so lucky and privileged that an obscure, eccentric poet reads his unpublished verse to you and you are foolish enough—a foolishness solely intending to boost optimism about the future of literature—to pass the good news on to a friend, you are simply left looking stupid. The mysterious verse is well known and highly regarded.

I am not very receptive to surprises—because, naturally, I don't ex-pect any. Now, when you find someone in Barcelona who is genuinely unaware of this or that, or is behind the times, it is a great joy. We live our lives among people who are remarkably knowledgeable.

Writing...

I find the following sentence in the Mercure de France collection in the Athenaeum library, in an article by Rémy de Gourmont: "*On n'écrit bien que ce qu'on n'a pas vécu*" (You only write well about things you haven't lived). A strange proposition. It seems like an obvious paradox. Of course, it may simply be a boutade. In any case, it appears that when Marcel Proust heard it—according to one of Barcelona's best-informed admirers of Proust—he said straightaway, *"Cela, c'est toute mon oeuvre."* What was Proust implying when he apparently endorsed Gourmont's proposition?

I think it is self-evident—the examples are legion—that one can write extremely well about things one has lived and especially about a small selection of such experiences, because one would produce huge amounts of insubstantial writing if one transformed everything one has lived into literature. Would Muntaner's historical chronicle be as fascinating as it is if its author hadn't experienced—personally experienced—a large part of what he committed to paper? Though it is also undeniable that one can write very well by adopting the perspective of a writer of memoirs and recording what other people have lived, in other words, acting as witness for someone else.

A literary work of a significant length, like Proust's, for example, is a bottomless well. It contains things he has experienced personally and things experienced by a large number of people. Every sentence has a specific origin and every paragraph its own history. It is a work created out of an immense, confused morass—exactly like life itself. The author projects the light of his memory over this confusion, and his memory is the element that introduces order and is decisive within limits. Proust has a prodigious memory: He not only has the most vivid recollection of things and people he has seen or known or has heard about from others but also manages to remember the thoughts suggested by these contacts, how they reacted mentally or sensuously to these relationships.

So one can't say that Proust simply writes memoirs. I am not very familiar with Saint-Simon's *Memoirs*: I have only read fragments. Saint-Simon is, I would say, the scholarly essence of a writer of memoirs because his work contains mainly facts. Facts, events, men, women, situations. There is much more than that in Proust. Fragments of his work are overwhelmingly realist, a realistic naturalism that no writer of this school (I know them well) could ever achieve, even on their best days. In this sense one could say Proust is one of the greatest realist writers of all time. However, as well as his realism, there is a whole realm of thought and ideas suggested to the author sometimes by physical contact, sometimes by spiritual contact with the outside world, sometimes by society, and sometimes by the art that brings it all together. Proust is a great realist writer, but a highly superior realist, much more rounded and complex than this type of writer. In this respect he is a synthesis of contradictions that seemed insoluble for years and years and were the object of an endless polemic that apparently could never be resolved because everyone was so locked in his own perspective. Proust resolves the childish oversimplification of the realism of his time by bringing to the foreground, with unique insight and a fabulous means of expression, a reality that is infinitely richer in sensuous and spiritual elements. It is very likely that great writers are significant in that they function as a kind of crossroads—in their ability to overcome contradictions that human petty-mindedness had transformed into rigid structures. I think it is evident that Proust banished from his literary horizons petty, low-ceilinged, reductive realism. On the one hand, he is much more realist than the writers in this vein and, at the same time, succeeds in sublimating reality by getting much closer to its essence, by re-creating it in its essential entirety, in its immense, wondrous complexity.

Perhaps what we are suggesting will become clearer in regard to detail. In strictly realist writing the accumulation of detail is so great that it becomes tiresome. They become naturalists, photographers. The amount of detail in Proust's work is much greater than in these writers. Sometimes so great that it feels like a landslide—an extremely large, copious landslide. The quintessence of all written work is in the details. The interest of all literary work—the essential, primary interest we would say—is to be found in the details. An author with real potential always confronts a large quantity of details from which he must choose. Sometimes, a detail, an adjective can suggest a whole world to a reader. Details in formulaic naturalist or realist writing have barely any power, they are overly simple; they often try to be so precise they suggest nothing at all, they produce mere inertia in the mind of the reader. They are, to an extent, too Euclidean—too linear, too straightforward. In Proust's work the detail is different, denser—and that doesn't mean it is more obtuse or commonplace; it is different, goes more to the heart of the matter, is more complete. Life ceases to follow a linear pattern in his literary world; it is a world with greater, more profound dimensions and volume, with vaster, richer perspectives—endowed, above all, with iron necessity.

I have heard it said that the greatest character Proust created is Charlus, the great cultured, free, idiosyncratic aristocrat and homosexual. Possibly. One could argue, however, that the character of Françoise, the cook, is equally grandiose. Her portrait is much clearer in that her spiritual and outer lives are explained in a perfect, inimitable manner.

Proust is one of the highest peaks of contemporary literature. I want to record how grateful I am to Joaquim Borralleras for the efforts he has made to encourage me to read him.

It is curious to observe how, with all his realism, Proust always adheres to a line of ineffable good taste—good taste with a spirit that cannot be defined in terms of the art and fashion of his times, and that, according to Quim, stems from the way English Pre-Raphaelites and modernists influenced his development.

2 October. A glorious day: sunny, bright, and airy. It is a pleasure to walk along the street. Autumn weather tends to create days with such subtle light that things appear precise and clear-cut—even in Barcelona. In my country of the Ampurdan, this light enhances the tone of large swathes of the landscape, of entire vistas—however little the north wind blows—and the way things are defined and stand out is quite marvelous, sometimes obsessively so.

Autumn brings the most pleasant weather to this country. This is extremely visible in the Ampurdan. Winter there is long, endless, and uncomfortable; spring is short and unstable; summer is a blast of hot air; autumn is long and linear, though never sumptuous: It is truly worthwhile. All Saints' Day can introduce a cold sting to this season, which the shortening days seem to underscore. If that happens, then houses begin to cool down inside—gradually and on the sly. If it doesn't, the air in the sky stays mild and warm and is only dislodged slowly from the houses. One can even reach late December in that state. However, by then one is powerless. The saying couldn't be truer: longer days, colder days.

When winter in Barcelona starts to fray, the cold retreats inside apartments, the trees lining the streets bud, and spring begins to float in the air; women, naturally, tend to shed their clothes. It is a marvelous, unique moment...whatever the current fashion may be. The opposite movement is visible in the autumn, clothing gets thicker, and when the first person with a cold appears croaking and hoarse, the freedom of your mind and senses begins to shrink.

I sometimes think about the years I spent at the university and the general—dreadful—state the university is in. Its condition makes life horrible for students and can be very disheartening. It prompts predictable reactions from young people; they descend easily into clichés and excessive generalization. Like my friends, I have found excellent individuals in the faculty of university teachers and I am sure we could reach agreement on certain names. We couldn't quote them—well, some for sure, though our lack of enthusiasm and curiosity was so marked we barely differentiated between them. We swallowed everything—good and bad. The normal student response was basically: "My professor was the most pedantic person I ever knew; the most pompous, the worst-tempered, the most disorganized, the least interested, the most boring, the most lightweight, as well as...He must have been selected on purpose."

I don't know if they were. I don't think so. However, there were so many, it seemed they must have been. Everything was so inextricably linked, one couldn't discern any visible difference. In the end, it was the institution itself that took all the criticism: the university as such.

Conversation with others would be easier if everyone or almost everyone had an obvious, accepted, distinctive epithet. If it had a contemptuous ring, all better. To be able to say, when relevant, for example, that Sr. Pi i Margall was nice but pathetic; that such-and-such young lady is pleasant but slightly squint-eyed; that Frigola is more sociable when it rains than when it is dry; that our mutual friend is slightly tubercular; that Josep Carner is a great poet, etcetera—and it could be a very long list. It would spare us lots of words, large amounts of verbiage and meaningful gestures, things that are always risky, ambiguous, and can have untold consequences.

"What about those of us who don't have a distinguishing mark and are fated to remain gray, what the hell are we supposed to do?"

"Those of us who don't have a distinct trait must get used to being sacrificial victims offered up for the gossip that will inevitably flourish around us. Spied on and vilified. Of course, there will always be many such victims in a society that is set in its ways."

4 October. In the years I spent at the university before starting out as a journalist, I tried my hand at the occasional literary exercise, as they say in school; I mean that I tried to write something without thinking of any outcome that might ever be public or minimally presentable. I made my contacts with the Palafrugell weeklies—a town of weeklies—as an adolescent, and at the age of fourteen or fifteen was sending gossip columns to *Baix Empordà* from boarding school in Girona, embroidering items printed in that old city's *El Diario*, *El Norte*, or *L'Autonomista*. They were mere side products, secondhand goods, not at all significant, and though I was never happy with them, I found it to be an amusing way to pass my time. My friend Ferret posted the letters. There were anonymous society columns, which to my astonishment the daily paper published.

Later on when I settled in Barcelona, I wrote a lot of articles for *Baix Empordà*. These articles are an unreadable complete mess and bear the characteristic mark of youth: barely concealed pomposity. They are an admixture of the spirit informing adolescent intellectuals in Barcelona in the second decade of this century—a spirit dominated by *noucentisme*—and the gray matter of Palafrugell, which was at the time no ordinary thing. It was the friendships I established with Joan B. Coromina, Tomàs Gallart, Joan Linares, Josep Vergés, Josep Ferrer, Josep Miquel, Roldós the pianist, Lluís Medir, Josep Bofill de Carreres, Enric Frigola, Ramon Casabó, and others I can't remember now who encouraged me to write. All these people—pleasant, easygoing individuals—created a kind of exciting buzz in Palafrugell, lively and local yet at the same time interested in the international scene, which is hardly surprising given the mentality in the cork industry, almost universal in its perspective. The buzz manifested itself in two ways: in a skeptical, rather messy critique of our habits, and in wild praise of the local landscape—praise that is wholly justified. Even so, my articles for *Baix Empordà* were terrible and if the weekly published them, it was out of compassion and particularly because of the eternal dearth of original material for this kind of local publication.

These wretched initial attempts were the forerunners to my wish—as I have already said—to try my hand at more ambitious literary exercises, but I must admit right away that I never achieved any positive results. In my case, what is usually called the prodigy of youth—or adolescence—was notably absent. In Barcelona I was in contact with some of the literary youth of the day. I wrote the occasional piece of literary prose—as it was then called. We would send such a piece to *Ofrena*, *El Camí*, and *La Revista*. Nothing very much, naturally. I published what I imagined to be fragments of much longer works—of various works over which I labored for hours and hours though never to any visible effect. I tried to write about Girona—perhaps encouraged by *Diari*'s publication of a piece on the Sant Daniel valley, which Alexandre Plana read when I was doing my military service. I then tried to write something about Palafrugell and its landscape, which I thought would be easy at first and then found impossible, and later a piece on the sea that was to include descriptions of the port of Barcelona, and another entitled "Men Against the Landscape" that proved to be a fond hope with no substance. I worked at these things for year after year and never produced a piece that was at all coherent. Alexandre Plana, the only person to whom I dared show my manuscripts, was always encouraging. I still don't know why; he was extraordinarily generous. It was thanks to Plana that I met my first hypothetical publisher: the poet Josep M. López-Picó, the director of *La Revista*.

"Work at it!" he told me, when I visited him in his gloomy office in the Economic Society of Friends of Paris, in that big house on carrer de Sant Sever, if I remember correctly. "Work at it! Bring me a book and

I will publish it. We will publish it as part of *La Revista*'s list. Come to our circle at the Continental and we can talk about all this. I will introduce you to my friends. Bring whatever you are working on now."

Picó was very friendly and accessible. I felt proud when he said this and I worked as much as I could on my drafts, but never produced anything. I tore up a vast quantity of quarto pages—those wonderful quarto pages from the library of the Athenaeum that were made of such splendid paper. I should thank God for such destruction. They were a total disaster—no doubt about that.

I went to the circle Picó, Riba, and Obiols held before dinner at the Continental. Not very often. Almost never. Frankly I didn't go because I was so shy, because I was so embarrassed. I have never been the detached sort. When there is a good crowd, I am always at a loss and cannot string two words together. My basic shyness is compatible with occasional audacious outbursts, particularly if the people I am with are total strangers or people I know only by sight.

All the same, such a continuous literary failure must have had a specific cause. But what was it? I discussed the matter with Alexandre Plana, the only person who had really looked at my manuscripts.

"What do you think?" I asked him. "It isn't going well at all."

"True, it's not going well at all. It is probably worse than you imagine ... I'll tell you why in a few words: You are too *noucentista*."

"What on earth do you mean?"

"I mean it seriously. You aren't a real convinced *noucentista*. I don't think you know enough to be one and the way you are certainly doesn't incline you to be that way. However, the fact is you are using a *noucentista* style. You hold a pen and write in this style. You use these archaic words, these medieval expressions, simply because you have read such things."

"You're absolutely right."

"It's obvious! So why do you use these Gallicisms, these neologisms, these localisms that no one understands? Why don't you write as Sr. Fabra is always telling the circle, naturally, as people speak ... as people speak in the circles you move in? Do you understand me?"

"Yes, I understand. But I thought *that* was the path to follow if you wanted to write literature."

"What literature?"

"The literature being written today in this country."

"The literature being written in this country today is *noucentista*. It may pass muster when Sr. d'Ors does it. When his disciples do it, it is literally appalling. You must put such things behind you."

"Which things?"

"You must break with rhetoric, precious subtlety, verbosity, with highfalutin literature. When you read what you have written, you don't even like it yourself. If you ever published it, who would like it apart from the four friends who belong to your clique? Believe me. Forget the cliques. Don't write with your mind on what you have read: follow your own temperament."

Alexandre was generally affable, imperturbable, and measured (at least on the outside), and now he seemed quite agitated and visibly irritated. Initially I imagined this change was caused by an outbreak of bad temper prompted by my reticence when it came to his advice and my constant requests for him to read my wretched writing. However, I was forced to revise that impression as he talked. No, he wasn't annoyed by the issue of my resistance and insistence. The central literary issues were driving him crazy—that is, he'd suggested a way forward and I'd never taken any notice, had never followed his advice at any stage.

After a short pause, Plana went on: "Conversely, the state of our literature doesn't allow for French-style stuff. Our language is very hard, very unelaborated and difficult to handle. Many things have been lost: However, one thing has never been lost, the spirit of the language. I don't mean the spirit of the thirteenth century—I don't think anyone knows what that is—but the elements of that spirit that have been brought up-to-date. That is the spirit we must preserve. We must adhere to a minimum of intelligibility, clarity, and simplicity. We must not be so tremendously vain as to wish to rebuff the people who approach our books or magnify the headaches and problems they already have. The moment hasn't yet arrived—we are a long ways off—to make minority literature: We must make a literature for everybody. Minority literature isn't necessarily good simply because it is so. One experiences so many disappointments on that front. In any case, let's leave such minority literature to languages that are sophisticated and developed. Ours isn't. I know that preaching these notions to the young is like flogging a dead horse. It may even be counterproductive. But no matter. It's what has to be done. If young people can't take responsibility for things as they really are, and display a certain spirit of self-sacrifice, you can be sure we won't have much joy, probably none at all."

I thought at length about everything Alexandre Plana said in this conversation—which inevitably I have much abridged—and must confess that what he said really struck home. I tore up sheaves of paper, everything I'd written over all those years, with such difficulty, in *noucentista* style, shall we say, as one way of describing it. As soon as I could, I started writing this notebook—*The Gray Notebook*. It was the natural consequence of the destruction of all that paper. It is never great fun tearing up your own efforts, particularly when you have worked hard at them, as in my case. But I did so and with little hesitation. I am sure it was the right thing to do, at least as far as I was concerned.

This notebook has been a struggle and hard work. And it has been written following other criteria. One thing encouraged me from the start: the realization that it was much more difficult to write in this way than the way I had tried to write before, the style Jules Renard calls *tarabiscoté*, which was exactly what I was about. In any case, I have persevered this far and I confess that I've even surprised myself. I can't say anything about the possible value of this notebook. Maybe it has none. I am almost sure that is true. If it is eventually published in its entirety—which is very different from publishing fragments—we will see how readers receive it. I sometimes suspect this notebook should contain more everyday things and should have ignored literary-artistic matters. I have a spontaneous, almost automatic resistance to anything artistic. At other times I think there is too much of the ordinary in the notebook. The fact is, I don't know one way or the other.

I rarely returned to the pre-supper circle at the Continental held by López-Picó, Riba, Obiols, and sometimes Estelrich, etcetera. If I'm walking down the Rambla and see their gathering in the distance, I stop for a moment and watch Carles Riba's rather tense face. If I walk up or down the pavement in front of the café—the gathering is held around one of the front tables—I wave at those in attendance, take my hat off, and walk on, up or down, happy to mingle with passersby. The truth is that my change of style—curiously—gives me a much more precise idea of my position on this earth: of my absolute, outright insignificance. In previous years, with the illusions of youth and my pretentious, entangled style, I had lost sight of that notion. It had more or less disappeared into the murky recesses of my mind. Now it was beginning to reemerge clearly, with some definition, and it did me a world of good. I even found it soothing. When I realized that I had the resources to lead a solitary life and found it preferable not to pester others with my presence, I sensed that I had taken a turn for the better.

7 October. In the early evening, just before the streetlamps were lit, Barcelona was hit by a heavy downpour of rain and a gusty wind— very autumnal. Tomorrow the newspapers will describe the cloudburst with their usual hyperboles. I watched from my boardinghouse window looking over rambla de Catalunya.

The moment the gale-force wind seemed most out of control, blowing chaotically and unpredictably, it began to rain cats and dogs. A gust even lashed the window with a flurry of rain. Raindrops hit the pane in a strange rage. Suddenly a door in the house slammed. The wind hissed through the leaves on the trees and made the wooden balcony shutters creak. Water streamed off the trams as they drove down. A young woman walked across the Rambla in light-colored clothes, displaying magnificent long calves and gripping a paltry umbrella. The raindrops made big bubbles on the ground. A cart passed pulled by a steaming horse. Its master was leading it by its bridle, under a huge umbrella that gleamed iridescently in the lamplight on the pavement. The wind couldn't blow away a thick, dust-colored cobweb that seemed to hang in the sky. Although the wind did finally sweep everything away and an autumnal sky appeared with bright, sparkling, sharply defined stars. The languid, white haze of summer nights is no more. The wind finally dropped and ushered in a still, static, rather cold night.

All in all it must have rained half an hour.

8 October. Dr. Borralleras often mentions a writer friend of his by the name of Sr. Girbal Jaume. He doesn't come to the circle, but they are close friends. Although he has written and published several books, I am unfamiliar with his work and person, so I asked him to fill me in—if his usual hypochondria will allow him to express himself.

"Girbal," he tells me today, "is simply rather an unfortunate case. The literature he is producing is almost entirely focused on the description of visible objects. He is inclined to believe that only material reality can have any substance. He writes on rural topics. He cultivates a naturalist vein within his love of the rural. As a naturalist, he tends to get lost in detail, to be a systematic photographer. After listing these features of his, I hardly need to tell you that he was and is the bête noire of the *noucentistes* who, as you know, are city-centered and professorial. They don't attack him; they simply ignore him, greet him with standoffish silence, In my view, this attitude is wholly unjust. Ors is a lifelong acquaintance: Girbal is a great character, pleasant, agreeable, and an excellent friend despite his irresistible desire to be the star. Although a French-style skeptic, when it comes to cultural or literary affairs, he is dogmatic, prescriptive, and tyrannical. He is convinced that he, and he alone, possesses the truth. He is intolerable. You can understand why Girbal feels so wretched: They have destroyed him."

Quim pauses before continuing: "I have little time for what Girbal writes. He is a man who can write, with a gift for language and a rich vocabulary he deploys well. But he doesn't appeal to me, I don't like what... As I am a friend of his, I sometimes allow myself to criticize him mercilessly—something I wouldn't allow anyone to do in my presence who wasn't in my position. After all, Girbal exists, and when things settle down, Girbal will be the most representative writer of a particular literary tendency, wrong-headed no doubt but with an undeniable presence. We don't have that many currents. We can't afford to neglect any one. We need them all. At the present time, rural literature, in this country, seems like past history. Our ruralists have perhaps overmined the vein. Their minds have a limited time span. But don't think this kind of literature is over and done with elsewhere. Not for one minute. It is bursting with life."

When I read the newspapers, my head goes into a spin. The chaos in Europe—on every front—is beyond words. States remain fiercely nationalistic and there is complete disunity. It becomes clearer by the day that France went to war solely to regain possession of Alsace and Lorraine. They have them. Now they want Germany to pay for the war. How can it? Where will it find the funds? The mere suggestion of such a plan and the economic collapse of Germany is a foregone conclusion. In any case, and despite the flourishing of Communism in the USSR, it seems that after the war the West is content to leave things as they were. It is an absolutely grotesque prospect. Even so, there are no initiatives to improve the economy, let alone improve the political situation. Wilson and his overall plan (the only one on the table) are a complete failure. The national political classes throughout Europe seem exhausted and have nothing to offer in words or deeds. Italy wants to right itself alone. The Italians are saying, "*L'Italia farà da se.*" That means they will help spread anarchy. The devaluation of the political class means the bourgeoisie is more anemic by the day. An anemic bourgeoisie! How is that possible? If the bourgeoisie isn't strong, audacious, and red in the face, what is the point of it?

"We Francophiles," Pujols was saying today in the circle, "are very down in the dumps. We understand nothing; we know nothing. We are complete country bumpkins."

He said that with such a wicked grin and so naturally I thought it was a delightful performance.

"How so, France is a great country," retorted Aguilar, stiffening.

"Yes, a great country that is behaving very badly."

"Why so? It doesn't seem possible," Dr. Dalí replied ingenuously.

"In the land of empiricism, anything *is* possible," replies Pujols dryly. "Don't make me laugh... France is a great country that has behaved very badly for the same reasons that Oller married a Rabassa, if you get my drift."

Everybody bust out laughing, but the reaction was short-lived and hardly sweet—it was anxious laughter.

Pujols is fortunate in this respect. He has his own philosophical system that is perhaps not fully established, but he is getting there. He seems happy with his system. Philosophical systems probably contribute little to the happiness of humanity; one can't deny they contribute to the happiness and contentment of those who construct them. I don't think Pujols is interested in anything else apart from his system.

10 October, Friday. I have been very lucky, so far, with my good health. I strongly believe in inheritance. Is it possible not to? If I had to choose my parents, I would choose mine again. My inheritance has worked positively so far. To be honest, I have never suffered from grievous physical pain. The occasional toothache has made me see stars. My mouth has caused me pain. So far I've only had toothaches. Obviously worries, headaches, upsets, inevitable blows to one's pride, disappointments, failures, failed expectations had and still have an impact, but I can't complain too much: I am reluctant to be seen as glib and unaware. I have lived without suffering any major crises. I have lived away from home practically since I was ten—I am now twenty-one—I have slept in many different beds and chewed and consumed a variety of (often very unappetizing) food, but for the moment I've not had to make any great effort to cope with any of it. I have been very lucky and must be grateful to the somewhat cold upbringing I experienced with my family (delivered without the usual commonplaces and tales that float across dining-room tables). I've been fortunate in life (apart from moments of erotic frenzy or great thirst) and have always acted in a natural, cautious manner. People say that southerners—an opinion you read every day—are passionate to the point of blindness. In principle I don't believe this to be the case. At the very least it's highly debatable. We are generally too frail to rescue ourselves from definitions that are constantly being imposed. We should examine every case. It must be because we are so ancient historically (the country gives the impression that it's very old and has been trampled over by all kinds of people), and this has left us with an irresistible tendency to systematically mistrust ourselves. In the body of clearly imprecise information about people from the south, we, the inhabitants of the Ampurdan, are held to be scatterbrained and eccentric. One finds this kind of person everywhere. On the other hand, the Ampurdan is perhaps the least conventional and most individualistic area within what the "Protectress" of Catalan education, and Estelrich, who is part of it, call the "linguistic area," and perhaps its inhabitants *are* more easygoing. Anyway I don't agree that the characteristics we just mentioned are the general rule where I come from. People in the Ampurdan are mostly discreet and ingenuous, wary and quick to be suspicious. I don't believe it could be any different. Our history is that of a frontier people, with a frontier that has been historically contentious and, consequently, we are people who are used to being on the defensive. That is why we are adaptable rather than dogmatic. One completely endorses what the historian Pella i Forgas wrote about our character as a creation of history. There are still sentry points on the new façade of the Pla farmhouse. I have often told my father we should remove them because they bear witness to a past era that is better forgotten. However, perhaps such a perspective is simply an illusion. Yes, of course, we ought to remove them. In the meantime these additions to the corners of the façade, with slits for firing guns in self-defense, demonstrate how insecure the lives of our ancestors were and indicate their only defense against what their geographical location kept throwing at them. The fortified towers of the walls of Palafrugell remained sturdy and in place until a few days ago. I remember seeing the last one. The fin-de-siècle manufacturers of bottle corks demolished them in the name of progress. It was well-intentioned, but perhaps the towers shouldn't have been lost entirely. The town would have had a reminder that's now gone forever. Conversely, we of the fourth estate have had to defend ourselves against the invasive, deeply rooted feudalism of nobles and prelates, which only slowly became extinct. This situation has existed for centuries and has shaped the way people are. It has produced ironic, individualistic, cautious countryfolk who aren't at all straightforward. One sees that at every social level, but it's particularly noticeable in people with a long, unbroken line of rural forebears—as in my case, for example. I can't deny that from time to time the odd countryman won't appear who is rather mad—countryman or whatever. I am also prepared to accept—as the pantarchy wrote to the *Almanac dels Noucentistas*—that in our heart of hearts we are *all* mad. In any case, some are more and some are less so. Thus, indigenous lunatics, like any others, are interchangeable and quite normal. And as those of us who are in this situation are the majority, exceptional lunatics think we are living sages. This is the state of play in the Ampurdan as seen by someone born here, with a youngish but inquiring mind. It is a situation that's very similar to what one finds elsewhere.

After this excursus—which seemed to come out of nowhere—I think it should be very clear that we ordinary locals are rather wary of the official representatives of the Ampurdan, the ones in the display cabinet, the ones newspapers and magazines always describe using the same adjectives, whenever they talk about their Greek origins or voice the opinion that they wear their hearts on their sleeves, when they're portrayed as being under the influence of the north wind, or disorganized and very progressive. All such formula are completely unfounded and constitute worthless clichés that people inject into facile, inept, lyrical prose uninformed by any contact with reality.

In any case, I have probably experienced more than my fair share of toothaches. My mother has suffered similarly. She is in her early forties and her mouth has that depopulated look. In the little one can deduce from photos of her as a young girl, she enjoyed fine teeth, which is what she has gradually lost, and quite irrevocably. She belongs to an era when physical pain was deemed inseparable from the normal progress of human life. Dentists, of all the healing professions, seemed the most ready to act irrespective of the pain produced by their actions. People said: Dentists hurt. They believed it was natural for them to inflict pain. I don't think they could do anything else. What could they have done to mollify the impact of their trade, apart from quoting the catechism or taking more care with their hands? There were dentists—even I have met some—who ignored these instruments of persuasion. They dreamed they were Napoleons of the pincer. My mother would be strangely cautious when walking past a dentist's practice—even though the best-known dentist came from Sant Feliu every week in his trap. At the time everything from Sant Feliu was believed to be highly important in Palafrugell. She always refused to go. She let the pain follow its natural course and would only use homespun remedies. When aspirins were put on sale, she was one of the first in town to buy them. Aspirin helped her resist the dentist. And that was the point of the exercise. The same happened to me. When I went off to boarding school, I did so with suitable tooth-paste and a toothbrush. That was unusual at the time. It was a line of business that was only just starting. My God! I have brushed so much! My toothpastes and liquids usually had a pleasant taste and left my mouth refreshed and sweet-smelling. They very possibly helped pre-serve my mouth, but even so one day I'd feel a decay drilling a hole into a tooth and on another a small abscess swelling my gums—at the bottom of one tooth or another. It might become inflamed; hour after hour I could feel my blood pounding in that inflamed spot and I suf-fered excruciating pain—a blend of pus and high temperatures com-bined with the usual cold shivers. I rarely went to dentists. Whenever I have gone, it was always to have a tooth extracted. Extractions were always accompanied by that atmosphere created by the seats in these practices—the adjacent seat with the basin to spit into, both white—and the white gown of the expert with the pincers. These extrac-tions—which lasted only a second—created unbearable mental tension that was much worse than any physical pain. When they in-troduced the first injections to deaden the pain—as they put it—things improved. These injections, along with aspirins taken before and after, were the first developments to improve these dreadful trials. I continued to brush my teeth every morning and evening and went to the dentist as little as possible—and only to have a tooth extracted. I couldn't break with the conventions of my era. I was completely wrong. In the course of my short life my mouth has already lost quite a few items. I don't know if I will have the strength to change my cri-teria. I doubt it. I will invent all manner of childish arguments to keep on as before. I will spend my whole life intermittently seeing stars and finish up with an emptied mouth. For the moment, I chew tremendously well. Perhaps that's how I'm misled.

12 October, Sunday. When friends gather in Palafrugell (or even acquaintances or enemies—there are always people who can't stand the sight of each other), almost total freedom exists in terms of the words used and judgments voiced. The same is true of our circle at the Athenaeum. All or almost all conversational circles in Barcelona are similar.

I have often wondered whether this freedom can last, whether it isn't excessive. "You can never have too much freedom," some people write or say. This is untrue. Let everyone think as he wishes as an individual. In social terms, freedom must have its boundaries. I doubt that today's freedom can last. Speech has no prompter. People today talk about anything under the sun, as garrulously as they like—as if they're bound to get it right by hook or by crook. Nothing is held in abeyance. Everything depends on the quip of the moment. One has to admit that torrents of words can be extremely amusing. The general tone of any conversation is quite charming. Pere Ynglada, who comes and goes from Barcelona to Paris and London, says conversations in Barcelona are unique at the moment. Not even social tensions introduce a more pensive vein—a hint of necessary seriousness. It creates the impression of a country of timid folk overawed by the endless opportunities they enjoy to be free and daring (with words).

"This situation," Enric Jardí was saying today in the circle, "will last as it long as it lasts. Another government will come along and all this chitchat will be swept away. People will abandon ship like rats. Everybody will become stiff, discreet, and lethally morose. Words will become more oblique and cautious; the frenzy will wane. We will go from one extreme to another. It has ever been so."

I think this verbal diarrhea has made no impact on the general levels of hypocrisy. Hypocrisy has held its ground. Hypocrisy is the hidden weapon—held in reserve for when the bad times come.

It was Sunday—a gentle, slightly cloudy afternoon, a warm autumnal afternoon. Autumn in Barcelona is pure joy. There were lots of people in the clubroom. On Sundays members appear who don't come on other days of the week: old Dalmau from his art galleries, doctors who have to work during the week, teachers, and artists. Dense smoke clouds the room. Many circle members smoke splendid Havana cigars. Josep M. Albinyana's cigars are spectacularly long, made from first-rate leaves, the size of which seem to grow in contrast to his body and long, thin, ascetic face. Some smokers (Albinyana) seem to inhale; others (Sagarra) puff pompously. Everyone follows his own fancy. Enric Jardí's words stop the flow of thoughts in the Sunday uproar. They are a shower of cold water—though they provoke little by way of reaction. Jardí is highly regarded in the circle and universally respected; he constantly argues against the frivolity and lack of seriousness in the air. He is no hard-line backwoodsman, like so many in the country. The variety among his closest friends fully attests to that—Quim, Eugeni d'Ors, Camps Margarit, and Josep Maria Junoy. Nonetheless, Jardí's full-blown pessimism leaves people cold. He generally irritates them. Whenever he is brief in what he says on the matter, they seem more interested in listening. If he goes on and on, they find it hard to hide their annoyance, whether great or small. If he speaks, deploying an argument that is evidently premeditated, eyes glaze over. It is boring and inopportune to speak of such things on a Sunday afternoon, on an autumnal Sunday afternoon that is so mellow, amid this blue smoke that smells so adorably of shit! What a bore! Quite beyond the pale!

Jardí uses the confusion generated by his words to take his hat and leave. He likes to stroll. He likes soccer, but not attending games. On the other hand, he likes watching people leave the stadium—people on foot—and listening to what they say as they disperse through the city. He once heard a man who was carrying a child on his shoulders tell him in a very affectionate accent from Valencia: "You are a tetchy little Zamora..."

15 October. I review what I wrote a few days ago about the Ampurdan and its people and conclude that the opinions expressed about this place seem more peculiar by the day. Those of us who live in the Ampurdan have experienced great danger in recent decades, namely because people consider this area and subject worthy of investigation not on human terms but—mark the word—scientifically. There is a lot of archaeology in the Ampurdan. Everything is dilapidated. It is quite natural this all should be researched. No one can complain about what the Barcelona Diputació did first, followed by the Mancomunitat in Ampurias. The lack of money, however, and resources is very evident. But it is perhaps rather far-fetched to want to project fatally fake light from twenty or twenty-five centuries ago on today's world. Local scholars—a picturesque crew—have contributed positively to this tendency. It is their way of having fun.

The truth is we are always on the point of being transformed into archaeological guinea pigs and objects for museum display cabinets. The mere fact that four seasick Greeks landed on the small promontory of Sant Martí d'Empúries makes us all Greeks—not flesh-and-blood Greeks, that is, identical or similar to Greeks of today, the ones who must vaguely resemble Greeks of antiquity, but the Greeks created by academic tomes, fake Greeks fashioned by scholars, wax-museum Greek figures with Hellenic noses. According to this superficial, clap-handed way of seeing things, everything we do in the Ampurdan, the way we eat, dance, sing, or fool around, is Greek, though not, I repeat, really and truly Greek, simply copies of fake amphora or whims in moribund erudite papers. Then, after observing how the Romans invaded the Peninsula via these lands, through some conscious strategic principle and with no little help from the weather, other gentlemen came along and placed uncomfortable firemen's helmets on our heads so we looked like the chorus from a postcard version of an epic *Quo Vadis* on celluloid, or some similar great production. However, the Roman element that still survives in this country—the legal system—was systematically scorned. Then they mounted us on Hannibal's elephants and gave us a glimpse of harems from theater wardrobes. They have tried—in a word—to reconstruct us, but have done so with dog-eared cardboard, stuffing our insides with straw and plastering over the cracks.

I think one should react to all this intelligently, with common sense, which would be a better way of seeing things than from the merely professorial or scholarly angle. The Greeks didn't come here to give future professors a pretext to deliver solemn, obscure, and pompous lectures but to trade and earn their living as best they could. Nor did they settle on this geographical terrain to embody any ethical, social, or aesthetic ideal; they didn't even commit to paper what they did here, thus providing academics with a wonderful opportunity to create conjectures, hypotheses, and fantasies. The handful of ragamuffin Greeks—ragamuffin though alive enough—who landed on this coast could never have imagined how their existence would become the object of boring, scholarly polemics. All the same, it is probably a good idea to strip the plaster and dross not only from Ampurias but from all of our ruins, and bring to the surface what is lurking under that literary crust, namely the spontaneous movement of ancient life, about which we haven't a clue in our country because the human realities of those people, their needs, passions, and instincts, have been distorted and misrepresented. An inevitably human vein—of basic passions—always reappears. This doesn't mean that ancient Greeks here lived like textile or engineering workers nowadays. Conversely, perhaps they did live like poor fishermen today or tinkers who hawk mirrors from village to village. In this respect there is no difference at all, they were exactly similar: They were completely insignificant, and that is precisely what people who write about this country and the people of the Ampurdan can never accept. They portray us as unique characters because we inherited this or that. If there is anything we inherited, it is modern: It has to do with the place's frontier, its insecurity, and country people's cautious, wary manner. This *is* a solid fact.

So we are presented with a cardboard cultural charade based, in the best of scenarios, on scraps of paper and, more often than not, on nonsense with no basis in truth. It is simply one more way of wasting time and replacing real sensibility with an artistic-literary sensibility (a cartoon caricature of paganism) that is completely fictitious. The arguments Sr. Maragall uses to establish a poetics based on living language might come in handy when investigating the traces of antiquity that are generally buried in this country if we are ever to decipher, inasmuch as it is possible, what they reveal about real human life. But please, let's have no more museum displays!

18 October. When I worked on *Las Noticias*, Sr. Miró i Folguera, the newspaper's editor, who was responsible for writing the opinion columns on the political situation, would sometimes say (when he was too busy), "Go to Cafè Catalunya. You know where it is off Vergara and the square. Listen in on Dr. Turró's circle and try to catch up on the latest political news."

The same thing happened at *La Publicidad*. Jori, the boss, sometimes said, "Go to Cafè Catalunya. Listen in on Dr. Turró's club. You might find out something new about what's going on politically. If you do, take it straight to Fontdevila. Don't leave it far too late, obviously."

The café gathering referred too was really something. It took place in the afternoon and at night—after lunch and dinner—and if there was something important showing at the theater, it rarely got going until after the curtain came down. The reputation held by the gathering convened by Dr. Turró, the director of the Municipal Laboratory and an eminent scientist, didn't assign it any specific features. It was completely political in character. In attendance were Sr. Moles, one of the sharpest commentators of the day; Pere Rahola; Juli Marial, the big cheese in Sants; Sr. Granyer, an impressive friars' cat; Sr. Mir i Miró, the young politician; and Professor Josep M. Trias de Bes, etcetera. Some of these gentlemen traveled from Madrid every week and sometimes brought news back—about which they often spoke in a flood of words or maintained complete silence. In any case, this café conversation was one of the places in Barcelona where one had direct access to the latest news. Introduced by Pere Rahola, whom I already knew from the circle at the Athenaeum, I tried to hover in the background as was appropriate, and often emerged with real information—though it was frequently underexploited—without ever causing the least conflict.

It was a gathering of strong personalities. Moles was witty and didn't hold back his opinions, as is the case now. This freedom is pointless when people have nothing to say or prefer to say nothing, but Moles's interventions were incisive and sparkling. Turró was quite remarkable and I don't understand why nobody has studied him as a conversationalist. Turró was unique and quite different from Moles. The latter was inclined to be fond of details and tangible references. Turró immediately focused his arguments or monologues on general ideas and a philosophical, scientific vision of things. Moles was a whirlwind who could make your hair stand on end; Turró immediately hit the right note when the debate became ponderous—he could introduce an air of passionate concern and his knowledge was always in evidence. Moles was so amusing he became tiresome; Turró was never tiresome—his mind was a constant stream of tremendous good sense.

Naturally in my visits to that café, I heard Dr. Turró speak on many different topics. The present political and social situation has brought considerable tension into these café conversations. I have heard Dr. Turró defend four different positions, depending on the issue he happened to be addressing. Here are his positions, as I observed them:

Dr. Turró was a severe judge of anything that upset the bourgeois social order, whatever the cause or form it took. He was an out-and-out reactionary. The Civil Guard is always right, systematically.

He is a dualist in philosophy—spirit and matter—rabidly anti-Kantian, and a Thomist, a *huge* admirer of Saint Thomas Aquinas. For him Saint Thomas's *Summa* is the highest point ever reached by philosophy. He dismisses German philosophical idealism as infantile.

In the realm of scientific thought, he is a pure freethinker and has no prejudices at all. A scientist with prejudices is the negation of research or thought in this respect. A scientist must be objective in his methods. That method constitutes his discipline.

He is a pragmatist in politics. His ideal would be a government of the left, though he regards them as fools. He thinks that men of the right are too driven by the most sordid and base instincts. He believes that you should react in politics according the needs of the moment.

The complexity of Dr. Turró's reactions is stunning and strikes a strange note in a country where almost everyone seems rigidly fixed in their ways, where reactionaries are consistently reactionary and always perform according to type.

Dr. Turró has a real thinker's face—in the most precise sense of that word. It is as if thought has shaped his features, which are particularly remarkable when he says nothing.

19 October. October weather in Barcelona can change dramatically. Sometimes, it seems late spring; at other times, early winter. It rains and is sunny. Twilights, however, are different, take on another color, another look. When afternoons end in hazy light and one is at the top of Passeig de Gràcia, one sees over Collserola a muted drama of red-embered twilights that give way to gloomy black-blue skies. If the wind from Montseny settles in, the clear sky to the north takes on a glassy, sapphire, fish-eyed aspect. Sometimes a noisy downpour of large raindrops sweeps the yellow leaves off the trees, chills the air, streams down carriages and trams, releases a smell of mushrooms from the earth, and causes people to huddle in lobbies—where the temperature drops. Shivering in autumn is the custom in Barcelona, the first sign of a change in the weather. Meanwhile, as the days go by, rooms in apartments grow imperceptibly colder—the cold begins with the rains of the Mercè—but the time comes when one can't deny reality: It is quite cold in the apartment. Blankets are spread over beds...noses start to stream and people's voices change. Bouts of loud sneezing can be heard in the most surprising places. I've spent October in Barcelona over a number of years. My memories aren't particularly pleasant. I mean, of the times when freezing temperatures reached the places where I've lived. My God! What a nightmare! The times I've frozen in Barcelona! The efforts I make to convince myself I am simply oversensitive to cold come to nothing. If I rub my hands nervously together to warm up, my skin turns red, but the impact is nonexistent, it makes no difference. In fact, you only feel good in the street, going for a stroll or doing this or that outside. Temperatures inside are horrendous.

When I think of my years in Barcelona studying to become a lawyer in autumnal and wintry weather, I can only ever remember feeling wretched. What a waste of time! What squandered opportunities! I wasn't a student with adequate means. The boarding and lodging houses where I stayed were humble—not to say poverty-stricken—and simply picturesque. Could one ever have studied peacefully, with minimal physical comfort, in this kind of establishment? I doubt it. In my book, the very few, extremely rare students who achieved good results in their studies are truly heroic. I don't include in this very small band those who worked without discomfort or cold—generally in their own homes—because of their individual circumstances. If you don't include the latter, you are left with a microscopically tiny number. I believe they are the real heroes.

In the system then established at the university one kind of student was destined to be successful. That was the student with a very good memory—the one who could read a text and repeat it word for word, even though he'd understood nothing. This psychological phenomenon is a gift from Providence, a striking personal attribute, but I cannot bring myself to include individuals with such a purely mechanical skill among my heroic students. I prefer intelligent students, particularly if they are also sensitive, to those endowed with good memories. Studying isn't simply about reading and regurgitating. Studying is about reading and also reflecting, relating, integrating, specifying, clarifying, absorbing, rejecting, and deciding—knowing what is important and what isn't. It is an activity that is hugely complex yet at the same time very natural. Studying means activating the mind, sometimes starting from within the mind itself or spurred on by things that provoke curiosity: that is, things that appeal positively. Something that is unappealing, that doesn't arouse a degree of fascination cannot be the object of reflection and study. It is impossible to focus or retain interest. Studying is a form of love—in truth, a form of sensuality: the most subtle, delicate caress the mind can produce. I am now twenty-two. I've studied and have devoted myself to study from the age of four or five. In fact, I have never done anything else. I have thought a little—very little—about these things. I am sure the conclusions I have reached are ones that many, many others share. As a consequence I wonder: How is it possible that something that should have given me so much pleasure, that I should have enjoyed so much, can have given me so many headaches, so much distress, so much hassle? A genuine student can only enjoy studying the substance of his vocation or elective affinity—in the same way a businessman or industrialist, a farmer or fisherman, or worker enjoys the activity he has chosen. This being the case, how can my life as a student have afforded me so few moments of pleasure?

The word *study* was rarely used in the years at the university that I am referring to. In fact, the favored word was *cram* or *empollar*, a loan from Spanish (the Catalan is *covar*) that refers to the incubation of eggs by a broody hen. A broody hen incubates eggs for three weeks without interruption—a sufficiently long amount of time to suggest the patience and persistence necessary for this kind of operation. In the university context, *empollar* didn't mean "to study" but "to stay put" (in this case, to stay put with one's butt on a chair), to have patience and staying power. An *empollón* or *grind* was a student who could stay seated for an inordinate number of hours. This attribute was a gift one couldn't buy or sell. Anyone who couldn't maintain this position for very long was a mediocre, average student. Cramming was like putting a collar or a muzzle on a young animal—a kind of dressage. But this isn't studying: Studying for a genuine student is about enjoyment, and, in the end, about freedom.

In lodging houses, *empollar*, in the tangible meaning of the word, involved sitting at a table in a bedroom that contained a bed (a bed that was sometimes still unmade in the afternoon), a wardrobe, and a washbowl. There were books on the table—textbooks. To the right of the course materials, a cup of coffee with a saucer full of butts, ash, and matches. On the left there was usually a forty-five-cent packet and a five-cent box of matches. Half a peseta, all told. The coffee in Barcelona was good and one could smoke black tobacco. Crouched in his chair, sometimes wearing his overcoat, sometimes his overcoat and scarf, the student would read a textbook open on his desk. The room was cold and the floor tiles freezing. Sometimes the student read with his hands in his pockets and an extinguished cigarette between his lips. Meanwhile songs by Nito-Jo drifted in from the apartments' inner yard or kitchens, sung by invisible domestic servants, especially the translation of the most popular lines—"*C'est la valse brune des chevaliers de la lune...*"—as the afternoon proceeded, the atmosphere in the air would become saturated with the stench from the cauliflower or greens being boiled on one stove or another. It reeked a smell that the cold air spread with incredible intensity. A penetrating odor that impregnated everything, the most improbable things; at a given moment it seemed to have soaked your brain. Time passed and suddenly you were hit with an additional bitter stench from frying-pan oil. That was the moment people started frying hake, the hake that bites its tail, the hake that in Barcelona is called "trawl" in natural hyperbole, one of the most insipid, worthless items you can imagine, one of the greatest nonevents in the human food chain. Meanwhile the cold that had been biting in the afternoon intensified with twilight. Floor tiles were like blocks of ice. The time would come when the atmosphere was so inimical and unpleasant that you stopped reading whatever the book had to say about long leases or repurchase or the articles of the Civil Code or letters of exchange. *Empollar*, keeping your butt firmly on a chair opposite an open textbook for the longest amount of time possible, was really difficult. You had to contend with a range of generally unpleasant, hellishly persistent external pressures that made concentration impossible. Conversely, the cold also meant you couldn't focus for a moment or even attempt to read coherently. It wasn't a dramatic, spectacular polar cold that might have forced you to burn whatever you had at hand. It was worse than that kind of cold: It was a ten-degree cold that stubbornly and insidiously filtered through to your bones and brought on the shivers, a cold that was so pure it was entirely sterile. It was a cold that sterilized mind and body. There was only one way out: escape. That was what most students in lodging houses did. At the start of the degree, when you still had the energy, escape was to the public libraries. However, the one that would really have been of use, the university library, was open only in the mornings, coinciding with our lectures. The system the university adopted was strange: It was about keeping students away from their alma mater for as long as possible. The way it was organized it was impossible to use the university library. It was a look-but-don't-touch library that drove a wall between readers and the books it held—a derisory, inaccessible, indeed archaic and ancient library. Thus students taking shelter from their lodging houses went to the College of Lawyers library, established in the Casa de l'Ardiaca, a dark, solitary, ghostly place, and the Library of Catalunya or the institute's, that was on carrer del Bisbe and was magnificent—and heated, naturally. But these establishments didn't meet the bibliographic needs of most students who required easier, less restricted access, which was precisely what they didn't have. And so most students in this category engaged in a different kind of escape. Apart from the few with great strength of will, most opted for the billiard halls and gambling tables on plaça de la Universitat or carrer de Gravina or the cafés with young ladies and the music halls on the Paral·lel that were shamelessly pornographic in a way that was perhaps never seen publicly. This was when dances and hedonistic-looking cafés began to move to the lower reaches of Aribau and Muntaner. Other students went to the cinema that was gloomy and pitch black and, as such, favorable to all manner of fleetingly pleasant adventures that were possibly not so amusing in the end. Eroticism was rife and took many off to the cemetery. Syphilis and gonorrhea were the order of the day. They were a constant topic of conversation. After gambling at seven and a half, the students who could feel the bitter rub of small change on their fingers could be happy. They'd survived. It could have been worse, for Christ's sake! And that's how people spent most of the university year. The university made a minimal, almost negligible impact on its students. It was an absurd, crazy situation. But that is how people got a degree.

The final strait of the year started at the end of April, beginning of May, once the examinations were in sight—they began on 20 May. Students who aspired to pass the year—some ruled that possibility out in advance—had no choice but to begin cramming continuously, despairingly. There was a leveler for the intellects and memories that began that exercise: coffee. We crammed drinking coffee—and smoking, naturally. As I have said, coffee in Barcelona, at the time, was excellent. You could drink such splendid, aromatic, delicious coffee at the Suís and the Continental! Waiters would bring trays of coffee up to the lodging houses from nearby cafés. The student drink de rigueur everywhere. I've even had the student's ruin recently: a glass of coffee, rum, sugar, and water. The mixture created a liquid that was the color of a Franciscan friar: an ashen gray. Later on, rum disappeared and was replaced in the best of cases by Domecq, three-star cognac, and in the worst case by undrinkable rotgut. As I lived in Barcelona when these establishments and concoctions were experiencing their swan song, I can attest to the great impact they had on goliardic minds and students intent on understanding the two kinds of law. Coffee aroused and enervated us, kept us in a state of tachycardia that, they said, helped students soak up the subjects that remained. I never really believed this, but as it was a commonplace, I had no choice but to follow the crowd. It was also thought to be axiomatic that coffee gave you verbal fluency in the viva voce that led to recognition of your merits. That was another fantasy. In fact, when the professors in the tribunal—paterfamilias to a man!—saw us troop in looking so pale and trembling with bags under our eyes, they took pity on us in a way that was sometimes theoretical but at others could show an active, fleeting kind of compassion, especially aimed at relieving the distress these things caused in our respective families. In any case, we were indefatigable drinkers of coffee, of coffee plus liquor, and tenacious chain smokers.

After finishing my degree and registering the decrease in the quality of life as a result of the recent war, I sometimes wonder how students manage to resolve their problems in mathematics, law, archaeology, or medicine with the coffee served today, which is like chestnut water. It is very likely that we were insignificant pigmies and that today's students are genuine geniuses. We must believe in progress, and increasingly so, even though these ideas may lead us to stake all our hopes for the future on the next round of children in diapers.

26 October, Saturday. I have been reading many articles by Joan Sardà (in the Athenaeum library), in the three volumes that were dedicated to his memory after he died. One of these volumes contains an excellent prologue by Maragall that is unfortunately not as comprehensive as the one he wrote for Mañé i Flaquer. In my humble opinion, one of Sardà's best articles is the one he wrote for *La Vanguardia* when *Diario de Barcelona* celebrated its hundredth year of existence.

Today very few people read *Diario de Barcelona*. It must have a very small circulation. Its social importance is minimal. It continues to come out because it was such a voice in the last century and the first few years of the twentieth. In 1892, when it was a hundred, it was still very influential. Mañé i Flaquer was still in charge. Mañé i Flaquer is a great nineteenth-century figure in this country. This gentleman's writing and the newspaper he edited for so many years had a profound impact on the outlook of Catalans.

Joan Sardà noted a few facts on the occasion of *El Brusi*'s first centenary. Basically, they are the following:

Diario's editorial board, at least what we might call its inner circle, has always been comprised of mainly, if not exclusively, university professors: Piferrer, Cortada, Reynals, Coll i Vehí, Àngel Bas, Damas Calvet, Duran i Bas, Flaquer, Gaietà Vidal, Milà i Fontanals, Miquel i Badia, and Mañé, a professor himself as well, if I remember correctly, in his youth... Its sternly doctoral air has been the cornerstone of *Diario*'s popularity in this region and the undoubted influence it has wielded. Barcelona and its *Diario* have experienced years and years of close interpenetration, fostering and reproducing each other in turn.

Diario was the true representative of what people have dubbed doctrinairism. Roughly defined, doctrinairism meant the promotion and defense in a purely abstract mode of a closed, extreme doctrine and the simultaneous relinquishing of the inflexibility of that doctrine in the practical, applied world by adapting it to the more or less objective needs of the present moment.

Diario has always propounded conservative doctrine, and its in-depth articles, when it was a case of explaining ideas, have always embodied an enlightened, well-argued exposition in the scientific, pedagogical tone of the great principles of the conservative school. In this exposition of ideas *Diario* has distinguished its own by giving them a particular hue, a regional one, that came naturally to its writers who were affiliated with a historical strand, which here formed a sub-strand of the great European school of conservatism.

In practical life, however, in the application of its doctrines to day-to-day political judgments, *Diario* has been one of the fiercest defenders, the firmest supporters of political parties that may have been described as conservative from a more or less technical perspective but that have disregarded the doctrinaire dogmas *Diario* professed.

Hence, for example, some priests and even bishops almost excommunicated *Diario*, while liberals and freethinkers have considered it to be neo-Catholic. Politically it has joined ranks with the right and the left, has been feared by all sides and almost repudiated by everyone. And what else? Even in economic matters *Diario*, the great champion of protectionism, would be attacked one day by Don Joan Güell i Ferrer, the great high priest of that policy, and become embroiled in a tremendous battle with him as an individual.

Another feature of *Diario* was the constant subordination of all its judgments to what it called ethics or morality, the single set of rules that underpinned its criticism of every area of life. The most important division made by *Diario* in respect of every event that passed before its iron gaze was its division of everything into what it considered moral and immoral. Nonetheless, the newspaper has perhaps sometimes overly narrowed its criteria in this regard, which generally speaking are just, healthy, and honorable, and everyone has to make divisions, especially those who pose as spiritual directors of society. Its concept of what is moral and immoral seems to have been poured into very narrow molds, and thus it often proclaims and applies a petty law of morality, subservient to a single commandment, the one that burns, servile obedience to which represses inspirational impulses in areas of intellectual life and in a lackluster society like ours that is hostile to new insights and madcap brainwaves, and thus strengthens mediocrity of judgment, its characteristic feature, that, depending on how you position yourself, reeks of hypocrisy and sanctimoniousness.

Joan Sardà was very, very perceptive. He knew what he was talking about. I would like to own the three volumes of his selected work, but they are not easy to find.

2 November. The Day of the Dead. After the rain that fell, the wind from the Montseny settled in and cleared the sky, creating a bright, glittering afternoon. It is cold in the evening—our first cold snap in fact. The citizens of Barcelona struggle to imagine it can be cold. It is futile; they want to keep quiet about it. When they find it is cold indoors and out, they look sour. I have seen lots of people in the street who are more or less well wrapped up, and seem tense—in protest.

I haven't seen a single Madrid cloak as I strolled along the streets today. This kind of cloak has been disappearing from sight over the last few years. It's a species that has become practically extinct. When I was a child a lot of people wore them—even in Palafrugell. Around 1904 or 1905, almost all the well-off friends of my father and grandfather were people who wore cloaks. I remember catching sight of that sinister character by the name of Pompeu Gener on the Rambla wearing a Madrid cloak. I am not sure if the garment keeps out the cold; perhaps the top part, with the wide collar, does; I think the bottom half, that always looks as if it is about to fly off, is quite ineffectual.

I have heard that the disappearance of the Madrid cloak is one positive result of Catalan nationalism. I think that may be perfectly possible, an accurate observation, if one also reasonably takes into consideration the fact that the garment offered poor protection against the elements.

In my modest opinion, the best piece to come from the pen of the novelist Narcís Oller is called "The September Revolution," included in the volume *Appearance and Landscape*. Sr. Oller has written excellent pages in his vast output that is perhaps excessively photographic in my view, probably because of the fashion at the time. "The September Revolution" is an exemplary, perfect, sensitive, and very intelligent story, which doesn't suffer from the influence of anything too immediate.

3 November. Sr. Pere Rahola has played a key political role in recent years and particularly in pro-French politics during the war. He always holds a different representative post. He is extremely well known in Barcelona and much admired when he walks down the street, coming or going from his house to shows and to circles of friends at the Athenaeum, Turró's circle, etcetera. He always seems optimistic, cheerful, and generously sociable. He seems a contented man, a spectacularly contented man. He welcomes people with howls of delight. He knows lots of anecdotes, many of which are quite saucy, and tells them with roars of laughter. He belongs to the era of the great Paris vaudevilles with long, pink bloomers. However, he sometimes seems sad and out of joint. He will suddenly become hesitant and perplexed, taciturn, twirl his mustache, brush his side curls—like small coat hangers—from his large baldpate with an anxious, thoughtful air. At other times he takes his beard in his hand and tugs at it, with gentle melancholy in his eyes as his thoughts wander far afield. All the Raholas I have known—whether from Roses or Cadaqués—have had large, melancholy, bulging eyes. The last time I saw Sr. Víctor Rahola in the house of Llimona the sculptor, I told myself, this family's eyes are like the eyes of a sad but fresh fish.

Despite my youthful years I have spent many hours in café conversations with Sr. Pere Rahola i Molinas. I have had the opportunity to observe him at length and follow his line of thought. I believe one of the turning points in his life was studying at the École de Sciences Politiques in Paris, during the fin-de-siècle heyday of the Third Republic—between the Dreyfus trial and Combes's policies on the religious orders. French culture entered the marrow of Rahola's bones and he is a complete rationalist, which manifests itself in his political practice through the skills he deploys defending the middle ground. He commands all the relevant clichés. His solutions are always French: He never concedes that the right or left are completely right, or the rich or the poor, he always suggests going slightly more rapidly or gradually, according to the needs of the moment... and *ça y est*! He gives the impression he carries this formula under his arm, like a veterinary of old with his syringes. He brings a solution to the issue at any given moment, accompanies his declaration with a rhetorical sweep aimed at smoothing over and softening the sharp conflicts within the different positions and interests at play... but the status quo often remains unchanged. Compromise isn't forthcoming and his impressive speech remains on the table like a large bouquet of paper flowers. The first to be aware of the outcome is Sr. Rahola himself and he shows his annoyance. His reaction may be one of irritation, if not contemptuous silence. However, sometimes he can be loud and violent and his bass voice can be useful. When his eyes bulge out of their sockets and his voice thunders "This is a country of idiots!," he inspires fear rather than joy, and looks like a figure from Mount Sinai. Sr. Moles, who has a poisonous tongue, usually responds to his close friend's tendency to exalt mediocrity (when no one is listening to him) by saying that Rahola is a man who likes to get drunk on béchamel sauce.

Sr. Rahola has so far always been a supporter of the Lliga, probably because he is a normal kind of man, that is, because he has never liked being on the losing side. However, not everything was flowers and roses in the Lliga, or so one gathers. Like a man who professes to being an agnostic in private, he has seen himself as someone to the left of Prat and Cambó. However, as he has always been guided by the formula of the middle ground, he has always thought Prat and Cambó were really less conservative and positive than himself. These contradictions (that are more or less apparent and about which much could be said) have often upset Rahola's feelings and triggered many amusing comic opera scenes—at least, to judge by what one hears people say who are interested in politics. In votes for positions in the Lliga, Sr. Rahola always receives the most votes and is the first to be elected.

When King Alfonso XIII came to Barcelona and Sr. Maragall wrote his "Royal Days," his commentary on their stay, Rahola was a highly influential lawyer and already fully dedicated to politics. He sported a large black beard, a mustache à la bourguignonne; his gestures were as broad as the brim of his Rembrandt hat, and his loud voice was permanently trapped in the vice of grandiloquence. He wasn't a man for sudden insights but an orator who preferred to elaborate his arguments. He was a rationalist. He wore a wide tie and a pearl tiepin that set off his magnificent chest. He dressed in the latest fashion, though the mannered, languishing forms of modernist fashion could never erase his male, virile air. It was then that Pujols remarked that he looked like an adulterer disguised as a financier. When Sr. Maura, who accompanied the king, heard him speak, he commented in Spanish, "Rahola is a young man who has a great facility with words."

Later on this comment has been attributed, frivolously, to a host of people. Uttered, in praise, by Sr. Maura—a fluent, baroque, difficult, specifically Mount Sinai kind of orator—it is witty in the positive sense.

After listening to Sr. Rahola at length, I concluded it would be very pleasant to live in the world this gentleman advocates—especially if you had a good income.

7 November. When I joined the editorial board of *Las Noticias*, Sr. Miró i Folguera made me attend a lot of the public meetings or rallies held by the different political parties. I had to do the same for *La Publicidad*. It isn't the most pleasant work, but it is work every journalist should have to do. Sr. Miró often said that and I think he was quite right. At this juncture, in any case, I don't think I wasted my time. I heard many orators—almost all the orators with any kind of reputation in the country and in particular political orators.

For a journalist who must write a report on a speech he has just heard, there are two kinds of orators: easy ones and difficult ones. The first are those who elucidate what they are trying to say by following a clear, precise line, who have the speech in their heads and set out the argument or inner structure it contains and formulate what they mean in a tangible, connected, balanced way that leads to a specific climax. Such speeches are easy to transcribe; they are striking, unforgettable, and follow what seems to be iron necessity.

However, there is another kind of orator: those who disperse themselves in a confused mess like a tangled skein, who are impossible to clarify and understand, full of digressions—endless digressions—that are incoherent, shapeless, and impossible to pin down and report. I don't mean that this kind of orator may not have his brilliant, amusing moments or second of success, but such moments make their speeches seem even murkier and wobblier. One can try to make them clear, if possible, to organize them, but that rarely works. It gives the impression that once the orator has finished blasting, he has said absolutely nothing to the people listening.

At the present time, Sr. Cambó is the kind of orator whose speeches are the easiest to report: perfectly easy. There are second-line orators who make an effort to follow his approach. Very few. All the other countless orators belong to the opaque, diffuse variety; their speeches have no inner thread, they are creators of darkness, of inanity, of nothing at all. However intrigued a journalist may be, their speeches are literally unreportable.

When listening to a speech by Cambó, the reporter following it, pencil and paper in hand, may or may not be in agreement, may feel indignant or persuaded, but he will never feel indifferent. The oratory is tangible. The report can be easily written—however slapdash—and it will seem perfectly decent. So this kind of work for a journalist can bring diverse results. If one is unfortunate enough to have to report on one of those confused, incoherent blasts of hot air, the final outcome will seem at best neither one thing nor the other; at worse, it will be pure rubbish that will be difficult to give shape to. When you come to the newspaper offices in the early hours and are forced to fill the space left in the columns for last-minute news, you must work your socks off to do so. On the other hand, when you listen to a coherent, organic, fluent orator, the tip of your pen assumes an unusual fluency, what you write is immediately coherent, and there is never enough room in the relevant section to take what you have written.

It was on one of my first assignments as a journalist that I could observe the figure of Sr. Cambó at length. Initially he seemed a unique, exceptional orator, and I didn't understand why a man possessed with this gift could have so many enemies in Barcelona and the places he visited. In the course of those public meetings, I had the opportunity to observe the way Cambó established contact with people. When he was with people he didn't know, Cambó's attitude was always silent, distant, and cold—unlike so many politicians who in such situations adopt a friendly air and tend to act like a buffoon. With people he knew, the forceful, dominant Cambó emerged, the man who argues to the end. This was the man displaying his real temperament: a force of nature. Sometimes, in the midst of the argument, a woman with genuine presence would come over or walk by. Cambó would look at her, sometimes for a split second. He had a striking way of looking at women! How natural, how free and personal his gaze, how directly he focused his eyes! Cambó had fascinating eyes that were extraordinarily complex and unusual. I am sure all men with strong personalities have unusual eyes.

10 November. Lluís Llimona, known as Titus in the Athenaeum circle, is generally very well liked. (He is a really amusing young man, who is even amusing physically, perhaps because he is so tall and slightly awkward.) And he is somewhat of a budding hunter. Once he was hunting in Tavertet (Collsacabra, near Vic) and presented to the usual members of the circle a hare, several partridges, and a good number of woodcocks. As always happens in this situation (which is not uncommon), Dr. Rafael Dalí took it upon himself to organize a collective dinner in the clubroom and cook the game on offer. Dr. Rafael Dalí, an undisputed gourmet, weighs in at two hundred and sixty pounds—a generous count, according to Camps Margarit. He is the best person to be charged with this task.

The dinner took place today and was excellent. Twenty-one members attended. Faced by Titus's woodcocks, Pompeu Fabra decided not to return home to Badalona that night.

Something unexpected occurred in the course of dinner. As a result of a rather stale though racy story, recounted by Pujols, Dr. Dalí started to guffaw nonstop, thus reducing himself to tears for a few seconds and finally sparking an incredibly spasmodic, continuous, persistent attack of hiccups. Dr. Dalí is paunchy and the spectacle of his paunch shaking with every hiccup was quite astonishing. If a man is thin and little, an attack of hiccups shifts nothing; if a man weighs two hundred and sixty pounds (at a generous count) his paunch is put under terrible pressure. Initially the Majorcan Antoni Homar (the doctor's big friend) said the hiccups had been triggered by a crust of bread that had made him choke. It was his way of trying to make it seem unimportant. The doctors present thought differently: They thought it *was* dangerous and suggested various ways to stop it and bring relief to their troubled colleague. As a result the apothecary nearest to the Athenaeum (on the corner of the Rambla and Bonsuccés) appeared with a battery of medicaments. Then I listened to what they said. I thought it was an unusual circumstance, but it transpired that, according to Borralleras, Dr. Dalí is prone to attacks of hiccups depending how he laughs—when he laughs, we might say, excessively. At any rate, he had experienced these onsets at other times, and they were particularly onerous and unpleasant because of his paunch. Time passed and finally, as he continued in that state, the decision was made to take him home. Quim Borralleras and Antoni Homar accompanied Dr. Dalí in a taxi to his private residence on carrer del Bisbe.

Dinner was resumed, rather more subdued, and when it was time for dessert, Alexandre Plana and Josep M. de Sagarra wrote, as they have at similar repasts, substantial occasional literary pieces, in verse, naturally, to praise the generosity of Lluís Llimona and his ability as a hunter with the predictable allusions to rifle and cartridge belt mythology, the quality of the cooking, and, evidently, the humans from the circle who were embroiled. Plana and Sagarra showed once again that they are two exceptional talents. They can write about anything, as long and substantially as they'd like to. They improvise like a fountain in full flow. They fashion their verse absolutely at will. Plana can write prose or verse and encounters few obstacles. Sagarra is wonderfully fertile when writing verse. Plana perhaps writes in a plainer way, with less color and beauty. Sagarra's poetry, so often ingenuous and superficial, is always full of character. Plana is hazy; Sagarra is clear. Pen in hand, they always find the right result.

The sight of a man writing almost without breathing—intelligible things, naturally—disconcerts, stuns, and fills me with admiration. Perhaps such an act is the source of all potential literature. To see this happen among a people—I hear Fabra say—that has made so much effort not to write is both amusing and inspiring.

I don't know if anyone collects the poems that are improvised in these suppers held by the circle. I imagine someone must. Perhaps Solé de Sojo, who sometimes participates in these positive activities (without making much fuss)? I am not sure. In any case, it is right that someone should. During dessert at these suppers, Sagarra (above all) has written copious amounts of poetry, a stream of magnificent lines, which one day will be published because this poet is unrivaled when it comes to improvisation.

12 November. Romà Jori, the director of the morning edition of *La Publicidad*, suggested I go to Paris as the paper's correspondent there, and did so without a fuss. It means seven hundred and fifty pesetas a month, which, at the present rate of exchange, is about nine hundred French francs.

As they wanted a quick reply, I accepted straightaway—presuming my family will react favorably (though they know nothing yet). I ask Jori to accept my thanks. He isn't sure which day I should go but assures me it will be very soon. I would be lying if I didn't say that I am pleased—though I'm afraid I won't do it well. I'm sure I won't.

Friends in the circle and on the editorial board don't seem at all reticent and if they are, I don't notice. Quim Borralleras tells me he is about to go to Paris and will be there to welcome me at the station on the Quai d'Orsay the day I arrive.

13 November. I quickly go to Palafrugell and speak to my family.

I never imagined the news would have been accepted so well. Everybody is visibly pleased.

On this visit, I would have liked to walk around the town, say goodbye to my friends, and go to our farmhouse, if possible. But no chance! It has been a sleepy, rainy, dull day with intermittent showers that have turned the streets to mud and closeted people inside their houses. The way small towns sometimes react so as to seem completely deserted. I thus spent the whole afternoon at home talking to my family—always with the same reserve induced by our upbringing—of this, that, and the other thing. Even though we spent a good long time together, neither my father nor my mother had any advice to give me. One of the pleasanter sides of our family seems to be the inability to turn any situation—big or small—into a spectacle. My mother announced she would make me a present of a set of sweaters—perhaps three or four. My father said he would give me money to buy a thick, comfortable overcoat and a large, very large suitcase made of genuine leather because, in his opinion, small suitcases are of no use on this kind of trip.

"Are you sure it must really be that large?" I asked.

"Yes, of course, the larger the better, provided you can carry it, even though you find it a struggle. On the other hand, you must learn how to pack a case. You can fit lots of things into a suitcase. You just see."

My father kept to his normal routine; after dinner he went to the café and returned at midnight, on the dot, as usual.

15 November. Make preparations for my journey. My passport will be ready tomorrow. A messenger will bring my set of sweaters and the money to buy an overcoat and a suitcase. Alexandre Plana and I will go shopping in the afternoon. The suitcase is particularly important.

I go to Paris the day after tomorrow.

OTHER NEW YORK REVIEW CLASSICS

For a complete list of titles, visit www.nyrb.com or write to:
Catalog Requests, NYRB, 435 Hudson Street, New York, NY 10014

* *Also available as an electronic book.*

Rick Steves'

PARIS
2007

Rick Steves, Steve Smith & Gene Openshaw